117898

S0-BLT-770

The Renaissance New Testament

Randolph O. Yeager

VOLUME THIRTEEN

I Cor. 11:1-16:24
II Cor. 1:1-13:14
Gal. 1:1-24

PELICAN PUBLISHING COMPANY

GRETNA 1983

Library of Congress Cataloging in Publication Data

Yeager, Randolph O.
    The Renaissance New Testament.

    Volumes 1-4 originally published in 1976-1978 by
Renaissance Press, Bowling Green, Ky.
        1. Bible. N.T.—Concordances, Greek. 2. Greek
language, Biblical. I. Title.
BS2302.Y4   1981   225.4'8'0321   79-28652
ISBN 0-88289-958-9 (v. 13)

Manufactured in the United States of America

Published by Pelican Publishing Company, Inc.
1101 Monroe Street, Gretna, Louisiana 70053

What's Past is Prologue

This observation of Antonio, the Duke of Milan (William Shakespeare, *The Tempest*, II, 1) has been alluded to often, especially by philosophers and historians. It is inscribed above the door of the National Archives in Washington, D.C. George Santayana, the Harvard poet and philosopher has warned us that he who does not remember the past is condemned to relive it.

Sir John Robert Seeley in his *Growth of British Policy* said, "History is past politics, and politics present history." It can also be said that history is past theology and present theological views drift along the same lines, from one error to another greater error, as they have always done in the past. In a letter to a member of the National Assembly a citizen warned that "You can never plan the future by the past." Perhaps not, but we can avoid future mistakes by looking at the way in which the same mistakes contributed to the evolution of political and theological thought.

In the past fifty years, since Fosdick issued his famous statement to the effect that the fundamentalists could not win, we have seen ample evidence that he was mistaken. The current best definition of a fundamentalist which I have seen says that he is one who is

iii

"comfortable with the term 'fundamentalist' over alternatives such as 'evangelical' or 'Protestant,' " (Stephen Board, *Fresh Air on the Right*, "Eternity," March, 1983, 9). Board adds that fundamentalists are those "whose doctrine and ethics are basically lists of things" and that they "tend to be independent Baptists." Finally he says, "That crowd is a-changin."

There is no doubt that "that crowd is a-changin'." Whether it is changing for better or for worse is debateable. It is true that some well known names who in the past have displayed some of the less savory features are now displaying some slight evidence that temperance is one of the fruits of the Holy Spirit. Thus Falwell's publication tips his hat with respect to such worthies as John Bunyan, Martin Luther, John and Charles Wesley, George Whitefield and Charles Spurgeon and goes on to deplore the fact that "by the standards of fellowship we observe with our brethren today, none of these men would be allowed in our pulpits or schools if they were alive." With reference to which observation the writer adds, "It is strange." (Truman Dollar in "Fundamentalist Journal" as cited in *Ibid.*) Indeed it is strange. On this, the year that marks the five hundredth anniversary of the birth of the man who dared to place his own opinion as an exegete of the New Testament above that of popes, councils, bishops, with or without an arch, prelates, indulgence salesmen, executive secretaries and television preachers, every preacher in America should be happy to invite Martin Luther to preach in his pulpit despite the fact that Lutherans sprinkle babies. They should also be willing to sit at the feet of Charles Haddon Spurgeon, whose ministry was used of the Holy Spirit to shake London for Christ. But Spurgeon was a five-point Calvinist and he rejected pretribulation rapture as something that, after 1800 years, was added to the New Testament by the charismatics, who would rather derive their theology out of an intuitive appeal to thin air, than from the New Testament, and who then preach what they have derived with unctuous dogma. John Wesley was an Arminian. That is "a grievous fault" as Mark Antony observed (William Shakespeare, *Julius Caesar*, III, 2) and "grievously (will the Arminians answer it)" but John Wesley led a lot of sinners to Jesus Christ, though according to his theology they could not then be sure that they had anything that they could keep. The Scotch Methodists were in a much better position because Charles Wesely, who led them to Christ, preached that one could receive salvation by grace through faith and that, though he could not keep it, it had "already been reserved in heaven" for those who by the power of God are kept through faith unto the glorification which had been made ready to be revealed at the second coming of our Lord. Thus Scotch Methodists have more assurance than American Methodists, because Charles understood his Bible better than John, who never could have written

Father, I stretch my hands to Thee; No other help I know:
If Thou withdraw Thyself from me, Ah! whither shall I go?
What did Thine only Son endure; Before I drew may breath!
What pain, what labor, to secure My soul from endless death!
Surely Thou canst not let me die; O speak, and I shall live;
And here I will unwearied lie, Till Thou Thy Spirit give.
Author of faith! to Thee I lift My weary, longing eyes:
O let me now receive that gift! My soul without it dies.

or

How can a sinner know His sins on earth forgiven?
How can my gracious Saviour show My name inscribed in heaven?
And publish to the sons of men The signs infallible,
We who in Christ believe That He for us hath died,
We all His unknown peace receive, And feel His blood applied.
We by His spirit prove And know the things of God,
The things which freely of His love He hath on us bestowed.

But Charles did, because he and his young friend Augustus M. Toplady were Calvinists. And Toplady wrote

Rock of Ages, cleft for me, Let me hide myself in Thee;
Let the water and the blood, From thy wounded side which flowed,
Be of sin the double cure, Save from wrath and make me pure.
Could my tears forever flow, Could my zeal no languor know,
These for sin could not atone; Thou must save, and Thou alone:
In my hand no price I bring: Simply to Thy cross I cling.
While I draw this fleeting breath, When my eyes shall close in death
When I rise to worlds unknown, And behold Thee on Thy throne:
Rock of Ages cleft for me, Let me hide myself in Thee.

If the criterion by which we are to select the term by which we choose to be known is that we must feel comfortable with it, some of us are hard put to it to choose a name. Most people who throw these terms around loosely have never given much thought to their denotation, but connotations are a dime a dozen. The word conservative denotes one who conserves. If you go by the dictionary few would fear to be known as a conservative? Is there anyone, except perhaps an extreme existentialist, who does not see the value in keeping things? I keep paper clips, old sermon notes that I would not care to be caught dead with now, fifty years later, copies of the National Geographic and the American Scholar, my old Scofield Bible, but only for sentimental reasons, since my sister gave it to me as a High School graduation present, before I was saved, and I have four empty bottles of Liquid Paper on my desk. I just do not have the heart to throw them away. Perhaps I am an extreme conservative, though not as far to the right as my neighbor who keeps fetid garbage, though he is looked upon in the community as a bit irrational.

But the trouble with capital letter Conservatives in the view of those of us who are small letter conservatives is that they are trying to conserve things that ought to have been scrapped in the theological, philosophical and political garbage cans of history millenia ago. The reason they insist upon conserving garbage is that they are not Liberal Conservatives (!). This use of Liberal as an adjective to modify the noun Conservative will be looked upon by many who read these lines, as a case of one who *darkeneth counsel by words without knowledge* (Job 38:2; 42:3). Since this is a quotation from the lips of our Sovereign Lord, Who applied the rebuke to Job, and of Job to himself in his humble confession of ignorance, I make bold to point out the difference between me and Job.

A conservative in the proper sense is one who wishes to conserve that which is eternally worth saving. (*On Canning Peaches,* The Renaissance New Testament, 8, iii-xxiv). The problem is not easily solved, because it calls for a series of value judgments. Propositions come easily, for they consist of simple statements in which we predicate about subjects. "It is a nice day," "The score is tied," "Old Blue Eyes sings off pitch." These are examples. They need not be true. They need only to say something, whether true or false. Mature people should give voice only to judgments. These are true propositions. A false proposition bears false witness and the Bible is against that. Thus the Christian should either speak only judgments or remain silent. A value judgment is a judgment that is worth fighting for. Caesar's wife was said to have been above reproach. If indeed she was, then the statement was a judgment to all in Rome, but it was a value judgment to the Emperor, who

vi

thought that Calpurnia's reputation was worth fighting for. And that is why he would have cheerfully knocked the block off anyone who slandered his wife, if in fact he did not feed him to the lions in the Colosseum.

If a conservative has an ounce of intellectual humility in his makeup he is aware that his desire to conserve only the good and to reject the evil is hindered by his inability in many cases to tell the difference. Which peaches do we can and which do we feed to the pigs? The best way to determine this question is to engage in dialogue with those whose views are somewhat different from our own. A Calvinist who is firmly convinced that the Reformed Theology is taught in the New Testament should test the strength of his conviction by submitting his views to the Arminian who is just as firmly convinced that the New Testament teaches the view of Jacobus Arminius. If the talks that ensue are conducted with proper Christian grace, tolerance, intellectual humility and mutual respect and love they are certain to be profitable. When Hegel advocated the dialectical method, by which thesis is confronted with antithesis to develop synthesis, his driving force was spirit, by which Hegel meant, not the Holy Spirit, but the human spirit - the pure reason of the unaided human intellect that Kant had spoken of a century earlier. DesCartes, Spinoza and Leibnitz had insisted that Locke, Hume and Berkeley were wrong when they said that man could advance no further in knowledge than the point to which his senses could take him. When Locke said that there was nothing in the intellect without first of all being in the senses, Leibnitz replied by saying, "Nothing indeed, except the intellect itself." And Immanuel Kant expanded upon Leibnitz's rejoinder to Locke with his *Critique of Pure Reason* and *Critique of Practical Reason*.

But when two Christians sit down together as liberals in an attempt to determine what the Bible really teaches, in order that they may also as conservatives conserve only that which must be conserved, they have at their disposal, not only DesCartes' human reason, by which they compute their income tax, but also the Holy Spirit, Who dwells within each and Who is committed to the task of making clear what He means by what He said in the New Testament, of which He is the Author. Thus Christians are privileged to conduct a Holy Spirit dialectic, which utilizes Hegel's human spirit but also enjoys the guidance of the Holy Spirit of God.

If we think of the word "liberal" as an adjective which suggests one whose heart is right, but who has doubts about the validity of his own thought processes, we will stop using it with a capital L to refer to the "Liberal" who does not believe in the virgin birth, blood atonement, bodily resurrection, divine and therefore inerrant revelation, but who believes only in evolution, situation ethics, secular humanism, abortion, women's rights, civil rights for gays and the Democratic Party. By analogy then a Conservative is a Republican who believes all of the "fundamental" theology and rejects all of that other garbage. Yet most Liberals and Conservatives who receive media treatment are among the most illiberal people one would ever care to meet. Do you know of an evolutionist who is willing to listen to a creationist without entertaining an attitude of tolerant accommodation? Or an Arminian willing to talk with a Calvinist? Or a Calvinist willing to talk to an Arminian? Or a premillenialist, or a postmillenialist, or an amillenialist, or a charismatic or a non-charismatic who reveals these admirable qualities of humility and a genuine desire to know the truth? Do not most of us hope that what we have always been taught, or what we have come to believe, and/or what we have become associated with in our public addresses or books, is the truth? Are we really interested in the truth? Or in our reputations? If the former, then we are liberal conservatives. If the latter than we are conservatives determined to can the peaches, whether they are ripe, fresh and viable or rotten, fetid and sure to blow up the can.

Thus I do not wish to be called a fundamentalist unless you are willing to spell it with a small letter and go by the denotation in the dictionary. And since few, if any, people are willing to think about it that much, I would rather find another term.

The term Evangelical is ruled out because many of the most prominent, whose names and pictures we see most often in the press, like to say that they are not interested in doctrine but in witnessing for Christ and winning the lost, as though one can witness for Christ without teaching that certain things are true. There is a current movement among capital E Evangelicals to ridicule and repudiate Calvinism. If they were true liberal evangelicals they would have the grace to entertain the thought that at least there is a possibility, however slight! that they could be wrong and that the Reformed Theologians, Machen, Van Til, Hodge, Spurgeon, Calvin, Toplady, Charles Wesley, Luther and Augustine might be right. One prominent radio personality is reported to have said that though he believed in Calvinism he dared not preach it since it was not conducive to the attraction of great crowds at services and wide radio and television audiences.

The word "Modernist" as it is applied in the field of religion has become a term of contempt, used to describe a disciple of Antichrist, bent upon the destruction of all that is high and holy. That description will fit the illiberal modernist who has already made up his mind and does not wish to be annoyed with any further discussion, but the liberal modernist possesses more intellectual humility than we credit to him and he may return to the faith of our fathers, if in fact he has ever deserted it.

It is significant and a bit sad to note that there is more intellectual humility among some scientists, even among those who are not Christians, and that in some notable cases, further thought and investigation on their part has led them to repudiate former positions in favor of others which are less popular. Recently some English former evolutionists have confessed that in previous days they had been hoodwinked.

It is not necessary to discuss in turn the official names given to the main line denominations. The Catholics, Lutherans, Presbyterians, Methodists, Baptists (57 varieties), Disciples of Christ, Churches of God, Churches of Christ, Churches of whatever, Assemblies of this and that - these are institutional name tags worn by various persons who have a social, political or economic interest in remaining with their present connections. These names generally mean whatever ten thousand butchers, bakers and candlestick makers say they mean.

But there is one name which has escaped the tar brush of the connotation. A Berean was a citizen of Berea who heard Paul and Silas preach the gospel of Christ, from the Old Testament scriptures. He heard that the Messiah of the Old Testament, long promised to Abraham, Isaac and David, and toward Whose coming, both the law and the prophets looked, had been born in a manger in Bethlehem. His name was Jesus. His mother had borne Him without benefit of husband, and He declared that He was the Son of God - a declaration that was supported, not only by His magnificent teaching, like unto which no man had ever heard, but also by His breathtaking miracles and most of all by His resurrection from the dead - a fact to which more than five hundred persons, most of whom were still living could attest. The Bereans were further told that even though they were Gentiles, this Galilean carpenter had made it clear that they could have a place in His eternal kingdom of peace and righteousness, if they would only repent and believe.

This message they heard and could scarcely believe, especially when a company of Jews from Thessalonica came to town intent upon running Paul and Silas out of Berea as they had previously run them out of Thessalonica. But these Bereans were as skeptical of Paul's Jewish critics, who were intent upon killing him, as they were of Paul himself. It takes a mature mind to be skeptical in the right sense. Immaturity manifests itself in the eager willingness of the naive to believe what they are told upon the first hearing. These are the people who regularly buy the Brooklyn Bridge and send their money to the television prophets. The Bereans were not naive. They did not immediately accept what Paul and Silas preached. Nor were they so skeptical that they rejected out of hand the new gospel which they had heard. They were noble people - "more noble than those in Thessalonica, in that they received the word with all readiess of mind, and searched the scriptures daily whether those things were so" (Acts 17:11).

There are some Bereans in the world today. Thank God, we are not organized. We are not structured into an institution. We have no logo. There are no cryptic signs, hand grips or signals which must be kept from the unwashed. Bereans are Bible students. They have a large dose of skepticism for any and all preachers who seem to be too eager that they should accept the message. They look in the poke before they buy the pig. They do not ignore what the salesman has said, but they reserve their opinion until they have conducted their own research to ascertain whether or not what he said is in line with what the Bible says.

This kind of research calls for a little more scholarship than many persons, who have the spirit of the Bereans, possess. Many of them have never learned to read the Scriptures in the original Hebrew and Greek. If they are true Bereans they will go looking for help. A class, currently meeting for an hour every Sunday night, numbering more than a score are taking elementary New

x

Testament Greek. They are typical upper-middle class people with average intelligence, but far more than average determination to learn how to read the Greek New Testament for themselves. They are civil servants for the federal government, military personnel, technicians, computer operators, school teachers, business men, college students and housewives. They range in age from early twenties to mid-sixties. Within another three months they will be studying intermediate and advanced Greek grammar and exegeting the orginal text of the Greek New Testament. They are determined to be enslaved by no Bible teacher, not even by their pastor, whom they love and respect and who is a better-than-average Greek student, with a constructive expository ministry.

The first purpose which the author had in mind when he began the study which has resulted, after fifty-two years, in The Renaissance New Testament, was to be a Berean myself. Not until the longhand manuscript was more than half finished, thirty years ago, did I dream that what I have written would ever be published. Thus there is now a second purpose for this work. It is that others may also be Bereans, even though they have not had the opportunity to learn the language which our Lord and the Apostles spoke and in which they wrote the New Testament.

There is no danger that independent exegesis of the Word of God will lead to a fragmentation of the Body of Christ, although it may not contribute to the solidity of institutional religion. Paul wrote about the unity of the Spirit and the bond of peace, and predicted that Bible study would result in a building "built upon the foundation of the apostles and prophets, Jesus Christ himself being the chief corner stone, in whom all the building fitly framed together groweth unto an holy temple in the Lord, in whom ye also are builded together for an habitation of God through the Spirit." (Eph.2:20-22). He added that when "we all come in the unity of the faith, and of the knowledge of the Son of God unto a perfect man, unto the measure of the stature of the fulness of Christ . . . we would be no more children tossed to and fro, and carried about with every wind of doctrine, by the sleight of men and cunning craftiness, whereby they lie in wait to deceive, but speaking the truth in love may grow up into him in all things, which is the head, even Christ, from whom the whole body fitly joined together and compacted by that which every joint supplieth,according to the effectual working of every part, maketh increase of the body unto the edifying of itself in love" (Eph.4:13-16).

This will never be accomplished until Bereans who disagree with other Bereans sit down together with their Bibles and examine with calm objectivity their own positions and those of their opponents. In this discussion, if it can be had, it will be apparent that one side or the other is wrong about any given issue. Otherwise we must conclude that the Holy Spirit has contradicted Himself in the New Testament. No Christian Berean can accept that. Sound exegesis, based on diction, grammar and syntax, which views every passage in the light of its context, with due regard to the time when it was written, the place where it was written and the circumstances under which it was written, will make the message of the Holy Spirit clear and unmistakable. Right views will become clear. Wrong views, both in doctrine and in practice will be revealed as such.

Sessions like these in which Bereans match scripture with scripture, (for no scripture is of its own interpretation) must begin with an understanding that everyone present loves everyone else present. If this is not understood those who have been confronted with evidence from the Word that their views are not scriptural will resort to a sermon about how all members of the Body of Christ should love all other members. Woe betide the skillful exegete who has the scriptures, rightfully exegeted at his command. He will not meet with a sound refutation of his views, but he is likely to hear a sermon about loving his brethren. Real Bereans love all others who are in the Body of Christ, however wrong they may be in their doctrinal views. Bereans love heretics. It is their heresy which they cannot tolerate.

We said at the beginning of this piece that we would do well to look backward and see how bad theology gave rise to worse. If we do not learn the lessons of church history what is past is certain to be prologue.

A fruitful field of enquiry for this research is found in the experience of the New England Puritans who came to Massachusetts in the seventeenth century. They were staunch five-point Calvinists. They had not yet been touched by the Enlightenment which developed in France more than one hundred years later. The influence of Rene DesCartes, the father of modern rationalism, had not yet been felt. He died in 1650. The Pilgrims had little communication with Europe during the early years, due to the long and hazardous passage across the Atlantic. This isolation from European society which they had felt it necessary for them to leave was unfortunate in many ways, but it shielded them from intellectual developments in Europe that tended to strike at their rock-ribbed Calvinism. Isaac Newton demonstrated that the mind of man, however depraved the Calvinists might consider it, was still able, with the help of DesCartes' three-dimensional mathematics, to figure out some things that were very important if we are to understand how the universe works. But he was not born until 1642. By the time of his death in 1727 the seeds of the Enlightenment had been sown in Europe and some had been carried westward across the Atlantic to New England. Jean Jacques Rousseau was born too late to corrupt the early Puritans in Massachusetts with his philosophy that man was "born free" not "in sin" as the Calvinists believe and that it was the fault of a corrupt society that "everywhere he is in chains." But his *Social Contract* was the daily intellectual bread and meat of the Founding Fathers who borrowed their philosophy of natural rights from him and from other deists and atheists who set 18th century France afire in 1789 and destroyed the Ancien Regime of the Bourbons.

Those who have not studied American history carefully are surprized to learn that the Declaration of Independence in 1776 stood exactly halfway in time between the landing of the Mayflower at Plymouth in 1620 and the great American depression on the eve of the American New Deal in 1932-33. During those 156 years New England Calvinism was assailed with the blasts of Enlightenment winds and New England's rock bound coasts were pounded with the thundering waves of European infidelity.

The Calvinists who came to an unexploited wilderness in 1620 applied what for them was a very practical application of their theology to the task of exploiting the vast lands with their rich resources. Their Protestant Ethic, borrowed a page from Martin Luther, who had taught that every Christian is called of God to make his living at some specific task for which Providence had equipped him. All he needed therefore was good health, a right relationship with God through Jesus Christ and an opportunity. The Yankees were healthy and they were saved, thanks to their doctrine of predestination, election and atonement. And they had all of the opportunity that anyone could wish. The frontier stretched away westward to and beyond the Great Lakes and "beyond the wide Missouri" to California. Land was dear and wages were low back east, but on the frontier land was cheap, even free in some areas and wages were at a premium. Calvinists found Ephesians 4:28 which speaks of working with our hands and making a profit. Thus the Protestant Ethic preached that every man become a small entrepreneur. There was no need for the welfare state except in cases of invalidism. The able bodied pauper was regarded as one who deserved his fate, since he did not lack the opportunity to work and become rich. Thus it was thought to be against the will of God to give him anything.

It was this idea that every man should be his own entrepreneur in a small capitalistic enterprise, that Thomas Jefferson understood as he envisaged America as a nation of small farmers and/or small business men in small towns, each of whom could contribute the products of his labor to the common good, but no one of whom would be big enough in relation to the free market to affect the competitive price. This is the heart of the *laissez faire* political philosophy of the classical economics of Adam Smith. Jefferson, immersed in the philosophy of the Enlightenment rejected the view that man is depraved and selfish and he also overlooked the psychology of individual differences that dictates that men are not created equal, except in the Jeffersonian sense that they are equal before the law. The New England Calvinists insisted that man was born a fallen creature, but Jefferson said that he was born a rising creature, whose taint of sin was only the superficial result of his contact with a society that could be made constructive. If Jefferson could have foreseen the coming of the Industrial Revolution, with its banking, transportation and manufacturing and marketing monopolies he might have been less optimistic about the future.

There appeared in New England both the Arminians and the charismatics to challenge the view that the mind and will of man is too depraved to make free choices. Thus arose rationalism, unitarianism, universalism and deism to challenge the old order. Also Anne Hutchinson the unstable psychic who was certain that the Holy Spirit had not written His final word in the New Testament but had reserved special additions which He communicated only to her and her friends. Harvard, William and Mary, the College of New Jersey, Dartmouth and the "log colleges" gradually forsook the faith and America was on her way to a secular society.

Antonio was right. "What's Past is Prologue."

1 Corinthians 11:1 - "Be ye followers of me, even as I also am of Christ."

μιμηταί μου γίνεσθε, καθὼς κἀγὼ Χριστοῦ.

"Be imitators of me, as I am of Christ." . . . RSV

μιμηταί (nom.pl.masc.of μιμητής, predicate nominative) 4132.
μου (gen.sing.masc.of ἐγώ, objective genitive) 123.
γίνεσθε (2d.per.pl.pres.mid.impv.of γίνομαι, entreaty) 113.
καθὼς (compound comparative particle) 1348.
κἀγὼ (adjunctive particle and first personal pronoun, crasis) 178.
Χριστοῦ (gen.sing.masc.of Χριστός, objective genitive) 4.

Translation - "Be followers of me as I also am a follower of Christ."

Comment: Paul never asked the saints for a standard of ethics higher than the goal he set for himself. The order is: Christ, the Leader, followed by Paul, the Apostle followed by the Corinthian Christians and all other saints.

In summary, Chapter 10 has told us that national Israel was an object of God's elective grace and love. Redeemed by blood and power, they were provided with the miraculous gifts of water and food while they worshipped the Rock, Christ Jesus, Who followed them. But many of them backslid and were punished by death in the wilderness. They lusted after evil; they were idolaters, fornicators, murmerers. Their experiences provide God's object lesson to individual Christians. We too are saved, as Israel was, and we can escape temptation if we seek the escape routes which are provided. We are to flee idolatry, separate ourselves from the devil's world. Though we have liberty in Christ, we must take care not to allow our liberty to become license. Our weak Christian brethren are our responsibility. We must give up practices which are not sinful for us but questionable in the minds of others. Living without offense we must serve others in order to win them to Christ. Finally we are to imitate Christ.

The eleventh chapter concerns relations between men and women, with a long passage about hair styles, followed by instructions about the administration of the Communion service.

Covering the Head in Worship

(1 Corinthians 11:2-16)

Verse 2 - "Now I praise you, brethren, that ye remember me in all things, and keep the ordinances, as I delivered them to you."

Ἐπαινῶ δὲ ὑμᾶς ὅτι πάντα μου μέμνησθε καὶ καθὼς παρέδωκα ὑμῖν τὰς παραδόσεις κατέχετε.

"I commend you because you remember me in everything and maintain the traditions even as I have delivered them to you." . . . RSV

Ἐπαινῶ (1st.per.sing.pres.act.ind.of ἐπαινέω, aoristic) 2568.

δὲ (explanatory conjunction) 11.

ὑμᾶς (acc.pl.masc.of σύ, direct object of Ἐπαινῶ) 104.

ὅτι (conjunction introducing a subordinate causal clause) 211.

πάντα (acc.pl.neut.of πᾶς, direct object of μέμνησθε) 67.

μου (gen.sing.masc.of ἐγώ, reference) 123.

μέμνησθε (2d.per.pl.perf.act.ind.of μιμνήσκω, consummative) 485.

καὶ (adjunctive conjunction joining verbs) 14.

καθὼς (compound comparative particle) 1348.

παρέδωκα (1st.per.sing.aor.act.ind.of παραδίδωμι, culminative) 368.

ὑμῖν (dat.pl.masc.of σύ, indirect object of παρέδωκα) 104.

τὰς (acc.pl.fem.of the article in agreement with παραδόσεις) 9.

παραδόσεις (acc.pl.fem.of παράδοσις, direct object of παρέδωκα) 1140.

κατέχετε (2d.per.pl.pres.act.ind.of κατέχω, present progressive retroactive) 2071.

Translation - "Now I heap praise upon you because you have been remembering everything about me and you have been keeping the ordinances just as I delivered them to you."

Comment: ἐπαινέω (#2568) is a heightened form of αἰνέω (#1881). ὅτι is regarded by some as declarative, but can just as well be considered causal. The perfect tense in μέμνησθε indicates consistent action by the Corinthians. They had always been and were still continuing to be mindful of all that Paul had taught them. Note the plural in τὰς παραδόσεις - baptism and the Lord's Supper. Paul's instructions, which follow, concern the latter, with particular emphasis upon proper hair styling (vss.3-16) and proper spiritual discipline when coming to the Lord's table (vss.17-34).

Verse 3 - "But I would have you know, that the head of every man is Christ; and the head of the woman, is the man; and the head of Christ is God."

θέλω δὲ ὑμᾶς εἰδέναι ὅτι παντὸς ἀνδρὸς ἡ κεφαλὴ ὁ Χριστός ἐστιν, κεφαλὴ δὲ γυναικὸς ὁ ἀνήρ, κεφαλὴ δὲ τοῦ Χριστοῦ ὁ θεός.

"But I want you to understand that the head of every man is Christ, the head of a woman is her husband, and the head of Christ is God." . . . RSV

θέλω (1st.per.sing.pres.act.ind.of θέλω, aoristic) 88.

δὲ (adversative conjunction) 11.

ὑμᾶς (acc.pl.masc.of σύ, general reference) 104.

εἰδέναι (perf.inf.of οἶδα, noun use, object of θέλω) 144b.

ὅτι (conjunction introducing an object clause in indirect discourse) 211.

παντὸς (gen.sing.masc.of πᾶς, in agreement with ἀνδρὸς) 67.

ἀνδρὸς (gen.sing.masc.of ἀνήρ, relationship) 63.

ἡ (nom.sing.fem.of the article in agreement with κεφαλή) 9.

κεφαλὴ (nom.sing.fem.of κεφαλή, predicate nominative) 521.

ὁ (nom.sing.masc.of the article in agreement with Χριστός) 9.

Χριστός (nom.sing.masc.of Χριστός, subject of ἐστιν) 4.

ἐστιν (3d.per.sing.pres.ind.of εἰμί, static) 86.

κεφαλὴ (nom.sing.fem.of κεφαλή, predicate nominative) 521.

δὲ (continuative conjunction) 11.

γυναικὸς (gen.sing.fem.of γυνή, relationship) 103.

ὁ (nom.sing.masc.of the article in agreement with ἀνήρ) 9.

ἀνήρ (nom.sing.masc.of ἀνήρ, subject of ἐστιν, understood) 63.

κεφαλὴ (nom.sing.fem.of κεφαλή, predicate nominative) 521.

δὲ (continuative conjunction) 11.

τοῦ (gen.sing.masc.of the article in agreement with Χριστοῦ) 9.

Χριστοῦ (gen.sing.masc.of Χριστός, relationship) 4.

ὁ (nom.sing.masc.of the article in agreement with θεός) 9.

θεός (nom.sing.masc.of θεός, subject of ἐστιν understood) 124.

Translation - "But I hope that you have come to understand that the head of every man is the Messiah and the man (is) head of the woman and God (is) the head of the Messiah."

Comment: The rule is that normally the subject has the article while the predicate does not, despite the word order. However, for particular emphasis the predicate can also have the article. Thus we have ἡ κεφαλὴ ὁ Χριστός ἐστιν, but κεφαλὴ δὲ γυναικὸς ὁ ἀνήρ and κεφαλὴ τοῦ Χριστοῦ ὁ θεός. Christ is the head of every man in a greater sense than the husband is head of his wife. The anarthrous substantive is the predicate nominative. *Cf.* Eph.5:23 - ὡς καὶ ὁ Χριστὸς κεφαλὴ τῆς ἐκκλησίας.

Paul's argument which follows with regard to how men and women shall pray or prophesy in public (private worship at home is not in view) is based upon a clear understanding of the ranking order of God, Christ, a Christian man and his

Christian wife, as the relationship of husband and wife is to be viewed in the church. He is not teaching that there is any subordination of any member of the Body of Christ to any other member. *Au contraire cf.* Gal.3:27,28. He is teaching that in the home and in the local church congregation there is a heirarchy of authority that runs from top to bottom thus: God, Christ, the Christian husband and his Christian wife. This subordination of a wife to her husband came over to Christianity from Judaism. Verses 7-9 alludes to the creation of Adam and Eve in the Garden of Eden. The Jewish tradition was that in synagogue worship, Jewish women symbolized their subordination to the husbands by praying or prophesying with a veil over their heads. The Hellenic tradition was not so. The Greeks went into the temples of their pagan deities uncovered to show their contempt for subordination and their love for liberty. Thus a Christian Greek man found the practice of praying or prophesying at church with uncovered head consistent with Christian teaching that he was head of his wife, while his act of praying and what he said in his prophetic utterance gave evidence that he was subordinate to Christ and God; but a Christian Greek woman found that her former practice of praying in a Greek temple without a covering upon her head was inconsistent with the Christian view that she was subordinate to her husband. Jewish Christian women had no problem. They had always prayed in the synagogue with covered heads, while Jewish Christian men prayed uncovered, but with a veil over the face.

The doctrine of liberty and equality in Christ was attractive to the women in the Christian congregation, and the question arose at Corinth whether Christian women should pray covered or uncovered. To pray covered seemed to some to deny the equality of Gal.3:28. To pray uncovered seemed to deny a Christian wife's subordination to her husband. The problem was solved by distinguishing between the husband/wife relationship as it relates to the Body of Christ and as it relates to society. In the former relationship they are equal. In the latter the husband comes first, but this superordinate/subordinate man/wife relationship applies only sociologically, and only in time, not spiritually nor for eternity.

Until recently commentators have said that the problem was a local one which applied only in the first century, and in the Hellenic communities where Christian church congregations existed. But the so-called "Women's Liberation" movement may focus attention again upon the importance of the teaching.

To the extent that the Women's Liberation movement pretends to be Christian there are two things to say: (a) In Christ's mystic Body there is no difference between the position of a Christian male and a Christian female (Gal.3:27,28). (b) In social, political and economic relationships under a democratic philosophy of government they are equal. Civil rights, politically, socially and economically must be maintained between the sexes on a coordinate basis. Equal pay for equal work, equal right to vote, seek and hold public office, and own and convey property must be maintained in a democratic society. In the home and in the church, however, if both husband and wife are Christian, the Scriptures impose the rule of verse 3. The Christian wife is subject to her husband. If in the late 20th century she recognizes this fact and duly observes it, there is no need to symbolize it by a head covering at church. Indeed we have seen some women who wore their head coverings at church, symbolically to say that they accepted their subordination, only to take them off at home and dominate their husbands and children like matriarchs. Thus the symbol said what the policy and practice denied. Apparently women's liberation of the wrong sort was prevalent in the Corinthian church. Thus Paul says in

Verse 4 - "Every man praying or prophesying, having his head covered, dishonoreth his head."

πᾶς ἀνὴρ προσευχόμενος ἢ προφητεύων κατὰ κεφλαῆς ἔχων καταισχύνει τὴν κεφαλὴν αὐτοῦ.

"Any man who prays or prophesies with his head covered dishonors his head,"
... RSV

πᾶς (nom.sing.masc.of πᾶς, in agreement with ἀνὴρ) 67.

ἀνὴρ (nom.sing.masc.of ἀνὴρ, subject of καταισχύνει) 63.

προσευχόμενος (pres.mid.part.nom.sing.masc.of προσεύχομαι, adjectival, restrictive, predicate position) 544.

ἢ (disjunctive) 465.

προφητεύων (pres.act.part.nom.sing.masc.of προφητεύω, adjectival, restrictive, predicate position) 685.

κατὰ (preposition with the genitive, "down upon") 98.

κεφαλῆς (gen.sing.fem.of κεφαλή, "down upon") 521.

ἔχων (pres.act.part.nom.sing.masc.of ἔχω, adverbial, circumstantial) 82.

καταισχύνει (3d.per.sing.pres.act.ind.of καταισχύνω, present progressive) 2505.

τὴν (acc.sing.fem.of the article in agreement with κεφαλὴν) 9.

κεφαλὴν (acc.sing.fem.of κεφαλή, direct object of καταισχύνει) 521.

αὐτοῦ (gen.sing.masc.of αὐτός, possession) 16.

Translation - "Every man, praying or prophesying with something on his head is bringing shame down upon his head."

Comment: The participles προσευχόμενος and προφητεύων are restrictive adjectives, modifying ἀνὴρ. The participle ἔχων is a circumstantial adverb. Paul is speaking only (restrictive adjectives) of a man who prays or prophesies with something hanging down upon and from his head. When a man is praying or speaking to a Christian congregation with a covering upon his head he is disgracing his head. He is saying in symbol that his position *vis-a-vis* his wife is one of subordination. This is not true. Within the church fellowship he is her superordinate (verse 3). The Jewish man in the synagogue prayed with a veil hanging down from his face, despite his Old Testament teaching that Adam was created first. This no Christian man should do. In Corinth these symbols meant the propagation of a principle. In modern society they do not, at least they do not at present (August 31, 1982). If they ever again come to mean what they meant in Corinth in the first century, Paul's teaching will apply again because the principle of verse 3 has not changed. If society disobeys it, we do so at our social peril. Modern atheistic and/or deistic women's liberation spells the downfall of western civilization because it means the destruction of the Christian home. Only in a Christian home are children taught by their parents the principles of Christian morality. Destroy the home environment where little children learn their first lessons in Bible morality at their mother's knee and we are only one generation away from paganism. Even Lenin, an atheistic Communist, who masterminded the Russian revolution in 1917 was forced to give up women's liberation in Russia to rescue the country. A part of his NEP (New Economic Policy) in 1921 involved the re-establishment of the home as the basic unit of society. Today it is harder to get a divorce in Russia than it is in the United States. Children born and reared in Russia during the 1920's and early 1930's were subject to more parental discipline than many in the United States in the same period. If the collapse of the home continues with its inevitable result in terms of juvenile delinquency women had better put on their veils when they go to church and men had better take them off. The symbols mean nothing and can be disregarded but the principle which they represent must be kept.

The New Testament does not say that male superordination gives the husband the right to became a "male chauvinist pig." *Au contraire cf.* Eph.5:25-27. It does say that in home and church relations, a Christian wife should defer to the judgment of her husband.

The κατὰ κεφαλῆς ἔχων construction is interesting. ἔχων is intransitive. There is no object expressed. κατά literally means "down" and κεφαλῆς is a genitive which serves to accent the person or thing affected - thus, "having (something) down upon his head."

The principle involved in this context is applied, appropriately in reverse in verse 5, with an added observation about the uncovered head of a woman.

Verse 5 - "But every women that prayeth or prophesieth with her head uncovered dishonoreth her head: for that is even all one as if she were shorn."

πᾶσα δὲ γυνὴ προσευχομένη ἢ προφητεύουσα ἀκατακαλύπτῳ τῇ κεφαλῇ καταισχύνει τὴν κεφαλὴν αὐτῆς. ἓν γάρ ἐστιν καὶ τὸ αὐτὸ τῇ ἐξυρημένῃ.

"... but any woman who prays or prophesies with her head unveiled dishonors her head — it is the same as if her head were shaven." ... RSV

πᾶσα (nom.sing.fem.of πᾶς, in agreement with γυνή) 67.

δὲ (adversative conjunction) 11.

γυνή (nom.sing.fem.of γυνή, subject of καταισχύνει) 103.

προσευχομένη (pres.mid.part.nom.sing.fem.of προσεύχομαι, adjectival, restrictive, predicate position in agreement with γυνή) 544.

ἢ (disjunctive) 465.

προφητεύουσα (pres.act.part.nom.sing.fem.of προφητεύω, adjectival, restrictive, predicate position in agreement with γυνή) 685.

#**4201** ἀκατακαλύπτῳ (instru.sing.neut.of ἀκατακάλυπτος, manner).

King James Version

uncovered - 1 Cor.11:5,13.

Revised Standard Version

unveiled - 1 Cor.11:5.
uncovered - 1 Cor.11:13.

Meaning: α privative plus κατακαλύπτω (#4202). Hence, not thoroughly covered. Uncovered. Unveiled - 1 Cor.11:5,13.

τῇ (instru.sing.fem.of the article in agreement with κεφαλῇ) 9.

κεφαλῇ (instru.sing.fem.of κεφαλή, manner) 521.

καταισχύνει (3d.per.sing.pres.act.ind.of καταισχύνω, present progressive) 2505.

τὴν (acc.sing.fem.of the article in agreement with κεφλαὴν) 9.

κεφαλὴν (acc.sing.fem.of κεφαλή, direct object of καταισχύνει) 521.

αὐτῆς (gen.sing.fem.of αὐτός, possession) 16.

ἐν (nom.sing.neut.of εἷς, predicate adjective) 469.

γάρ (causal conjunction) 105.

ἐστιν (3d.per.sing.pres.ind.of εἰμί, static) 86.

καὶ (emphatic conjunction) 14.

τὸ (nom.sing.neut.of the article in agreement with αὐτὸ) 9.

αὐτὸ (nom.sing.neut.of αὐτός, intensive, predicate adjective) 16.

τῇ (instru.sing.fem.of the article in agreement with ἐξυρημένη) 9.

ἐξυρημένη (perf.pass.part.instru.sing.fem.of ξυράω, substantival, likeness and identity) 3556.

Translation - "But every woman praying or prophesying with the head uncovered dishonors her head, because it is in fact the same as though she had been shaved."

Comment: Note that here Paul uses an instrumental of manner construction, ἀκατακαλύπτῳ τῇ κεφαλῇ, instead of the circumstantial participle, κατὰ κεφαλῆς ἔχων as he did in verse 4, to say the same thing.

When a woman prays or prophesies in the chucrh with her head uncovered (the opposite procedure from that of the man in verse 4) she dishonors her head, for two reasons. First she says in symbol that she rejects the idea that she is subordinate to her husband. Yet the divine order was set forth in verse 3. Few proponents of the modern women's liberation movement would accept the divine order. The uncovered head of the woman in the church service said to the Corinthian audience that she was asserting her authority, which her husband would be surrendering under the opposite circumstances. But there was another reason why she should pray and prophesy only with her head covered. To do otherwise suggested the same as if she had her head shorn - ἐν γάρ ἐστιν καὶ τὸ αὐτὸ τῇ ἐξυρημένη - "Because it (the uncovered head) is one and the same thing as having been shorn." The participle is an instrumental of likeness or identity.

The female head bereft of her long tresses adverstized her profession as a prostitute. This was true in Corinth in the first century. It is not true in modern American society. If she left off her head covering, not as her protest against the divine order in the church and in the home, but as a symbol of her liberty, as a coordinate with all other members of the Body of Christ, the symbolism of her uncovered head would be likely to be misinterpreted as an advertisement that she was a courtesan. That this does not apply in the 20th century is obvious. The short hair-cut today does not identify the women with the underworld of illicit sex. Nor does the lack of a hat at the church service carry this suggestion. In the interest of good taste, however, it would seem proper to suggest that the hair style be such, for both sexes, as to indicate whether the individual involved is male or female. In fact, any hair style or mode of dress, either for men or women that serves to call undue attention to oneself is considered boorish. Christian humility will dictate that we "be not the first by whom the new is tried, nor yet the last to lay the old aside." If the Christian is conspicuous let it be because of his dedication to the will of the Holy Spirit and in the exercise of his gifts, not in the way he dresses or wears his hair.

Verse 6 - "For if the woman be not covered, let her also be shorn: but if it be a shame for a woman to be shorn or shaven, let her be covered."

εἰ γὰρ οὐ κατακαλύπτεται γυνή, καὶ κειράσθω. εἰ δὲ αἰσχρὸν γυναικὶ τὸ κείρασθαι ἢ ξυρᾶσθαι, κατακαλθπτέσθω.

"For if a woman will not veil herself, then she should cut off her hair; but if it is disgraceful for a woman to be shorn or shaven, let her wear a veil." . . . *RSV*

εἰ (conditional particle in a first-class condition) 337.
γὰρ (inferential conjunction) 105.
οὐ (negative conjunction with the indicative) 130.

#**4202** κατακαλύπτεται (3d.per.sing.pres.mid.ind.of κατακαλύπτω, first-class condition).

　　　King James Version

be covered - 1 Cor.11:6,6.
cover - 1 Cor.11:7.

　　　Revised Standard Version

veil herself - 1 Cor.11:6a.
wear a veil - 1 Cor.11:6b.
cover - 1 Cor.11:7.

Meaning: A combination of κατά (#98) and καλύπτω (#753). Hence, to cover "down." To cover by wearing a veil that hangs down around the head - 1 Cor.11:6,6,7.

γυνὴ (nom.sing.fem.of γυνή, subject of κατακαλύπτεται) 103.

καὶ (emphatic conjunction) 14.
κειράσθω (3d.per.sing.1st aor.mid.impv.of κείρω, command) 3176.
εἰ (conditional particle in an elliptical first-class condition) 337.
δὲ (adversative conjunction) 11.

#4203 αἰσχρὸν (nom.sing.neut.of αἰσχρός, predicate adjective).

King James Version

filthy - Titus 1:11.
a shame - 1 Cor.11:6; 14:35; Eph.5:12.

Revised Standard Version

disgraceful - 1 Cor.11:6.
shameful - 1 Cor.14:35.
shame - Eph.5:12.
base - Titus 1:11.

Meaning: Cf. αἶσχος - baseness, disgrace. Hence, shameful, disgraceful, base, low. *Cf.* αἰσχροκερδής (#4739), αἰσχροκερδῶς (#5216), αἰσχρολογία (#4630), αἰσχρότης (#4507). To cut a woman's hair - 1 Cor.11:6; to speak at church - 1 Cor.14:35; to speak of sinful things - Eph.5:12; to take money - Titus 1:11.

γυναικὶ (dat.sing.fem.of γυνή, personal disadvantage) 103.
τὸ (nom.sing.neut.of the article in agreement with κείρασθαι) 9.
κείρασθαι (1st.aor.pass.inf.of κείρω, noun use, subject of ἐστιν understood) 3176.
ἢ (disjunctive) 465.
ξυρᾶσθαι (1st.aor.pass.inf.of ξυράω, noun use, subject of ἐστιν understood) 3556.
κατακαλυπτέσθω (3d.per.sing.pres.pass.impv.of κατακαλύπτω, command) 4202.

Translation - "So if a woman will not wear a veil let her in fact cut her hair. But since it is disgraceful for a woman to have her hair cut or her head shaved, let her be covered with a veil."

Comment: The first εἰ conditional clause assumes as true what may be untrue. Paul is not saying that he is certain that some of the Corinthian Christian women would refuse to wear a veil, but his command in the apodosis is certain. *If* she refuses to wear a veil, then his order is that she cut her hair. Why? Because her refusal to wear a veil, however sincere and for whatever pure motive in her own mind, will be misinterpreted. Others will suppose that her refusal to wear a veil is her protest to the rule of verse 3. She may in fact be symbolizing her equality with men in the Body of Christ, but that will not be generally known. So she may as well come to church with her hair cut short. In either case she will be looked upon as a woman of the street.

The second εἰ clause is a first-class condition with no doubt about the premise.

Prostitutes in Corinth advertized their services either by wearing their hair short or by shaving their heads. Public opinion would therefore leap to an unwarranted conclusion if a Christian woman appeared in church without her veil. Her motive no doubt would be pure. She, like the Greek pagan women, would be saying in symbol that she was equal to all others, although her ground for equality with men would be her position as a member of the Body of Christ, while theirs was their philosophy of democracy. But the public would not understand this. Thus Paul orders her to avoid the appearance of evil (1 Thess.5:22) and wear her veil, thus to symbolize that as a Christian woman she was subject to her husband.

Verse 7 - "For a man indeed ought not to cover his head, forasmuch as he is the image and glory of God: but the woman is the glory of the man."

ἀνὴρ μὲν γὰρ οὐκ ὀφείλει κατακαλύπτεσθαι τὴν κεφαλήν, εἰκὼν καὶ δόξα θεοῦ ὑπάρχων. ἡ γυνὴ δὲ δόξα ἀνδρός ἐστιν.

"For a man ought not to cover his head, since he is the image and glory of God; but woman is the glory of man." . . . *RSV*

ἀνὴρ (nom.sing.masc.of ἀνήρ, subject of ὀφείλει) 63.
μὲν (particle of affirmation) 300.
γὰρ (adversative conjunction) 105.
οὐκ (negative conjunction with the indicative) 130.
ὀφείλει (3d.per.sing.pres.act.ind.of ὀφείλω, static) 1277.
κατακαλύπτεσθαι (pres.mid.inf.of κατακαλύπτω, epexegetical) 4202.
τὴν (acc.sing.fem.of the article in agreement with κεφαλήν) 9.
κεφαλήν (acc.sing.fem.of κεφαλή, direct object of κατακαλύπτεσθαι) 521.
εἰκὼν (nom.sing.fem.of εἰκών, predicate nominative) 1421.
καὶ (adjunctive conjunction joining nouns) 14.
δόξα (nom.sing.fem.of δόξα, predicate nominative) 361.
θεοῦ (gen.sing.masc.of θεός, description) 124.
ὑπάρχων (pres.act.part.nom.sing.masc.of ὑπάρχω, adjectival, restrictive, predicate position, in agreement with ἀνὴρ) 1303.
ἡ (nom.sing.fem.of the article in agreement with γυνὴ) 9.
γυνὴ (nom.sing.fem.of γυνή, subject of ἐστιν) 103.
δὲ (adversative conjunction) 11.
δόξα (nom.sing.fem.of δόξα, predicate nominative) 361.
ἀνδρός (gen.sing.masc.of ἀνήρ, description) 63.
ἐστιν (3d.per.sing.pres.ind.of εἰμί, static) 86.

Translation - "But in fact the man who bears the image and glory of God ought not to cover his head. But the woman is man's glory."

Comment: The μὲν . . . δὲ sequence is common, *Cf.*#300. μεν is emphatically affirmative and δὲ is emphatically adversative. γὰρ depends for its force on the argument of verses 3-6. The basic principle is in verse 3. The practical results of its policy follow in verse 4-6, both for Christian men and women. ὑπάρκων can be construed either as an adjective modifying ἀνήρ as I have done, or as a causal adverb. *Because* the man who possesses the image and glory of God has that honor, for the reason that is stated in verse 8, he ought not to cover his head. His position of superordination applies only in the human realm. In Christ all are coordinate, just as God, Christ and the believer are coordinate in the spiritual realm. It is because of our Lord's incarnation, by which He emptied Himself and became a man (Phil.2:6-8) that in the human realm He is subordinate to God the Father. This arrangement brings glory to God if it is observed, both in practice and in symbol, although the practice is more important than the symbol. That is why the presence or absence of a head covering in a culture that does not recognize the symbol, is not significant. In Corinth the male head, uncovered in church, symbolized the headship of the husband over his wife, but not his dictatorship (Eph.5:25-27). In the same way the women, in proper subjection to her husband, bring glory both to him and to God. In more recent cultures both men and women bring glory to God by recognizing the principle and living their lives in conformity with it. Though, even in modern society, some Christian fellowships require women to cover their heads at church, most do not. Thus the woman with a distinctive head cover (not a hat) may attract unwarranted attention to herself, attention which may glorify her, rather than either God or her husband. And a man who sat in a Christian church service with his hat on would be sure to be noticed and branded as some kind of fanatic.

Lest Paul be accused of teaching male dominance in an extreme form, he hastens to show the interdependence of man and woman in verses 11-12. In verses 8-10 he explains the reason for the order set forth in verse 3.

Verse 8 - "For the man is not of the woman; but the woman of the man."

οὐ γάρ ἐστιν ἀνὴρ ἐκ γυναικός, ἀλλὰ γυνὴ ἐξ ἀνδρός.

"(For man was not made from woman, but woman from man." . . . *RSV*

οὐ (negative conjunction with the indicative) 130.
γάρ (causal conjunction) 105.
ἐστιν (3d.per.sing.pres.ind.of εἰμί, static) 86.
ἀνὴρ (nom.sing.masc.of ἀνήρ, subject of ἐστιν) 63.
ἐκ (preposition with the ablative of source) 19.
γυναικός (abl.sing.fem.of γυνή, source) 103.
ἀλλὰ (alternative conjunction) 342.
γυνὴ (nom.sing.fem.of γυνή subject of ἐστιν understood) 103.
ἐξ (preposition with the ablative of source) 19.
ἀνδρός (abl.sing.masc.of ἀνήρ, source) 63.

Translation - "Because man was not created from woman, but woman from man."

Comment: ἐκ γυναικός and ἐξ ἀνδρός are ablatives of source. Eve was not the source of Adam, but she came from Adam (Gen.2:21-25). Modern skeptics sneer at the Adam and Eve story, but Paul believed it and he uses it to reinforce the principle of verse 3. Darwinists, in the event that they have the mental ability to enjoy a modicum of consistency, will reject the notion that the male is dominant in society. They may even teach that the female is dominant, since only the fittest survive to pass the evolutionary process on to the next generation! It is not difficult to see the results in society of the evolutionary hypothesis, which in the thinking of the unsaved is no longer in the realm of the hypothetical. Only the Bible believer who accepts at face value the Adam and Eve story will accept Paul's analysis which is based upon it. Thus the role of women as homemakers, producers and teachers of the next generation is repudiated in some extreme circles and played down in others. Yet such women must have sex, and resort either to lesbianism or to illicit heterosexuality and in the event of pregnancy to abortion of the unwanted fetus. Thus marriage as a Christian institution which God established in the Garden of Eden is destroyed and the concept of the Christian home, so essential to social viability, is repudiated.

This does not mean that all Christian women who are forced by economics to work outside the home, have abandoned their duties as homemakers and mothers. Many at great sacrifice and some danger to their health play the double role. But many others pursue a "career" which in some cases is only an evidence of their personal insecurity, and leave their unwanted children to shift for themselves, while sociologists and psychiatrists deplore and seek to explain the reasons for juvenile delinquency and crime in the streets.

So far from putting down women as inferior creatures (could anything that God created be inferior?) the Bible glorifies them and has assigned to them a function without which population growth would be negative and the human race would disappear from the face of the earth and from God's historical scenario. Furthermore upon her shoulders rests the responsibility and in her heart is found the motivation for caring for her children when they are helpless and teaching them the precepts of Biblical morality without which society tends to dig its own grave and write it own dismal epitaph. The Christian woman who understands her role as set forth in Scripture will never feel inferior. Nothing and no one created by God is inferior.

Verse 9 - "Neither was the man created for the woman; but the woman for the man."

καὶ γὰρ οὐκ ἐκτίσθη ἀνὴρ διὰ τὴν γυναῖκα, ἀλλὰ γυνὴ διὰ τὸν ἄνδρα.

"Neither was man created for woman, but woman for man)." . . . RSV

καὶ (emphatic conjunction) 14.

γὰρ (causal conjunction) 105.

οὐκ (negative conjunction with the indicative) 130.

ἐκτίσθη (3d.per.sing.aor.pass.ind.of κτίζω, constative) 1284.

ἀνὴρ (nom.sing.masc.of ἀνήρ, subject of ἐκτίσθη) 63.

διὰ (preposition with the accusative, cause) 118.

τὴν (acc.sing.fem.of the article in agreement with γυναῖκα) 9.

γυναῖκα (acc.sing.fem.of γυνή, cause) 103.

διὰ (preposition with the accusative of cause) 118.

τὸν (acc.sing.masc.of the article in agreement with ἄνδρα) 9.

ἄνδρα (acc.sing.masc.of ἀνήρ, cause) 63.

Translation - "Because in fact man was not created because of the woman, but woman because of the man."

Comment: διά with the accusative is a causal construction. That Adam was not created because of Eve is obvious. Adam was created first. Adam's creation was cause; Eve's result. Result always follows cause. That Eve was created in order to meet a need for Adam is clear from Gen.2:18. Had there been no creation of Eve there would have been no human race and God's eternal plan of redemption, as long conceived before the creation as God Himself (!) could not have been effected. Thus Paul reinforces his argument about the priority of man over woman, a priority in the economy of God, to be symbolized at the Corinthian church service by a bareheaded man and a veiled woman.

God the Father, God the Son and God the Holy Spirit took counsel with themselves and said, "Let us make man in our image, after our likeness" (Gen.1:26). And so they did. In what sense is man created in the image of God? Not in the physical sense, because God never had a physical body until Mary had a baby. It is more correct to say that God in incarnation was made in the image of man, not man in the image of God, when we are speaking of the physical. To say that God had a human body before the incarnation is to indulge the error of anthropomorphism which is at the bottom of the Mormon heresy. But God created a man whom He called Adam and endowed him with procreative capacity in order that he might father the human race, every member of which is made "in the image of God." Thus man is unique among the animals in that he has intellectual powers of reason by which he can arrive at some certitude and he also has an inner sense of the difference between right and wrong. The definition of right and wrong may differ in different cultures in which societal pressures have dictated the one or the other. In some native cultures it is considered sinful for a man to have only one wife, just as in others it is considered sinful if he has more than one. But both cultures agree that there is a difference between right and wrong. Man is not by nature amoral. The animals are. Thus man is made "in the image of God" and all of Adam's race, the sons and daughters of Adam and Eve have inherited this same image. That is why man possesses the image and glory of God (verse 7).

There would have been no human race - only Adam, the prototype, had God not created Eve, and the entire plan of God for the redeemed human race would have failed.

Eve was not Adam's slave. She was his eager sex partner, destined to become the mother of his children. "Her desire was unto her husband" (Gen.3:16) and it was God's order that he should rule over her. The women in the Corinthian church are asked to recognize this fact by what they wore on their head.

Verse 10 - "For this cause ought the women to have power on her head because of the angels."

διὰ τοῦτο ὀφείλει ἡ γυνὴ ἐξουσίαν ἔχειν ἐπὶ τῆς κεφαλῆς διὰ τοὺς ἀγγέλους.

"That is why a woman ought to have a veil on her head, because of the angels."

. . . *RSV*

διὰ (preposition with the accusative, cause) 118.

τοῦτο (acc.sing.neut.of οὗτος, cause) 93.

ὀφείλει (3d.per.sing.pres.act.ind.of ὀφείλω, static) 1277.

ἡ (nom.sing.fem.of the article in agreement with γυνὴ) 9.

γυνὴ (nom.sing.fem.of γυνή, subject of ὀφείλει) 103.

ἐξουσίαν (acc.sing.fem.of ἐξουσία, direct object of ἔχειν) 707.

ἔχειν (pres.act.inf.of ἔχω, epexegetical) 82.

ἐπὶ (preposition with the genitive, metaphorical "over") 47.

τῆς (gen.sing.fem.of the article in agreement with κεφαλῆς) 9.

κεφαλῆς (gen.sing.fem.of κεφαλή, metaphorical "over") 521.

διὰ (preposition with the accusative, cause) 118.

τοὺς (acc.pl.masc.of the article in agreement with ἀγγέλους) 9.

ἀγγέλους (acc.pl.masc.of ἄγγελος, cause) 96.

Translation - *"This is why the woman ought to have authority over what she wears on her head, because of the messengers."*

Comment: A variant reading has κάλυμμα (#4291) instead of ἐξουσίαν (#707). Another reads κάλυμμα καὶ ἐξουσίαν, but the overwhelming manuscript authority reads ἐξουσίαν. It is a difficult passage. On its face it says that a woman ought to have authority over her head, *i.e.* with reference to what she wears upon it, if anything. "The angels" (τοὺς ἀγγέλους) can refer to heavenly angels who attend the saints (Mt.18:10; Ps.91:11,12; Heb.1:13,14), but note #96 and the fact that in seven places in the New Testament it refers to human messengers. Goodspeed opts for heavenly angels and takes liberties with the text to translate, "That is why she ought to wear upon her head something to symbolize her subjection, out of respect to the angels, *if to nobody else.*"

The gloss κάλυμμα, which occurs only in "versional and patristic witnesses" (Metzger, *A Textual Commentary on the Greek New Testament*, 562) replaces the difficult ἐξουσίαν and would indicate that the passage means that the woman should wear upon her head a veil to symbolize her subjection to the superior authority of her husband, and to the Lord who ordained in creation that it should be so. However Paul is not teaching that women are inferior to men. Mature women who are committed to obedience to the Word of God and are superior in intellect to their husbands, will recognize the fact, and, because of their spiritual maturity will not make an issue out of it. Less mature women, who, though regenerate have not grown in grace, may recognize the fact and resent their subordinate position. They are the ones who create the trouble, both in the home and in the church and they may reap the evil harvest of their disobedience in the tragic failure in the lives of their children.

It is possible that Paul is using τοὺς ἀγγέλους here to refer to messengers from other Christian churches who are likely to visit in Corinth and who will note with benefit the behavior of the Corinthian women.

Verse 11 - *"Nevertheless, neither is the man without the woman, neither the woman without the man, in the Lord."*

πλὴν οὔτε γυνὴ χωρὶς ἀνδρὸς οὔτε ἀνὴρ χωρὶς γυναικὸς ἐν κυρίῳ.

"(Nevertheless, in the Lord woman is not independent of man nor man or woman;" . . . RSV

πλὴν (adversative conjunction) 944.
οὔτε (negative copulative conjunction) 598.
γυνὴ (nom.sing.fem.of γυνή, subject of the verb understood) 103.
χωρὶς (preposition with the ablative, separation) 1077.
ἀνδρὸς (abl.sing.masc.of ἀνήρ, separation) 63.
οὔτε (negative copulative conjunction) 598.
ἀνὴρ (nom.sing.masc.of ἀνήρ, subject of verb understood) 63.
χωρὶς (preposition with the ablative, separation) 1077.
γυνικὸς (abl.sing.fem.of γυνή, separation) 103.
ἐν (preposition with the locative of sphere) 80.
κυρίῳ (loc.sing.masc.of κύριος, sphere) 97.

Translation - "However neither is a woman independent of a man, nor a man independent of a woman in the Lord."

Comment: In Christ Jesus, where every believer is a member of His Body, neither sex can claim superiority or independent status from the other. The superordination of man over woman is wholly a sociological arrangement, to be observed only in time, not in eternity. Women have no reason to feel discrimination because of this passage. In the spiritual realm all are alike in Christ.

In verse 12 the additional point is made that no woman can declare herself independent of man, for had it not been for Adam and one of his descendants, her father, she would not exist. Nor can a man declare himself independent of women, for without Eve and one of her daughters, his mother, he too would not exist.

Verse 12 - "For as the woman is of the man, even so is the man also by the woman: but all things of God."

ὥσπερ γὰρ ἡ γυνὴ ἐκ τοῦ ἀνδρός, οὕτως καὶ ὁ ανὴρ διὰ τῆς γυναικός, τὰ δὲ πάντα ἐκ τοῦ θεοῦ.

"for as woman was made from man, so man is now born of woman. And all things are from God.)" . . . RSV

ὥσπερ (intensive comparative particle) 560.
γὰρ (causal conjunction) 105.
ἡ (nom.sing.fem.of the article in agreement with γυνή) 9.
γυνὴ (nom.sing.fem.of γυνή, subject of ἐστιν understood) 103.
ἐκ (preposition with the ablative of source) 19.
τοῦ (abl.sing.masc.of the article in agreement with ἀνδρός) 9.
οὕτως (demonstrative adverb) 74.
καὶ (adjunctive conjunction joining clauses) 14.

ὁ (nom.sing.masc.of the article in agreement with ἀνὴρ) 9.

ἀνὴρ (nom.sing.masc.of ἀνήρ, subject of ἐστιν understood) 63.

διὰ (preposition with the ablative, intermediate agent) 118.

τῆς (abl.sing.fem.of the article in agreement with γυναικός) 9.

γυναικός (abl.sing.fem.of γυνή, intermediate agent) 103.

τὰ (nom.pl.neut.of the article in agreement with πάντα) 9.

δὲ (adversative conjunction) 11.

πάντα (nom.pl.neut.of πᾶς, subject of ἐστιν understood) 67.

ἐκ (preposition with the ablative of source) 19.

τοῦ (abl.sing.masc.of the article in agreement with θεοῦ) 9.

θεοῦ (abl.sing.masc.of θεός, source) 124.

Translation - "*Therefore just as the woman has her source in the man, in the same way also the man exists through the agency of the woman. But everything is from God.*"

Comment: περ in ὥσπερ intensifies the comparison. We have source and agency both expressed by the ablative. Woman originally came from Adam's rib. And in the same way every man was born of a woman. But both men and women, and all else beside have their source in God.

With verses 12 and 13 Paul elevates the woman to her rightful place of equality with man before God, which again spotlights the point that her subjection to her husband is only temporary and for sociological reasons.

Paul seems to have made his point, but as he did in Chapter 7 with reference to sex, he finds it necessary to labor the point for four more verses.

Verse 13 - "*Judge in yourselves: is it comely that a woman pray unto God uncovered?*"

ἐν ὑμῖν αὐτοῖς κρίνατε. πρέπον ἐστὶν γυναῖκα ἀκατακάλυπτον τῷ θεῷ προσεύχεσθαι;

"*Judge for yourselves; is it proper for a woman to pray to God with her head uncovered?*" . . . RSV

ἐν (preposition with the locative, with plural pronouns) 80.

ὑμῖν (loc.pl.masc.of σύ, place) 104.

αὐτοῖς (loc.pl.masc.of αὐτός, intensive) 16.

κρίνατε (2d.per.pl.aor.act.impv.of κρίνω, command) 531.

πρέπον (pres.act.part.nom.sing.neut.of πρέπω, adjectival, predicate adjective) 321.

ἐστὶν (3d.per.sing.pres.ind.of εἰμί, direct question) 86.

γυναῖκα (acc.sing.fem.of γυνή, general reference) 103.

ἀκατακάλυπτον (acc.sing.neut.of ἀκατακάλυπτος, adverbial accusative) 4201.

τῷ (dat.sing.masc.of the article in agreement with θεῷ) 9.

θεῷ (dat.sing.masc.of θεός, indirect object of προσεύχεσθαι) 124.

προσεύχεσθαι (pres.mid.inf.of προσεύχομαι, noun use, subject of ἐστιν) 544.

Translation - "Think it over for yourselves. Is it proper for a woman to be praying to God without a veil?"

Comment: αὐτοῖς in the predicate position is intensive. Note the participial predicate adjective in πρέπον. Cf. Mt.3:15. Paul has raised the question and asks the Corinthians to discuss it among themselves and come to a conclusion. He supports his own implied position that it would be highly improper in verses 14 and 15. τῷ θεῷ is really superfluous, but is added for emphasis.

Paul's question, asked of the Corinthians, who were products of that culture, expects "No" for an answer. For if the woman prayed without a veil her act would be construed, either as the protest of the pagan Greeks in favor of democracy for women or as a protest of a Christian that she opposed the divine order set forth in verse 3. The context says nothing about the length of her hair. We assume that she was neither shaved nor shorn - only praying with bowed head without a veil. Verse 6 seems to make it clear that the covering in this context is not to be interpreted as the long hair of the woman. To say that if she has no veil she should cut off her long hair, but that if that is unacceptable she should keep her long hair and wear a veil, makes no sense if the veil and her long hair are the same thing.

Verse 14 - "Doth not even nature itself teach you, that, if a man have long hair, it is a shame unto him?"

οὐδὲ ἡ φύσις αὐτὴ διδάσκει ὑμᾶς ὅτι ἀνὴρ μὲν ἐὰν κομᾷ ἀτιμία αὐτῷ ἐστιν,

"Does not nature itself teach you that for a man to wear long hair is degrading to him," . . . RSV

οὐδὲ (disjunctive particle) 452.
ἡ (nom.sing.fem.of the article in agreement with φύσις) 9.
φύσις (nom.sing.fem.of φύσις, subject of διδάσκει) 3811.
αὐτὴ (nom.sing.fem.of αὐτός, intensive, predicate position) 16.
διδάσκει (3d.per.sing.pres.act.ind.of διδάσκω, present progressive retroactive) 403.
ὑμᾶς (acc.pl.masc.of σύ, direct object of διδάσκει) 104.
ὅτι (conjunction introducing an object clause in indirect discourse) 211.
ἀνὴρ (nom.sing.masc.of ἀνήρ, subject of κομᾷ) 63.
μὲν (particle of affirmation) 300.
ἐὰν (conditional particle with the subjunctive in a third-class condition) 363.

#4204 κομᾷ (3d.per.sing.pres.act.subj.of κομάω, third-class condition).

King James Version

have long hair - 1 Cor.11:14.

Revised Standard Version

wear long hair - 1 Cor.11:14.

has long hair - 1 Cor.11:15.

Meaning: Cf. κόμη (#4205). Hence, the let the hair grow; to have long hair - 1 Cor.11:14,15.

ἀτιμία (nom.sing.fem.of ἀτιμία, predicate nominative) 3808.
αὐτῷ (dat.sing.masc.of αὐτός, personal disadvantage) 16.
ἐστιν (3d.per.sing.pres.ind.of εἰμί, aoristic) 86.

Translation - "Does not even nature itself teach us that if a man wears long hair it is degrading to him?"

Comment: μὲν here belongs to the μὲν . . . δὲ sequence with verse 15. αὐτή in the predicate position is intensive. The object clause in indirect discourse is a third-class condition with ἐὰν and the subjunctive κομᾷ in the protasis and the present indicative in the apodosis. "If a man wears his hair long (Paul had some doubt that he would, but if he did) it is a disgrace to him."

Why should this be true? The answer lies in social psychology. Paul means that if a man wears his hair as a woman normally does, he will be ashamed, since he will appear effeminate. God in creation made Adam to be manly, not effeminate, and a normal man will not wish to appear in any style of dress or coiffure which appears feminine. On the contrary he will wish it apparent that he is a man.

The late 20th century fad of long hair for young men is fast fading among those who are normal. Abnormal types, caught up in the drug culture, may persist and pay the social price as they advertize their abnormality. We may not soon go back to the crew cut but men's hair styles are definitely such as to distinguish them from those of women. The argument that 18th century men wore long hair misses the point. They did indeed wear their hair longer than early 20th century man, but there was a distinct difference between their coiffure and that of their female contemporaries. Hence they were not ashamed. Male hair styles may differ from others from century to century, but all normal hair styles in whatever century differ from female hair styles in the same century.

The same is true of skirts. Scotch gentlemen wear kilts, but there is never any difficulty in distinguishing a Scotchman from his wife.

Paul's protest stands since what he really means to say is that nature demands that men look masculine and that women look feminine. Nature teaches us that a man who is a "sissy" should be ashamed. If he lacks embarrassment, a lack which proves the point against him, he is sure to merit only pity or contempt in the eyes of normal people.

Male homosexuals who are aware of the contempt which society naturally feels toward their type often make extra effort to appear *macho* in coiffure and dress style and with verbal accounts of their prowess as football players or prize fighters.

The same natural law that makes a man ashamed of a feminine coiffure makes the woman proud of it.

Verse 15 - "But if a woman have long hair, it is a glory to her: for her hair is given her for a covering."

γυνὴ δὲ ἐὰν κομᾷ δόξα αὐτῇ ἐστιν; ὅτι ἡ κόμη ἀντὶ περιβολαίου δέδοται (αὐτῇ)."

". . . but if a woman has long hair, it is her pride? For her hair is given to her for a covering." . . . RSV

γυνὴ (nom.sing.fem.of γυνή, subject of κομᾷ) 103.
δὲ (adversative conjunction) 11.
ἐὰν (conditional particle with the subjunctive in a third-class condition) 363.
κομᾷ (3d.per.sing.pres.act.subj.of κομάω, third-class condition) 4204.
δόξα (nom.sing.fem.of δόξα, predicate nominative) 361.
αὐτῇ (dat.sing.fem.of αὐτός, personal advantage) 16.
ἐστιν (3d.per.sing.pres.ind.of εἰμί, aoristic) 86.
ὅτι (conjunction introducing a subordinate causal clause) 211.
ἡ (nom.sing.fem.of the article in agreement with κόμη) 9.

#4205 κόμη (nom.sing.fem.of κόμη, subject of δέδοται).

King James Version

hair - 1 Cor.11:15.

Revised Standard Version

hair - 1 Cor.11:15.

Meaning: Cf. κομάω (#4204). Hair. It differs from θρίξ (#261), which is the term for hair in the anatomical sense. κόμη means hirsute adornment. Hair as a bodily adornment, an aid to beauty. There is nothing in the word itself to suggest length. With reference to feminine hair in 1 Cor.11:15.

ἀντὶ (preposition with the genitive - "instead of") 237.

#4206 περιβολαίου (gen.sing.neut.of περιβόλαιον, "instead of").

King James Version

covering - 1 Cor.11:15.
vesture - Heb.1:12.

Revised Standard Version

covering - 1 Cor.11:15.
mantle - Heb.1:12.

Meaning: Cf. περιβάλλω (#631) from περί (#173) and βάλλω (#299). Hence, something to wrap around one's person. A synonym for ἱμάτιον in the synonymous parallelism of Heb.1:11,12, which is quoted from Ps.102:26. A woman's hair if allowed to grow would be long enough to provide a "wrap around" covering for her body, which otherwise might be naked. Thus the figure speaks of the becoming modesty of the woman - 1 Cor.11:15.

δέδοται (3d.per.sing.perf.pass.ind.of δίδωμι, intensive) 362.
(αὐτῇ) (dat.sing.fem.of αὐτός, indirect object of δέδοται) 16.

Translation - "But if a woman has long hair it is a glory to her; because the hair has been given to her instead of a robe."

Comment: The μὲν . . . δὲ sequence is completed here. That which is true of men in verse 14 is countered by the opposite in verse 15. Men are ashamed of long hair. Women would be ashamed without it. The third-class condition indicates some doubt in Paul's mind that some Corinthian women would wear long hair, but if they did it would contribute to their feminine modesty and would therefore be a source of pride. Why? The ὅτι clause is causal. God gave long hair to women instead of clothing. We get a picture of Eve in the Garden of Eden before she transgressed His commandment. Her long tresses, luxuriant enough to serve as a garment to cover her body and maintain a proper modesty, only enhanced her femininity. She was more desireable for being elusive.

Paul is not speaking here of the veil which he had mentioned before in this chapter. The word is not κατακαλύπτος but περιβόλαιον (#4206). The KJV rendering "her hair is given her for a covering" is misleading. Paul is not saying that long hair is a substitute for the veil which women wore when they prayed and/or prophesied. Her hair glorifies her because it could serve as a robe to cover her entire body, and thus enhance her feminine charms.

That the Apostle expected some of the Corinthians to argue the point is clear from the abrupt way in which he closes the discussion in

Verse 16 - "But if any man seem to contentious, we have no such custom, neither the churches of God."

Εἰ δέ τις δοκεῖ φιλόνεικος εἶναι, ἡμεῖς τοιαύτην συνήθειαν οὐκ ἔχομεν, οὐδὲ αἱ ἐκκλησίαι τοῦ θεοῦ.

"If any one is disposed to be contentious, we recognize no other practice, nor do the churches of God." . . . RSV

Εἰ (conditional particle in a first-class condition) 337.
δὲ (adversative conjunction) 11.
τις (nom.sing.masc.of τις, indefinite pronoun, subject of δοκεῖ) 486.
δοκεῖ (3d.per.sing.pres.act.ind.of δοκέω, aoristic) 287.

#4207 φιλόνεικος (nom.sing.masc.of φιλόνεικος, predicate adjective).

King James Version

contentious - 1 Cor.11:16.

Revised Standard Version

contentious - 1 Cor.11:16.

Meaning: A combination of φίλος (#932) and νεῖκος - "strife." Hence, fond of strife; disposed to be contentious; controversial; argumentative. With reference to hair styles for Christians - 1 Cor.11:16.

εἶναι (pres.inf.of εἰμί, epexegetical) 86.
ἡμεῖς (nom.pl.masc.of ἐγώ, subject of ἔχομεν) 123.
τοιαύτην (acc.sing.fem.of τοιοῦτος, in agreement with συνήθειαν) 785.
συνήθειαν (acc.sing.fem.of συνήθεια, direct object of ἔχομεν) 2843.
οὐκ (negative particle with the indicative) 130.
ἔχομεν (1st.per.pl.pres.act.ind.of ἔχω, customary) 82.
οὐδὲ (disjunctive particle) 452.
αἱ (nom.pl.fem.of the article in agreement with ἐκκλησίαι) 9.
ἐκκλησίαι (nom.pl.fem.of ἐκκλησία, subject of ἔχομεν) 1204.
τοῦ (gen.sing.masc.of the article in agreement with θεοῦ) 9.
θεοῦ (gen.sing.masc.of θεός, possession) 124.

Translation - "But if anyone appears to be disposed to argue about it, we have no other practice, nor do the churches of God."

Comment: The assumption in the protasis may or may not be true. Paul was not certain - "If anyone is disposed to argue the point . . . κ.τ.λ." Paul had taught all of the churches which he had established to follow the same rule which he laid down for the Corinthians. In this somewhat arbitrary manner he closes the discussion.

In the modern church, where the sociological issue is not long or short hair or the presence or absence of a veil, the fundamental principle is still present. In family and church life, wives are to be subject to their husbands. Any undue assertion of female authority in in poor taste. But this is not to say that ἐν Χριστῷ there is any subordination of any member of the Body of Christ to any other. Attitudes and the behavior which result from them, both in men and women, are the important thing. In a modern audience whether the woman's hair is long or short, or whether she does or does not wear a hat or other head covering has nothing to do with the assertion or the lack of it of her civil rights. But nature has always taught and still does teach us that men who wear their hair like a woman are suffering some sort of aberration.

Abuses at the Lord's Supper

(1 Corinthians 11:17-22)

Verse 17 - "Now in this that I declare unto you I praise you not, that ye come together not for the better, but for the worse."

Τοῦτο δὲ παραγγέλλων οὐκ ἐπαινῶ ὅτι οὐκ εἰς τὸ κρεῖσσον ἀλλὰ εἰς τὸ ἧσσον συνέρχεσθε.

"But in the following instructions I do not commend you, because when you

come together it is not for the better but for the worse."

Τοῦτο (acc.sing.neut.of οὗτος, direct object of παραγγέλλων) 93.

δὲ (adversative conjunction) 11.

παραγγέλλων (pres.act.part.nom.sing.masc.of παραγγέλλω, adverbial, temporal) 855.

    οὐκ (negative particle with the indicative) 130.

    ἐπαινῶ (1st.per.sing.pres.act.ind.of ἐπαινέω, aoristic) 2568.

    ὅτι (conjunction introducing a subordinate causal clause) 211.

    οὐκ (negative conjunction with the indicative) 130.

    εἰς (preposition with the accusative, result) 140.

    τὸ (acc.sing.neut.of the article in agreement with κρεῖσσον) 9.

    κρεῖσσον (acc.sing.neut.of κρείσσων, result) 4157.

    ἀλλὰ (alternative conjunction) 342.

    εἰς (preposition with the accusative, result) 140.

    τὸ (acc.sing.neut.of the article in agreement with ἧσσον) 9.

#4208 ἧσσον (acc.sing.neut.of ἥττων, result).

    King James Version

less - 2 Cor.12:15.
worse - 1 Cor.11;17.

    Revised Standard Version

less - 2 Cor.12:15.
worse - 1 Cor.11:17.

Meaning: An adjective - inferior. In the neuter, used adverbially. In 2 Cor.12:15 opposed to περισσοτέρως and in a result construction, εἰς τὸ ἧσσον - "with the result that you are worse" where it is opposed to τὸ κρεῖσσον - 1 Cor.11:17.

συνέρχεσθε (2d.per.pl.pres.mid.ind.of συνέρχομαι, present progressive retroactive) 78.

Translation - "*But in what I am about to say I am not heaping praise upon you, because you have been coming together not to improve but to become worse.*"

Comment: The participle παραγγέλλων is a temporal adverb. It introduces Paul's next section in which he points to bad practices in the observance of the Lord's Supper. *Cf. contra,* in 1 Cor.11:2, where he only means that he praises them for observing the ordinance, not for the manner in which they do so. Their observances which they had been holding regularly (present progressive retroactive tense in συνέρχεσθε) were doing more harm than good. It is not likely that εἰς τὸ κρεῖσσον and εἰς τὸ ἧσσον are purpose, though some may have been deliberately trying to disrupt the congregation. It is more likely that Paul meant that the result of their practicing the Communion service as they had been doing was bad rather than good. In the remainder of the chapter he points out the flaws in their observance and what they should do to eliminate them.

Verse 18 - "For first of all, when ye come together in the church, I hear that there be divisions among you; and I partly believe it."

πρῶτον μὲν γὰρ συνερχομένων ὑμῶν ἐν ἐκκλησίᾳ ἀκούω σχίσματα ἐν ὑμῖν ὑπάρχειν, καὶ μέρος τι πιστεύω.

"For, in the first place, when you assemble as a church, I hear that there are divisions among you; and I partly believe it," . . . RSV

πρῶτον (acc.sing.neut.of πρῶτος, adverbial) 487.

μὲν (particle of affirmation) 300.

γὰρ (causal conjunction) 105.

συνερχομένων (pres.mid.part.gen.pl.masc.of συνέρχομαι, genitive absolute) 78.

ὑμῶν (gen.pl.masc.of σύ, genitive absolute) 104.

ἐν (preposition with the locative, pregnant usage) 80.

ἐκκλησίᾳ (loc.sing.fem.of ἐκκλησία, pregnant use of ἐν, place) 1204.

ἀκούω (1st.per.sing.pres.act.ind.of ἀκούω, present iterative retroactive) 148.

σχίσματα (acc.pl.neut.of σχίσμα, general reference) 807.

ἐν (preposition with the locative with plural pronouns) 80.

ὑμῖν (loc.pl.masc.of σύ, place) 104.

ὑπάρχειν (pres.inf.of ὑπάρχω, noun use, direct object of ἀκούω) 1303.

καὶ (continuative conjunction) 14.

μέρος (acc.sing.neut.of μέρος, adverbial) 240.

τι (acc.sing.neut.of τις, indefinite pronoun, direct object of πιστεύω) 486.

πιστεύω (1st.per.sing.pres.act.ind.of πιστεύω, aoristic) 734.

Translation - "Because first of all I have been hearing that when you come to church there are divisions among you, and in part I believe it."

Comment: Blass (*Grammar of New Testament Greek,* 267, as cited in Robertson, *Grammar,* 1152) takes μέν is its original use, as emphasizing πρῶτον. Thus he translates "from the very outset" meaning that this sad situation of division had characterized the Corinthian church since its inception. This may indeed be the meaning, but it is difficult to believe that the Corinthians, during the first days of Paul's revival there were so plagued with division. The usual rendering is to take πρῶτον as indicating that the accusation of division is the subject of the first of two which Paul will mention, the second being mentioned in 1 Cor.12:1ff.

συνερχομένων ὑμῶν is a genitive absolute in the present tense. ἐν ἐκκλησίᾳ here means the church in its physical form as assembled together, not in its spiritual sense as the mystic Body of Christ. The text does not tell us where they met for worship - whether in the home of one of them or in some other building.

In ἀκούω we have an effective aoristic present, similar to an intensive perfect or it can be construed as I have as a present iterative retroactive - "I have been told again and again in the past (present iterative retroactive) and as a result I understand (effective aoristic present) that you are having trouble in the church.

The Corinthians were faithfully observing the ordinance of the Lord's Supper as Paul had taught them (1 Cor.11:2) but they were ignoring the need for spiritual preparation before they approached the Lord's table (*cf.* Mt.5:23,24; Gal.6:1; Mt.18:15-17). To continue to observe in a formal manner while ignoring the deeper spiritual significance of the Communion is only to make a bad spiritual condition in the church worse (verse 17). It is scant wonder that many formal church services which feature Communion only as a ritual and ignore the need for spiritual preparation are virtually beyond spiritual help. Better not to observe the Lord's Supper than to come to the table with unconfessed and unforsaken sin.

Verse 19 - *"For there must be also heresies among you, that they which are approved may be made manifest among you."*

δεῖ γὰρ καὶ αἱρέσεις ἐν ὑμῖν εἶναι, ἵνα (καὶ) οἱ δόκιμοι φανεροὶ γένωνται ἐν ὑμῖν.

"for there must be factions among you in order that those who are genuine among you may be recognized." . . . *RSV*

δεῖ (3d.per.sing.pres.ind.impersonal of δεῖ) 1207.
γὰρ (causal conjunction) 105.
καὶ (adjunctive conjunction) 14.
αἱρέσεις (acc.pl.fem.of αἵρεσις, general reference) 3058.
ἐν (preposition with the locative with plural pronouns) 80.
υἱμῖν (loc.pl.masc.of σύ, place) 104.
εἶναι (pres.inf.of εἰμί, complementary) 86.
ἵνα (conjunction with the subjunctive, result) 114.
καὶ (adjunctive conjunction joining substantives) 14.
οἱ (nom.pl.masc.of the article in agreement with δόκιμοι) 9.
δόκιμοι (nom.pl.masc.of δόκιμος, subject of γένωνται) 4042.
φανεροὶ (nom.pl.masc.of φανερός, predicate adjective) 981.
γένωνται (3d.per.pl.aor.mid.subj.of γίνομαι, result) 113.
ἐν (preposition with the locative with plural pronouns) 80.
ὑμῖν (loc.pl.masc.of σύ, place) 104.

Translation - *"Because there must be differences of opinion among you since the result is that those among you who are approved are so designated."*

Comment: Paul's argument is that sects or parties of differeing opinion must exist at Corinth since only some of the members are approved and others are not. Otherwise all would be approved and none would stand out as more qualified to serve in the church, since all alike would be of the same mind. It requires differences to bring about elections.

The proper observance of the Communion, if carried on in complete conformity to the rules that regulate it, will correct this situation of division within the church. That the Corinthians were not observing it properly is apparent from what follows.

Verse 25 - "When you come together therefore into one place, this is not to eat the Lord's supper."

Συνερχομένων οὖν ὑμῶν ἐπὶ τὸ αὐτὸ οὐκ ἔστιν κυριακὸν δεῖπνον φαγεῖν,

"When you meet together, it is not the Lord's supper that you eat." . . . RSV

Συνερχομένων (pres.mid.part.gen.pl.masc.of συνέρχομαι, genitive absolute) 78.
    οὖν (causal conjunction) 68.
    ὑμῶν (gen.pl.masc.of σύ, genitive absolute) 104.
    ἐπὶ (preposition with the accusative of extent) 47.
    τὸ (acc.sing.neut.of the article in agreement with αὐτὸ) 9.
    αὐτὸ (acc.sing.neut.of αὐτός, extent) 16.
    οὐκ (negative particle with the indicative) 130.
    ἔστιν (3d.per.sing.pres.ind.of εἰμί, aoristic) 86.

#4209 κυριακὸν (acc.sing.neut.of κυριακός, in agreement with δεῖπνον).

    King James Version

Lord's - 1 Cor.11:20; Rev.1:10.

    Revised Standard Version

Lord's - 1 Cor.11:20; Rev.1:10.

Meaning: an adjective meaning "of" or "for" the Lord. The Lord's supper - 1 Cor.11:20; the Lord's day - Rev.1:10, upon which *cf.* comment.

    δεῖπνον (acc.sing.neut.of δεῖπνον, direct object of φαγεῖν) 1440.
    φαγεῖν (aor.act.inf.of ἐσθίω, noun use, predicate nominative) 610.

Translation - "Because when you assemble your purpose is not to eat the Lord's Supper."

Comment: The prepositional phrase ἐπὶ τὸ αὐτὸ (with τόπον elided) is redundant since to "come together" (Συνερχομένων ὑμῶν) is to come "to the same place." Their purpose was not to eat the simple meal as Jesus and the disciples did in the upper room in commemoration of the Passove. It was *after* they had eaten that Jesus instituted the Communion of bread and wine, which is distinct from the supper itself (Mt.26:20-30).

    The Corinthians were meeting frequently to eat a large meal - the love feast which is a Jewish feast to be eaten only once a year at the Passover. Paul says here that that is not the Communion. The Corinthian church apparently had turned what was designed to be a worship service of deep personal introspection, repentance and forsaking of known sin, into a feast, replete with gorging and gluttony, including some intoxication.

    Before Paul describes in detail (verses 23-26) what belongs properly in the Communion service, he points out in further detail (verses 21-22) their evil practices.

Verse 21 - "For in eating every one taketh before other his own supper: and one is hungry, and another is drunken."

ἕκαστος γὰρ τὸ ἴδιον δεῖπνον προλαμβάνει ἐν τῷ φαγεῖν, καὶ ὃς μὲν πεινᾷ, ὃς δὲ μεθύει.

"For in eating, each one goes ahead with his own meal, and one is hungry and another in drunk." . . . RSV

ἕκαστος (nom.sing.masc.of ἕκαστος, subject of προλαμβάνει) 1217.
γὰρ (emphatic conjunction) 105.
τὸ (acc.sing.neut.of the article in agreement with δεῖπνον) 9.
ἴδιον (acc.sing.neut.of ἴδιος, in agreement with δεῖπνον) 778.
δεῖπνον (acc.sing.neut.of δεῖπνον, direct object of προλαμβάνει) 1440.
προλαμβάνει (3d.per.sing.pres.act.ind.of προλαμβάνω, present iterative progressive) 2746.
ἐν (preposition with the locative of time point) 80.
τῷ (loc.sing.neut.of the article, in agreement with φαγεῖν) 9.
φαγεῖν (aor.act.inf.of ἐσθίω, articular infinitive, locative of time point) 610.
καὶ (continuative conjunction) 14.
ὃς (nom.sing.masc.of ὅς, demonstrative, subject of πεινᾷ) 65.
μὲν (particle of affirmation) 300.
πεινᾷ (3d.per.sing.pres.ind.of πεινάω, iterative) 335.
ὃς (nom.sing.masc.of ὅς, demonstrative, subject of μεθύει) 65.
δὲ (adversative conjunction) 11.
μεθύει (3d.per.sing.pres.act.ind.of μεθύω, iterative) 1527.

Translation - "In fact each one, when he eats, rushes ahead to get his own supper and (the result is that) one is hungry and another gets drunk."

Comment: It is not a favorable picture of the social graces of the Corinthians.
γὰρ is emphatic. In verse 20 Paul has said that the Communion service is not the occasion to eat a large meal (Lord's Supper Love Feast) but only a worship of communion of common participation of bread and wine, preceded by sincere heart-searching and repentance. The fact was, however (emphatic γὰρ) that there was a lot of pushing and shoving as each one tried to get to the head of the line in order to eat his fill. The result of this undignified chaos was that some got nothing to eat and the others got drunk! It is scant wonder that these meetings were killing the spiritual life of the church!
The articular infinitive with ἐν (τῷ φαγεῖν) is a locative of time point. They behaved in this boorish manner "when they ate." Note that ὃς is demonstrative, not relative.
Meyer thinks that ἕκαστος γὰρ τὸ ἴδιον δεῖπνον προλαμβάνει means that each one brought his own food to the supper and that each ate what he brought without sharing. Thus the rich ate too much and the poor saints ate little or nothing since they were too poor to bring food. In any case the manner in which the Corinthians were conducting this service was far out of line with Christ's

policy and purpose for the Communion. Verse 22 seems to militate against Meyer's view.

Verse 22 - "What? Have ye not houses to eat and to drink in? Or despise ye the church of God, and shame them that have not? What shall I say to you? Shall I praise you in this? I praise you not."

μὴ γὰρ οἰκίας οὐκ ἔχετε εἰς τὸ ἐσθίειν καὶ πίνειν; ἢ τῆς ἐκκλησίας τοῦ θεοῦ καταφρονεῖτε, καὶ καταισχύνετε τοὺς μὴ ἔχοντας; τί εἴπω ὑμῖν; ἐπαινέσω ὑμᾶς; ἐν τούτῳ οὐκ ἐπαινῶ.

"What! Do you not have houses to eat and drink in? Or do you despise the church of God and humiliate those who have nothing? What shall I say to you? Shall I commend you in this? No, I will not." . . . RSV

μὴ (negative interrogative particle) 87.

γὰρ (emphatic conjunction) 105.

οἰκίας (acc.pl.fem.of οἰκία, direct object of ἔχετε) 186.

οὐκ (negative particle with the indicative in rhetorical question expecting a positive reply) 130.

ἔχετε (2d.per.pl.pres.act.ind.of ἔχω, rhetorical question expecting a positive reply) 82.

εἰς (preposition with the accusative, purpose) 140.

τὸ (acc.sing.neut.of the article in agreement with ἐσθίειν) 9.

ἐσθίειν (pres.act.inf.of ἐσθίω, articular infinitive of purpose) 610.

καὶ (adjunctive conjunction joining infinitives) 14.

πίνειν (pres.act.inf.of πίνω, articular infinitive of purpose) 611.

ἢ (disjunctive) 465.

τῆς (gen.sing.fem.of the article in agreement with ἐκκλησίας) 9.

ἐκκλησίας (gen.sing.fem.of ἐκκλησία, objective genitive) 1204.

τοῦ (gen.sing.masc.of the article in agreement with θεοῦ) 9.

θεοῦ (gen.sing.masc.of θεός, possession) 124.

καταφρονεῖτε (2d.per.pl.pres.act.ind.of καταφρονέω, direct question) 607.

καὶ (adjunctive conjunction joining verbs) 14.

καταισχύνετε (2d.per.pl.pres.act.ind.of καταισχύνω, direct question) 2505.

τοὺς (acc.pl.masc.of the article in agreement with ἔχοντας) 9.

μὴ (negative particle with the participle) 87.d

ἔχοντας (pres.act.part.acc.pl.masc.of ἔχω, substantival, direct object of καταισχύνετε) 82.

τί (acc.sing.neut.of τίς, interrogative pronoun, in direct question) 281.

εἴπω (1st.per.sing.aor.act.subj.of εἶπον, deliberative) 155.

ὑμῖν (dat.pl.masc.of σύ, indirect object of εἴπω) 104.

ἐπαινέσω (1st.per.sing.fut.act.ind.of ἐπαινέω, deliberative) 2568.

ὑμᾶς (acc.pl.masc.of σύ, direct object of ἐπαινέσω) 104.

ἐν (preposition with the locative of sphere) 80.

τούτῳ (loc.sing.neut.of οὗτος, sphere) 93.

οὐκ (negative particle with the indicative) 130.

ἐπαινῶ (1st.per.sing.pres.act.ind.of ἐπαινέω, futuristic) 2568.

Translation - *"Really! You do have houses for eating and drinking do you not? Or do you want to show contempt for the house of God and embarrass the poor? What shall I say to you? Shall I heap praise upon you in reference to this? I shall not!*

Comment: The rhetorical question expects "Yes" for an answer. μή is the interrogative particle, while οὐκ is the negative joined to the verb. εἰς τὸ ἐσθίειν καὶ πίνειν is normally final, but here it seems to carry the sense of the consecutive (result) - "You do have homes for the purpose and with the result that . . . you eat and drink at home?" Robertson (*Grammar*, 1072) also points to a dative idea in εἰς τὸ here. There is some sarcasm from Paul here. What is their motive for coming to church to eat and drink since obviously they could eat and drink at home? Were they delibertely showing contempt for the church and/or trying to humiliate the poor who may have had no homes? Paul does not say that these were their motives, but he challanges them to deny it. He praised them for keeping the ordinances (1 Cor.11:2), but for the way in which they had turned its sacred purposes over to the function of a riotous and selfish orgy, he certainly did not intend to heap praise upon them. ἐπαινῶ can be construed both as aoristic and futuristic. He was not praising them then and he would never praise them for such behavior.

He now procedes to explain to them how the Communion service was introduced by Jesus, as a model which they should follow.

The Institution of the Lord's Supper

(1 Cor.11:23-26; Mt.26:26-29; Mk.14:22-25; Lk.22:14-20)

Verse 23 - *"For I have received of the Lord that which also I delivered unto you. That the Lord Jesus the same night in which he was betrayed took bread."*

Ἐγὼ γὰρ παρέλαβον ἀπὸ τοῦ κυρίου, ὃ καὶ παρέδωκα ὑμῖν, ὅτι ὁ κύριος Ἰησοῦς ἐν τῇ νυκτὶ ᾗ παρεδίδετο ἔλαβεν ἄρτον.

"For I received from the Lord what I also delivered unto you, that the Lord Jesus on the night when he was betrayed took bread, . . ." . . . RSV

Ἐγὼ (nom.sing.masc.of ἐγώ, subject of παρέλαβον) 123.
γὰρ (causal conjunction) 105.
παρέλαβον (1st.per.sing.aor.act.ind.of παραλαμβάνω, culminative) 102.
ἀπὸ (preposition with the ablative of source) 70.
τοῦ (abl.sing.masc.of the article in agreement with κυρίου) 9.
κυρίου (abl.sing.masc.of κύριος, source) 97.
ὃ (acc.sing.neut.of ὅς, relative pronoun, direct object of παρέλαβον and παρέδωκα) 65.
καὶ (adjunctive conjunction joining verbs) 14.

παρέδωκα (1st.per.sing.aor.act.ind.of παραδίδωμι, constative) 368.

ὑμῖν (dat.pl.masc.of σύ, indirect object of παρέδωκα) 104.

ὅτι (conjunction introducing an apposition clause in indirect discourse) 211.

ὁ (nom.sing.masc.of the article in agreement with κύριος) 9.

κύριος (nom.sing.masc.of κύριος, subject of ἔλαβεν) 97.

Ἰησοῦς (nom.sing.masc.of Ἰησοῦς, apposition) 3.

ἐν (preposition with the locative, time point) 80.

τῇ (loc.sing.fem.of the article in agreement with νυκτὶ) 9.

νυκτὶ (loc.sing.fem.of νύξ, time point) 209.

ᾗ (loc.sing.fem.of ὅς, relative pronoun, adjectival, in agreement with νυκτὶ) 65.

παρεδίδετο (3d.per.sing.imp.pass.ind.of παραδίδωμι, inceptive) 368.

ἔλαβεν (3d.per.sing.aor.act.ind.of λαμβάνω, constative) 533.

ἄρτον (acc.sing.masc.of ἄρτος, direct object of ἔλαβεν) 338.

Translation - "Because I got from the Lord that which I also gave to you, that the Lord Jesus on the night on which he was about to be betrayed, took bread ... "

Comment: Paul's justification for his critical attitude toward the Corinthians is now given. He will not praise, but rather censure them, because (causal γὰρ) they know better. He had told them what the Lord had told him. Thus his message to them was an indirect revelation from Christ through Paul. He does not tell us when he got this information from the Lord. Perhaps it was when he got the rest of his theology (2 Cor.12:1-4). Note the relative clause serving as an adjective to modify νυκτὶ. The imperfect tense in παρεδίδετο indicates that the Lord instituted the Communion service on the night when He was about to be betrayed. This is the force of the inceptive imperfect. Judas left during the supper and negotiated his betrayal and He was arrested in the Garden shortly after.

Verse 24 - "And when he had given thanks he broke it and said, Take, eat: this is my body, which is broken for you: this do in remembrance of me."

καὶ εὐχαριστήσας ἔκλασεν καὶ εἶπεν, Τοῦτό μού ἐστιν τὸ σῶμα τὸ ὑπὲρ ὑμῶν. τοῦτο ποιεῖτε εἰς τὴν ἐμὴν ἀνάμνησιν.

"and when he had given thanks, he broke it, and said, 'This is my body which is for you. Do this in remembrance of me.' " ... RSV

καὶ (adjunctive conjunction joining verbs) 14.

εὐχαριστήσας (aor.act.part.nom.sing.masc.of εὐχαριστέω, adverbial, temporal) 1185.

ἔκλασεν (3d.per.sing.aor.act.ind.of κλάω, constative) 1121.

καὶ (adjunctive conjunction joining verbs) 14.

εἶπεν (3d.per.sing.aor.act.ind.of εἶπον, constative) 155.

Τοῦτό (nom.sing.neut.of οὗτος, predicate nominative) 93.

μού (gen.sing.masc.of ἐγώ, possession) 123.

ἐστιν (3d.per.sing.pres.ind.of εἰμί, aoristic) 86.

τὸ (nom.sing.neut.of the article in agreement with σῶμα) 9.

σῶμα (nom.sing.neut.of σῶμα, subject of ἐστίν) 507.

τό (nom.sing.neut.of the article in agreement with σῶμα) 9.

ὑπὲρ (preposition with the ablative, "in behalf of") 545.

ὑμῶν (abl.pl.masc.of σύ, substitution) 104.

τοῦτο (acc.sing.neut.of οὗτος, direct object of ποιεῖτε) 93.

ποιεῖτε (2d.per.pl.pres.act.impv.of ποιέω, command) 127.

εἰς (preposition with the accusative, purpose) 140.

τὴν (acc.sing.fem.of the article in agreement with ἀνάμνησιν) 9.

ἐμὴν (acc.sing.fem.of ἐμός, in agreement with ἀνάμνησιν) 1267.

ἀνάμνησιν (acc.sing.fem.of ἀνάμνησις, purpose) 2774.

Translation - "And after He had given thanks He broke it and said, 'This is my body, the one (broken, given, crucified) for you. Do this in my remembrance.'"

Comment: Though the text presented has the best evidence to support it, κλώμενον, θρυπτόμενον and διδόμενον are added by variant readings to complete τό in the emphatic attribution after σῶμα. These participles explain more fully what is easily inferred without them. Metzger says that "τὸ ὑπὲρ ὑμῶν . . . is characteristic of Paul's style." (Metzger, *A Textual Commentary on the Greek New Testament*, 562). *Cf.* Luke 22:19 which adds διδόμενον. τοῦτο is deictic. The second τοῦτο is anaphoric. The εἰς phrase is purpose.

Never did self-denial in sacrifice for others reach the heights that Jesus reached on the cross. This symbolic communion is enjoined upon the saints for the purpose of allowing its inherent character (#2774) to always remind us of Christ on the cross. The boorish behavior of the Corinthians (verses 21-22) spoke with compelling eloquence of their selfishness. Their observance was a complete negation of the spirit of love and self-denial, as expressed at Calvary, that the Communion was designed to recall and promote. As the rich crowded forward boisterously and gorged themselves on rich food and wine, the poor stood aside in deep humiliation. What a flagrant disregard for the very essence of Christianity! It is no great wonder that Paul told them that every time they met they made matters worse (verse 17).

It is wholly appropriate that offerings for poor relief are taken in many Communion services. If we are to catch and exemplify the spirit of the Communion service we will make the offering for the poor far greater than the few coins or single dollar bills which normally find their way into the envelope as we hasten for the exit in order to be on the first tee by one o'clock.

Verse 25 - "After the same manner also he took the cup, when he had supped, saying, This cup is the new testament in my blood; this do ye, as oft as ye drink it, in remembrance of me."

ὡσαύτως καὶ τὸ ποτήριον μετὰ τὸ δειπνῆσαι, λέγων, Τοῦτο τὸ ποτήριον ἡ καινὴ διαθήκη ἐστὶν ἐν τῷ ἐμῷ αἵματι. τοῦτο ποιεῖτε, ὁσάκις ἐὰν πίνητε, εἰς τὴν ἐμὴν ἀνάμνησιν.

"In the same way also the cup, after supper, saying, 'This cup is the new covenant in my blood. Do this, as often as you drink it, in remembrance of me.".

. . RSV

ὡσαύτως (comparative intensive adverb) 1319.
καὶ (adjunctive conjunction joining nouns) 14.
τὸ (acc.sing.neut.of the article in agreement with ποτήριον) 9.
ποτήριον (acc.sing.neut.of ποτήριον, direct object of ἔλαβεν understood) 902.
μετὰ (preposition with the accusative of time extent) 50.
τὸ (acc.sing.neut.of the article, time extent in an articular infinitive) 9.
δειπνῆσαι (aor.act.inf.of δειπνέω, noun use, time extent) 2595.
λέγων (pres.act.part.nom.sing.masc.of λέγω, adverbial, circumstantial, introducing direct discourse) 66.
Τοῦτο (nom.sing.neut.of οὗτος, in agreement with ποτήριον) 93.
τὸ (nom.sing.neut.of the article in agreement with ποτήριον) 9.
ποτήριον (nom.sing.neut.of ποτήριον, subject of ἐστιν understood) 902.
ἡ (nom.sing.fem.of the article in agreement with διαθήκη) 9.
καινὴ (nom.sing.fem.of καινός, in agreement with διαθήκη) 812.
διαθήκη (nom.sing.fem.of διαθήκη, predicate nominative) 1575.
ἐστὶν (3d.per.sing.pres.ind.of εἰμί, aoristic) 86.
ἐν (preposition with the locative, metaphorical place) 80.
τῷ (loc.sing.neut.of the article in agreement with αἵματι) 9.
ἐμῷ (loc.sing.neut.of ἐμός, in agreement with αἵματι) 1267.
αἵματι (loc.sing.neut.of αἷμα, metaphorical place) 1203.
τοῦτο (acc.sing.neut.of οὗτος, direct object of ποιεῖτε) 93.
ποιεῖτε (2d.per.pl.pres.act.impv.of ποιέω, command) 127.

#4210 ὁσάκις (temporal conjunction).

        King James Version

as oft as - 1 Cor.11:25.
as often as - 1 Cor.11:26; Rev.11:6.

        Revised Standard Version

as often as - 1 Cor.11:25,26; Rev.11:6.

Meaning: Temporal conjunction indicating indefinite repetition. With ἐάν and the subjunctive in 1 Cor.11:25,26; Rev.11:6.

ἐὰν (conditional particle in a third-class condition) 363.
πίνητε (2d.per.pl.pres.act.subj.of πίνω, third-class condition) 611.
εἰς (preposition with the accusative, purpose) 140.
ἐμὴν (acc.sing.fem.of ἐμός, in agreement with ἀνάμνησιν) 1267.
ἀνάμνησιν (acc.sing.fem.of ἀνάμνησις, purpose) 2774.

Translation - "In the same way also the cup after he had eaten saying, 'This cup is the new covenant in my blood. If you drink it, as often as you do, do it in order to remember me.' "

Comment: The new covenant is ratified and made operative by means of the blood of our Lord Jesus. *Cf.* comment on Mt.26:26-29; Heb.8:6-10; 9:14-28. The apodosis of the third-class condition τοῦτο ποιεῖτε precedes the protasis ὁσάκις ἐὰν πίνητε. "Drink only when you like, but when you do and as often as you do, in a series of indefinite repetitions, drink it for the purpose of remembering that your salvation depends wholly upon my sacrifice."

Once again, as in verse 24, the thoughts that should arise in the Christian heart when he partakes of bread and wine in Communion are not the thoughts that conduce to the behavior of the Corinthians described in verse 21.

As we eat the bread and drink the wine our thoughts are directed backward to Calvary and forward to the Second Coming of the One who died and rose again. This is the thought of

Verse 26 - "For as often as ye eat this bread, and drink this cup, ye do shew the Lord's death till he come."

ὁσάκις γὰρ ἐὰν ἐσθίητε τὸν ἄρτον τοῦτον καὶ τὸ ποτήριον πίνητε, τὸν θάνατον τοῦ κυρίου καταγγέλλετε, ἄχρις οὗ ἔλθῃ.

"For as often as you eat this bread and drink the cup, you proclaim the Lord's death until he comes." . . . RSV

ὁσάκις (temporal conjunction) 4210.
γὰρ (causal conjunction) 105.
ἐὰν (conditional particle with the subjunctive in a third-class condition) 363.
ἐσθίητε (2d.per.pl.pres.act.subj.of ἐσθίω, third-class condition) 610.
τὸν (acc.sing.masc.of the article in agreement with ἄρτον) 9.
ἄρτον (acc.sing.masc.of ἄρτος, direct object of ἐσθίητε) 338.
τοῦτον (acc.sing.masc.of οὗτος, in agreement with ἄρτον) 93.
καὶ (adjunctive conjunction joining verbs) 14.
τὸ (acc.sing.neut.of the article in agreement with ποτήριον) 9.
ποτήριον (acc.sing.neut.of ποτήριον, direct object of πίνητε) 902.
πίνητε (2d.per.pl.pres.act.subj.of πίνω, third-class condition) 611.
τὸν (acc.sing.masc.of the article in agreement with θάνατον) 9.
θάνατον (acc.sing.masc.of θάνατος, direct object of καταγγέλλετε) 381.
τοῦ (gen.sing.masc.of the article in agreement with κυρίου) 9.
κυρίου (gen.sing.masc.of κύριος, description) 97.
καταγγέλλετε (2d.per.pl.pres.act.ind.of καταγγέλλω, futuristic) 3023.
ἄχρις (preposition with genitive of time description) 1517.
οὗ (gen.sing.neut.of ὅς, time description) 65.
ἔλθῃ (3d.per.sing.aor.mid.subj.of ἔρχομαι, indefinite temporal clause) 146.

Translation - "Because as often as you eat this bread and drink this cup, you will be demonstrating the death of the Lord until such time as He comes."

Comment: ἄχρις followed by the relative οὗ, a genitive of time description (#1517) in an indefinite temporal clause. The time of the Lord's coming is in doubt, though not the fact of His coming. While we wait we will demonstrate His death by partaking of the elements. Thus the Communion service looks back to

Calvary and forward to Coronation. The partaking Christian therefore is in the role of the pilgrim; an ambassador in a foreign country representing the interests of the heavenly city. He is a citizen in the world only in the political sense. He marches to a heavenly drum and he need not expect to be understood by any except those in whom the Holy Spirit dwells.

What should be his ethical attitude on such an occasion? He should reflect upon the fact that by His grace he is a member of the Body of Christ. The student should review here the comment on 1 Cor.10:14-17. As we are partakers of the true bread from heaven, of which the physical elements are symbols, we are incorporated into one body (1 Cor.12:13). Our divine Head is in heaven with His resurrected body. His spiritual body consists of all true believers. The intimacy of the Christian's relation to Christ and to each other is the point to remember at the Communion table. Looking backward in time to Calvary where He redeemed us, we join all other members of His body in a look forward to the second coming when He will glorify us. Therefore to come to the Lord's Table in anything less than an attitude of deep personal devotion and commitment is a blasphemous miscarriage of propriety. The penalty for such blasphemy is indeed great.

Partaking of the Supper Unworthily

(1 Corinthians 11:27-34)

Verse 27 - "Wherefore whosoever shall eat this bread and drink this cup of the Lord, unworthily, shall be guilty of the body and blood of the Lord."

Ὥστε ὃς ἂν ἐσθίῃ τὸν ἄρτον ἢ πίνῃ τὸ ποτήριον τοῦ κυρίου ἀναξίως, ἔνοχος ἔσται τοῦ σώματος καὶ τοῦ αἵματος τοῦ κυρίου.

"Whoever, therefore, eats the bread or drinks the cup of the Lord in an unworthy manner will be guilty of profaning the body and blood of the Lord."..
                                                                          RSV

Ὥστε (conjunction with the indicative in a result clause) 752.

ὃς (nom.sing.masc.of ὅς, relative pronoun, with the subjunctive in a more probable condition) 65.

ἂν (contingent particle with the subjunctive in a more probable condition) 205.

ἐσθίῃ (3d.per.sing.pres.act.subj.of ἐσθίω, more probable condition) 610.

τὸν (acc.sing.masc.of the article in agreement with ἄρτον) 9.

ἄρτον (acc.sing.masc.of ἄρτος, direct object of ἐσθίῃ) 338.

ἢ (disjunctive) 465.

πίνῃ (3d.per.sing.pres.act.subj.of πίνω, more probable condition) 611.

τὸ (acc.sing.neut.of the article in agreement with ποτήριον) 9.

ποτήριον (acc.sing.neut.of ποτήριον, direct object of πίνῃ) 902.

τοῦ (gen.sing.masc.of the article in agreement with κυρίου) 9.
κυρίου (gen.sing.masc.of κύριος, description) 97.

#4211 ἀναξίως (adverbial).

King James Version

unworthily - 1 Cor.11:21.

Revised Standard Version

in an unworthy manner - 1 Cor.11:27.

Meaning: α privative plus ἀξίως (#4064). An adverb - in an unworthy manner. With reference to the Communion elements without proper spiritual preparation - 1 Cor.11:27.

ἔνοχος (nom.sing.masc.of ἔνοχος, predicate adjective) 477.
ἔσται (3d.per.sing.fut.ind.of εἰμί, predictive in a result clause) 86.
τοῦ (gen.sing.neut.of the article in agreement with σώματος) 9.
σώματος (gen.sing.neut.of σῶμα, descriptive genitive with an adjective) 507.
καὶ (adjunctive conjunction joining nouns) 14.
τοῦ (gen.sing.neut.of the article in agreement with αἵματος) 9.
αἵματος (gen.sing.neut.of αἷμα, descriptive genitive with an adjective) 1203.
τοῦ (gen.sing.masc.of the article in agreement with κυρίου) 9.
κυρίου (gen.sing.masc.of κύριος, description) 97.

Translation - "The result is that whoever eats the bread or drinks the cup of the Lord unworthily shall be guilty of the body and blood of the Lord."

Comment: *Cf.*#477 for the various cases used after this adjective. Mt.26:66; Mk.14:64; 1 Cor.11:27; Jam.2:10; Mk.3:29 and Heb.2:15 with the genitive; Mt.5:21,22a,b with the instrumental, but Mt.5:22c with the accusative. ὥστε with the indicative for result is rare in the New Testament, where it expresses actual result. *Cf.*John 3:16. "But actual result may also be expressed by the infinitive with ὥστε (Mt.8:24; 12:22; Lk.5:7)." (Mantey, *Manual,* 286).

The result of participation in the Communion without a proper spiritual recognition of its great significance and consequent spiritual preparation, in terms of objective introspection, repentance, request for forgiveness and a new yielding to the Holy Spirit is great.

The relative pronoun ὅς followed by ἄν and the subjunctive in ἐσθίῃ and πίνῃ indicate that Paul had no one in mind specifically who might be unfortunate enough to appear at the Lord's table without spiritual preparation. It is a more probable conditional clause. Paul did not predict that it would happen, but the chances were great that it would. If anyone ate or drank unworthily he would be subject to judgment. To eat or drink unworthily is to symbolize his utter dependence upon Christ and to say in symbol that he is a member of the Body of Christ when he has known and unconfessed sin in his life. The wrath of God poured out without measure upon Christ's murderers, who shed His blood and broke His body would, to some degree fall upon the unworthy Christian who had mocked the intimacy of the relationship, but this chastening is not to be confused with the wrath of God which falls upon the unsaved, "for God hath not appointed us unto wrath, but to obtain salvation by our Lord Jesus Christ." (1 Thess.5:9). There is a distinction between the chastisement of a loving Father upon an erring child and the wrath of the Judge of all the earth upon His enemies.

The disjunctive ἤ between ἐσθίῃ and πίνῃ does not mean that some Christians ate while others drank, but that any Christian, whether he ate or drank unworthily would be punished. The penalties are set forth in verse 30. The way to avoid punishment is suggested in

Verse 28 - "But let a man examine himself, and so let him eat of that bread, and drink of that cup."

δοκιμαζέτω δὲ ἄνθρωπος ἑαυτόν, καὶ οὕτως ἐκ τοῦ ἄρτου ἐσθιέτω καὶ ἐκ τοῦ ποτηρίου πινέτω.

"Let a man examine himself, and so eat of the bread and drink of the cup." . . . RSV

δοκιμαζέτω (3d.per.sing.pres.act.impv.of δοκιμάζω, command) 2493.
δὲ (adversative conjunction) 11.
ἄνθρωπος (nom.sing.masc.of ἄνθρωπος, subject of δοκιμαζέτω) 341.
ἑαυτόν (acc.sing.masc.of ἑαυτοῦ, direct object of δοκιμαζέτω) 288.
καὶ (adjunctive conjunction joining verbs) 14.
οὕτως (demonstrative adverb) 74.
ἐκ (preposition with the ablative of source) 19.
τοῦ (abl.sing.masc.of the article in agreement with ἄρτου) 9.
ἄρτου (abl.sing.masc.of ἄρτος, source) 338.
ἐσθιέτω (3d.per.sing.pres.act.impv.of ἐσθίω, command) 610.
καὶ (adjunctive conjunction joining verbs) 14.
ἐκ (preposition with the ablative of source) 19.
τοῦ (abl.sing.neut.of the article in agreement with ποτηρίου) 9.
ποτηρίου (abl.sing.neut.of ποτήριον, source) 902.
πινέτω (3d.per.sing.pres.act.impv.of πίνω, command) 611.

Translation - "But let a man examine himself and only then let him eat of the bread and drink from the cup."

Comment: οὕτως here carries the idea in the context that self-examination is prerequisite to participation in the Communion. A Christian who often comes to the Communion table and looks back to Calvary and forward to the second coming will think about the sure return of the King. He will reflect upon the terrible price which our Lord paid for his salvation. He will exalt in the fact that our Lord arose from the grave and conquered death once for all. He will anticipate the glories of the coming kingdom of God on earth. He will also consider that just as he and other Christians at the table eat of the same bread, so they all are partakers of the spiritual Bread of Life (John 6:48) and united as members of Christ's Body. All of this should lead him carefully to scrutinize his own life style in terms of 1 Cor.6:19,20 and Mt.5:23,24. If he does he will not behave as the Corinthians are described to have behaved in 1 Cor.11:21.

Thus the Communion is the ordinance designed to keep the child of God in full communion with Christ in terms of a victorious life. Immersion in water symbolizes our *union* with Christ and as we eat the bread and drink the wine at the Lord's table we symbolize our *communion* with Him.

Self examination reveals personal sins before they become apparent to others. We pray with David, not only for the forgiveness for sins which we know about, but we also pray with him, "Cleanse thou me from secret faults" (Psalm 19:12).

Happy is the child of God who understands and utilizes to the fullest extent the privileges of the Lord's Supper. Unfortunately the negative side of the picture is seen in

Verse 29 - "For he that eateth and drinketh unworthily, eateth and drinketh damnation to himself, not discerning the Lord's body."

ὁ γὰρ ἐσθίων καὶ πίνων κρίμα ἑαυτῷ ἐσθίει καὶ πίνει μὴ διακρίνων τὸ σῶμα.

"For any one who eats and drinks without discerning the body eats and drinks judgment upon himself." . . . RSV

ὁ (nom.sing.masc.of the article in agreement with ἐσθίων) 9.

γὰρ (causal conjunction) 105.

ἐσθίων (pres.act.part.nom.sing.masc.of ἐσθίω, substantival, subject of ἐσθίει) 610.

καὶ (adjunctive conjunction joining participles) 14.

πίνων (pres.act.part.nom.sing.masc.of πίνω, substantival, subject of πίνει) 611.

κρίμα (acc.sing.neut.of κρίμα, direct object of ἐσθίει and πίνει) 642.

ἑαυτῷ (dat.sing.masc.of ἑαυτοῦ, personal disadvantage) 288.

ἐσθίει (3d.per.sing.pres.act.ind.of ἐσθίω, iterative) 610.

καὶ (adjunctive conjunction joining verbs) 14.

πίνει (3d.per.sing.pres.act.ind.of πίνω, iterative) 611.

μὴ (negative particle with the participle) 87.

διακρίνων (pres.act.part.nom.sing.masc.of διακρίνω, adverbial, conditional) 1195.

τὸ (acc.sing.neut.of the article in agreement with σῶμα) 9.

σῶμα (acc.sing.neut.of σῶμα, direct object of διακρίνων) 507.

Translation - "Because if he does not reflect upon the body he who eats and drinks, eats and drinks judgment upon himself."

Comment: Paul now identifies the Christian whose participation at the Communion table brings down God's judgment upon him, with the sad results of verse 30. He is the eater and drinker who repeatedly eats and drinks (iterative present in ἐσθίει and πίνει) without giving thought to the spiritual significance of this very special food and drink, and reacting accordingly, in terms of a fresh commitment to Christ. The Communion is a most blessed ordinance for the Christian who approaches the table worthily. He has examined himself, recognized his failures as a Christian, repented, asked forgiveness and forsaken his sins and he has rectified wrongs which he has perpetrated against his neighbor (1 Cor.6:19; 1 John 1:9; Mt.5:23, etc.). It is a most dangerous ordinance for those who approach the table and ignore its significance.

The participle διακρίνων is involved in an implied condition. The apodosis is here - he eats and drinks judgment down upon himself. The protasis is implied by the negative adverbial condition - μὴ διακρίνων. Robertson says, "The condition is hinted at, not stated." (*Grammar*, 1023). Some MSS have ἀναξίως after πίνων, though the context indicates that this is what Paul means. Others add τοῦ κυρίου after σῶμα, while Ψ adds Ἰησοῦ. 1241 adds αἷμα τοῦ κυρίου. There is no good reason to explain why these word(s) should have been omitted had they been in the original text (*A Textual Commentary on the Greek New Testament*, 562,3). The same sense is perfectly clear without the glosses.

Unfortunately some of the Corinthian saints had already violated the sanctity of the communion table with the sad results of

Verse 30 - *"For this cause many are weak and sickly among you, and many sleep."*

διὰ τοῦτο ἐν ὑμῖν πολλοὶ ἀσθενεῖς καὶ ἄρρωστοι καὶ κοιμῶνται ἱκανοί.

"That is why many of you are weak and ill, and some have died." . . . RSV

διὰ (preposition with the accusative, cause) 118.

τοῦτο (acc.sing.neut.of οὗτος, cause) 93.

ἐν (preposition with the locative with plural pronouns) 80.

ὑμῖν (loc.pl.masc.of σύ, place) 104.

πολλοὶ (nom.pl.masc.of πολύς, subject of verb understood) 228.

ἀσθενεῖς (nom.pl.masc.of ἀσθενής, predicate adjective) 1551.

καὶ (adjunctive conjunction joining adjectives) 14.

ἄρρωστοι (nom.pl.masc.of ἄρρωστος, predicate adjective) 1117.

καὶ (continuative conjunction) 14.

κοιμῶνται (3d.per.pl.pres.mid.ind.of κοιμάω, present progressive retroactive) 1664.

ἱκανοί (nom.pl.masc.of ἱκανός, subject of κοιμῶνται) 304.

Translation - *"This is why many among you are weak and sick and a large number have died."*

Comment: διὰ τοῦτο is a common causal construction - "on account of this" with τοῦτο used in an anaphoric sense, as it points back to verse 29.

Why should ill health, debilitation and even physical death be the punishment for the misuse of the Lord's table? Because the body of the Christian is the temple of the Holy Spirit (1 Cor.6:19,20; 3:16). Thus the sinning Christian forces the Holy Spirit into a compromising position. He cannot leave, contrary to Arminius, since by Him we are sealed until the resurrection (Eph.1:13,14; 4:30). Thus if we defile the temple (our bodies) God will destroy the temple (1

Cor.3:16,17). It is the sin unto physical death sometimes visited upon the backslidden and *persistently* rebellious Christian. *Cf.* Acts 5:1-11; 1 Cor.5:1-5; 1 John 5:16. The unrepentant saint who sits at the Lord's table is particularly sinful because of the lofty spiritual significance of the Communion. Here the unity of the Body of Christ, characterized by the mystical union of all Christians with the Head, is set forth in symbol. We eat and drink, in order to say that just as the bread and wine become a part of our organic chemistry to sustain us physically, so, in the spiritual realm, Christ's death, in which His body, the Bread of Life, was broken for us and His blood was shed for our redemption, is our only source of life. Yet His death was selfless - the supreme example of self-denial, while the behavior of the Corinthians at the table was utterly selfish.

A backslidden Christian can usher, pass the offering plates, sing a solo or even preach a sermon without incurring God's judgment, but the Communion service is the very heart of Christianity.

If it be asked why, then, there are so many healthy church members who live long lives, the answer may be that they were never regenerated. God does not punish the devil's children (John 8:44) before the time, but He does chastize His own (Heb.12:5-8). While the Communion table is a dangerous place for the careless Christian, it is indeed the safest possible place for the Christian who observes the ordinance as he should.

Verse 31 - "For if we would judge ourselves, we should not be judged."

εἰ δὲ ἑαυτοὺς διεκρίνομεν, οὐκ ἂν ἐκρινόμεθα.

"But if we judged ourselves truly, we should not be judged." . . . RSV

εἰ (conditional particle in a second-class, contrary to fact, condition) 337.
δὲ (adversative conjunction) 11.
ἑαυτοὺς (acc.pl.masc.of ἑαυτοῦ, direct object of διεκρίνομεν) 288.
διεκρίνομεν (1st.per.pl.imp.act.ind.of διακρίνω, progressive duration, second-class condition) 1195.
οὐκ (negative particle with the indicative) 130.
ἂν (contingent particle in a second-class condition) 205.
ἐκρινόμεθα (1st.per.pl.imp.pass.ind.of κρίνω, second-class condition) 531.

Translation - "But if we had really been judging ourselves we should not now be condemned."

Comment: The second-class condition assumes that the premise in the protasis is contrary to fact. This may or may not be true, but the conclusion follows logically from the assumption that they had not thoroughly judged themselves. When the imperfect is used both in the protasis and the apodosis, it indicates present time in the protasis. Other examples are Luke 7:39; John 5:46; 8:42; 9:41; 15:19; 18:36; Gal.1:10; Heb.8:4,7. Had they done so they would not now be the objects of God's chastening. Thus the ordinance when properly observed demands spiritual introspection and a readiness to admit fault, repent and forsake sin before we approach the Lord's table. If we do this we keep our relationships acceptable both vertically (with God) and horizontally (with man) (Mt.5:23,24).

The so-called "closed communion" view is based upon the assumption that if a Christian refuses to repent of and forsake sin, he should be dismissed from local church fellowship (Mt.18:15-17) and thus denied the elements, since the ordinance is admininstered by the local church only to those who are in fellowship. Thus the backsliding saint is barred from the act of eating and drinking and thus he is protected from the dire effects of eating and drinking unworthily. If the local congregation continues to preach and practice "closed communion" but neglects or refuses to discipline members, it has negated the only reason for its position. Otherwise observed it is only an empty dogma, such as characterizes so much that we find in the institutional church.

Verse 32 - "But when we are judged, we are chastened of the Lord, that we should not be condemned with the world."

κρινόμενοι δὲ ὑπὸ (τοῦ) κυρίου παιδευόμεθα, ἵνα μὴ σὺν τῷ κόσμῳ κατακριθῶμεν.

"But when we are judged by the Lord, we are chastened so that we may not be condemned along with the world." . . . RSV

κρινόμενοι (pres.pass.part.nom.pl.masc.of κρίνω, adverbial, condition) 531.
δὲ (adversative conjunction) 11.
ὑπὸ (preposition with the ablative of agent) 117.
(τοῦ) (abl.sing.masc.of the article in agreement with κυρίου) 9.
κυρίου (abl.sing.masc.of κύριος, agent) 97.
παιδευόμεθα (1st.per.pl.pres.pass.ind.of παιδεόω, aoristic) 2838.
ἵνα (conjunction with the subjunctive in a negative sub-final clause) 114.
μὴ (negative particle with the subjunctive in a negative sub-final clause) 87.
σὺν (preposition with the instrumental of association) 1542.
τῷ (instru.sing.masc.of the article in agreement with κόσμῳ) 9.
κόσμῳ (instru.sing.masc.of κόσμος, association) 360.
κατακριθῶμεν (1st.per.pl.aor.pass.subj.of κατακρίνω, sub-final) 1012.

Translation - "But if we are judged by the Lord we are disciplined in order (and with the result) that we will not be utterly condemned with the world."

Comment: The difference is between the judgment by the Lord (κρινόμενοι), which is the required discipline which the sinning Christian needs (Heb.12:5-7) and the condemnation to hell (κατακριθῶμεν) which is the fate of the unsaved world. One of the marks of identification of the child of God is the fact that he receives periodic discipline from the Father for his sin. The Scriptures do not teach that God judges the unsaved until the final judgment. Violation of natural law will work its retribution upon the sinner - if he violates the law of gravity, falls out of a tree and breaks his leg - but that is not a judgment personally visited by God. The chastening of the believer is God's way of maintaining the distinction between the regenerate sinner and the sinner who is unregenerate.

Verse 33 - *"Wherefore, my brethren, when ye come together to eat, tarry one for another."*

ὥστε, ἀδελφοί μου, συνερχόμενοι εἰς τὸ φαγεῖν ἀλλήλους ἐκδέχεσθε.

"So then, my brethren, when you come together to eat, wait for one another — " . . . *RSV*

ὥστε (inferential conjunction) 752.

ἀδελφοί (voc.pl.masc.of ἀδελφός, address) 15.

μου (gen.sing.masc.of ἐγώ, relationship) 123.

συνερχόμενοι (pres.mid.part.nom.pl.masc.of συνέρχομαι, adverbial, temporal) 78.

εἰς (preposition with the accusative, purpose) 140.

τὸ (acc.sing.neut.of the article, articular infinitive, purpose) 9.

φαγεῖν (aor.act.inf.of ἐσθίω, purpose) 610.

ἀλλήλους (acc.pl.masc.of ἀλλήλων, direct object of ἐκδέχεσθε) 1487.

ἐκδέχεσθε (2d.per.pl.pres.mid.impv.of ἐκδέχομαι, command) 3398.

Translation - *"So, my brethren, when you come together to eat, wait upon one another."*

Comment: ὥστε here is only inferential, like οὖν. As Paul closes this section he alludes to their behavior described in verse 21, which he found to be so offensive. Now, in order that they conduct themselves in keeping with the essential significance of the Communion he lays down the rule that when they arrive at the place of meeting, they are to wait until all have arrived and have been served before they eat. In any social situation this is only proper behavior, but in view of the significance of the Lord's Supper, to violate this rule is a total negation of the Spirit of Christ.

In the last verse of the chapter he anticipates an objection which might be made. Suppose that a man is exceptionally hungry? Does the rule still apply? Paul answers that objection in

Verse 34 - *"And if any man hunger, let him eat at home; that ye come not together unto condemnation. And the rest will I set in order when I come."*

εἴ τις πεινᾷ, ἐν οἴκῳ ἐσθιέτω, ἵνα μὴ εἰς κρίμα συνέρχησθε. Τὰ δὲ λοιπὰ ὡς ἂν ἔλθω διατάξομαι.

". . . if any one is hungry, let him eat at home — lest you come together to be condemned. About the other things I will give directions when I come." . . . *RSV*

εἴ (conditional particle in a first-class condition) 337.

τις (nom.sing.masc.of τις, indefinite pronoun, subject of πεινᾷ) 486.

πεινᾷ (3d.per.sing.pres.act.ind.of πεινάω, aoristic, first-class condition) 335.

ἐν (preposition with the locative of place) 80.

οἴκῳ (loc.sing.masc.of οἶκος, place) 784.

ἐσθιέτω (3d.per.sing.pres.act.impv.of ἐσθίω, command) 610.

ἵνα (conjunction with the subjunctive, negative result) 114.

μή (negative particle with the subjunctive, result) 87.

εἰς (preposition with the predicate accusative) 140.

κρίμα (acc.sing.neut.of κρίμα, predicate use) 642.

συνέρχησθε (2d.per.pl.pres.mid.subj.of συνέρχομαι, negative result) 78.

Τὰ (acc.pl.neut.of the article in agreement with λοιπὰ) 9.

δὲ (continuative conjunction) 11.

λοιπὰ (acc.pl.neut.of λοιπός, direct object of διατάξομαι) 1402.

ὡς (temporal particle with the subjunctive in an indefinite temporal clause) 128.

ἄν (contingent particle in an indefinite temporal clause) 205.

ἔλθω (1st.per.sing.2d.aor.mid.subj.of ἔρχομαι, indefinite temporal clause) 146.

διατάξομαι (1st.per.sing.fut.mid.ind.of διατάσσω, predictive) 904.

Translation - "If any one is hungry let him eat at home in order that you do not assemble and be condemned. And the other matters I will set in order when I come."

Comment: The first-class condition has εἰ and the present indicative in the protasis and the present imperative in the apodosis. Paul is not making any statement that any one will or will not be hungry, but if any one is, the instruction is explicit - "let him eat at home." There is a hint here that they had served a full meal before, and that Paul is saying that they were to restrict the service to the bread and wine only. In any event they were not to turn the Lord's Supper observance into a banquet. Thus only could they avoid the judgment discussed in verses 29-32.

Paul ends his discussion of the problem with a promise that he will deal with the other questions which, apparently, they had asked about, when he comes again to Corinth. ὡς with ἄν and the subjunctive are also found in Rom.15:24 and Phil.2:23.

Chapters 12-14 are devoted to a full discussion of the gifts of the Holy Spirit which He gives to the members of the Body of Christ.

Spiritual Gifts

(1 Corinthians 12:1-11)

1 Cor.12:1 - "Now concerning spiritual gifts, brethren, I would not have you ignorant."

Περὶ δὲ τῶν πνευματικῶν, ἀδελφοί, οὐ θέλω ὑμᾶς ἀγνοεῖν.

"Now concerning spiritual gifts, brethren, I do not want you to be uninformed." . . . RSV

Περὶ (preposition with the genitive of reference) 173.

δέ (explanatory conjunction) 11.

τῶν (gen.pl.neut.of the article in agreement with πνευματικῶν) 9.

πνευματικῶν (gen.pl.neut.of πνευματικός, in agreement with δώρων understood, reference) 3791.

ἀδελφοί (voc.pl.masc.of ἀδελφός, address) 15.

οὐ (negative particle with the indicative) 130.

θέλω (1st.per.sing.pres.act.ind.of θέλω, aoristic) 88.

ὑμᾶς (acc.pl.masc.of σύ, general reference) 104.

ἀγνοεῖν (pres.act.inf.of ἀγνοέω, noun use, direct object of θέλω) 2345.

Translation - "Now with reference to spiritual matters, brethren, I do not want you to be misinformed."

Comment: δέ is explanatory as Paul begins a new section. The Greek does not have δώρων after πνευματικῶν, as some translators supply. *Cf.* Rom. 1:11 and 1 Cor. 14:1. ἀγνοεῖν is the object infinitive after θέλω with ὑμᾶς the accusative of general reference. The word ἀγνοέω (#2345) can either mean uninformed or misinformed. To be misinformed is to have false information which precludes the true. The Corinthians knew about the gifts but they were misusing them. Hence the translation has "misinformed" rather than "uninformed" or "ignorant."

There is great need in the late 20th century for the church to look humbly, carefully and thoroughly into the charismatic question. Some whom I believe are misinformed as the Corinthians were have captured the word "charismatic" and given to it an aura which speaks of emotional excess and fanaticism, often associated with the term "holy roller." At best this development has alienated many sincere and genuinely regenerated Christians, who are thus making the mistake of writing off the entire subject, rather than looking at it with renewed zeal and disciplined objectivity, while at worst the so-called charismatic movement threatens to substitute experience, which can only be imperfectly interpreted, for the scientific exegesis of the Word of God. It is this development, exploited by certain electronic evangelists, who profess to have the gifts of prophecy, special knowledge and "tongues" which justifies our calling the movement an antiscriptural cult, on the level of the Mormons and the Watchtower Bible and Tract Society.

The Scriptures seem clearly to teach that the Holy Spirit has indeed enriched every member of the Body of Christ with one or more gifts as it has pleased Him in His sovereign wisdom to bestow, but that at least two of these gifts, prophecy and knowledge were *ad hoc* gifts, especially needed by the church in the first century before the New Testament canon of Scripture was written, and phased out when the Holy Spirit wrote *Finis* to the New Testament, while the gift of the ability to speak a language not previously known to the speaker has "ceased" because it is no longer needed.

The Body of Christ could not function in the world in pursuit of the worldwide missionary enterprise if there were no gifts, and the Scripture is clear that there has never been a Christian in any age who did not have at least one gift.

Verse 2 - "Ye know that ye were Gentiles, carried away unto these dumb idols, even as ye were led."

Οἴδατε ὅτι ὅτε ἔθνη ἦτε πρὸς τὰ εἴδωλα τὰ ἄφωνα ὡς ἂν ἤγεσθε ἀπαγόμενοι.

"You know that when you were heathen, you were led astray to dumb idols, however you may have been moved." . . . RSV

Οἴδατε (2d.per.pl. perf.ind.of οἶδα, intensive) 144b.
ὅτι (conjunction introducing an object clause in indirect discourse) 211.
ὅτε (conjunction with the indicative in a definite temporal clause) 703.
ἔθνη (nom.pl.neut.of ἔθνος, predicate nominative) 376.
ἦτε (2d.per.pl.imp.ind.of εἰμί, progressive duration) 86.
πρὸς (preposition with the accusative of extent) 197.
τὰ (acc.pl.neut.of the article in agreement with εἴδωλα) 9.
εἴδωλα (acc.pl.neut.of εἴδωλον, extent) 3138.
τὰ (acc.pl.neut.of the article in agreement with ἄφωνα) 9.
ἄφωνα (acc.pl.neut.of ἄφωνος, in agreement with εἴδωλα) 3177.
ὡς (particle introducing a causal participle) 128.
ἂν (contingency particle) 205.
ἤγεσθε (2d.per.pl.imp.pass.ind.of ἄγω, progressive duration) 876.
ἀπαγόμενοι (pres.pass.part.nom.pl.masc.of ἀπάγω, adverbial, causal) 665.

Translation - "You are now aware that when you were pagans, presumably because you were motivated to do so, you were led to the idols that could not speak."

Comment: There are two main points in verse 2. Before they became Christians the Corinthians were pagans who worshipped inarticulate idols which could not communicate to them in any way. An idol is totally passive. It can only receive worship. It is incapable of producing thought, emotion or action in the experience of the worshipper. It is never an active force in the life of the devotee.

The second thought is that the pagan Corinthians worshipped these idols because (causal participle in ἀπαγόμενοι in the present tense) in their unregenerate days they were being constantly seduced and led away to their stupid pagan worship. The presence of ἂν with ὡς and the temporal clause in the indicative means that Paul was presuming that the reason for their idol worship was that they were influenced by a force or forces outside themselves. By whom? Not by the idols themselves, for Paul has already said that they are inarticulate. He emphasizes this by placing τὰ ἄφωνα in the emphatic attributive position.

The seducer of course is Satan (2 Cor.4:4; Eph.2:2,3; 1 John 5:19; John 10:10). Note ἀπάγω (#665) in the seductive sense in Mt.7:13. Thus the Corinthians were passive, being acted upon by Satan, who was leading them away at all times to an empty and fake worship of an inarticulate stick or stone. The Corinthians knew this now having become aware of it at the time of their regeneration. This is the force of the intensive perfect in Οἴδατε. Note ὡς ἂν ἤγεσθε. ὡς with ἂν in the temporal clause. "When you were led to the pagan idol altar it was probably because you were being motivated to do so by a force outside yourself - a force diabolical and malignant." The thought of verse 3 is that, whatever the force that victimized the Corinthians in their pagan days and motivated their heathen worship it was not the Holy Spirit of God.

Verse 3 - "Wherefore I give you to understand, that no man speaking by the Spirit of God calleth Jesus accursed: and that no man can say that Jesus is the Lord, but by the Holy Ghost."

διὸ γνωρίζω ὑμῖν ὅτι οὐδεὶς ἐν πνεύματι θεοῦ λαλῶν λέγει, Ἀνάθεμα Ἰησοῦς, καὶ οὐδεὶς δύναται εἰπεῖν, Κύριος Ἰησοῦς, εἰ μὴ ἐν πνεύματι ἁγίῳ.

"Therefore I want you to understand that no one speaking by the Spirit of God ever says, 'Jesus be cursed!' and no man can say 'Jesus is Lord' except by the Holy Spirit." . . . RSV

διὸ (inferential particle) 1622.
γνωρίζω (1st.per.sing.pres.act.ind.of γνωρίζω, aoristic) 1882.
ὑμῖν (dat.pl.masc.of σύ, indirect object of γνωρίζω) 104.
ὅτι (conjunction introducing an object clause in indirect discourse) 211.
οὐδεὶς (nom.sing.masc.of οὐδείς, subject of λέγει) 446.
ἐν (preposition with the instrumental of means) 80
πνεύματι (instru.sing.neut.of πνεῦμα, means) 83.
θεοῦ (gen.sing.masc.of θεός, description) 124.
λαλῶν (pres.act.part.nom.sing.masc.of λαλέω, adverbial, temporal) 815.
λέγει (3d.per.sing.pres.act.ind.of λέγω, aoristic) 66.
Ἀνάθεμα (exclamation) 3597.
Ἰησοῦς (nom.sing.masc.of Ἰησοῦς, subject of ἐστιν understood) 3.
καὶ (continuative conjunction) 14.
οὐδεὶς (nom.sing.masc.of οὐδείς, subject of δύναται) 446.
δύναται (3d.per.sing.pres.mid.ind.of δύναμαι, aoristic) 289.
εἰπεῖν (aor.act.inf.of εἶπον, epexegetical) 155.
Κύριος (nom.sing.masc.of κύριος, predicate nominative) 97.
Ἰησοῦς (nom.sing.masc.of Ἡσοῦς, subject of ἐστιν understood) 3.
εἰ (conditional particle in an elliptical first-class condition) 337.
μὴ (negative particle in an elliptical first-class condition) 87.
ἐν (preposition with the instrumental of means) 80.
πνεύματι (instru.sing.neut.of πνεῦμα, means) 83.
ἁγίῳ (instru.sing.neut.of ἅγιος, in agreement with πνεύματι) 84.

Translation - "So I am telling you that no one when he is speaking under the influence of the Spirit of God ever says, 'Cursed Jesus', and no one is able to say 'Lord Jesus' except by the Holy Spirit."

Comment: The two facts of verse 2 are now matched by two more facts in verse 3. The Corinthians had been motivated to go to the idol temple and say, 'Cursed Jesus,' but the motivation did not come from the idol itself. Now Paul says that when they said, "Cursed Jesus" they were not being motivated by the Holy Spirit of God. And when they said, "Jesus is Lord" at the time of their regeneration they were motivated by no one else except the Holy Spirit of God. If the idol itself did not put the curse in the minds and upon their lips, and if the Holy Spirit did not, who did? We have already answered that in comment upon verse 2. It was Satan. Now who motivated them to repent and replace the epithet "Cursed Jesus" with the confession "Jesus is Lord"? It was not the dumb idol. It was not Satan. It was not even themselves. It was the Holy Spirit. When one speaks by the Holy Spirit he cannot curse Jesus. When he speaks by the Holy Spirit, and only when he speaks by the Holy Spirit can he say, "Jesus is Lord."

Thus we have Paul setting forth the tenet which Calvinists later called effectual call and divine enabling. It is the Holy Spirit (John 3:8; Rom.8:14) who enables the lost sinner, previously seduced by Satan to curse Jesus (2 Cor.4:4; Eph.2:2,3) now to call upon His name and be saved (Rom.10:9,10,13). Paul thus begins his discussion of the gifts of the Spirit by pointing out that the Christian experience begins with the Holy Spirit (John 16:7-11). The implication is that any capabilities which the Christian may have, which he did not have before the Holy Spirit enabled him to say, "Jesus is Lord", capabilities which Satan, who motivated him to say, "Curse Jesus" did not give to him, and which the inarticulate idol did not give to him, are gifts of the Holy Spirit. Did he have these gifts when he stood before an idol and cursed Jesus? Obviously not. Does he have them now, since the moment that he was enabled to call Jesus his Lord? Obviously yes. Then Who is the Giver of these gifts?

We call attention now to the fact that by $\pi\nu\epsilon\hat{\upsilon}\mu\alpha$ Paul means the Holy Spirit of God, the third person of the Godhead. This fact is important when we exegete verse 13.

The Pelagian and Arminian contentions that unregenerate man is capable, in and of himself, to choose Christ or to deny Him, is denied by this verse. Every sinner who, in repentance, called Jesus his Lord did so because prior to his utterance he was enabled to do so by the Holy Spirit.

One is struck with the prominence which the Holy Spirit has chosen to give to Himself in this epistle. It is the Spirit who reveals to us the things "which God hath prepared for them that love him" (1 Cor.2:10). It is the Spirit Who has researched the "deep things of God" (1 Cor.2:10,11). It is the Holy Spirit Who teaches us as He compares "spiritual things with spiritual" (1 Cor.2:13). He it is Who regenerates the "natural" man and then who changes the "carnal" Christian into a "spiritual" Christian (1 Cor.2:14-3:3). It is His guidance that enables us to build upon the foundation a Christian superstructure of "gold, silver and precious stones" (1 Cor.3:10-14). He guides Christians to peaceful solutions of legal disputes without recourse to secular courts (1 Cor.6). He guides us in matters relating to marriage and the family (1 Cor.7). He guides us to the answers to questions about eating certain meats and directs our life styles that they do not hinder the growth of other saints (1 Cor.8). He directs our methods of personal evangelism (1 Cor.9). It is His guidance which helps us avoid Israel's backslidings in the wilderness (1 Cor.10), since it is the body of the Christian which is His temple (1 Cor.6:19,20). He directs what we wear and how we should conduct ourselves at the Lord's Supper. And now in chapter 12 He enriches us with His gifts. In chapter 13 He tells us that though His gifts are great and greatly to be treasured they are worse than useless without the love which, though not one of His gifts is one of His fruits. He also tells us in chapter 13 that one of His gifts would *cease* and that two others would be phased out when their *ad hoc* function was completed. In chatper 14 He lays down strict orders as to how the linguistic ability is to be regulated.

Finally He devotes the 15th chapter to the resurrection of the physical bodies of all of those who are incorporated into the mystical Body of Christ. It was His baptism that brought the elect into that Body (1 Cor.12:13). It is His witness that reassures us that we are members of the Body (Rom.8:16-17) and it is His presence in our bodies that guarantees that we will be glorified when the Head of the Body comes again (Rom.8:11). All of this is true because when we believed He sealed us as God's property (Eph.1:13,14; 4:30). At the time of our regeneration He moved in and made our bodies His temple (1 Cor.6:19) and, though we grieve Him, we cannot grieve Him away, because He is the "down payment" that secures the transaction until at glorification we are totally redeemed (Eph.4:30).

During the Old Testament period God the Father spoke unto the fathers through the mouths of the Prophets. During the first thirty-three years of the "last days" He spoke unto us through His Son. Throughout the remainder of the "last days" He has spoken unto us through the Holy Spirit. When the "last days" (Heb.1:1-2) are over and the mystery is completed (Eph.3:1-13; Rev.10:7) our Lord will return and establish the kingdom that will never be overthrown. Sinners rejected God the Father in the Old Testament period; they rejected God the Son when He was here in incarnation; if they reject God the Holy Spirit now, there remains no fourth member of the Godhead to appeal to them. That is why the sin of attributing to   Beelzeboul the ministry of the Holy Spirit is the sin for which there is no forgiveness. His offer of salvation is the last escape hatch from the world which is under judgment and is soon to be set on fire.

The Holy Spirit's revelation consists of the literature of the New Testament. It is complete (John 16:12-14). It goes beyond the revelation which our Lord gave to the Apostles. Jesus could not tell them more, not because He did not know more to say to them, but because at that point they were unable to grasp what He had to say. When they were filled with the Holy Spirit (Acts 2:1-4) they began to be receptive to the remainder of the revelation, which the Holy Spirit gave to them and which they committed to writing. This writing we call the New Testament. It was completed when the Apostle John finished his gospel and epistles. The Holy Spirit has had nothing to say to the Body of Christ since the first century, because He has said all in the literature which, through the gifts of prophecy and knowledge, He enabled the writers of the New Testament to understand and record. When He had written *Finis* to the revelation, the gifts of prophecy and knowledge were phased out. *Cf.* our comment on 1 Cor.13:8-13. Those who, since the close of the first century of the Christian era, claim heavenly supernatural powers to add to the revelation which the Holy Spirit gave to the Apostles are mistaken. The fact that they are mistaken does not impugn their sincerity nor suggest that they are unregenerate, but it does establish that they are perhaps unwitting tools in the hands of Satan as he unleashes upon the world his hellish campaign of deception.

There can be no doubt that the Holy Spirit has given His gifts to the children of God and that each gift has been given to be used in the performance of specific functions in the Body of Christ, as He directs. It is the duty of the child of God to find his gift and to use it as our Lord, Who is Head over all things to His church (Eph.1:22,23) directs. It is also his duty to avoid imagining that he possesses gifts which were indispensable in the ministry of the church in the first century before the New Testament literature was written.

Verse 4 - "Now there are diversities of gifts, but the same spirit."

Διαιρέσεις δὲ χαρισμάτων εἰσίν, τὸ δὲ αὐτὸ πνεῦμα.

"Now there are varieties of gifts, but the same Spirit;" . . . *RSV*

#4212 Διαιρέσεις (nom.pl.fem.of διαίρεσις, subject of εἰσίν).

King James Version

difference - 1 Cor.12:5.
diversity - 1 Cor.12:4,6.

Revised Standard Version

varieties - 1 Cor.12:4,5,6.

Meaning: Cf. διαιρέω (#2545). Hence, different types, varieties. Followed by a genitive of description - χαρισμάτων in 1 Cor.12:4; by διακονιῶν in 1 Cor.12:5; by ἐνεργημάτων in 1 Cor.12:6. These gifts were given in keeping with the sovereign will of the Holy Spirit - διαιροῦν ἰδίᾳ ἑκάστῳ καθὼς βούλεται - 1 Cor.12:11.

δὲ (explanatory conjunction) 11.
χαρισμάτων (gen.pl.neut.of χάρισμα, description) 3790
εἰσίν (3d.per.pl.pres.ind.of εἰμί, static) 86.
τὸ (nom.sing.neut.of the article in agreement with πνεῦμα) 9.
δὲ (adversative conjunction) 11.
αὐτὸ (nom.sing.neut.of αὐτός, in agreement with πνεῦμα) 16.
πνεῦμα (nom.sing.neut.of πνεῦμα, subject of ἐστιν understood) 83.

Translation - "Now there are various kinds of gifts, but the same Spirit."

Comment: The fact that one Christian has one gift and another a different gift, while a third and a fourth are enriched in other ways, does not speak of a multiplicity of gods or spirits as animism teaches. There is only one Holy Spirit, but He is God and He is capable of dividing among the saints whom He calls a variety of capabilities. The saints are *one* in that they are all enriched by the same divine Benefactor. The saints are *many* in that each has his own gift peculiar to himself. Even those with the same gift may possess varying degrees of ability to exercise it, due to differing cultural backgrounds. All of these details are known to God and taken into account as the Holy Spirit enriches the Body of Christ. Just as it is the function of the Holy Spirit to bestow the gifts, so it is the function of Jesus Christ, the Head over all things to His church to direct how, when, where and to what extent each member of His body will exercise it.

Since the saints are all members of the same Body of Christ, the Body, thanks to the wise distribution of gifts to the several members by the Holy Spirit, is a many splendored organism, fully capable of fulfilling the total will of Christ, the Head (Eph.1:22,23). The extent to which the Church fails to perform in keeping with the perfect will of God is the extent to which the individual saints fail to be filled with the Holy Spirit.

Verse 5 - "And there are differences of administrations, but the same Lord."

καὶ διαιρέσεις διακονιῶν εἰσιν, καὶ ὁ αὐτὸς κύριος.

"And there are varieties of service, but the same Lord:" . . . RSV

καὶ (continuative conjunction) 14.
διαιρέσεις (nom.pl.fem.of διαίρεσις subject of εἰσιν) 4212.
διακονιῶν (gen.pl.fem.of διακονία, description) 2441.
εἰσιν (3d.per.pl.pres.ind.of εἰμί, static) 86.
καὶ (adversative conjunction) 14.
ὁ (nom.sing.masc.of the article in agreement with κύριος) 9.
αὐτὸς (nom.sing.masc.of αὐτός, intensive, in agreement with κύριος) 16.
κύριος (nom.sing.masc.of κύριος, subject of ἐστιν, understood) 97.

Translation - "And there are various kinds of duties to perform but the same Lord."

Comment: In verse 4 He is called the Spirit. In verse 5 He is called the Lord. In verse 6 He is called God. Indeed the Holy Spirit is both Lord and God. χάρισμα (verse 4) is a general term applied to all of the capabilities with which the saints are equipped by the Holy Spirit. διακονία (#2441) in verse 5 is also a general term indicating that the gifts are useful. They provide services. The word "administration" of the KJV has come to mean institutional direction and supervision, such as the function of the president of a corporation who makes and directs policy. διακονία (#2441) means any kind of service - doing anything that needs to be done for the good of the operation of the Body of Christ. Study #2441 for a list of services mentioned in the New Testament, though this list is not exhaustive. The church custodian and he/she who passes out the hymn books performs a service.

Verse 6 - "And there are diversities of operations, but it is the same God which worketh all in all."

καὶ διαιρέσεις ἐνεργημάτων εἰσίν, ὁ δὲ αὐτὸς θεός, ὁ ἐνεργῶν τὰ πάντα ἐν πᾶσιν.

"and there are varieties of working, but it is the same God who inspires all in every one." . . . RSV

καὶ (continuative conjunction) 14.
διαιρέσεις (nom.pl.fem.of διαίρεσις, subject of εἰσίν) 4212.

#4213 ἐνεργημάτων (gen.pl.neut.of ἐνέργημα, description).

King James Version

operation - 1 Cor.12:6.
working - 1 Cor.12:10.

Revised Standard Version

working - 1 Cor.12:6,10.

Meaning: Cf. ἐνέργεια (#4466), ἐνεργέω (#1105); ἐνεργής (#4260). Hence, the result of energy at work. Workings; operations. Absolutely in 1 Cor.12:6; followed by δυνάμεων in 1 Cor.12:10.

εἰσίν (3d.per.pl.pres.ind.of εἰμί, static) 86.
ὁ (nom.sing.masc.of the article in agreement with θεός) 9.
δὲ (adversative conjunction) 11.
αὐτὸς (nom.sing.masc.of αὐτός, intensive, in agreement with θεός) 16.
θεός (nom.sing.masc.of θεός, subject of ἐστιν understood) 124.
ὁ (nom.sing.masc.of the article in agreement with ἐνεργῶν) 9.
ἐνεργῶν (pres.act.part.nom.sing.masc.of ἐνεργέω, apposition) 1105.
τὰ (acc.pl.neut.of the article in agreement with πάντα) 9.
πάντα (acc.pl.neut.of πᾶς, direct object of ἐνεργῶν) 67.
ἐν (preposition with the locative, place) 80.
πᾶσιν (loc.pl.masc.of πᾶς, place) 67.

Translation - "And there are all kinds of operations, but it is the same God, the One who manipulates all of the gifts in everybody."

Comment: The division of labor in the Godhead is clear. The legislative function is performed by God the Father. He is the universal Lawmaker. The Lord Jesus Christ is the Judge (John 5:22). The Holy Spirit is the Executive. He has the function of carrying out the will of the Father as adjudicated by the Lord Jesus Christ. He directs the working of every gift which He has given to each member of the Body of Christ. Note the article τὸ with πάντα, but not with πᾶσιν. He activates each of the gifts in the Body of Christ as a whole. Of course he also activates each gift in each member individually, for He dwells within the physical body of every Christian and it is at His direction and by His inspiration that each child of God exercises his special gift. The Holy Spirit never asks any Christian to do that which he cannot do. Educational directors in churches should remember this. No one should be asked to teach a Sunday School class who does not have the gift of teaching. The gift of teaching is far more important than the knowledge of the subject to be taught, though the gifted teacher sins grievously against the Giver of his gift, if he does not prepare himself as thoroughly as possible in the field of academe with a knowledge of the subject to be taught. No one is justified in saying that since he has the gift of teaching he need not have a knowledge of that which is to be taught. On the other hand, the thorough scholar without the Holy Spirit's gift of teaching is ineffective in the classroom, while the less well informed person with the gift of teaching will do better.

This verse gives us a picture of a perfectly coordinated body, subject to one will, with each member used to exercise his specific skills, with the result that what is done innures to the personal benefit of all. A professional symphony orchestra under the direction of a perfect director or a football team coached by a professional demonstrates a team of highly skilled players, each with the ability to function so that a perfect meshing of coordinate abilities brings the result desired. The Body of Christ, as she goes about in the world in obedience to His divine command, in promotion of the worldwide missionary enterprise, is God's ideal symphony and God's ideal team.

In contrast the local church where stubborn members at best leave unused, or at worst, misuse their gifts, makes sin hideous. The play on Saturday afternoon that goes awry because a lineman missed his block or a pass receiver failed to run the pattern, or the cachophony of the symphony or village choir because the strings were out of tune or the altos sang flat, are pitiable illustrations of the ineptitude of a local church in which worldly unconcern and sin have prevented God's plan from being executed. But when the Head of the Body is in perfect control of every member because the Holy Spirit, Who is always resident is also regnant, the efficiency, grace and beauty of the Body is marvelous to behold.

Verse 7 — "But the manifestation of the Spirit is given to every man to profit withal."

ἑκάστῳ δὲ δίδοται ἡ φανέρωσις τοῦ πνεύματος πρὸς τὸ συμφέρον.

"To each is given the manifestation of the Spirit for the common good." . . .
RSV

ἑκάστῳ (dat.sing.masc.of ἕκαστος, indirect object of δίδοται) 1217.
δὲ (continuative conjunction) 11
δίδοται (3d.per.sing.pres.pass.ind.of δίδωμι, customary) 362.
ἡ (nom.sing.fem.of the article in agreement with φανέρωσις) 9.

#4214 φανέρωσις (nom.sing.fem.of φανέρωσις, subject of δίδοται).

King James Version

manifestation - 1 Cor.12:7; 2 Cor.4:2.

Revised Standard Version

manifestation - 1 Cor.12:7.
open statement - 2 Cor.4:2.

Meaning: Cf. φανερόω (#1960); φανερός (#981); φανερῶς (#2072). Hence, manifestation; disclosure; display; indication. Followed by a genitive of description in 1 Cor.12:7; followed by τῆς ἀληθείας in 2 Cor.4:2.

τοῦ (gen.sing.neut.of the article in agreement with πνεύματος) 9.
πνεύματος (gen.sing.neut.of πνεῦμα, description) 83.
πρὸς (preposition with the accusative, purpose) 197.
τὸ (acc.sing.neut.of the article in agreement with συμφέρον) 9.
συμφέρον (pres.act.part.acc.sing.neut.of συμφέρω, substantival, purpose) 505.

Translation - "And to each one is given the evidence of the Spirit for the purpose of achieving the common good."

Comment: Paul again speaks in terms of the one and the many. There are many members. Each is saved. Each gets a gift. The confirmation that he feels in his heart that the Holy Spirit has saved him and has given him a gift also tells him that he is to use his gift, at the direction of the Lord Jesus Christ, for the common good of the body. Note πρὸς and the articular substantival participle in the accusative case - "For the purpose of putting it all together for the advantage of everyone." There was never ἡ φανέρωσις τοῦ εἰδώλου. The idol could bestow no gift upon the pagan worshipper, nor could it witness within his darkened and silent heart, because it is τὸ εἴδωλον τὸ ἄφωνον - "an inarticulare idol." But the Holy Spirit is not inarticulate. He calls, regenerates, quickens, teaches, gives His gifts, indwells, asks that He may infill and assures and reassures each child of God that he is important because he has a task assigned to him which is assigned to no other and he has the ability to do what the task requires. The result is that the Body of Christ is perfectly coordinated and will function to be profitable for all - or at least it would be if the Holy Spirit were *president* in every temple where He is *resident* (1 Cor.6:19,20).

The various gifts and the manner in which they are distributed is the subject of verses 8-10.

Verse 8 - "For to one is given by the Spirit the word of wisdom; to another the word of knowledge by the same Spirit."

ᾧ μὲν γὰρ διὰ τοῦ πνεύματος δίδοται λόγος σοφίας, ἄλλῳ δὲ λόγος γνώσεως κατὰ τὸ αὐτὸ πνεῦμα.

"To one is given through the Spirit the utterance of wisdom, and to another the utterance of knowledge according to the same Spirit," . . . RSV

ᾧ (dat.sing.masc.of ὅς, relative pronoun, indirect object of δίδοται) 65.
μὲν (particle of affirmation) 300.
γὰρ (inferential conjunction) 105.
διὰ (preposition with the ablative of agent) 118.
τοῦ (abl.sing.neut.of the article in agreement with πνεύματος) 9.
πνεύματος (abl.sing.neut.of πνεῦμα, agent) 83.

δίδοται (3d.per.sing.pres.pass.ind.of δίδωμι, customary) 362.

λόγος (nom.sing.masc.of λόγος, subject of δίδοται) 510.

σοφίας (gen.sing.fem.of σοφία, description) 934.

ἄλλῳ (dat.sing.masc.of ἄλλος, indirect object of δίδοται) 198.

δὲ (adversative conjunction) 11.

λόγος (nom.sing.masc.of λόγος, subject of δίδοται) 510.

γνώσεως (gen.sing.fem.of γνῶσις, description) 1856.

κατὰ (preposition with the accusative, standard) 98.

τὸ (acc.sing.neut.of the article in agreement with πνεῦμα) 9.

αὐτὸ (acc.sing.neut.of αὐτός, in agreement with πνεῦμα, intensive) 16.

πνεῦμα (acc.sing.neut.of πνεῦμα, standard) 83.

Translation - "So to one a wise message is given by the Spirit, but to another a knowledgeable message (is given) in accord with the same Spirit."

Comment: ᾧ here is demonstrative, not relative. *Cf.*#65. Note its use with ἄλλῳ (verse 8) and ἑτέρῳ (verse 9) - "To one . . . to another. . . to the other . . . κ.τ.λ." Note the μὲν . . . δὲ sequence. The Holy Spirit is the divine Agent Who dispenses the gifts. λόγος σοφίας - "the message of holistic thinking." *Cf.* comment on previous uses of σοφία in 1 Corinthians, as listed under #934. σοφία is not one of the gifts which is scheduled to be phased out. *Cf.* comment on 1 Cor. 13:8-11. But γνῶσις is. The early church had members with the gift of knowledge (γνῶσις) who knew what to tell the churches about matters which were covered later in the Apostolic writings and which became the New Testament canon of inspired Scripture. What the Apostles had imparted to them by the Holy Spirit in the exercise of their gift of γνῶσις they recorded in the New Testament. As knowledge of these matters became common property as a part of revelation, the gift of knowledge was no longer needed and hence withdrawn (1 Cor. 13:8, at which reference, more on this subject). This λόγος γνῶσις - "knowledgeable utterance" is not the prerogative of any Christian today, nor has it been since the New Testament canon of Scripture was finished in the first century.

λόγος γνῶσις as used here is not synonymous with science in the sense that we think of a highly educated person with great academic accomplishments and superior intellectual powers. The "knowledge" which we possess now is either that which we acquired in pursuit of the scientific method of research or which we derived from a study of the Bible. Nothing new has been added to the divine revelation which the Holy Spirit gave the Body of Christ in the first century. Neither Joseph Smith and the Mormons, nor the Watchtower Bible and Tract Society, nor Mary Baker Eddy, nor the self-appointed prophets of the so-called "Charismatic" groups are inspired mouth pieces of the Holy Spirit in the inerrant sense in which the Apostles were.

Meyer has suggested the following outline:

Charismata which have reference to intellectual power

    (1). λόγος σοφίας.

    (2). λόγος γνώσεως.

Charismata which depend upon special energy of faith

(1). The πίστις itself.
(2). It's agency in deeds,namely

    (a). ἰάματα.
    (b). δυνάμεις.

(3). Its agency in words, namely, the προφητεία.
(4). Its critical agency, the διάκρισις πνευμάτων.

Charismata which have reference to the γλῶσσαι

(1). Speaking with tongues.
(2). Interpretation of tongues.

(Meyer, 1st Corinthians, p.280).

The New Testament lists twenty gifts which Christ the Head over all things to His church and the Holy Spirit have given:

They are wisdom, knowledge (1 Cor.12:8) faith (1 Cor.12:9), healing (1 Cor.12:9,28), miracles (1 Cor.12:10,28); prophecy, discering of spirits (1 Cor.12:10), tongues (1 Cor.12:10,28), interpretation of tongues (1 Cor.12:10), helps and governments (1 Cor.12:28). In Romans 12:6, Paul mentions prophecy, ministering and teaching (Romans 12:7), exhorting, giving, ruling and showing mercy (Romans 12:8). Apostles, prophets and teachers are mentioned in 1 Cor.12:28 and Apostles, prophets, evangelists and pastor-teachers are listed in Ephesians 4:11. This is a total of twenty. Languages are said to cease and prophecy and knowledge are said to have been scheduled to be phased out (1 Cor.13:8). If the ability to speak in a language other than one in which one is naturally fluent is to cease, the gift of interpretation of the language is also no longer needed. There were only twelve men designated as Apostles by our Lord in the first century, to whom the Holy Spirit gave the special gifts of prophecy and knowledge which they utilized to guide the early churches in their infancy before the New Testament was written, and to record their knowledge in the divine record.

To affirm that the possession of certain designated gifts such as tongues, prophecies and knowledge is evidence of salvation and that those who lack these gifts are not saved is to say, in the absence of all Scripture whatsoever, that these designated gifts are more important than the others, and it is also to imply that there are no other gifts or that the Holy Spirit has given the other gifts, not on the favorite list, to the unsaved. Thus there is dissension in the Body of Christ and some are found to occupy the Judgment Throne which is reserved only to our Lord (John 5:22).

Verse 9 - "To another faith by the same Spirit: to another the gifts of healing by the same Spirit."

ἑτέρῳ πίστις ἐν τῷ αὐτῷ πνεύματι, ἄλλῳ δὲ χαρίσματα ἰαμάτων ἐν τῷ ἑνὶ πνεύματι,

". . . to another faith by the same Spirit, to another gifts of healing by the one Spirit." . . . RSV

ἑτέρῳ (dat.sing.masc.of ἕτερος, indirect object of δίδοται) 605.
πίστις (nom.sing.fem.of πίστις, subject of δίδοται) 728.
ἐν (preposition with the instrumental of means) 80.
τῷ (instru.sing.neut.of the article in agreement with πνεύματι) 9.
αὐτῷ (instru.sing.neut.of αὐτός, in agreement with πνεύματι) 16.
πνεύματι (instru.sing.neut.of πνεῦμα, means) 83.
ἄλλῳ (dat.sing.masc.of ἄλλος, indirect object of δίδοται) 198.
δὲ (continuative conjunction) 11.
χαρίσματα (nom.pl.neut.of χάρισμα, subject of δίδοται) 3790.

#4215 ἰαμάτων (gen.pl.neut.of ἴαμα, description).

King James Version

healing - 1 Cor.12:9,28,30.

Revised Standard Version

healing - 1 Cor.12:9,30.
healers - 1 Cor.12:28.

Meaning: Cf. ἰάομαι (#721); ἴασις (#2514); ἰατρός (#793). The act of healing; remedy; medicine; medical care. One of the gifts of the Spirit - 1 Cor.12:9,28,30.

ἐν (preposition with the instrumental of means) 80.
τῷ (instrumental sing.neut.of the article in agreement with πνεύματι) 9.
ἑνὶ (instru.sing.neut.of εἷς, in agreement with πνεύματι) 469.
πνεύματι (instru.sing.neut.of πνεῦμα, means) 83.

Translation - *"To another faith by the same Spirit, and to another gifts for a healing ministry by the one Spirit."*

Comment: Note the change from διὰ τοῦ πνεύματος in verse 8 to ἐν τῷ αὐτῷ πνεύματι in verse 9 - "through the agency of" and "by means of." ἰαμάτων is plural, indicating a ministry of healing in which the healer moves from one stricken patient to another.

Some Mss. have ἐν τῷ αὐτῷ πνεύματι in the last clause as in the first. p46 has ἐν τῷ πνεύματι, while Ψ omits ἰαμάτων . . . πνεύματι, but Aland, *et al* with B confidence, because of "the diversified support of ἑνὶ (A B 33 81 104 1739 etc.) "have retained ἑνὶ as *supra*.

The gift of healing is indeed a blessed gift when used scripturally in keeping with the procedure laid down in James 5:14. It is regrettable that some evangelists have used it as a prominent feature in a production which has Barnum and Bailey overtones and which often contributes to their estate. The true healer, with the genuine gift of the Holy Spirit, who carries on his ministry in keeping with James 5:14-16 is not an empire builder.

Verse 10 - "To another the working of miracles; to another prophecy; to another the discerning of spirits; to another divers kinds of tongues; to another the interpretation of tongues."

ἄλλῳ δὲ ἐνεργήματα δυνάμεων, ἄλλῳ δὲ) προφητεία, ἄλλῳ (δὲ) διακρίσεις πνευμάτων, ἑτέρῳ γένη γλωσσῶν, ἄλλῳ δὲ ἑρμηνεία γλωσσῶν.

". . . to another the working of miracles, to another prophecy, to another the ability to distinguish between spirits, to another various kinds of tongues, to another the interpretation of tongues." . . . RSV

ἄλλῳ (dat.sing.masc.of ἄλλος, indirect object of δίδοται) 198.
δὲ (continuative conjunction) 11.
ἐνεργήματα (nom.pl.neut.of ἐνέργημα, subject of δίδοται) 4213.
δυνάμεων (gen.pl.fem.of δύναμις, description) 687.
ἄλλῳ (dat.sing.masc.of ἄλλος, indirect object of δίδοται) 198.
(δὲ) (continuative conjunction) 11.
προφητεία (nom.sing.fem.of προφητεία, subject of δίδοται) 1041.
ἄλλῳ (dat.sing.masc.of ἄλλος, indirect object of δίδοται) 198.
(δὲ) (continuative conjunction) 11.
διακρίσεις (nom.pl.fem.of διάκρισις, subject of δίδοται) 4040.
πνευμάτων (gen.pl.neut.of πνεῦμα, description) 83.
ἑτέρῳ (dat.sing.masc.of ἕτερος, indirect object of δίδοται) 605.
γένη (nom.pl.neut.of γένος, subject of δίδοται) 1090.
γλωσσῶν (gen.pl.fem.of γλῶσσα, description) 1846.
ἄλλῳ (dat.sing.masc.of ἄλλος, indirect object of δίδοται) 198.
δὲ (continuative conjunction) 11.

#4216 ἑρμηνεία (nom.sing.fem.of ἑρμηνεία, subject of δίδοται).

King James Version

interpretation - 1 Cor.12:10; 14:26.

Revised Standard Version

interpretation - 1 Cor.12:10; 14:26.

Meaning: Cf. ἑρμηνεύω (#1965). Hence, an interpretation. In the New Testament of that which has been spoken in a language other that which could naturally be understood by those present - 1 Cor.12:10; 14:26. The Greek New Testament knows nothing of an *unknown* tongue (language).

γλωσσῶν (gen.pl.fem.of γλῶσσα, description) 1846.

Translation - "And to another miraculous deeds, and to another prophecy, and to another distinction between spirits, to another various languages and to another their translation.

Comment: Prophecy (προφητεία), along with γνῶσις are the two gifts of the

Holy Spirit which were phased out when the New Testament canon of Scripture became complete (1 Cor. 13:8). The Body of Christ needs nothing further in the way of supernatural revelation of truth than that which the Holy Spirit placed in the New Testament. This is not to say that we do not need His constant help to sharpen our skills in exegesis of that which He has written. He will help us, if we ask Him, to avoid reading into the text our preconceptions and He will save us from errors of translation and interpretation which arise from ignorance of grammar and syntax and He will help us to put all that He has written in context and view it in *zeitgeist*. Exegesis of what He has already written is essential, but we need pay no attention to self-appointed "prophets" and "holy men" who tell us that they have a message from the Lord which is supplemental to that which He has already caused to be recorded.

The ability to discriminate between spirits is a marvelous gift. Some Christians can "sense" heresy and the presence of heretics, long before their intellectual analysis of what is being taught bears out their purely subjective impression. Christians with this gift often identify books as having been produced by Watchtower Bible and Tract Society writers or by Mormons without opening them for examination or noting the color and type face on the outside.

There is danger in the church that those who possess certain gifts will think themselves superior to others who do not. It must be kept in mind that the capabilities listed are "gifts" given by the Sovereign Holy Spirit for a purpose and that no special merit attaches to the recipient. Every member of the Body of Christ has some gift. As we shall see in Chapter 14 the gift of languages would be useless unless the Holy Spirit gave the gift of interpretation to another Christian. The ability to perform miracles apparently ceased with the Apostolic age. While it existed it served to give authenticity to the message of the Apostles, at a time when there was no written New Testament. The full revelation of the incarnation of Jesus Christ, His virgin birth, sinless life, matchless teachings, super-scientific miracles, atoning death, bodily resurrection and ascension is now with us in the Greek New Testament. It is the full revelation of truth, of which the gospel accounts, which deal with the earthly ministry of Jesus, is only partial (John 16:12-15). It is a "more sure word of prophecy" than that possessed by Peter, James and John on the Mount of Transfiguration as they stood transfixed by the metamorphosis of Jesus (Mt. 17:2; Mk. 9:2; 2 Pet. 1:16-21). What need we with any more? It is a wicked and adulterous generation that seeks for a sign (Mt. 12:38-40). No other sign will be given to the world than that of our Heavenly Jonah. That story is told in its fullness in the New Testament. The unsaved must reach their conclusions about Jesus Christ on the basis of what the New Testament says. If they will not believe Moses, the Prophets and the Apostles who wrote the New Testament they would not believe even if one rose from the dead.

Satan will have his miracle workers at work in the last days of the last days (Rev. 13:13-15) and the chaos that will result is characteristic of the confusion that now follows the self-appointed miracle worker who, in the name of Christ, claims special powers. If anyone had the gift of miracles today he could preach anything he wished, however extra/unscriptural, authenticate his message with a "miracle" and gain a following. The unsaved will believe the devil's lies if they see a miracle, but they will not believe the truth even though the greatest miracle of all, the incarnation of Jesus Christ, is presented to them.

Verse 11 - "But all these worketh that one and the selfsame Spirit, dividing to every man severally as he will."

πάντα δὲ ταῦτα ἐνεργεῖ τὸ ἓν καὶ τὸ αὐτὸ πνεῦμα, διαιροῦν ἰδίᾳ ἑκάστῳ καθὼς βούλεται.

"All these are inspired by the same Spirit, who apportions to each one individually as he wills." . . . RSV

πάντα (acc.pl.neut.of πᾶς, in agreement with ταῦτα) 67.
δὲ (continuative conjunction) 11.
ταῦτα (acc.pl.neut.of οὗτος, direct object of ἐνεργεῖ) 93.
ἐνεργεῖ (3d.per.sing.pres.act.ind.of ἐνεργέω, customary) 1105.
τὸ (nom.sing.neut.of the article in agreement with πνεῦμα) 9.
ἓν (nom.sing.neut.of εἷς, in agreement with πνεῦμα) 469.
καὶ (adjunctive conjunction joining modifiers) 14.
τὸ (nom.sing.neut.of the article in agreement with πνεῦμα) 9.
αὐτὸ (nom.sing.neut.of αὐτός, in agreement with πνεῦμα) 16.
πνεῦμα (nom.sing.neut.of πνεῦμα, subject of ἐνεργεῖ) 83.
διαιροῦν (pres.act.part.nom.sing.neut.of διαιρέω, adverbial, modal) 2545.
ἰδίᾳ (instru.sing.fem.of ἴδιος, manner) 778.
ἑκάστῳ (dat.sing.masc.of ἕκαστος, indirect object of διαιροῦν) 1217.
καθὼς (compound comparative particle) 1348.
βούλεται (3d.per.sing.pres.mid.ind.of βούλομαι, aoristic) 953.

Translation - "And one and the same Spirit does all of these things, parcelling out to each of us individually, just as He wishes."

Comment: πάντα δὲ ταῦτα, the object of ἐνεργεῖ is in emphasis. *Cf.* Phil.2:13 and Eph.1:11 for other uses of ἐνεργέω (#1105). The sovereign power of the Holy Spirit is demonstrated. He dispenses His gifts καθὼς βούλεται - "precisely as He wishes," which is parallel to κατὰ τὴν βουλὴν τοῦ θελήματος αὐτοῦ in Eph.1:11 and also Phil.2:13 - ὑπὲρ τῆς εὐδοκίας. The Holy Spirit, the sovereign Dispenser of gifts is the divine Executive of the Godhead, Who is putting together by regeneration and Spirit baptism the Body of Christ, as he adds in verse 12,13.

One Body with Many Members

(1 Corinthians 12:12-31)

Verse 12 - "For as the body is one, and hath many members, and all the members of that one body, being many, are one body: so also is Christ."

Καθάπερ γὰρ τὸ σῶμα ἕν ἐστιν καὶ μέλη πολλὰ ἔχει, πάντα δὲ τὰ μέλη τοῦ σώματος πολλὰ ὄντα ἕν ἐστιν σῶμα, οὕτως καὶ ὁ Χριστός.

"For just as the body is one and has many members, and all the members of the body, though many, are one body, so it is with Christ." . . . RSV

Καθάπερ (intensive comparative particle) 3883.
γὰρ (causal conjunction) 105.
τὸ (nom.sing.neut.of the article in agreement with σῶμα) 9.
σῶμα (nom.sing.neut.of σῶμα, subject of ἐστιν) 507.
ἕν (nom.sing.neut.of εἷς, predicate adjective) 469.
ἐστιν (3d.per.sing.pres.ind.of εἰμί, static) 86.
καὶ (concessive conjunction) 14.
μέλη (acc.pl.neut.of μέλος, direct object of ἔχει) 506.
πολλὰ (acc.pl.neut.of πολύς, in agreement with μέλη) 228.
ἔχει (3d.per.sing.pres.act.ind.of ἔχω, static) 82.
πάντα (nom.pl.neut.of πᾶς, in agreement with μέλη) 67.
δὲ (continuative conjunction) 11.
τὰ (nom.pl.neut.of the article in agreement with μέλη) 9.
μέλη (nom.pl.neut.of μέλος, subject of ἐστιν) 506.
τοῦ (gen.sing.neut.of the article in agreement with σώματος) 9.
σώματος (gen.sing.neut.of σῶμα, possession) 507.
πολλὰ (nom.pl.neut.of πολύς, predicate adjective) 228.
ὄντα (pres.part.nom.pl.neut.of εἰμί, adverbial, concessive) 86.
ἕν (nom.sing.neut.of εἷς, predicate adjective) 469.
ἐστιν (3d.per.sing.pres.ind.of εἰμί, static) 86.
οὕτως (demonstrative adverb) 74.
καὶ (adjunctive conjunction joining substantives) 14.
ὁ (nom.sing.masc.of the article in agreement with Χριστός) 9.
Χριστός (nom.sing.masc.of Χριστός, subject of ἐστιν understood) 4.

Translation - *"Because precisely as the body is a unit, even though it has many parts, and all the parts, though they are many are one body, so also is Christ."*

Comment: Paul presented the same analogy to the Romans (Romans 12:4-8) and in the same connection - spiritual gifts. Note the Καθάπερ. . . οὕτως sequence - "Precisely as . . . even so. . . " Note the rare use of concessive καὶ. Despite the fact that the human body has many organs it is neverthelsss a coordinated unit, with each member functioning properly only as it depends upon the other members. This human analogy finds it likeness in the Body of Christ, mystically uniting every believer as a member united to the Head, who is Christ. Here is Paul's use of the famous "one and the many" model in philosophy.

Now we are to learn that the Holy Spirit, Who is Lord (verse 5) and God (verse 6) and Who is sovereign (verse 11), Who is the Dispenser of spiritual gifts, is also responsible for forming the Body of Christ (verse 13). He Who produced the physical body of Jesus in Mary's womb (Lk.1:35; Mt.1:20,21) is also engaged in producing the spiritual Body of Christ.

Verse 13 - "For by one Spirit are we all baptized into one body, whether we be Jews or Gentiles, whether we be bond or free: and have been all made to drink into one Spirit."

καὶ γὰρ ἐν ἑνὶ πνεύματι ἡμεῖς πάντες εἰς ἓν σῶμα ἐβαπτίσθημεν, εἴτε Ἰουδαῖοι εἴτε Ἕλληνες, εἴτε δοῦλοι εἴτε ἐλεύθεροι, καὶ πάντες ἓν πνεῦμα ἐποτίσθημεν.

"For by one Spirit we were all baptized into one body — Jews or Greeks, slaves or free — and all were made to drink of one Spirit." . . . RSV

καὶ (continuative conjunction) 14.

γὰρ (causal conjunction) 105.

ἐν (preposition with the instrumental of means) 80.

ἑνὶ (instru.sing.neut.of εἷς, in agreement with πνεύματι) 469.

πνεύματι (instru.sing.neut.of πνεῦμα, means) 83.

ἡμεῖς (nom.pl.masc.of ἐγώ, subject of ἐβαπτίσθημεν) 123.

πάντες (nom.pl.masc.of πᾶς, in agreement with ἡμεῖς) 67.

εἰς (preposition with the accusative, extent, metaphorical) 140.

ἓν (acc.sing.neut.of εἷς, in agreement with σῶμα) 469.

σῶμα (acc.sing.neut.of σῶμα, metaphorical extent) 507.

ἐβαπτίσθημεν (1st.per.pl.aor.pass.ind.of βαπτίζω, culminative) 273.

εἴτε (disjunctive) 4016.

Ἰουδαῖοι (nom.pl.masc.of Ἰουδαῖος, predicate nominative) 143.

εἴτε (disjunctive) 4016.

Ἕλληνες (nom.pl.masc.of Ἕλλην, predicate nominative) 2373.

εἴτε (disjunctive) 4016.

δοῦλοι (nom.pl.masc.of δοῦλος, predicate nominative) 725.

εἴτε (disjunctive) 4016.

ἐλεύθεροι (nom.pl.masc.of ἐλεύθερος, predicate nominative) 1245.

καὶ (continuative conjunction) 14.

πάντες (nom.pl.masc.of πᾶς, subject of ἐποτίσθημεν) 67.

ἓν (acc.sing.neut.of εἷς, in agreement with πνεῦμα) 469.

πνεῦμα (acc.sing.neut.of πνεῦμα, accusative of the things with a passive voice verb) 83.

ἐποτίσθημεν (1st.per.pl.aor.pass.ind.of ποτίζω, culminative) 900.

Translation - "Because all of us were immersed by one Spirit into one body, whether Jews or Greeks, slaves or free men, and all have been saturated with one Spirit."

Comment: That this is not water baptism is clear since the instrumental clause ἐν ἑνὶ πνεύματι says that the medium is the Spirit, not water. That the Holy Spirit is meant is clear from the context. Paul has made the Holy Spirit the theme of the chapter since verse 1. This in rebuttal to the old-time view that interprets the verse to mean, "Every member of a local church was baptized in water on the authority of the voting members present who, in a spirit of unity, voted to receive the candidate into full fellowship upon his immersion in water."

Verse 12 makes clear that σῶμα means the Body of Christ, not a local autonomous church body. The school of the baptismal regenerationists who must hold that all references to baptism in the Scripture must mean water, should consult the plain text and research #273 for other passages in which the context is clear that Spirit baptism is meant. The unity that exists in the minds of a congregation is indeed the fruit of the Spirit, but the πνεῦμα of this verse means the third person of the Godhead, not a psychological state of unanimity in a congregation.

The Holy Spirit Who led us (Rom.8:14), convicted us (John 16:8-11), and breathed upon us (John 3:8) has also immersed (overwhelmed) us and incorporated us into Christ's mystical body (1 Cor.12:13). He has also sealed us (Eph.1:13; 4:30), given us gifts (1 Cor.12:1-11) and produced His fruit in our lives (Gal.5:22,23). He is the Agent through Whom Christ's prayer of John 17:21 is answered.

The accusative in ἐν πνεῦμα is an example of a passive voice verb retaining an accusative of the thing. Other examples are Acts 18:25; 2 Thess.2:15; Mt.22:11; Mk.1:6; Rev.1:13; 15:6; 19:14; Lk.16:19; Rev.16:9; Lk.12:47,48; Mk.10:38; Heb.6:9; Phil.1:11; Col.1:9. This is a part of Robertson's list (*Grammar*, 485). "Saturated with the Spirit" - "imbued" - "filled with." *Cf.* John 7:38,39.

Thus the Holy Spirit calls the elect for whom Christ died and incorporates them into His Body.

Verse 14 - "For the body is not one member, but many."

καὶ γὰρ τὸ σῶμα οὐκ ἔστιν ἓν μέλος ἀλλὰ πολλά.

"For the body does not consist of one member but of many." . . . RSV

καὶ (emphatic conjunction) 14.
γὰρ (causal conjunction) 105.
τὸ (nom.sing.neut.of the article in agreement with σῶμα) 9.
σῶμα (nom.sing.neut.of σῶμα, subject of ἔστιν) 507.
οὐκ (negative particle with the indicative) 130.
ἔστιν (3d.per.sing.pres.ind.of εἰμί, static) 86.
ἓν (nom.sing.neut.of εἷς, in agreement with μέλος) 469.
μέλος (nom.sing.neut.of μέλος, predicate nominative) 506.
ἀλλὰ (alternative conjunction) 342.
πολλά (nom.pl.neut.of πολύς, predicate nominative) 228.

Translation - "Because in fact the body is not one member but many."

Comment: This is Paul's statement about the Body of Christ, as verse 12 was his description of the human body, which he used to introduce the analogy. The Holy Spirit, in His divine unity with Father and Son, acted in union with the Godhead to bring a common experience to every member of the Body of Christ. We have all been baptized by Him into one body. The cooperation of all of the various members of the Body, the mutual respect for each other and the common interests of all is the theme of the remainder of the chapter.

Verse 15 - "If the foot shall say, Because I am not the hand, I am not of the body; is it therefore not of the body?"

ἐὰν εἴπῃ ὁ πούς,"Ὅτι οὐκ εἰμὶ χείρ, οὐκ εἰμὶ ἐκ τοῦ σώματος, οὐ παρὰ τοῦτο οὐκ ἔστιν ἐκ τοῦ σώματος.

"If the foot should say, 'Because I am not a hand, I do not belong to the body,' that would not make it any less a part of the body." . . . RSV

ἐὰν (conditional particle in a third-class condition) 363.
εἴπῃ (3d.per.sing.aor.act.subj.of εἶπον, third-class condition) 155.
ὁ (nom.sing.masc.of the article in agreement with πούς) 9.
πούς (nom.sing.masc.of πούς, subject of εἴπῃ) 353.
Ὅτι (conjunction introducing a subordinate causal clause) 211.
οὐκ (negative particle with the indicative) 130.
εἰμὶ (1st.per.sing.pres.ind.of εἰμί, static) 86.
χείρ (nom.sing.fem.of χείρ, predicate nominative) 308.
οὐκ (negative conjunction with the indicative) 130.
εἰμὶ (1st.per.sing.pres.ind.of εἰμί, static) 86.
ἐκ (preposition with the genitive, partitive) 19.
τοῦ (gen.sing.neut.of the article in agreement with σώματος) 9.
σώματος (gen.sing.neut.of σῶμα, partitive genitive) 507.
οὐ (negative conjunction with the indicative) 130.
παρὰ (preposition with the accusative, cause) 154.
τοῦτο (acc.sing.neut.of οὗτος, cause) 93.
οὐκ (negative conjunction with the indicative) 130.
ἔστιν (3d.per.sing.pres.ind.of εἰμί, static) 86.
ἐκ (preposition with the partitive genitive) 19.
τοῦ (gen.sing.neut.of the article in agreement with σώματος) 9.
σώματος (gen.sing.neut.of σῶμα, partitive genitive) 507.

Translation - "If the foot says, 'Because I am not a hand I am not a part of the body,' it is not on that account not a part of the body, is it?"

Comment: The third-class condition is for purposes of illustration. Paul is not saying that the foot would ever say that, but if it did . . . ? It is a hypothetical question. The adverbial phrase παρὰ τοῦτο has the preposition with the accusative indicating cause like *propter*. This is not common in the New Testament.

Paul pursues this line of argument through verse 17. Form relates to function as every engineer knows. The form and function of a member of the body has nothing to do with whether or not it is a part of the body. Christians who deprecate their gifts and the functions assigned to them are missing the point. So also are Christians who make odious comparisons between their superior gifts and those of others who are less fortunate. The Christian who is tone deaf and because of that fact, not invited to sing in the choir, should draw only one conclusion from that circumstance. He cannot sing. It does not mean that he is not a Christian; nor does it mean that he does not belong in the church. There are many Christians who cannot sing, as all will attest who have ever attended a Baptist revival meeting! What that Christian should remember is that there are members in the choir who cannot teach, and others who have not the special gift of faith, and others who do not have the gift of ministering to the sick. Perhaps a choir member feels inferior because, though he can sing, he is not invited to usher.

It is ludicrous to imagine how the body would get along if all of the functions assigned to the hand were attempted by the foot. Who ever crocheted with her feet?! What surgeon ever performed brain surgery with his toes? Acrobats walk on their hands but it is not the method suggested by the form, nor the intention of the divine Creator.

We have another illustration in

Verse 16 - "And if the ear shall say, Because I am not the eye, I am not of the body; is it therefore not of the body?"

καὶ ἐὰν εἴπῃ τὸ οὖς, Ὅτι οὐκ εἰμὶ ὀφθαλμός, οὐκ εἰμὶ ἐκ τοῦ σώματος, οὐ παρὰ τοῦτο οὐκ ἔστιν ἐκ τοῦ σώματος.

"And if the ear should say, 'Because I am not an eye, I do not belong to the body,' that would not make it any less a part of the body." . . . RSV

καὶ (continuative conjunction) 14.
ἐὰν (conditional particle in a third-class condition) 363.
εἴπῃ (3d.per.sing.aor.act.subj.of εἶπον, third-class condition) 155.
τὸ (nom.sing.neut.of the article in agreement with οὖς) 9.
οὖς (nom.sing.neut.of οὖς, subject of εἴπῃ) 887.
Ὅτι (conjunction introducing a subordinate causal clause) 211.
οὐκ (negative particle with the indicative) 130.
εἰμὶ (1st.per.sing.pres.ind.of εἰμί, static) 86.
ὀφθαλμός (nom.sing.masc.of ὀφθαλμός, predicate nominative) 501.
οὐκ (negative particle with the indicative) 130.
εἰμὶ (1st.per.sing.pres.ind.of εἰμί, static) 86.
ἐκ (preposition with the partitive genitive) 19.
τοῦ (gen.sing.neut.of the article in agreement with σώματος) 9.
σώματος (gen.sing.neut.of σῶμα, partitive genitive) 507.
οὐ (negative particle with the indicative) 130.
παρὰ (preposition with the accusative, adverbial, cause) 154.
τοῦτο (acc.sing.neut.of οὗτος, adverbial, cause) 93.
οὐκ (negative particle with the indicative) 130.
ἔστιν (3d.per.sing.pres.ind.of εἰμί, static) 86.
ἐκ (preposition with the partitive genitive) 19.
τοῦ (gen.sing.neut.of the article in agreement with σώματος) 9.
σώματος (gen.sing.neut.of σῶμα, partitive genitive) 507.

Translation - *"And if the ear says, 'Because I am not an eye I am not a part of the body,' it is not on that account not a part of the body is it?"*

Comment: The same point as in verse 15.

Verse 17 - *"If the whole body were an eye, where were the hearing? If the whole were hearing, where were the smelling?"*

εἰ ὅλον τὸ σῶμα ὀφθαλμός, ποῦ ἡ ἀκοή; εἰ ὅλον ἀκοή, ποῦ ἡ ὄσφρησις;

"If the whole body were an eye, where would be the hearing? If the whole body were an ear, where would be the sense of smell?" . . . RSV

εἰ (conditional particle in a second-class condition) 337.
ὅλον (nom.sing.neut.of ὅλος, in agreement with σῶμα) 112.
τὸ (nom.sing.neut.of the article in agreement with σῶμα) 9.
σῶμα (nom.sing.neut.of σῶμα, subject of ἦν understood) 507.
ὀφθαλμός (nom.sing.masc.of ὀφθαλμός, predicate nominative) 501.
ποῦ (interrogative local adverb) 142.
ἡ (nom.sing.fem.of the article in agreement with ἀκοή) 9.
ἀκοή (nom.sing.fem.of ἀκοή, subject of ἦν understood) 409.
εἰ (conditional particle in a second-class condition) 337.
ὅλον (nom.sing.neut.of ὅλος, in agreement with σῶμα understood) 112.
ἀκοή (nom.sing.fem.of ἀκοή, predicate nominative) 409.
ποῦ (interrogative local adverb) 142.

#4217 ὄσφρησις (nom.sing.fem.of ὄσφρησις, subject of ἦν understood).

King James Version

smelling - 1 Cor.12:17.

Revised Standard Version

sense of smell - 1 Cor.12:17.

Meaning: Cf. ὀσφραίνομαι - "to smell." Hence, the olfactory function - 1 Cor.12:17.

Translation - *"If the entire body were an eye, where would the auditory perception be? If all were auditory where would the olfactory be?"*

Comment: The verbs are omitted. We are to supply ἦν, both in the protasis and apodosis, since it is a second-class, contrary to fact condition, dealing with time present to Paul at the time of writing. Thus the imperfect. It is a hypothetical contrary-to-fact question.

Note that when Paul pursued his analogy, using both foot/hand and eye/ear functions, he chose the eye/ear illustration, and even involved the nose in his question, since it is possible, though not efficient, for hand and foot to substitute for each other. We have alluded to acrobats walking on their hands, but they have never won the hundred yard dash at the Olympics. People without hands do some things normally manual in function with their feet, though not very well. Houdini could write with his toes! But no one sees with the ear, hears with the eye or nose, nor smells with the eye or ear. The body has many varied functions to perform and hence is equipped with many members having varied forms.

When a Christian in the Body of Christ wishes to possess some gift other than that which the Holy Spirit has given to him, he deprecates the importance of the function which his gift equips him to perform. If he has no musical talent but is a great accountant he should not envy the organist who plays beautifully but has no capacity for bookkeeping. This suggests that the proper keeping of financial records in the church is of less importance than the music program.

The Christian who complains, either that he has no gifts, or that his gift is not the one which he would like to have is criticizing the Holy Spirit. This is a wicked presumption. No member of the Body of Christ is bereft of all gifts (verse 11). It is the Christian's duty to find out what his gift is and then to look to the Lord Jesus, the Head over all things to His church (Eph.1:22,23) for direction as to where, when and how to use it. If he does this he allows God to exploit it for His glory and the church's good (verse 7).

Note that Paul suggests in hypothesis that the entire body might be either eye or ear. Is he gently chiding some Corinthian saint who believed that his particular function was the only function in the congregation? Occasinally one sees a deacon who thinks this!

Verse 18 - "But now hath God set the members every one of them in the body, as it hath pleased him."

νυνὶ δὲ ὁ θεὸς ἔθετο τὰ μέλη, ἐν ἕκαστον αὐτῶν, ἐν τῷ σώματι καθὼς ἠθέλησεν.

"But as it is, God arranged the organs in the body, each one of them, as he chose." . . . RSV

νυνὶ (temporal adverb) 1497.

δὲ (adversative conjunction) 11.

ὁ (nom.sing.masc.of the article in agreement with θεὸς) 9.

θεὸς (nom.sing.masc.of θεός, subject of ἔθετο) 124.

ἔθετο (3d.per.sing.2d.aor.mid.ind.of τίθημι, culminative) 455.

τὰ (acc.pl.neut.of the article in agreement with μέλη) 9.

μέλη (acc.pl.neut.of μέλος, direct object of ἔθετο) 506.

ἐν (acc.sing.neut.of εἷς, in agreement with ἕκαστον) 469.

ἕκαστον (acc.sing.neut.of ἕκαστος, apposition) 1217.

αὐτῶν (gen.pl.neut.of αὐτός, partitive genitive) 16.

ἐν (preposition with the locative of place) 80.

τῷ (loc.sing.neut.of the article in agreement with σώματι) 9.

σώματι (loc.sing.neut.of σῶμα, place) 507.

καθὼς (compound comparative particle) 1348.

ἠθέλησεν (3d.per.sing.aor.act.ind.of θέλω, constative) 88.

Translation - "But now God has placed the members - each one of them, in the body exactly as He wanted them."

Comment: Paul brushes aside the ignorant criticisms of those who were complaining. God has already determined how the human body should be created, the forms of its various organs and what they functions were to be. This is His divine prerogative as Creator. Our Lord has total authority to do the same thing in His Body,the church (Eph.1:22,23; 1 Cor.12:11; Col.1:18; 2:19). It is His body. He has given personal attention to "each one of them" - ἐν ἕκαστον αὐτῶν. And He consulted no one but Himself. Paul might with some asperity have asked the critics, "If you do not like the anatomical structure of your body, what are you going to do about it?" Or, "Would you like to have been present at the creation in order to give advice to the Lord about how He should create Adam and Eve?" This sarcasm is not in the text, but it is between the lines.

What gifts are given and to whom and for what purpose is none of the critic's business. To complain that one has no gifts denies verse 6 and charges God with nonfeasance; to complain that one does not have the proper gift charges Him with malfeasance. The time and energy spent in complaining would be better spent in developing and using the gift(s) God has given.

What is to be said about the Christian who obviously possesses skills and aptitudes which are not normally thought of as useful in the programs which are considered proper activities of the local church as she pursues her task in carrying out the Great Commission? Can the Holy Spirit use all the skills which people have? Suppose the auto mechanic has no other gift? Do we not need him to keep the church buses running? Aviators, with natural ability to fly, are found on mission fields where there are no access surface roads to remote areas which otherwise could not be reached with the gospel. The Christian woman whose only skill is culinary is indispensable to the success of the church summer camp for the children and for the fellowship suppers on prayer meeting night. There is no child of God who possesses a gift which the Holy Spirit cannot use in a church that is awake to this great truth.

Further it is a mistake to suppose that the only time the Christian serves the Lord is when he is working at a task in direct connection with a church program. We are to glorify God with our skills at all times (1 Cor.10:31), whether we are working in the ecclesiastical or in the secular spheres. The Christian university professor who teaches in a state university exerts a greater influence on his students for Christ because he is also a good history or economics professor. Does a mediocre high school football coach who should have driven a taxicab win as many high school students to Christ as the coach with natural ability to lead his teams to victory?

Wherever a member of the Body of Christ goes, whatever he does and how he does it, whether in pursuit of a church function or one in the secular world, he will be directed by the indwelling Holy Spirit to glorify God and to promote, perhaps in ways that he least suspects, the program of calling out from among the Gentiles a people for His name (Acts 15:14).

Verse 19 - "And if they were all one member, where were the body?"

εἰ δὲ ἦν τὰ πάντα ἓν μέλος, ποῦ τὸ σῶμα;

"If all were a single organ, where would the body be?" . . . RSV

εἰ (conditional particle in a second-class, contrary to fact condition) 337.
δὲ (adversative conjunction) 11.
ἦν (3d.per.sing.imp.ind.of εἰμί, second-class, contrary to fact condition) 86.
τὰ (nom.pl.neut.of the article in agreement with πάντα) 9.
πάντα (nom.pl.neut.of πᾶς, subject of ἦν) 67.
ἓν (nom.sing.neut.of εἷς, in agreement with μέλος) 469.
μέλος (nom.sing.neut.of μέλος, predicate nominative) 506.
ποῦ (interrogative local adverb) 142.
τὸ (nom.sing.neut.of the article in agreement with σῶμα) 9.
σῶμα (nom.sing.neut.of σῶμα, subject of verb understood) 507.

Translation - "But if all were one organ, where would the body be?"

Comment: Another elliptical condition as in verse 17. The context alone can tell us that it is a second-class condition. It is another hypothetical question, with the premise contrary to fact. A body composed only of one organ - be it eye, ear,hand,foot - is not a body at all, but a monstrosity - something put together by a committee! But God did not create a monstrosity. His creation is an example of the one and the many - unity in diversity. His work is described in verse 20. Here in verse 19 Paul describes what he hinted at in verse 17 - that some may have imagined that their gift was the only one of importance.

Verse 20 - "But now are they many members, yet but one body."

νῦν δὲ πολλὰ μὲν μέλη, ἓν δὲ σῶμα.

"As it is, there are many parts, yet one body." . . . RSV

νῦν (temporal adverb) 1497.
δὲ (adversative conjunction) 11.
πολλὰ (nom.pl.neut.of πολύς, in agreement with μέλη) 228.
μὲν (particle of affirmation) 300.
μέλη (nom.pl.neut.of μέλος, subject of ἐστιν, understood) 506.
ἓν (nom.sing.neut.of εἷς, in agreement with σῶμα) 469.
δὲ (adversative conjunction) 11.
σῶμα (nom.sing.neut.of σῶμα, subject of verb understood) 507.

Translation - "But now although there are many members, yet there is one body."

Comment: The monstrosity of verse 19 exists only in hypothesis. That is how some Christians might have done it, being careful to declare that their own gifts were the only ones necessary. On the contrary God indeed (μὲν) has drawn together many individual personal units from many diverse cultural and ethnic backgrounds - Jews, Greeks, black, white, yellow, brown, red, male, female, slave, free man, educated, ignorant - products of all sorts of environmental conditioning and has coalesced them into a harmoniously coordinated unit, in which the skills of each mesh with the total model construction for the benefit of all. Here is the divine sociology of the Body of Christ - something that the social planners could never produce in a million years.

The Body of Christ, which is the Church, while still short of the sinlessness of glorification, does not give a perfect performance consistent with her potential, but she is constructed in such a way that, given the complete sanctification of glorification at the rapture, she will be conformed to the image of her Head, and Christ, the Head will have a perfect body (Eph.4:11-13).

The interdependence of all upon the performance of each is the theme of verses 21-26.

Verse 21 - "And the eye cannot say unto the hand, I have no need of thee: nor again the head to the feet, I have no need of you."

οὐ δύναται δὲ ὁ ὀφθαλμὸς εἰπεῖν τῇ χειρί, Χρείαν σου οὐκ ἔχω, ἢ πάλιν ἡ κεφαλὴ τοῖς ποσίν, Χρείαν ὑμῶν οὐκ ἔχω.

"The eye cannot say to the hand, 'I have no need of you,' nor again the head to to the feet, 'I have no need of you.' " . . . RSV

οὐ (negative particle with the indicative) 130.
δύναται (3d.per.sing.pres.mid.ind.of δύναμαι, static) 289.
δὲ (continuative conjunction) 11.
ὁ (nom.sing.masc.of the article in agreement with ὀφθαλμὸς) 9.
ὀφθαλμὸς (nom.sing.masc.of ὀφθαλμός, subject of δύναται) 501.
εἰπεῖν (aor.act.inf.of εἶπον, complementary) 155.
τῇ (dat.sing.fem.of the article in agreement with χειρί) 9.
χειρί (dat.sing.fem.of χείρ, indirect object of εἰπεῖν) 308.
Χρείαν (acc.sing.fem.of χρεία, direct object of ἔχω) 317.
σου (gen.sing.masc.of σύ, objective genitive) 104.
οὐκ (negative particle with the indicative) 130.
ἔχω (1st.per.sing.pres.act.ind.of ἔχω, present progressive retroactive) 82.
ἢ (disjunctive) 465.
πάλιν (adverbial) 355.
ἡ (nom.sing.fem.of the article in agreement with κεφαλή) 9.
κεφαλὴ (nom.sing.fem.of κεφαλή, subject of δύναται understood) 521.
τοῖς (dat.pl.masc.of the article in agreement with ποσίν) 9.
ποσίν (dat.pl.masc.of πούς, indirect object of εἰπεῖν understood) 353.
Χρείαν (acc.sing.fem.of χρεία, direct object of ἔχω) 317.
ὑμῶν (gen.pl.masc.of σύ, objective genitive) 104.
οὐκ (negative particle with the indicative) 130.
ἔχω (1st.per.sing.pres.act.ind.of ἔχω, present progressive retroactive) 82.

Translation - "And the eye cannot say to the hand, 'I have no need of you', neither again the head to the feet, 'I have no need of you.' "

Comment: Direct discourse without recitative ὅτι. Note ἤ πάλιν together - "Or, to use a parallel example . . . " However exalted and important one member may be, however indispensable to the proper function of the whole, he is dependent upon the functioning of the other members or he cannot perform his function. The eye sees what must be done, but the hand must do it, because the eye cannot. The head knows where we must go, but the feet must carry us. A cotter pin, worth only fifty cents, was broken and a United States Navy airplane, worth ten million dollars was grounded. This teaching is necessary in order to show the saints with an inferiority complex how important they are in the successful operation of the Body of Christ. When one knows that his services are indispensable to the Holy Spirit he will regain his confidence and stop shouting to attract attention.

Verse 22 - "Nay, much more those members of the body, which seem to be more feeble, are necessary."

ἀλλὰ πολλῷ μᾶλλον τὰ δοκοῦντα μέλη τοῦ σώματος ἀσθενέστερα ὑπάρχειν ἀναγκαῖά ἐστιν.

"On the contrary, the parts of the body which seem to be weaker are indispensable," . . . RSV

ἀλλὰ (adversative conjunction) 342.

πολλῷ (instru.sing.neut.of πολύς, measure) 228.

μᾶλλον (adverbial) 619

τὰ (nom.pl.neut.of the article in agreement with μέλη) 9.

δοκοῦντα (pres.act.part.nom.pl.neut.of δοκέω, adjectival, attributive position, ascriptive, in agreement with μέλη) 287.

μέλη (nom.pl.neut.of μέλος, subject of ἐστιν) 506.

τοῦ (gen.sing.neut.of the article in agreement with σώματος) 9.

σώματος (gen.sing.neut.of σῶμα, description) 507.

ἀσθενέστερα (nom.pl.neut.of ἀσθενής, comparative, predicate adjective, in agreement with μέλη) 1551.

ὑπάρχειν (pres.inf.of ὑπάρχω, completes δοκοῦντα) 1303.

ἀναγκαῖά (nom.pl.neut.of ἀναγκαῖος, predicate adjective) 3225.

ἐστιν (3d.per.sing.pres.ind.of εἰμί, static) 86.

Translation - "Quite the contrary! The parts of the body which appear to be weaker are indispensable."

Comment: πολλῷ μᾶλλον - "to a greater extent by much." *Cf.#*'s 228 and 619 for other uses of this idiom. Note the adjectival participle δοκοῦντα, modifying μέλη, and completed by the infinitive ὑπάρχειν. Members of the body which appear to superficial observation to be weak and unnecessary are indispensable. A medical scientist or an engineer can appreciate this verse perhaps more than others.

Verse 23 - "*And those members of the body, which we think to be less honourable, upon these we bestow more abundant honor; and our uncomely parts have more abundant comeliness.*"

καὶ ἃ δοκοῦμεν ἀτιμότερα εἶναι τοῦ σώματος, τούτοις τιμὴν περισσοτέραν περιτίθεμεν, καὶ τὰ ἀσχήμονα ἡμῶν εὐσχημοσύνην περισσοτέραν ἔχει,

"and those parts of the body which we think less honorable we invest with the greater honor, and our unpresentable parts are treated with greater modesty,"..
. *RSV*

καὶ (continuative conjunction) 14.

ἃ (acc.pl.neut.of ὅς, general reference) 65.

δοκοῦμεν (1st.per.pl.pres.act.ind.of δοκέω, customary) 287.

ἀτιμότερα (acc.pl.neut.comparative of ἄτιμος, predicate adjective) 1102.

εἶναι (pres.inf.of εἰμί, noun use, direct object of δοκοῦμεν) 86.

τοῦ (gen.sing.neut.of the article in agreement with σώματος) 9.

σώματος (gen.sing.neut.of σῶμα, description) 507.

τούτοις (dat.pl.masc.of οὗτος, indirect object of περιτίθεμεν) 93.

τιμὴν (acc.sing.fem.of τιμή, direct object of περιτίθεμεν) 1619.

περισσοτέραν (acc.sing.fem.comparative, of περισσός, in agreement with τιμὴν) 525.

περιτίθημεν (1st.per.pl.pres.act.ind.of περιτίθημι, customary) 1376.

καὶ (continuative conjunction) 14.

τὰ (nom.pl.neut.of the article in agreement with ἀσχήμονα) 9.

#4218 ἀσχήμονα (nom.pl.neut.of ἀσχήμων, subject of ἔχει).

King James Version

uncomely - 1 Cor.12:23.

Revised Standard Version

unpresentable - 1 Cor.12:23.

Meaning: α privative plus σχῆμα (#4163). Hence, not properly formed; indecent; unseemly; misshapen; indecorous; ugly; unpresentable. With reference to parts of the body not normally displayed to the public - 1 Cor.12:23.

ἡμῶν (gen.pl.masc.of ἐγώ, possession) 123.

#4219 εὐσχημοσύνην (acc.sing.fem.of εὐσχημοσύνη, direct object of ἔχει).

King James Version

comeliness - 1 Cor.12:23.

Revised Standard Version

modesty - 1 Cor.12:23.

Meaning: Cf. εὐσχήμων (#2872). Hence, charm, elegance of form, external beauty, decorum, modesty, seemliness - 1 Cor.12:23.

περισσοτέραν (acc.sing.fem.comp.of περισσός, in agreement with εὐσχημοσύνην) 525.

ἔχει (3d.per.sing.pres.act.ind.of ἔχω, customary) 82.

Translation - "And those parts of the body which we regard as less dignified, upon them we bestow greater honor and our unpresentable parts have greater care bestowed upon them."

Comment: We do not eliminate the less honorable parts of the body as though they were unnecessary and unimportant, but we cover them with clothing to make them more presentable. That is the essence of what Paul is saying.

Verse 24 - "For our comely parts have no need: but God hath tempered the body together, having given more abundant honor to that part which lacked."

τὰ δὲ εὐσχήμονα ἡμῶν οὐ χρείαν ἔχει. ἀλλὰ ὁ θεὸς συνεκέρασεν τὸ σῶμα, τῷ ὑστερουμένῳ περισσοτέραν δοὺς τιμήν.

"which our more presentable parts do not require. But God has so adjusted the body, giving the greater honor to the inferior part, . . . " . . . RSV

τὰ (nom.pl.neut.of the article in agreement with εὐσχήμονα) 9.
δὲ (adversative conjunction) 11.
εὐσχήμονα (nom.pl.neut.of εὐσχήμων, subject of ἔχει) 2872.
ἡμῶν (gen.pl.masc.of ἐγώ, possession) 123.
οὐ (negative particle with the indicative) 130.
χρείαν (acc.sing.fem.of χρεία, direct object of ἔχει) 317.
ἔχει (3d.per.sing.pres.act.ind.of ἔχω, static) 82.
ἀλλὰ (adversative conjunction) 342.
ὁ (nom.sing.masc.of the article in agreement with θεὸς) 9.
θεὸς (nom.sing.masc.of θεός, subject of συνεκέρασεν) 124.

#4220 συνεκέρασεν (3d.per.sing.aor.act.ind.of συγκεράννυμι, constative).

King James Version

temper together - 1 Cor.12:24.
be mixed with - Heb.4:2.

Revised Standard Version

adjust - 1 Cor.12:24.
meet with - Heb.4:2.

Meaning: A combination of σύν (#1542) and κεράννυμι (#5390). Hence, to pour out together; to mix; to bring together various elements. God has constructed the Body of Christ by bringing together in Him various types of people - 1 Cor.12:24. The Word of God must be "mixed" with faith in the hearers in order to bring salvation - Heb.4:2.

τὸ (acc.sing.neut.of the article in agreement with σῶμα) 9.

σῶμα (acc.sing.neut.of σῶμα, direct object of συνεκέρασεν) 507.

τῷ (dat.sing.masc.of the article in agreement with ὑστερουμένῳ) 9.

ὑστερουμένῳ (pres.mid.part.dat.sing.masc.of ὑστερέω, substantival, indirect object of δούς) 1302.

περισσοτέραν (acc.sing.fem.of περισσός, in agreement with τιμήν) 525.

δούς (aor.act.part.nom.sing.masc.of δίδωμι, adverbial, modal) 362.

τιμήν (acc.sing.fem.of τιμή, direct object of δούς) 1619.

Translation - "But our beautiful parts do not need this: but God has put the body together by giving more honor to the part which needed it.

Comment: The thrust of the entire passage is that each part of the body has its own indispensable function. Without it the body could not do what it was designed by the Creator to do. Since form relates to function, as the latter is unique so is the former. Unfortunately society has its standards, which are not necessarily the standards of the Creator, and by its standards some parts of the body have forms which are less attractive than others. There is danger therefore that such persons will suffer a loss of prestige, despite the fact that their form relates to a function which is just as important in the operation of the body as those functions which have more beautiful and more honorable forms. Thus the less attractive members require extra adornment which the more attractive do not need. For example the Christian cook in the kitchen who prepares the delicious food which is enjoyed by all after the eloquent sermon by the pastor-teacher is as essential to the success of the day as the preacher. The auto mechanic who keeps the church bus running is as important as the preacher. If it were not for him the bus could not have brought the people to the service and the sermon would have been preached to empty pews.

God will not allow the prejudices of people who have been brainwashed by society to frustrate His design. He has adjusted the parts of the Body of Christ (#4220) to make it perfect - that is, the perfect realization of the Creator's intention. The result — ?

Verse 25 - "That there should be no schism in the body: but that the members should have the same care one for another."

ἵνα μὴ ᾖ σχίσμα ἐν τῷ σώματι, ἀλλὰ τὸ αὐτὸ ὑπὲρ ἀλλήλων μεριμνῶσιν τὰ μέλη.

"that there may be no discord in the body, but that the members may have the same care of one another." . . . RSV

ἵνα (conjunction with the subjunctive in a sub-final clause) 114.

μὴ (negative particle with the subjunctive in a negative sub-final clause) 87.

ᾖ (3d.per.sing.pres.subj.of εἰμί, sub-final clause) 86.

σχίσμα (nom.sing.neut.of σχίσμα, subject of ᾖ) 807.
ἐν (preposition with the locative of place) 80.
τῷ (loc.sing.neut.of the article in agreement with σώματι) 9.
σώματι (loc.sing.neut.of σῶμα, place) 507.
ἀλλά (alternative conjunction) 342.
τὸ (acc.sing.neut.of the article in agreement with αὐτό) 9.
αὐτὸ (acc.sing.neut.of αὐτός, adverbial, intensive - "to the same extent") 16.
ὑπὲρ (preposition with the ablative, "in behalf of") 545.
ἀλλήλων (abl.pl.masc.of ἀλλήλων, "in behalf of") 1487.
μεριμνῶσιν (3d.per.pl.pres.act.subj.of μεριμνάω, positive sub-final clause) 609.
τὰ (nom.pl.neut.of the article in agreement with μέλη) 9.
μέλη (nom.pl.neut.of μέλος, subject of μεριμνῶσιν) 506.

Translation - "In order (and with the result) that there be no split in the church, but that the members may always care for each other to the same extent."

Comment: We have a negative sub-final clause followed by a positive sub-final clause, but note that Paul did not repeat ἵνα with the subjunctive μεριμνῶσιν. The second clause may be only final, if we are thinking of the church as she is still in the world, because there are splits in the church now, many of which are caused by a failure of the members to have the same regard for all, but when we think of the glorified church in heaven, we can take the second clause also as sub-final - both purpose and result. God will work in and through His body until the genius of His creative plan will be demonstrated. This perfect harmony could be achieved within the body now, even before glorification at the rapture if the Holy Spirit Who indwells every member were allowed also to overwhelm each of us. He is not at odds with Himself. Each member, if he is under the control of the Holy Spirit will care to the same extent (τὸ αὐτό) for every other member of the body.

It is God's will that every member of the Body of Christ recognize and respect the dignity of every other member, thus to be concerned for all as much as we are for any one. There is no special privilege in the Body of Christ. In Him egalitarian philosophy is the rule. None of us would be there but by His grace; all would be in hell if justice were handed down apart from His love which was demonstrated in His atoning death. Each has his indispensable place; each has been given his gift(s) with which he is perfectly equipped to perform the function assigned to him. Where then is there any room for friction?

When the Holy Spirit is in control within the Body there is love, joy, peace, longsuffering, gentleness, goodness, faith, meekness and self-control (Gal.5:22,23). This is why Paul told the Colossians to "let the peace of God rule" (Col.3:15). If there is a divided vote on a motion to buy a new broom, it is obvious that somebody is out of touch with the Holy Spirit, since it is obvious either that the Holy Spirit wants to buy a new broom or that He does not.

The mutual care of verse 25 yields the results described in

Verse 26 - "And whether one member suffer, all the members suffer with it; or one member be honored, all the members rejoice with it."

καὶ εἴτε πάσχει ἓν μέλος, συμπάσχει πάντα τὰ μέλη, εἴτε δοξάζεται ἐν μέλος, συγχαίρει πάντα τὰ μέλη.

"If one member suffers, all suffer together; if one member is honored, all rejoice together." . . . RSV

καὶ (inferential conjunction) 14.

εἴτε (disjunctive) 4016.

πάσχει (3d.per.sing.pres.act.ind.of πάσχω, first-class condition) 1208.

ἓν (nom.sing.neut.of εἷς, in agreement with μέλος) 469.

μέλος (nom.sing.neut.of μέλος, subject of πάσχει) 506.

συμπάσχει (3d.per.sing.pres.act.ind.of συμπάσχω, first-class condition) 3936.

πάντα (nom.pl.neut.of πᾶς, in agreement with μέλη) 67.

τὰ (nom.pl.neut.of the article in agreement with μέλη) 9.

μέλη (nom.pl.neut.of μέλος, subject of συμπάσχει) 506.

εἴτε (disjunctive) 4016.

δοξάζεται (3d.per.sing.pres.pass.ind.of δοξάζω, first-class condition) 461.

ἐν (nom.sing.neut.of εἷς, in agreement with μέλος) 469.

μέλος (nom.sing.neut.of μέλος subject of δοξάζεται) 506.

συγχαίρει (3d.per.sing.pres.act.ind.of συγχαίρω, first-class condition) 1840.

πάντα (nom.pl.neut.of πᾶς, in agreement with μέλη) 67.

τὰ (nom.pl.neut.of the article in agreement with μέλη) 9.

μέλη (nom.pl.neut.of μέλος, subject of συγχαίρει) 506.

Translation - "Therefore if one member is suffering all the members suffer with him; and if one member is honored, all the members rejoice with him."

Comment: εἴτε, the disjunctive is εἰ and the correlative τε, and in this sentence serves in both instances to introduce a first-class condition - "If in fact . . . and if . . . κ.τ.λ." Two correlated clauses are tied together - "If one suffers . . . if one is honored." The parts of the body are so closely correlated that pain or joy for one is pain or joy for all. Who with a toothache can doubt this?

God has orchestrated the experiences of the members into a perfect score that presents a divine symphony in both minor and major keys. Alas, the average church congregation presents some members playing in the major while others play the same passage in the minor key. The deacons rejoice while the pastor weeps! *Cf.* Lk.1:58; 15:6,9; Phil.2:17,18; 1 Cor.13:6; Rom.12:15.

Verse 27 - "Now ye are the body of Christ, and members in particular."

Ὑμεῖς δέ ἐστε σῶμα Χριστοῦ καὶ μέλη ἐκ μέρους.

"Now you are the body of Christ and individually members of it." . . . RSV

Ὑμεῖς (nom.pl.masc.of σύ, subject of ἐστε) 104.

δέ (explanatory conjunction) 11.

ἐστε (2d.per.pl.pres.ind.of εἰμί, static) 86.

σῶμα (nom.sing.neut.of σῶμα, predicate nominative) 507.

Χριστοῦ (gen.sing.masc.of Χριστός, description) 4.

καὶ (adjunctive conjunction joining nouns) 14.
μέλη (nom.pl.neut.of μέλος, predicate nominative) 506.
ἐκ (preposition with the genitive, adverbial) 19.
μέρους (gen.sing.neut.of μέρος, adverbial prepositional phrase) 240.

Translation - "Now you are the Body of Christ and as individuals members of it."

Comment: Note the plural Ὑμεῖς as subject with ἐστε, but the predicate nominative σῶμα is a collective singular. Collectively the saints comprise a unit known as the Body of Christ. The adverbial prepositional phrase ἐκ μέρους says that each individual Christian is one of the members. For other examples of prepositional phrases used adverbially *cf.* ἐκ μέτρου (John 3:34); ἐξ ἀνάγκης (2 Cor.9:7), ἐκ συμφώνου (1 Cor.7:5). (Robertson, *Grammar*, 597). Thus we have the one and the many. With the loss of one member, the Body of Christ would be mutilated and truncated. Not a single sheep from the flock of the Good Shepherd (John 10:11), nor a single member of the Body of Christ (1 Cor.12:27), nor a single two-by-four from the building (Eph.2:21,22) will be missing at the rapture. Thus the P in the Tulip.

Other offices and gifts are mentioned in

Verse 28 - "And God hath set some in the church, first apostles, secondarily prophets, thirdly teachers, after that miracles, then gifts of healing, helps, governments, diversities of tongues."

καὶ οὓς μὲν ἔθετο ὁ θεὸς ἐν τῇ ἐκκλησίᾳ πρῶτον ἀποστόλους, δεύτερον προφήτας, τρίτον διδασκάλους, ἔπειτα δυνάμεις, ἔπειτα χαρίσματα ἰαμάτων, ἀντιλήμφεις, κυβερνήσεις, γένη γλωσσῶν.

"And God has appointed in the church first apostles, second prophets, third teachers, then workers of miracles, then healers, helpers, administrators, speakers in various kinds of tongues." . . . *RSV*

καὶ (continuative conjunction) 14.
οὓς (acc.pl.masc.of ὅς, demonstrative, direct object of ἔθετο) 65.
μὲν (particle of affirmation) 300.
ἔθετο (3d.per.sing.2d.aor.mid.ind.of τίθημι, culminative) 455.
ὁ (nom.sing.masc.of the article in agreement with θεός) 9.
θεὸς (nom.sing.masc.of θεός, subject of ἔθετο) 124.
ἐν (preposition with the locative of place) 80.
τῇ (loc.sing.fem.of the article in agreement with ἐκκλησίᾳ) 9.
ἐκκλησίᾳ (loc.sing.fem.of ἐκκλησία, place) 1204.
πρῶτον (acc.sing.neut.of πρῶτος, adverbial) 487.
ἀποστόλους (acc.pl.masc.of ἀπόστολος, direct object of ἔθετο) 844.
δεύτερον (acc.sing.neut.of δεύτερος, adverbial) 1371.
προφήτας (acc.pl.masc.of προφήτης, direct object of ἔθετο) 119.
τρίτον (acc.sing.neut.of τρίτος, adverbial) 1209.
διδασκάλους (acc.pl.masc.of διδάσκαλος, direct object of ἔθετο) 742.
ἔπειτα (ordinal adverb) 2566.
δυνάμεις (acc.pl.fem.of δύναμις, direct object of ἔθετο) 687.

ἔπειτα (ordinal adverb) 2566.
χαρίσματα (acc.pl.neut.of χάρισμα, direct object of ἔθετο) 3790.
ἰαμάτων (gen.pl.neut.of ἴαμα, description) 4215.

#4221 ἀντιλήμφεις (acc.pl.fem.of ἀντίλημφις, direct object of ἔθετο).

King James Version

helps - 1 Cor.12:28.

Revised Standard Version

helpers - 1 Cor.12:28.

Meaning: In profane Greek, mutual acceptance; a laying hold of. *Cf.* ἀντιλαμβάνομαι (#1837). Apprehension, perception, objection of a disputant (Thayer). In the New Testament, help, assistance, such as a deacon might give - 1 Cor.12:28. Not synonymous however with διακονία. Frequent in petitions to the Ptolemies (pap.), Cf. P. Par. 26 (B.C. 163-2). (Robertston, *Grammar* 574). διακονία is the help of an inferior to a superior, but ἀντίλημφις is the help of a superior to any other where a special skill is needed.

#4222 κυβερνήσεις (acc.pl.fem.of κυβέρνησις, direct object of ἔθετο).

King James Version

government - 1 Cor.12:28.

Revised Standard Version

administrators - 1 Cor.12:28.

Meaning: Cf. κυβερνάω - "to govern." Also κυβερνήτης (#3696). Hence, government; administration of affaris; wise counsel; sage advice on policy matters - 1 Cor.12:28.

γένη (acc.pl.neut.of γένος, direct object of ἔθετο) 1090.
γλωσσῶν (gen.pl.fem.of γλῶσσα, description) 1846.

Translation - *"And God has established certain ones in the church - first, apostles; secondly, prophets; thirdly, teachers; then those with special powers; then gifts of healing, helps, administrations, those with various language skills."*

Comment: οὓς μὲν is demonstrative. There is no corresponding οὓς δὲ. The gifts seem to be listed in a pattern of descending ordinal importance. There were only twelve Apostles, who, along with the Old Testament Prophets provided the foundation of the church (Eph.2:20) with Christ as the Cornerstone. They were as indispensable to the establishment of the first century churches as the Old Testament Prophets who had foreseen as prophecy what the Apostles preached as history. The power to speak authoritatively under inspiration, and lay down certain principles of faith and practice which were later written into the New Testament is the gift of prophecy. This is one of the gifts, granted on an *ad hoc* basis for the purpose of guiding the early churches in matters of faith and practice before the New Testament literature was written. What the first century Apostles, prophets and those with special knowledge taught they later recorded. The written record in the New Testament made their continued function unnecessary. That is why they were phased out. *Cf.* comment on 1 Cor.13:8. There have been no prophets or those with special knowledge in this sense since the first century.

Teaching is listed here as a gift, something that education courses may indeed improve upon in some cases, but in no case bestow. "Only those who can teach." Teachers are born, not made.

The distribution of gifts is according to the sovereign will of the Holy Spirit (verse 11). Obviously therefore the list of rhetorical questions in verses 29 and 30 is unnecessary, but Paul asks them for emphasis.

Verse 29 - "Are all apostles? Are all prophets? Are all teachers? Are all workers of miracles?"

μὴ πάντες ἀπόστολοι; μὴ πάντες προφῆται; μὴ πάντες διδάσκαλοι; μὴ πάντες δυνάμεις;

"Are all apostles? Are all prophets? Are all teachers? Do all work miracles?"..
                                                                                        RSV

μὴ (negative particle with the indicative understood in rhetorical question expecting a negative reply) 87.

πάντες (nom.pl.masc.of πᾶς, subject of εἰσίν understood) 67.

ἀπόστολοι (nom.pl.masc.of ἀπόστολος, predicate nominative) 844.

μὴ (negative particle with the indicative in rhetorical question expecting a negative reply) 87.

πάντες (nom.pl.masc.of πᾶς, subject of εἰσίν understood) 67.

προφῆται (nom.pl.masc.of προφήτης, predicate nominative) 119.

μὴ (negative particle with the indicative understood, in rhetorical question expecting a negative reply) 87.

παντες (nom.pl.masc.of πᾶς, subject of εἰσίν, understood) 67.

διδάσκαλοι (nom.pl.masc.of διδάσκαλος, predicate nominative) 742.

μὴ (negative particle with the indicative understood in rhetorical question expecting a negative reply) 87.

πάντες (nom.pl.masc.of πᾶς, subject of εἰσίν, understood) 67.

δυνάμεις (nom.pl.masc.of δύναμις, predicate nominative) 687.

Translation - "Not all are Apostles, are they? Not all are prophets? Not all are teachers? Not all are miracle workers are they?"

Comment: These are rhetorical questions which demand a negative response as are the three in verse 30.

Verse 30 - "Have all the gifts of healing? Do all speak with tongues? Do all interpret?"

μὴ πάντες χαρίσματα ἔχουσιν ἰαμάτων; μὴ πάντες γλώσσαις λαλοῦσιν;
μὴ πάντες διερμηνμεύουσιν;

"Do all possess gifts of healing? Do all speak with tongues? Do all interpret?" .
. . *RSV*

μὴ (negative particle with the indicative in rhetorical question expecting a negative reply) 87.

πάντες (nom.pl.masc.of πᾶς, subject of ἔχουσιν) 67.

χαρίσματα (acc.pl.neut.of χάρισμα, direct object of ἔχουσιν) 3790.

ἔχουσιν (3d.per.pl.pres.act.ind.of ἔχω, in rhetorical question expecting a negative reply) 82.

ἰαμάτων (gen.pl.neut.of ἴαμα, description) 4215.

μὴ (negative particle with the indicative in rhetorical question expecting a negative reply) 87.

πάντες (nom.pl.masc.of πᾶς, subject of λαλοῦσιν) 67.

γλώσσαις (loc.pl.fem.of γλῶσσα, sphere) 1846.

λαλοῦσιν (3d.per.pl.pres.act.ind.of λαλέω, present iterative, in rhetorical question expecting a negative reply) 815.

μὴ (negative particle with the indicative in rhetorical question expecting a negative reply) 87.

πάντες (nom.pl.masc.of πᾶς, subject of διερμηνεύουσιν) 67.

διερμηνεύουσιν (3d.per.pl.pres.act.ind.of διερμηνεύω, present iterative, in rhetorical question expecting a negative reply) 2906.

Translation - "Not all have gifts of healing do they? Not all speak in foreign languages do they? Not all translate do they?"

Comment: To respond to these questions with "Yes" is like saying that every organ of the human body has as its function those of all of the others. The Body of Christ is a divinely selected group of believers who, collectively, can do it all, because individually each can do something. Not all gifts have the same value but all are indispensable and therefore very important.

Verse 31 - "But covet earnestly the best gifts: and yet shew I unto you a more excellent way."

ζηλοῦτε δὲ τὰ χαρίσματα τὰ μείζονα. Καὶ ἔτι καθ' ὑπερβολὴν ὁδὸν ὑμῖν
δείκνυμι.

"But earnestly desire the higher gifts. And I will show you a still more excellent way." . . . *RSV*

ζηλοῦτε (2d.per.pl.pres.act.impv.of ζηλόω, command) 3105.
δὲ (adversative conjunction) 11.
τὰ (acc.pl.neut.of the article in agreement with χαρίσματα) 9.
χαρίσματα (acc.pl.neut.of χάρισμα, direct object of ζηλοῦτε) 3790.
τὰ (acc.pl.neut.of the article in agreement with μείζονα) 9.

μείζονα (acc.pl.neut.comp.of μέγας, in agreement with χαρίσματα) 184.
καὶ (adversative conjunction) 14.
ἔτι (temporal adverb) 448.
καθ' (preposition with the accusative, in an adverbial phrase) 98.
ὑπερβολὴν (acc.sing.fem.of ὑπερβολή, in agreement with ὁδὸν) 3923.
ὁδὸν (acc.sing.fem.of ὁδός, direct object of δείκνυμι) 199.
ὑμῖν (dat.pl.masc.of σύ, indirect object of δείκνυμι) 104.
δείκνυμι (1st.per.sing.pres.act.ind.of δείκνυμι, futuristic) 359.

Translation - *"But you must be more concerned about the greater gifts. And yet I am going to show you a way that is far better."*

Comment: "Greater than what?" The context demands that he is speaking of gifts greater than those he has mentioned in verses 28-30. Note that γλῶσσαι and their translation are listed last in the descending order of importance. Yet there are those who seek them more earnestly and display them more proudly than any others - even to the point of suggesting that those who do not possess these gifts at worst are not saved, or at best are living on an inferior spiritual level. We are to put the most emphasis upon those gifts which do most to edify the Body of Christ. The Apostles are no longer needed since they recorded their contributions of prophetic knowledge in the pages of the Greek New Testament. Prophets were phased out when they had completed their *ad hoc* assignments. Teachers are still with us, and are needed in the fulfillment of the Great Commission (Mt.28:18-20). After the elect have been discipled and immersed in water they are to be taught. Miracle workers, healers, helpers, administrators and foreign language experts complete the list. Paul is saying that Christians are to put these matters in the same perspective as did the Holy Spirit and our Lord, the Head over all things to His church (1 Cor.12:1-11; Eph.1:22,23).

But there is even a more excellent road to follow which will take you further on your journey to the victorious life. This is the force of the adverbial prepositional phrase καθ' ὑπερβολὴν ὁδόν.

Gifts are good for God is the giver of every good and perfect gift (James 1:17), but love, one of the fruits of the Spirit (Gal.5:22,23) is better. The motivation for seeking the better gifts must have love, not self-serving as the determining and compelling principle (Meyer, *First Corinthians*, 297). It is appropriate to ask the Christian who is seeking the "gift of tongues" or boasting that he already has it, why?

Paul is not saying that if we have love, we do not need the gifts which are appropriate, but he is saying that our interest in the gifts should be a loving desire to most helpful to others in the Body of Christ. The better way to get the gifts, whatever they may be, is to seek them in love.

Love

(1 Corinthians 13:1-13)

1 Cor.13:1 - *"Though I speak with the tongues of men and of angels, and have not charity, I am become as sounding brass, or a tinkling cymbal."*

Ἐὰν ταῖς γλώσσαις τῶν ἀνθρώπων λαλῶ καὶ τῶν ἀγγέλων, ἀγάπτην δὲ μὴ ἔχω, γέγονα χαλκὸς ἠχῶν ἢ κύμβαλον ἀλαλάζον.

"If I speak in the tongues of men and of angels, but have not love, I am a noisy gong or a clanging cymbal." . . . RSV

Ἐὰν (conditional particle with the subjunctive in a third-class condition) 363.
ταῖς (loc.pl.fem. of the article in agreement with γλώσσαις) 9.
γλώσσαις (loc.pl.fem. of γλῶσσα, sphere) 1846.
τῶν (gen.pl.masc. of the article in agreement with ἀνθρώπων) 9.
ἀνθρώπων (gen.pl.masc. of ἄνθρωπος, description) 341.
λαλῶ (1st.per.sing.pres.act.subj. of λαλέω, third-class condition) 815.
καὶ (adjunctive conjunction joining nouns) 14.
τῶν (gen.pl.masc. of the article in agreement with ἀγγέλων) 9.
ἀγγέλων (gen.pl.masc. of ἄγγελος, description) 96.
ἀγάπην (acc.sing.fem. of ἀγάπη, direct object of ἔχω) 1490.
δὲ (adversative conjunction) 11.
μὴ (negative particle with the subjunctive, in a third-class condition) 87.
ἔχω (1st.per.sing.pres.act.subj. of ἔχω, third-class condition) 82.
γέγονα (1st.per.sing.2d.perf.ind. of γίνομαι, intensive) 113.
χαλκὸς (nom.sing.masc. of χαλκός, predicate nominative) 861.

#4223 ἠχῶν (pres.act.part.nom.sing.masc. of ἠκέω, adjectival, predicate position, restrictive, in agreement with χαλκὸς).

King James Version

sounding - 1 Cor. 13:1.

Revised Standard Version

noisy - 1 Cor. 13:1.

Meaning: Cf. ἦχος (#2064). To emit a sound. A participial adjective - a noisy piece of brass, like a gong or a bell - 1 Cor. 13:1.

ἢ (disjunctive) 465.

#4224 κύμβαλον (nom.sing.neut. of κύμβαλον, predicate nominative).

King James Version

cymbal - 1 Cor. 13:1.

Revised Standard Version

cymbal - 1 Cor. 13:1.

Meaning: Cf. κύμβος - "a hollow." A hollow basin of brass, producing a musical sound when two are struck together - 1 Cor.13:1.

ἀλαλάζον (pres.act.part.nom.sing.neut.of ἀλαλάζω, adjectival, restrictive, predicate position, in agreement with κύμβαλον) 2241.

Translation - "If I speak with the tongues of men and of angels but if I do not have love, I have become a noisy gong or a clanging cymbal."

Comment: Ἐὰν with the subjunctive in λαλῶ and ἔχω in a third-class condition. Paul is not saying that he has or that he has not great linguistic ability or that he has or lacks love, but he is saying that if he has the former and lacks the latter the exercise of his linguistic gift will turn him into a noisy irritation for all who are unfortunate enough to hear him. *Cf.*#2064 for the mournful roar of the waves at sea and #2241 for the howling and wailing of the insincere paid mourner at a funeral. Add to this the nerve shattering sound of a brass gong and the clash of cymbals. The effect is totally upsetting.

Paul begins with the gift of languages which apparently was being given too much status in Corinth, but he procedes to say that all of the other gifts, however important, are also to no avail, if not administered with love.

The fact that he associates γλώσσαις with those spoken in the human and also in the angelic spheres hints that he did not mean incomprehensible gibberish which is often heard in current "tongues" meetings and described as "heavenly language." There is no evidence in the New Testament that γλῶσσα ever means anything other than the physical organ of speech in the human mouth, in its proper sense, as in Mark 7:33,35; Luke 16:24; Rev.16:10; James 3:5,6,6,8 (*cf.*#1846) or some language or dialect understood by men on earth or angels in heaven. The adjective *unknown* is never applied to it in the New Testament. No language was spoken at Pentecost that was not recognized as the native language of someone present. The adjective in Acts 2:4 is ἑτέραις - "other" languages, not unknown. The languages heard at Pentecost were those other than the current Hebrew and/or Κοινή Greek. *Cf.* our discussion of the reason why this gift "ceased" in 1 Cor.13:8.

Verse 2 - "And though I have the gift of prophecy, and understand all mysteries, and all knowledge; and though I have all faith, so that I could remove mountains, and have not charity, I am nothing.

καὶ ἐὰν ἔχω προφητείαν καὶ εἰδῶ τὰ μυστήρια πάντα καὶ πᾶσαν τὴν γνῶσιν, κἂν ἔχω πᾶσαν τὴν πίστιν ὥστε ὄρη μεθιστάναι, ἀγάπην δὲ μὴ ἔχω οὐθέν εἰμι.

"And if I have prophetic powers, and understand all mysteries and all knowledge, and if I have all faith, so as to remove mountains, but have not love, I am nothing." . . . RSV

καὶ (continuative conjunction) 14.
ἐὰν (conditional particle with the subjunctive in a third-class condition) 363.
ἔχω (1st.per.sing.pres.act.subj.of ἔχω, third-class condition) 82.
προφητείαν (acc.sing.fem.of προφητεία, direct object of ἔχω) 1041.
καὶ (adjunctive conjunction joining verbs) 14.
εἰδῶ (1st.per.sing.aor.act.subj.of ὁράω, third-class condition) 144b.

τὰ (acc.pl.neut.of the article in agreement with μυστήρια) 9.

μυστήρια (acc.pl.neut.of μυστήριον, direct object of εἰδῶ) 1038.

πάντα (acc.pl.neut.of πᾶς, in agreement with μυστήρια) 67.

καὶ (adjunctive conjunction joining nouns) 14.

πᾶσαν (acc.sing.fem.of πᾶς, in agreement with γνῶσιν) 67.

τὴν (acc.sing.fem.of the article in agreement with γνῶσιν) 9.

γνῶσιν (acc.sing.fem.of γνῶσις, direct object of εἰδῶ) 1856.

κἄν (adjunctive conjunction joining verbs and conditional particle in a third-class condition, crasis) 1370.

ἔχω (1st.per.sing.pres.act.subj.of ἔχω, third-class condition) 82.

πᾶσαν (acc.sing.fem.of πᾶς, in agreement with πίστιν) 67.

τὴν (acc.sing.fem.of the article in agreement with πίστιν) 9.

πίστιν (acc.sing.fem.of πίστις, direct object of ἔχω) 728.

ὥστε (conjunction with the infinitive introducing a result clause) 752.

ὄρη (acc.pl.neut.of ὄρος, direct object of μεθιστάναι) 357.

μεθιστάναι (pres.act.inf.of μεθίστημι, result) 2564.

ἀγάπην (acc.sing.fem.of ἀγάπη, direct object of ἔχω) 1490.

δὲ (adversative conjunction) 11.

μὴ (negative particle with the subjunctive) 87.

ἔχω (1st.per.sing.pres.act.subj.of ἔχω, third-class condition) 82.

οὐθέν (nom.sing.neut.of οὐδείς, predicate nominative) 446.

εἰμί (1st.per.sing.pres.ind.of εἰμί, static) 86.

Translation - "And if I have the prophetic gift and understand all the mysteries and all the knowledge, and if I have all the faith, with the result that I move mountains, but if I do not have love, I am nothing."

Comment: Note the articles here with qualities γνῶσιν and πίστιν. Paul is exaggerating in order to make the point. *All* the mysteries, *all* the knowledge and *all* the faith. It does not take *all* the faith to move a mountain - only a little (Mt.17:20), but Paul says that if he had it all, but lacked love, all of the preaching ability, a knowledge of all of the mysteries, all of the scientific data and all of the faith would add up to nothing. Why? Because only love dictates that these other vast resources will be used for the benefit of the Body of Christ. If Paul were the only member of the Body of Christ then love would be unimportant. In that case his talents and intellectual brilliance would be used for himself alone. But Paul was only one member in the fellowship. One so richly endowed, who used his talents only selfishly would be a curse to everyone associated with him.

We have only to reflect upon the impact upon society of the "mad genius" who used his superior talents to inflict misery upon the human race - Ghengis Khan, Tamerlane, Attila the Hun, Lenin, Stalin, Adolf Hitler and the supreme example - Satan.

Even an outward show of "love" for others is not proof that real love in present as we see in

Verse 3 - "And though I bestow all my goods to feed the poor, and though I give my body to be burned, and have not charity, it profiteth me nothing."

κἄν φωμίσω πάντα τὰ ὑπάρχοντά μου, καὶ ἐὰν παραδῶ τὸ σῶμά μου ἵνα καυχήσωμαι, ἀγάπην δὲ μὴ ἔχω, οὐδὲν ὠφελοῦμαι.

"If I give away all I have, and if I deliver my body to be burned, but have not love, I gain nothing." . . . RSV

κἀν (adjunctive conjunction joining verbs and conditional particle in a third-class condition, crasis) 1370.

φωμίσω (1st.per.sing.aor.act.subj.of φωμίζω, third-class condition) 4030.

πάντα (acc.pl.neut.of πᾶς, in agreement with ὑπάρχοντά) 67.

τὰ (acc.pl.neut.of the article in agreement with ὑπάρχοντά) 9.

ὑπάρχοντά (pres.act.part.acc.pl.neut.of ὑπάρχω, substantival, direct object of φωμίσω) 1303.

μου (gen.sing.masc.of ἐγώ, possession) 123.

καὶ (continuative conjunction) 14.

ἐὰν (conditional particle with the subjunctive in a third-class condition) 363.

παραδῶ (1st.per.sing.2d.aor.mid.subj.of παραδίδωμι, third-class condition) 368.

τὸ (acc.sing.neut.of the article in agreement with σῶμά) 9.

σῶμά (acc.sing.neut.of σῶμα, direct object of παραδῶ) 507.

μου (gen.sing.masc.of ἐγώ, possession) 123.

ἵνα (conjunction with the subjunctive in a purpose clause) 114.

καυχήσωμαι (1st.per.sing.1st.aor.subj.of καυχάομαι, purpose) 3847.

ἀγάπην (acc.sing.fem.of ἀγάπη, direct object of ἔχω) 1490.

δὲ (adversative conjunction) 11.

μὴ (negative particle with the subjunctive) 87.

ἔχω (1st.per.sing.pres.act.subj.of ἔχω, third-class condition) 82.

οὐδὲν (acc.sing.neut.of οὐδείς, accusative of the thing) 446.

ὠφελοῦμαι (1st.per.sing.pres.pass.ind.of ὠφελέω, aoristic) 1144.

Translation - "And if I parcel out all my property and if I give my body in order to glory, but if I do not have love it is not profitable to me."

Comment: *Cf.*#4030 for the basic meaning - "If I give away my property bit by bit — " thus to develop a reputation for being magnanimous, which is not a proper motive. The ἵνα clause is in dispute. Because the resolution of the difficulty in the text is not important, since both readings support the general thrust of the passage and Paul's point is not destroyed, whether we accept the one or the other, the problem is an interesting example of the challenge which the text sometimes offers the science of textual criticism. We offer the Metzger explanation in full:

"Did Paul write ἵνα καυχήσωμαι ("that I may glory") or ἵνα καυθήσομαι ("that I should be burned")? To answer this question requires the evaluation of several very evenly balanced considerations.

In support of the reading καυχήσωμαι one can appeal to external evidence that is both early and weighty (p46 Sinaiticus A B 6 33 69 1739* copsa,bo gothmg Clement Greek mssacc to Jerome). Transcriptional considerations likewise favor καυχήσωμαι, for copyists, uncertain of Paul's meaning in linking the idea of glorying or boasting to the preceding clause about the giving up of one's body, may well have sought to improve the sense by substituting the similar sounding word καυθήσομαι. Intrinsic considerations likewise seem to favor καυχήσωμαι, for this verb occurs frequently in the letters traditionally attributed to Paul (a total of 35 times).

On the other hand, in support of κανθήσομαι (—σωμαι) here is an impressive number of witnesses, including C D F G K L Ψ most minuscules it vg syrp,h gothtxt arm ethpp, and numerous patristic writers, including Tertullian Aphraates Cyprian Origen Basil Chryssotom Cyril Theodoret Euthalius Maximus-Confessor John-Damascus. It has been argued that in the context κανθήσομαι is as appropriate as καυχήσωμαι is inappropriate, for the reference to burning, whether by martyrdom (as the Three Hebrew Youths in Daniel 3.15ff.) or by voluntary self-burning, is particularly suitable as the strongest example of sacrifice; whereas, if the motive for giving up life is pride and self-glory, there is no need to declare that such sacrifice is worthless, and therefore Paul's following statement, ἀγάπην δὲ μὴ ἔχω, becomes superfluous.

A majority of the Committee preferred καυχήσωμαι for the following reasons. (*a*). After the Church entered the epoch of martyrdom, in which death by fire was not rare, it is easier to understand how the variant κανθήσομαι for καυχήσωμαι would creep into the text, than the opposite case. Likewise the passage in Daniel was well known in the Church and might easily have induced a copyist to alter καυχήσωμαι into κανθήσομαι. On the other hand, if the latter reading were original, there is no good reason to account for its being replaced in the oldest copies by the other reading.

(*b*) The expression παραδῶ τὸ σῶμά μου ἵνα κανθήσομαι, though certainly tolerable in itself, is noticebly cumbersome ("I give up my body, that I may be burnt"); one would have expected, as a more natural expression, ἵνα κανθῇ ("... that it may be burnt"). But in the case of καυχήσωμαι this difficulty disappears.

(*c*) The reading κανθήσωμαι (future subjunctive!), while appearing occasionaly in Byzantine times, is a grammatical monstrosity that cannot be attributed to Paul (Blass-Debrunner-Funk, paragraph 28; Moulton-Howard, p.219); occasionally, however, the future indicative after ἵνα occurs (Ga.2:4; Php.2.10,11).

(*d*) The argument that the presence of the statement, "that I may glory," destroys the sense of the passages loses some of its force when one observes that for Paul "glorying" is not invariably reprehensible; sometimes he regards it as justified (2 Cor.8.24; Php.2.16; 1 Th 2.19; 2 Th 1.4). (Metzger, *A Textual Commentary on the Greek New Testament*, 563, 564).

The thrust of the passage is that any exercise of a spiritual gift or any other meritorious Christian service which is not done for the sheer love of the Lord and the brethren, and is therefore self-serving, is done for an unworthy reason and thus not spiritually profitable. This sense is not destroyed whether we read καυχήσωμαι or κανθήσομαι. The strongest argument for καυχήσωμαι is that there was no such form as a future subjunctive (!) in the first century. Paul never would have made this egregious error.

Verse 4 - "Charity suffereth long, and is kind; charity enviety not; charity vaunteth not itself, is not puffed up."

Ἡ ἀγάπη μακροθυμεῖ, χρηστεύεται ἡ ἀγάπη, οὐ ζηλοῖ, οὐ περπερεύεται, οὐ φυσιοῦται,

"Love is patient and kind; love is not jealous or boastful;" . . . RSV

Ή (nom.sing.fem.of the article in agreement with ἀγάπη) 9.
ἀγάπη (nom.sing.fem.of ἀγάπη, subject of μακροθυμεῖ) 1490.
μακροθυμεῖ (3d.per.sing.pres.act.ind.of μακροθυμέω, customary) 1274.

#4225 χρηστεύεται (3d.per.sing.pres.mid.ind.of χρηστεύομαι, customary).

> King James Version

be kind - 1 Cor.13:4.

> Revised Standard Version

kind - 1 Cor.13:4.

Meaning: Cf. χρηστός (#959); to show oneself to be kind, good and gracious - 1 Cor.13:4.

ἡ (nom.sing.fem.of the article in agreement with ἀγάπη) 9.
ἀγάπη (nom.sing.fem.of ἀγάπη, subject of χρηστεύεται) 1490.
οὐ (negative particle with the indicative) 130.
ζηλοῖ (3d.per.sing.pres.act.ind.of ζηλόω, customary) 3105.
οὐ (negative particle with the indicative) 130.

#4226 περπερεύεται (3d.per.sing.pres.mid.ind.of περπερεύομαι customary).

> King James Version

vaunt one's self - 1 Cor.13:4.

> Revised Standard Version

boastful - 1 Cor.13:4.

Meaning: Cf. πέρπερος — "vainglorious", "boastful." Hence, to boast; to call attention to one's virtues; to be arrogant - 1 Cor.13:4.

οὐ (negative particle with the indicative) 130.
φυσιοῦται (3d.per.sing.pres.mid.ind.of φυσιόω, customary) 4122.

Translation - *"Love is longsuffering; love is always gracious; it is never envious; it is not arrogant; it is not conceited."*

Comment: Note the lack of copulative paratactic conjunctions. We find only δὲ is verse 6 which is adversative. Patient, longsuffering, kind, good, gracious, not envious, neither boastful nor conceited. Goodspeed has "it does not put on airs." The implication is that the Corinthians were not overflowing with love. That is why they were so concerned about demonstrating that they possessed the "best" gifts and were eager to show that they were more heavily endowed with the gifts of the Holy Spirit than others less fortunate.

One who is overwhelmed with the love of God, which is the result of being filled with the Holy Spirit (Eph.5:18) and blessed with all of His fruits (Gal.5:22,23) has no time to consider the possibility that he is insecure, for indeed he is not insecure, and therefore he displays none of the behavior that telegraph to society that he is.

Verse 5 - "Doth not behave itself unseemly, seeketh not her own, is not easily provoked, thinketh no evil;"

οὐκ ἀσχημονεῖ, οὐ ζητεῖ τὰ ἑαυτῆς, οὐ παροξύνεται, οὐ λογίζεται τὸ κακόν.

"it is not arrogant or rude. Love does not insist on its own way; it is not irritable or resentful;" . . . RSV

οὐκ (negative particle with the indicative) 130.
ἀσχημονεῖ (3d.per.sing.pres.act.ind.of ἀσχημονέω, customary) 4168.
οὐ (negative particle with the indicative) 130.
ζητεῖ (3d.per.sing.pres.act.ind.of ζητέω, customary) 207.
τὰ (acc.pl.neut.of the article, direct object of ζητεῖ) 9.
ἑαυτῆς (gen.sing.fem.of ἐμαυτοῦ, possession) 288.
οὐ (negative particle with the indicative) 130.
παροξύνεται (3d.per.sing.pres.pass.ind.of παροξύνω, customary) 3399.
οὐ (negative particle with the indicative) 130.
λογίζεται (3d.per.sing.pres.mid.ind.of λογίζομαι, customary) 2611.
τὸ (acc.sing.neut.of the article in agreement with κακόν) 9.
κακόν (acc.sing.neut.of κακός, direct object of λογίζεται) 1388.

Translation - "Is not rude; does not seek her own; is never provoked to a paroxysm of rage; does not continue to think about evil."

Comment: The present tenses indicate that ἀγάπη, is never guilty of the excesses mentioned. The text does not say that love is never provoked. It does say that the provocation does not lead to a fit of rage. Love often thinks of evil. To be otherwise is to be naive. But love does not spend all of its time in thinking about evil.

Verse 6 - "Rejoiceth not in iniquity, but rejoiceth in the truth."

οὐ χαίρει ἐπὶ τῇ ἀδικίᾳ, συγχαίρει δὲ τῇ ἀληθείᾳ,

"it does not rejoice at wrong, but rejoices in the right." . . . RSV

οὐ (negative particle with the indicative) 130.
χαίρει (3d.per.sing.pres.act.ind.of χαίρω, customary) 182.
ἐπὶ (preposition with the instrumental of cause) 47.
τῇ (instru.sing.fem.of the article in agreement with ἀδικίᾳ) 9.
ἀδικίᾳ (instru.sing.fem.of ἀδικία, cause) 2367.
συγχαίρει (3d.per.sing.pres.act.ind.of συγχαίρω, customary) 1840.
δὲ (adversative conjunction) 11.
τῇ (instru.sing.fem.of the article in agreement with ἀληθείᾳ) 9.
ἀληθείᾳ (instru.sing.fem.of ἀλήθεια, cause) 1416.

Translation - *"Does not rejoice because of iniquity, but rejoices in the truth."*

Comment: Love can never be happy with iniquity because ἀδικία (#2367) is opposed to truth (John 7:18; Rom.2:8). ἀδικία is associated with ἀσεβεία (#3794). *Cf.* Rom.1:18. God is love (1 John 4:8) and God is truth (John 14:6). Hence love is happy with truth and unhappy with truth's enemies, including ἀδικία and ἀσεβεία. The empiricist, in love with his scientific propensity to doubt, may ask how love can rejoice over truth since no one can know truth. The child of God's love has an epistemology that transcends the world's doubt (1 Cor.2:9).

In Christ are hid "all of the treasures of wisdom and knowledge" (Col.2:3). The more truth the Christian understands the greater is the area of his fellowship with Christ. Since ἀδικία and ἀσεβεία, militate against truth, and thus prevent the intimate association with Christ which the child of God otherwise would enjoy, he cannot be happy about them. And conversely that is why he rejoices in the truth.

Verse 7 - *"Beareth all things, believeth all things, hopeth all things, endureth all things."*

πάντα στέγει πάντα πιστεύει, πάντα ἐλπίζει, πάντα ὑπομένει.

"Love bears all things, believes all things, hopes all things, endures all things."

... RSV

πάντα (acc.pl.neut.of πᾶς, direct object of στέγει) 67.
στέγει (3d.per.sing.pres.act.ind.of στέγω, customary) 4177.
πάντα (acc.pl.neut.of πᾶς, direct object of πιστεύει) 67.
πιστεύει (3d.per.sing.pres.act.ind.of πιστεύω, customary) 734.
πάντα (acc.pl.neut.of πᾶς, direct object of ἐλπίζει) 67.
ἐλπίζει (3d.per.sing.pres.act.ind.of ἐλπίζω, customary) 991.
πάντα (acc.pl.neut.of πᾶς, direct object of ὑπομένει) 67.
ὑπομένει (3d.per.sing.pres.act.ind.of ὑπομένω, customary) 880.

Translation - *"Bears everything in silence; believes everything; hopes for everything; endures everything."*

Comment: Forbearing, trustful, hopeful, patient. These are marks of optimism and characteristics that make for good mental health and personality equilibrium. *Cf.* James 3:17 - "the wisdom that is from above is first pure, then peaceable, gentle, and *easily persuaded* . . . " Paul does not mean that the Christian who has love believes everything he hears, or even sees. He does mean that he believes everything in God's word. The child with perfect love for his father knows that his father loves him with perfect love and therefore that his father will not lie to him.

Verse 8 - *"Charity never faileth; but whether there be prophecies,they shall fail; whether there be tongues, they shall cease; whether there be knowledge, it shall vanish away."*

Ἡ ἀγάπη οὐδέποτε πίπτει. εἴτε δὲ προφητεῖαι, καταργηθήσονται, εἴτε γλῶσσαι, παύσονται, εἴτε γνῶσις, καταργηθήσεται.

"Love never ends; as for prophecies, they will pass away; as for tongues, they will cease; as for knowledge, it will pass away." . . . RSV

Ἡ (nom.sing.fem.of the article in agreement with ἀγάπη) 9.
ἀγάπη (nom.sing.fem.of ἀγάπη, subject of πίπτει) 1490
οὐδέποτε (intensive negative temporal adverb) 689.
πίπτει (3d.per.sing.pres.act.ind.of πίπτω, static) 187.
εἴτε (disjunctive) 4016.
δὲ (adversative conjunction) 11.
προφητεῖαι (nom.pl.fem.of προφητεία, subject of καταργηθήσονται) 1041.
καταργηθήσονται (3d.per.pl.fut.pass.ind.of καταργέω, predictive) 2500.
εἴτε (disjunctive) 4016.
γλῶσσαι (nom.pl.fem.of γλῶσσα, subject of παύσονται) 1846.
παύσονται (3d.per.pl.fut.pass.ind.of παύω, predictive) 2044.
εἴτε (disjunctive) 4016.
γνῶσις (nom.sing.fem.of γνῶσις, subject of καταργηθήσεται) 1856.
καταργηθήσεται (3d.per.sing.fut.pass.ind.of καταργέω, predictive) 2500.

Translation - "Love will never fall, but as for prophecies, they will be superseded; as for tongues, they will cease; as for knowledge it will be replaced."

Comment: The key words of this passage, without the proper contextual force of which we are sure to go astray, are καταργηθήσονται/καταργηθήσεται (#2500) and τέλειον of verse 10 (#553). What precisely does Paul mean when he says that prophecies and knowledge will "be superseded," "be replaced," "fail" and "vanish away"? Whatever it means it will happen only ὅταν . . . ἔλθη τὸ τέλειον (verse 10). What is this perfection that is to come? We must also understand the phrase ἐκ μέρους in verses 9,10.

An exhaustive look at #2500 is a must.

Since this verse has become a battleground on which is fought the controversy with reference to the gifts of the Holy Spirit - a difference of opinion between those who, on the one hand, believe in charismata, but insist that some are claiming gifts which are no longer being given, and others who claim possession of the gifts of "tongues," prophecy and knowledge, the student must conduct his own research and reach his own conclusions. Above all, "let brotherly love continue" (Heb. 13:1) and may all "let (our) moderation be known unto all men" (Phil.4:5).

It is the current view of *The Renaissance New Testament* that καταργέω (#2500) refers to the act of being superseded by something better. The automobile is a better mode of transportation than the horse and buggy. Therefore when autos were invented the horse and buggy were phased out. Electricity as a means of providing light replaced the kerosene lamp.

In other contexts καταργέω refers to the destruction of something. In all contexts when the καταργέω experience occurs the thing has ceased to exist or it has become ineffective.

We have καταργέω in some one of its forms in 2 Cor.3:7,11,13 and 14, where the context has Moses on Mount Sinai receiving the tablets of stone on which were written the Mosaic Law. In verse 7 Paul writes, "But if the administration of death, written and engraven in stones, was glorious, so that the children of Israel could not stedfastly behold the face of Moses for the glory of his countenance, which glory *was to be done away:*"

In verse 11, he continues, "For if that which *is done away* was glorious, much more that which remaineth is glorious."

And in verse 13 - "And not as Moses, which put a vail over his face, that the children of Israel could not stedfastly look to the end of *that which is abolished:*"

In verse 14 - "But their minds were blinded: for until this day remaineth the same vail untaken away in the reading of the old testament; *which vail is done away in Christ.*"

What is the glory that was *done away*? (verse 7,11). What was the vail which is *done away* in Christ? (verse 14). What was *abolished*? (verse 13). The glory light of the presence of God which transfigured Moses' face was superseded by a greater glory as Jesus Christ fulfilled the law (Mt.7:21) and died to save those who had transgressed it. The vail was *abolished* in Christ.

In Romans 7:6 we are *delivered* from the law. Does this not mean that the covenant of grace has ended the death "wherein we were held" and now that we are *delivered* "we serve in newness of spirit, and not in the oldness of the letter"?

What was the "middle wall of partition" between Jews and Gentiles? What was the enmity between us? It is defined in Eph.2:14-18 as "the law of commandments contained in ordinances." Again we have a reference to the Mosaic and Levitical codes of 2 Cor.3:7,11,13,14 and Rom.7:6. What happened to this enmity? It was *abolished*. (Eph.2:15). In Christ there is no more enmity as Hebrew Christians and Gentile Christians share in the fellowship of John 17:21.

In Romans 4:14 "if they which are of the law be heirs, faith is made void and the promise *made of none effect.*"

In Gal.3:17 we learn that the Abrahamic covenant which was confirmed of God in Christ four hundred and thirty years before the Mosaic Law was given, cannot be disannuled, that it should *make the promise of none effect.*" *(*Romans 3:3).

In Rom.3:31 we do not *make void* the law through faith, in the sense that our salvation was provided by our substitute, the man, Christ Jesus (1 Tim.2:5), Who established the law by fulfilling it (Mt.5:17) and then died as though He had broken every part, in order to impute to us the righteousness of the law.

What happens to death?   2 Tim.1:10 says that "our Saviour Jesus Christ (has) *abolished* death" and 1 Cor.15:26 says that "the last enemy that shall *be destroyed* is death."

An interesting application of καταργέω is found in Luke 13:7 where a fruitless tree, which remained fruitless, despite much care from the gardener was ordered cut down with the question, "Why *cumbereth* it the ground?" Does this mean that the tree still had some years of fruitbearing or does it mean that in the judgment of the owner it had outlived its usefulness?

In the following passages καταργέω is translated in the King James Version by the word "destroy." Let the student decide whether or not something that has been "destroyed" (καταργέω) has any further usefulness.

"Knowing this first, that our old man is crucified with him, that the body of sin might be *destroyed*. . . " (Rom.6:6).

"Meats for the belly and the belly for meats: but God shall *destroy* both it and them. . . " (1 Cor.6:13).

"And then shall that Wicked be revealed, whom the Lord shall consume with the spirit of his mouth and *shall destroy* with the brightness of his coming." (2 Thess.2:8). Does this mean that Antichrist will be out of business for good, or do we want to give him another period of activity?

"Forasmuch then as the children are partakers of flesh and blood, he also himself likewise took part of the same; that through death he might *destroy* him that had the power of death, that is, the devil. . . " (Heb.2:14).

What is *brought to nought* in 1 Cor.1:28?

What does Romans 7:2 mean when Paul says that when a woman's husband dies "she is *loosed* from the law of her husband?" Is it still in force or not?

Is Christ really going to *put down* all rule and all authority and power (1 Cor.1:24) or are we to expect our Lord's enemies to continue to oppose Him?

For those who are justifed by the law, "Christ *is become of none effect*" (Gal.5:4)

If Paul had told his audiences that circumcision saves, "then is the offence of the cross *ceased.*" (Gal.5:11).

What did Paul mean when he said that he spoke not the wisdom of this world, nor of the princes of this world "that *come to nought*"? (1 Cor.2:6).

When Paul became a man he *put away* his toys (1 Cor.13:11). Does this mean that they held no further attraction for him or that he still played with them?

This is a complete list of the places in the New Testament where the Holy Spirit led the writers to use the verb καταργέω, except the two that are involved in 1 Cor.13:8. There he says that "whether there be prophecies, they shall *fail*, and that "whether there be knowledge it shall *vanish away.*"

Every student of the Word of God is a charismatic. How could we be otherwise as we exegete 1 Corinthians 12-14; Romans 12:6-8 and Eph.4:11? There can be no doubt that the Holy Spirit has given gifts to all of the members of the Body of Christ.

But some charismatics insist that *all* of the gifts which the Holy Spirit gave in the first century, as recorded in the Acts of the Apostles, are still being given today. And they insist that He has given these gifts to them. Thus they feel free to advertize over the television ether waves that they are in a position to give "a word of knowledge" to one and a "prophetic message" to another, always of course in return for a cash offering to help pay expenses.

Has the student in a close and prayerful examination of any of the passages cited above in which καταργέω is used, found an instance where what is said to have been terminated (καταργέω) had any further existence after the termination? If so, which one? If not, why then should we say that καταργέω in 1

Cor. 13:8 means that the gifts of prophecy and knowledge are still being given and exercised when the passage clearly says that they have been phased out?

Because, say the brethren, the verbs καταργηθήσονται and καταργηθήσεται in verse 8 are future tense and thus point to a future time when these gifts will be phased out. Further that this phasing out of these gifts is tied to the indefinite temporal clause ὅταν . . . ἔλθῃ τὸ τέλειον. -"That which is in part will be phased out *when that which is perfect is come.*" They further argue that since this is an indefinite temporal clause (ὅταν with the subjunctive in ἔλθῃ) there is no way to tell when the perfect thing (τὸ τέλειον) will come. Some look forward to the Second Coming of our Lord as the time when "the perfect" shall have come. Thus, they conclude that the gifts of prophecy and knowledge are still in vogue.

It is quite correct to say that we cannot date the termination of these gifts from the grammar of the passage. The future tenses point us forward in time and the temporal clause is indeed indefinite. But this grammar, as all grammatical constructions is related to a context. Let us look therefore to the context of 1 Cor. 13:8-13 and relate the grammar to it.

Paul is clearly talking about gifts of communication. The Apostles in the first century had the gifts of prophecy and knowledge. How else could they have guided the early churches in matters of faith and practice at a time when they had not yet committed their special knowledge to paper? To prophesy is to communicate knowledge from heaven. What they said was divinely inspired and when they wrote it down Paul could say that "all writing which is Godbreathed is profitable . . . " (2 Tim. 3:16,17) He was talking about the writings of the Apostles, not the writings of the Gnostics and Jewish Legalists, who were preaching another gospel "which was not another" (Gal. 1:6,7). These prophecies and bits and pieces of special knowledge were fragmentary. Paul says this clearly in 1 Cor. 13:9 and 10, where he also adds that the "in part" knowledge (ἐκ μέρους) will be phased out. When? When the perfect knowledge has been given by the Holy Spirit (τὸ τέλειον). Τὸ τέλειον means the completed canon of inspired New Testament literature.

That this cannot mean the perfection of the Second Coming or of the eternal heavenly realm should be apparent when we study, as we did before *in re* καταργέω the word τέλειος (#553).   The list is available in *The Renaissance New Testament*, 1, 444). A partial study will demonstrate the method and the point to be made:

Paul speaks to some in the Philippian church who were *perfect* (τέλειοι). They were in Philippi in the first century A.D. not present at the second coming of Christ nor in heaven. They were not perfect and τέλειος does not refer to moral perfection. They were mature Christians. This is what Jesus meant by it in Mt. 5:48. Note this sense in James 1:4 - "Let patience have her *perfect work* (ἔργον τέλειον) that ye may be *perfect* (τέλειοι) and entire, lacking nothing." Thus to be τέλειος is to be complete - to lack nothing. Thus, in 1 Cor. 13:10 when the complete revelation of God's truth came, the partial bits and pieces of revelation which the Holy Spirit gave to the Apostles from time to time, as they had need, were phased out. In 1 Cor. 14:20 we have, "Brethren, be not children in understanding: howbeit in malice be ye children, but in understanding be *men* (τέλειοι γίνεσθε)." Paul was telling the Corinthians to grow up. See the same idea of maturity, not moral perfection, in 1 Cor.2:6 - ". . . we speak wisdom among them that are *perfect* (ἐν τοῖς τελείοις).

We have seen that the exegesis of verses 8-10 with their future tenses and the indefinite temporal clause must depend, not upon the grammar and syntax alone, but upon the context in which these constructions occur. We must also understand the *zeitgeist* ("the spirit of the times") of the passage. Paul wrote this passage in A.D.55-56 and used the future tense to say that the gifts of prophecy and special knowledge would be terminated sometime in *his* future. There is nothing in the indefinite temporal clause to say that the complete revelation of New Testament truth must wait for a time in *our* future in A.D. 1982. The tenth decade of the first century of the Christian era saw the last of the New Testament revelation committed to parchment, when the Apostle John finished his Gospel. Thus "that which is perfect" (τὸ τέλειον) came forty years after Paul wrote 1st Corinthians, although it was almost 1800 years before the current date. To point to those future tenses in verses 8 and 10 and relate them to us in the late 20th century, rather than to Paul in A.D.55-56 is to ignore the *zeitgeist.*

But there is more evidence to support the notion that τὸ τέλειον refers to the completion of the New Testament revelation in the first century and not to the Second Coming of Christ or some other later event.

God spoke in times past unto the fathers by the prophets on various occasions and in various ways. But the Old Testament revelation was not complete. He added to this revelation in "these last days" when He spoke unto us, who already had the partial Old Tesament revelation, by His Son (Heb.1:1,2). But though the revelation which Jesus gave was a notable addition to the partial revelation which the Old Testament prophets gave, it was still a partial revelation when Jesus went back to glory and sat down at the Father's right hand (Heb.1:3). The original installment, given to us in bits and pieces by the Holy Spirit through the Old Testament prophets (2 Peter 1:21), and supplemented by our Lord Jesus in the Gospels was completed by the Holy Spirit, Who used the Apostles, to whom He gave the gifts of propecy and special knowledge. And this completion of the divine revelation was made after our Lord ascended to the Father (Acts 1:11).

We have Jesus' own words for this statement. He could have given the total revelation to the Apostles, but for their inability to receive what He had to say. They were regenerated as they sat with Him at the Last Supper (Judas Iscariot had already left the room), but they did not have the fullness of the Holy Spirit. That experience was to be theirs at Pentecost, a little more than seven weeks later (Acts 2:1-4). Let us listen to Jesus:

"I have yet many things to say unto you, but ye cannot bear them now. Howbeit when he, the Spirit of truth, is come, he will guide you into **all truth**: *for he shall not speak of himself; but whatsoever he shall hear, that shall he speak: and he will shew you things to come. He shall glorify me: for he shall receive of mine, and shall shew it unto you.* **All things** *that the Father hath are mine: therefore said I, that he shall take of mine, and shall shew it unto you." (John 16:12-15).*

Here is a promise given by Jesus to a group of men all of whom were dead before the end of the first century. Yet Jesus promised that after they had been filled with the Holy Spirit (they were soon to be indwelt, John 20:22), which promise was redeemed at Pentecost, He would guide them into *all truth* and that *all things* in the Father's care which were related to the revelation of Ὁ Λόγος, would be taken by the Holy Spirit and revealed unto them.

Yet there are those who would seem to be attempting to monopolize the charismatic truth who tell us that the revelation of God is not yet total, but is still being supplemented, as it was in the Old Testament period, "on various occasions and in various ways" as they, self-appointed prophets of God and special knowledge dispensors, speak with the same inspiration that the Old Testament prophets and the New Testament Apostles had, and thus with the same authority. And this they expect to continue until some indefinite time in *our* future. The logic of this is that the Holy Spirit has not yet finished writing the Bible. If that were true, those of us who understand that "no scripture is of its own interpretation," (2 Pet. 1:20) but must be interpreted only after all of the light of every other scripture which is germane to the point, has been allowed to shine its light upon it, must abandon all Bible study until the revelation is complete. Nothing definite can be said about any scripture passage until the Holy Spirit has placed a period at the end of the last sentence which He intends to write and has written *FINIS*. Then and only then can we begin to examine this wonderful set of documents and discover what God has had to say to us.

Long experience in Bible teaching and preaching yields the expectation that someone in the audience is going to put upon words and phrases extreme interpretations, either deliberately to obscure the point, or in an honest effort to understand it better. When Jesus said that the Holy Spirit would reveal to the Apostles before they died *all the truth*, He did not mean all the truth there is, but all of the truth that is involved in the revelation of Ὁ Λόγος that God wants us to have. There is nothing in the New Testament to say that Columbus discovered America, or if he did not, who did. The Pythagorean theorem is not found in the New Testament, nor the fact that Henry Ford invented an automobile. One of the truths (and there are many!) that is true is that Charles Darwin propounded an hypothesis that organic evolution of all species, as well as the life which they possess, developed quite by random from resident nonrational forces in the primeval soup, and that the reason why Christians cannot understand this is because the process has required untold billions of centuries. That is the truth, but it is not in the New Testament, but that Darwin was wrong about his uniformitarianism is the truth and that truth is discussed in the New Testament, as Peter tells us why the evolutionists are wrong. They are "willingly ignorant" of the truth that fully explains that for which they have a fallacious explanation (2 Peter 3:3-6). The reason why evolutionists do not believe in Noah's Flood is because they do not wish to believe in it, since it provides the scientific answer to the fossil-strata record, upon which they base their "proof" of evolution.

Now that we have satisfied the sophomores about how much of all of the truth the Holy Spirit wishes us to have in the New Testament, we return to the question as to whether or not the New Testament as we have it now, without the additions which the "charismatics" are constantly imposing upon us, is the final authority. If it is, let us study it "to show ourselves approved unto God" with the promise that we will not "be ashamed" because we have put it together properly (2 Timothy 2:15). If it is not, let us abandon all attempts to find out what it says until we are assured that the Holy Spirit has said the last word that He wishes to say. When we are assured that what Jesus promised the Apostles at the Last Supper in a promise that He did not keep for them, has been in fact been given to us, then we will be justified in examining it. One should never try to evaluate what someone else has said until he stops speaking.

When we face the "charismatics" with this kind of logic we find it interesting to note their confusion. The following is the essence, if not the exact words, of a conversation with a dear, sincere man who says that he and others in his congregation have the gifts of "tongues" and their translation, prophecy and special knowledge. I say "special" knowledge for he did not deny that I had some knowledge - for example I know what kind of car I drive.

He: "I believe in the gifts because Mark 16:20 says that "the signs follow."
I: "The last twelve verses of the last chapter of Mark are not a part of the divinely inspired text."
He: "Indeed. I did not know that."
I: "The textual critics who are qualified to have an opinion agree. But let us suppose that they are wrong. If they are wrong and the text is genuine do you accept and follow all of it?"

He: "I believe everything that is in the Bible."
I: "Do you believe that water baptism is essential to salvation? Mark 16:16 says that it is. Are there any Presbyterians in heaven?"
He: "I do not believe in immersion in water as a prerequisite to salvation."
I: "Do you handle snakes in your services?"
He: "Of course not."
I: "Do you drink poison?"
He: "No."
I: "Why not? Those matters are discussed in Mark 16:18."
He: "I have no answer to that."
I: "Let it pass. Do you have those in your congregation who "speak in tongues?"
He: "Yes."
I: "And are there those who interpret what was said?"
He: "Yes."
I: "When they translate what was said into English, do you check the interpretation against the New Testament?"
He: "Yes."
I: "In the event that the interpretation conflicts with the New Testament, which has the priority?"
He: "The New Testament."
I: "If the interpretation conforms to the New Testament, what then?"
He: "There is no problem."
I: "In other words in that case the Holy Spirit has only repeated what He had already said in the New Testament. Is that not true?"
He: "I suppose so."

I: "And in the event that there is a clash between the interpretation of the tongues and the New Testament, then the Holy Spirit has contradicted Himself?

He: "The Holy Spirit is God. He cannot contradict Himself."

I: "Amen, brother. Then in the event of a clash, since someone has to be wrong, it is either the tongues speaker or his interpreter, since it cannot be the Holy Spirit?"

He: "That is right."

I: "Have you ever heard an interpreter say that the tongues speaker said something that was out of harmony with the New Testament?"

He: "Not that I recall."

I: "But if the New Testament as we have it now is the final arbiter of what is true and what is not, and if the Holy Spirit has already written the New Testament, why should He say it again in a charismatic meeting?"

He: "Perhaps He wants to emphasize something that He has already said."

I: "Could He not do that by leading us to read what He has already written? Is it not true that if one goes to church expecting to be titillated by a supernatural message from heaven, he will find it easier to listen to the voice of God in that manner and not spend time reading what God has already written?"

He: "That may be true?"

I: "In the event that what is said is not contradictory to the message of the New Testament, is it ever supplemental?

He: "I do not recall. I do not know everything that is in the New Testament. Perhaps I should."

I: "Should not we all and shame upon us that we do not!

I: "Can you give me a sample of those things which are said which do not contradict but emphasize what is in the New Testament? Suppose that the message from heaven is that Jesus Christ is a good man?"

He: "Everyone knows that anyhow.But suppose the message is that we ought to live better Christian lives?

I: "Everyone knows that too if he reads the New Testament. Does anyone ever say that the coming of the Lord will take place during the lifetime of the current generation?

He: "Yes, and I believe that that is true."

I: "Can you prove that by the New Testament?"

He: "I do not know."

I: "Suppose He doesn't?"

It seems clear that what is said in a "tongues" meeting as interpreted by another consists either of that which is in clear violation of what the Holy Spirit has already said in the New Testament, or is a repetition of what He has already said. The danger results in lessening the importance that we put upon scholarly exegesis and hermeneutics. One "charismatic" wrote that Biblical exegesis is a waste of time, since the Holy Spirit will tell us all that we want to know. Perhaps he did not mean to go that far, but that is what he wrote.

Another danger is that we will accept without question what is said in such meetings and lock ourselves in with a prejudicial mind-set that it is true, and then go to the New Testament to read into the text what is not there, having never been put there by the Holy Spirit in the first century. Thus the curse of eisegesis, the bane of sound Biblical interpretation and the death knell of Christian theology.

An example is the "revelation" of the charismatic woman in England, one hundred fifty years ago, that the church would be raptured before the tribulation - a classic piece of eisegesis, promoted since by Irving, J.N.Darby, W.E.Blackstone, the Plymouth Brethren and the Bible Institutes in America, with a zeal that has demanded in some circles that acceptance of the doctrine be made a test of Christian fellowship.

All Christians with the spirit of the Bereans (Acts 17:11) will give attention to all of these matters. It is obvious that being wrong about anything can do nothing to make it right, and that constant assertion that a doctrine is true does not change what the Holy Spirit has said about it already in the New Testament. No sincere child of God wishes to be wrong about anything that He has put in His love letter to us. Prerequisite to a fruitful study of the Word is a deep sense of one's own inadequacy and an assumption that those who disagree with us are as sincere about it as we are. With that in mind we must remember that if we want the filling of the Holy Spirit and His guidance as we study the Book of which He is the Author, all we need do is to ask Him for it (Luke 11:9-13).

Our verse also says that "tongues shall cease." The word for cease ($\pi\alpha\dot{\upsilon}\sigma\text{ο}\nu\tau\alpha\iota$) is the ordinary word for "stop" (#2044). In 1 Cor.13:8 it is a future passive. "tongues shall be brought to an end sometime in the future" - *i.e.* future to Paul at the time of this writing in A.D. 55-56.

It is obvious that by tongues ($\gamma\lambda\hat{\omega}\sigma\sigma\alpha$ #1846) Paul did not mean the physical organ in the mouth, although it occurs in this proper use in Mk.7:33,35; Lk.16:24; Rev.16:10 and James 3:5,6,6,8. In all other passages it means a language or dialect which can be understood without the services of a translator by someone present. To have the gift of interpretation ($\dot{\epsilon}\rho\mu\eta\nu\epsilon\acute{\iota}\alpha\ \gamma\lambda\omega\sigma\sigma\hat{\omega}\nu$) is to be endowed by the Holy Spirit with a special aptitude for translating from one language into another. Those who have acquired this skill by much study of the language are not necessarily endowed with this gift. If they had been they would not have needed to study.

There is nothing in the New Testament about "unknown" tongues. The adjective adjoined is $\dot{\epsilon}\tau\acute{\epsilon}\rho\alpha\iota\varsigma$ (Acts 2:4). Note that the King James Version presents the word "unknown" in italics to indicate that it is not in the original text. If it is unknown it is unknown only to some in the audience, not to all. If French is spoken in Kokomo, Indiana it is an "other" language which is also likely to be "unknown" by most of the natives, though some of the local sophisticates, including indeed some of the children who have studied it in school will understand it. English in Paris is another language, in the sense that it is "other" than French, but it will be unknown only to a few Parisians, since most are bi-lingual.

That what was spoken at Pentecost was not "unknown" is clear from Acts 2:8-11. There was no need for interpretation on that occasion. The miracle was that some among the 120 Christians present were supernaturally enabled to witness to the saving power of Jesus Christ in a language which they had never learned and which was clearly understood by some of those who listened. Thanks to this miracle the good news of the gospel of Christ was carried back home by those who heard it for the first time, and thus the seed was planted throughout the Mediterranean and Mid-Eastern world.

It is interesting to note that Paul did not say that the gift of languages would be superseded. He did say that the exercise of the gift would cease, but this does not deny that it may be exercised again. Indeed end-time events will see the revival of the gift in the fulfillment of Joel 2:28-32. When Peter said at Pentecost, in reference to Joel's prophecy, "This is that . . . " he did not say, "This is all of that. . . " But current charistmatics can find no support for their views here, since we are not yet in the period known as Daniel's 70th week (Daniel 9:27).

The gift of languages has not been superseded ($\kappa\alpha\tau\alpha\rho\gamma\dot{\epsilon}\omega$) but its exercise has ceased ($\pi\alpha\acute{u}\omega$), because it is no longer essential to communication. If everyone in the meeting speaks and understands the language which is native to the speaker, there is no need for him to speak in another language. Indeed if he does so he is manifesting a childish desire to show off his linguistic ability. Paul deals with this problem in 1 Corinthians 14. Judged by these Biblical standards and the canons of common sense, the current glossalalia wave of fleshly enthusiasm has little to commend it. We may expect a return of the phenomenon when Joel's prophecy is fulfilled at the Second Coming of our Lord. If we see it before that time it will be because of a special case in which the gift is necessary for communication of the gospel. For example, the writer has spent some time in Mexico, witnessing for Christ. I did not speak Spanish with sufficient fluency to be an effective preacher, and the Holy Spirit did not give me the supernatural ability to speak it without having learned it. But I learned it well enough to get the gospel story across to the audience, in services where there was no Mexican to interpret my English into Spanish. Ultimately, with much practice and hard work, I learned to speak Spanish without an interpreter. But if I were the only Christian in Moscow and the Holy Spirit wanted me to preach the gospel He would have to give me the gift of the Russian language because I know no Russian except *da* and *nyet*. But this situation is not likely to arise, since there are Russian Christians who are able to preach the gospel in Russian and there are also Russians who understand English well enough to appreciate my sermon, even though I spoke to them in English. No one doubts that the sovereign God can do anything He wishes to do, except that He cannot contradict Himself. That is why we can trust what He has said in His word, if only we can interpret it properly.

In verse 9 Paul, speaking in A.D.55,56 wrote that the knowledge which he then possessed was only partial.

Verse 9 - "For we know in part, and we prophesy in part."

ἐκ μέρους γὰρ γινώσκομεν καὶ ἐκ μέρους προφητεύομεν.

"For our knowledge is imperfect and our prophecy is imperfect;" . . . RSV

ἐκ (preposition with the objective genitive) 19.

μέρους (gen.sing.neut.of μέρος, objective genitive) 240.

γὰρ (causal conjunction) 105.

γινώσκομεν (1st.per.pl.pres.act.ind.of γινώσκω, aoristic) 131.

καὶ (adjunctive conjunction joining verbs) 14.

ἐκ (preposition with the objective genitive) 19.

μέρους (gen.sing.neut.of μέρος, objective genitive) 240.

προφητεύομεν (1st.per.pl.pres.act.ind.of προφητεύω, aoristic) 685.

Translation - "Because we know a part (of God's revelation) and we prophesy a part."

Comment: Here Paul is pointing to the situation at the time of his writing. In verse 10 he points to his (not ours) future. In verse 9 he admits that his knowledge and the content of his preaching and teaching is not complete. The word "imperfect" is unfortunate for ἐκ μέρους if it implies that which is "faulty" or "inaccurate." What Paul and the other Apostles knew and preached was sound, in so far as it went in scope, but its scope was limited. The limits on the scope of his knowledge were to be removed in the future revelation which will be τὸ τέλειον. That God's revelation of truth is given in gradual unfolding is clear from John 16:12, 13, 14; 2 Pet.1:16; 1 Pet.1:10-12, etc. That God would ultimately complete His revelation to us is also clear in 1 Cor.2:9-13. Paul was writing to the Corinthians before the revelation of *all truth* (John 16:13) had been made. Thus though he recognized the gifts of special knowledge and prophecy as true spiritual gifts, indispensable for the development of the first century Christians and churches, he also saw them in an *ad hoc* capacity, due to be phased out when the full revelation of the New Testament literature was in hand. At that time the partial revelation was included in the full revelation. In other words, we know more about Christianity now than Paul did then, and we are in a better position to appreciate the glories of the Lord Jesus in His incarnation now than the disciples were, even though they knew Him in the sense that they associated with him in physical time and space relations. The reason for our greater knowledge is that we have the entire New Testament to study. They did not. The student should try to imagine what his knowledge of Christian theology would be like if we did not have the Gospel of John. Paul did not have John's gospel, nor did any of the Christians who died before it was written.

If the gifts of prophecy and special knowledge were now being exercised, the Holy Spirit could only say what He has already written into the New Testament. Otherwise He did not put into the New Testament all that He had to tell us. But Jesus promised the Apostles that the Holy Spirit would reveal all to them, that He Himself would have revealed to them except for the fact that at that point they were unable to "bear it." (John 16:12).

Verse 10 - "But when that which is perfect is come, then that which is in part shall be done away."

ὅταν δὲ ἔλθῃ τὸ τέλειον, τὸ ἐκ μέρους καταργηθήσεται.

"but when the perfect comes, the imperfect will pass away." . . . RSV

ὅταν (conjunction introducing the subjunctive in an indefinite temporal clause) 436.

δὲ (adversative conjunction) 11.

ἔλθῃ (3d.per.sing.aor.subj.of ἔρχομαι, indefinite temporal clause) 146.

τὸ (nom.sing.neut.of the article in agreement with τέλειον) 9.

τέλειον (nom.sing.neut.of τέλειον, subject of ἔλθῃ) 553.

τὸ (nom.sing.neut.of the article, joined with the prepositional phrase ἐκ μέρους as the subject of καταργηθήσεται) 9.

ἐκ (preposition with the partitive genitive) 19.

μέρους (gen.sing.neut.of μέρος, partitive genitive) 240.

καταργηθήσεται (3d.per.sing.fut.pass.ind.of καταργέω, predictive) 2500.

Translation - "But when that which is complete has come, the partial will be needed no longer."

Comment: Paul uses the indefinite temporal clause, with ὅταν and the subjunctive in ἔλθῃ, not because he doubted that God would complete the revelation of His truth to the Church, but because he did not know the precise date when it would become complete. If God had told Paul in advance that the last writing of the New Testament would be that of the Apostle John and that he would write his gospel in the tenth decade, then Paul could have said, "When John has finished his gospel forty years from now then the partial knowledge which we have now will be forgotten in the joy of perusing the New Testament which will contain all of the revelation."

We have already discussed at length the meaning of καταργέω (#2500), in our comment on verse 8. If the student has not already done so, it is imperative that he turn to that analysis now.

Some interpret τὸ τέλειον to mean ἀγάπη, one of the fruits of the Holy Spirit and say that Paul is saying that ἀγάπη is the perfect gift (τὸ τέλειον), while the other gifts - prophecy, tongues, healing, etc. are imperfect, hence that Christians should pay less attention to the gifts and seek ἀγάπη. This interpretation falls before the fact that Paul says that the imperfect gifts, knowledge and prophecy, do not coexist with τὸ τέλειον (verses 9,10), whereas ἀγάπη, as a fruit of the Spirit had already been given to the Christians. The passage demands that the ἐκ μέρους precedes τὸ τέλειον, and that when the latter comes, the former is phased out.

The view that τὸ τέλειον means heaven, strikes at the doctrine that the New Testament is the final word of God to the church, a view that is in conflict with what Jesus told the disciples in John 16:12-15. The ἄρτι clause in verse 12 cannot be stretched chronologically to include 1800 years of church history after Paul's death. That Paul is teaching that love is better than gifts cannot be denied, or at least that the gifts without the love are worse than useless, but that τὸ τέλειον means ἡ ἀγάπη is not good exegesis.

Paul both approves and disapproves of the gifts. They were good in their time era and in pursuit of their purpose. Two were due to be phased out, one was to cease, while the others were to continue to bless the Body of Christ even after the

New Testament was completed. They are bad when they tarry after they have outlived their usefulness to compete with τὸ τέλειον.

For example the current glossalalia and the exercise of the gifts of prophecy and special knowledge, as practised by self-appointed "Apostles," with its emphasis upon the "baptism of the Holy Spirit" as a second work of grace, "prophecy," "knowledge," "tongues" and their interpretation, "revelations," "dreams" and "visions" is diabolically indifferent to what the New Testament teaches. An exegete with an open Greek New Testament in such a meeting could not compete with what "the Holy Spirit has revealed" to some wild-eyed fanatic. At Yeddo, Indiana, during a revival meeting, one of the local "charismatics" got a vision from the Lord that the devil was under the church where the author was preaching, whereupon a large number of men and boys tore down a telephone pole, much to the dismay of the local telephone company, and used it as a battering ram to rout the enemy from under the building. They were unimpressed with the passage of Scripture which was pointed out to them that "this kind goeth not out but by prayer and fasting" (Mt.17:21). They preferred telephone poles.

If the sign gifts are still with us or, having been withheld for a time, are with us again, who needs a New Testament? There are no imaginable limits to what may be "revealed" once we admit that the New Testament is not the final word. Who is to say Joseph Smith, Brigham Young, Charles Russell, Mary Baker Eddy, Ellen White, the Reverend James Jones, the Reverend Moon or the "Jesus Freaks" are not inspired, whatever their revelations may be, if there is no complete record of "Thus saith the Lord?" The lost generation of the 1960's told us that their sexual promiscuity, which was nothing less than ἔρος on the loose, was a manifestation of the divine ἀγάπη.

The current movement of the "charismatics" puts the emphasis upon experience rather than upon the Word of God. No one can deny that God's truth will lead to human experience and that experience when examined in the light of the Word of God and with reason brings consistency, coherence and correspondance with reality. The Renaissance mind sees the need for faith, reason and experience *in proper balance*. When faith in the Word of God and reason are neglected if not abandoned, we are left only with experience which can be interpreted only imperfectly. Thus the ship is at the mercy of the elements over which it has no control, without chart, compass or rudder.

Paul gives us an illustration of what he means in

Verse 11 - "When I was a child, I spake as a child, I understood as a child, I thought as a child: but when I became a man, I put away childish things."

ὅτε ἤμην νήπιος, ἐλάλουν ὡς νήπιος, ἐφρόνουν ὡσ νήπιος, ἐλογιζόμην ὡς νήπιος.ὅτε γέγονα ἀνήρ, κατήργηκα τὰ τοῦ νηπίου.

"When I was a child, I spoke like a child, I thought like a child, I reasoned like a child; when I became a man, I gave up childish ways." . . . RSV

ὅτε (conjunction with the indicative in a definite temporal clause) 703.
ἤμην (1st.per.sing.imperf.ind.of εἰμί, progressive duration) 86.

νήπιος (nom.sing.masc.of νήπιος, predicate nominative) 951.

ἐλάλουν (1st.per.sing.imp.act.ind.of λαλέω, progressive duration) 815.

ὡς (comparative particle) 128.

νήπιος (nom.sing.masc.of νήπιος, subject of λαλεῖ understood) 951.

ἐφρόνουν (1st.per.sing.imp.act.ind.of φρονέω, progressive duration) 1212.

ὡς (comparative particle) 128.

νήπιος (nom.sing.masc.of νήπιος, subject of φρονεῖ understood) 951.

ἐλογιζόμην (1st.per.sing.imp.mid.ind.of λογίζομαι, progressive duration) 2611.

ὡς (comparative particle) 128.

νήπιος (nom.sing.masc.of νήπιος, subject of λογίζεται understood) 951.

ὅτε (conjunction with the indicatve in a definite temporal clause) 703.

γέγονα (1st.per.sing.2d.perf.ind.of γίνομαι, intensive) 113.

ἀνήρ (nom.sing.masc.of ἀνήρ, predicate nominative) 63.

κατήργηκα (1st.per.sing.perf.act.ind.of καταργέω, intensive) 2500.

τὰ (acc.pl.neut.of the article, direct object of κατήργηκα) 9.

τοῦ (gen.sing.masc.of the article in agreement with νηπίου) 9.

νηπίου (gen.sing.masc.of νήπιος, description) 951.

Translation - *"When I was a child I always talked as a child, I always understood as a child, I always thought as a child. By the time I had become a man, I had put away childish things."*

Comment: Note ὅτε meaning "when" in the past, when it is joined with the imperfect, but meaning "when" in the present with the 2d. perfect and hence translated "now" as in "Now that I have become a man. . . " The imperfects are progressive duration constructions. When Paul was a child he always talked "baby talk." Note that the word is λαλέω (#815) not λέγω (#66). The words are synonymous in some contexts, but when there is a difference, λαλέω, can mean the call of a bird, the cry of an animal or the prattle of a baby, whereas λέγω means to speak with clear communication of thought. Because as a child he understood and thought like a child he also talked like a child.

But childhood patterns of thought and speech were superseded by the maturity of manhood. *Cf.*#2500, where we have καταργέω again in the same sense in which we used it in verse 8.

We have an interesting clue here as to the meaning of τέλειον. Note in 1 Cor.14:20 that "in malice" they were to be children (νηπιάζετε, the verb form of νήπιος), but in understanding they were to be *men* (τέλειοι γίνεσθε), - another evidence that τέλειος means "maturity" or "full development." When Paul became a man (1 Cor.13:11) he became τέλειος (1 Cor.14:20).

Thus again the point is made that the verb καταργέω (#2500) refers to a policy of phasing out one policy which is no longer appropriate in favor of another which is designed to meet the needs in the new situation. Just as men do not play with the toys that entertained them when they were children, but put them aside for other things, so prophecies and special knowledge were of no further utility once the mature (total, complete) revelation of God's truth was made known in Greek New Testament.

That the Corinthians were being childish as they vaunted themselves with puffed up arrogance because of their gifts rather than looking forward to the full revelation which would supersede partial knowledge is clear. Their childish behavior demonstrated a notable lack of the love which is the mark of Christian maturity. But the thrust of verse 11 is that partial gifts are opposed to τὸ τέλειον. The point is that Paul and all Christians in the sixth decade of the Christian era lacked the full revelation of God's truth. But the Apostles at least understood that the complete revelation was forthcoming within their lifetime. This was our Lord's promise to them in John 16:12-15. This point of view is reinforced by what he says in

Verse 12 - "For now we see through a glass darkly; but then face to face; now I know in part; but then shall I know, even as also I am known."

βλέπομεν γὰρ ἄρτι δι᾽ ἐσόπτρου ἐν αἰνίγματι, τότε δὲ πρόσωπον πρὸς πρόσωπον. ἄρτι γινώσκω ἐκ μέρους, τότε δὲ ἐπιγνώσομαι καθὼς καὶ ἐπεγνώσθην.

"For now we see in a mirror dimly, but then face to face. Now I know in part; then I shall understand fully, even as I have been fully understood." . . . RSV

βλέπομεν (1st.per.pl.pres.act.ind.of βλέπω, present progressive retroactive) 499.

γὰρ (causal conjunction) 105.

ἄρτι (temporal adverb) 320.

δι᾽ (preposition with the genitive, "through") 118.

#4227 ἐσόπτρου (gen.sing.neut.of ἔσοπτρον, "through").

King James Version

glass - 1 Cor.13:12; James 1:23.

Revised Standard Version

mirror - 1 Cor.13:12; James 1:23.

Meaning: A combination of ἐν and ὄπτω - "to see into." Hence a mirror. The ancient mirrors were not made of glass but of burnished iron or other shining metal - 1 Cor.13:12; James 1:23.

ἐν (preposition with the instrumental in an adverbial sense) 80.

#4228 αἰνίγματι (instru.sing.neut.of αἴνιγμα, adverbial).

King James Version

darkly - 1 Cor.13:12.

Revised Standard Version

dimly - 1 Cor.13:12.

Meaning: from αἰνίσσομαι - "to express something obscurely." Hence, an obscure saying; an enigma. Adverbially with ἐν in 1 Cor.13:12.

τότε (temporal adverb) 166.
δὲ (adversative conjunction) 11.
πρόσωπον (acc.sing.neut.of πρόσωπον, adverbial accusative) 588.
πρὸς (preposition with the accusative of extent) 197.
πρόσωπον (acc.sing.neut.of πρόσωπον, extent, adverbial) 588.
ἄρτι (temporal adverb) 320.
γινώσκω (1st.per.sing.pres.act.ind.of γίνωσκω, present progressive retroactive) 131.
ἐκ (preposition with the genitive) 19.
μέρους (gen.sing.neut.of μέρος, partitive) 240.
τότε (temporal adverb) 166.
δὲ (adversative conjunction) 11.
ἐπιγνώσομαι (1st.per.sing.fut.mid.ind.of ἐπιγινώσκω, predictive) 675.
καθὼς (compound comparative adverb) 1348.
καὶ (emphatic conjunction) 14.
ἐπεγνώσθην (1st.per.sing.aor.pass.ind.of ἐπιγινώσκω, constative) 675.

Translation - "Because now we see through a mirror obscurely, but then face to face. Now I know in part, but then I shall know fully, just as in fact I have always been known."

Comment: Let us not forget to view this passage in *zeitgeist*. It is the statement of a Christian in the sixth decade of the first century of the Christian era. He is partially enlightened by that part of the Christian revelation which had at that time already been given. He had the Markan document and possibly those written by Matthew and Luke. He did not have John's gospel, his epistles, nor the Revelation. He himself had written only a small portion of the literature of the New Testament which ultimately he was to contribute. Thus he had not had available the complete document which we call the Greek New Testament. His gifts of prophecy and special knowledge, the sources of ἐπίγνωσις (#3817) (as distinct from γνῶσις - #1856) were yet to be exercised to the fullest extent. This is how we interpret ἄρτι in both clauses. Note how γὰρ ἄρτι opposes τότε δὲ - "because now . . . but then" - Paul's knowledge at the time of the writing as opposed to his future full understanding at a later time when the canon of New Testament literature would be available. Paul did not live to see it, but other Christians did.

Gestalt psychology understands well that partial knowledge is enigmatic. Paul was crying out for closure. The jigsaw puzzle makes little sense until it is complete. That is why the "charismatics" who tell us that they are still adding to the New Testament are in the dark. They must wait until they get another new revelation, and another and another, another, anoth, an, a a!

The phrase πρόσωπον πρὸς πρόσωπον is in contrast to δι' ἐσόπτρου ἐν αἰνίγματι. In the same way ἐπιγνώσομαι καθὼς καὶ ἐπεγνώσθη contrasts with γινώσκω ἐκ μέρους. Partial knowledge gives way to total knowledge. Obscurity fades before clear vision. The gestaltist's confusion is gone when closure is achieved. Christians who have lived and studied since the New Testament was completed are living in the days of the τότε clauses. Paul was living in the day of the ἄρτι clauses. Paul is not talking in the τότε clauses about the Second Coming or about heaven. The Christian now who still sees obscurely rather than clearly and who only knows in part must explain his ignorance and confusion with reference to his own mental shortcomings or his intellectual laziness. He cannot blame the textbook. It is finished and it is clear. In fact it is a better source of knowledge than the sense perception which Peter, James and John enjoyed on the mount of transfiguration, as Peter was careful to tell us. It is a "more sure word" - more sure than what? More sure than what Peter saw as Moses and Elijah came back to talk personally with their transfigured Lord. (2 Peter 1:17-19). There is no problem about the textbook which we have to study as we try to "show (ourselves) approved" (2 Tim.2:15). The Author lives inside the body of each of us and He uses it as His temple (1 Cor.6:19,20; John 14:17). Now we need no prophets nor those who profess to have been given gifts of special knowledge. That is why the Holy Spirit has given no such gifts to the church, since He completed the New Testament. The problem with Biblical studies now lies in the fact that some are more interested in the additions which self-appointed prophets and holy men are making to the New Testament than in the New Testament itself.

As the need for *zeitgeist* (looking at the passage in the light of the time, place and circumstance in which it was written) has been pointed out before, we say again that verse 13 must be so viewed, with special emphasis upon the temporal adverb.

Verse 13 - "And now abideth faith, hope, charity, these three: but the greatest of these is charity."

νυνὶ δὲ μένει πίστις, ἐλπίς, ἀγάπη, τὰ τρία ταῦτα. μείζων δὲ τούτων ἡ ἀγάπη.

"So faith, hope, love abide, these three; but the greatest of these is love."

νυνὶ (temporal adverb) 1497.
δὲ (continuative conjunction) 11.
μένει (3d.per.sing.pres.act.ind.of μένω, present progressive retroactive) 864.
πίστις (nom.sing.fem.of πίστις, subject of μένει) 728.
ἐλπίς (nom.sing.fem.of ἐλπίς, subject of μένει) 2994.
ἀγάπη (nom.sing.fem.of ἀγάπη, subject of μένει) 1490.
τὰ (nom.pl.neut.of the article in agreement with τρία) 9.
τρία (nom.pl.neut.of τρεῖς, apposition) 1010.
ταῦτα (nom.pl.neut.of οὗτος, anaphoric) 93.
μείζων (nom.sing.neut.comp.of μέγας - #184, predicate adjective) 916.

δὲ (adversative conjunction) 11.

τούτων (gen.pl.neut.of οὗτος, partitive genitive) 93.

ἡ (nom.sing.fem.of the article in agreement with ἀγάπη) 9.

ἀγάπη (nom.sing.fem.of ἀγάπη, subject of ἐστιν understood) 1490.

Translation - "And now faith, hope,love remain — these three. But the greatest of these is love."

Comment: There as been much about how the Holy Spirit has equipped the Body of Christ with the various capabilities, without which she could never do His will in the world. Some of these are specifically called gifts (δῶρα). They are exotic empirical evidences of the Holy Spirit's presence in the Corinthians saints, some of whom were unduly excited about it. Paul spent the entire 12th chapter discussing this question, only to say, in 1 Cor.13:8-11 that two of them (prophecy and special knowledge) were only *ad hoc* expedients, to be withdrawn as the divine revelation became complete. Prophecies, linguistic ability, special knowledge, healing, helps and administrtions all were to have their day only to be superseded. The completed revelation in the New Testament would make prophecies and special knowledge obsolete; the spread of a common language or linguistic skills acquired by missionaries would make tongues unnecessary; the glorification of the church at the rapture will leave the divine healers with nothing to do. When the church is raptured the administrators and helpers, who were so important in her operations while she was still on the earth can be retired to pursue other interests for the glory of God.

Three gifts remain - faith, hope and love. What sermon on this text has not said love is greater than faith and hope and that it always be greater because faith will become sight and hope will be realized at the Second Coming? This may be true, but the text does not say that. What it says is that in A.D.55,56 as Paul was writing to the Corinthian church — a group of people who had manifested so much interest in their gifts that they had demonstrated very little love, love was the "better way."

Paul did not say that love would always be greater than faith and hope. To be sure faith was essential then and it is still essential and will continue to be until the rapture, when faith will become sight. But that does not say that faith is less important in the economy of God and in the life of the Christian than love.

So also with hope (Rom.8:24,25).

Love is eternal because God is love (1 John 4:8). Were it not for God's love redemption would not have been provided. But were it not for faith, God's gift, redemption could not have been appropriated. Were it not for hope the church could not survive in a world where empirical evidence for a brighter future is lacking. Since love is the remedy for all ills (1 Cor.13:4-7) it is obviously a better way (ὑπερβολὴν ὁδόν 1 Cor.12:31). Better than what? Better than the exercise of the gifts of which the Corinthians had become so inordinately proud that love was in scant evidence. Love far exceeds the other gifts in producing the victorious life while the church is still in the world, but Paul does not say that love will be greater than faith and hope in eternity.

Tongues and Prophecy

(1 Corinthians 14:1-25)

1 Cor.14:1 - "Follow after charity, and desire spiritual gifts, but rather that ye may prophesy."

Διώκετε τὴν ἀγάπην, ζηλοῦτε δὲ τὰ πνευματικά, μᾶλλον δὲ ἵνα προφητεύητε.

"Make love your aim, and earnestly desire the spiritual gifts, especially that you may prophesy." . . . RSV

Διώκετε (2d.per.pl.pres.act.impv.of διώκω, command) 434.
τὴν (acc.sing.fem.of the article in agreement with ἀγάπην) 9.
ἀγάπην (acc.sing.fem.of ἀγάπη, direct object of Διώκετε) 1490.
ζηλοῦτε (2d.per.pl.pres.act.impv.of ζηλόω, command) 3105.
δὲ (continuative conjunction) 11.
τὰ (acc.pl.neut.of the article in agreement with πνευματικά) 9.
πνευματικά (acc.pl.neut.of πνευματικός, direct object of ζηλοῦτε) 3791.
μᾶλλον (adverbial) 619.
δὲ (adversative conjunction) 11.
ἵνα (conjunction with the subj. in a purpose clause) 114.
προφητεύητε (2d.per.pl.pres.act.subj.of προφητεύω, purpose) 685.

Translation - "Pursue love and zealously seek spiritual blessings, but especially that you may prophesy."

Comment: It was Leopold von Ranke, the great German historian, the centennial anniversary of whose birth will be celebrated at Syracuse University in 1986, who insisted that if the historian is to be objective he must "divorce the study of the past as much as humanly possible from the passions of the present. . . " (G.P.Gooch, *History and Historians in the Nineteenth Century*, 96,97). When, consciously or subconsciously, we look at what was written in the past through the spectacles of the present, we are sure to miss some and perhaps all of the point. Thus Ranke preached *wie es eigentlich gewesen*. The historian must tell it exactly as it was. This is the *zeitgeist* principle that must guide all who seek to interpret that which was written and read in earlier times and under other circumstances.

If we are to understand Paul's chapter on the regulation of the use of foreign languages and their relation to prophecy in Corinth we must have his perspective. Dr.Wilber T. Dayton's discussion of the problem Paul faced in the Corinthian church and his attempts to correct it is particularly helpful in taking us back to Corinth and seeing the problem as though we were in fact present in the first century.

There is still the haunting question of "What is Corinthian tongues?" Why don't the tongues really communicate? Why are interpreters needed? Why must tongues be restricted in public service? Are the tongues not really languages as would be indicated by the plain literal meaning of γλῶσσαι? *The translator has no other option but to call them "tongues." That was the old English word for languages. And nothing else would convey the meaning of the Greek word. With all the confusion, distortion, and perversion that may have characterized the Corinthian tongues, it was still speech uttered in languages. And the function of language is to convey thought from one mind to another. Where is the breakdown of communication? The translators concluded that the fault was in the lack of knowledge. Not enough people present knew the language. Therefore the message fell on deaf ears. So the translator inserted the word "unknown," implying that the languages were real but simply not known.*

This does explain some things fairly well if the ambiguity is not pressed too far. If a Cappadocian is speaking or praying in his own language in a Greek-speaking Corinthian congregation, God hears him but man does not understand what he is saying. The language is unknown to them. That in no way denies the work of the Spirit in the Cappadocian speaker. He may be speaking profound mysteries by divine revelation. But it simply leaves the audience untouched because the language is unknown -- by them, that is. God knows the language and so does the speaker. Otherwise he couldn't edify himself (14:4). If he wants to edify others, of course, the thoughts must be expressed in a way that they understand. Paul can imagine an ideal solution. If there were no language barrier, there would be no problem. Paul just wishes we all knew each other's languages and could speak in them (14:5). Then we could all understand each other as was the case before the Tower of Babel and will be the case in Heaven. What an advantage that would be in witnessing, especially in a foreign land! But that kind of tongues seems not to be available to us now. However, if one really desires a valuable ability, it is more important to speak from God (i.e., to prophesy) than to be able to say it in different languages -- unless, of course, one is able to bridge the gap and to translate his own messages into the language of his hearers (verse 5).

In effect, Paul says, "Let us be reasonable now. If I come unto you speaking with languages, what good will it do you unless there is a meeting of the minds so that I really speak to your very ears the matter of revelation, knowledge, proclamation, or doctrine?" (14:6).

Wilber T. Dayton, *Charismatics and the New Testament*, 16,17.

Above all things the Christian should be in hot pursuit of the greatest of the gifts which is love. It is the crowning achievement of Christian growth in grace (*cf.* comment on 2 Peter 1:1-11). The pursuit of ἀγάπη begins with faith and in the following order acquires excellence in the pursuit of knowledge, knowledge, temperance, patience, godliness and brotherly kindness, which then introduces the seeker to love itself. To acquire love in boundless measure is to experience Christianity at its highest possible level of efficiency. Thus as we follow Peter's suggested path on the road to "growth in grace" (2 Pet.1:1-11; 3:18) we reach the point where soul winning is the natural result of the abundant life.

Meanwhile the first century Christian should also seek the spiritual gifts, since he lived during the time when the New Testament was being written and before it was complete. It is important to note that tongues are never said to be one of the gifts of the Holy Spirit, though they are included in passages in which Paul is speaking of spiritual matters (πνευματικῶν, in 1 Cor.12:1 and πνευματικά in 1 Cor.14:1). Love was indeed superior to them all, but this is not to say that the gifts in the first century were not important. However of all of the gifts prophecy is the most important.

Paul devotes the entire 14th chapter to his proof that this is so. Why? Because he who prophesies edifies the church and therefore contributes to the exercise of love. If the gift one possesses, however miraculous it may be, and however titilative its effect upon those present, does not display one's love for his brethren and contribute to their edification it is inferior. Healing passes the test. How wonderful to be able to pray the prayer of faith that will heal the sick and suffering! What better way to show one's love than to alleviate his suffering? Helps and administrations do. But the one which was most popular with the Corinthians edified no one except the one who was speaking, unless of course there was one present able to translate from the foreign language of the speaker to the native language of the listener. But interpretation is a form of prophecy because, if it is genuine, it edifies the church.

It has been said that Paul did not forbid the Corinthians to speak in a foreign language that nobody present understood. This statement results from a mistranslation of 1 Cor.14:39, with reference to which Dayton says, "This is perhaps the most mistranslated verse in the New Testament." (*Ibid.*22). Those who may not agree that Paul forbade the Corinthians to display their linguistic abilities before the public in a church service, in an act which he interpeted as a childish attempt to show off, will still agree that he practically regulated the practice out of existence. Who today in the typical Pentecostal meeting pays any attention to the regulations which Paul includes in this chapter?

A study of διώκω (#434) reveals a list of Christian virtues to be pursued. Here is material for a sermon. If we pursue and apprehend love we shall have got all of the others.

Paul now sets out to show that prophecy is a much superior gift to the practice of making a speech in a language that no one present understands.

Verse 2 - "For he that speaketh in an unknown tongue speaketh not unto men, but unto God: for no man understandeth him; howbeit in the spirit he speaketh mysteries."

ὁ γὰρ λαλῶν γλώσσῃ οὐκ ἀνθρώποις λαλεῖ ἀλλὰ θεῷ, οὐδεὶς γὰρ ἀκούει, πνεύματι δὲ λαλεῖ μυστήρια.

"For one who speaks in a tongue speaks not to men but to God; for no one understands him, but he utters mysteries in the Spirit." . . . *RSV*

ὁ (nom.sing.masc.of the article in agreement with λαλῶν) 9.
γὰρ (causal conjunction) 105.

λαλῶν (pres.act.part.nom.sing.masc.of λαλέω, substantival, subject of λαλεῖ) 815.

γλώσσῃ (instru.sing.fem.of γλῶσσα, means) 1846.

οὐκ (negative particle with the indicative) 130.

ἀνθρώποις (dat.pl.masc.of ἄνθρωπος, indirect object of λαλεῖ) 341.

λαλεῖ (3d.per.sing.pres.act.ind.of λαλέω, static) 815.

ἀλλὰ (alternative conjunction) 342.

θεῷ (dat.sing.masc.of θεός, indirect object of   λαλεῖ) 124.

οὐδεὶς (nom.sing.masc.of οὐδείς, subject of ἀκούει) 446.

γὰρ (causal conjunction) 105.

ἀκούει (3d.per.sing.pres.act.ind.of ἀκούω, aoristic) 148.

πνεύματι (instru.sing.neut.of πνεῦμα, means) 83.

δὲ (adversative conjunction) 11.

λαλεῖ (3d.per.sing.pres.act.ind.of λαλέω, aoristic) 815.

μυστήρια (acc.pl.neut.of μυστήριον, direct object of   λαλεῖ) 1038.

Translation - "Because the one who speaks in a foreign language is not speaking to men, but to God, because no one understands; but by means of the Spirit he is speaking unintelligible material."

Comment: The point to be demonstrated is that prophecy is a better medium of communication that a foreign language. Paul now sets out to prove it. The speaker who uses a foreign language is talking to God, Who understands him, since He is speaking by means of the Holy Spirit. What he says is not nonesense since there is someone in the world who understands the language that he is speaking, but those people are not present. Hence, despite the quality of what he may be saying, he is not speaking to the church assembled since no one understands. ἀκούει is used without an object, but if it were present it would be in the accusative case - "No one hears with understanding." The audience would hear the sound of his voice (ἀκούω with the genitive) but they would not be able to tell what he was saying (ἀκούω with the accusative). Thus the church is not edified; he is not helping them however much he may be receiving help for himself. This is a selfish demonstration of his linguistic ability, and it is not consistent with ἀγάπη.

The proper way to speak in the assembly of the saints in set forth in

Verse 3 - "But he that prophesieth speaketh unto men to edification, and exhortation, and comfort."

ὁ δὲ προφητεύων ἀνθρώποις λαλεῖ οἰκοδομὴν καὶ παράκλησιν καὶ παραμυθίαν.

"On the other hand, he who prophesies speaks to men for their upbuilding and encouragement and consolation." . . . RSV

ὁ (nom.sing.masc.of the article in agreement with προφητεύων) 9.

δὲ (adversative conjunction) 11.

προφητεύων (pres.act.part.nom.sing.masc.of προφητεύω, substantival, subject of λαλεῖ) 685.

ἀνθρώποις (dat.pl.masc.of ἄνθρωπος, indirect object of λαλεῖ) 341.

λαλεῖ (3d.per.sing.pres.act.ind.of λαλέω, static) 815.

οἰκοδομὴν (acc.sing.fem.of οἰκοδομή, direct object of λαλεῖ) 1481.

καὶ (adjunctive conjunction joining nouns) 14.

παράκλησιν (acc.sing.fem.of παράκλησις, direct object of λαλεῖ) 1896.

καὶ (adjunctive conjunction joining nouns) 14.

#4229 παραμυθίαν (acc.sing.fem.of παραμυθία, direct object of λαλεῖ).

King James Version

comfort - 1 Cor.14:3.

Revised Standard Version

consolation - 1 Cor.14:3.

Meaning: cf. παραμυθέομαι (#2602). Hence, comfort, consolation, counselling, general conversation designed to strengthen one - 1 Cor.14:3.

Translation - "But the prophet is saying that which edifies and encouragement and good counsel to men.

Comment: Here is Paul's definition of the gift of prophecy. The student should run all of the references under #'s 1481, 1896 and 4229 (only here). Prophecy therefore must be intelligible to the audience and cannot therefore be in a language which the hearers do not understand. The prophet speaks not to God but for God to his brethren. But when he speaks in a language foreign to his audience, he is speaking only to God (verse 2), Who cannot be edified and Who needs no comfort, counsel or consolation. Thus he edifies only himself. This is a selfish, loveless practice. But the prophet speaks to men and hence what he says is helpful to the church. This is what the next verse says.

Verse 4 - "He that speaketh in an unknown tongue edifieth himself; but he that prophesieth edifieth the church."

ὁ λαλῶν γλώσσῃ ἑαυτὸν οἰκοδομεῖ. ὁ δὲ προφητεύων ἐκκλησίαν οἰκοδομεῖ.

"He who speaks in a tongue edifies himself, but he who prophesies edifies the church." . . . *RSV*

ὁ (nom.sing.masc.of the article in agreement with λαλῶν) 9.

λαλῶν (pres.act.part.nom.sing.masc.of λαλέω, substantival, subject of οἰκοδομεῖ) 815.

γλώσσῃ (instru.sing.fem.of γλῶσσα, means) 1846.

ἑαυτὸν (acc.sing.masc.of ἑαυτοῦ, direct object of οἰκοδομεῖ) 288.

οἰκοδομεῖ (3d.per.sing.pres.act.ind.of οἰκοδομέω, static) 694.

ὁ (nom.sing.masc.of the article in agreement with προφητεύων) 9.

δὲ (adversative conjunction) 11.

προφητεύων (pres.act.part.nom.sing.masc.of προφητεύω, substantival, subject of οἰκοδομεῖ) 685.

ἐκκλησίαν (acc.sing.fem.of ἐκκλησία, direct object of οἰκοδομεῖ) 1204.
οἰκοδομεῖ (3d.per.sing.pres.act.ind.of οἰκοδομέω, static) 694.

Translation - *"He who speaks in a foreign language is edifying himself, but the prophet is edifying a church."*

Comment: The participial substantives in the nominative case are the subjects of the verbs - the one who speaks unintelligibly and the one who speaks so that the audience knows what he is saying. The function of the former is self-serving; the latter is performing a needed service. The New Testament no where says that the former is exercising a gift (δῶρον). The latter has one of the gifts of the Holy Spirit - a gift which was indispensable for the edification of the Christians of the first century who did not have the entire New Testament available. Indeed before Mark wrote his gospel in the fifth decade they did not have any divine guidance except that which came from those who had the prophetic gift.

To speak to an audience in a language that one knows the listeners cannot understand is a childish public display of one's linguistic virtuosity, unless it happens to be the only language that the speaker can use, in which case he should remain silent. This same principle can be applied to the preacher who is indeed speaking in the native language of his audience, but who uses technical terms and polysyllabic creations designed not to convey thought but to impress the audience. The preacher who is speaking "over the heads" of his audience is as guilty of self-serving as though he spoke in a foreign tongue.

Though Paul does not say so the prophet whose purpose is to build up, console, encourage and counsel the church also in the process builds up himself. How often God-called preachers who try humbly to speak under the inspiration of the Holy Spirit have felt the blessing of their own edification as they spoke. Some of the greatest applications of Scripture in the preacher's repertoire may have come to him as he spoke. Holy Spirit motivated Biblical exegesis in a public service contributes to closure, as the jigsaw puzzle of Biblical revelation adds another piece in a connection never perceived before. This is the ideal situation in which the Holy Spirit is really the preacher, expounding the book which He wrote and using the preacher only as His mouthpiece. A good sermon will edify the preacher more than it does the people in the audience. There is no thrill for the student like that of being creative!

But preachers since the close of the apostolic period are not prophets in the sense that the Apostles were. They are not adding to the divine revelation, for there is nothing to add. The Holy Spirit wrote *Finis* to the production when the Apostle John penned his last line. The inspired utterance of the modern preacher results from his exposition of a book that is already complete. Modern exegetes know only that which is already in the record. Though what we say may be new to us and to the audience, we are only discovering connections in the Word which have been there all of the time, although we were unaware of it.

There is however the possibility that the modern preacher can make new applications of principles already revealed in the Word as he discusses them in a culture that has made scientific advances which were unknown to preachers in former days. Paul did not write that E equals MC squared. Einstein did. If we assume that Einstein was correct (the author cannot speak from personal research!) it is likely that this principle can be connected with something in the New Testament. If so, to discover the connection and to expound it for the edification of the church is to be creative, but not prophetic. It is creative because it is a connection never perceived before, but the preacher is not the original contributor, either of what Paul or Einstein said

The first century church had many problems, both theoretical and practical, which only the prophets and those with the gift of special knowledge could solve. The solutions which they gave are available to modern Christians in the New Testament, a book only partially available then.

Corinth, due to her geographical location, was an entrepot of commerce. Ships from cities throughout the Mediterranean littoral called at her ports regularly. The result was that there was a communication problem. The Corinthians spoke κοινή Greek. Some of them were bilingual. The Jews in the city probably also spoke their native Yiddish, and others some other language. But there were few, probably none, in Corinth so versatile that they understood all of the languages spoken by those who came to the city. This is the problem that Paul addresses in

Verse 5 - "I would that ye all spoke with languages, but rather that ye prophesied: for greater is he that prophesieth than he that speaketh with foreign languages, except he interpret, that the church may receive edifying."

θέλω δὲ πάντας ὑμᾶς λαλεῖν γλώσσαις, μᾶλλον δὲ ἵνα προφητεύητε. μείζων δὲ ὁ προφητεύων ἢ ὁ λαλῶν γλώσσαις, ἐκτὸς εἰ μὴ διερμηνεύῃ, ἵνα ἡ ἐκκλησία οἰκοδομὴν λάβῃ.

"Now I want you all to speak in tongues, but even more to prophesy. He who prophesies is greater than he who speaks in tongues, unless someone interprets, so that the church may be edified." . . . RSV

θέλω (1st.per.sing.pres.act.ind.of θέλω, aoristic) 88.

δὲ (explanatory conjunction) 11.

πάντας (acc.pl.masc.of πᾶς, in agreement with ὑμᾶς) 67.

ὑμᾶς (acc.pl.masc.of σύ, general reference) 104.

λαλεῖν (pres.act.inf.of λαλέω, noun use, direct object of θέλω) 815.

γλώσσαις (instru.pl.fem.of γλῶσσα, means) 1846.

μᾶλλον (adverbial) 619.

δὲ (adversative conjunction) 11.

ἵνα (conjunction with the subjunctive, result) 114.

προφητεύητε (2d.per.pl.pres.act.subj.of προφητεύω, consecutive) 685.

μείζων (nom.sing.neut.comp.of μέγας #184, predicate adjective) 916.

δὲ (causal conjunction) 11.

ὁ (nom.sing.masc.of the article in agreement with προφητεύων) 9.

προφητεύων (pres.act.part.nom.sing.masc.of προφητεύω, substantival, subject of ἐστιν understood) 685.

ἤ (disjunctive) 465.

ὁ (nom.sing.masc.of the article in agreement with λαλῶν) 9.

λαλῶν (pres.act.part.nom.sing.masc.of λαλέω, substantival, subject of ἔστιν understood) 815.

γλώσσαις (instru.pl.fem.of γλῶσσα, means) 1846.

ἐκτὸς (adverbial) 1461.

εἰ (conditional particle in a third-class condition) 337.

μὴ (negative particle with the subjunctive in a third-class condition) 87.

διερμηνεύῃ (3d.per.sing.pres.act.subj.of διερμηνεύω, third-class condition) 2906.

ἵνα (conjunction with the subjunctive in a purpose clause) 114.

ἡ (nom.sing.fem.of the article in agreement with ἐκκλησία) 9.

ἐκκλησία (nom.sing.fem.of ἐκκλησία, subject of λάβῃ) 1204.

οἰκοδομὴν (acc.sing.fem.of οἰκοδομή, direct object of λάβῃ) 1481.

λάβῃ (3d.per.sing.2d.aor.act.subj.of λαμβάνω, purpose) 533.

Translation - "Now I wish that all of you were multi-lingual, but I would rather that you propesied, because if the linguist does not translate in order that the church may receive edification the prophet is greater than he."

Comment: δὲ is first explanatory, then adversative and finally causal. Note πάντας ὑμᾶς with ὑμᾶς, the accusative of general reference with the infinitive λαλεῖν, instead of πάντος ὑμῶν, a partitive genitive construction. The prophet who speaks intelligibly to the people is of greater benefit than the one who speaks a dialect that no one understands, unless he translates what he has said for them, in which case the question is this: If he has the ability to translate into the language of those present, why does he not use their language in the first place? The only answer seems to be that he wishes to show off his great linguistic prowess. Preachers who tell the audience of English speaking people what the Greek word in the New Testament is, unless it is necessary to do so in order to make the English clear, is guilty of this same self-serving gimmick. It is only when we communicate that we help anyone.

Note the pleonastic ἐκτὸς εἰ μὴ. ἐκτός means "except" or "unless" without the third-class condition. We have the same idiom in 1 Cor.15:2; 1 Tim.5:19.

Paul could have pointed out the lack of logic in the use of a foreign language which is then translated by the same speaker into the local dialect, but he did not, because he was being careful not to offend those who did so. He only sought to help the Corinthians to see the problem in perspective. It is likely that the Corinthians got the point. If the Cappadocian stood up in church and addressed the Corinthians in his own tongue, which they could not understand, and then proceded to translate what he had just said into κοινή Greek, he has indeed edified them after they found out what he said, but in the process he has demonstrated his skill as a linguist and he has probably telegraphed to his audience that he is so insecure that he felt the need to place himself in the spotlight.

Paul pursues the point relentlessly in

Verse 6 - "Now, brethren, if I came unto you speaking with tongues, what shall I profit you, except I speak to you either by revelation, or by knowledge, or by prophesying or by doctrine?"

Νῦν δέ, ἀδελφοί ἐὰν ἔλθω πρὸς ὑμᾶς γλώσσαις λαλῶν, τί ὑμᾶς ὠφελήσω, ἐὰν μὴ λαλήσω ἢ ἐν ἀποκαλύψει ἢ ἐν γνώσει ἢ ἐν προφητείᾳ ἢ ἐν διδαχῇ;

"Now, brethren, if I come to you speaking in tongues, how shall I benefit you unless I bring you some revelation or knowledge or prophecy or teaching?" . . .
RSV

Νῦν (explanatory) 1497.

δὲ (adversative conjunction) 11.

ἀδελφοί (voc.pl.masc.of ἀδελφός, address) 15.

ἐὰν (conditional particle with the subjunctive in a third-class condition) 363.

ἔλθω (1st.per.sing.pres.mid.subj.of ἔρχομαι third-class condition) 146.

πρὸς (preposition with the accusative of extent) 197.

ὑμᾶς (acc.pl.masc.of σύ, extent) 104.

γλώσσαις (instru.pl.fem.of γλῶσσα, means) 1846.

λαλῶν (pres.act.part.nom.sing.masc.of λαλέω, adverbial, complementary) 815.

τί (acc.sing.neut.of τίς, interrogative pronoun, direct object of ὠφελήσω) 281.

ὑμᾶς (acc.pl.masc.of σύ, double accusative) 104.

ὠφελήσω (1st.per.sing.fut.act.ind.of ὠφελέω, deliberative) 1144.

ἐὰν (conditional particle with the subjunctive in a third-class condition) 363.

μὴ (negative particle with the subjunctive) 87.

ὑμῖν (dat.pl.masc.of σύ, indirect object of λαλήσω) 104.

λαλήσω (1st.per.sing.aor.act.subj.of λαλέω, third-class condition) 815.

ἢ (disjunctive) 465.

ἐν (preposition with the locative of sphere) 80.

ἀποκαλύψει (loc.sing.fem.of ἀποκαλύψις, sphere) 1902.

ἢ (disjunctive) 465.

ἐν (preposition with the locative of sphere) 80.

γνώσει (loc.sing.fem.of γνῶσις, sphere) 1856.

ἢ (disjunctive) 465.

ἐν (preposition with the locative of sphere) 80.

προφητείᾳ (loc.sing.fem.of προφητεία, sphere) 1041.

ἢ (disjunctive) 465.

ἐν (preposition with the locative of sphere) 80.

διδαχῇ (loc.sing.fem.of διδακή, sphere) 706.

Translation - "But now, brethren, if I come to you speaking in a foreign language how can I help you if I do not speak to you either in the role of one with a revelation, or with knowledge or with prophecy or with teaching?"

Comment: An interesting syntax arrangement here has two protases, each with ἐὰν and the subjunctive, completed by a single apodosis with the deliberative future indicative.

The Corinthians were unduly excited about the practice which was least able to edify the church and most likely to contribute to sinful pride. Paul says to them, "Suppose I return to Corinth speaking to you in a language that you do not understand instead of speaking plainly of some new revelation of truth, or in a message of enlightenment, comfort, consolation, counsel, encouragements or instruction. What benefit would result for you?" His teaching is centered in the fact that all believers are incorporated into the Body of Christ by the baptism of the Holy Spirit (1 Cor.12:13) so that each member should help all of the others, as each member of the physical body cooperates with all the rest. The speaker who addresses the audience in a foreign tongue helps no one but himself. This is not a manifestation of love (1 Cor.13:4-8). Communication is essential to edification. There is no communication when the sounds heard are not associated with thoughts in transit. This is the thought of

Verse 7 - "And even things without life giving sound, whether pipe or harp, except they give a distinction in the sounds, how shall it be known what is piped or harped?"

ὅμως τὰ ἄφυχα φωνὴν διδόντα, εἴτε αὐλὸς εἴτε κιθάρα, ἐὰν διαστολὴν τοῖς φθόγγοις μὴ δῷ, πῶς γνωσθήσεται τὸ αὐλούμενον ἢ τὸ κιθαριζόμενον;

"If even lifeless instruments, such as the flute or harp, do not give distinct notes, how shall any one know what is played?" . . . RSV

ὅμως (adversative particle) 2710.

τὰ (nom.pl.neut.of the article in agreement with διδόντα) 9.

#**4230** ἄφυχα (nom.pl.neut.of ἄφυχος, in agreement with διδόντα).

King James Version

things without life - 1 Cor.14:7.

Revised Standard Version

lifeless instruments - 1 Cor.14:7.

Meaning: α privative and φυχή (#233); lifeless; without a soul. Inanimate - 1 Cor.14:7 with reference to a musical instrument.

φωνὴν (acc.sing.fem.of φωνή, direct object of διδόντα) 222.
διδόντα (pres.act.part.nom.pl.neut.of δίδωμι, substantival, subject of δῷ) 362.
εἴτε (disjunctive) 4016.

#**4231** αὐλὸς (nom.sing.masc.of αὐλός, nominative absolute).

King James Version

pipe - 1 Cor.14:7.

Revised Standard Version

flute - 1 Cor.14:7.

Meaning: cf. αὐλέω (#926); αὐλητής (#824). Hence a flute - 1 Cor.14:7.

εἴτε (disjunctive) 4016.

#4232 κιθάρα (nom.sing.fem.of κιθάρα, nominative absolute).

King James Version

harp - 1 Cor.14:7; Rev.5:8; 14:2; 15:2.

Revised Standard Version

harp - 1 Cor.14:7; Rev.5:8; 14:12; 15:2.

Meaning: a harp; generally in 1 Cor.14:7; a heavenly misical instrument in Rev.5:8; 14:2; 15:2.

ἐὰν (conditional particle in a third-class condition) 363.
διαστολὴν (acc.sing.fem.of διαστολή, direct object of δῷ) 3872.
τοῖς (dat.pl.masc.of the article in agreement with φθόγγοις) 9.
φθόγγοις (dat.pl.masc.of φθόγγος, reference) 3875.
μὴ (negative particle with the subjunctive) 87.
δῷ (3d.per.sing.aor.act.subj.of δίδωμι, third-class condition) 362.
πῶς (interrogative adverb in direct question) 627.
γνωσθήσεται (3d.per.sing.1st.fut.pass.ind.of γινώσκω, deliberative) 131.
τὸ (acc.sing.neut.of the article in agreement with αὐλούμενον) 9.
αὐλούμενον (pres.pass.part.acc.sing.neut.of αὐλέω, substantival, direct object of γνωσθήσεται) 926.
ἢ (disjunctive) 465.
τὸ (acc.sing.neut.of the article in agreement with κιθαριζόμενον) 9.

#4233 κιθαριζόμενον (pres.pass.part.acc.sing.neut.of κιθαρίζω, substantival, direct object of γνωσθήσεται).

King James Version

harped - 1 Cor.14:7; Rev.14:2.

Revised Standard Version

played - 1 Cor.14:7; Rev.14:2.

Meaning: Cf. κιθάρα (#4232); κιθαρωδός (#5389). To play upon a harp - generally in 1 Cor.14:7; in the heavenly scene - Rev.14:2.

Translation - "Even though inanimate things such as a flute or a harp give a sound, if they do not make a distinction with reference to the sounds, how shall what is played on flute or harp be recognized?"

Comment: ὅμως brings out the concessive force of the participle διδόντα. A symphony is recognized by contrapuntal and harmonic arrangements of notes on a scale that are distinct. Any rendition that blurs the distinction between sounds obscures the melody until the listener cannot tell what is being played. Nor can anyone tell what is being said when another is speaking in a languge that is foreign to him. Thus there is no communication and no mutual blessing - only a self-serving display of linguistic ability. That is not love.

Paul's next illustration takes his reader from the orchestra hall to the battlefield.

Verse 8 - "For if the trumpet give an uncertain sound, who shall prepare himself to the battle."

καὶ γὰρ ἐὰν ἄδηλον σάλπιγξ φωνὴν δῷ, τίς παρασκευάσεται εἰς πόλεμον;

"And if the bugle gives an indistinct sound, who will get ready for battle?"

καὶ (continuative conjunction) 14.

γὰρ (emphatic conjunction) 105.

ἐὰν (conditional particle with the subjunctive in a third-class condition) 363.

ἄδηλον (acc.sing.fem.of ἄδηλος, in agreement with φωνὴν) 2465.

σάλπιγξ (nom.sing.fem.of σάλπιγξ, subject of δῷ) 1507.

φωνὴν (acc.sing.fem.of φωνή, direct object of δῷ) 222.

δῷ (3d.per.sing.aor.act.subj.of δίδωμι, third-class condition) 362.

τίς (nom.sing.masc.of τίς, interrogative pronoun, direct question) 281.

παρασκευάσεται (3d.per.sing.fut.mid.ind.of παρασκευάζω, deliberative) 3217.

εἰς (preposition with the accusative, purpose) 140.

πόλεμον (acc.sing.masc.of πόλεμος, purpose) 1483.

Translation - "And indeed if a bugle emits an uncertain sound who is going to prepare himself for battle?"

Comment: Note continuative καὶ with emphatic γὰρ. ἐὰν and the subjunctive gives us another third-class condition with a deliberative future indicative in the apodosis. Note the repetition of these hypothetical questions in verses 6,7,8 - "If I come speaking a foreign language . . . ?" "If an orchestra plays indistinctly . . . ?" "If a bugle call is indistinct . . . ?" Preachers, orchestras and buglers on battlefields had better communicate clearly whatever they have to say.

Having illustrated the point Paul now drives it home emphatically in

Verse 9 - "So likewise ye, except ye utter by the tongue words easy to be understood, how shall it be known what is spoken? For ye shall speak into the air."

οὕτως καὶ ὑμεῖς διὰ τῆς γλώσσης ἐὰν μὴ εὔσημον λόγον δῶτε, πῶς γνωσθήσεται τὸ λαλούμενον; ἔσεσθε γὰρ εἰς ἀέρα λαλοῦντες.

"So with yourselves; if you in a tongue utter speech that is not intelligible, how will any one know what is said? For you will be speaking into the air." . . . RSV

οὕτως (demonstrative adverb) 74.
καὶ (adjunctive conjunction) 14.
ὑμεῖς (nom.pl.masc.of σύ, nominative absolute) 104.
διὰ (preposition with the ablative, intermediate agent) 118.
τῆς (abl.sing.fem.of the article in agreement with γλώσσης) 9.
γλώσσης (abl.sing.fem.of γλῶσσα, intermediate agent) 1846.
ἐὰν (conditional particle with the subjunctive in a third-class condition) 363.
μὴ (negative particle with the subjunctive) 87.

#4234 εὔσημον (acc.sing.masc.of εὔσημος, in agreement with λόγον).

King James Version

easy to be understood - 1 Cor.14:9.

Revised Standard Version

intelligible - 1 Cor.14:9.

Meaning: εὖ (#1536) and σῆμα - "a sign." *Cf.* σημαίνω (#2708). Hence, good sign, one that is well marked, distinct, definite, precise. Joined with λόγον - hence a well understood speech - 1 Cor.14:9.

λόγον (acc.sing.masc.of λόγος, direct object of δῶτε) 510.
δῶτε (2d.per.pl.aor.act.subj.of δίδωμι, third-class condition) 362.
πῶς (interrogative adverb in rhetorical question) 627.
γνωσθήσεται (3d.per.sing.fut.pass.ind.of γινώσκω, future periphrastic) 131.
τὸ (nom.sing.neut.of the article in agreement with λαλούμενον) 9.
λαλούμενον (pres.pass.part.nom.sing.neut.of λαλέω, substantival, subject of γωνσθήσεται) 815.
ἔσεσθε (2d.per.pl.fut.ind.of εἰμί, future periphrastic) 86.
γὰρ (causal conjunction) 105.
εἰς (preposition with the accusative of extent) 140.
ἀέρα (acc.sing.masc.of ἀήρ, extent) 3584.
λαλοῦντες (pres.act.part.nom.pl.masc.of λαλέω, adverbial, causal) 815.

Translation - "It is the same with you. If you do not deliver an intelligible message in a language that can be understood, how shall that which is being spoken be understood? Because you will be speaking into the air."

Comment: οὕτως refers to verses 7 and 8 which presented the out-of-tune orchestra and the confused bugler. "In the same way (οὕτως) also (καὶ) you . . ." The protasis has ἐὰν with the subjunctive in δῶτε and the apodosis has the future periphrastic in a question. Note δῶτε with λόγον as its object - "give a word" or "make a speech." The question is rhetorical. No one can understand the sense of an unintelligible speech. If it is German and the audience knows no German it is no better than the gibberish which one hears which is affirmed to be the language of the Holy Spirit. He has already said in the Greek New Testament all that He has to say, but if He had something more to add we may be sure that He would say it in a language that could be understood without the services of some self-appointed interpreter who professes to be able to listen to a language that is not spoken anywhere on this planet and translate it into the dialect of those present. Is there an interpreter who knows no French or German who could go to Paris or Berlin, listen to the gibberish of a local Pentecostal charismatic and then translate it into the dialect of Frenchmen or Germans?

Verse 10 - "There are, it may be, so many kinds of voices in the world, and none of them is without signification."

τοσαῦτα εἰ τύχοι γένη φωνῶν εἰσιν ἐν κόσμῳ, καὶ οὐδὲν ἄφωνον.

"There are doubtless many different languages in the world, and none is without meaning." . . . RSV

τοσαῦτα (nom.pl.neut.of τοσοῦτος, in agreement with γένη) 727
εἰ (conditional particle with the potential optative in a fourth-class condition) 337.
τύχοι (3d.per.sing.2d.aor.optative of τυγχάνω, potential, fourth-class condition) 2699.
γένη (nom.pl.neut.of γένος, subject of εἰσιν) 1090.
φωνῶν (gen.pl.fem.of φωνή, description) 222.
εἰσιν (3d.per.pl.pres.ind.of εἰμί, aoristic) 86.
ἐν (preposition with the locative of place) 80.
κόσμῳ (loc.sing.masc.of κόσμος, place) 360.
καὶ (continuative conjunction) 14.
οὐδὲν (nom.sing.neut.of οὐδείς, subject of ἐστιν understood) 446.
ἄφωνον (nom.sing.neut.of ἄφωνος, predicate adjective) 3177.

Translation - "It may well be, if in fact there are, so many kinds of voices in the world, and not one is without meaning."

Comment: εἰ τύχοι (*cf.* 1 Cor.15:37) is a fourth-class conditional protasis with no apodosis. "No example of this condition complete in both protasis and apodosis is to be found in the New Testament. Indeed, Robertson denies that a complete example occurs in the LXX or papyri 'so far as examined.' . . . 'It is an ornament of the cultured class and was little used by the masses save in a few set phrases.' (R.1020)" (Mantey, *Manual*, 290). We have here a potential optative serving "in a clause which implies a condition. . . Expressed fully" our verse would read as I have translated it (*Ibid.,*174).

Paul was not sure how many different languages and dialects were in the world or whether any lacked the power to communicate thought. He assumes that all of them do, since the function of speech is to communicate thought. The other requirement, if thought is indeed transmitted, is that both the speaker and the listener must understand the language being spoken.

It is to be noted that Paul does not use γλώσσων (languages) here but φωνῶν (voices, sounds). Study carefully #222. It can mean the cry of an animal or bird or even the sound of an inanimate object, such as a squeak of a wheel that needs grease, the report of a gun or the majestic roar of a Niagra as in Rev.1:15b, where φωνή is used in Rev.1:15a to refer to the voice of our Lord. He has a voice with which He was about to speak to John in dictation of epistles to seven churches, in a language that John understood. And His voice sounded like the roar of a mighty waterfall. This sound also signifies something. Paul had already said in verse 8 that a bugle call, if properly sounded, communicated thought to soldiers, whether it be to attack or to retreat.

It is necessary therefore that whatever the sound may be, whether that of a voice speaking a language or of a sound giving a signal and leading to an intelligent conclusion, it must be interpreted properly. This is his thought in

Verse 11 - "Therefore if I know not the meaning of the voice, I shall be unto him that speaketh a barbarian, and he that speaketh shall be a barbarian unto me."

ἐὰν οὖν μὴ εἰδῶ τὴν δύναμιν τῆς φωνῆς, ἔσομαι τῷ λαλοῦντι βάρβαρος καὶ ὁ λαλῶν ἐν ἐμοὶ βάρβαρος.

"but if I do not know the meaning of the language, I shall be a foreigner to the speaker and the speaker a foreigner to me." . . . RSV

ἐὰν (conditional particle with the subjunctive in a third-class condition) 363.
οὖν (inferential conjunction) 68.
μὴ (negative particle with the subjunctive) 87.
εἰδῶ (1st.per.sing.aor.act.subj.of ὁράω, third-class condition) 144b.
τὴν (acc.sing.fem.of the article in agreement with δύναμιν) 9.
δύναμιν (acc.sing.fem.of δύναμις, direct object of εἰδῶ) 687.
τῆς (gen.sing.fem.of the article in agreement with φωνῆς) 9.
φωνῆς (gen.sing.fem.of φωνή, description) 222.
ἔσομαι (1st.per.sing.fut.mid.ind.of εἰμί, predictive) 86.
τῷ (dat.sing.masc.of the article in agreement with λαλοῦντι) 9.
λαλοῦντι (pres.act.part.dat.sing.masc.of λαλέω, substantival, reference) 815.
βάρβαρος (nom.sing.masc.of βάρβαρος, predicate nominative) 3755.
καὶ (continuative conjunction) 14.
ὁ (nom.sing.masc.of the article in agreement with λαλῶν) 9.
λαλῶν (pres.act.part.nom.sing.masc.of λαλέω, substantival, subject of ἔσται understood) 815.
ἐν (preposition with the dative of reference) 80.
ἐμοὶ (dat.sing.masc.of ἐμός, reference) 1267.
βάρβαρος (nom.sing.masc.of βάρβαρος, predicate nominative) 3755.

Translation - "So if I do not understand the meaning of the voice I will seem to the speaker to be a foreigner and he will seem to be a foreigner to me."

Comment: τὴν δύναμιν τῆς φωνῆς means, of course, "the meaning of the voice." But it is not the voice (φωνή) that transmits meaning but the words (λόγοι) which the voice speaks. Thus the voice (φωνή) has power (δύναμις) to use words which transmit thought only if the words used are understood. The voice can only transmit sound. This happens when someone speaks gibberish, the sound of which is heard, despite the fact that the sound is devoid of meaning. In such a case the speaker and his listener with reference to each other are mere babblers (*cf.*#3755). Neither is the one an edifier nor the other edified.

Note the difference between λέγω (#66) and λαλέω (#815) which the context *sometimes* (not always) demands. *Cf.* our comment on Heb.5:11.

The ἐάν clause with the subjunctive is a third-class condition. Paul is talking about a hypothetical situation. If he understands the language spoken no babbling occurs. If not, there is no benefit to the listener. The test of spiritual merit is the degree of good which the speaker does for the other members of the Body of Christ, not the degree of good which he imagines that he receives for himself (verse 4). In fact he who speaks to an audience in a language that he knows no one in the audience understands is doing for himself a disservice. Psychologists present will see in his childish display of linguistic virtuosity an evidence that he is afflicted with a deep sense of inferiority. Why else should he show off?

Verse 12 - "Even so ye, forasmuch as ye are zealous of spiritual gifts, seek that ye may excel to the edifying of the church."

οὕτως καὶ ὑμεῖς, ἐπεὶ ζηλωταί ἐστε πνευμάτων, πρὸς τὴν οἰκοδομὴν τῆς ἐκκλησίας ζητεῖτε ἵνα περισσεύητε.

"So with yourselves; since you are eager for manifestations of the Spirit, strive to excel in building up the church."

οὕτως (demonstrative adverb) 74.
καὶ (adjunctive conjunction) 14.
ὑμεῖς (nom.pl.masc.of σύ, subject of ἐστε, ζητεῖτε and περισσεύητε) 104.
ἐπεὶ (subordinating conjunction in a causal clause) 1281.
ζηλωταί (nom.pl.masc.of ζηλωτής, predicate nominative) 2120.
ἐστε (2d.per.pl.pres.ind.of εἰμί, aoristic) 86.
πνευμάτων (gen.pl.neut.of πνεῦμα, description) 83.
πρὸς (preposition with the accusative, purpose) 197.
τὴν (acc.sing.fem.of the article in agreement with οἰκοδομὴν) 9.
οἰκοδομὴν (acc.sing.fem.of οἰκοδομή, purpose) 1481.
τῆς (gen.sing.fem.of the article in agreement with ἐκκλησίας) 9.
ἐκκλησίας (gen.sing.fem.of ἐκκλησία, description) 1204.
ζητεῖτε (2d.per.pl.pres.act.impv.of ζητέω, command) 207.
ἵνα (conjunction with the subjunctive in a purpose clause— 114.
περισσεύητε (2d.per.pl.pres.act.subj.of περισσεύω, purpose) 473.

Translation - "So also you since you are zealots for spiritual matters, try always to edify the church in order that you may work to the best possible advantage."

Comment: When barbarians shout at each other nothing but chaos results. This is no way to edify the church. Paul may have his tongue in cheek as he commends them for being quite properly ambitious to promote spiritual values. Note that the King James Version "gifts" is not in the Greek. If indeed they were sincere in seeking to improve the rapport between the saints and the Holy Spirit and thus promote the cause of the gospel of Christ in Corinth, they should try to achieve the greatest possible efficiency. Let them become spiritual efficiency experts. In their quest for the best (περισσεύητε) they will abandon policies and practices which at best are of questionable value and at worst destructive to growth in grace.

Verse 13 - "Wherefore let him that speaketh in an unknown *tongue pray that he may interpret."*

διὸ ὁ λαλῶν γλώσσῃ προσευχέσθω ἵνα διερμηνεύῃ.

"Therefore, he who speaks in a tongue should pray for the power to interpret."
                                                                    . . . RSV

διὸ (inferential particle) 1622.

ὁ (nom.sing.masc.of the article in agreement with λαλῶν) 9.

λαλῶν (pres.act.part.nom.sing.masc.of λαλέω, substantival, subject of προσευχέσθω) 815.

γλώσσῃ (instru.sing.fem.of γλῶσσα, means) 1846.

προσευχέσθω (2d.per.sing.pres.impv.of προσεύχομαι, command) 544.

ἵνα (conjunction with the subjunctive in a purpose clause) 114.

διερμηνεύῃ (3d.per.sing.pres.act.subj.of διερμηνεύω, purpose) 2906.

Translation - "Therefore let him who speaks in a foreign language pray that he may be able to translate what he says."

Comment: We will never understand Paul's meaning here if we divorce this passage from the *zeitgeist*. We must remember that Corinth was a city with many visitors from many different parts of the Mediterranean who spoke many different dialects. Not all of them were able to speak the κοινή Greek. When these foreigners came to Corinth many of them may have come to church. The speaker who was a Christian and who felt led by the Holy Spirit to testify to the glory of God might possibly be unilingual - able to speak only in his native language. Suppose that no one present understands? In such a case his message, however sincere and however eloquent in his language could do nothing to edify the church, unless he was able to translate what he had said into the language(s) of those present. Assuming that he was not an accomplished liguist, like Paul, he could translate his Cappadocian (for example) into κοινη or Latin only if the Lord performed a miracle. So his choice was either to pray for a linguistic miracle or to remain silent.

But if he could pray for the ability to speak what to him was a foreign language, in order that he might translate what he had just said, which was foreign to his audience, why not pray for the ability to speak *their* language(s) in the first place? Why go through the procedure of saying what he had to say in his own language (foreign to the audience but not to him) first if when he finished he intended to pray for the ability to tell the audience what he had just said in their language(s)?

Let us suppose that the Cappadocian could in fact speak both his language and the κοινή, but not the patois of some rural church in Galatian country, and that a Galatian christian was present. Further that there were Romans present who understood nothing but Latin. In that case he would speak first in κοινή and then pray for the ability to translate both into the Galatian provincial dialect and into Latin in order that when the exercise was finished all present would know what he said and thus be edified. It would be childish for him to speak first in Cappadocian, and then transalte into κοινή for the benefit of the Corinthians after which he would translate again both into Latin and the Galatian dialect. Would it not be better for him to remain silent? One demonstrates his fluency in a foreign language only when it is necessary to communicate.

The scenarios which we have presented, in an attempt to make sense out of verse 13, apply in few American audiences where the "gift of tongues" is exploited by the "charismatics." Seldom if ever is one present who does not understand English. Thus what Paul says in our passage does not apply to the present situation.

There are some Christians on the current American scene who wish to escape the odium attached to the position of the extreme charismatics. They disclaim any desire supernaturally to speak to the audience in a foreign language, but say that in their private devotions they often pray in a language which they do not understand. Paul deals with this matter in verses 14 and 15 and concludes that for his part he will pray in a language which both he and God understands.

Verse 14 - "For if I pray in an unknown *tongue, my spirit prayeth, but my understanding is unfruitful."*

ἐὰν (γὰρ) προσεύχωμαι γλώσσῃ, τὸ πνεῦμά μου προσεύχεται, ὁ δὲ νοῦς μου ἄκαρπός ἐστιν.

"For if I pray in a tongue, my spirit prays but my mind is unfruitful." ... RSV

ἐὰν (conditional particle in a third-class condition) 363.

(γὰρ) (inferential conjunction) 105.

προσεύχωμαι (1st.per.sing.pres.mid.subj.of προσεύχομαι, third-class condition) 544.

γλώσσῃ (instru.sing.fem.of γλῶσσα, means) 1846.

τὸ (nom.sing.neut.of the article in agreement with πνεῦμα) 9.

πνεῦμά (nom.sing.neut.of πνεῦμα, subject of προσεύχεται) 83.

μου (gen.sing.masc.of ἐγώ, possession) 123.

προσεύχεται (3d.per.sing.pres.mid.ind.of προσεύχομαι, present iterative) 544.

ὁ (nom.sing.masc.of the article in agreement with νοῦς) 9.

δὲ (adversative conjunction) 11.

νοῦς (nom.sing.masc.of νοῦς, subject of ἐστιν) 2928.

μου (gen.sing.masc.of ἐγώ, possession) 123.

ἄκαρπος (nom.sing.masc.of ἄκαρπος, predicate adjective) 1052.
ἐστιν (3d.per.sing.pres.ind.of εἰμί, futuristic) 86.

Translation - "Therefore if I pray in a foreign language my spirit is praying but my mind will bear no fruit."

Comment: We are dealing with a third-class condition. Paul is suggesting a hypothetical situation. He is not saying that he or anyone else should pray in a foreign language. When the Holy Spirit "bears witness with our spirit that we are the children of God" (Rom.8:16) there can be no doubt that there is rapport between His mind and ours. Also when He prays for us because we do not know how to pray for ourselves His "groanings cannot be uttered" (Rom.8:26). Thus neither of these passages has anything to do with the text before us. Paul is not saying whether when he prays he is alone or with others present, but verse 16 suggests the latter. To be sure when we are praying we are talking to God Who already knows what we have in mind whether we speak aloud to Him or not. But when we pray aloud to God when others are present our prayer is also edifying to them if we pray in a language that they understand. So there is no more reason to pray than to preach in a foreign language, and the same objections that have been urged against the latter can be urged against the former. Our worship, whether we pray, preach, play an instrument and sing *a cappella* must edify the church as well as ourselves. Otherwise the gifts are used for selfish purposes. Thus to pray in a foreign language when one knows that others are listening is not love. And to pray in a foreign language when one is alone makes no sense at all. God is fairly difficult to impress!

Note how Paul implies that edification of the intellect is not inconsistent with edification of the spiritual nature of the Christian. For Paul there could never be any conflict between intellectual growth and spiritual health. Some who are interested in the ecstatic are not notably concerned with the development of intellectual power, as though the intellect is an evil force that militates against spiritual development. *Contra* Paul who told the Romans to be "transformed" by the renewing of the mind (Rom.12:2). The word is μεταμορφοῦσθε (#1222) and is applied to Jesus in Mt.17:2 and Mark 9:2 and suggested as a goal for the believer in Romans 12:2 and 2 Cor.3:18. Paul wanted his mind to bear fruit in the lives of others as he prayed.

Verse 15 - "What is it then? I will pray with the spirit, and i will pray with the understanding also: I will sing with the Spirit and I will sing with the understanding also."

τί οὖν ἐστιν; προσεύξομαι τῷ πνεύματι, προσεύξομαι δὲ καὶ τῷ νοΐ. φαλῶ τῷ πνεύματι, φαλῶ δὲ καὶ τῷ νοΐ.

"What am I to do? I will pray with my spirit and I will pray with the mind also; I will sing with the spirit and I will sing with the mind also."   RSV

τί (nom.sing.neut.of τίς, interrogative pronoun, subject of ἐστιν) 281.
οὖν (inferential conjunction) 68.

ἐστιν (3d.per.sing.pres.ind.of εἰμί, futuristic, deliberative) 86.
προσεύξομαι (1st.per.sing.fut.mid.ind.of προσεύχομαι, predictive) 544.
τῷ (loc.sing.neut.of the article in agreement with πνεύματι) 9.
πνεύματι (loc.sing.neut.of πνεῦμα, sphere) 83.
προσεύξομαι (1st.per.sing.fut.mid.ind.of προσεύχομαι, predictive) 544.
δὲ (adversative conjunction) 11.
καὶ (adjunctive conjunction joining nouns) 14.
τῷ (loc.sing.masc.of the article in agreement with νοΐ) 9.
νοΐ (loc.sing.masc.of νοῦς, sphere) 2928.
φαλῶ (1st.per.sing.fut.act.ind.of φάλλω, predictive) 4047.
τῷ (loc.sing.neut.of the article in agreement with πνεύματι) 9.
πνεύματι (loc.sing.neut.of πνεῦμα, sphere) 83.
φαλῶ (1st.per.sing.fut.act.ind.of φάλλω, predictive) 4047.
δὲ (adversative conjunction) 11.
καὶ (adjunctive conjunction joining nouns) 14.
τῷ (loc.sing.masc.of the article in agreement with νοΐ) 9.
νοΐ (loc.sing.masc.of νοῦς, sphere) 2928.

Translation - "What then is my decision? I will pray in the Spirit and I will also pray with the understanding. i will play and sing with the spirit and I will also play and sing with the understanding."

Comment: Why should Paul pray, play an instrument and sing only with his spirit in some ecstatic frenzy when he can also bring his mind (intellectual faculty, understanding, rationale) into the function of his worship? To pray and sing with a lyre or harp is good even if the words are strange, but it is better to pray, sing and play with an intelligent grasp of what is being said, as this engages the mind of the Christian with the mind of the Spirit of God. *Cf.*#4047 for the true meaning of φάλλω in the first century. The future tenses are volitive as well as pointing to the future.

Verse 16 suggests that the prayer of verse 15 which Paul had in mind was not being prayed alone, but with others present.

Verse 16 - "Else when thou shalt bless with the spirit, how shall he that occupieth the room of the unlearned say Amen at thy giving of thanks, seeing he understandeth not what thou sayest?"

ἐπεὶ ἐὰν εὐλογῆς ἐν πνεύματι, ὁ ἀναπληρῶν τὸν τόπον τοῦ ἰδιώτου πῶς ἐρεῖ τὸ Ἀμήν ἐπὶ τῇ σῇ εὐχαριστίᾳ, ἐπειδὴ τί λέγεις οὐκ οἶδεν;

ἐπεὶ (subordinating conjunction in a causal clause introducing a third-class condition) 1281.
ἐὰν (conditional particle with the subjunctive in a third-class condition) 363.
εὐλογῆς (2d.per.sing.pres.act.subj.of εὐλογέω, third-class condition) 1120.
ἐν (preposition with the locative of sphere) 80.
πνεύματι (loc.sing.neut.of πνεῦμα, sphere) 83.
ὁ (nom.sing.masc.of the article in agreement with ἀναπληρῶν) 9.

ἀναπληρῶν (pres.act.part.nom.sing.masc.of ἀναπληρόω, substantival, subject of ἐρεῖ) 1040.

τὸν (acc.sing.masc.of the article in agreement with τόπον) 9.

τόπον (acc.sing.masc.of τόπος, direct object of ἀπαπληρῶν) 1019.

τοῦ (gen.sing.masc.of the article in agreement with ἰδιώτου) 9.

ἰδιώτου (gen.sing.masc.of ἰδιώτης, description) 3032

πῶς (interrogative adverb in rhetorical question) 627.

ἐρεῖ (3d.per.sing.fut.act.ind.of ἐρῶ, deliberative) 155.

τὸ (acc.sing.neut.of the article in agreement with Ἀμήν) 9.

Ἀμήν (explicative) 466.

ἐπὶ (preposition with the instrumental of cause) 47.

τῇ (instru.sing.fem.of the article in agreement with εὐχαριστίᾳ) 9.

σῇ (instru.sing.fem.of σός, in agreement with εὐχαριστίᾳ) 646.

εὐχαριστίᾳ (instru.sing.fem.of εὐχαριστία, cause) 3616.

ἐπειδή (compound causal conjunction) 2148.

τί (acc.sing.neut.of τίς, interrogative pronoun, direct object of οἶδεν) 281.

λέγεις (2d.per.sing.pres.act.ind.of λέγω, aoristic) 66.

οὐκ (negative particle with the indicative) 130.

οἶδεν (3d.per.sing.perf.act.ind.of οἶδα, intensive) 144b.

Translation - "Otherwise if you give a testimony by the spirit, how shall the one who is in the place of the unlearned respond with 'Amen' because of your testimony, in view of the fact that he does not know what you are saying?"

Comment: Note the conjunction ἐπεί with ἐὰν and ἐπειδή in a causal sense. Such confusion as Paul suggests could not occur as a result of Paul's worship since what he does at church is understood by all, whether he prays, sings or plays a musical instrument. However constructive the testimony may be, if it is spoken in a foreign language, it means nothing to the unlearned who is not an accomplished linguist in his own right and does not have the ability to translate for himself. He cannot empathize with the worshipper. He does not know when to say 'Amen" since he does not know what the speaker is talking about.

Indeed preachers who depend more upon the excitement of aroused emotion than upon an appeal to the mind of the audience often interject expletives at inopportune times. The results can sometimes be so illogical as to excite hilarity. A preacher in the midst of an emotion charged passage, which he often, and without premeditation punctuated with exclamations of praise to God, assured his audience that "This old world is going to hell. Praise the Lord!" One cannot imagine the Apostle Paul being carried away like that.

He takes care not to denigrate the peformance of the worshipper in question, although he points to a better way to worship, in

Verse 17 - "For thou verily givest thanks well, but the other is not edified."

σὺ μὲν γὰρ καλῶς εὐχαριστεῖς, ἀλλ' ὁ ἕτερος οὐκ οἰκοδομεῖται.

σὺ (nom.sing.masc.of σύ, subject of εὐχαριστεῖς, emphatic) 104.

μὲν (particle of affirmation) 300.

γὰρ (concessive conjunction) 105.

καλῶς (adverbial) 977.

εὐχαριστεῖς (2d.per.sing.pres.act.ind.of εὐχαριστέω, aoristic) 1185.

ἀλλ' (adversative conjunction) 342.

ὁ (nom.sing.masc.of the article in agreement with ἕτερος) 9.

ἕτερος (nom.sing.masc.of ἕτερος, subject of οἰκοδομεῖται) 605.

οὐκ (negative particle with the indicative) 130.

οἰκοδομεῖται (3d.per.sing.pres.pass.ind.of οἰκοδομέω, aoristic) 694.

Translation - *"Although in fact you are giving thanks beautifully the other man is not being edified."*

Comment: The μὲν ... δὲ constrast shows up here - "On the one hand ... but on the other. . . " It can be handled by construing γὰρ in a concessive sense, as it is in a few places. Despite the fact that the one Christian is giving eloquent thanks to God as he addresses the Deity, in a language that both he and God understand, the other man, sitting in the seat of the unlearned derives no spiritual edification from the worship.

Every member of the body can worship in a way that edifies himself and all the other members at the same time. Since he can do so, he should.

Lest Paul be accused of objecting to something that he was unable to do he describes his own policy in verses 18 and 19.

Verse 18 - *"I thank my God, I speak with tongues more than ye all."*

εὐχαριστῶ τῷ θεῷ, πάντων ὑμῶν μᾶλλον γλώσσαις λαλῶ.

"I thank God that I speak in tongues more than you all;" . : . RSV

εὐχαριστῶ (1st.per.sing.pres.act.ind.of εὐχαριστέω, aoristic) 1185.

τῷ (dat.sing.masc.of the article in agreement with θεῷ) 9.

θεῷ (dat.sing.masc.of θεός, indirect object of εὐχαριστῶ) 124.

πάντων (abl.pl.masc.of πᾶς, in agreement with ὑμῶν) 67.

ὑμῶν (abl.pl.masc.of σύ, comparison) 104.

μᾶλλον (adverbial) 619.

γλώσσαις (loc.pl.fem.of γλῶσσα, sphere) 1846.

λαλῶ (1st.per.sing.pres.act.ind.of λαλέω, aoristic) 815.

Translation - *"I thank God that I speak in foreign languages more than all of you."*

Comment: Paul does not mean that his linguistic versatility is greater than that of the combined Corinthian congregation, but it is greater than that of any one of the people. He was a well educated man who had the advantage of travel in his missionary trips and he had applied himself with diligence. The result was that he was multilingual. This skill had been acquired. It was not a gift of the Holy Spirit, except perhaps in the sense that he had a natural aptitude for languages.

Verse 19 - *"Yet in the church I had rather speak five words with my understanding, that by my voice I might teach others also, than ten thousand words in an* unknown *tongue."*

ἀλλὰ ἐν ἐκκλησίᾳ θέλω πέντε λόγους τῷ νοΐ μου λαλῆσαι, ἵνα καὶ ἄλλους κατηχήσω, ἢ μυρίους λόγους ἐν γλώσσῃ.

"nevertheless, in church I would rather speak five words with my mind, in order to instruct others, than ten thousand words in a tongue." . . . RSV

ἀλλὰ (adversative conjunction) 342.
ἐν (preposition with the locative of place) 80.
ἐκκλησίᾳ (loc.sing.fem.of ἐκκλησία, place) 1204.
θέλω (1st.per.sing.pres.act.ind.of θέλω, aoristic) 88.
πέντε (numeral) 1119.
λόγους (acc.pl.masc.of λόγος, direct object of λαλῆσαι) 510.
τῷ (instru.sing.masc.of the article in agreement with νοΐ) 9.
νοΐ (instru.sing.masc.of νοῦς, manner) 2928.
μου (gen.sing.masc.of ἐγώ, possession) 123.
λαλῆσαι (aor.act.inf.of λαλέω, noun use, direct object of θέλω) 815.
ἵνα (conjunction with the subjunctive, purpose) 114.
καὶ (adjunctive conjunction) 14.
ἄλλους (acc.pl.masc.of ἄλλος, direct object of κατηχήσω) 198.
κατηχήσω (1st.per.sing.pres.act.subj.of κατηχέω, purpose) 1714.
ἢ (disjunctive) 465.
μυρίους (acc.pl.masc.of μύριοι, in agreement with λόγους) 1272.
λόγους (acc.pl.masc.of λόγος, direct object of λαλῆσαι) 510.
ἐν (preposition with the locative of sphere) 80.
γλώσσῃ (loc.sing.fem.of γλῶσσα, sphere) 1846.

Translation - *"But at church I prefer to speak five words with my understanding in order that I also may instruct others than innumerable words in a foreign language."*

Comment: Paul distinguished between his policy when he was involved in his missionary travels and when he was present in a church service where everyone spoke the same language. As he travelled throughout the Mediterranean world he found it necessary to resort to his linguistic skills as he preached the gospel. In one area he spoke one dialect; in another area, another. He always sought to adapt to the needs of the moment, for there is no witness for Christ where there is no communication. In a local church service there might still be some need for him to adapt the medium of his remarks to the needs of the people. In no case would he speak in a language which they did not understand. Rather he would speak in the native tongue of the listener. If this meant that he would need to repeat in a different dialect for the benefit of a part of the audience what he had just said in another dialect for another part, he would, of course, do so. These situations might arise and he was able to meet the exigencies of the time and place, but to speak in a foreign language at church with others present, when one could speak to them intelligibly, was a callous disregard of one's obligation to help them. Five words that they could understand were better than ten thousand foreign words since the latter were worth nothing to the saints.

Only an insecure man acting like a child would take advantage of a local church congregation and seize the opportunity to speak to them at length in order to display his skill as a linguist, when he knew that they could only sit silently and endure it until he had finished his charade.

In verse 20 he tells them to grow up.

Verse 20 - *"Brethren be not children in understanding: howbeit in malice be children, but in understanding be men."*

'Αδελφοί, μὴ παιδία γίνεσθε ταῖς φρεσίν, ἀλλὰ τῇ κακίᾳ νηπιάζετε, ταῖς δὲ φρεσὶν τέλειοι γίνεσθε.

"Brethren, do not be children in your thinking; be babes in evil, but in thinking be mature." . . . RSV

'Αδελφοί (voc.pl.masc.of ἀδελφός, address) 15.
μὴ (negative particle with the imperative in a prohibition) 87.
παιδία (nom.pl.neut.of παιδίον, predicate nominative) 174.
γίνεσθε (2d.per.pl.pres.mid.impv.of γίνομαι, command) 113.
ταῖς (loc.pl.fem.of the article in agreement with φρεσίν) 9.

#4235 φρεσίν (loc.pl.fem.of φρήν, sphere).

King James Version

understanding - 1 Cor.14:20,20.

Revised Standard Version

thinking - 1 Cor.14:20,20.

Meaning: Liddel & Scott list four meanings: (1) midriff, (2) heart, as the seat of the passions,(3) mind, as seat of the mental faculties, perceptions, thought, and (4) will or purpose. In 1 Cor.14:20,20 the mind and will seem to be Paul's thought.

ἀλλὰ (adversative conjunction) 342.
τῇ (loc.sing.fem.of the article in agreement with κακίᾳ) 9.
κακίᾳ (loc.sing.fem.of κακία, sphere) 641.

#4236 νηπιάζετε (2d.per.pl.pres.act.impv.of νηπιάζω, command).

King James Version

be a child - 1 Cor.14:20.

Revised Standard Version

be babes - 1 Cor.14:20.

Meaning: cf. νήπιος (#951). Hence to have the characteristics of a baby; be naive. With the locative of sphere τῇ κακίᾳ in 1 Cor.14:20. It is the mark of high Christian achievement to be unskilled and inexperienced in the realm of evil. Opposed to τέλειος (#553).

τᾱῖς (loc.pl.fem.of the article in agreement with φρεσὶν) 9.
δὲ (adversative conjunction) 11.
φρεσὶν (loc.pl.fem.of φρήν, sphere) 4235.
τέλειοι (nom.pl.masc.of τέλειος, predicate adjective) 553.
γίνεσθε (2d.per.pl.pres.mid.impv.of γίνομαι, command) 113.

Translation - *"Brethren, stop being naive in your thinking, but in the sphere of wickedness be a child; but with reference to thinking be mature."*

Comment: μή with the present imperative - "Do not go on being a child." Grow up. This order has to do with their intellectual development. The Corinthians were acting like babies (*cf.*#174 for the age range of παιδίον). They were not thinking logically about the question of foreign languages and their communication problems.

But with reference to κακία (general evil - #641) they were to be always like babies. δὲ is adversative as he adds, "But always be mature in intellectual matters." Like children with a new toy the Corinthians were fascinated with the various languages which could be heard. The city was overrun with evil and it is highly possible that some of the gibberish which they heard was demon inspired. Some were misapplying Isaiah 28:11-12 and Paul deals with this passage in verses 21 and 22.

Verse 21 - *"In the law it is written, With men of other tongues and other lips will I speak unto this people; and yet for all that will they not hear me, saith the Lord."*

ἐν τῷ νόμῳ γέγραπται ὅτι Ἐν ἑτερογλώσσοις καὶ ἐν χείλεσιν ἑτέρων λαλήσω τῷ λαῷ τούτῳ, καὶ οὐδ' οὕτως εἰσακούσονταί μου, λέγει κύριος.

"In the law it is written, 'By men of strange tongues and by the lips of foreigners will I speak to this people, and even then they will not listen to me, says the Lord." . . . RSV

ἐν (preposition with the locative of place) 80.
τῷ (loc.sing.masc.of the article in agreement with νόμῳ) 9.
νόμῳ (loc.sing.masc.of νόμος, place) 464.
γέγραπται (3d.per.sing.perf.pass.ind.of γράφω, intensive) 156.
ὅτι (recitative) 211.
ἐν (preposition with the locative of sphere) 80.

#4237 ἑτερογλώσσοις (loc.pl.masc.of ἑτερόγλωσσος, sphere).

King James Version

of another tongue - 1 Cor.14:21.

Revised Standard Version

of strange tongues - 1 Cor.14:21.

Meaning: A combination of ἕτερος (#605) and γλῶσσα (#1846). Hence, one who speaks a foreign language. In 1 Cor.14:21 of those at Pentecost who had the ability to speak in languages other than their own.

καὶ (adjunctive conjunction, joining nouns) 14.

χείλεσιν (instrumental pl.neut.of χεῖλος, means) 1146.

ἑτέρων (gen.pl.masc.of ἕτερος, possession) 605.

λαλήσω (1st.per.sing.fut.act.ind.of λαλέω, predictive) 815.

τῷ (dat.sing.masc.of the article in agreement with λαῷ) 9.

λαῷ(dat.sing.masc.of λαός, indirect object of λαλήσω) 110.

τούτῳ (dat.sing.masc.of οὗτος, in agreement with λαῷ) 93.

καὶ (adversative conjunction) 14.

οὐδ' (disjunctive particle) 452.

οὕτως (demonstrative adverb) 74.

εἰσακούσονται (3d.per.pl.fut.mid.ind.of εἰσακούω, predictive) 574.

μου (gen.sing.masc.of ἐγώ, objective genitive) 123.

λέγει (3d.per.sing.pres.act.ind.of λέγω, aoristic) 66.

κύριος (nom.sing.masc.of κύριος, subject of λέγει) 97.

Translation - "In the law it is written, 'With other languages and with lips of others I will speak to this people; but despite all of that they will not hear me,' says the Lord."

Comment: "The quotation is from Isaiah 28:11-12 and Deut.28:49. Paul cites the passages to support his point in verse 22 that this phenomenon was originally designed as a supernatural sign to unbelievers that the early church at Pentecost was genuine. What happened at Pentecost (Acts 2;1-13) was a fulfillment of Isa.28:11-12.

The Corinthians may have known of the passage and if so, were probably misapplying it. The sign was not to be used for a toy for the entertainment and amusement of the early church, but for the purpose which he sets forth in

Verse 22 - "Wherefore tongues are for a sign, not to them that believe, but to them that believe not; but prophesying serveth not for them that believe not but for them which believe."

ὥστε αἱ γλῶσσαι εἰς σημεῖόν εἰσιν οὐ τοῖς πιστεύουσιν ἀλλὰ τοῖς ἀπίστοις, ἡ δὲ προφητεία οὐ τοῖς ἀπίτοις ἀλλὰ τοῖς πιστεύουσιν.

"Thus, tongues are a sign not for believers but for unbelievers, while prophecy is not for unbelievers but for believers." . . . RSV

ὥστε (inferential conjunction) 752.

αἱ (nom.pl.fem.of the article in agreement with γλῶσσαι) 9.

γλῶσσαι (nom.pl.fem.of γλῶσσα, subject of εἰσιν) 1846.

εἰς (preposition with the accusative, purpose) 140.

σημεῖον (acc.sing.neut.of σημεῖον, purpose) 1005.
οὐ (negative particle with the indicative) 130.
τοῖς (dat.pl.masc.of the article in agreement with πιστεύουσιν) 9.
πιστεύουσιν (pres.act.part.dat.pl.masc.of πιστεύω, substantival, personal advantage) 734.
ἀλλὰ (alternative conjunction) 342.
τοῖς (dat.pl.masc.of the article in agreement with ἀπίστοις) 9.
ἀπίστοις (dat.pl.masc.of ἄπιστος, personal advantage) 1231.
ἡ (nom.sing.fem.of the article in agreement with προφητεία) 9.
δὲ (adversative conjunction) 11.
προφητεία (nom.sing.fem.of προφητεία, subject of ἐστιν understood) 1041.
οὐ (negative particle with the indicative) 130.
τοῖς (dat.pl.masc.of the article in agreement with ἀπίστοις) 9.
ἀπίστοις (dat.pl.masc.of ἄπιστος, personal advantage) 1231.
ἀλλὰ (alternative conjunction) 342.
τοῖς (dat.pl.masc.of the article in agreement with πιστεύουσιν) 9.
πιστεύουσιν (pres.act.part.dat.pl.masc.of πιστεύω, substantival, personal advantage) 734.

Translation - "We conclude that the foreign languages are for a sign, not to those who already believe but for the unbelievers; but prophecy is not for the unbelievers, but for those who believe."

Comment: ὥστε is used inferentially here like οὖν. The miracle that occurred at Pentecost (Acts 2:1-13), at Caesarea (Acts 10:44-46) and at Ephesus (Acts 19:1-7) was for the purpose of convincing those present that the message which had been preached, to which the Christians were committed, was genuine. In the home of Cornelius the miracle also served to convince the Jews present who had accompanied Peter that God indeed intended to include the Gentiles in His church, while the twelve at Ephesus, who had previously been committed to a garbled message from Apollos and who now understood it better, thanks to Paul, gave evidence that they had been truly born again, thanks to their faith in the death, burial and resurrection of Jesus. Thus the practice of speaking in a foreign language in a church service where all present are Christians is out of place. It is also futile, even when the unsaved are present, since they have no idea what the speaker is saying. At Ephesus, it was the twelve who had just been saved, who spoke in tongues, not Paul. At Caesarea it was Cornelius and his family and friends who were saved who spoke in tongues, not Peter and the other Christians present.

The Pentecost experience was especially dramatic. One hundred twenty Christians, all of whom were Jews were waiting in Jerusalem in obedience to our Lord's command (Acts 1:1-8) for the filling of the Holy Spirit, which was so essential to their effective witness. They said that Jesus of Nazareth was alive and that He was the Jewish Messiah. Thousands of unbelieving Jews were present, totally prejudiced against the Christian message. They had come from many points throughout the Mediterranean littloral, as well as from their homes in the city. Though many in the audience were at home with the κοινή Greek, some were not. Thus if the gospel message of the 120 Christians was to be understood by all present the miracle was needed. The miracle occurred. The Galileans preached so that every man heard "in our own tongue, wherein we were born" (Acts 2:7,8), and then in verses 9-11 the areas represented are listed. It was this miracle that impressed them, but not all. Three thousand were saved, but just as Isa.28:11-12 says, even though God spoke to them in other languages and with other lips, some scoffed and explained away the miracle as an evidence of too much wine. Thus God's purpose was accomplished in that His elect were impressed with the phenomenon and came to Christ, while His prophecy was also fulfilled in that others rejected the gospel. The ability to speak languages which they had never studied nor had ever spoken was not a sign to the Christians. It was a sign to the unbelievers.

It is also important to note that there were no translators present at Pentecost, nor in the home of Cornelius nor at Ephesus. None were needed. Every one who was supposed to hear heard, without interpretation. But when a Corinthian Christian in the church, totally on his own responsibility and without a "gift" displayed his linguistic versatility in a childish bid for attention, an interpreter was needed - otherwise no one gained benefit from what he said.

It is significant that δῶρον (#191) is never associated in the New Testament with the ability to speak a foreign language and that δωρεά (#2004) occurs only twice (Acts 10:45; 11:17) in this connection in both of which passages the "gift" (δωρεά) is not that of tongues, as such, but of the Holy Spirit. The student may wish to run the references on the verb δίδωμι (#362) to note its contextual affiliations as they relate to the "gift of tongues."

Having set the stage in verses 21 and 22, Paul procedes to give his instructions in verses 23-25.

Verse 23 - "If therefore the whole church be come together into one place, and all speak with tongues, and there come in those that are unlearned, or unbelievers, will they not say that ye are mad?"

Ἐὰν οὖν συνέλθῃ ἡ ἐκκλησία ὅλη ἐπὶ τὸ αὐτὸ καὶ πάντες λαλῶσιν γλώσσαις, εἰσέλθωσιν δὲ ἰδιῶται ἢ ἄπιστοι, οὐκ ἐροῦσιν ὅτι μαίνεσθε;

"If, therefore, the whole church assembles and all speak in tongues, and outsiders or unbelievers enter, will they not say that you are mad?" . . . RSV

Ἐὰν (conditional particle with the subjunctive in a third-class condition) 363.

οὖν (inferential conjunction) 68.

συνέλθῃ (3d.per.sing.aor.mid.subj.of συνέρχομαι, third-class condition) 78.

ἡ (nom.sing.fem.of the article in agreement with ἐκκλησία) 9.

ἐκκλησία (nom.sing.fem.of ἐκκλησία, subject of συνέλθῃ) 1204.

ὅλη (nom.sing.fem.of ὅλος, in agreement with ἐκκλησία) 112.

ἐπὶ (preposition with the accusative of extent) 47.

τὸ (acc.sing.neut.of the article in agreement with αὐτὸ) 9.

αὐτὸ (acc.sing.neut.of αὐτός, in agreement with τόπον understood, extent) 16.

καὶ (continuative conjunction) 14.

πάντες (nom.pl.masc.of πᾶς, subject of λαλῶσιν) 67.

λαλῶσιν (3d.per.pl.pres.act.subj.of λαλέω, third-class condition) 815.

γλώσσαις (loc.pl.fem.of γλῶσσα, sphere) 1846.

εἰσέλθωσιν (3d.per.pl.aor.mid.subj.of εἰσέρχομαι, third-class condition) 234.

δὲ (continuative conjunction) 11.

ἰδιῶται (nom.pl.masc.of ἰδιώτης, subject of εἰσέλθωσιν) 3032.

ἢ (disjunctive) 465.

ἄπιστοι (nom.pl.masc.of ἄπιστος, subject of εἰσέλθωσιν) 1231.

οὐκ (negative particle with the indicative in rhetorical question expecting a positive reply) 130.

ἐροῦσιν (3d.per.pl.fut.act.ind.of ἔρω, deliberative, in rhetorical question) 155.

ὅτι (conjunction introducing an object clause in indirect discourse) 211.

μαίνεσθε (2d.per.pl.pres.ind.of μαίνομαι, aoristic) 2408.

Translation - "So if the entire church assembles at the same place and everyone speaks in a foreign language, and if unlearned men or unbelievers come in, will they not say that you are insane?"

Comment: Here we have a third-class condition with three if-clauses and the deliberative future indicative in the apodosis, in a rhetorical question where the reply expected in "Yes." Paul is not saying that this will occur. It is a hypothetical scenario with three elements: (1) the entire church assembles, (2) every Christian present makes a speech in a foreign language, (3) uneducated and unbelieving persons come in, who cannot understand what is being said by anyone. It is difficult to imagine the uproar and confusion of this bedlam. It would seem obvious that the visitors would conclude that the Christians were crazy. Why should people who are already saved speak in foreign languages when no unbelievers are present. Paul's question assumes that the orators (!) were already in full cry *before* the visitors came in. If no one was present at the beginning of the service except Christians they should have been edifying each other. And that requires prophecy, couched in the local dialect, not a speech that no one can understand.

Note ἐπὶ τὸ αὐτό (with τόπον understood) in Acts 1:15; 2:1,44,47; 4:26; 1 Cor. 14:23.

What should the saints do when they come together? In verses 24 and 25 Paul describes a scenario with a happier ending.

Verse 24 - "But if all prophesy, and there come in one that believeth not, or one unlearned, he is convinced of all, he is judged of all."

ἐὰν δὲ πάντες προφητεύωσιν, εἰσέλθῃ δέ τις ἄπιστος ἢ ἰδιώτης, ἐλέγχεται ὑπὸ πάντων, ἀνακρίνεται ὑπὸ πάντων,

"But if all prophesy, and an unbeliever or outsider enters, he is convicted by all, he is called to account by all," . . . RSV

ἐὰν (conditional particle with the subjunctive in a third-class condition) 363.

δὲ (adversative conjunction) 11.

πάντες (nom.pl.masc.of πᾶς, subject of προφητεύωσιν) 67.

προφητεύωσιν (3d.per.pl.pres.act.subj.of προφητεύω, third-class condition) 685.

εἰσέλθῃ (3d.per.sing.aor.mid.subj.of εἰσέρχομαι, third-class condition) 234.

δὲ (continuative conjunction) 11.

τις (nom.sing.masc.of τις, indefinite pronoun, in agreement with ἄπιστος and ἰδιώτης) 486.

ἄπιστος (nom.sing.masc.of ἄπιστος, subject of εἰσέλθῃ) 1231.

ἤ (disjunctive) 465.

ἰδιώτης (nom.sing.masc.of ἰδιώτης, subject of εἰέλθῃ) 3032.

ἐλέγχεται (3d.per.sing.pres.pass.ind.of ἐλέγχω, futuristic) 1261.

ὑπὸ (preposition with the ablative of agent) 117.

πάντων (abl.pl.masc.of πᾶς, agent) 67.

ἀνακρίνεται (3d.per.sing.pres.pass.ind.of ἀνακρίνω, futuristic) 2837.

ὑπὸ (preposition with the ablative of agent) 117.

πάντων (abl.pl.masc.of πᾶς, agent) 67.

Translation - "But if everyone is prophesying and some unbeliever or unlearned person comes in, he will be convicted by all; he will be called to account by all."

Comment: Note the difference in the reactions of the visitors of verses 23 and 24. The former conclude that the Christians are insane; the latter become Christians. Why the difference? In the former case the Christians are all talking at once, each in a language that none of the visitors, and probably none of the local gentry understands. In the latter case they are preaching the inspired Word of the gospel of Christ. The visitor hears first one Holy Spirit inspired utterance and then another and another. He finds himself being convinced that what they are saying is true (John 16:7-11). When the Holy Spirit effectually calls the elect He does it by leading some Christian to "preach the Word" (2 Tim.4:2) - in a language that the prospect can understand. *Cf.*#1261 for a list of agents who "convince" their listeners.

Not only does the unbeliever find himself convinced (convicted) but he also finds his own philosophical and theological rationale put to the acid test of thorough analysis (#2837). His objections to Christ are answered; his own fallacies become apparent to him; the blank spots in his own knowledge are filled in. He is "called to account" (Goodspeed). He is "sifted" (Weymouth). He "feels himself judged" (Montgomery).

Note also that the Holy Spirit uses every saint who has the gift of prophecy to accomplish this work - the unbeliever is convinced ὑπὸ πάντων - "by all." This is not the quantitative all but everyone who is speaking under the motivation of the Holy Spirit.

Two common errors are corrected by this passage: (1) that the preacher should do all of the talking in a worship service, as though he alone had the call to preach, and (2) that every Christian present should speak, as though everyone was called to preach. Perhaps the fallacy also is exposed that women must always remain silent in church, as though the Holy Spirit had never given the gift of prophecy to a woman despite the record of Acts 21:8,9. *Cf.* also 1 Cor.12:11 where ἰδίᾳ means "every person" not "every male." The attempted "testimony" meeting in which the leader scolds the silent saints until everyone is bored, rests upon the fallacy that every Christian has the gift of prophecy. The conclusion that only the Christians who "testified" are consecrated to the Lord, on the sole grand that the others had nothing to say is palpably false.

The convicting impact of the combined utterances of the gifted speakers is devastating.

Verse 25 - "And thus are the secrets of his heart made manifest; and so falling down on his face he will worship God, and report that God is in you of a truth."

τὰ κρυπτὰ τῆς καρδίας αὐτοῦ φανερὰ γίνεται, καὶ οὕτως πεσὼν ἐπὶ πρόσωπον προσκυνήσει τῷ θεῷ, ἀπαγγέλλων ὅτι Ὄντως ὁ θεὸς ἐν ὑμῖν ἐστιν.

"the secrets of his heart are disclosed; and so, falling on his face, he will worship God and declare that God is really among you." . . . RSV

τὰ (nom.pl.neut.of the article in agreement with κρυπτὰ) 9.
κρυπτὰ (nom.pl.neut.of κρυπτός, subject of γίνεται) 565.
τῆς (gen.sing.fem.of the article in agreement with καρδίας) 9.
καρδίας (gen.sing.fem.of καρδία, description) 432.
αὐτοῦ (gen.sing.masc.of αὐτός, possession) 16.
φανερὰ (nom.pl.neut.of φανερός, predicate adjective) 981.
γίνεται (3d.per.sing.pres.ind.of γίνομαι, futuristic) 113.
καὶ (continuative conjunction) 14.
οὕτως (demonstrative adverb) 74.
πεσὼν (aor.act.part.nom.sing.masc.of πίπτω, adverbial, temporal) 187.
ἐπὶ (preposition with the accusative of extent) 47.
πρόσωπον (acc.sing.neut.of πρόσωπον, extent) 588.
προσκυνήσει (3d.per.sing.fut.act.ind.of προσκυνέω, predictive) 147.
τῷ (dat.sing.masc.of the article in agreement with θεῷ) 9.
θεῷ (dat.sing.masc.of θεός, personal advantage) 124.
ἀπαγγέλλων (pres.act.part.nom.sing.masc.of ἀπαγγέλλω, adverbial, circumstantial) 176.
ὅτι (recitative) 211.
Ὄντως (adverbial) 2386.
ὁ (nom.sing.masc.of the article in agreement with θεὸς) 9.
θεὸς (nom.sing.masc.of θεός, subject of ἔτιν) 124.
ἐν (preposition with the locative in plural pronouns) 80.
ὑμῖν (loc.pl.masc.of σύ, place) 104.
ἐστιν (3d.per.sing.pres.ind.of εἰμί, aoristic) 86.

Translation - "The secret thoughts of his heart will be laid bare and so, having fallen down on his face, he will worship God as he says, 'Truly God is in your midst."

Comment: The Holy Spirit searches hearts (Rom.8:27) and therefore He knows all the thoughts that the unsaved visitor thinks are known only to him. Since the Holy Spirit is the Giver of the gift of prophecy He motivates the prophet to say things that he may not have known, but unlike the foreign language speaker, he says them in the language that the sinner can understand. The Christian may wonder why he is saying what he says (1 Pet.1:9-12). The unsaved sinner meanwhile is thinking, "How does he know what my secret thoughts are?" He doesn't but the Holy Spirit does. Thus the prospect finds himself philosophically "undressed" by Christians whom he does not even know. His repentance is total. οὔτως tells us why he repents. It is because of the revelation of his secret thoughts. How many times evangelists have not permitted the gifted prophets in the congregation to speak, have preached eloquently but ineffectively, only because they did not uncover the secret thoughts of the unsaved - a feat that can be accomplished only by the Holy Spirit Who might choose to use some uneducated saint who nevertheless had the gift of prophet.

Repentance is followed by worship and a full confession.

All Things to be Done in Order

(1 Corinthians 14:26-40)

Verse 26 - "How is it then, brethren? When ye come together, every one of you hath a psalm, hath a doctrine, hath a tongue, hath a revelation, hath an interpretation. Let all things be done unto edifying."

Τί οὖν ἐστιν, ἀδελφοί; ὅταν συνέρχησθε, ἕκαστος ψαλμὸν ἔχει, διδαχὴν ἔχει, ἀποκάλυψιν ἔχει, γλῶσσαν ἔχει, ἑρμηνείαν ἔχει. πάντα πρὸς οἰκοδομὴν γινέσθω.

"What then, brethren? When you come together, each one has a hymn, a lesson, a revelation, a tongue, or an interpretation. Let all things be done for edification." . . . RSV

τί (nom.sing.neut.of τίς, interrogative pronoun, subject of ἐστιν) 281.

οὖν (inferential conjunction) 68.

ἐστιν (3d.per.sing.pres.ind.of εἰμί, futuristic) 86.

ἀδελφοί (voc.pl.masc.of ἀδελφός, address) 15.

ὅταν (temporal adverb with the subjunctive in an indefinite temporal clause) 436.

συνέρχησθε (2d.per.pl.pres.mid.subj.of συνέρχομαι, indefinite temporal clause) 78.

ἕκαστος (nom.sing.masc.of ἕκαστος, subject of ἔχει) 1217.

ψαλμὸν (acc.sing.masc.of ψαλμός, direct object of ἔχει) 2703.

ἔχει (3d.per.sing.pres.act.ind.of ἔχω, futuristic) 82.

διδαχὴν (acc.sing.fem.of διδαχή, direct object of ἔχει) 706.

ἔχει (3d.per.sing.pres.act.ind.of ἔχω, futuristic) 82.

ἀποκάλυφιν (acc.sing.fem.of ἀποκάλυφις, direct object of ἔχει) 1902.
ἔχει (3d.per.sing.pres.act.ind.of ἔχω, futuristic) 82.
γλῶσσαν (acc.sing.fem.of γλῶσσα, direct object of ἔχει) 1846.
ἔχει (3d.per.sing.pres.act.ind.of ἔχω, futuristic) 82.
ἑρμηνείαν (acc.sing.fem.of ἑρμηνεία, direct object of ἔχει) 4216.
ἔχει (3d.per.sing.pres.act.ind.of ἔχω, futuristic) 82.
πάντα (acc.pl.neut.of πᾶς, direct object of γινέσθω) 67.
πρὸς (preposition with the accusative, purpose) 197.
οἰκοδομὴν (acc.sing.fem.of οἰκοδομή, purpose) 1481.
γινέσθω (3d.per.sing.pres.impv.of γίνομαι, command) 113.

Translation - "What then, brethren is the proper procedure? When you come to church each one will have a musical number, a doctrine, a new idea, a tongue, an interpretation. Do everything with a view to edification."

Comment: οὖν - "in the light of the foregoing" (verses 24,25) τί . . . ἐστιν - "what ought to be done? How should you procede? What order of service is proper?" ὅταν with the subjunctive points forward to a time when they will have another church service which they will all attend. The time is indefinite, but that there will be another service is not.

The Corinthians were a gifted people (1 Cor.1:4-7). Note that every Corinthian Christian had a specific contribution to make to the meeting. This is the force of ἕκαστος (#1217). The Holy Spirit has enriched every Christian with some gift (1 Cor.12:11). No one present is unimportant. Everyone therefore should be free to make his contribution to the meeting, whether it be a musical number - a solo accompanied on an instrument (#'s 2703; 4047), a bit of teaching, a new idea revealed by the Holy Spirit which he wishes to make known to one who does not speak the local dialect or a translation of something said in a foreign language.

The modern stereotyped formal worship service, with its dictatorial order of worship bulletin, precludes all of this. There must be an "Order of Worship" which serves to lock the Holy Spirit out of His own assembly. They even tell the ushers when not to seat the people. The dreary homogeneity of it - one boring Sunday morning after another, is enough to drive intelligent people away. Prelude, introit, doxology, invocation, choral response, hymn, greeting to visitors, who raise their hands, then stand in embarrassment while ushers fumble with long, complicated, nosey demands for information, announcements - "the prayer meeting on Wednesday evening *as usual* (unfortunately)" another hymn, the offering, special number, sermon (introduction, three points and a poem), invitation, benediction, choral response, postlude, mad exit to the first tee.

When does the Holy Spirit ever have an opporunity to direct such a service? Is it reasonable that He is consulted before the Bulletin goes to press? Or is He consulted and does He choose to do it every Sunday in exactly the same way? Whatever is done, Paul demands, is expressly done for the purpose of edification of all (πρὸς οἰκοδομὴν).

The Society of Friends (Quakers) have made some progress in conducting a service that allows the freedom of the Holy Spirit that Paul here insists upon.

It is important to remember that Paul was writing before the canon of New Testament literature was complete, at a time when first century apostolic gifts were an indispensable part of the service. At that time (sixth decade) the Corinthian pastor-teacher had little of the Greek New Testament available to him for guidance as he spoke. The gifts of prophecy and special knowledge have been phased out and the custom of speaking in a foreign language is said to have ceased (1 Cor.13:8-13). The modern church does not need the gifts of prophecy and special knowledge, since we have something better - the Greek New Testament which is the product of them. There is no need for Christians to speak in a foreign language in a church service. But the musical contributions, both vocal and instrumental, and the new insights into the Scriptures are still in order.

Paul now guards against the confusion that would result if the foreign language artists are not regulated, in

Verse 27 - "If any man speak in an unknown tongue, let it be by two, or at most by three, and that by course; and let one interpret."

εἴτε γλώσσῃ τις λαλεῖ, κατὰ δύο ἢ τὸ πλεῖστον τρεῖς, καὶ ἀνὰ μέρος, καὶ εἷς διερμηνευέτω.

"If any speak in a tongue, let there be only two or at most three, and each in turn; and let one interpret." . . . RSV

εἴτε (compound particle in a first-class condition) 4016.

γλώσσῃ (instrumental sing.fem.of γλῶσσα, means) 1846.

τις (nom.sing.masc.of τις, indefinite pronoun, subject of λαλεῖ) 486.

λαλεῖ (3d.per.sing.pres.act.ind.of λαλέω, first-class condition) 815.

κατὰ (preposition with the accustive, standard) 98.

δύο (numeral) 385.

ἤ (disjunctive) 465.

τὸ (acc.sing.neut.of the article in agreement with πλεῖστον) 9.

πλεῖστον (acc.sing.neut.of πλεῖστος, extent) 935.

τρεῖς (numeral) 1010.

ἀνὰ (preposition with the accusative, "in turn") 1059.

μέρος (acc.sing.neut.of μέρος - "in turn") 240.

καὶ (continuative conjunction) 14.

εἷς (nom.sing.masc.of εἷς, subject of διερμηνευέτω) 469.

διερμηνευέτω (3d.per.sing.pres.act.impv.of διερμηνεύω, command) 2906.

Translation - "And if anyone is going to speak in a foreign language, let it. be by two or at the most three, and in turn, and let one translate."

Comment: εἴτε here (εἰ plus τε) introduces the first-class condition. Paul is assuming that some one present will wish to show off his linguistic capabilities. If, in the midst of all of the constructive activity as the Corinthians seek to edify each other, some one must speak unintelligibly, at least the practice must be regulated. There is scant need ever in the modern "charismatic" meeting for the policy of speaking in a foreign language in order to communicate thought. If a German, Frenchman, Italian, Mexican or Russian is present who understands no English and if no one present speaks German, French, Italian, Spanish or Russian the visitor must remain unenlightened unless the Professor of Foreign Languages from the local university is called in and asked to tell him what is being said. As Paul has said repeatedly in this chapter the use of a foreign language in a meeting where everyone understands the local dialect is a childish bid for attention - a self-serving stratagem employed, unconsciously perhaps, to promote the notion that one is an intellectual. This "sophistication on parade" will be discerned by mature people and the result is that the "tongues" speaker will be down graded. But if it must be, Paul sighed, the ground rules follow:

(1) Not more than three (preferably two, one or none) will participate.

(2) They should speak one at a time (ἀνὰ μέρος) - never two or more at the same time.

(3) After one, two or three have spoken, each in his turn, a translation shall be given.

For example, if one should say ἵππος, the translator should then tell the Englishman present who knew no Greek that the speaker said, "Horse." The speaker may have been talking about Job's horse, who, like himself "smelleth the battle afar off" (Job 39:25).

τὸ πλεῖστον is a superlative, used adverbially.

There is a fourth rule to be observed, implicit in the last clause of verse 27 and stated clearly in

Verse 28 - "But if there be no interpreter, let him keep silence in the church; and let him speak to himself, and to God."

ἐὰν δὲ μὴ ᾖ διερμηνευτής, σιγάτω ἐν ἐκκλησίᾳ, ἑαυτῷ δὲ λαλείτω καὶ τῷ θεῷ.

"But if there is no one to interpret, let each of them keep silence in church, and speak to himself and to God." . . . RSV

ἐὰν (conditional particle with the subjunctive in a third-class condition) 363.
δὲ (adversative conjunction) 11.
μὴ (negative particle with the subjunctive) 87.
ᾖ (3d.per.sing.pres.subj.of εἰμί, third-class condition) 86.

#4238 διερμηνευτής (nom.sing.masc.of διερμηνευτής, subject of ᾖ).

King James Version

interpreter - 1 Cor.14:28.

Revised Standard Version

one to interpret - 1 Cor.14:28.

Meaning: Cf. διερμηνεύω *(#2906). Hence, an interpreter; a translator - 1 Cor.14:28.*

σιγάτω (3d.per.sing.pres.act.impv.of σιγάω, command) 2330.
ἐν (preposition with the locative, place) 80.
ἐκκλησία (loc.sing.fem.of ἐκκλησία, place) 1204.
ἑαυτῷ (dat.sing.masc.of ἑαυτοῦ, indirect object of λαλείτω) 288.
δὲ (continuative conjunction) 11.
λαλείτω (3d.per.sing.pres.act.impv.of λαλέω, command) 815.
καὶ (adjunctive conjunction joining a pronoun with a noun) 14.
τῷ (dat.sing.masc.of the article in agreement with θεῷ) 9.
θεῷ (dat.sing.masc.of θεός, indirect object of λαλείτω) 124.

Translation - "But if no translator is present, let him keep silence in church, and let him speak to himself and to God."

Comment: δὲ is adversative. One set of rules applies if a translator is present. But (adversative δὲ) another rule applies if he is not. The third-class condition with ἐὰν and the subjunctive ᾖ sets up the hypothetical situation. Paul does not know whether a translator will be present on any given occasion or not. He only knows what they should do if he is not - "Let him maintain his silence in church." If he still wants to talk in a foreign language let him go home and talk to himself or to God (1 Cor.14:2,4). What possible personal edification results when one talks to himself in a foreign language? It is always helpful to talk to God, but most people who talk to themselves need the kind of help that linguistic skills cannot provide.

There is a clear implication here that the "tongues" speaker has self-control. He can exercise his will either to speak or to remain silent. This clashes with the statements of the modern Pentecostalist who speaks of a "baptism of the Holy Spirit" which is alleged to carry him into a state of ecstatic euphoria beyond his control - a statement which leads many to conclude that the modern movement is motivated by spiritual forces less than heavenly in origin. Why, otherwise, do such persons spend more time talking about the Holy Spirit than they do talking about the Lord Jesus Christ, despite the fact that He said that the Holy Spirit would not talk about Himself, but would show us things to come that would glorify our Lord? (John 16:13,14). Why also should the extreme cults of this persuasion deny the essential deity of Jesus? (1 John 4:3).

The ability to speak in more than one language is not a gift, but an accomplishment which rewards hard work and diligent application to detail. But the Scripture does not say that it is phased out as are the gifts of prophecy and special knowledge (1 Cor.13:8). It does say that they will cease (παύσονται), without specifying when this will happen. Indeed they will, if not before we get to heaven, at least then, because in heaven the communication barrier that has divided the human race since the Tower of Babel will be forever broken down. There will be no foreign languages in heaven. Everyone there will understand everyone else. In the meantime linguistic abilities are useful where communication is hindered because of the language barrier.

A godly woman of great personal charm and humility, but with little formal education was forbidden by her pastor to exercise what she considered her "gift of tongues." She graciously complied. There was no malice nor diminution of love and respect for her pastor. She also had the ability to testify in English in a manner that was most uplifting to all, even to those sophisticated people in the congregation who would be quick to resent a show of emotionalism, if it were, to the slightest degree a staged performance. This godly saint often said things in testimony to the church that very much needed to be said, but which, if the pastor had said them, would have caused division in the church. A situation arose that demanded (a) that something scriptural be said clearly and with authority and, (b) that the pastor was not the one to say it. In the course of a Sunday morning sermon the woman arose, held up her hands, giving praise to the Lord and came down the aisle. The pastor's first impression was to stop her, but the Holy Spirit clearly said, "Let her talk." She faced the congregation and, in an exhortation she said all that was needed to resolve the difficulty. Her message carried all of the authority of the Holy Spirit and was supported by the widespread acceptance of her godly character and sincerity. She was the woman in the church that young parents always called in to pray when the baby got sick. When she finished speaking, amid the hush that fell upon the congregation, she walked quietly and humbly back to her seat and the pastor resumed his sermon.

The woman's speech was not prophecy in the sense in which Paul used the word in the first century, for she did not add anything to the message of the Greek New Testament. She had exercised her gift of teaching and the result was a total resolution of the difficulty in the church which otherwise might have caused a serious division. The woman did not often intervene as she did on that occasion, but the pastor often prayed, "Lord, lead Mrs. D— to say something."

Paul now suggests regulations for those with the gift of prophecy in

Verse 29 - "Let the prophets speak two or three, and let the other judge."

προφῆται δὲ δύο ἢ τρεῖς λαλείτωσαν, καὶ οἱ ἄλλοι διακρινέτωσαν.

"Let two or three prophets speak, and let the others weigh what is said." . . .
RSV

προφῆται (nom.pl.masc.of προφήτης, subject of λαλείτωσαν) 119.
δὲ (continuative conjunction) 11.
δύο (numeral) 385.
ἢ (disjunctive) 465.
τρεῖς (numeral) 1010.
λαλείτωσαν (3d.per.pl.pres.act.impv.of λαλέω, command) 815.
καὶ (adjunctive conjunction) 14.
οἱ (nom.pl.masc.of the article in agreement with ἄλλοι) 9.
ἄλλοι (nom.pl.masc.of ἄλλος, subject of διακρινέτωσαν) 198.
διακρινέτωσαν (3d.per.pl.pres.act.impv.of διακρίνω, command) 1195.

Translation - "And let two or three prophets speak, and the rest should thoroughly analyze what is said."

Comment: Just as those who spoke in a foreign language were to take their turn, not more than three in a series, after which they were to pause for translation, so those who claimed to possess the gift of prophecy, whether by divine or self-appointment, were ordered to take their turn, and then wait until other "prophets" considered whether what was said was correct. That Paul was aware that the church in Corinth had "prophets by presumption" just as she had linguistic "experts" seems clear from his demand that the prophecies be analyzed by others. If he had been certain that only the true prophets would speak, his conclusion would have been that what they said was the message of the Holy Spirit. This he doubted. Thus his demand for a multiple-check. In the spirit of Abraham Lincoln, Paul apparently believed that "you can fool some of the people all of the time, and all of the people some of the time, but you cannot fool all of the people all of the time."

The same procedure should be followed in the modern church. The first century gift of prophecy has been phased out, since the prophets then were the source of the material of the New Testament, and when that revelation was completed there was no further need for them. Indeed those since who have claimed to be prophets have confused the Body of Christ with their additions and have corrupted the Word of God. But the gift of teaching was not withdrawn, and the modern church is blessed with many God-called and Holy Spirit inspired teachers of the Word. However, these teachers are human and still subject to the disabilities of the flesh. They still harbor their prejudicial ideas and they tend to insist upon their views, since the confession that they have been mistaken is hard on their sinful pride. Thus we still need the multi-check of what they say by the other teachers. This is why the Berans were "more noble than those in Thessalonica, in that they received the word with all readiness of mind, and searched the scriptures (the Old Testament) daily, whether those things were so" (Acts 17:11).

Dialogue among the members of the Body of Christ who are possessed of the proper intellectual humility, who eschew error, demand only the truth, and in whom "brotherly love continue(s)" (Heb.13:1) will filter out error from the offerings of the teachers and result in total edification for all. This is what Paul wanted for the Corinthians and that is why he ordered that those who professed to be prophets should submit their "revelations" to the judgment of their peers.

The dialogue which Paul demands is predicated upon the *a priori* position that the Holy Spirit cannot be inconsistent. What He has said to one cannot conflict with what He has said to others. Thus conflicting messages indicate that the problem is not in the divine Source of the prophecy but in the human medium. Thus the dialogue will have at least a two-fold purpose.(1) If the speaker is in error, however sincere he may be, the others will detect the difference between what he said and what may have been revealed to them. Since the Holy Spirit does not give conflicting revelations all of the prophets should be inclined to agree with what the others had to say. (2) Perhaps the content of one prophet's discourse would contribute supplementary light upon what another was thinking. This is an application of the closure psychology of the gestalt school - a concession to the Hegelian method.

The revelations of the Spirit of God are protean, not contradictory, and the angle of exposition of one prophet might shed light on the thoughts of others to enable them to develop their own rationale more completely. If one of the silent judges has his own thought advanced by what is being said, he should ask the speaker to yield the floor to him. Thus what is said by one prophet cross-fertilizes concepts understood by another. This recalls the insight learning by which Sultan, Wolfgang Kohler's ape, discovered how to put the sticks together, thus to have one long enough to reach the banana outside the cage. The difference is that the monkey discovered this quite by chance and the saints of God, if their attitude is right, are subject to the guidance of the Holy Spirit.

Verse 30 - "If anything be revealed to another that sitteth by, let the first hold his peace."

ἐὰν δὲ ἄλλῳ ἀποκαλυφθῇ καθημένῳ, ὁ πρῶτος σιγάτω.

"If a revelation is made to another sitting by, let the first be silent." . . . RSV

ἐὰν (conditional particle with the subjunctive in a third-class condition) 363.
δὲ (continuative conjunction) 11.
ἄλλῳ (dat.sing.masc.of ἄλλος, indirect object of ἀποκαλυφθῇ) 198.
ἀποκαλυφθῇ (3d.per.sing.aor.pass.subj.of ἀποκαλύπτω, third-class condition) 886.
καθημένῳ (pres.mid.part.dat.sing.masc.of καθημαι, adjectival, predicate position, restrictive, in agreement with ἄλλῳ) 377.
ὁ (nom.sing.masc.of the article in agreement with πρῶτος) 9.
πρῶτος (nom.sing.masc.of πρῶτος, subject of σιγάτω) 487.
σιγάτω (3d.per.sing.pres.act.impv.of σιγάω, command) 2330.

Translation - "And if one who has seated himself there has a new insight, let the first speaker yield the floor."

Comment: What the Holy Spirit reveals to any prophet (or in the modern church, to any teacher) must be given to all present forthwith, even if he must interrupt the speaker. Thus the Holy Spirit is the director of the worship as He orchestrates the symphony of divine revelation. In the church in Corinth in the first century the Holy Spirit was contributing to the text of the New Testament, which at that time was not yet finished. What He contributes now to the teachers in the modern church is the proper insights and interconnections of that which has already been written. But the method is the same.

Apparently Paul intended that those prophets who were seated in the congregation, engaged in critical evaluation of the content of the message of the speaker, and who suddenly received new light from heaven, perhaps as a result of something that the speaker said, should raise his hand, stand, or in some other way indicate his desire to speak. Whereupon the speaker should immediately yield the floor. Of course if the critic disagreed with something said, or if he honestly had a problem with it, he should also interrupt to involve those present in a discussion of the point.

Verse 31 - "For ye may all prophesy one by one, that all may learn, and all may be comforted."

δύνασθε γὰρ καθ' ἕνα πάντες προφητεύειν, ἵνα πάντες μανθάνωσιν καὶ πάντες παρακαλῶνται,

"For you can all prophesy one by one, so that all may learn and all be encouraged." . . . RSV

δύνασθε (2d.per.pl.pres.mid.ind.of δύναμαι, futuristic) 289.
γὰρ (inferential conjunction) 105.
καθ' (preposition with the accusative, distributive) 98.
ἕνα (acc.sing.masc.of εἷς, distributive) 469.
πάντες (nom.pl.masc.of πᾶς, subject of δύνασθε) 67.
προφητεύειν (pres.act.inf.of προφητεύω, epexegetical) 685.
ἵνα (conjunction with the subjunctive in a double purpose clause) 114.
μανθάνωσιν (3d.per.pl.pres.act.subj.of μανθάνω, purpose) 794.
καὶ (adjunctive conjunction joining verbs) 14.
πάντες (nom.pl.masc.of πᾶς, subject of παρακαλῶνται) 67.
παρακαλῶνται (3d.per.pl.pres.pass.subj.of παρακαλέω, purpose) 230.

Translation - "*Thus all of you will be able to prophesy, one at a time, in order that all may learn and all may be motivated.*"

Comment: γὰρ is inferential in the sense of "thus." If they follow Paul's instructions about how to procede the result will be that all of the prophets will have an opportunity to exercise their gift. πάντες refers to all of the prophets, not to "all" present in the total quantitative sense. Apparently in previous Corinthian meetings some of the brethren who thought they had the gift of prophecy had never been able to exercise his gift because of the confusion as they all tried to talk at once. But if all are given the opportunity to speak the purpose will be achieved. Everyone in the meeting (πάντες is the last two clauses means everyone) will learn something more about the faith and everyone will be motivated, comforted, encouraged and stimulated. παρακαλέω (#230) can mean any and all of these, according to context.

If this ideal plan is followed all of the spiritual and intellectual resources in a congregation will be used to the advantage of all. The modern service, tied in homogeneous conformity to social custom, suppresses the urge to participate that might otherwise be obeyed. The modern church goer is forced always to take and never given an opportunity to give. Thus his spiritual faculties atrophy for lack of exercise and the unsaved world gets only one point of view - that of the pastor. This criticism in no way denigrates the function of the pastor-teacher. He is also a learner and if he has the right spirit he will welcome the light which the Holy Spirit may wish to give through someone else. The degree to which a listener is compelled always to listen to another, with never the opportunity to talk back is the degree of the danger that he will become an intellectual slave, who always expresses ideas which are not really his own.

The foreign language experts were able to control their impulses (verses 27,28). So also the prophets need not yield to compulsion as we see in

Verse 32 - '*And the spirits of the prophets are subject to the prophets.*"

καὶ πνεύματα προφητῶν προφήταις ὑποτάσσεται.

"and the spirits of prophets are subject to prophets." . ... RSV

καὶ (continuative conjunction) 14.
πνεύματα (nom.pl.neut.of πνεῦμα, subject of ὑποτάσσεται) 83.
προφητῶν (gen.pl.masc.of προφήτης, descriptive) 119.
προφήταις (dat.pl.masc.of προφήτης, person) 119.
ὑποτάσσεται (3d.per.sing.pres.mid.ind.of ὑποτάσσω, static) 1921.

Translation - "And prophetic spirits subordinate themselves to prophets."

Comment: *Cf.*#1921. If those who have been given prophetic and other gifts are such compulsive personalities that they are unable to exercise control over their use, there would be no point in the regulation of the gifts. Thus the Holy Spirit, Who bestows the gift, also with it gives to the recipient the power of will to control its use, and then issues ground rules for its exercise, so that the gifts may be exercised for their intended purpose, *viz.* the edification of the Body of Christ. If this were not true God would be the author of confusion. This Paul denies in

Verse 33 - "For God is not the author of confusion, but of peace, as in all churches of the saints."

οὐ γάρ ἐστιν ἀκαταστασίας ὁ θεὸς ἀλλὰ εἰρήνης. Ὡς ἐν πάσαις ταῖς ἐκκλησίαις τῶν ἁγίων,

"For God is not a God of confusion but of peace. As in all the churches of the saints, . . . RSV

οὐ (negative particle with the indicative) 130.
γάρ (causal conjunction) 105.
ἐστιν (3d.per.sing.pres.ind.of εἰμί, static) 86.
ἀκαταστασίας (gen.sing.fem.of ἀκαταστασία, description) 2718.
ὁ (nom.sing.masc.of the article in agreement with θεὸς) 9.
θεὸς (nom.sing.masc.of θεός, subject of ἐστιν) 124.
ἀλλὰ (alternative conjunction) 342.
εἰρήνης (gen.sing.fem.of εἰρήνη, description) 865.
Ὡς (comparative particle) 128.
ἐν (preposition with the locative of place) 80.
πάσαις (loc.pl.fem.of πᾶς, in agreement with ἐκκλησίαις) 67.
ταῖς (loc.pl.fem.of the article in agreement with ἐκκλησίαις) 9.
ἐκκλησίαις (loc.pl.fem.of ἐκκλησία, place) 1204.
τῶν (gen.pl.masc.of the article in agreement with ἁγίων) 9.
ἁγίων (gen.pl.masc.of ἅγιος, description) 84.

Translation - ". . . because God is not a God of confusion but of peace. As in all of the assemblies of the saints . . . "

Comment: ἀκαταστασία is a predicate genitive. It is in the predicate rather than in an attributive position modifying ὁ θεὸς. Thus "God is not one (or a God of) confusion." On the contrary (strong adversative in ἀλλὰ) He is a God of peace.

Whether Ὡς ἐν πάσαις ταῖς ἐκκλησίαις τῶν ἁγίων belongs in verse 33 or is the opening of verse 34 is a matter of editing. The original autographs were uncial and there was neither space between words nor accent and breathing marks. If the phrase belongs with verse 33, Paul is saying that the same instructions which he has given to the church in Corinth with reference to their use of foreign languages and their translation on the one hand, and the exercise of the gift of prophecy on the other, is the same instructions which he has given to all of the other churches. If the phrase belongs with verse 34 he is saying that the instruction about women speaking in the church is the same as in the other churches.

Verse 34 - "Let your women keep silence in the churches; for it is not permitted unto them to speak: but they are commanded to be under obedience, as also saith the law."

αἱ γυναῖκες ἐν ταῖς ἐκκλησίαις σιγάτωσαν, οὐ γὰρ ἐπιτρέπεται αὐταῖς λαλεῖν, ἀλλὰ ὑποτασσέσθωσαν, καθὼς καὶ ὁ νόμος λέγει.

"the women should keep silence in the churches. For they are not permitted to speak, but should be subordinate, as even the law says." . . . RSV

αἱ (nom.pl.fem.of the article in agreement with γυναῖκες) 9.
γυναῖκες (nom.pl.fem.of γυνή, subject of σιγάτωσαν) 103.
ἐν (preposition with the locative of place) 80.
ταῖς (loc.pl.fem.of the article in agreement with ἐκκλησίαις) 9.
ἐκκλησίαις (loc.pl.fem.of ἐκκλησία, place) 1204.
σιγάτωσαν (3d.per.pl.pres.act.impv.of σιγάω, command) 2330.
οὐ (negative particle with the indicative) 130.
γὰρ (causal conjunction) 105.
ἐπιτρέπεται (3d.per.sing.pres.pass.ind.of ἐπιτρέπω, static) 747.
αὐταῖς (dat.pl.fem.of αὐτός, indirect object of ἐπιτρέπεται) 16.
λαλεῖν (pres.act.inf.of λαλέω, epexegetical) 815.
ἀλλὰ (alternative conjunction) 342.
ὑποτασσέσθωσαν (3d.per.pl.pres.mid.impv.of ὑποτάσσω, static) 1921.
καθὼς (compound comparative adverb) 1348.
καὶ (ascensive conjunction) 14.
ὁ (nom.sing.masc.of the article in agreement with νόμος) 9.
νόμος (nom.sing.masc.of νόμος, subject of λέγει) 464.
λέγει (3d.per.sing.pres.act.ind.of λέγω, static) 66.

Translation - "The women should always keep silent in the churches because the privilege of speaking is not given to them, but they must subordinate themselves just as even the law says."

Comment: There is nothing in the Mosaic law that places women in a subordinate position. Other passages make clear that the Holy Spirit gives gifts to all the saints. The daughters of Philip, the evangelist, were prophetesses (Acts 21:8,9). That Paul means that women should never speak at church under any circumstances is hardly consistent with other scriptures. Women are indeed to be subordinate to their husbands in matters of church life and family administration, but this subordination does not impose silence upon them. Verse 35 seems to add the idea that the Corinthian women had an argumentative voice in church matters. It is probable that this restriction was imposed to meet a peculiar local situation in the Corinthian church not necessarily found elsewhere. Other churches with the same problem would, of course, be subject to the same restriction.

The pagan priestesses in the temples were prostitutes, and it may be for this reason that Paul lays down such strict rules in an effort to protect the reputation of the Christian women, and thus protect the influence of their witness for Christ. That the restriction was temporally and geographically localized seems evident. *Cf.* 1 Cor.11:3, where some speaking is permitted if the woman is properly attired. *Cf.* also 1 Tim.2:12 and Titus 2:5, in which passages Paul forbids women to exercise authority over the man and is required to be submissive to their husbands. What Paul seems to teach is that women should not be imperiously arrogant and dominant, either at home or at church.

The text does not tell us what law Paul cited. It may have been a part of the civil code in Corinth. If so the Christians in the city would be obligated to obey it (Romans 13:1-7).

Verse 35 - "And if they will learn anything, let them ask their husbands at home: for it is a shame for women to speak in the church."

εἰ δέ τι μαθεῖν θέλουσιν, ἐν οἴκῳ τοὺς ἰδίους ἄνδρας ἐπερωτάτωσαν, αἰσχρὸν γάρ ἐστιν γυναικὶ λαλεῖν ἐν ἐκκλησίᾳ.

"If there is anything they desire to know, let them ask their husbands at home. For it is shameful for a woman to speak in church."

εἰ (conditional particle in a first-class condition) 337.

δέ (continuative conjunction) 11.

τι (acc.sing.neut.of τις, indefinite pronoun, direct object of μαθεῖν) 486.

μαθεῖν (aor.act.inf.of μανθάνω, epexegetical) 794.

θέλουσιν (3d.per.pl.pres.act.ind.of θέλω, first-class condition) 88.

ἐν (preposition with the locative of place) 80.

οἴκῳ (loc.sing.masc.of οἶκος, place) 784.

τοὺς (acc.pl.masc.of the article in agreement with ἄνδρας) 9.

ἰδίους (acc.pl.masc.of ἴδιος, in agreement with ἄνδρας) 778.

ἄνδρας (acc.pl.masc.of ἀνήρ, direct object of ἐπερωτάτωσαν) 63.

ἐπερωτάτωσαν (3d.per.pl.pres.act.impv.of ἐπερωτάω, command) 973.

αἰσχρὸν (acc.sing.neut.of αἰσχρός, predicate accusative, adverbial) 4203.

γάρ (causal conjunction) 105.

ἐστιν (3d.per.sing.pres.ind.of εἰμί, static) 86.

γυναικὶ (dat.sing.fem.of γυνή, personal disadvantage) 103.
λαλεῖν (pres.act.inf.of λαλέω, noun use, subject of ἐστιν) 815.
ἐν (preposition with the locative of place) 80.
ἐκκλησίᾳ (loc.sing.fem.of ἐκκλησία, place) 1204.

Translation - *"And if they wish to be informed about something let them ask their own husbands at home; because to speak in church is disgraceful for a woman."*

Comment: The εἰ clause is a first-class condition. Christian women naturally wish to learn as much about the Christian faith as their husbands. To suppose otherwise is to imply that women have no interest in Christian growth or proper church administration. The contrary fact is evident. That Paul teaches that a Christian woman is to be subordinate to her husband is clear from 1 Cor.11:3*ff*, Eph.5:22,23; 1 Tim.2:12 and Titus 2:5. She is to ask "her own husband" - τοὺς ἰδίους ἄνδρας - and this question should be asked in the home - ἐν οἴκῳ. She may pray or prophesy at church if she is properly attired. This attire is to indicate her subordination. *Cf.* our discussion of 1 Cor.11:5. But she may not argue a point at church. Why? Paul only says that it is disgraceful for her to do so. Why? The answer must be in the local Corinthian customs. *Cf.* our comment on verse 34. Pagan prostitues held forth with eloquence and exercised great authority in the pagan temples. Social control in Corinth thus demanded that Christian women should behave otherwise. If Paul were directing instructions to a modern church where no such social control existed, while he would still insist upon the Christian woman's subordination to her husband, in the spirit of Ephesians 5:22-25, he would not insist on silence at church. In fact he did not insist upon *total* silence, even in Corinth.

Doctor Dayton's observation is very much to the point.

"In your exercise of spiritual liberty, beware that you do not violate local standards and sensibilities in a way that unnecessarily offends and alienates the people from your testimony. Don't let women be boisterous and loud where they are expected to be refined and helpful. You don't win people to the Lord by conduct that is shameful to them." (Wilber T. Dayton, *Charismatics and the New Testament*, 21).

Verse 36 - *"What? Came the word of God out from you? Or came it unto you only?"*

ἢ ἀφ' ὑμῶν ὁ λόγος τοῦ θεοῦ ἐξῆλθεν, ἢ εἰς ὑμᾶς μόνους κατήντησεν;

"What! Did the word of God originate with you, or are you the only ones it has reached?" . . . RSV

ἢ (disjunctive) 465.
ἀφ' (preposition with the ablative of source) 70.
ὑμῶν (abl.pl.masc.of σύ, source) 104.
ὁ (nom.sing.masc.of the article in agreement with λόγος) 9.
λόγος (nom.sing.masc.of λόγος, subject of ἐξῆλθεν) 510.

τοῦ (gen.sing.masc.of the article in agreement with θεοῦ) 9.

θεοῦ (gen.sing.masc.of θεός, description) 124.

ἐξῆλθεν (3d.per.sing.aor.ind.of ἐξέρχομαι, rhetorical question, expecting a negative reply) 161.

ἤ (disjunctive) 465.

εἰς (preposition with the accusative of extent) 140.

ὑμᾶς (acc.pl.masc.of σύ, extent) 104.

μόνους (acc.pl.masc.of μόνος, predicate accusative, adverbial) 339.

κατήντησεν (3d.per.sing.aor.act.ind.of καταντάω, rhetorical question, expecting a negative reply) 3353.

Translation - "Did the Word of God perhaps originate with you?! Or has He appeared face to face only to you?!"

Comment: *Cf.* 1 Cor.6:19 for ἤ in this introduction that expresses surprize. Paul is being sarcastic. Apparently he anticipated objections to his directives and decided to put them in their place. The two questions are sarcastically rhetorical, and as such they serve emphatically to state the opposite. Our Lord did not visit Corinth in His incarnation, nor did He visit the Corinthians face to face. Nor did the Corinthians write the New Testament.

Paul is asserting his apostolic authority and saying with some emphasis that the Corinthians are pupils and not teachers. His stern rebuke apparently did some good (2 Cor.2:1-5).

Verse 37 - "If a man think himself to be a prophet, or spiritual, let him acknowledge that the things I write unto you are the commandments of the Lord."

Εἴ τις δοκεῖ προφήτης εἶναι ἢ πνευματικός, ἐπιγινωσκέτω ἃ γράφω ὑμῖν ὅτι κυρίου ἐστὶν ἐντολή.

"If any one thinks that he is a prophet, or spiritual, he should acknowledge that what I am writing to you is a command of the Lord." . . . RSV

εἰ (conditional particle in a first-class condition) 337.

τις (nom.sing.masc.of τις, indefinite pronoun, subject of δοκεῖ) 486.

δοκεῖ (3d.per.sing.pres.act.ind.of δοκέω, first-class condition) 287.

προφήτης (nom.sing.masc.of προφήτης, predicate nominative) 119.

εἶναι (pres.inf.of εἰμί, noun use, direct object of δοκεῖ) 86.

ἤ (disjunctive) 465.

πνευματικός (nom.sing.masc.of πνευματικός, predicate adjective) 3791.

ἐπιγινωσκέτω (3d.per.sing.pres.act.impv.of ἐπιγινώσκω, command) 675.

ἃ (nom.pl.neut.of ὅς, relative pronoun, subject of ἐστὶν) 65.

γράφω (1st.per.sing.pres.act.ind.of γράφω, historical) 156.

ὑμῖν (dat.pl.masc.of σύ, indirect object of γράφω) 104.

ὅτι (conjunction introducing an object clause in indirect discourse) 211.

κυρίου (gen.sing.masc.of κύριος, description) 97.

ἐστὶν (3d.per.sing.pres.ind.of εἰμί, static) 86.

ἐντολή (nom.sing.fem.of ἐντολή, predicate nominative) 472.

Translation - "If any one considers himself a prophet or a spiritual man, let him understand that that which I have written to you is a commandment of the Lord."

Comment: For those trouble makers in Corinth who may have thought of themselves more highly than they ought, there is a challenge. Paul flatly asserts the divine reliability of what he has written. Let them challenge him if they dare. Those who are more inclined to concentrate on the ecstatic in the Christian experience often develop a sense of spiritual superiority to a degree greater than the facts warrant.

Verse 38 - "But if any man be ignorant, let him be ignorant."

εἰ δέ τις ἀγνοεῖ, ἀγνοεῖται.

"If any one does not recognize this, he is not recognized." . . . RSV

εἰ (conditional particle in a first-class condition) 337.
δέ (adversative conjunction) 11.
τις (nom.sing.masc.of τις, indefinite pronoun, subject of ἀγνοεῖ) 486.
ἀγνοεῖ (3d.per.sing.pres.act.ind.of ἀγνοέω, first-class condition) 2345.
ἀγνοεῖται (3d.per.sing.pres.mid.ind.of ἀγνοέω, present progressive) 2345.

Translation - "But if any one does not know it, he is ignorant by his own choice."

Comment: Some Mss authority can be gathered to support the imperative ἀγνοείτω, which translates "let him be ignorant" or "pay no attention to him" (Goodspeed). But the present middle indicative ἀγνοεῖται, is supported by "several important representatives of the Alexandrian, the Western, and the Palestinian texts (which) unite to support (it)." (Metzger, *A Textual Commentary on the Greek New Testament*, 566). "The alteration between active and passive forms of the same verb accords with Paul's usage in 8.2-3, whereas the use of the imperative form may have been suggested by Re 22.11. In any case the imperative gives a less forceful meaning than ἀγνοεῖται." (*Ibid.*).
    Anyone who ignores the Word of God, denies it or does not know that it is final authority in a rational universe is contributing to his own ignorance. Indeed there is no ultimate truth apart from the acceptance of the propositional revelation of the Bible. To reject the Word of God is to will oneself ignorant. Men who do not know, do not, because they do not choose to know. Those who profess themselves to be wise become fools (Romans 1:22).

Verse 39 - "Wherefore, brethren, covet to prophesy, and forbid not to speak with tongues."

ὥστε, ἀδελφοί (μου), ζηλοῦτε τὸ προφητεύειν, καὶ τὸ λαλεῖν μὴ κωλύετε γλώσσαις.

"So, my brethren, earnestly desire to prophesy, and do not forbid speaking in tongues."

ὥστε (inferential conjunction) 752.

ἀδελφοί (voc.pl.masc.of ἀδελφός, address) 15.

(μου) (gen.sing.masc.of ἐγώ, relationship) 123.

ζηλοῦτε (2d.per.pl.pres.act.impv.of ζηλόω, command) 3105.

τό (acc.sing.neut.of the article in agreement with προφητεύειν, articular infinitive) 9.

προφητεύειν (pres.act.inf.of προφητεύω, noun use, articular infinitive, direct object of ζηλοῦτε) 685.

καί (adjunctive conjunction joining verbs) 14.

τό (acc.sing.neut.of the article in agreement with λαλεῖν, articular infinitive) 9.

λαλεῖν (pres.act.inf.of λαλέω, noun use, direct object of κωλύετε) 815.

μή (negative particle with the imperative) 87.

κωλύετε (2d.per.pl.pres.act.impv.of κωλύω, command) 1296.

γλώσσαις (instru.pl.fem.of γλῶσσα, means) 1846.

Translation - "Therefore, brethren, be eager to prophesy, and stop hindering your communication with the use of foreign languages."

Comment: Before we defend the translation on grounds of diction, grammar and syntax, let me defend it on grounds of context.

There is no reason to translate γλῶσσα as heavenly language that no one on earth has ever spoken, or as the result of ecstatic loss of control, or as the gibberish that is heard in the typical "tongues" meeting. The concept "foreign language," - one that is spoken somewhere, but not spoken locally, and thus not understood by those present - fits every context where the word occurs. We must keep in mind the *zeitgeist* of the Corinthian situation, which we have discussed *supra* (pages 105,106). *Cf.* Dr. Dayton's excellent statement. Thus we have a clear picture of the problem which the Christians faced at Corinth and only thus can we understand Paul's instructions.

The gift of prophecy, in the exercise of which the prophet speaks under the inspiration of the Holy Spirit *in language which the audience understands*, is always held to be superior to the ability to speak in a foreign language, since prophecy edifies while foreign language discourse mystifies, confuses, frustrates and bores the audience. To speak in a foreign language is a self-serving practice. One gains the reputation for being sophisticated, in that he has extensive linguistic capability, and selfish, in that he refuses to speak in a way that helps other people. If music is played on an instrument that is out of tune, the audience breaks out in hives. The people are not edified. If the bugler on a battlefield blows the wrong signal the troops are misled.

In an audience where some linguist shows off those present become barbarians. To speak in French when no one in the audience knows French is to go back to the Tower of Babel.

The same principle applies in a prayer meeting, and there is no advantage in praying when he is alone in a language which one does not understand. Prayer is communication between the Christian and the Lord. God knows all of the languages so it does not make any difference to Him which one you choose, so why not talk to him in the language that you know best? Or are you trying to tell God, not only that you need money to pay the rent, but also that you, who learned English as a child and regard it as your native language also know French or German or Swahili? If you are as smart as you think you are, God is likely already to be aware of the fact. You need not try to impress Him, for God is not easily impressed with human achievements, linguistic or otherwise. Paul therefore said that he would pray in the spirit and also with his understanding.

Paul was an accomplished linguist and he thanked God for it, for otherwise he could not have preached the good news about our Lord in every crossroads town in Asia Minor, Macedonia and Achaia, but he did not regard it as a gift, but rather the result of his own effort, but he quickly added that five words which could be understood were better than thousands which could not, since the five resulted in edification of the saints, while the flood of incomprehensibility was a stupid exercise in futility.

Paul then tells us what happened on the three New Testament occasions when Christians spoke languages which they did not know, and he tells us the purpose for the miracle. At Pentecost they were for a sign for the benefit of the unbelievers present, who otherwise would never have heard the gospel, and in the cases of the Ephesian twelve (Acts 19:1-7) and Cornelius and his family and friends (Acts 10:44-48) the miracle convinced Paul at Ephesus and Peter and his Hebrew-Christian friend at Caesarea that the work of regeneration was genuine. Paul also told the Corinthians what would happen in their meetings if they spoke in foreign languages and also what would happen if they preached so that the audience could understand. In the former case the people would conclude that the Christians were crazy, and in the latter case, they would be convicted by the Holy Spirit, repent, believe, be saved and witness to the truth of what was said.

The remainder of chapter 14 is concerned with the order of service which should be followed where the use of a foreign language was imperative, if, in fact, it was ever the last resort, and also how the prophets should preach. Double and triple checks were to be provided to guard against false prophecies.

And now, after all of that argument, none of which defends the use of a foreign language in any sort of meeting where communication is important, be it a church service, a sewing circle or a political rally, and all of which extols the superiority of prophecy, with its clear communication, over foreign language with its confusion, the King James Version asks us to believe that Paul nevertheless told the Corinthians *not* to forbid the use of a foreign language!

So much for the logic of the context. What do the diction, the grammar and the syntax of verse 39 say?

The key verb is κωλύω (#1296). Let the student examine each of the contexts where it occurs. There are only 23 of them. Does it mean "to forbid" or "to hinder"? The former is normally construed as a vocal prohibition, as in "I forbid you to . . . " The word "hinder" means to prevent (interfere with, obstruct, oppose, resist, impede, inhibit, curb, interrupt, intercept, frustrate). If Caspar Milquetoast, who weighs 120 pounds plays linebacker for the Washington Redskins, he may forbid the ball carrier for the Dallas Cowboys to come through his side of the line, but it is not likely that he will hinder him from doing so. When the little children were trying to get past the disciples in order to sit on our Lord's lap and receive His blessing (Mt.19:14; Mk.10:14; Lk.18:16) the disciples were blocking their path. Jesus said, "Get out of the way of the children (step aside -῎Αφετε, #319) and do not hinder them ... μὴ κωλύετε)..." Note μὴ κωλύετε, the same prohibition (μὴ with the imperative) that occurs in 1 Cor.14:39, though in Mt.19:14 it is followed by a complementary infinitive, whereas in 1 Cor.14:39 the prohibition has an direct object in the articular infinitive τὸ λαλεῖν. The impediment which the disciples were trying to impose in῎Αφετε was designed to prevent the coming of the children to Jesus. Our Lord ordered them to "step aside" and "not to hinder." Thus His postive command and His prohibition meant the same thing. In 1 Cor.14:29 there is a positive command and a prohibition which would, if ignored, hinder the success of the thing commanded. Paul tells the Corinthians to "seek to prophesy" - *i.e.* to preach or teach in the language of the people, and in order that their prophecy be not hindered, that they are not to hinder (μὴ κωλύετε) it with the interjection of languages which could not be understood. Thus, when properly translated, verse 39 teaches exactly the opposite of the translation of the King James Version.

Baalam's loquacious ass did not *forbid* the prophet to procede, but he *hindered* him from doing so, first by wandering into the field and then by crushing Baalam's foot against the vineyard wall, and finally by lying down beneath his burden (Numbers 22:21-27). Thus the ass hindered the progress of the madness of the prophet (2 Pet.2:16).

In Hebrews 7:23 the Levitical priests were not *forbidden* to continue in the priesthood by death (θανάτῳ) but they were *hindered* from doing so (τὸ κωλύεσθαι). Death did not order them to cease, but it prevented them from continuing.

In Acts 8:36 the man from Ethiopia did not ask who would *forbid* him to be immersed in water, but what unfulfilled requirement would *hinder* him. And since there was nothing to hinder his immersion, Philip did not forbid it.

Paul was not forbidden to go to Rome, but he was hindered from doing so by circumstances over which he had no control - (Rom.1:13).

When the soldiers aboard the sinking ship at Malta determined to kill the prisoners on board to prevent their escape, the centurion, who was determined to rescue Paul, prevented the soldiers from carrying out their plan. Did he issue an order forbidding the slaughter or did he stand between the prisoners and the soldiers? Perhaps he did both.

When a robber takes your cloke by force you are not to seek to prevent him from taking your coat also (Luke 6:29). To translate the prohibition μὴ κωλύσῃς here as "do not forbid" makes no sense. When one is being mugged he does not summon all of his authority and say to the assailant, "I forbid you to take my coat," although he may try to hinder him from taking it, by fighting back or by flight. As we apply both "forbid" and "hinder" to κωλύω in the 23 contexts where it occurs (#1296) we find that the idea of hindrance is always present, whereas the idea of verbal prohibition makes no sense in some of the contexts and is there only by implication in the others.

Now that the diction problem is solved, let us examine the grammar and syntax of the passage. There is a mandate followed by a prohibition. The mandate (ζηλοῦτε τὸ προφητεύειν) consists of the verb and an articular infinitive in the accusative case, as its direct object. The Corinthians were ordered to prophesy. This means, of course, as the context of chapter 14 abundantly attests, to teach or preach in a language which the people in the audience can understood. The prohibition also consists of an imperative with μὴ and an articular infinitive in the accusative case, as its direct object (καὶ τὸ λαλεῖν μὴ κωλύετε γλώσσαις). Just as they were told to seek the gift of prophecy in the first clause, they were forbidden to *hinder* something. What were they not to hinder? That which they spoke - τὸ λαλεῖν. It is necessary to talk when one prophesies, and if you want the prophecy to have its intended edifying effect, do not prevent (hinder, inhibit, decrease the efficiency of, etc.) what you have to say from having its full beneficient impact upon the people whom you are trying to help. τὸ λαλεῖν is the direct object of μὴ κωλύετε, just as τὸ προφητεύειν is the direct object of ζηλοῦτε - "seek to prophesy" and "do not hinder what you say." Now how could a speaker who enjoyed rapport with his audience because he was speaking a language that they understood, reduce the efficiency of his discourse? By the use of a foreign language that they did not understand. And we have it in verse 39 in γλώσσαις which is the instrumental plural feminine of γλῶσσα, which in this context means a foreign language. Thus our translation - "*Therefore, brethren, be eager to prophesy, and stop hindering your communication with the use of foreign languages.*"

This is precisely what we would expect Paul to say at the close of his discussion of the problem which had turned the Corinthian church services into chaotic bedlam and reduced its effectiveness to the vanishing point.

What sincere Christian whose only desire is to participate in a worship service for the glory of our Lord and who noted with delight that his message was receiving eager attention from his audience with whom he enjoyed rapt rapport, and whom he was holding spellbound, would be foolish enough to stop speaking in the prophetic language that they all understood, and by which they were being helped, and resort to a foreign language the use of which turned you from an inspired prophet into a barbarian?

It is altogether fitting therefore that Paul should close this chapter with

Verse 40 — "Let all things be done decently and in order."

πάντα δὲ εὐσχημόνως καὶ κατὰ τάξιν γινέσθω.

"*but all things should be done decently and in order.*" . . . RSV

πάντα (nom.pl.neut.of πᾶς, subject of γινέσθω) 67.

δὲ (adversative conjunction) 11.

εὐσχημόνως (adverbial) 4038.

καὶ (adjunctive conjunction joining an adverb and an adverbial prepositional phrase) 14.

κατά (preposition with the accusative, standard) 98.

τάξιν (acc.sing.fem.of τάξις, standard, adverbial) 1786.

γινέσθω (3d.per.sing.pres.impv.of γίνομαι, command) 113.

Translation - "But all things should be done with dignity and in an orderly way."

Comment: *Cf.* #'s 2872 and 4038 for the basic meaning. We can imagine the mayhem of the typical Corinthian "charismatic" meeting with everyone talking at once, each in a different medium and with extreme emotional expression, and then imagine the opposite. Paul did not oppose emotion in religious expression but it was the emotion which is inspired by the Holy Spirit which is never divorced from intellectual activity. The service which is under the guidance of the Holy Spirit is peaceful and without confusion (verse 33). The presence of disorder which in some circles is evidence of the Holy Spirit's presence, is in fact indicative of the opposite. Where God the Holy Spirit is there is never confusion, but there is life and the heavenly activity that accompnies it. On the other hand the formal worship of the structured service may be an evidence of spiritual death.

A discussion of the charismatic question is in the nature of the case controversial. It is therefore imperative that objectivity be our rule. There should never be a determination to "prove" views which we have always held and there should be rejoicing at the entrance of new light. Above all "brotherly love must continue" (Heb.13:1).

In concluding his excellent study Dr. Dayton has said,

"It must be admitted that many do not agree that Paul used γλῶσσας literally to mean "languages" in the Corinthian Epistle. But it is a growing conviction with the present writer that the Scriptures require it. It is a fundamental rule of hermeneutics that the literal rendering of a word is the correct rendering when the concept is possible. When the literal is not possible, the inconsistency points the way to the correct figurative use. Since the literal is understandable, I conclude that it is the intended meaning. If so, whoever in ancient Corinth or in our day seeks authority for the use of tongues for other than intelligible and edifying discourse to facilitate and enlarge communication must look elsewhere than in the Corinthian Epistle. This is not to deny that historically there may have been bizarre emotional or even frenzied accompaniments of the use of languages in Corinth. There could have been swooning and trances as some strained for effect. There could have been even demonic and blasphemous tirades in the languages that were not common to the group. Paul indicates that some came from a background of demonic paganism and may not yet be out of danger of relapse, especially if they were putting on an exhibition of piety by signs (12:2,3). And it is certain that abuses of language have been perpetrated in many places since apostolic times. The present writer does not profess to understand or account for all of the phenomena. The ability of God to lift one above the language barrier for the communication of the Gospel ought not to be denied. But it is seriously doubted that all so-called "tongues" has that same divine origin. What of the hypnotic, psychological, induced motor responses, power of suggestion, and even demonic activity? Whatever these variants are, they lack Scriptural authority. It cannot be proved that they are of God by the Holy Spirit. Then it would be unwise to grant to them the terms Pentecostal, charismatic, gift of tongues, or perhaps even manifestation of the Spirit, and certainly not "the evidence" of the abiding presence of the Holy Spirit. This is not to pass judgment on the piety of other believers. It is simply to fail to find Scriptural support for an idea and practice that has caused much confusion by its uses and certainly by its abuses."

Wilber T. Dayton, *Charismatics and the New Testament*, 23,24

The Resurrection of Christ

(1 Corinthians 15:1-11)

1 Cor.15:1 - "Moreover, brethren, I declare unto you the gospel which I preached unto you, which also ye have received, and wherein ye stand."

Γνωρίζω δὲ ὑμῖν, ἀδελφοί, τὸ εὐαγγέλιον ὃ εὐηγγελισάμην ὑμῖν, ὃ καὶ παρελάβετε, ἐν ᾧ καὶ ἑστήκατε,

"Now I would remind you, brethren, in what terms I preached to you the gospel, which you received, in which you stand, . . . " . . . RSV

Γνωρίζω (1st.per.sing.pres.act.ind.of γνωρίζω, futuristic) 1882.

δὲ (explanatory conjunction) 11.

ὑμῖν (dat.pl.masc.of σύ, indirect object of γνωρίζω) 104.

ἀδελφοί (voc.pl.masc.of ἀδελφός, address) 15.

τὸ (acc.sing.neut.of the article in agreement with εὐαγγέλιον) 9.

εὐαγγέλιον (acc.sing.neut.of εὐαγγέλιον, direct object of γνωρίζω) 405.

ὃ (acc.sing.neut.of ὅς, relative pronoun, in agreement with εὐαγγέλιον, adjectival) 65.

εὐηγγελισάμην (1st.per.sing.1st.aor.mid.ind.of εὐαγγελλίζω, constative) 909.

ὑμῖν (dat.pl.masc.of σύ, indirect object of εὐηγγελισάμην) 104.

ὃ (acc.sing.neut.of ὅς, relative pronoun, in agreement with εὐαγγέλιον, adjectival) 65.

καὶ (adjunctive conjunction joining verbs) 14.

παρελάβετε (2d.per.pl.aor.act.ind.of παραλαμβάνω, constative) 102.

ἐν (preposition with the locative of sphere) 80.

ᾧ (loc.sing.neut.of ὅς, relative pronoun, sphere, adjectival) 65.

καὶ (adjunctive conjunction joining verbs) 14.

ἑστήκατε (2d.per.pl.perf.act.ind.of ἵστημι, intensive) 180.

Translation - "Now I declare to you, brethren, the good news which I preached to you, which you also received, in the truth of which also you have been standing, . . . "

Comment: γνωρίζω (#1882) does not mean "remind" or "renew". It only means to tell, declare, relate, etc. However, since Paul follows it with the three relative clauses, "which I preached," "which you received" (both aorists) and "in which you have been standing" (perfect tense), in this context it is clear that he means that he is repeating something which he had already preached. Therefore for contextual reasons we can translate "remind" or "repeat."

The gospel which Paul preached when he came to Corinth the first time (Acts 18:1-20) has not changed in historical fact or in theological content. When he preached it, they accepted it, stood upon it and had been standing upon the truth of it since. The problem in the Corinthian church was not that they had rejected the essence of the gospel for another system as had the churches in Galatia (Gal.1:6,7). Rather they had got carried away in their emphasis to an exaggerated importance of the spiritual gifts. They imagined that one of these gifts was the ability to speak a foreign language, having never studied it, and pointed to ecstatic utterances which they witnessed and heard in their services, without once questioning whether these manifestations were from the Holy Spirit or from demonic forces. They also found it amusing to argue about women's rights, as they related to her position of authority in the church, her dress and hair style.

Thus they needed a reemphasis upon what the real essence of the gospel of Christ is and the conclusions in terms of faith and practice which can be drawn from it. These truths were infinitely more important than the problems with which Paul had been dealing in chapters 12-14. It is likely that it was with a sigh of relief that the Apostle turned from his section on the gifts to the thrilling statement about the resurrection of our Lord in chapter fifteen.

We have two constative aorists in verse one. Paul preached the gospel and they received it. "This use of the aorist contemplates the action in its entirety. It takes an occurrence and, regardless of its extent of duration, gathers it into a single whole. We have here the basal, unmodified force of the aorist tense." (Mantey, *Manual*, 196).

This use of the aorist tells us nothing about how long the action referred to lasted. In Acts 5:5 it points to an action that lasted only a moment. Ananias died. In Ephesians 2:4 we learn that God has loved us forever, but it is not the onset of His love (ingressive aorist), nor the current results (culminative or effective aorist) of it that we see. It is the grand fact that ever and always (constative aorist) He has loved us and loves us still. In 2 Cor.11:25, Paul tells us that he was beaten three times, stoned once, in three shipwrecks and a day and a night in danger of drowning, yet his reference is to these experiences as a whole. Thus the constative aorist there covers a succession of acts or events. For the constative with reference to a momentary event, *cf.* Mt.8:3; for the constative for an extended time *cf.* Acts 28:30; a series of acts viewed as a single act by the constative can be found in Mt.22:28. (Burton, *New Testament Moods and Tenses*, 19,20).

Verse 2 - "By which also ye are saved, if ye keep in memory what I preached unto

unto you, unless ye have believed in vain."

δι' οὗ καὶ σώζεσθε, τίνι λόγῳ ⟨εὐηγγελισάμην ὑμῖν εἰ κατέχετε, ἐκτὸς εἰ μὴ εἰκῇ ἐπιστεύσατε.

"by which you are saved, if you hold it fast — unless you believed in vain."...
RSV

δι' (preposition with the ablative, means) 118.

οὗ (abl.sing.neut.of ὅς, relative pronoun, means) 65.

καὶ (adjunctive conjunction joining verbs) 14.

σώζεσθε (2d.per.pl.pres.pass.ind.of σώζω, present progressive retroactive) 109.

τίνι (instru.sing.masc.of τίς, interrogative pronoun, in agreement with λόγῳ) 281.

λόγῳ (instru.sing.masc.of λόγος, means) 510.

εὐηγγελισάμην (1st.per.sing.1st.aor.mid.ind.of εὐαγγελίζω, constative) 909.

ὑμῖν (dat.pl.masc.of σύ, indirect object of εὐηγγελισάμην) 104.

εἰ (conditional particle in a first-class condition) 337.

κατέχετε (2d.per.pl.pres.act.ind.of κατέχω, first-class condition) 2071.

ἐκτὸς (pleonastic adverb) 1461.

εἰ (conditional particle in a second-class condition) 337.

μὴ (negative particle with the indicative in a second-class condition) 87.

εἰκῇ (adverbial) 4034.

ἐπιστεύσατε (2d.per.pl.aor.act.ind.of πιστεύω, constative, second-class condition) 734.

Translation - "By means of which you are saved, if you are keeping in mind what message I preached to you, unless you made an insincere commitment."

Comment: We have the fourth relative clause - all relating to τὸ εὐαγγέλιον of verse 1. It is the gospel (1) which Paul preached, (2) which they received, (3) to the truths of which they were committed, and (4) through which they were saved. Paul's gospel gave them the rationale for their faith and it is the source of their salvation. Paul then abandoned the use of another relative for τίνι λόγῳ in indirect question in a first-class condition. "If you are holding fast to whatever the message was which I preached unto you." Then he adds a qualifying clause with pleonastic ἐκτος. It isn't needed since it is followed by a conditional sentence. We have the same construction in 1 Cor.14:5 and 1 Tim.5:19.

In view of the behavior and attitudes of some of the Corinthians Paul may have wondered if some of them had believed in a farcical, insept, insincere and capricious way. Paul had some ground for thinking that the professed faith of some was spurious, though he makes no direct accusation. In view of Paul's implied thought that some of the Corinthians may have been insincere, he follows with the most logical presentation of the basic truth of the gospel to be found in the New Testament.

Verse 3 - "For I delivered unto you first of all that which I also received, how that Christ died for our sins, according to the scriptures."

παρέδωκα γὰρ ὑμῖν ἐν πρώτοις , ὃ καὶ παρέλαβον, ὅτι Χριστὸς ἀπέθανεν ὑπὲρ τῶν ἁμαρτιῶν ἡμῶν κατὰ τὰς γραφάς.

"For I delivered to you as of first importance what I also received, that Christ died for our sins in accordance with the scriptures,. . . " . . . RSV

παρέδωκα (1st.per.sing. 1st.aor.act.ind.of παραδίδωμι, constative) 368.
γὰρ (causal conjunction) 105.
ὑμῖν (dat.pl.masc.of σύ, indirect object of παρέδωκα) 104.
ἐν (preposition with the locative of time point) 80.
πρώτοις (loc.pl.neut.of πρῶτος, time point, adverbial) 487.
ὃ (acc.sing.neut.of ὅς, relative pronoun, direct object of παρέλαβον) 65.
καὶ (adjunctive conjunction joining verbs) 14.
παρέλαβον (1st.per.sing.aor.act.ind.of παραλαμβάνω, constative) 102.
ὅτι (declarative conjunction) 211.
Χριστὸς (nom.sing.masc.of Χριστός, subject of ἀπέθανεν) 4.
ἀπέθανεν (3d.per.sing.aor.act.ind.of ἀποθνήσκω, constative) 774.
ὑπὲρ (preposition with the ablative, "in behalf of") 545.
τῶν (abl.pl.fem.of the article in agreement with ἁμαρτιῶν) 9.
ἁμαρτιῶν (abl.pl.fem.of ἁμαρτία, in behalf of) 111.
ἡμῶν (gen.pl.masc.of ἐγώ, possession) 123.
κατὰ (preposition with the accusative, standard) 98.
τὰς (acc.pl.fem.of the article in agreement with γραφάς) 9.
γραφάς (acc.pl.fem.of γραφή, standard) 1389.

Translation - "Because I gave to you at first that which I also received, that Christ died for our sins according to the Scriptures."

Comment: Paul is anxious to show that the gospel which he preached at Corinth was more than a philosophy of human origin - his or that of anyone else. His message at first (*i.e.* when he first came to Corinth) was not something that he concocted. It was that which he had previously received.

In his second epistle to Corinth he gives a detailed account of this introduction to the gospel (2 Cor. 12:1-4). Now he only states that he received it and relayed its message to the Corinthians. It is difficult, if not impossible, to say whether ἐν πρώτοις means first in point of time or in point of importance. Both ideas are true. The central fact of the gospel is the death of Jesus Christ for our sins. *Cf.*#545 for ὑπέρ and the ablative in passages which teach substitutionary atonement. Christ's death was not an accident; nor was it a misfortune. It was planned before the foundation of the world (Rev.13:8), announced in Eden (Gen.3:15), predicted by Jesus Himself (Mt.16:21), carried out at the precise hour (John 12:27-33). It was in keeping with the prophecies of many Old Testament Scriptures (Isa.53; Psalm 22, etc.). Thus Paul links the gospel story of

Christianity together with the prophetic Scriptures of Judaism and makes it impossible to separate the two (Romans 3:21). Note how Peter, Stephen and Philip tied together what the Old Tesament says with the history of the person and work of Jesus (Acts 2:14*ff*, 3:13-19; 7:2-53; 8:26-39).

"The New is in the Old contained; the Old is in the new explained."

That Paul's gospel was not contrary to what had been taught before he came, he here declares. His message, like that of the other Apostles and like that of Jesus Himself was κατὰ τὰ γραφάς.

Cf. our comment on 1 Cor.2:1-5.

Verse 4 - "And that he was buried, and that he rose again the third day, according to the Scriptures."

καὶ ὅτι ἐτάφη, καὶ ὅτι ἐγήγερται τῇ ἡμέρᾳ τῇ τρίτῃ κατὰ τὰς γραφάς.

"that he was buried, that he was raised on the third day in accordance with the scriptures, . . . " . . . RSV

καὶ (continuative conjunction) 14.
ὅτι (declarative conjunction) 211.
ἐτάφη (3d.per.sing.2d.aor.pass.ind.of θάπτω, constative) 748.
καὶ (continuative conjunction) 14.
ὅτι (declarative conjunction) 211.
ἐγήγερται (3d.per.sing.perf.pass.ind.of ἐγείρω, intensive) 125.
τῇ (loc.sing.fem.of the article in agreement with ἡμέρᾳ) 9.
ἡμέρᾳ (loc.sing.fem.of ἡμέρα, time point) 135.
τῇ (loc.sing.fem.of the article in agreement with τρίτῃ) 9.
τρίτῃ (loc.sing.fem.of τρίτος, in agreement with ἡμέρᾳ) 1209.
κατὰ (preposition with the accusative, standard) 98.
τὰς (acc.pl.fem.of the article in agreement with γραφάς) 9.
γραφάς (acc.pl.fem.of γραφή, standard) 1389.

Translation - "And that he was buried and that He was raised on the third day according to the Scriptures."

Comment: Note ὅτι in verse 3, joined by καὶ ὅτι . . . καὶ ὅτι . . . καὶ ὅτι in verses 4 and 5. "He died . . . He was buried . . . He was raised . . He was seen. . . " Paul puts the intensive present perfect ἐγήγερται between the two aorists ἐτάφη and ὤφθη, to say that "Christ, being raised from the dead, dieth no more. Death hath no more dominion over Him. For in that He died, He died unto sin once, but in that He liveth, He liveth unto God" (Rom.6:9,10).

The fact of His burial proves the reality of His death. The phrase "three days and three nights" (Mt.12:40) and "the third day" (Mt.16:21; 1 Cor.15:4) is discussed at length in A.T.Robertson, *A Harmony of the Gospels,*289-291. We are not concerned here with the details of this controversy, but rather with the fact that the same Scriptures that foretold Christ's death (Isaiah 53) also foretold His resurrection (Psalm 16:10). *Cf.* John 10:17,18; Mt.16:21; John 2:19-21.

Infidelity staggers before the astounding supernatural character of a bodily resurrection and makes vapid and vacuous efforts to reduce it to something that the unregenerate mind can accept. That a "spiritual" resurrection cannot mean a "noncorporeal" resurrection is evident.If the resurrection was noncorporeal then there was no resurrection at all since His spirit never died. Resurrection of the spirit is nonesense. That he arose in the same tangible corporeal body in which He suffered is attested by verses 5-8, as Paul adds the empircal evidence.

Verse 5 - "And that he was seen of Cephas, then of the twelve."

καὶ ὅτι ὤφθη Κηφᾷ, εἶτα τοῖς δώδεκα.

"and that he appeared to Cephas, then to the twelve." . . . RSV

καὶ (adjunctive conjunction joining declarative clauses) 14.
ὅτι (declarative conjunction) 211.
ὤφθη (3d.per.sing.aor.pass.ind.of ὁράω, constative) 144.
Κηφᾷ (instru.sing.masc.of Κεφᾶς, agent) 1964.
εἶτα (temporal adverb) 2185.
τοῖς (instru.pl.masc.of the article in agreement with δώδεκα) 9.
δώδεκα (instru. indeclin. of δώδεκα, agent) 820.

Translation - "And that he was seen by Cephas, then by the twelve."

Comment: Here is a historical statement to the effect that there was empirical evidence that our Lord arose. Cephas (Peter) saw the resurrected Jesus (Luke 24:34). It is natural to assume that by τοῖς δώδεκα Paul meant the twelve disciples, including Judas Iscariot. If so, he was in error, if we assume that Judas hanged himself before the resurrection. The story in Matthew 27:1-6 does not tell us when he died. The assumption is that Judas was already dead before our Lord arose. If Paul meant the disciples he should have said "the eleven" (Mt.28:16). Note that John was still referring to the disciples as "the twelve" after Judas' death (John 20:24). Actually Jesus' first appearance to the disciples as a group was to only ten, since Judas was dead and Thomas was absent. Paul's point is not concerned with precise numbers. He is talking about witnesses, and he could have spoken of many more than twelve, as indeed he did in the next verse. He is piling up scientific evidence that Jesus arose, a fact that is demonstrated by the fact that He was seen after His resurrection by Peter, Mary, the ten disciples, then the eleven, plus the two disciples from Emmaus and finally by many, many others. Here we have the historical document that gives empirical evidence, based not upon hearsay but upon sight. The testimonies of these people would be admissible in any court of law.

Let infidels attack the resurrection of our Lord on the ground that the Scriptural record is false, for it is upon the *a priori* assumption that the Scriptural record is true that the Christian bases his faith. But let him not deny the resurrection on the ground that the Bible does not teach that He arose. It is not a matter of exegesis and hermeneutics.

Verse 6 - "After that, he was seen of above five hundred brethren at once; of whom the greater part remain unto this present, but some are fallen asleep."

ἔπειτα ὤφθη ἐπάνω πεντακοσίοις ἀδελφοῖς ἐφάπαξ, ἐξ ὧν οἱ πλείονες μένουσιν ἕως ἄρτι, τινὲς δὲ ἐκοιμήθησαν.

"Then he appeared to more than five hundred brethren at one time, most of whom are still alive, though some have fallen asleep." . . . RSV

ἔπειτα (temporal adverb) 2566.

ὤφθη (3d.per.sing.aor.pass.ind.of ὁράω, constative) 144.

ἐπάνω (adverb of numerical superiority) 181.

πεντακοσίοις (dat.pl.masc.of πεντακόσιος, in agreement with ἀδελφοῖς) 2171.

ἀδελφοῖς (dat.pl.masc.of ἀδελφός, personal interest) 15.

ἐφάπαξ (adverbial) 3913.

ἐξ (preposition with the paritive genitive) 19.

ὧν (gen.pl.masc.of ὅς, partitive genitive) 65.

οἱ (nom.pl.masc.of the article in agreement with πλείονες) 9.

πλείονες (nom.pl.masc.of πλείων, subject of μένουσιν) 474.

μένουσιν (3d.per.pl.pres.act.ind.of μένω, present progressive) 864.

ἕως (preposition with the genitive in a time expression) 71.

ἄρτι (temporal adverb) 320.

τινὲς (nom.pl.masc.of τις, indefinite pronoun, subject of ἐκοιμήθησαν) 486.

δὲ (adversative conjunction) 11.

ἐκοιμήθησαν (3d.per.pl.aor.pass.ind.of κοιμάω, constative) 1664.

Translation - "A little later he was seen by more than five hundred brothers at the same time, of whom the majority are still alive, though some have died."

Comment: Study #'s 2566 and 3913. ἔπειτα does not suggest that Paul is listing these post-resurrection appearances of Jesus in their proper ordinal, but rather in their proper chronological order. A study of the gospel records reveals that there were others who saw Jesus after He arose whom Paul does not mention since it would not serve his purpose. He is only interested in convincing the reader beyond all cavil that Jesus actually arose. Of the number, in excess of five hundred who saw Jesus at the same time prior to His ascension (Acts 1:1-11) a few had died by the time Paul wrote, though most had not. Thus it would have been possible for Paul to assemble a great number of witnesses to testify in a court of law, in which rules of evidence are observed, that they saw Jesus alive after His death (Acts 1:3).

Note in ἐκοιμήθησαν a constative aorist which describes a succession of events in the past. *Cf.*2 Cor.11:25; Mt.22:28. The perfect tense would have meant that all died at the same time. ἐφάπαξ (#3913) destroys the infidel argument that those who said they saw Jesus were sincere but deluded by some hallucination or optical illusion. Possible for one or two or a few, but five hundred identical hallucinations simultaneously?!

None of the arguments against the resurrection, when submitted to rigorous analysis, are worthy of serious consideration. But it serves no purpose to argue with the unsaved. They only rearrange their prejudices. The faith which saves is not contingent upon a rationale. Sinners who are effectually called by the Holy Spirit are not deterred by intellectual difficulties (Mt.11:25-27). The time for Christian Education follows discipleship and immersion (Mt.28:19-20).

Verse 7 - "After that, he was seen of James; then of all the apostles."

ἔπειτα ὤφθη Ἰακώβῳ, εἶτα τοῖς ἀποστόλοις πᾶσιν.

"Then he appeared to James, then to all the apostles." . . . RSV

ἔπειτα (temporal adverb) 2566.
ὤφθη (3d.per.sing.aor.pass.ind.of ὁράω, constative) 144.
Ἰακώβῳ (instru.sing.masc.of Ἰάκωβον, agent) 397.
εἶτα (temporal adverb) 2185.
τοῖς (instru.pl.masc.of the article in agreement with ἀποστόλοις) 9.
ἀποστόλοις (instru.pl.masc.of ἀπόστολος, agent) 844.
πᾶσιν (instru.pl.masc.of ἀπόστολος, in agreement with ἀποστόλοις) 67.

Translation - "After that He was seen by James; then by all the Apostles."

Comment: Paul's order, chronological though not ordinal, for post-resurrection appearances is (1) Cephas, (2) the Twelve, (3) more than five hundred Christians, (4) James, (5) all the Apostles and (6) Paul himself on the Damascus road. He has omitted appearances to Mary, the Emmaus disciples and others. But he has made his point. A great many people saw the resurrected Lord on a great many different occasions, scattered across forty days. There is more evidence for the resurrection of Jesus than for the fact that Julius Caesar crossed the Rubicon.

Verse 8 - "And last of all he was seen of me also, as of one born out of due time."

ἔσχατον δὲ πάντων ὡσπερεὶ τῷ ἐκτρώματι ὤφθη κἀμοί.

"Last of all, as to one untimely born, he appeared also to me." . . . RSV

ἔσχατον (acc.sing.neut.of ἔσχατος, adverbial) 496.
δὲ (continuative conjunction) 11.
πάντων (gen.pl.neut.of πᾶς, partitive genitive) 67.

#4239 ὡσπερεὶ (combination intensive conditional particle).

King James Version

as - 1 Cor.15:8.

Revised Standard Version

as - 1 Cor.15:8.

Meaning: A combination of ὡς (#128), περ, the intensive suffix and εἰ (#337). Precisely as if - 1 Cor.15:8, followed by τῷ ἐκτρώματι.

τῷ (instru.sing.masc.of the article in agreement with ἐκτρώματι) 9.

#4240 ἐκτρώματι (instru.sing.masc.of ἔκτρωμα, apposition).

King James Version

be born out of due time - 1 Cor.15:8.

Revised Standard Version

one untimely born - 1 Cor.15:8.

Meaning: Cf. ἐκτιτρώσκω - "to abort." To suffer or induce an abortion. Hence, one aborted. With reference to Paul whose regeneration and appointment to the Apostleship came in point of time after (not at the proper time) that of the other eleven Aposltes - 1 Cor.15:8.

ὤφθη (3d.per.sing.aor.pass.ind.of ὁράω, constative) 144.
κἀμοί (instru.sing.masc.of κἀγώ, agent) 178.

Translation - "And last of all He was seen also by me, as if I were untimely born."

Comment: ἔσχατον here in a chronological sense, and used adverbially. *Cf.* Mk.12:6,22. Paul calls himself an "abortion" (#4240) since he was saved, not during Jesus' public ministry before His death, as were the other eleven Apostles, but after Jesus' ascension.

But, though he was the last of the Apostles chosen, like them Paul had met Jesus face to face, so that he could testify personally as to the fact of the resurrection. He also saw Jesus in the experience which he describes in 2 Cor.12:1-4. Due to his late introduction to the Apostolic ministry he willingly takes the low place in the company, as we learn in

Verse 9 - "For I am the least of the apostles, that am not meet to be called an apostle, because I persecuted the church of God."

Ἐγὼ γάρ εἰμι ὁ ἐλάχιστος τῶν ἀποστόλων, ὅς οὐκ εἰμὶ ἱκανὸς καλεῖσθαι ἀπόστολος, διότι ἐδίωξα τὴν ἐκκλησίαν τοῦ θεοῦ.

"For I am the least of the apostles unfit to be called an apostle, because I persecuted the church of God." . . . RSV

Ἐγὼ (nom.sing.masc.of ἐγώ, subject of εἰμι) 123.
γάρ (inferential conjunction) 105.
εἰμι (1st.per.sing.pres.ind.of εἰμί, aoristic) 86.
ὁ (nom.sing.masc.of the article in agreement with ἐλάχιστος) 9.
ἐλάχιστος (nom.sing.masc.of ἐλάχιστος, predicate nominative) 159.
τῶν (gen.pl.masc.of the article in agreement with ἀποστόλων) 9.
ἀποστόλων (gen.pl.masc.of ἀπόστολος, partitive genitive) 844.
ὅς (nom.sing.masc.of ὅς, relative pronoun, subject of εἰμὶ, adjectival) 65.
οὐκ (negative particle with the indicative) 130.

εἰμὶ (1st.per.sing.pres.ind.of εἰμί, aoristic) 86.
ἱκανὸς (nom.sing.masc.of ἱκανός, predicate adjective) 304.
καλεῖσθαι (pres.pass.inf.of καλέω, complementary) 107.
ἀπόστολος (nom.sing.masc.of ἀπόστολος, predicate nominative) 844.
διότι (compound particle introducing a causal clause) 1795.
ἐδίωξα (1st.per.sing.aor.act.ind.of διώκω, constative) 434.
τὴν (acc.sing.fem.of the article in agreement with ἐκκλησίαν) 9.
ἐκκλησίαν (acc.sing.fem.of ἐκκλησία, direct object of ἐδίωξα) 1204.
τοῦ (gen.sing.masc.of the article in agreement with θεοῦ) 9.
θεοῦ (gen.sing.masc.of θεός, description) 124.

Translation - "Therefore I am the least of the Apostles, who am not worthy to be called an Apostle, because I persecuted the church of God."

Comment: Not only was Saul of Tarsus last chosen to be an Apostle but when he was chosen he was engaged in a concentrated effort to exterminate the church of Christ (Acts 9:1-9). These facts, he felt, were sufficient to rate him last in importance among those chosen.

ἐλάχιστος is a true superlative. There is an interesting deescalation of Paul's opinion of himself, beginning with this passage. "The least of the Apostles" (1 Cor.15:9) later called himself "less than the least of all saints" (Eph.3:8) and finally said that he was "the chief of sinners" (1 Tim.1:15). The closer we get to God the less highly we evaluate ourselves. But though, in himself, Paul was unworthy by the grace of God he was an Apostle.

Verse 10 - "But by the grace of God I am what I am: and his grace which was bestowed upon me was not in vain: but I laboured more abundantly than they all; yet not I, but the grace of God which was with me."

χάριτι δὲ θεοῦ εἰμι ὃ εἰμι, καὶ ἡ χάρις αὐτοῦ ἡ εἰς ἐμὲ οὐ κενὴ ἐγενήθη, ἀλλὰ περισσότερον αὐτῶν πάντων ἐκοπίασα, οὐκ ἐγὼ δὲ ἀλλὰ ἡ χάρις τοῦ θεοῦ (ἡ) σὺν ἐμοί.

"But by the grace of God I am what I am, and his grace toward me was not in vain. On the contrary, I worked harder than any of them, though it was not I, but the grace of God which is with me." . . . RSV

χάριτι (instru.sing.fem.of χάρις, means) 1700.
δὲ (adversative conjunction) 11.
θεοῦ (abl.sing.masc.of θεός, source) 124.
εἰμι (1st.per.sing.pres.ind.of εἰμί, aoristic) 86.
ὃ (nom.sing.neut.of ὅς, relative pronoun, subject of εἰμί, predicate nominative) 65.
καὶ (continuative conjunction) 14.
ἡ (nom.sing.fem.of the article in agreement with χάρις) 9.
χάρις (nom.sing.fem.of χάρις, subject of ἐγενήθη) 1700.
αὐτοῦ (gen.sing.masc.of αὐτός, possession) 16.
ἡ (nom.sing.fem.of the article in agreement with χάρις) 9.

εἰς (preposition with the accusative, locative, static use) 140.
ἐμέ (acc.sing.masc.of ἐμός, static use) 1267.
οὐ (negative particle with the indicative) 130.
κενή (nom.sing.fem.of κενός, predicate adjective) 1836.
ἐγενήθη (3d.per.sing.aor.ind.of γίνομαι, culminative) 113.
ἀλλά (adversative conjunction) 342.
περισσότερον (acc.sing.neut.comp.of περισσός, adverbial) 525.
αὐτῶν (gen.pl.masc.of αὐτός, partitive genitive) 16.
πάντων (abl.pl.masc.of πᾶς, comparison) 67.
ἐκοπίασα (1st.per.sing.aor.act.ind.of κοπιάω, constative) 629.
οὐκ (negative particle with the indicative understood) 130.
ἐγώ (nom.sing.masc.of ἐγώ, predicate nominative) 123.
δέ (concessive conjunction) 11.
ἀλλά (adversative conjunction) 342.
ἡ (nom.sing.fem.of the article in agreement with χάρις) 9.
χάρις (nom.sing.fem.of χάρις, subject of verb understood) 1700.
τοῦ (abl.sing.masc.of the article in agreement with θεοῦ) 9.
θεοῦ (abl.sing.masc.of θεός, source) 124.
ἡ (nom.sing.fem.of the article in agreement with χάρις) 9.
σύν (preposition with the instrumental of association) 1542.
ἐμοί (instru.sing.masc.of ἐμός, association) 1267.

Translation - *"But by means of divine grace, I am what I am and His grace, which is in me was not in vain; on the contrary I worked harder than all of them, although it was not I, but the grace of God which was with me."*

Comment: The clause εἰμι ὃ εἰμι is not the same idea as ὅς οὐ εἰμί of verse 9, which was 1st.person, although of course the relative pronoun has no person. In verse 10 ὃ is third person. It is not "who" but "what I am." Whatever Paul was, it was because of divine grace. This grace had not been ineffectual. Because of it Paul worked harder than all of the other Apostles, yet (concessive δέ) he is quick to disclaim any credit for his performance. It was not Paul's effort but the work of abiding grace. *Cf.*#629 for the other places where Christian hard work and sacrifice, Paul's and that of others, are mentioned. Minor variations in other MSS for ἡ σύν ἐμοί do not affect the exegesis.

Verse 11 - *"Therefore whether it were I or they, so we preach, and so ye believed."*

εἴτε οὖν ἐγώ εἴτε ἐκεῖνοι, οὕτως κηρύσσομεν καὶ οὕτως ἐπιστεύσατε.

"Whether then it was I or they, so we preach and so you believed." . . . RSV

εἴτε (disjunctive) 4016.
οὖν (inferential conjunction) 68.
ἐγώ (nom.sing.masc.of ἐγώ, nominative absolute) 123.
εἴτε (disjunctive) 4016.
ἐκεῖνοι (nom.pl.masc.of ἐκεῖνος, anaphoric) 246.
οὕτως (demonstrative adverb) 74.

κηρύσσομεν (1st.per.pl.pres.act.ind.of κηρύσσω, customary) 249.
καὶ (continuative conjunction) 14.
οὕτως (demonstrative adverb) 74.
ἐπιστεύσατε (2d.per.pl.aor.act.ind.of πιστεύω, constative) 734.

Translation - "Therefore whether it is I or they - that is what we preach and that is what you have believed."

Comment: It really does not matter that Paul's conversion was a tardy "abortion" which from Paul's point of view made him inferior in prestige (verse 9) though superior in effort (verse 10). The point is that what the other eleven Apostles were preaching and what he was preaching was the same message. Note the customary present action in κηρύσσομεν and the constative aorist in ἐπιστεύσατε. "We (the Apostles) customarily preach what we have always preached and you have believed it." ἐκεῖνοι is anaphoric, referring to τῶν ἀποστόλων of verse 9.

But Paul had thought it necessary to define with precision what this gospel is. It is Christ's death, burial and resurrection, all of which was foretold by the Jewish Scriptures of the Old Testament. It was *not* sex relations, male dominance, the liberation of women, ladies' hair styles at church, the use of foreign languages in worship and any other peripheral matters that have taken so much space in this epistle.

But perhaps the Corinthians do not believe in the resurrection of Jesus. Verses 12-19 prove that if we do not accept the resurrection as a fact, logic demands that we reject the entire Christian model.

The Resurrection of the Dead

(1 Corinthians 15:12-34)

Verse 12 - "Now if Christ be preached that he rose from the dead, how say some among you that there is no resurrection of the dead?"

Εἰ δὲ Χριστὸς κηρύσσεται ὅτι ἐκ νεκρῶν ἐγήγερται, πῶς λέγουσιν ἐν ὑμῖν τινες ὅτι ἀνάστασις νεκρῶν οὐκ ἔστιν;

"Now if Christ is preached as raised from the dead, how can some of you say that there is no resurrection of the dead?"

Εἰ (conditional particle in a first-class condition) 337.
δὲ (explanatory conjunction) 11.
Χριστὸς (nom.sing.masc.of Χριστός, subject of κηρύσσεται) 4.
κηρύσσεται (3d.per.sing.pres.pass.ind.of κηρύσσω, first-class condition) 249.
ὅτι (conjunction introducing an object clause in indirect discourse) 211.
ἐκ (preposition with the ablative of separation) 19.
νεκρῶν (abl.pl.masc.of νεκρός, separation) 749.
ἐγήγερται (3d.per.sing.perf.pass.ind.of ἐγείρω, intensive) 125.

πῶς (interrogative adverb in direct question) 627.

λέγουσιν (3d.per.pl.pres.act.ind.of λέγω, present iterative retroactive) 66.

ἐν (preposition with the locative with plural pronouns) 80.

ὑμῖν (loc.pl.masc.of σύ, place) 104.

τινες (nom.pl.masc.of τις, indefinite pronoun, subject of λέγουσιν) 486.

ὅτι (conjunction introducing an object clause in indirect discourse) 211.

ἀνάστασις (nom.sing.fem.of ἀνάστασις subject of ἔστιν) 1423.

νεκρῶν (gen.pl.masc.of νεκρός, definition) 749.

οὐκ (negative particle with the indicative) 130.

ἔστιν (3d.per.sing.pres.ind.of εἰμί, aoristic) 86.

Translation - "Now since Christ is being represented as having been raised from the dead, how is it that some of you have been saying that there is no resurrection of the dead?"

Comment: The εἰ clause is a first-class condition with no doubt about the truth of the premise in the protasis. Christ had indeed been preached as having risen from the dead. The message had not changed. All of the Apostles were preaching it. They also supported their message with the empirical evidence of their own experiences of physical sight, sound and touch. "Since then that was being preached . . . " the apodosis has the question, with πῶς and ὅτι in indirect discourse. Not all of the Corinthians were saying that the physical resurrection of the dead body could not occur. But some of them were saying this. Note the present iterative retroactive force of λέγουσιν. Time and again in the past and also still in the present these skeptics had rejected the doctrine.

Greek philosophy with its extreme idealism, a concept which had been reinforced by the Gnostics from the Middle East, held that physical resurrection of the body was neither to be expected nor indeed desired. It is probable that some of the Corinthian Christians had been influenced by Plato and others. Of course the Gnostic view, which is A.D.55 was only in its inchoate stage, looked upon all matter as evil and could not accept the notion that a material body could live forever in heaven.

The denial of the resurrection of the body of Jesus Christ is the first step in a logical chain of thought that ultimately shows that if any part of the Christian rationale is rejected, the rest of it cannot be true. If Jesus Christ of Nazareth is alive then every issue, be it moral, philosophical, political, social, economic, aesthetic or psychological is settled and there is ground for optimism. If He is dead then nothing is settled, we have lived always in a random universe and no one can predict when and how the end will come - or indeed if there is any end to this exercise in futility which we call life.

There follows in verses 13-19 what has been called the greatest demonstration of formal logic ever written.

Verse 13 - "But if there be no resurrection of the dead, then is Christ not risen."

εἰ δὲ ἀνάστασις νεκρῶν οὐκ ἔστιν, οὐδὲ Χριστὸς ἐγήγερται.

"But if there is no resurrection of the dead, then Christ has not been raised;"..
. *RSV*

εἰ (conditional particle in a first-class condition) 337.

δὲ (adversative conjunction) 11.

ἀνάστασις (nom.sing.fem.of ἀνάστασις, subject of ἔστιν) 1423.

νεκρῶν (gen.pl.masc.of νεκρός, definition) 749.

οὐκ (negative particle with the indicative) 130.

ἔστιν (3d.per.sing.pres.ind.of εἰμί, aoristic) 86.

οὐδὲ (disjunctive particle) 452.

Χριστὸς (nom.sing.masc.of Χριστός, subject of ἐγήγερται) 4.

ἐγήγερται (3d.per.sing.perf.pass.ind.of ἐγείρω, intensive) 125.

Translation - "But if there is no resurrection of the dead then Christ has not been raised."

Comment: The first-class condition with εἰ and the indicative in the protasis *assumes* for the sake of the argument that the premise is true, although Paul has already said that it is false. The premise in a first-class condition may or may not be true, but it is always assumed to be true. In verse 12 it was indeed true. In verse 13 it is in fact false. There is a resurrection of the dead. But if the premise in verse 13 were true (it is not) then the conclusion in the apodosis would also be true, which it is not. If resurrection from the dead is not a fact, then obviously Christ has not arisen (perfect tense in ἐγήγερται) and therefore He will remain dead.

But Paul and the other Apostles had always preached that He did arise (vss.4,12). Where does this logic lead us?

Verse 14 - "And if Christ be not risen, then is our preaching vain, and your faith is also vain."

εἰ δὲ Χριστὸς οὐκ ἐγήγερται, κενὸν ἄρα (καὶ) τὸ κήρυγμα ἡμῶν, κενὴ καὶ ἡ πίστις ὑμῶν,

"if Christ has not been raised, then our preaching is in vain and your faith is in vain." . . . RSV

εἰ (conditional particle in a first-class condition) 337.

δὲ (continuative conjunction) 11.

Χριστὸς (nom.sing.masc.of Χριστός, subject of ἐγήγερται) 4.

οὐκ (negative particle with the indicative) 130.

ἐγήγερται (3d.per.sing.perf.pass.ind.of ἐγείρω, intensive) 125.

κενὸν (nom.sing.neut.of κενός, predicate adjective) 1836.

ἄρα (illative particle) 995.

καὶ (emphatic conjunction) 14.

τὸ (nom.sing.neut.of the article in agreement with κήρυγμα) 9.

κήρυγμα (nom.sing.neut.of κήρυγμα, subject of ἔστιν understood) 1013.

ἡμῶν (gen.pl.masc.of ἐγώ, possession) 123.

κενὴ (nom.sing.fem.of κενός, predicate adjective) 1836.

καὶ (continuative conjunction) 14.

ἡ (nom.sing.fem.of the article in agreement with πίστις) 9.

πίστις (nom.sing.fem.of πίστις, subject of ἐστιν understood) 728.

ὑμῶν (gen.pl.masc.of σύ, possession) 104.

Translation - "And if Christ has not been raised (and is therefore not now alive) then in fact our preaching is without substance and so is your faith."

Comment: Again we have the first-class condition assuming that the premise in the if clause is true, although Paul was insisting that it was false. If it were true, which it is not, that Christ had not been raised and was therefore still dead, then it would also be true, which it is not, that the Apostles' preaching was false (vain, empty, worthless, without substance) and also that the faith of the Corinthian Christians was also without foundation in fact. Thus their faith would be a belief in something that was unreal.

Modernists who reject the literal bodily resurrection of Jesus should take note and stop preaching. Any preacher who is preaching about a dead Jesus is wasting his effort and the time of the audience.

The 15th verse has another first-class condition but with the apodosis first and the protasis following it.

Some MSS read ἡμῶν for ὑμῶν. "Although several important witnesses (including B Dᵍʳ· 33 81 330 1739) read ἡμῶν, this may be either itacism for ὑμῶν or mechanical assimilation to the previous ἡμῶν. In any case, the context seems to require "your faith" as a correlative to "our preaching;" compare also ἡ πίστις ὑμῶν in verse 17, where the reading is firm." (Metzger, *A Textual Commentary on the Greek New Testament*, 567, 568).

Whether ὑμῶν or ἡμῶν, Paul's point is the same.

Verse 15 - "Yea, and we are found false witnesses of God: because we have testified of God that he raised up Christ, whom he raised not up, if so be that the dead rise not."

εὑρισκόμεθα δὲ καὶ φευδομάρτυρες τοῦ θεοῦ, ὅτι ἐμαρτυρήσαμεν κατὰ τοῦ θεοῦ ὅτι ἤγειρεν τὸν Χριστόν, ὃν οὐκ ἤγειρεν εἴπερ ἄρα νεκροὶ οὐκ ἐγείρονται.

"We are even found to be misrepresenting God, because we testified of God that he raised Christ, whom he did not raise if it is true that the dead are not raised." . . . RSV

εὑρισκόμεθα (1st.per.pl.pres.pass.ind.of εὑρίσκω, aoristic) 79.

δὲ (continuative conjunction) 11.

καὶ (ascensive conjunction) 14.

φευδομάρτυρες (nom.pl.masc.of φευδομάρτυρ, predicate nominative) 1602.

τοῦ (gen.sing.masc.of the article in agreement with θεοῦ) 9.

θεοῦ (gen.sing.masc.of θεός, reference) 124.

ὅτι (conjunction introducing a subordinate causal clause) 211.

ἐμαρτυρήσαμεν (1st.per.pl.aor.act.ind.of μαρτυρέω, culminative) 1471.

κατὰ (preposition with the genitive with a verb of swearing) 98.

τοῦ (gen.sing.masc.of the article in agreement with θεοῦ) 9.

θεοῦ (gen.sing.masc.of θεός, with a verb of swearing) 124.

ὅτι (conjunction with an object clause in indirect discourse) 211.

ἤγειρεν (3d.per.sing.1st.aor.act.ind.of ἐγείρω, constative) 125.

τὸν (acc.sing.masc.of the article in agreement with Χριστόν) 9.

Χριστόν (acc.sing.masc.of Χριστός, direct object of ἤγειρεν) 4.

ὅν (acc.sing.masc.of ὅς, relative pronoun, direct object of ἤγειρεν) 65.

οὐκ (negative particle with the indicative) 130.

ἤγειρεν (3d.per.sing.aor.act.ind.of ἐγείρω, constative) 125.

εἴπερ (intensive conditional particle in a first-class condition) 3879.

ἄρα (emphatic particle) 995.

νεκροὶ (nom.pl.masc.of νεκρός, subject of ἐγείρονται) 749.

οὐκ (negative particle with the indicative) 130.

ἐγείρονται (3d.per.pl.pres.pass.ind.of ἐγείρω) 125.

Translation - "*And furthermore we are demonstrated to be false witnesses with reference to God, because we swore, calling God to witness that He raised up Christ, Whom He did not raise, if in fact it is true that dead people are not raised.*"

Comment: Here the result in the apodosis is given first and the assumption in the protasis upon which it is contingent follows. The assumption, introduced by εἴπερ ἄρα is assumed true for the sake of the argument, though it is false. If indeed it is true (it isn't) that dead men are never raised from the dead, then we are liars. Why? Because we said, as we called God to witness, that He raised Christ, which He did not do. *Cf.#98* for κατά with the genitive with verbs of swearing. Paul is not only a liar; he is a perjurer. He testified falsely under oath.

How then could the Corinthians believe anything else in the gospel story if Paul lied about the most important part? The credibility gap created by the conclusion that Paul lied about the resurrection is such as to call in question everything else that he said.

εἴπερ is intensified εἰ, strengthened by ἄρα. *Cf. #'s* 3879 and 995.

Verse 16 - "*For if the dead rise not, then is not Christ raised.*"

εἰ γὰρ νεκροὶ οὐκ ἐγείρονται, οὐδὲ Χριστὸς ἐγήγερται.

"*For if the dead are not raised, then Christ has not been raised.*" . . . *RSV*

εἰ (conditional particle in a first-class condition) 337.

γὰρ (causal conjunction) 105.

νεκροὶ (nom.pl.masc.of νεκρός, subject of ἐγείρονται) 749.

οὐκ (negative particle with the indicative) 130.

ἐγείρονται (3d.per.pl.pres.pass.ind.of ἐγείρω, first-class condition) 125.

οὐδὲ (disjunctive particle) 452.

Χριστὸς (nom.sing.masc.of Χριστός, subject of ἐγήγερται) 4.

ἐγήγερται (3d.per.sing.perf.pass.ind.of ἐγείρω, intensive) 125.

Translation - "*Because if dead men are not raised, neither has Christ been raised.*"

Comment: Another first-class condition as in verses 13,14 and 15. Paul has already made his point, and repeats it only for emphasis. *Cf.* verse 13.

Verse 17 - "And if Christ be not raised, your faith is vain; ye are yet in your sins."

εἰ δὲ Χριστὸς οὐκ ἐγήγερται, ματαία ἡ πίστις ὑμῶν, ἔτι ἐστὲ ἐν ταῖς ἁμαρτίαις ὑμῶν.

"If Christ has not been raised, your faith is futile and you are still in your sins."

. . . RSV

εἰ (conditional particle in a first-class condition) 337.
δὲ (continuative conjunction) 11.
Χριστὸς (nom.sing.masc.of Χριστός, subject of ἐγήγερται) 4.
οὐκ (negative particle with the indicative) 130.
ἐγήγερται (3d.per.sing.perf.pass.ind.of ἐγείρω, intensive) 125.
ματαία (nom.sing.fem.of μάταιος, predicate adjective) 3321.
ἡ (nom.sing.fem.of the article in agreement with πίστις) 9.
πίστις (nom.sing.fem.of πίστις, subject of ἐστιν understood) 728.
ὑμῶν (gen.pl.masc.of σύ, possession) 104.
ἔτι (temporal adverb) 448.
ἐστὲ (2d.per.pl.pres.ind.of εἰμί, aoristic) 86.
ἐν (preposition with the instrumental of cause) 80.
ταῖς (instrumental pl.fem.of the article in agreement with ἁμαρτίαις) 9.
ἁμαρτίαις (instru.pl.fem.of ἁμαρτία, cause) 111.
ὑμῶν (gen.pl.masc.of σύ, possession) 104.

Translation - "And if Christ has not been raised, your faith is void of significance. You are still dead because of your sins."

Comment: Note verse 14 where Paul used κενή (#1836), a close synonym of ματαία (#3321). We can supply νενεκρωμένον with ἐστὲ and translate "you are yet dead (perfect periphrastic) because of your sins." *Cf.* John 8:21,24 where we have ἐν ταῖς ἁμαρτίαις in a causal sense as here.

The force of Romans 4:25 is lost, unless Christ arose. *Cf.* comment on Romans 4:25 - "raised again *because of* our justification." If He is not raised, then there is no justification. The doctrine of justification, forgiveness, redemption, pardon - it all depends upon the fact of the bodily resurrection of our Lord, for only if He arose, as He predicted, can we be sure that the man on the cross was God incarnate. The Romans crucified many people - two others on that same day. What was unique about Jesus of Nazareth?

Thus Paul stands like Gibraltar against the demythologization of Rudolf Karl Bultmann, the German theologian, who sought to rid the Scriptures, especially those in the Gospels of what he called mythical elements that he said had no application or relevance to contemporary concerns. Strongly influenced by the existentialism of Martin Heidegger, Bultmann is proof that when we allow existentialism, with its emphasis upon the present, to destroy our faith in the objectivity of the historical record, our faith becomes an empty exercise in religious cant, with no power to save either the individual or society. Neither Bultmann at the University of Marburg nor any other German theologian of his persuasion was able to guard the German people from the deceptions of Adolf Hitler. The fruit was said by our Lord to be an accurate guide to the type of tree which produces it. There were some German Christians who rejected Bultmann and the redactors of Higher Criticism with their documentary hypothesis who also raised their voices in protest against the Nazis. One of them, Dietrich Bonhoeffer, died before a Nazi firing squad in 1945. Bultmann's theology, bereft of its supernaturalism, offered no effective opposition to the philosophy of Hitler. He died in 1976, having lived out his days.

Verse 18 - "Then they also which are fallen asleep in Christ are perished."

ἄρα καὶ οἱ κοιμηθέντες ἐν Χριστῷ ἀπώλοντο.

"Then those also who have fallen asleep in Christ have perished." . . . *RSV*

ἄρα (illative particle) 995.
καὶ (continuative conjunction) 14.
οἱ (nom.pl.masc.of the article in agreement with κοιμηθέντες) 9.
κοιμηθέντες (aor.pass.part.nom.pl.masc.of κοιμάω, substantival, subject of ἀπώλοντο) 1664.
ἐν (preposition with the instrumental of association) 80.
Χριστῷ (instru.sing.masc.of Χριστός, association) 4.
ἀπώλοντο (3d.per.pl.2d.aor.mid.ind.of ἀπόλλυμι, constative) 208.

Translation - "And therefore they who have fallen asleep in Christ have perished."

Comment: *Cf.*#1664 for κοιμάω in the sense of physical death and #208 for ἀπόλλυμι in the sense of spiritual condemnation. Note that those who are still alive and who believe that Christ is alive, though in fact He is dead, are no different from those who regard the gospel as foolishness (1 Cor.1:18), those who think that the gospel smells like death (2 Cor.2:15,16), those who do not understand the gospel (2 Cor.4:3) and those who are deceived by Antichrist (2 Thess.2:10). All men alike are doomed (ἀπόλλυμι), the Christian "believer" no less than the unbeliever, if Christ is dead, since the Christian "believes" something that is not true. The conclusion to which this line of logic leads us in stated in

Verse 19 - "If in this life only we have hope in Christ, we are of all men most miserable."

εἰ ἐν τῇ ζωῇ ταύτῃ ἐν Χριστῷ ἠλπικότες ἐσμὲν μόνον, ἐλεεινότεροι πάντων ἀνθρώπων ἐσμέν.

"If for this life only we have hoped in Christ, we are of all men most to be pitied." . . . *RSV*

εἰ (conditional particle in a first-class condition) 337.

ἐν (preposition with the locative of time point) 80.

τῇ (loc.sing.fem.of the article in agreement with ζωῇ) 9.

ζωῇ (loc.sing.fem.of ζωή, time point) 668.

ταύτῃ (loc.sing.fem.of οὗτος, in agreement with ζωῇ) 93.

ἐν (preposition with the locative of sphere) 80.

Χριστῷ (loc.sing.masc.of Χριστός, sphere) 4.

ἠλπικότες (perf.act.part.nom.pl.masc.of ἐλπίζω, perfect periphrastic) 991.

ἐσμὲν (1st.per.pl.pres.ind.of εἰμί, perfect periphrastic) 86.

μόνον (acc.sing.neut.of μόνος, adverbial) 339.

#4241 ἐλεεινότεροι (nom.pl.masc.of ἐλεεινός, comparative, predicate adjective).

King James Version

miserable - 1 Cor.15:19; Rev.3:17.

Revised Standard Version

most to be pitied - 1 Cor.15:19.
piteable - Rev.3:17.

Meaning: cf.ἐλεέω (#430) and ἐλεήμων (#429). Subject to pity; pitiable; in a miserable state, such as to elicit pity. With reference to the Christian whose hope of eternal life is not soundly based - 1 Cor.15:19; of the unregenerate church member in the tribulation - Rev.3:17.

πάντων (abl.pl.masc.of πᾶς, in agreement with ἀνθρώπων) 67.

ἀνθρώπων (abl.pl.masc.of ἄνθρωπος, comparison) 341.

ἐσμέν (1st.per.pl.pres.ind.of εἰμί, present progressive retroactive) 86.

Translation - "If in this life only we are to indulge a hope in Christ, we are more to be pitied than all men."

Comment: The εἰ clause with the perfect periphrastic in the indicative in the protasis assumes as true what Paul knows is false. The key word is the adverb μόνον. If a continuous trust (perfect periphrastic in ἠλπικότες ἐσμέν) in Christ as incarnate God Who actually rose from the dead (locative of sphere in ἐν Χριστῷ) can be entertained only during this life at the end of which it will be hopelessly dashed and shown to be a cruel hoax, then Christians will be more pitiable than unbelievers who have never believed in immortality and have therefore stoically resigned themselves to the fact that this life is the only life man has. It is better to know the truth, even if to know it is to be robbed of the joy of expectation of life eternal which will never be ours, than it is to have false hopes built up, only to have them dashed. Thus Christians are more to be pitied than sinners if it be true (which it is not) that faith in immortality is only an earthly error to be indulged until we know better.

The apodosis ἐλεεινότεροι πάντων ἀνθρώπων ἐσμέν is true only if the

the premise in the protasis is true. But it is not true that our hope in Christ is disappointed at our death. On the contrary it will be rewarded as we receive the empirical evidence that what we have believed in life is supported by reality.

Paul's lesson in logic (verses 12-19) is finished and he will assail us with no more "if clauses" for a while except for the one in verse 21 where the premise is true and the conclusion is also true. He now asserts the fact of the resurrection of Jesus Christ in the same body in which He suffered.

Verse 20 - "But now is Christ risen from the dead, and become the firstfruits of them that slept."

Νυνὶ δὲ Χριστὸς ἐγήγερται ἐκ νεκρῶν, ἀπαρχὴ τῶν κεκοιμημένων.

"But in fact Christ has been raised from the dead, the first fruits of those who have fallen asleep." . . . *RSV*

Νυνὶ (emphatic conjunction) 1497.
δὲ (adversative conjunction) 11.
Χριστὸς (nom.sing.masc.of Χριστός, subject of ἐγήγερται) 4.
ἐγήγερται (3d.per.sing.perf.pass.ind.of ἐγείρω, intensive) 125.
ἐκ (preposition with the ablative of separation) 19.
νεκρῶν (abl.pl.masc.of νεκρός, separation) 749.
ἀπαρχὴ (nom.sing.masc.of ἀπαρχή, apposition) 3946.
τῶν (gen.pl.masc.of the article in agreement with κεκοιμημένων) 9.
κεκοιμημένων (perf.mid.part.gen.pl.masc.of κοιμάω, substantival, description) 1664.

Translation - "But in fact Christ has been raised from the dead, the first fruit of those who have been sleeping."

Comment: The fact of Christ's resurrection is now categorically stated. Having been raised (ἐγήγερται, a perfect tense) from the dead in a completed action in the past, the present continuous result is that He is now alive, and will always remain alive. Paul says in Romans 6:9 the same thing that he says here with the perfect tense in ἐγήγερται.

Our ever living Lord is the Sovereign Conqueror over death, both spiritual and physical. As such He is the ἀπαρχή (#3946). He was the choice part of the harvest. The harvester takes the best first. He is the evidence that the vine, having borne the first fruit will also bear other fruit which will be harvested later. Thus the first fruit is the evidence of a full harvest. All fruit depends upon the emergence of the ἀπαρχή. He is the root of resurrection. His resurrection guarantees that there will be others.

In point of time Christ's resurrection was not first. There were resurrections in the Old Testament (1 Kings 17:17-24; 2 Kings 4:18-37). Lazarus (John 11:1-46), the daughter of Jairus (Mt.9:18-26; Mark 5:22-43) and the son of the widow of Nain (Lk.7:11-17) were raise before Christ, but also because of His resurrection. The power of His resurrection extended backward as well as forward in time. Both Enoch and Elijah are examples of victory over death, thanks to the first fruit. They are suggestive of all of the saints who will survive until the Second Coming. Not all of the members of the Body of Christ will "sleep," as Paul will tell us in verse 51 (1 Thess.4:17).

"O joy, O delight, should we go without dying!"

Those who do will escape death because He arose from the dead. Those who do not will be rescued from death.

Verse 21 - "For since by man came death, by man came also the resurrection of the dead."

ἐπειδὴ γὰρ δι᾽ ἀνθρώπου θάνατος, καὶ δι᾽ ἀνθρώπου ἀνάστασις νεκρῶν.

"For as by a man came death, by a man has come also the resurrection of the dead." . . . RSV

ἐπειδὴ (compound conditional conjunction, in a first-class condition) 2148.
γὰρ (inferential conjunction) 105.
δι᾽ (preposition with the ablative of agent) 118.
ἀνθρώπου (abl.sing.masc.of ἄνθρωπος, agent) 341.
θάνατος (nom.sing.masc.of θάνατος, subject of verb understood) 381.
καὶ (adjunctive conjunction joining nouns) 14.
δι᾽ (preposition with the ablative of agent) 118.
ἀνθρώπου (abl.sing.masc.of ἄνθρωπος, agent) 341.
ἀνάστασις (nom.sing.fem.of ἀνάστασις, subject of verb understood) 1423.
νεκρῶν (abl.pl.masc.of νεκρός, separation) 749.

Translation - "So since death came through a man, resurrection from death also will come through a man."

Comment: The copulas are not necessary. We can supply ἦν in the first clause and ἔσται in the second. ἐπειδή (#2148) is both causal and conditional - in this case introducing a first-class condition, where the truth of the premise is not in doubt. *Cf.* Luke 7:1 where ἐπειδή is temporal as well as causal.

It was the deliberate disobedience of Adam that brought death, spiritual and physical to the human race (Genesis 2:17; 1 Timothy 2:14). Adam did not die physically on the day that he deliberately disobeyed God, but lived on for 930 years and then died (Genesis 5:5). But the seeds of physical death worked in his body without fail every day of his long life. Physical death passed genetically to the race through Adam's genes (Gen.5:8,11,14,17,20,27,31, etc.) But Adam died spiritually that day, becaue his deliberate transgression of the rule which he understood perfectly separated him from God until he was regenerated, at which time the broken fellowship was restored. Indeed Adam's relationship to God was greater and better after his regeneration than that which he enjoyed before he fell. So with all of Adam's race (Eph.2:1; Rom.3:23; 5:12-14).

Our passage teaches what some theologians call "federal headship" theology. But God does not condemn the entire race because of Adam's sin. Men since have been born with sinful natures, because they are genetically descended from

Adam. Thus they are sinners by nature from the moment of conception, but they are not sinners by choice until that first moment, when, having reached the age of discretion they deliberately disobey that which they clearly understand to be the command of God. Then they sin "after the similitude of Adam's transgression" (Romans 5:14). Then they become transgressors. God does not condemn sinners; He does condemn transgressors. Since sin is any want of conformity to the holy nature of God, little children, by that definition are sinners, but they are not transgressors. It is not the fault of a baby that, like David, he was "shapen in iniquity and conceived in sin" (Psalm 51:5) and God does not hold the baby morally responsible, but it is his fault when he does what he knows is contrary to the will of God. Eve was deceived by Satan. She thought that she was doing the right thing when she ate the forbidden fruit. But Adam was not deceived. He walked into that situation and ate the fruit with his eyes wide open. He could not plead that although he was mistaken, he was sincerely mistaken. If "federal headship" theology teaches that infants who die in infancy are lost because they are members of the race it is wrong. Whether theologians of this school have ever taught this is in dispute. When we consider that a large percentage of the human race have died in infancy, and that although little babies who die are not saved, they are *safe* we reach the conclusion that heaven will be more densely populated than hell. This fact serves to make Calvinism a little more palatable. It goes a long way to rescue the system from the image, falsely conceived and falsely described that says that the vast majority of Adam's fallen race will find their eternal destiny in hell and that only a few will be saved.

Just as those born in the first Adam are sinners by nature and certain to transgress God's law when they understand it, so the members of the Body of the last Adam are "born from above" (John 3:3,7) with sinless natures, which cannot sin because they are born of God. The members of the new body constitute a new race, made up of God's regenerated people. Through Him Who died for them and rose again because on the cross He gained their justification (Rom.4:25) comes the resurrection life now, in terms of its superior quality and the glorification of physical resurrection when He comes again.

Cf. our comments on Romans 5:18.

Verse 22 - "For as in Adam all die, even so in Christ shall all be made alive."

ὥσπερ γὰρ ἐν τῷ Ἀδὰμ πάντες ἀποθνῄσκουσιν, οὕτως καὶ ἐν τῷ Χριστῷ πάντες ζῳοποιηθήσονται.

"For as in Adam all die, so also in Christ shall all be made alive." . . . RSV

ὥσπερ (intensive particle introducing a comparative clause) 560.
γὰρ (inferential conjunction) 105.
ἐν (preposition with the locative of sphere) 80.
τῷ (loc.sing.masc.of the article in agreement with Ἀδὰμ) 9.
Ἀδὰμ (loc.sing.masc.of Ἀδάμ, sphere) 1774.
πάντες (nom.pl.masc.of πᾶς, subject of ἀποθνῄσκουσιν) 67.
ἀποθνῄσκουσιν (3d.per.pl.pres.act.ind.of ἀποθνῄσκω, static) 774.

οὗτως (demonstrative adverb) 74.

καὶ (adjunctive conjunction joining prepositional phrases) 14.

ἐν (preposition with the locative of sphere) 80.

τῷ (loc.sing.masc.of the article in agreement with Χριστῷ) 9.

Χριστῷ (loc.sing.masc.of Χριστός, sphere) 4.

πάντες (nom.pl.masc.of πᾶς, subject of ζωοποιηθήσονται) 67.

ζωοποιηθήσονται (3d.per.pl.fut.pass.ind.of ζωοποιέω, predictive) 2098.

Translation - "So exactly as it is that all those in Adam die, even so also all those in Christ will always live."

Comment: Note the intensifying force of περ in ὥσπερ (#560), and the correlative οὗτως (#74). "In precisely the same way as . . . just so will . . . "

It is man's genetic relationship with Adam that produced his propensity to sin as a baby and transgress as a man. The result is death. But there is another sphere of redemptive activity operating in the universe thanks to the incarnation of our Lord. It is also the believer's relationship with Christ that brings his salvation with its result of everlasting life.

The prepositional phrases ἐν τῷ ʼΑδὰμ and ἐν τῷ Χριστῷ are locatives of sphere. Note that Paul is careful to add the article in both phrases to accentuate the fact that there is one Adamic sphere and there is also another sphere in Jesus Christ. Those is the sphere of Adam share his sinful nature, his guilt and his death as transgression's penalty. Those in the sphere of Christ share His sinless nature, His intimate fellowship with the Father and the Holy Spirit (John 17:21; 1 Cor.6:19,20) and His victory over death and life everlasting. The articles make both Adam and Christ definite. Thus the two men of verse 21 are identified.

Universalists have tried hard, without success to make this passage teach their view that just as the quantitative whole died in Adam, so the same quantitative whole will live in Christ. The substantive πάντες in the first clause does indeed include the entire human race. We were all born physically ἐν τῷ ʼΑδάμ, and in him we sinned, transgressed and died. But the substantive πάντες in the second clause refers only to all of those who are ἐν τῷ Χριστῷ. These are those who shall live in glory. These are the elect (1 Peter 1:2; Romans 8:29-30; Eph.1:4).

Notice that the Son makes alive those οὓς θέλει - "whom He will," (John 5:21). The Son treats the elect exactly as the Father treated Him. *Cf.* 1 Tim.6:13; 1 Cor.15:45.

The first fruit (ἀπαρχή, verse 20) gives assurance that the remainder of the harvest will be forthcoming in God's good time.

Verse 23 - "But every man in his own order: Christ, the firstfruits: afterward they that are Christ's at his coming."

ἕκαστος δὲ ἐν τῷ ἰδίῳ τάγματι. ἀπαρχὴ Χριστός, ἔπειτα οἱ τοῦ Χριστοῦ ἐν τῇ παρουσίᾳ αὐτοῦ.

"But each in his own order; Christ the first fruits, then at his coming those who belong to Christ." . . . RSV

ἕκαστος (nom.sing.masc.of ἕκαστος, nominative absolute) 1217.
δὲ (adversative conjunction) 11.
ἐν (preposition with the locative of time point) 80.
τῷ (loc.sing.neut.of the article in agreement with τάγματι) 9.
ἰδίῳ (loc.sing.neut.of ἴδιος, in agreement with τάγματι) 778.

#4242 τάγματι (loc.sing.neut.of τάγμα, time point).

King James Version

order - 1 Cor.15:23.

Revised Standard Version

order - 1 Cor.15:23.

Meaning: Cf. τάσσω (#722). Hence the result of an arrangement. That which has been arranged. A body of soldiers; a corps assembled. In the New Testament of the groups or individuals to be resurrected. First Christ, then believers - 1 Cor.15:23.

ἀπαρχή (nom.sing.fem.of ἀπαρχή, nominative absolute) 3946.
Χριστός (nom.sing.masc.of Χριστός, apposition) 4.
ἔπειτα (temporal adverb) 2566.
οἱ (nom.pl.masc.of the article, nominative absolute) 9.
τοῦ (gen.sing.masc.of the article in agreement with Χριστοῦ) 9.
Χριστοῦ (gen.sing.masc.of Χριστός, relationship) 4.
ἐν (preposition with the locative of time point) 80.
τῇ (loc.sing.fem.of the article in agreement with παρουσίᾳ) 9.
παρουσίᾳ (loc.sing.fem.of παρουτσία, time point) 1482.
αὐτοῦ (gen.sing.masc.of αὐτός, possession) 16.

Translation - "But each one in his own order: the first fruits, Christ; afterward those belonging to Christ at His coming."

Comment: The resurrection process is the work of Christ (verse 23). But He is demonstrated to be "the resurrection and the life" (John 11:25) only by the fact of His own resurrection (Rom.4:25; Heb.5:1-10; John 14:19 *q.v.*). Thus the entire issue of immortality, life beyond this present life and victory over death was not resolved until the Firstfruits was raised. Had He not risen neither would those who believe upon Him rise, and we would be the victims of a cruel hoax and a pious fraud (verse 19).

The time point of ἔπειτα is defined by the locative phrase ἐν τῇ παρουσίᾳ αὐτοῦ. *Cf.*#1482 for παρουσία in connection with His Second Coming. His disciples asked about it (Mt.24:3) and associated it with the end of the age; it will not be a secret event (Mt.24:27); it will follow a time of great moral decline upon the earth (Mt.24:37); the unsaved will not believe in it (Mt.24:39; 2 Pet.3:4). The saints will be there with Him (1 Thess.2:19); all of the saints will be there (1 Thess.3:13); some Christians will not die before He comes (1 Thess.4:15). Paul nraved for all saints to be preserved blameless until His coming (1 Thess.5:23). He will destroy the Antichrist when He comes (2 Thess.2:8). Saints should wait patiently for it (James 5:7), for it is not long remote (James 5:8). It will be a glorious event (2 Pet.1:16). The saints will never again be ashamed (1 John 2:28).

Many passages tie the παρουσία of Christ to the last day of Daniel's 70th week, which is the last day of the Great Tribulation. To expect a παρουσία at the beginning of the tribulation, which results in the position, often heard, that it is imminent is pure eisegesis and is doing incalculable harm in the 20th century evangelical circles in which it is being taught. The παρουσία *may be* very near at the time this is written (18 September 1982), perhaps not much more than seven years in the future. There is no way to tell precisely at this point, but it is *not* imminent, in the sense that it is the next scheduled prophetic event.

Verse 24 - "Then cometh the end, when he shall have delivered up the kingdom of God, even the Father; when he shall have put down all rule and all authority and power."

εἶτα τὸ τέλος, ὅταν παραδιδῷ τὴν βασιλείαν τῷ θεῷ καὶ πατρί, ὅταν καταργήσῃ πᾶσαν ἀνρχὴν καὶ πᾶσαν ἐξουσίαν καὶ δύναμιν.

"Then comes the end, when he delivers the kingdom to God the Father after destroying every rule and every authority and power." . . . RSV

εἶτα (temporal adverb) 2185.
τὸ (nom.sing.neut.of the article in agreement with τέλος) 9.
τέλος (nom.sing.neut.of τέλος, subject of verb understood) 881.
ὅταν (conjunction with the subjunctive in an indefinite temporal clause) 436.
παραδιδῷ (3d.per.sing.pres.act.subj.of παραδίδωμι, indefinite temporal clause) 368.
τὴν (acc.sing.fem.of the article in agreement with βασιλείαν) 9.
βασιλείαν (acc.sing.fem.of βασιλεία, direct object of παραδιδῷ) 253.
τῷ (dat.sing.masc.of the article in agreement with θεῷ) 9.
θεῷ (dat.sing.masc.of θεός, indirect object of παραδιδῷ) 124.
καὶ (ascensive conjunction) 14.
πατρί (dat.sing.masc.of πατήρ, indirect object of παραδιδῷ) 238.
ὅταν (conjunction with the subjunctive in an indefinite temporal clause) 436.
καταργήσῃ (3d.per.sing.aor.act.subj.of καταργέω, indefinite temporal clause) 2500.
πᾶσαν (acc.sing.fem.of πᾶς in agreement with ἀρχὴν) 67.
ἀρχὴν (acc.sing.fem.of ἀρχή, direct object of καταργήσῃ) 1285.
καὶ (adjunctive conjunction joining nouns) 14.
πᾶσαν (acc.sing.fem.of πᾶς, in agreement with ἐξουσίαν) 67.
ἐξουσίαν (acc.sing.fem.of ἐξουσία, direct object of καταργήσῃ) 707.
καὶ (adjunctive conjunction joining nouns) 14.
δύναμιν (acc.sing.fem.of δύναμις, direct object of καταργήσῃ) 687.

Translation - "Then the end, when He shall have completed the delivery of the kingdom to God, even the Father, when He shall have put an end to all government and all authority and power."

Comment: Three events are being listed in the order of their occurrence: (1) the resurrection of Jesus Christ, (2) His second coming and the resurrection of the dead in Christ and the rapture of the living and (3) the final overthrow of all human opposition to God and the final delivery of the kingdom to the Father.

The first event took place on the third day after the crucifixion. The second is posttribulational and premillenial. The third is postmillenial. More than nineteen centuries have already separated the first from the second, and at this point there is no way to tell how much more time will elapse before the second coming. Exactly one thousand years will separate the second from the third. Verse 24 describes the postmillenial picture. τὸ τέλος is the end of time as counted by human beings. Christ will then have delivered (culminative aorist in παραδῷ) all the power given to Him at His resurrection (Mt.28:18) which He will have exercised during the millenium (Rev.20:4,6) to the Father. He will also have (culminative aorist in καταργήσῃ) put down (overcome, defeated, phased out) all opposition to the divine order. This makes clear that this is a postmillenial picture since Satan's last revolt against God, which will be speedily destroyed, will come at the end of the thousand year reign of Christ (Rev.20:7-10). The last indefinite temporal clause could not be said to have described an event at the second coming.

His coming (ἐν τῇ παρουσίᾳ) of verse 23 is premillenial, though posttribulational. Verse 24 is postmillenial, at the end of time and the beginning of eternity future.

Paul continues to explain all of this through verse 28.

Verse 25 - "For he must reign, till he hath put all enemies under his feet."

δεῖ γὰρ αὐτὸν βασιλεύειν ἄχρι οὗ θῇ πάντας τοὺς ἐχθροὺς ὑπὸ τοὺς πόδας αὐτοῦ.

"For he must reign until he has put all his enemies under his feet.". . . RSV

δεῖ (pres.ind.of δεῖ, impersonal) 1207.

γὰρ (causal conjunction) 105.

αὐτὸν (acc.sing.masc.of αὐτός, general reference) 16.

βασιλεύειν (pres.act.inf.of βασιλεύω, epexegetical) 236.

ἄχρι (preposition with the genitive of time description) 1517.

οὗ (gen.sing.neut.of ὅς, relative pronoun, time description) 65.

θῇ (3d.per.sing.2d.aor.act.subj.of τίθημι, in an indefinite temporal clause) 455.

πάντας (acc.pl.masc.of πᾶς, in agreement with ἐχθροὺς) 67.

τοὺς (acc.pl.masc.of the article in agreement with ἐχθροὺς) 9.

ἐχθροὺς (acc.pl.masc.of ἐχθρός, direct object of θῇ) 543.

ὑπὸ (preposition with the accusative of extent) 117.

τοὺς (acc.pl.masc.of the article in agreement with πόδας) 9.

πόδας (acc.pl.masc.of πούς, extent) 353.

αὐτοῦ (gen.sing.masc.of αὐτός, possession) 16.

Translation - "Because it is necessary for Him to reign until he shall have put all the enemies under His feet."

Comment: The quotation is from Psalm 8:6 and Psalm 110:1. If our Lord gave back to the Father the authority of the Kingdom of God (verse 24) before the end of the millenium, He would be relinquishing His power at a time when there was still unfinished business, for Satan's last revolt, another unsuccessful *coup d' etat*, will terminate the Kingdom Age (the millenium) and mark the end of time, as men count time, and the beginning of eternity. Thus what Lucifer attempted and failed (Isaiah 14:12-15; Ezek.28:11-19; Luke 10:18) at the beginning of his diabolical career he will attempt and fail to achieve again as his last act of rebellion. Then he will be thrown into hell, bag and baggage, not to assume his role as King of Hell but honored with the dubious distinction of being hell's chief victim. He will enjoy a tenure in his position never to be taken from him. There will be no retirement nor retirement benefits.

Cast out of heaven for his pains in his first attempt to seize power, Satan attacked Eve with deception and through her, brought about the fall of God's crowning achievement in creation (Genesis 3:1-6), only to be told that he had overplayed his hand again and that just as he had used the woman to bring about the downfall of the human race, God would use her to bring about its redemption (Genesis 3:15) in the process of which Satan's head would be bruised. And so it was that "through death (Jesus) destroyed him that had the power of death, that is the devil, and delivered them who through all of their lifetime were subject to bondage" (Heb.2:14).

The devil has really been out of business since Calvary insofar as his control over the elect, for whom Christ died, and who are destined to be incorporated into the Body of Christ, is concerned. He is still the "god of this world" (2 Cor.4:4) and "the spirit that works in the children of disobedience" (Eph.2:2), and he will drag down to his own miserable fate those who insist upon believing his lies, but he is only the "strong man" armed, he thinks to the teeth and therefore able to secure the goods in his palace, who met at a place called Golgotha, a "stronger man" who came in, overcame him, disarmed him and took all that He wanted (Luke 11:21,22). And since the "stronger man" is "greater than he that is in the world" (1 John 4:4) there is not a chance that the devil will ever be able to recover what he lost in the divine robbery, which he was unable to prevent.

Satan will have his little day - a brief three and one half years - to enjoy his incarnation as king of the earth, when he will reign supreme over his doomed subjects (Rev.13:1-18), but during this time he will be unable to prevent the "stronger man" from taking the rest of his goods which our Lord bought at the cross (Rev.10:7), and at the end of his brief tenure, Antichrist will be cast into the lake of fire (Rev.19:19-21) there to await the coming of the devil himself one thousand years later (Rev.20:7-10).

The judgments visited upon Satan, the Antichrist, the False Prophet , the demons and their victims are only the implementations of God's decree which was issued at the time of our Lord's second advent. He could not descend from His position at the Father's right hand in glory until God had "made His enemies His footstool" (Psalm 110:1). The student should keep in mind that God is not a creature of time and space relations. God ruled that Christ was supreme over all His foes when the last elect soul for whom He died became the last member to be incorporated into His body. This will occur "in the days of the voice of the seventh angel when he shall begin to sound . . . " (Rev. 10:7). Then the "mystery of God (will) be finished, as he hath declared to his servants the prophets" and as He revealed in total clarity to Paul (Eph. 3:1-11).

The alert student will note that the seventh trumpet of Rev. 10:7 and Rev. 11:15-19 will be "the last trump" of 1 Cor. 15:52) - (when will we hear a later one?) and that it will signal our Lord's descent "from heaven, with a shout with the voice of the archangel and with the trumpet of God" (1 Thess. 4:16-18). He cannot leave the Father's right hand a single moment, nor three and one half years, nor seven years *before* this time, because His enemies, though potentially judged will not be actually placed beneath His feet until His redemptive work is implemented by the regeneration of the last elect soul whom He purchased at the cross. Indeed Satan will never have enjoyed his hellish dominance over the earth as he will during this seven years, (with these powers of control intensified during the last half of the period), and he will never enjoy this power again, after his incarnations (Antichrist and the False Prophet) are thrown headlong into hell and he is locked up in the abyss for one thousand years.

Thus the position that the rapture of the living saints and the resurrection of those who have died cannot occur until the fulfillment of Psalm 110:1 is not threatened by those who argue that if we take Psalm 110:1 literally we cannot have a return of Christ until the end of the millenium. What God has decreed in His eternal plan is carried out in historic time. God decreed the salvation of the reader of these lines, if in fact the reader is a Christian, but His decree was not implemented until that day when the Holy Spirit called him to repentance and faith. The indefinite temporal clause ἕως ἂν ϑῶ τοὺς ἐχϑρούς σου ὑποπόδιον in Heb. 1:13 "has an actual future reference" (Mantey, *Manual*, 281). This is reinforced by the presence of ἄν. Thus it is indefinite (subjunctive in ϑῶ) only with reference to the precise time point, but it is definite in that it points to an event that is certain to occur. Thus we are justified in locating the fulfillment of Psalm 110:1 at a definite point in time, and it has nothing to do with the eternal decree of God that finds its implementation in time. Our Lord will descend from heaven at some definite point in time which is still future to the time of this writing (20 September 1982), but He must remain at the Father's right hand *until* an actual future time point has been reached. This takes the interpretation out of the realm of the eternal, in which God's operates and places it within the realm of our temporal reckoning.

Verse 26 - "The last enemy that shall be destroyed is death."

ἔσχατος ἐχϑρὸς καταργεῖται ὁ ϑάνατος.

"The last enemy to be destroyed is death." . . . RSV

ἔσχατος (nom.sing.masc.of ἔσχατος, in agreement with ἐχϑρὸς) 496.
ἐχϑρὸς (nom.sing.masc.of ἐχϑρός, predicate nominative) 543.
καταργεῖται (3d.per.sing.pres.pass.ind.of καταργέω, futuristic) 2500.
ὁ (nom.sing.masc.of the article in agreement with ϑάνατος) 9.
ϑάνατος (nom.sing.masc.of ϑάνατος, subject of καταργεῖται) 381.

Translation - "Death is the last enemy that will be overthrown."

Comment: καταργεῖται is a futuristic present. Just as all three kinds of action are found in the present, *viz.* punctiliar, durative, perfective, so all three kinds of time are found in the present indicative. Thus the historical present (the past) and the futuristic present (the future) as well as the immediate present. (Robertson, *Grammar*, 869). The point involved is certainty of expectation. One uses it when he is certain that the predicted event will take place. Paul was in no doubt about it. Death, the enemy of mankind, because sin, of which it is the payment (Rom.6:23) is also the enemy of mankind, will be the last enemy of God and man to be overthrown (Rev.20:13-14). Thus in His last official act as Messiah, Jesus Christ, Who is life (John 11:25) will abolish (banish, overthrow, phase out, terminate) death in His own eternal kingdom and consign it to hell where it belongs. Since καταργέω (#2500) means to be rendered totally inoperative, death, in the sense of annihilation of consciousness, will be unable to rescue the lost whose punishment in hell will be eternal. Death in that sense, if it in fact functioned in that manner, would be a boon to the lost (Rev.9:6) if it were available to them.

Verse 27 - "For he hath put all things under his feet. But when he saith all things are put under him, it is manifest that he is excepted, which did put all things under him."

πάντα γὰρ ὑπέταξεν ὑπὸ τοὺς πόδας αὐτοῦ.ὅταν δὲ εἴπῃ ὅτι πάντα ὑποτέτακται, δῆλον ὅτι ἐκτὸς τοῦ ὑποτάξαντος αὐτῷ τὰ πάντα.

" 'For God has put all things in subjection under his feet.' But when it says, 'All things are put in subjection under him,' it is plain that he is excepted who put all things under him." . . . RSV

πάντα (acc.pl.neut.of πᾶς, direct object of ὑπέταξεν) 67.
γὰρ (causal conjunction) 105.
ὑπέταξεν (3d.per.sing.aor.act.ind.of ὑποτάσσω, culminative) 1921.
ὑπὸ (preposition with the accusative of extent) 117.
τοὺς (acc.pl.masc.of the article in agreement with πόδας) 9.
πόδας (acc.pl.masc.of πούς, extent) 353.
αὐτοῦ (gen.sing.masc.of αὐτός, possession) 16.
ὅταν (conjunction introducing an indefinite temporal clause) 436.

δὲ (adversative conjunction) 11.

εἴπῃ (3d.per.sing.aor.act.subj.of εἶπον, indefinite temporal clause) 155.

ὅτι (conjunction introducing an object clause in indirect discourse) 211.

πάντα (nom.pl.neut.of πᾶς, subject of ὑποτέτακται) 67.

ὑποτέτακται (3d.per.sing.perf.pass.ind.of ὑποτάσσω, culminative) 1921.

δῆλον (acc.sing.neut.of δῆλος, predicate adjective) 1612.

ὅτι (conjunction introducing an object clause in indirect discourse) 211.

ἐκτὸς (preposition with the ablative) 1461.

τοῦ (abl.sing.masc.of the article in agreement with ὑποτάξαντος) 9.

ὑποτάξαντος (1st.aor.act.part.abl.sing.masc.of ὑποτάσσω, separation) 1921.

αὐτῷ (dat.sing.masc.of αὐτός, personal advantage) 16.

τὰ (acc.pl.neut.of the article in agreement with πάντα) 9.

πάντα (acc.pl.neut.of πᾶς, direct object of ὑποτάξαντος) 67.

Translation - "Because He put all things under His feet. But when He said that **all things** *are to be subjected, it is obvious that the One who subjected all things to Him is not included."*

Comment: The aorist ὑπέταξεν is effective (culminative) as is the perfect passive ὑποτέτακται. God has decreed that, before the divine plan of redemption has been completed, everything will be subordinated to Jesus Christ. This is potential and it is certain to be fulfilled, since it it God's decree. Empirically it had not been carried out in Paul's day, nor has it in ours. *Cf.* Acts 2:35; Mt.22:44; Mk.12:36; Lk.20:43; Heb.1;13 and Heb.10:13 all of which quote Psalm 110:1.

Our Lord is now at the Father's right hand in an anthroporphic and spatial sense, although "the right hand of the Father" can never be interpreted anthropomorphically, since God the Father has no hands in the physical sense (Heb.1:3; Rom.8:34; Mt.26:64; Mk.14:62; Lk.22:69; Acts 2:33; 5:31; 7:55,56; Eph.1:20; Col.3:1; Heb.8:1; 10:12; 12:2; 1 Pet.3:22). He will leave that position to return to earth one thousand years before the ultimate empirical subjection of His enemies referred to in 1 Cor.15:25. To say that Christ will remain physically at the "right hand of God the Father" in heaven until His enemies are all subjected to Him in an empirical sense, is to postpone the second coming, with its judgment upon Antichrist, until the end of the millenium. Thus we have either postmillenialism or amillenialism, both of which are embarrassed by Revelation 20 in which the phrase "a thousand years" occurs six times (vss. 2, 3, 4, 5, 6 and 7). *Cf.* our comment on verse 25. And yet in verse 27 it seems proper to interpret Psalm 110:1 to mean that God regards the resurrected Jesus as his "right hand man" whom He fully supports and in behalf of Whom the Father subjugates all His enemies under His feet, after which the Son surrenders the Kingdom to the Father (verse 28). This interpretation does not preclude the physical departure of Jesus from the Father's right hand and descent to David's throne in Jerusalem at the beginning of the millenium. Our Lord will still be sitting "at the right hand of God" during the Kingdom Age (though physically upon the earth in Jerusalem) as God's Vice-Regent.

Paul adds that the statement "He put all things under His (Christ's) feet" obviously does not mean that the Father is not included in the phrase "all things." Everything and everyone else except the Father, is subordinate to Christ, and our Lord's total superordinate control over all His enemies will have been exercised in full when the judgments of the Great White Throne at the end of the millenium will have been carried out. Then He will take His place at the Father's disposal. This is the thought of

Verse 28 - "And when all things shall be subdued unto him, then shall the Son also himself be subject unto him that put all things under him, that God may be all in all."

ὅταν δὲ ὑποταγῇ αὐτῷ τὰ πάντα, τότε (καὶ) αὐτὸς ὁ υἱὸς ὑποταγήσεται τῷ ὑποτάξαντι αὐτῷ τὰ πάντα, ἵνα ᾖ ὁ θεὸς (τὰ) πάντα ἐν πᾶσιν.

"When all things are subjected to him, then the Son himself will also be subjected to him who put all things under him, that God may be everything to every one." . . . RSV

ὅταν (conjunction with the subjunctive in an indefinite temporal clause) 436.

δὲ (continuative conjunction) 11.

ὑποταγῇ (3d.per.sing.2d.aor.pass.subj.of ὑποτάσσω, in an indefinite temporal clause) 1921.

αὐτῷ (dat.sing.masc.of αὐτός, personal advantage) 16.

τὰ (nom.pl.neut.of the article in agreement with πάντα) 9.

πάντα (nom.pl.neut.of πᾶς, subject of ὑποταγῇ) 67.

τότε (temporal adverb) 166.

καὶ (adjunctive conjunction joining substantives) 14.

αὐτὸς (nom.sing.masc.of αὐτός, in agreement with υἱὸς, intensive) 16.

ὁ (nom.sing.masc.of the article in agreement with υἱὸς) 9.

υἱὸς (nom.sing.masc.of υἱός, subject of ὑποταγήσεται) 5.

ὑποταγήσεται (3d.per.sing.2d.fut.mid.ind.of ὑποτάσσω, predictive) 1921.

τῷ (dat.sing.masc.of the article in agreement with ὑποτάξαντι) 9.

ὑποτάξαντι (aor.act.part.dat.sing.masc.of ὑποτάσσω, personal advantage) 1921.

αὐτῷ (dat.sing.masc.of αὐτός, personal advantage) 16.

τὰ (acc.pl.neut.of the article in agreement with πάντα) 9.

πάντα (acc.pl.neut.of πᾶς, direct object of ὑποτάξαντι) 67.

ἵνα (conjunction with the subjunctive in a sub-final clause) 114.

ᾖ (3d.per.sing.pres.subj.of εἰμί, sub-final clause) 86.

ὁ (nom.sing.masc.of the article in agreement with θεὸς) 9.

θεὸς (nom.sing.masc.of θεός, subject of ᾖ) 124.

τὰ (nom.pl.neut.of the article in agreement with πάντα) 9.

πάντα (nom.pl.neut.of πᾶς, predicate nominative) 67.

ἐν (preposition with the locative of sphere) 80.

πᾶσιν (loc.pl.neut.of πᾶς, sphere) 67.

Translation - "And when all things have been made subject to Him, then also the Son Himself will subject Himself to Him Who subjected all things to Him, in order (and with the result) that God may be supreme in all areas."

Comment: ὅταν with the subjunctive ὑποταγῇ implies no doubt that all will be subject to Christ. The doubt has to do only with the precise time when the millenial reign of Messiah will end. Nor do we know at the time of this writing when it will end, since we do not know the time of the beginning of Daniel's 70th week. Once that date is established, it is only a matter of counting forward 1007 years.

When the very short and very decisive battle which Satan will start and which our Lord will finish forthwith, at the close of the Kingdom Age, is over (Rev.20:7-10; 2 Pet.3:10), Christ will be supreme over all. On that day the Son Himself (intensive αὐτὸς in the predicate position) will voluntarily subject Himself (middle voice in ὑποταγήσεται) to the One Who subjected all to Him. Why? The ἵνα clause is both purpose and result - hence sub-final - "In order (and with the result) that God may be supreme in every sphere" of activity in the universe.

This subordination of Christ to the Father is not coerced. The verb is in the middle voice. The same spirit that made the Lamb of God submissive to the will of the Father before the foundation of the world (Rev.13:8) will again lead Him to His eternal position in the Godhead.

This creates problems for some who fear that the teaching is that since Jesus Christ will be subordinate to the Father in administrative activity throughout eternity, He is something less than Deity. Analogies are never totally helpful but they shed some light. Administration involves three functions: The law making function is carried out by the legislature. The function of adjudication of the law which the legislature enacts is the work of the Supreme Court. Once the law is enacted by the Congress and declared pursuant to the constitution by the Supreme Court, it is then executed by the Executive. Enactment of the law, its judicial review and the execution of its mandates are coordinate functions and are carried out by coordinate entities. The power balance between the three is not precise in the experience of the United States across time, but within the Godhead the balance of power in the division of labor is most precise. The Holy Spirit is inferior to the Son neither in power, intelligence, dignity, prestige nor in any other way. Nor is the Son in any sense inferior to the Father. Administratively their functions are different.

This completes Paul's analysis of the redemptive role of the Incarnate Son of God in the plan of salvation. The Last Adam rescued that which the First Adam lost. He died, He arose, He will reign and demonstrate before His suzerainty is over that He is supreme in executive power and administrative authority over all who would resist Him (Mt.28:18; Eph.1:17-23; Phil.2:5-11).

Now Paul, with a touch of whimsy needles his audience with a very logical question in

Verse 29 - "Else what shall they do which are baptized for the dead, if the dead

rise not at all? Why are they then baptized for the dead?"

Ἐπεὶ τί ποιήσουσιν οἱ βαπτιζόμενοι ὑπὲρ τῶν νεκρῶν; εἰ ὅλως νεκροὶ οὐκ ἐγείρονται, τί καὶ βαπτίζονται ὑπὲρ αὐτῶν;

"Otherwise, what do people mean by being baptized on behalf of the dead? If the dead are not raised at all, why are people baptized on their behalf?" . . . RSV

Ἐπεὶ (compound particle introducing direct question) 1281.

τί (acc.sing.neut.of τίς, interrogative pronoun, direct object of ποιήσουσιν) 281.

ποιήσουσιν (3d.per.pl.fut.act.ind.of ποιέω, deliberative) 127.

οἱ (nom.pl.masc.of the article in agreement with βαπτιζόμενοι) 9.

βαπτιζόμενοι (pres.pass.part.nom.pl.masc.of βαπτίζω, substantival, subject of ποιήσουσιν) 273.

ὑπὲρ (preposition with the ablative, "in behalf of") 545.

τῶν (abl.pl.masc.of the article in agreement with νεκρῶν) 9.

νεκρῶν (abl.pl.masc.of νεκρός, "in behalf of") 749.

εἰ (conditional particle introducing a first-class condition) 337.

ὅλως (adverbial) 517.

νεκροὶ (nom.pl.masc.of νεκρός, subject of ἐγείρονται) 749.

οὐκ (negative particle with the indicative) 130.

ἐγείρονται (3d.per.pl.pres.pass.ind.of ἐγείρω, first-class condition) 125.

τί (acc.sing.neut.of τίς, cause) 281.

καὶ (inferential conjunction) 14.

βαπτίζονται (3d.per.pl.pres.pass.ind.of βαπτίζω, customary) 273.

ὑπὲρ (preposition with the ablative, "in behalf of") 545.

αὐτῶν (abl.pl.masc.of αὐτός, "in behalf of") 16.

Translation - "Otherwise what should those who are being immersed for the dead do? If the dead do not rise at all, why then are they being immersed for them?"

Comment: The first question is direct; the second is rhetorical. If we construe ἐπεὶ as conditional we must supply the protasis. It is the same protasis as the one in the second question. The condition(s) are first-class, with the premise assumed as true in order to make the questions logical. "If the dead do not rise (but they do) what are you who are being immersed for them doing?" The question demands a sensible answer. Either affirm that the dead do in fact arise, or explain this strange rite.

This verse makes no sense at all unless we view it in *zeitgeist*. Apparently the Corinthians knew about some pagan custom in keeping with which the living were immersed in behalf of some one who had died without immersion. Some of them may have even practised this strange custom. Under the Christian system such a practice has no merit, but at the least it indicated that those who did so believed in immortality and also in the resurrection of the body. The Greeks believed in the immortality of the spirit, but rejected the idea of bodily resurrection. Christianity does not teach the immortality of the soul apart from the resurrection of the body, although the body is not essential to consciousness of the soul and spirit after death. Even those who believed in the resurrection of the body could not justify the practice of being immersed in water for the dead.

But even if it were proper Christian practice, it would be illogical if the dead do not rise. That is Paul's point.

It is possible to interpret the passage to mean that some one accepted Christ and was baptized in order to keep a promise made to another Christian who, now dead, had exacted the promise from the candidate when he was still alive. Suppose a Christian said to an unsaved loved one, "Meet me in heaven," and then died before the survivor accepted Christ and was baptized? In that sense it could be said that the candidate was being baptized "for the Christian who was now in heaven."

But there is nothing in Scripture to justify the practice of substitution of one's own faith and obedience in baptism for one who has died without faith and/or baptism. Indeed there is much in Scripture against it. If this was being done in Corinth by the Christians they were wrong, and Paul does not approbate the practice.

It is not known to the writer whether the Mormons point to this passage in support of their practice or whether they depend upon the writings of Joseph Smith or some other guru.

Verse 30 - "And why stand we in jeopardy every hour?"

τί καὶ ἡμεῖς κινδυνεύομεν πᾶσαν ὥραν;

"Why am I in peril every hour?" . . . RSV

τί (acc.sing.neut.of τίς, interrogative pronoun, cause) 281.

καὶ (continuative conjunction) 14.

ἡμεῖς (nom.pl.masc.of ἐγώ, subject of κινδυνεύομεν) 123.

κινδυνεύομεν (1st.per.pl.pres.act.ind.of κινδυνεύω, present iterative retroactive) 2212.

πᾶσαν (acc.sing.fem.of πᾶς, in agreement with ὥραν) 67.

ὥραν (acc.sing.fem.of ὥρα, time extent) 735.

Translation - "And why have we been in danger again and again?"

Comment: Paul is trying to show the Corinthians that the fact of the resurrection of the body and immortality alone is able to explain the rest of the Christian system. If it is not true the rest of the system collapses. (Verses 14-19; 29). The physical risks which the Apostles took in their ministry, as they invited persecution and death at the hands of unbelievers would never be taken, except for the fact that they preached the resurrection of Jesus, that judgment was coming after death for all and that Christ was the only way of salvation. Every hour brought new hazards to life and limb, because they preached that earthly life is only a prelude to eternity.

Verse 31 - "I protest by your rejoicing which I have in Christ Jesus our Lord, I die daily."

καθ᾽ ἡμέραν ἀποθνῄσκω, νὴ τὴν ὑμετέραν καύχησιν, (ἀδελφοί) ἥν ἔχω ἐν Χριστῷ Ἰησοῦ τῷ κυρίῳ ἡμῶν.

"I protest, brethren, by my pride in you which I have in Christ Jesus our Lord, I die every day!" . . . RSV

καθ᾽ (preposition with the accusative, distributive) 98.

ἡμέραν (acc.sing.fem.of ἡμέρα, distributive) 135.

ἀποθνῄσκω (1st.per.sing.pres.act.ind.of ἀποθνῄσκω, present iterative retroactive) 774.

#4243 νὴ (affirmative particle).

King James Version

I protest by - 1 Cor.15:31.

Revised Standard Version

protest - 1 Cor.15:31.

Meaning: a particle used in affirmations or oaths. Joined by an accusative of person or thing by which the oath is taken. "Νή is a peculiarity of the Attic dialect and is used in solemn asseverations   (oaths,etc.) and means 'truly,' 'yes.' It is probably the same word as ναί the affirmative adverb which occurs over thirty times in the N.T." (Robertson, *Grammar*. 1150). - 1 Cor.15:31.

τὴν (acc.sing.fem.of the article in agreement with καύχησιν) 9.

ὑμετέραν (acc.sing.fem.of ὑμέτερος, in agreement with καύχησιν) 2127.

καύχησιν (acc.sing.fem.of καύχησις, accusative of the thing, with an oath) 3877.

(ἀδελφοί) (voc.pl.masc.of ἀδελφός, address) 15.

ἥν (acc.sing.fem.of ὅς, relative pronoun, direct object of ἔχω) 65.

ἔχω (1st.per.sing.pres.act.ind.of ἔχω, aoristic) 82.

ἐν (preposition with the instrumental of association) 80.

Χριστῷ (instru.sing.masc.of Χριστός, association) 4.

Ἰησοῦ (instru.sing.masc.of Ἰησοῦς, apposition) 3.

τῷ (instru.sing.masc.of the article in agreement with κυρίῳ) 9.

κυρίῳ (instru.sing.masc.of κύριος, apposition) 97.

ἡμῶν (gen.pl.masc.of ἐγώ, relationship) 123.

Translation - "I risk death every day. I swear it, brethren, by the pride which I have in you, along with Christ Jesus our Lord."

Comment: Note the present iterative with its retroactive force in ἀποθνῄσκω. Paul had been putting his life in jeopardy every day for a long time by preaching a gospel that was unpopular. The pride which he has in his converts in Corinth is shared by the Lord Jesus. *Cf.* 2 Cor.4:10,11 for additional comment on καθ᾽ ἡμέραν ἀποθνῄσκω.

What good purpose is served if Paul risks his life every day preaching a message which is untrue? If Jesus Christ is alive no price is too great for the preacher of His gospel to pay. If Jesus is dead the preacher who gives up his life for Him is a fool.

Paul's philosophy was also false if Christ is dead. This he says in

Verse 32 - "If after the manner of men I have fought with beasts at Ephesus, what advantageth it me, if the dead rise not? Let us eat and drink; for tomorrow we die."

εἰ κατὰ ἄνθρωπον ἐθηριομάχησα ἐν Ἐφέσῳ, τί μοι τὸ ὄφελος; εἰ νεκροὶ οὐκ ἐγείρονται, Φάγωμεν καὶ πίωμεν, αὔριον γὰρ ἀποθνήσκομεν.

"What do I gain if, humanly speaking, I fought with beasts at Ephesus? If the dead are not raised, 'Let us eat and drink, for tomorrow we die.' " . . . RSV

εἰ (conditional particle in a second-class condition, contrary to fact) 337.
κατὰ (preposition with the accusative of standard) 98.
ἄνθρωπον (acc.sing.masc.of ἄνθρωπος, standard) 341.

#4244 ἐθηριομάχησα (1st.per.sing.aor.act.ind.of θηριομαχέω, in a second-class condition, contrary to fact).

King James Version

fight with beasts - 1 Cor.15:32.

Revised Standard Version

fight with beasts - 1 Cor.15:32.

Meaning: Cf. θηριομάχος - "a fight with wild beasts." The view that Paul means this literally and that at Ephesus he was forced into an arena to fight wild beasts can be objected to on the grounds that he would have been most unlikely to omit such a persecution from the list of 2 Cor.11:23-27. Most commentators believe that he means the Epicureans in Ephesus whose philosophy was pitched on the moral level of the pig sty. This view is strengthened by the quotations from Isaiah 22:13; 56:12 and by the fact that it recalls Luke 12:19,20. The quotation from Menander in verse 33 supports this conjecture also. It is also unlikely that Luke would have failed to report the event if it had occurred literally.

ἐν (preposition with the locative of place) 80.
Ἐφέσῳ (loc.sing.masc.of Ἔφεσος, place) 3452.
τί (nom.sing.neut.of τίς, interrogative pronoun, predicate nominative) 281.
μοι (dat.sing.masc.of ἐγώ, personal advantage) 123.
τὸ (nom.sing.neut.of the article in agreement with ὄφελος) 9.

#4245 ὄφελος (nom.sing.neut.of ὄφελος, subject of ἔστιν understood).

King James Version

it advantageth - 1 Cor.15:32.
it profiteth - James 2:14,16.

Revised Standard Version

gain - 1 Cor.15:32.
profit - James 2:14,16.

Meaning: Cf. ὀφέλλω - "to increase;" ὠφελέω (#1144); ὠφέλιμος (#4754). Hence, profit; gain; utility. Economists are familiar with Vilfredo Pareto's concept of ophelimity, in the economic sense of "utility" which derives from these Greek words. With reference to the supposed advantage of living a moral life, even though there is no resurrection - 1 Cor.15:32; of faith without works - James 2:14; of kind words without gracious deeds - James 2:16.

εἰ (conditional particle in a first-class condition) 337.
νεκροὶ (nom.pl.masc.of νεκρός, subject of ἐγείρονται) 749.
οὐκ (negative particle with the indicative) 130.
ἐγείρονται (3d.per.pl.pres.pass.ind.of ἐγείρω, first-class condition) 125.
Φάγωμεν (1st.per.pl.aor.act.subj.of ἐσθίω, hortatory) 610.
καὶ (adjunctive conjunction joining verbs) 14.
πίωμεν (1st.per.pl.aor.act.subj.of πίνω, hortatory) 611.
αὔριον (temporal adverb) 633.
γὰρ (causal conjunction) 105.
ἀποθνήσκομεν (1st.per.pl.pres.act.ind.of ἀποθνήσκω, futuristic) 774.

Translation - "If I had fought with the wild beasts at Ephesus what, from a human point of view, would I have gained if the dead are not raised? Let us eat and let us drink because tomorrow we are going to die."

Comment: κατὰ ἄνθρωπον puts Paul's struggle with the pagan philosophers at Ephesus into a purely human context. And that is the only point of view we have if the dead do not rise again. Thus Paul is saying that there is nothing for him to gain by arguing for righteousness, temperance and judgment to come (Acts 24:25), since the Epicureans were correct that this is the only life. Therefore we must fill it with pleasure and look to human reason alone as a guide to the extent to which we indulge ourselves.

The logical conclusion is "And behold joy and gladness, slaying oxen and killing sheep, eating flesh and drinking wine: let us eat and drink; for tomorrow we shall die." (Isa.22:13). *Cf.* also Isa.56:12. Any other philosophy must rest for its support upon the fact of resurrection life after death, judgment and immortality.

Attempts have been made to show that morals may be maintained independent of any theological views which speak of eternity and the resurrection. *Cf.* Walter Lippmann, *Preface to Morals.* Paul denies that the Judeo-Christian ethic is valid except as it is viewed in connection with the Judeo-Christian eschatology.

Paul uses a second-class contrary to fact condition in his first clause. Thus we are told that he did not fight in Ephesus, either with the wild beasts in the Ephesian arena or with the Epicurean philosophers. But if he had (he did not) there would have been no profit in it for him if it is true that there is no resurrection.

There is a definite connection between philosophy and morals. This is the thought of

Verse 33 - "Be not deceived: evil communications corrupt good manners."

μὴ πλανᾶσθε. Φθείρουσιν ἤδη χρηστὰ ὁμιλίαι κακαί.

"Do not be deceived: 'Bad company ruins good morals.' " . . . RSV

μὴ (negative particle with the imperative in a prohibition) 87.
πλανᾶσθε (2d.per.pl.pres.pass.impv.of πλανάω, prohibition) 1257.
Φθείρουσιν (3d.per.pl.pres.act.ind.of φθείρω, customary) 4119.

#4246 ἤδη (acc.pl.neut.of ἤθος, direct object of Φθείρουσιν).

King James Version

manner - 1 Cor.15:33.

Revised Standard Version

morals - 1 Cor.15:33.

Meaning: Cf. ἔθος (#1788). In classical Greek - a customary abode, dwelling place, haunt. In the New Testament only in 1 Cor.15:33. Custom, usage, morals, proper behavior, ethics, manners.

χρηστὰ (acc.pl.neut.of χρηστός, in agreement with ἤθη) 959.

#4247 ὁμιλίαι (nom.pl.fem.of ὁμιλία, subject of φθείρουσιν).

King James Version

communication - 1 Cor.15:33.

Revised Standard Version

company - 1 Cor.15:33.

Meaning: Cf. ὅμιλος (mgn.in Rev.18:17). Companionship; human association; communion; verbal exchange; social acculturation. *cf.* homily. Joined to κακαί in 1 Cor.15:33.

κακαί (nom.pl.fem.of κακός, in agreement with ὁμιλίαι) 1388.

Translation - "Stop being deceived. Evil conversations corrupt good morals."

Comment: Here and in Acts 17:28 and Titus 1:12 we have Paul's only resort to the writings of the Greek poets. Here it is Menander, *Thais,* (218). If a Christian engages in a useless debate with unbelievers, such idle mental sparring may be injurious to his own moral standards. For the unbeliever there is no harm. He has nothing to lose. But the Christian has much to lose. So he should avoid useless debate (1 Tim.1:4; Titus 3:9).

Verse 34 - "Awake to righteousness and sin not; for some have not the knowledge of God: I speak this to you shame."

ἐκνήφατε δικαίως καὶ μὴ ἁμαρτάνετε, ἀγνωσίαν γὰρ θεοῦ τινες ἔχουσιν. πρὸς ἐντροπὴν ὑμῖν λαλῶ.

"Come to your right mind, and sin no more. For some have no knowledge of God. I say this to your shame." . . . RSV

#4248 ἐκνήφατε (2d.per.pl.aor.act.impv.of ἐκνήφω, command).

King James Version

awake - 1 Cor.15:34.

Revised Standard Version

come to your right mind - 1 Cor.15:34.

Meaning: A combination of ἐκ (#19) and νήφω (#4668). Properly, to recover from drunkenness; become sober. In the New Testament with δικαίως - "to become intellectually and philosophically sober." To achieve intellectual rectitude. To return to a rationale consistent with the Christian revelation - 1 Cor.15:34.

δικαίως (adverbial) 2855.
καὶ (adjunctive conjunction joining verbs) 14.
μή (negative particle with the imperative in a prohibition) 87.
ἁμαρτάνετε (2d.per.pl.pres.act.impv.of ἁμαρτάνω, prohibition) 1260.

#4249 ἀγνωσίαν (acc.sing.fem.of ἀγνωσία, direct object of ἔχουσιν).

King James Version

ignorance - 1 Peter 2:15.
not knowledge - 1 Cor.15:34.

Revised Standard Version

no knowledge - 1 Cor.15:34.
ignorance - 1 Peter 2:15.

Meaning: α privative plus γνῶσις (#1856); want of knowledge; ignorance - 1 Cor.15:34 where it is followed by a genitive of reference; in 1 Peter 2:15 with a genitive of description.

γὰρ (causal conjunction) 105.

θεοῦ (gen.sing.masc.of θεός, reference) 124.

τινες (nom.pl.masc.of τις, indefinite pronoun, subject of ἔχουσιν) 486.

ἔχουσιν (3d.per.pl.pres.act.ind.of ἔχω, aoristic) 82.

πρὸς (preposition with the accusative, purpose) 197.

ἐντροπὴν (acc.sing.fem.of ἐντροπή, purpose) 4149.

ὑμῖν (dat.pl.masc.of σύ, personal interest) 104.

λαλῶ (1st.per.sing.pres.act.ind.of λαλέω, aoristic) 815.

Translation - "Return to sober thinking as you ought, and stop sinning, because some of you have no knowledge of God. I am saying this to make you ashamed."

Comment: δικαιώς is adverbial. Hence "wake up to righteousness" is incorrect. It was their duty to "sober up" for they had been in a state of mental stupor with too much speculation about the resurrection as a result of which their morals had been corrupted (verse 33). Paul orders them to recover their sobriety, as was their duty and to stop sinning ("do not go on sinning" - μὴ with the present imperative).

Why this great need for revival at Corinth? Because some of them had little or no knowledge of God. That Paul means some within the church is clear from the last clause. He wanted the Corinthians to see themselves as he saw them. Some of them knew little about God.

Greek philosophy with its view that the soul and spirit of man could be immortal only if they were made free from the body had challenged the Christian message that God is unwilling to allow Satan to have even a partial victory over man. The body is as much a part of God's creation as the intellect and emotion, and Christ came to rescue the entire man. He was unwilling to provide only a partial redemption. Thus He arose from the grave in the physical sense and became the "first fruits" of all of the members of His spiritual body. To counter the Corinthian error Paul has devoted this entire chapter to the resurrection of the body.

It is possible that the Greek view that there would be no resurrection of the body was the result of Gnostic influence, particularly as it was encountered after the conquest of Alexander the Great.

Paul now devotes the remainder of the chapter to answering the Gnostic objection that a material body, by virtue of the fact that it is material, cannot therefore be eternal.

The Resurrection Body

(1 Corinthians 15:35-58)

Verse 35 - "But some man will say, How are the dead raised up? And with what body do they come."

Ἀλλὰ ἐρεῖ τις, Πῶς ἐγείρονται οἱ νεκροί; ποίῳ δὲ σώματι ἔρχονται;

"But some one will ask, 'How are the dead raised? With what kind of body do they come?' " . . . *RSV*

'Αλλά (adversative conjunction) 342.

ἐρεῖ (3d.per.sing.fut.act.ind.of εἴρω, predictive) 155.

τις (nom.sing.masc.of τις, indefinite pronoun, subject of ἐρεῖ) 486.

πῶς (interrogative adverb) 627.

ἐγείρονται (3d.per.pl.pres.pass.ind.of ἐγείρω, futuristic) 125.

οἱ (nom.pl.masc.of the article in agreement with νεκροὶ) 9.

νεκροὶ (nom.pl.masc.of νεκρός, subject of ἐγείρονται) 749.

ποίῳ (instru.sing.neut.of ποῖος, in agreement with σώματι) 1298.

δὲ (continuative conjunction) 11.

σώματι (instru.sing.neut.of σῶμα, manner) 507.

ἔρχονται (3d.per.pl.pres.ind.of ἔρχομαι, futuristic, direct question) 146.

Translation - "But some one is going to say, 'How are the dead raised up?' and 'What kind of body are they going to have?' "

Comment: Paul anticipates the questions of the unbelievers. Modern Bible believing pastor-teachers and evangelists have heard all that Paul heard and more. The current crop of skeptics has imagined all manner of circumstances which, in their judgment, make the fact of bodily resurrection, in a corporeal sense, impossible.

Two examples from my own experience in a university class in New Testament Greek —

A sailor died and was buried at sea. The sharks ate him, each of which digested his portion of the repast. Thus the sailor's body was distributed among the bodies of the sharks who ate him. The sharks died and were eaten by other forms of aquatic life - devil fish, whales, etc. These died also. The skeptic now asks me to follow this pattern of life, death, ingestion, digestion, excretion, *ad infinitum, ad nauseam.* Ultimately the body of the dead sailor is thoroughly mixed with the waters of the seven seas and is circulated by ocean currents around the planet again and again. Some of it sinks to the floor of the ocean and becomes a part of the primeval ooze where the foot of man has never yet trod.

This scenario came from the professor.

A student who hoped to become a minister (!) declared that the professor's example was "as weak as a rained-on bee." He wanted to show off his knowledge of Torrence. He lived in Gary, Indiana. A neighbor worked in the steel mill. As he walked upon a narrow angle iron above a giant ladle he lost his balance and fell into ten tons of white hot molten steel. His body was never found, though they knew where it was - somewhere in chemical solution in the giant ladle. They dared not sell the steel because the media told the story and if they had, every one who bought a new car would imagine that the dead man was riding with him. So they gave the ten tons of steel Christian burial.

Now, demanded the professor and the students, "How can the bodies of the sailor and the steel worker be raised?" Every eye was focused upon me. I waited for the proper oratorical pause in order to make my reply more effective, and said,

"I don't know."

These people had cranked up their imaginations to produce the ultimate in incredibility, as though their cases were any more difficult, in the event that one is looking for difficulty to fuel his skepticism, than the case of any dead body, buried in the soil and returned by biodegradability to the original chemical elements.

It is scant wonder that Paul reacted as he did in

Verse 36 - "Thou fool, that which thou sowest is not quickened, except it die."

ἄφρων, σὺ δ σπείρεις οὐ ζῳοποιεῖται ἐὰν μὴ ἀποθάνῃ.

"You foolish man! What you sow does not come to life unless it dies." . . . RSV

ἄφρων (voc.sing.masc.of ἄφρων, address) 2462.
σὺ (nom.sing.masc.of σύ, subject of σπείρεις) 104.
δ (nom.sing.neut.of ὅς, relative pronoun, subject of ζῳοποιεῖται) 65.
σπείρεις (2d.per.sing.pres.act.ind.of σπείρω, aoristic) 616.
οὐ (negative particle with the indicative) 130.
ζῳοποιεῖται (3d.per.sing.pres.pass.ind.of ζῳοποιέω, futuristic) 2098.
ἐὰν (conditional particle with the subjunctive in a third-class condition) 363.
μὴ (negative particle with the subjunctive) 87.
ἀποθάνῃ (3d.per.sing.aor.act.subj.of ἀποθνήσκω, third-class condition) 774.

Translation - "Stupid! That which you plant does not germinate if it does not decompose."

Comment: The noun ἄφρων (stupid man) is here used in the vocative. The word means one who fails to understand (#2462). Though it is possible to take σὺ with ἄφρων - "you stupid man" - it is not necessary. It is more natural to consider it proleptically for emphasis - "That which *you yourself* plant . . . κ.τ.λ." (Robertson, *Grammar,*423. 678) *Cf.* Luke 12:20 where Ἄφρων is in the vocative case.

Here the apodosis comes before the protasis in the sentence. If what is planted does not die and decompose first, it will never germinate and grow. Thus Paul lays down a first principle. Resurrection is contingent upon death. Only those who have died can be resurrected. Death, therefore, so far from being a tragedy is the first necessary step to the glorious experience of resurrection. This is true in the world of botany. If a grain of wheat - ὁ κόκκος τοῦ σίτου - does not rot it will never grow (John 12:24) said Jesus with reference to His own death, burial and resurrection.

The Corinthians, like all Greeks, had the highest regard for the human body. Witness the sculpture of Phidias. For them death and decomposition of the body was a tragedy. How could a body, once subject to chemical decomposition, rise again? It was too early in the development of physics for them to understand that since E equals M it follows that M also equals E. Paul here says that only if it does die can it be resurrected. If it could escape death it would be forever destined to its inferior status - a status far inferior to that of the resurrected body. Thus to one who wishes to admire the human body as much as the Greeks did, let him admire it in its resurrected state, not in its pre-death state which is at best inferior. Thus death is a fortunate first and essential step to something far better. better.

In verse 37 Paul points to another principle with which any farmer is well familiar.

Verse 37 - "And that which thou sowest thou sowest not that body that shall be, but bare grain, it may chance of wheat, or of some other grain."

καὶ ὃ σπείρεις, οὐ τὸ σῶμα τὸ γενησόμενον σπείρεις ἀλλὰ γυμνὸν κόκκον εἰ τύχοι σίτου ἢ τινος τῶν λοιπῶν.

"And what you sow is not the body which is to be, but a bare kernel, perhaps of wheat or some other grain." . . . RSV

καὶ (continuative conjunction) 14.
ὃ (nom.sing.neut.of ὅς, relative pronoun, in agreement with σῶμα) 65.
σπείρεις (2d.per.sing.pres.act.ind.of σπείρω, aoristic) 616.
οὐ (negative particle with the indicative) 130.
τὸ (nom.sing.neut.of the article in agreement with σῶμα) 9.
σῶμα (nom.sing.neut.of σῶμα, subject of ἔστιν, understood) 507.
τὸ (nom.sing.neut.of the article in agreement with γενησόμενον) 9.
γενησόμενον (fut.part.nom.sing.neut.of γίνομαι, substantival, predicate nominative) 113.
σπείρεις (2d.per.sing.pres.act.ind.of σπείρω, aoristic) 616.
ἀλλὰ (alternative conjunction) 342.
γυμνὸν (acc.sing.masc.of γυμνός, in agreement with κόκκον) 1548.
κόκκον (acc.sing.masc.of κόκκος, direct object of σπείρεις) 1067.
εἰ (conditional particle with the optative in a fourth-class, less probable condition) 337.
τύχοι (3d.per.sing.2d.aor.optative of τυγχάνω, fourt-class less probable condition) 2699.
σίτου (gen.sing.masc.of σῖτος, description) 311.
ἢ (disjunctive) 465.
τινος (gen.sing.masc.of τις, indefinite pronoun, description) 486.
τῶν (gen.pl.masc.of the article in agreement with λοιπῶν) 9.
λοιπῶν (gen.pl.masc.of λοιπός, partitive genitive) 1402.

Translation - "And that which you sow is not the body that will grow; instead you plant a bare grain, whatever it may be - wheat or some one of the others."

Comment: The copula is supplied with τὸ σῶμα to which the relative ὃ is joined, and the participial substantive τὸ γενησόμενον is the predicate nominative.

"That seed which you sow is not the plant that will grow." On the contrary (ἀλλὰ) you sow naked kernels which germinate and push above the ground a plant entirely different in design and appearance. And yet it is not different. Wheat grows wheat, not corn. And corn grows corn, not wheat. Whatever is planted - that is the genus that grows. If a farmer wants Canadian winter wheat, which is a specific genus within the species to which all wheat belongs, he must plant Canadian winter wheat.

Note the rare fourth-class, less probable condition with εἰ and the optative τύχοι. We have only the protasis. The apodosis, if it were present would consist of the optative mode with ἄν. *Cf.* 1 Pet.3:14 and 1 Cor.14:10 for other examples. "No example of this condition complete in both protasis and apodosis is to be found in the New Testament. Indeed, Robertson denies that a complete example occurs in the LXX or papyri 'so far as examined.' . . . 'It is an ornament of the cultured class and was little used by the masses saved in a few set phrases.' " (Robertson, *Grammar*, 1020) as cited in Mantey, *Manual*, 290).

Thus the second principle is laid down. There is a difference in form between the seed planted and the harvest expected. It is not a difference in genus, but in form. To secure a stalk of corn, with leaves, tassles, corn silks and a cob that carries the grains, one does not plant a stalk of corn; nor to secure a grain of wheat does one plant a stalk of wheat. One grain of corn, lacking all of the botanical accouterments, if planted, will produce the stalk of corn in all of its glory. But a grain of corn will produce a stalk of corn, not a stalk of wheat or a kumquat. The genus within the species is the same, but the form and therefore the appearance is not the same.

It is here that Paul's analogy breaks down as all analogies must. Form relates to function. The final product of the stalk of corn is another grain of corn which is identical to the original grain which was planted. But there is no similarity in form between the original grain and the intermediate stages of growth. The stalk, tassels, corn silks and cob are necessary steps to the grain that grows on the cob, but the intermediate steps have a different function and therefore a different form and appearance. No farmer plants corn cobs and expects to get a crop of corn.

The resurrection of the body of the Christian produces the same genus within the same species, within the same family and, unlike the corn and wheat in Paul's analogy, it also has the same form and therefore the same appearance. The difference is in the condition. The resurrection body of the Christian is no longer depraved. It is glorified. It is capable of all of the normal functions. It is incapable of the abnormal function. In our resurrection bodies we will walk, run, jump, play, stand, sit, sing, laugh and work, to mention a few. We will not sin. Sin is not a normal function of the human body.

In γενησόμενον we have one of the infrequent future participles, used here as a substantive as predicate nominative. The future participle always indicates time subsequent to that of the main verb and is almost always punctilair ingressive, though it is possible to conceive of it as durative as here in 1 Cor.15:37. That which it will begin to be, at the point of germination (ingressive) it will continue to be (durative).

To ask, as some did, "With what body will they come?" is like asking a farmer what he expects to reap after he plants a grain of wheat or a kernel of corn! It is scant wonder that Paul called them "Stupid."

The third and fourth principles are laid down in

Verse 38 - "But God giveth it a body as it hath pleased him, and to every seed his own body."

ὁ δὲ θεὸς δίδωσιν αὐτῷ σῶμα καθὼς ἠθέλησεν, καὶ ἑκάστῳ τῶν σπερμάτων ἴδιον σῶμα.

"But God gives it a body as he has chosen, and to each kind of seed its own body." . . . RSV

ὁ (nom.sing.masc.of the article in agreement with θεὸς) 9.

δὲ (continuative conjunction) 11.

θεὸς (nom.sing.masc.of θεός, subject of δίδωσιν) 124.

δίδωσιν (3d.per.sing.pres.act.ind.of δίδωμι, futuristic) 362.

αὐτῷ (dat.sing.masc.of αὐτός, indirect object of δίδωσιν) 16.

σῶμα (acc.sing.neut.of σῶμα, direct object of δίδωσιν) 507.

καθὼς (compound particle in a comparative clause) 1348.

ἠθέλησεν (3d.per.sing.aor.act.ind.of θέλω, constative) 88.

καὶ (concessive conjunction) 14.

ἑκάστῳ (dat.sing.masc.of ἕκαστος, indirect object of δίδωσιν) 1217.

τῶν (gen.pl.neut.of the article in agreement with σπερμάτων) 9.

σπερμάτων (gen.pl.neut.of σπέρμα, partitive genitive) 1056.

ἴδιον (acc.sing.neut.of ἴδιος, in agreement with σῶμα) 778.

σῶμα (acc.sing.neut.of σῶμα, direct object of δίδωσιν) 507.

Translation - "And God will give to it a body, just as He has pleased, although to each of the seeds (he will give) its own body."

Comment: The first of the new principles added here is that since God is the God of resurrection, Who alone is capable of bringing resurrection life out of decomposing death, he will give to each seed whatever type of resurrection body He has pleased to give. There is a touch of asperity here, as Paul seems to be saying to the inquisitive and skeptical Corinthian of verse 35, "It is none of your usiness." Since no man can produce the miracle of resurrection, no man should question how it is done, nor should he criticize the result. Beggars should not be choosers. Would he rather have what God has pleased to give him or would he rather do without and stay dead? The sufficient answer to the question ποίῳ δὲ σώματι ἔρχονται is "Whatever body God wishes it to have."

Having made the point that the details of the resurrection are the prerogative of heaven, he now concedes that God has already established another principle. This is the force of concessive καὶ. God has already decided to give back in the resurrection to every seed its own body - like the one it had before death. In the case of the Christian it is the same in identity and the same in form, function and appearance, but it is not the same in condition. Human corpses will be raised up as human resurrected bodies, just as a kernel of corn, a grain of wheat or an apple seed ultimately reproduces itself.

Paul now teaches us how to classify the various species - human, zoological, ichthyological and ornithological.

Verse 39 - "All flesh is not the same flesh; but there is one kind of flesh of men, another flesh of beasts, another of fishes and another of birds."

οὐ πᾶσα σὰρξ ἡ αὐτὴ σάρξ, ἀλλὰ ἄλλη μὲν ἀνθρώπων, ἄλλη δὲ σὰρξ κτηνῶν, ἄλλη δὲ σὰρξ πτηνῶν, ἄλλη δὲ ἰχθύων.

"For not all flesh is alike, but there is one kind for men, another for animals, another for birds, and another for fish." . . . RSV

οὐ (negative particle with the indicative) 130.
πᾶσα (nom.sing.fem.of πᾶς, in agreement with σὰρξ) 67.
σὰρξ (nom.sing.fem.of σάρξ, subject of ἐστιν understood) 1202.
ἡ (nom.sing.fem.of the article in agreement with σάρξ) 9.
αὐτὴ (nom.sing.fem.of αὐτός, attributive position, intensive) 16.
σάρξ (nom.sing.fem.of σάρξ, predicate nominative) 1202.
ἀλλὰ (adversative conjunction) 342.
ἄλλη (nom.sing.fem.of ἄλλος, in agreement with σὰρξ) 198.
μὲν (particle of affirmation) 300.
ἀνθρώπων (gen.pl.masc.of ἄνθρωπος, description) 341.
ἄλλη (nom.sing.fem.of ἄλλος, in agreement with σὰρξ understood) 198.
δὲ (adversative conjunction) 11.
σὰρξ (nom.sing.fem.of σάρξ, subject of ἐστιν) 1202.
κτηνῶν (gen.pl.masc.of κτῆνος, description) 2430.
ἄλλη (nom.sing.fem.of ἄλλος, in agreement with σὰρξ) 198.
δὲ (adversative conjunction) 11.
σὰρξ (nom.sing.fem.of σάρξ, subject of ἐστιν) 1202.

#4250 πτηνῶν (gen.pl.neut.of πτηνός, description).

King James Version

birds - 1 Cor.15:39.

Revised Standard Version

birds - 1 Cor.15:39.

Meaning: Cf. πέτομαι (#5384). Furnished with wings; winged; flying. Hence, birds - 1 Cor.15:39.

ἄλλη (nom.sing.fem.of ἄλλος ιν αγρεεμεντ ςιτη σὰρξ understood) 198.
δὲ (adversative conjunction) 11.
ἰχθύων (gen.pl.masc.of ἰχθύς, description) 657.

Translation - "Not all flesh is the same, but one is human, and one is of animals, and another of birds and another of fish."

Comment: The Greek οὐ πᾶσα σάρξ says what Paul means - "not all flesh is the same" - which means some flesh is the same and some is different. The King James Version has "all flesh is not the same flesh" which means that every instance of fleshness is different from every other one. This is not what Paul said. The Madison Avenue writers apparently know as little English as the translators of the King James Version. They tell us that "All aspirins are not alike." But they do not mean that all aspirins are different.

Flesh comes in various categories, four of which Paul mentions. There are human beings, animals, birds and fish. He could have mentioned reptiles and worms, but he made his point. Note again αὐτή in the intensive attributive position meaning "the same" as in Rom.10:12; Heb.10:11. The substantive is omitted but understood in Mt.5:47; Heb.2:14; Lk.6:23.

Paul now teaches us astronomy with differentiation between that which is heavenly and that which is of the earth.

Verse 40 — "There are also celestial bodies, and bodies terrestrial: but the glory of the celestial is one, and the glory of the terrestrial is another."

καὶ σώματα ἐπουράνια, καὶ σώματα ἐπίγεια. ἀλλὰ ἑτέρα μὲν ἡ τῶν ἐπουρανίων δόξα, ἑτέρα δὲ ἡ τῶν ἐπιγείων.

"There are celestial bodies and there are terrestrial bodies; but the glory of the celestial is one, and the glory of the terrestrial is another." . . . RSV

καὶ (continuative conjunction) 14.
σώματα (nom.pl.neut.of σῶμα, subject of ἔστιν understood) 507.
ἐπουράνια (nom.pl.neut.of ἐπουράνιος, in agreement with σώματα) 1989.
καὶ (adjunctive conjunction joining nouns) 14.
σώματα (nom.pl.neut.of σῶμα, subject of ἔστιν understood) 507.
ἐπίγεια (nom.pl.neut.of ἐπίγειος, in agreement with σώματα) 1988.
ἀλλὰ (adversative conjunction) 342.
ἑτέρα (nom.sing.fem.of ἕτερος, predicate nominative) 605.
μὲν (particle of affirmation) 300.
ἡ (nom.sing.fem.of the article in agreement with δόξα) 9.
τῶν (gen.pl.fem.of the article in agreement with ἐπουρανίων) 9.
ἐπουρανίων (gen.pl.fem.of ἐπουράνιος, description) 1989.
δόξα (nom.sing.fem.of δόξα, subject of ἔστιν understood) 361.
ἑτέρα (nom.sing.fem.of ἕτερος, predicate nominative) 605.
δὲ (adversative conjunction) 11.
ἡ (nom.sing.fem.of the article in agreement with δόξα understood) 9.
τῶν (gen.pl.fem.of the article in agreement with ἐπιγείων) 9.
ἐπιγείων (gen.pl.fem.of ἐπίγειος, description) 1988.

Translation - "And there are heavenly bodies and earthly bodies; but the glory of the heavenly is one glory, but that of the earthly is a different glory."

Comment: Paul is pointing to the many different orders in creation. The botanical world has wheat, corn, barley, flowers, shrubs, etc. The world of zoology has men, animals, birds, fish, reptiles, insects and worms. Other things are classifed as heavenly or earthly. In verse 41 he adds the astronomical bodies - sun, moon and stars. Each order of creation remains within the confines assigned to it. So also is the resurrection of the dead (verse 42).

Verse 41 - "There is one glory of the sun, and another glory of the moon, and another glory of the stars; for one star differs from another star in glory."

ἄλλη δόξα ἡλίου, καὶ ἄλλη δόξα σελήνης, καὶ ἄλλη δόξα ἀστέρων. ἀστὴρ γὰρ ἀστέρος διαφέρει ἐν δόξῃ.

"There is one glory of the sun, and another glory of the moon, and another glory of the stars; for star differs from star in glory." . . . RSV

ἄλλη (nom.sing.fem.of ἄλλος, in agreement with δόξα) 198.
δόξα (nom.sing.fem.of δόξα, subject of ἔστιν understood) 361.
ἡλίου (gen.sing.masc.of ἥλιος, description) 546.
καὶ (adjunctive conjunction) 14.
ἄλλη (nom.sing.fem.of ἄλλος, in agreement with δόξα) 198.
δόξα (nom.sing.fem.of δόξα, subject of ἔστιν understood) 361.
σελήνης (nom.sing.fem.of σελήνη, description) 1505.
καὶ (adjunctive conjunction joining nouns) 14.
ἄλλη (nom.sing.fem.of ἄλλος, in agreement with δόξα) 198.
δόξα (nom.sing.fem.of δόξα, subject of ἔστιν understood) 361.
ἀστέρων (gen.pl.masc.of ἀστήρ, description) 145.
ἀστὴρ (nom.sing.masc.of ἀστήρ, subject of διαφέρει) 145.
γὰρ (concessive conjunction) 105.
ἀστέρος (abl.sing.masc.of ἀστήρ, comparison) 145.
διαφέρει (3d.per.sing.pres.act.ind.of διαφέρω, static) 620.
ἐν (preposition with the locative of sphere) 80.
δόξῃ (loc.sing.fem.of δόξα, sphere) 361.

Translation - "There is one glory of the sun and another glory of the moon and another glory of the stars, although one star surpasses another star in glory."

Comment: Paul continues to point to the varied nature and characteristics of that which God created. Each has its beauty of a different kind. Sun, moon and stars, and since to the observer on earth there is only one sun and one moon, but many stars he puts the latter in the plural. If Paul had written that there were many suns and moons the Corinthians would not have understood it.

Paul adds concessively that the stars each have their own unique characteristics - an astronomical fact well known to the modern astronomer who speaks of the various magnitudes of the stars.

In Paul's inspired rhetoric the copulas are all missing without the slightest hindrance to the obvious transmission of thought.

He has laid a careful foundation for his analogy. Now he builds upon it to teach the doctrine of the resurrection and to answer the question posed in verse 35.

In verses 39-41 God is cast in the role of the supreme creative artist, whose versatility is displayed is the variety of forms which He has created. Only an omnipotent Creator-God could turn E to M and only an omniscient Creator could plan the M forms which their classification reveals. He Who decreed that in the time period upon earth that men call History, certain functions would be performed, could relate form to function. Consider the contributions which every form which God has created make to what we call "the balance of nature." That we preserve this balance is the concern of the environmentalists. Every form has its function and every function is essential to the viability of life on this planet. This applies not only to living but also to inert forms. Paul talked about zoology in verse 39 - men, animals, birds and fish and he could have added reptiles, worms and insects. What a tragic blunder if the Creator had made all of these forms alike. But He did not. In verse 38 we learned that God gave to each the "body" ($\sigma\hat{\omega}\mu\alpha$) which He, in His creative wisdom, was pleased to give it. Thus corn grows corn and wheat grows wheat and they are not the same. Let the chemists tell us the contributions that each makes that the other fails to make and let us then decide how poor we would be if we had only one and not the other.

The same principle applies to the animals and man, who, zoologically speaking is also an animal. But as form relates to function thus man has the intelligence which is required if he is to understand from the things which are made "His eternal power and Deity" (Rom. 1:20). Non-rational animals (monkeys, elephants, bears, dogs, cats) do not have that kind of brain power because they do not need it. Thinking about God is not one of their functions. But the elephant who cannot run as fast as the tiger, his mortal enemy, must have his giant form in order to survive. The speed of the cheetah is his Creator's gift to him. He needs it in order to perform his assigned function and also to survive. Suppose there were no cows? There would be no milk, butter, cheese or beef steak! The uncanny homing instinct of the pigeon, the acute olfactory ability of the German Shepherd to sniff out the bomb which otherwise might kill the President of the United States, the acuity of the eagle and chicken hawk which permits him to see his prey upon the ground from his lofty flight and the speed with which he descends upon it and the ability of the dog to hear sounds that are beyond the vibration range of men - these are all examples of the difference in form of that which God created in keeping with the function which He has assigned to each. Together they make up "the balance of nature." Because man, in his superintelligent stupidity, has destroyed the balance of nature, he has decreed the doom of life on this planet, subject only to the supernatural intervention of the Son of God Who will be forced some day to return and rescue His experiment.

Natural scientists can give us many other fortunate examples of the necessary functions which demand different forms.

All birds are beautiful but are we not grateful to the Creator that He did not create them all to look alike? God in creation ordained that sound waves should differ in length and hence in frequency. Otherwise we could never enjoy a symphony orchestra concert. Light waves produce the colors which delight us as we gaze at the ceiling of the Sistine Chapel. Suppose that there had been only one color! What could Michelangelo have done? Suppose that there were no diatonic and chromatic scale! How could George Frederick Handel have written "The Hallelujah Chorus"? What would be the psychological cost to us if grass were red instead of green and if the sky were a bright orange instead of blue? Let the psychologists tell. Suppose God had forgotten to vary the taste buds on the tongue! How dreary life would be. As it is an apple is good because it is sour and candy is good because it is sweet. What would life be like if all was salt and there were no sugar? God in creation ordained what psychologists call homeostasis. Thus our appetites change to demand those foods which are rich in the chemicals in which our bodies at the moment are deficient. The little girl on record who drank ink and ate chalk needed the chemicals which ink and chalk provide. When a metabolism test revealed her chemical deficiency a prescribed change in diet met the need and she ate no more chalk and drank no more ink.

If God had not ordained that air pressures around the earth would differ there would be no change in the weather. Air currents move to low pressure areas, hindered only by the resistance of ground clutter and they carry the clouds full of water. Otherwise half of the earth would be a desert and the other half a watery waste where only fish could survive. Alfred Marshall was watching the rise and fall of the waves of the ocean when the concept of equilibrium dawned upon him and he rewrote the economics textbooks to add demand curves to the old classical supply analysis. The demand curve itself was the result of the discovery of Gossen and Stanley Jevons of the principle of diminishing marginal utility. And who was it that decreed in creation that the human animal would desire less and less of a product as, in the short run, he ate more and more? And why does man suffer greater and greater increments of pain as his spending reduces his remaining cash closer and closer to the vanishing point? Thus there comes the time when the increased pain of surrendering one more unit of money is exactly equal to the increased utility of eating one more hamburger. And that is the last sandwich that the economic man will buy at that time. Thus the negative slope of the demand curve must intersect the positive slope of the supply curve and we have the equilibrium in the market place which Alfred Marshall saw amidst the waves of the ocean. God had decreed that it should be so. If high waves in the ocean did not tend to come down while low waves rise, the waters of he sea would not remain in their places and there would be another flood, without the benefit of Noah's ark. Job was asked to ponder this question: "Who shut up the sea with doors, when it brake forth, as if it had issued out of the womb? When I made the cloud the garment thereof, and thick darkness a swaddling band for it, and brake up for it my decreed place, and set bars and doors, and said, Hitherto shalt thou come, but no further; and here shall thy proud waves be stayed?" (Job 38:8-11). The God of creation, that is Who? Thus the principle of equilibrium rules the winds and the weather, the waves of the sea and the demand and supply curves in the market place. This concept in economics is so sound, because it is the result of the Creator's decree that it is at the heart of the Keynesian analysis, which now has replaced the theories of the past. It supplemented the half-light of classical economics and provided the kind of economics that would bring the millenium to this earth, but for the fact that men are such vicious sinners and such spastic social scientists. Why can we not discover all of God's natural laws, which He ordained in creation and why can we not then have the intelligence and good judgment to apply them? Francis Bacon said that if man wished to be happy he need only discover natural law and obey it. Some natural law we have discovered. Some we have not yet perceived. But, because those who reject Christ choose to "walk in the night (and) stumble, because there is no light in (them)" (John 11:9,10), and because democracy, with its unjustified premise that man is good and rational, teaches that mass stupidity becomes wisdom when it is consulted between sunup and sundown on the second Tuesday in November on evennumbered years, we have not the good sense to obey the little bit of light we have. What democracy really proves is that the people and the politicians deserve each other.

As we see design in nature we are overwhelmed with the wisdom and knowledge of God who created it. And this is the final answer to the skeptic who is looking for something to criticize in the divine order. When the Corinthians asked, "Why should God raise the dead, and if He does, how is He going to do it?" they were told by Paul to look around them, observes the various forms, both in the inanimate and animate worlds, reflect upon the fact that form relates to function, and then note how that varied functions provide the balance of natural forces, which make it possible to believe in the ultimate viability of human society - now by the grace of God until His Son returns to solve the sin problem, and after that, throughout eternity. If God could do all of that, why should we worry about the little problem as to what the resurrection body is going to look like and how it is going to function?

Verse 42 - "So also is the resurrection of the dead. It is sown in corruption; it is raised in incorruption."

Οὕτως καὶ ἡ ἀνάστασις τῶν νεκρῶν. σπείρεται ἐν φθορᾷ, ἐγείρεται ἐν ἀφθαρσίᾳ.

"So it is with the resurrection of the dead. What is sown is perishable, what is raised is imperishable." . . . RSV

Οὕτως (demonstrative adverb) 74.
καὶ (adjunctive conjunction joining substantives) 14.
ἡ (nom.sing.fem.of the article in agreement with ἀνάστασις) 9.
ἀνάστασις (nom.sing.fem.of ἀνάστασις, subject of ἔστιν understood) 1423.
τῶν (gen.pl.masc.of the article in agreement with νεκρῶν) 9.
νεκρῶν (gen.pl.masc.of νεκρός, description) 749.
σπείρεται (3d.per.sing.pres.pass.ind.of σπείρω, customary) 616.
ἐν (preposition with the locative, accompanying circumstance) 80.
φθορᾷ (loc.sing.fem.of φθορά, accompanying circumstance) 3942.
ἐγείρεται (3d.per.sing.pres.pass.ind.of ἐγείρω, futuristic) 125.
ἐν (preposition with the locative, accompanying circumstance) 80.
ἀφθαρσίᾳ (loc.sing.fem.of ἀφθαρσία, accompanying circumstance) 3836.

Translation - "So also is the resurrection of the dead; the body is buried in a state of disintegration; it is raised in a viable condition."

Comment: Οὕτως connects what follows with what Paul said in verses 39-41. The Christian's body, although classified zoologically as an animal, is a unique animal. It is in a category all its own. It alone, of all of the animals, is the temple of the Holy Spirit (1 Cor.6:19,20; Rom.8:11,23; Eph.1:13,14). But physically it is dead. Before it died the chemical disintegration which we call katabolism was countered by the chemical restoration known as anabolism. Cells die in the mitotic process, but not until they have reproduced themselves. At death anabolism ceases but katabolism continues until through the process of entropy chemical equilibrium is complete. What was once a living body is reduced to its simplest chemical elements. That is what Paul meant when he said that when we bury a corpse it has already begun to disintegrate, and this disintegration will continue after burial until it is complete. Here is the equilibrium principle at work. During life anabolism balances katabolism. At death katabolism takes over because anabolism ceases. *Cf.*#3942.

What is happening to the dead body is also happening to the entire physical universe. The second law of thermodynamics dictates that Einstein's M is becoming Einstein's E. But the E, thanks to the first law, although still in existence is no longer available for work. This is what Paul says in Romans 8:21.

But the disintegration of the body which is going on at the funeral will be countered by the fact that the resurrection body will be one of integration. The locative of accompanying circumstance (ἐν φθορᾷ) is the opposite tendency from the locative of accompanying circumstance (ἐν ἀφθαρσίᾳ). *Cf.*#'s 3836 and 3942. They speak of opposite concepts. Now the student should follow the concordance and look at every place in the New Testament where each is used.

What is buried? A dead body. What is raised? The same body, no longer dead. It is the same in identity but it is not the same in condition, nor will it ever be again. Thus the contrast between the buried corpse and the living Christian on resurrection day (verse 53).

The fact that the resurrected body is the *same* body as the one previously dead and buried can be proved by examining the verbs σπείρεται and ἐγείρεται. Both are third person singular, although the subject "it" is supplied, since it is implicit in the verb. "*It* is sown . . . *it* is raised." Even stronger evidence however is found in John 2:19 where the pronoun αὐτόν can have only one antecedent - the noun ναόν. *Cf.* our discussion (*The Renaissance New Testament*, IV, 373, 374). Jesus said, "I will raise up the same thing that you destroy."

Two more contrasts are set forth in

Verse 43 - "It is sown in dishonour; it is raised in glory; it is sown in weakness; it is raised in power."

σπείρεται ἐν ἀτιμίᾳ, ἐγείρεται ἐν δόξῃ, σπείρεται ἐν ἀσθενείᾳ, ἐγείρεται ἐν δυνάμει.

"It is sown in dishonor, it is raised in glory. It is sown in weakness, it is raised in power." . . . RSV

σπείρεται (3d.per.sing.pres.pass.ind.of σπείρω, customary) 616.
ἐν (preposition with the locative of accompanying circumstance) 80.
ἀτιμίᾳ (loc.sing.fem.of ἀτιμία, accompanying circumstance) 3808.
ἐγείρεται (3d.per.sing.pres.pass.ind.of ἐγείρω, futuristic) 125.
ἐν (preposition with the locative of accompanying circumstance) 80.
δόξῃ (loc.sing.fem.of δόξα, accompanying circumstance) 361.
σπείρεται (3d.per.sing.pres.pass.ind.of σπείρω, customary) 616.
ἐν (preposition with the locative of accompanying circumstance) 80.
ἀσθενείᾳ (loc.sing.fem.of ἀσθένεια, accompanying circumstance) 740.
ἐγείρεται (3d.per.sing.pres.pass.ind.of ἐγείρω, futuristic) 125.
ἐν (preposition with the instrumental, means) 80.
δυνάμει (instru.sing.fem.of δύναμις, means) 687.

Translation - "It is buried in dishonour; it is raised in glory; buried in weakness it is raised by power."

Comment: Death is characterized by humiliation and weakness. Resurrection is accompanied by glory (accompanying circumstance) and accomplished by power (instrumental of means). The student should take the time and expend the effort to locate all of the passages in the New Testament where δύναμις (#687) is associated by the context with the resurrection of the body, either that of Jesus Christ or of the believer. An example is Phil.3:10.

The verbs σπείρεται in verses 42, 43 and 44 are customary presents. Robertson (*Grammar*, 866) calls this use the gnomic present and defines it as "... timeless in reality, true of all time." The customary practice, which is "true of all time" is to bury the dead (!) and the dead is always buried as corrupt, in dishonour, in weakness and as a natural body. The verbs ἐγείρεται of course are futuristic presents.

All that is sadly true at the cemetery - disintegration, humiliation and the total weakness of the natural body of death is to be countered by all that will be triumphantly true at the rapture and resurrection - viability, glory and power of the spiritual body.

Paul now defines the "natural" body and the "spiritual" body and destroys forever the Gnostic notion that if something is "spiritual" it must also be "immaterial."

Verse 44 - "It is sown a natural body; it is raised a spiritual body. There is a natural body, and there is a spiritual body."

σπείρεται σῶμα φυχικόν, ἐγείρεται σῶμα πνευματικόν. εἰ ἔστιν σῶμα φυχικόν, ἔστιν καὶ πνευματικόν.

"It is sown a physical body, it is raised a spiritual body. If there is a physical body, there is also a spiritual body." . . . RSV

σπείρεται (3d.per.sing.pres.pass.ind.of σπείρω, customary) 616.
σῶμα (nom.sing.neut.of σῶμα, subject of σπείρεται) 507.
φυχικόν (nom.sing.neut.of φυχικός, in agreement with σῶμα) 4112.

ἐγείρεται (3d.per.sing.pres.pass.ind.of ἐγείρω, futuristic) 125.

σῶμα (nom.sing.neut.of σῶμα, subject of ἐγείρεται) 507.

πνευματικόν (nom.sing.neut.of πνευματικός, in agreement with σῶμα) 3791.

εἰ (conditional particle in a first-class condition) 337.

ἔστιν (3d.per.sing.pres.ind.of εἰμί, first-class condition) 86.

φυχικὸν (nom.sing.neut.of φυχικός in agreement with σῶμα) 4112.

ἔστιν (3d.per.sing.pres.ind.of εἰμί, first-class condition) 86.

καὶ (adjunctive conjunction joining nouns) 14.

πνευματικόν (nom.sing.neut.of πνευματικός, in agreement with σῶμα understood) 3791.

Translation - "A natural body is buried; a spiritual body will be raised. Since there is a natural body, there is going to be a spiritual body."

Comment: The first clause states that there is a natural body and predicts that there will be a spiritual body. The second clause is a first-class condition with the premise in the protasis considered true. Hence our translation "Since" not "If." The existence of the body φυχικόν is adduced here as evidence that there is also to be the body πνευματικόν. *Cf.* carefully #'s 4112 and 3791, and convince yourself that these adjectives "natural" and "spiritual" have nothing to do with material, tangible corporeity. The "natural" (φυχικός) man is not that because he has a physical body, but because he cannot receive the revelation of God's Spirit (1 Cor.2:14). The "spiritual" (πνευματικός) man is no less spiritual because he too has a physical body, but he is spiritual because, unlike the natural man, he discerns all things (1 Cor.2:15). The city of Corinth had both types. All unsaved people are "natural" (φυχικός). They were not members of the church. The Corinthian church had "spiritual" people in it (πνευματικός) and there were also other Christians who, though no longer φυχικός, were not yet πνευματικός. Paul called them σάρκινος (#3924) or σαρκικός (#4058). They were "babes in Christ" - born again to be sure, but not fully developed in their growth in grace (2 Pet.3:18). But the πνευματικοί in Corinth were not ghosts who floated about the city and in and out of the church. To be πνευματμικός is not therefore to be without a physical body.

Similarly the Galatian Christians who were to be selected to provide guidance and counselling for the erring brother in the church had physical bodies, but spiritual attitudes; hence they are called "spiritual" (πνευματικός) in Gal.6:1. Paul did not tell the Galatians to send some ghost to pray and counsel with the backslidden brother/sister.

The fallacy that πνευματικός (#3791) means "ghostlike," "phantasmagorical," "immaterial" or "lacking in physical and chemical substance" is the reason why some do not believe in a bodily resurrection. How often do we hear, "But the Bible says that the resurrection body is a *spiritual* body." As though to be spiritual one must be immaterial, despite the fact that there were spiritual Corinthian and Galatian Christians who were still walking about in their physical bodies.

Our verse only means that the dead physical body of the Christian which was buried, was subject only to those impulses to which the unregenerate respond.

The φυχικοί "have not the Spirit" (Jude 19). Romans 8:9 tells us that if any man "have not the Spirit of Christ, he is none of His."

Now what is buried at the Christian's funeral? It is not the Christian himself, for he has departed from the body and is "present with the Lord" (2 Cor.5:8). We bury his body, which was "shapen in inquity and conceived in sin" (Psalm 51:5). It is the flesh for deliverance from which Paul prayed so earnestly (Rom.7:24,35); it is that part of the Christian while he was still alive which "profits nothing" (John 6:63). It militates against the Holy Spirit and its works reveal its depraved nature (Gal.5:17-21). It houses the child of God during the time when he still has something to do for the Lord (Eph.2:10), but he must fight it every step of the way, by the power of the indwelling Holy Spirit. It embarrasses him, sometimes defeats him and grieves the Holy Spirit. The Christian who wishes to be victorious in the Lord is jolly well delighted to be rid of it. This is what we bury. It is a φυχικός body, and its immediate fate is total chemical disintegration in a tomb, six feet down fortunately, by order of the public health authority, where the wretched and malodorous thing crumbles into dust.

But its ultimate destiny is resurrection. It will be the same body, but it will be totally dominated by the Holy Spirit, hence viable throughout eternity. The child of God in heaven will have a πνευματικός body to go along with his πνευματικός nature, both intellectual and emotional, which he received when he was "born from above" (John 3:3,7). This is why physical death for the Christian whose work on earth for the Lord is finished is such a great blessing. Who wants to be tied to this "body of death" (Romans 7:24) any longer than necessary? As he enjoys the fellowship with those in glory who have preceded him he can look forward to the second coming of our Lord when his old φυχικός body will be resurrected and he will rejoin it. The difference is that in that day it will be a πνευματικός body. There will be no more warfare between the flesh and the spirit (Gal.5:17).

Those Christians who survive upon earth until the second coming of our Lord will be spared the death, burial and disintegration in a grave of the old body. They will be "changed" (ἀλλαγησόμεθα) instantaneously as we learn in verse 52 and in Phil.3:21; 1 John 3:2. Paul's anguished cry for deliverance (Rom.7:24,25) will be answered at the resurrection and the rapture.

The important point in this verse is the difference between three Greek adjectives - φυχικός, σαρκικός and πνευματικός - #'s 4112, 4058, 3791 and 3924 (synonymous with 4112). The student should study these with care and *cf.* our comments on 1 Cor.2:14 - 3:3.

Verse 45 - "And so it is written, The first man Adam was made a living soul: the last Adam was made a quickening spirit."

οὔτως καὶ γέγραπται,Ἐγένετο ὁ πρῶτος ἄνθρωπος Ἀδὰμ εἰς φυχὴν ζῶσαν. ὁ ἔσχατος Ἀδὰμ εἰς πνεῦμα ζῳοποιοῦν.

   "Thus it is written, 'The first man Adam became a living being'; the last Adam became a life-giving spirit." . . . RSV

οὕτως (demonstrative adverb) 74.

καὶ (inferential conjunction) 14.

γέγραπται (3d.per.sing.perf.pass.ind.of γράφω, intensive) 156.

Ἐγένετο (3d.per.sing.aor.ind.of γίνομαι, ingressive) 113.

ὁ (nom.sing.masc.of the article in agreement with ἄνθρωπος) 9.

πρῶτος (nom.sing.masc.of πρῶτος, in agreement with ἄνθρωπος) 487.

ἄνθρωπος (nom.sing.masc.of ἄνθρωπος, subject of Ἐγένετο) 341.

Ἀδὰμ (nom.sing.masc.of Ἀδάμ, apposition) 1774.

εἰ (preposition with the accusative, purpose) 140.

φυχὴν (acc.sing.fem.of φυχή, purpose) 233.

ζῶσαν (pres.act.part.acc.sing.fem.of ζάω, adjectival, in agreement with φυχήν) 340.

ὁ (nom.sing.masc.of the article in agreement with Ἀδάμ) 9.

ἔσχατος (nom.sing.masc.of ἔσχατος, in agreement with Ἀδάμ) 496.

Ἀδὰμ (nom.sing.masc.of Ἀδάμ, subject of ἔστιν understood) 1774.

εἰς (preposition with the accusative, purpose) 140.

πνεῦμα (acc.sing.neut.of πνεῦμα, purpose) 83.

ζωοποιοῦν (pres.act.part.acc.sing.neut.of ζωοποιέω, adjectival, restrictive, predicate position) 2098.

Translation - *"So it stands written like this: The first man Adam was created in order to be a living soul. The last Adam is a life-giving Spirit."*

Comment: Since the physical body presupposes the existence of the spiritual body, we would expect to be introduced to the federal head of human natural life and the federal head of the supernatural spiritual life. This is the force of οὕτως καὶ - "so thus it is written..." Where is it written? Gen.2:7. Adam in Eden was created (ingressive aorist in ἐγένετο) for the purpose of being a self-conscious (φυχήν #233) human being endowed with the power to procreate human life. But sin came, though it was no surprize to God, Who in His wisdom permitted it, and the human life which Adam passed on to posterity was destined to die. Thus the last Adam (Christ) became necessary in God's redemptive plan. *Cf.* Gen.3:15; Heb.2:14.

Adam, the first, contributed his nature, which was sinful, to his posterity by genetics and so "death passed upon all men for that all have sinned" (Romans 5:12), and thus, though he was created both to live and to give life, he died and plunged the entire race into sin and death. But Adam, the Last, gives life of a spiritual type. It is important to distinguish these Adams in relation to their contribution to the race. This Paul does in verse 46. *Cf.* our comment on Romans 5:12-21.

Verse 46 - *"Howbeit that was not first which is spiritual, but that which is natural; and afterward that which is spiritual."*

ἀλλ᾽ οὐ πρῶτον τὸ πνευματικὸν ἀλλὰ τὸ φυχικόν, ἔπειτα τὸ πνευματικόν.

"But it is not the spiritual which is first but the physical, and then the spiritual"
                                                        ... RSV

ἀλλ' (adversative conjunction) 342.

οὐ (negative particle with the indicative) 130.

πρῶτον (acc.sing.neut.of πρῶτος, predicate accusative) 487.

τὸ (nom.sing.neut.of the article in agreement with πνευματικὸν) 9.

πνευματικὸν (nom.sing.neut.of πνευματικός, subject of verb understood) 3791.

ἀλλὰ (alternative conjunction) 342.

τὸ (nom.sing.neut.of the article in agreement with ψυχικόν) 9.

ψυχικόν (nom.sing.neut.of ψυχικός, subject of verb understood) 4112.

ἔπειτα (temporal adverb) 2566.

τὸ (nom.sing neut.of the article in agreement with πνευματικόν) 9.

πνευματικόν (nom.sing.neut.of πνευματικός, predicate accusative) 3791.

Translation - *"However, the spiritual is not the first, but the natural; after him the spiritual."*

Comment: In terms of human history the natural Adam, with the body which is described in verse 47 as being of the earth, antedates the spiritual Adam, the incarnate Son of God. His was a body fathered by the Holy Spirit in the womb of the virgin Mary.

This does not mean that the incarnation was an afterthought. God does not have afterthoughts. Our Lord was the "Lamb slain from the foundation of the earth" (Rev.13:8). The sublapsarian logical (not chronological) order of decrees is the decree to create, followed by the decree to permit the fall and that followed by the decree to redeem. But since God is not a creature of time, but the Father of Eternity He did not set His cross in the Garden of Eden, but just outside the Garden of Gethsemane. It appears to us who are subject to the categories of time and space as if God saved the Old Testament saints "on credit" since their justification was decreed before their debt was paid. There is no difficulty about this since as God sees the end from the beginning and views all that He has decreed as already accomplished, their debt was already paid, even though in historic time Jesus was not yet born, nor had He died.

Old Testament sinners who believed God's promise that salvation would be provided, and who thus became Old Testament saints, were saved by faith just as are New Testament saints. They looked forward in time to the cross, on the basis of God's promise, just as we have looked back to it on the basis of God's historical account. *Cf.* our comment on Romans 3:24-26.

Just as the father of our fallen nature came first in history, so in our experience the ψυχικός man with his depraved nature was born first. Born to sin, die and disintegrate in the grave, he was destined to be rescued by the Last Adam. Thus his salvation came as a result of a new birth "from above" (John 3:3,7; 1 Pet.1:23) which came later in time than his first birth. This new life came from Him Who is a life-giving Spirit. As a result, though the new spiritual man is housed temporarily in an old depraved natural body, it is destined in resurrection to have a spiritual body which will conform in all respects to his spiritual nature. Thus the born again child of God has everlasting life.

Verse 47 - "The first man is of the earth, earthy; the second man is the Lord from heaven."

ὁ πρῶτος ἄνθρωπος ἐκ γῆς χοϊκός, ὁ δεύτερος ἄνθρωπος ἐξ οὐρανοῦ.

"The first man was from the earth, a man of dust; the second man is from heaven." . . . RSV

ὁ (nom.sing.masc.of the article in agreement with ἄνθρωπος) 9.
πρῶτος (nom.sing.masc.of πρῶτος, in agreement with ἄνθρωπος) 487.
ἄνθρωπος (nom.sing.masc.of ἄνθρωπος, subject of ἦν understood) 341.
ἐκ (preposition with the ablative of source) 19.
γῆς (abl.sing.fem.of γῆ, source) 157.

#4251 χοϊκός (nom.sing.masc.of χοϊκός, predicate adjective).

King James Version

earthy - 1 Cor.15:47,48,48,49.

Revised Standard Version

man of dust - 1 Cor.15:47,48,48,49.

Meaning: Cf. χόος (#2250). Hence, dust, dirt, soil - 1 Cor.15:47,48,48,49. With reference to Adam's creation - 1 Cor.15:47,48a; with reference to the nature of unregenerate man - 1 Cor.15:48b, 49.

ὁ (nom.sing.masc.of the article in agreement with δεύτερος) 9.
δεύτερος (nom.sing.masc.of δεύτερος, in agreement with ἄνθρωπος) 1371.
ἄνθρωπος (nom.sing.masc.of ἄνθρωπος, subject of ἦν understood) 341.
ἐξ (preposition with the ablative of source) 19.
οὐρανοῦ (abl.sing.masc.of οὐρανός, source) 254.

Translation - "The first man was from the soil of the earth; the second man is from heaven."

Comment: *Cf.* Gen.2:7. The ψυχικός body of Adam, and ours, which is genetically derived from it, is a complex creation of basic chemical elements which are biodegradable, though during physical life, the chemical balance is maintained by metabolism. At the time of physical death the disintegration begins and ultimately becomes total. This Paul had already said in verse 42.

The author remembers a zoology professor at Syracuse University who defined physical death as chemical equilibrium of the body, in obedience to entropy, the second law of thermodynamics. The bodily functions of exercise, respiration, eating, drinking, etc. arrest entropy to keep us alive. These functions promote the chemical disequilibrium and thus result in negative entropy to sustain life, but eventually these functions fail and entropy procedes to the point that vital functions (heart beat, respiration) cannot continue, after which biodegradability continues in the grave until the complex body has returned to its basic chemical elements from which it came when God created Adam in the Garden of Eden.

But in the case of the Christian, a second birth, the new creation of 2 Cor.5:17, has occurred as the Man from Heaven saved us and implanted His new nature in the body of dust. The first man, a living soul, made out of the soil of the earth, is the father of the race naturally (ψυχικός). The second man from heaven is the life giving Spirit (πνευματικός).

A variant reading adds ὁ κύριος after ὁ δεύτερος ἄνθρωπος, which is an "obvious gloss added to explain 'the man from heaven.' " (Metzger, *A Textual Commentary on the Greek New Testament*, 568).

Verse 48 - "As is the earthy, such are they also that are earthy: and as is the heavenly, such are they also that are heavenly."

οἷος ὁ χοϊκός, τοιοῦτοι καὶ οἱ χοϊκοί, καὶ οἷος ὁ ἐπουράνιος, τοιοῦτοι καὶ οἱ ἐπουράνιοι.

"As was the man of dust, so are those who are of the dust; and as is the man of heaven, so are those who are of heaven." . . . RSV

οἷος (nom.sing.masc.of οἷος, predicate nominative) 1496.
ὁ (nom.sing.masc.of the article in agreement with χοϊκός) 9.
χοϊκός (nom.sing.masc.of χοϊκός, subject of εἰσίν, understood) 4251.
τοιοῦτοι (nom.pl.masc.of τοιοῦτος, predicate adjective) 785.
καὶ (adjunctive conjunction joining nouns) 14.
οἱ (nom.pl.masc.of the article in agreement with χοϊκοί) 9.
χοϊκοί (nom.pl.masc.of χοικός, subject of ἔστιν understood) 4251.
καὶ (continuative conjunction) 14.
οἷος (nom.sing.masc.of οἷος, predicate nominative) 1496.
ὁ (nom.sing.masc.of the article in agreement with ἐπουράνιος) 9.
ἐπουράνιος (nom.sing.masc.of ἐπουράνιος, subject of ἔστιν understood) 1989.
τοιοῦτοι (nom.pl.masc.of τοιοῦτος, predicate adjective) 785.
καὶ (adjunctive conjunction joining nouns) 14.
οἱ (nom.pl.masc.of the article in agreement with ἐπουράνιοι) 9.
ἐπουράνιοι (nom.pl.masc.of ἐπουράνιος, subject of εἰσίν, understood) 1989.

Translation - "As the man of dust was, so also are his children of dust; and as the heavenly man is, so also are the heavenly ones."

Comment: οἷος and its correlative τοιοῦτος are qualitative relative pronouns. Just as corn grows corn and wheat grows wheat, so depraved Adam, the man of dust, peopled the earth with men and women of dust - natural (ψυχικός) depraved, sinful and doomed to entropy (φθόρα).

But the Man from heaven, the Lord Jesus,the Last Adam also produced a spiritually reborn race of heavenly people. *Cf.* Romans 8:29 and comment. Adam, the first, of earth, sinned, died and decayed. Adam, the Second, of heaven, came, lived without sin, died for sinners, rose again without φθόρα (Psalm 16:10) and hence, we, the heavenly ones, though our ψυχικὸν σῶμα will succomb to φθόρα, yet it will rise a πνευματικὸν σῶμα, like Christ's. This is what Paul says in

Verse 49 - "And as we have borne the image of the earthy, we shall also bear the image of the heavenly."

καὶ καθὼς ἐφορέσαμεν τὴν εἰκόνα τοῦ χοϊκοῦ, φορέσομεν καὶ τὴν εἰκόνα τοῦ ἐπουρανίου.

"Just as we have borne the imagine of the man of dust, we shall also bear the image of the man of heaven."

καὶ (continuative conjunction) 14.
καθὼς (compound particle of comparison) 1348.
ἐφορέσαμεν (1st.per.pl.aor.act.ind.of φορέω, constative) 913.
τὴν (acc.sing.fem.of the article in agreement with εἰκόνα) 9.
εἰκόνα (acc.sing.fem.of εἰκών, direct object of ἐφορέσαμεν) 1421.
τοῦ (gen.sing.masc.of the article in agreement with χοϊκοῦ) 9.
χοϊκοῦ (gen.sing.masc.of χοϊκός, description) 4251.
φορέσομεν (1st.per.pl.fut.act.ind.of φορῶ, predictive) 913.
καὶ (adjunctive conjunction joining nouns) 14.
τὴν (acc.sing.fem.of the article in agreement with εἰκόνα) 9.
εἰκόνα (acc.sing.fem.of εἰκών, direct object of φορέσομεν) 1421.
τοῦ (gen.sing.masc.of the article in agreement with ἐπουρανίου) 9.
ἐπουρανίου (gen.sing.masc.of ἐπουράνιος, description) 1989.

Translation - "And as we formerly wore the body of dust we shall also wear forever the heavenly body."

Comment: The United Bible Societies' Committee has chosen the future indicative φορέσομεν over the hortatory subjunctive φορέσωμεν, though only with a C degree of confidence. Goodspeed, Montgomery and Weymouth, following the subjunctive have "let us also try to be like the man from heaven" (Goodspeed) or words to similar effect. I object to the subjunctive here since the context has to do with the condition of our bodies *after* resurrection (verse 35*ff*), not with admonitions about present standards of Christian living. Metzger agrees - "Exegetical considerations (*i.e.* the context is didactic, not hortatory) led the Committee to prefer the future indicative, despite its rather slender external support (B I 38 88 206 218 242 630 915 919 999 1149 1518 1872 1881 Syr_p cop_{sa} eth *al*). (Metzger, *A Textual Commentary on the Greek New Testament*, 569).

Paul indeed becomes hortatory in verse 58 after a long passage of teaching about the facts of the resurrection. Verse 49 is parallel to 1 John 3:2. *Cf.* also Romans 8:29. We shall be conformed ethically and physically. His spiritual body was none the less material (Luke 24:39, 41-43). So indeed shall ours be material and tangible though never gain subject to decay.

Verse 50 - "Now this I say, brethren, that flesh and blood cannot inherit the kingdom of God; neither doth corruption inherit incorruption."

Τοῦτο δέ φημι, ἀδελφοί, ὅτι σὰρξ καὶ αἷμα βασιλείαν θεοῦ κληρονομῆσαι οὐ δύναται, οὐδὲ ἡ φθορὰ τὴν ἀφθαρσίαν κληρονομεῖ.

"I tell you this, brethren: flesh and blood cannot inherit the kingdom of God, nor does the perishable inherit the imperishable." . . . RSV

Τοῦτο (acc.sing.neut.of οὗτος, direct object of φημι) 93.

δὲ (explanatory conjunction) 11.

φημι (1st.per.sing.pres.act.ind.of φημί, aoristic) 354.

ἀδελφοί (voc.pl.masc.of ἀδελφός, address) 15.

ὅτι (conjunction introducing an object clause in indirect discourse) 211.

σὰρξ (nom.sing.fem.of σάρξ, subject of δύναται) 1202.

καὶ (adjunctive conjunction joining nouns) 14.

αἷμα (nom.sing.neut.of αἷμα, subject of δύναται) 1203.

βασιλείαν (acc.sing.fem.of βασιλεία, direct object of κληρονομῆσαι) 253.

θεοῦ (gen.sing.masc.of θεός, description) 123.

κληρονομῆσαι (aor.act.inf.of κληρονομέω, epexegetical) 426.

οὐ (negative particle with the indicative) 130.

δύναται (3d.per.sing.pres.mid.ind.of δύναμαι, static) 289.

οὐδὲ (disjunctive) 452.

ἡ (nom.sing.fem.of the article in agreement with φθορὰ) 9.

φθορὰ (nom.sing.fem.of φθορά subject of κληρονομεῖ) 3942.

τὴν (acc.sing.fem.of the article in agreement with ἀφθαρσίαν) 9.

ἀφθαρσίαν (acc.sing.fem.of ἀφθαρσία, direct object of κληρονομεῖ) 3836.

κληρονομεῖ (3d.per.sing.pres.act.ind.of κληρονομέω, predictive) 426.

Translation - "Now I tell you this, brethren, that flesh and blood cannot inherit a divine kingdom, nor does that which is perishable succeed to that which is imperishable."

Comment: The first clause says essentially what the second clause repeats. Paul is showing in contrast the work of the first Adam as opposed to that of Christ, the last Adam. Every member of the human race is a child of Adam. We have his flesh and blood. Just as Adam could not participate in the kingdom of God after his fall and before his regeneration, so we cannot if all we have is his fallen nature (Rom.5:12; 1 Cor.15:22). But the Christian is the child of God because of his "birth from above" (John 3:3,7) which is not "out of bloods (plural), nor out of the will of the flesh, nor out of the will of man" (John 1:13). It is "out of God."

By "flesh and blood" Paul means those in Adam's fallen line. That line is subject to decay (φθορά #3942) and cannot therefore be imperishable (ἀφθαρσίαν #3836). The verse does not preclude the entry into God's kingdom of bodies of flesh in the anatomical sense, as some suppose. If the verse means that the resurrection body is not a fleshly body, then Christ Himself is not in heaven for He had flesh and bone after His resurrection (Luke 24:39).

Paul has yet to deal with the problem of the flesh and blood nature of the child of God. The fact that we have the new nature as a result of the new birth, and that our spirits are imperishable, however corrupt our flesh may be, means that something must be done for us physically at the resurrection and the rapture. The body of the Christian, still subject to decay cannot enter the kingdom of God. There must be some sort of transformation. And this is what Paul now explains in the remainder of the chapter.

Verse 51 - "Behold, I shew you a mystery: we shall not all sleep, but we shall all be changed."

ἰδοὺ μυστήριον ὑμῖν λέγω, πάντες οὐ κοιμηθησόμεθα, πάντες δὲ ἀλλαγησόμεθα,

"Lo! I tell you a mystery. We shall not all sleep, but we shall all be changed,"..
                                                                              . RSV

ἰδοὺ (exclamation) 95.

μυστήριον (acc.sing.neut.of μυστήριον, direct object of λέγω) 1038.

ὑμῖν (dat.pl.masc.of σύ, indirect object of λέγω) 104.

λέγω (1st.per.sing.pres.act.ind.of λέγω, futuristic) 66.

πάντες (nom.pl.masc.of πᾶς, subject of κοιμηθησόμεθα) 67.

οὐ (negative particle with the indicative) 130.

κοιμηθησόμεθα (1st.per.pl.fut.pass.ind.of κοιμάω, predictive) 1664.

πάντες (nom.pl.masc.of πᾶς, subject of ἀλλαγησόμεθα) 67.

δὲ (adversative conjunction) 11.

ἀλλαγησόμεθα (1st.per.pl.fut.pass.ind.of ἀλλάσσω, predictive) 3097.

Translation - "Look! I am going to explain a mystery to you. Not all of us will die, but all of us will be changed."

Comment: He had already said that the Christian who died and was buried, to undergo decay, would be raised in a new body that would be viable (verse 42). But what about the Christian who will never die, because he will still be alive when our Lord returns? They will still have their flesh and blood bodies which can never enter the Kingdom of God. How will they be rid of this Adamic nature? Though not all will die, all will be changed. In other words the change from φυχικός to πνευματικός, as these adjectives relate to the Christian's body will occur in resurrection for those who have died and in the rapture for those who survive until the Lord returns.

Cf. 1 John 3:2 and Phil.3:21.

Verse 52 - "In a moment, in the twinkling of an eye, at the last trump: for the trumpet shall sound and the dead shall be raised incorruptible, and we shall be changed."

ἐν ἀτόμῳ, ἐν ῥιπῇ ὀφθαλμοῦ, ἐν τῇ ἐσχάτῃ σάλπιγγι. σαλπίσει γάρ, καὶ οἱ νεκροὶ ἐγερθήσονται ἄφθαρτοι, καὶ ἡμεῖς ἀλλαγησόμεθα.

*"in a moment, in the twinkling of an eye, at the last trumpet. For the trumpet
will sound, and the dead will be raised imperishable, and we shall be changed."* . .

. *RSV*

ἐν (preposition with the locative of time point) 80.

#4252 ἀτόμῳ (loc.sing.masc.of ἄτομος, time point).

King James Version

moment - 1 Cor.15:52.

Revised Standard Version

moment - 1 Cor.15:52.

Meaning: α privative plus τέμνω - "to cut." Hence indivisible. In a temporal
sense of a moment of time - 1 Cor.15:52.

ἐν (preposition with the locative of time point) 80.

#4253 ῥιπῇ (loc.sing.fem.of ῥιπή, time point).

King James Version

twinkling - 1 Cor.15:52.

Revised Standard Version

twinkling - 1 Cor.15:52.

Meaning: Cf. ῥίπτω (#837); ῥιπτέω (#3583); ῥιπίζω (#5095). Hence, the action
of flipping, tossing or flinching. Followed by a genitive of description -
ὀφθαλμοῦ in 1 Cor.15:52. The flicker of an eyelid.

ὀφθαλμοῦ (gen.sing.masc.of ὀφθαλμός, description) 501.
ἐν (preposition with the locative of time point) 80.
τῇ (loc.sing.fem.of the article in agreement with σάλπιγγι) 9.
ἐσχάτῃ (loc.sing.fem.of ἔσχατος, in agreement with σάλπιγγι) 496.
σάλπιγγι (loc.sing.fem.of σάλπιγξ, time point) 1507.
σαλπίσει (3d.per.sing.fut.act.ind.of σαλπίζω, predictive) 559.
γὰρ (causal conjunction) 105.
καὶ (continuative conjunction) 14.
οἱ (nom.pl.masc.of the article in agreement with νεκροὶ) 9.
νεκροὶ (nom.pl.masc.of νεκρός, subject of ἐγερθήσονται) 749.
ἐγερθήσονται (3d.per.pl.fut.pass.ind.of ἐγείρω, predictive) 125.
ἄφθαρτοι (nom.pl.masc.of ἄφθαρτος, predicate adjective) 3802.
καὶ (continuative conjunction) 14.
ἡμεῖς (nom.pl.masc.of ἐγώ, subject of ἀλλαγησόμεθα) 123.
ἀλλαγησόμεθα (1st.per.pl.fut.pass.ind.of ἀλλάσσω, predictive) 3097.

*Translation - "In a moment, in the flick of an eyelid, at the last trumpet; because
it will sound, and the dead will be raised in incorruption and we will be changed."*

Comment: Note ἐν with the locative of time point, in three temporal phrases, two of which indicate time duration while the third identifies with another event. The dead will be raised and the living changed in the smallest amount of time - no longer than the time required to flick an eyelid, at the moment when the last trumpet is sounded. *Cf.*#1507. Paul mentions this trumpet in connection with the same event in 1 Thess.4:16 as did Jesus in Mt.24:31, where we have another identification of time point. It will be "immediately after the tribulation of those days . . . κ.τ.λ." (Mt.24:29-31).

Another trumpet sounded when Moses was given the law at Sinai (Heb.12:19). Thus sounds the voice of Christ (Rev.1:10; 4:1). There will be seven trumpet blasts - one each from seven trumpets (Rev.8:2,6,13; 9:14. Paul dates the resurrection with the last one, the sounding of which is recorded in Rev.11:15-19. In the days of that last (seventh) trumpet the "mystery of God will be complete" (Rev.10:7). This mystery, completed at the time of the last trumpet, is the Body of Christ, the Gentile church, called out from among the Gentiles in the age of grace (Eph.3:3-7). The church will not be complete until the end of the tribulation period and of course cannot be raptured and resurrected until that time.

Luke 14:12-14 identifies the judgment seat of Christ, where rewards will be awarded for believers' works, as taking place "at the resurrection of the just" (Luke 14:14), which is "at the last trump" (1 Cor.15:52), which also announces that the nations of earth are angry and that the wrath of the Lamb has come (Rev.11:11-19). It is quite to be expected therefore that we should find the judgment seat of Christ (Rev.11:18) at the "last trump," as indeed we do. Just as "things equal to the same things are equal to each other" so "events which occur at the same time as the same event occur simultaneously."

The judgment seat of Christ occurs at the resurrection of the just (Luke 14:14).

The resurrection of the just occurs at the same time as the rapture (1 Cor.15:52 ; 1 Thess.4:16,17).

The resurrection and rapture occur at the last trump (1 Cor.15:52).

The judgment seat of Christ occurs at the same time as the second coming (Mt.16:27).

Ergo: The rapture of the living saints, the resurrection of those who are asleep in Christ, the anger of the nations and the wrath of the Lamb (Psalm 2:1-5), the assumption of power upon the throne of David by Messiah and the beginning of the Kingdom Age, and the judgment seat of Christ all occur "at the last trump" (Rev.11:15-19).

That this trumpet is the last one and that it is sounded on the last day of the tribulation period is clear from Rev.11:15-19, when we study it with care with special attention to the tenses of the verbs. What is said at that time could not be said seven years or even seven days before the end. This is not the place for the detailed exegesis of Revelation 11:15-19. *Cf.* comment *en loc.*

The phrases ἐν ἀτόμῳ and ἐν ῥιπῇ ὀφθαλμοῦ refer, not to the ascension of the saints to meet the descending Lord, but to the changes from ψυχικός to πνευματικός and from φθαρτὸν to ἀφθαρσίαν in verse 53. The verb for "be caught up" (ἁρπαγησόμεθα) occurs in 1 Thess.4:17, not here.

The rapture is often represented as a sudden instantaneous translation into the sky. One second on earth; the next second beyond the clouds and in glory. Rather it is one second with a ψυχικὸν σῶμα - a corruptible body in the case of the living saints and with a body in the grave already corrupted, in the case of the dead in Christ, and the next second with an eternal πνευματικὸν σῶμα which is eternally viable.

Our ascent from earth into the clouds to meet the Lord will more likely be like Jesus' ascension, which was deliberate to watch and gloriously majestic (Acts 1:11). We will be the Bride of Christ rising to meet the descending Bridegroom. What bride at her wedding sprints madly down the aisle to the altar to meet her husband? Weddings normally are more dignified.

1 Corinthians 15:52 will correct, if we will permit it to do so, the fallacy of a rapture of the church seven (or three and one half) years before the second coming of our Lord in glory. The coming of the Lord is not divided into two phases, separated in time, and designated as His coming *for* His saints and His coming *with* His saints. This bit of eisegesis is the result of the "inspired prophecy" of an overwrought, hyper-emotional pentecostal woman in England one hundred, fifty years ago. She did not find this doctrine in the Greek New Testament, because the Holy Spirit did not write it into the Book. Christians since have read her insights, supposedly given with the assistance of the Holy Spirit, into the New Testament.

There are indeed two phases of the Second Coming. He will be coming to gather the members of His body and He will also be coming to judge the unsaved world and to take His place on David's throne (Luke 1:30-33) to begin His Kingdom Age, but these events will occur at the same time and on the same day. It is the day when the last trumpet will sound. It is the last day of Daniel's 70th week, neither 2520 nor 1260 days before. It is "the great day of His wrath" when none "shall be able to stand" (Rev.6:17).

Some will insist that we are in error when we identify the "last trump" of 1 Cor.15:52 with the seventh trumpet of Revelation 11:15-19. We do not necessarily identify the two trumpets. We only insist that if the two are not the same, then the resurection/rapture trumpet must be blown *after* the seventh trumpet of Revelation 11, since Paul says that it is the *last* trumpet. Pretribulation rapturists say that there will be seven trumpets sounded *after* the *last* one! Thus, in order to save face and support an early 19th century error, which received great circulation in America after the Civil War, with the rise of the Bible Institutes, they resort to eisegesis.

There have been premillenialists since the days of our Lord and the Apostles. Where were the pretribulation premillenialists before 1830?

Verse 53 - "For this corruptible must put on incorruption, and this mortal must put on immortality."

δεῖ γὰρ τὸ φθαρτὸν τοῦτο ἐνδύσασθαι ἀφθαρσίαν καὶ τὸ θνητὸν τοῦτο ἐνδύσασθαι ἀθανασίαν.

"For this perishable nature must put on the imperishable, and this mortal nature must put on immortality." . . . RSV

δεῖ (pres.ind.imperson. of δεῖ) 1207.

γὰρ (causal conjunction) 105.

τὸ (acc.sing.neut.of the article in agreement with φθαρτὸν) 9.

φθαρτὸν (acc.sing.neut.of φθαρτός, general reference) 3804.

τοῦτο (acc.sing.neut.of οὗτος, in agreement with φθαρτὸν) 93.

ἐνδύσασθαι (aor.mid.inf.of ἐνδύω, noun use, subject of δεῖ) 613.

ἀφθαρσίαν (acc.sing.fem.of ἀφθαρσία, direct object of ἐνδύσασθαι) 3836.

καὶ (adjunctive conjunction joining infinitives) 14.

τὸ (acc.sing.neut.of the article in agreement with θνητὸν) 9.

θνητὸν (acc.sing.neut.of θνητός, general reference) 3914.

τοῦτο (acc.sing.neut.of οὗτος, in agreement with θνητὸν) 93.

ἐνδύσασθαι (aor.mid.inf.of ἐνδύω, noun use, subject of δεῖ) 613.

#4254 ἀθανασίαν (acc.sing.fem.of ἀθανασία, direct object of ἐνδύσασθαι).

King James Version

immortality - 1 Cor.15:53,54; 1 Tim.6:16.

Revised Standard Version

immortality - 1 Cor.15:53,54; 1 Tim.6:16.

Meaning: α privative plus θάνατος (#381). Hence, no death; immortality. With reference to the resurrection body - 1 Cor.15:53,54; 1 Tim.6:16.

Translation - "Because this biodegradable body must be endued with viability and this body victimized by death must be given immortality."

Comment: ἐνδύσασθαι is the subject infinitive of δεῖ. What is necessary? What must be done? It is a necessity that lies in the nature of the case. Why must it be true that the corruptible and the mortal must change to incorruptible and immortal? Because we learned in verse 50 that flesh and blood in their corruptible and mortal state cannot enter heaven. If they could heaven would be a place of death, entropy and chemical equilibrium.

Some Christians are σαρκικός ("babies in spiritual development) and others are πνευματικός ("mature in spiritual development"). None are ψυχικός ("having not the Spirit" and therefore unsaved - Jude 19). But *all* Christians, living and dead, before the second coming, whether they are σαρκικοί or πνευματικοί are still living in physical bodies that were untouched by regeneration. At conversion the soul is saved and the intellect is quickened, but the body is the same old sin-infested body of flesh that it always had been, which can do nothing but work its sinful works (Gal.5:19-21). If our Lord raptured and resurrected that into heaven, we would spend eternity fighting it as we have since the day that we were saved (Gal.5:16,17). Where is the deliverance for which Paul prayed (Rom.7:24) and for which in advance he thanked God (Rom.7:25)?

If redeemed souls and spirits were forced to live throughout eternity in corrupt bodies, we would be forced to admit that Satan had gained at least a partial victory. Unable to prevent our going to heaven, he could still gloat over the fact that we would be miserable while there, fighting the inducement to evil and on occasion losing the fight. This says nothing about the physical pains and disabilities which we would still endure under this scenario. Is heaven to be a place where Christian men will grow too much hair on the chin and too little on the head? Are some to walk the streets of the New Jerusalem with wooden legs and crutches? Are Christian teeth to ache and rot forever? Is arthritis and cancer never to be conquered? The thought is preposterous, not only because it suggests an eternity of pain and tears, but more preposterous because it says that God must allow the devil to have at least a partial victory. This can never be, since at Calvary through His death He "destroyed him that hath the power of death and delivere(d) them who through fear of death were all their lifetime (on earth that is) subject to bondage" (Heb.2:14,15).

No, our Sovereign Lord has all the power there is, both in heaven and earth (Mt.28:18) and having saved our souls and enlightened our intellects, when the Holy Spirit called us, He promised then that the last thing that He would do for us on this earth would be to save our bodies as well. And the seal of this promise was the Holy Spirit, Who indwelt us from the day of our birth from above (John 3:3,7) and became the "down payment" on the redemption of our bodies (Eph.1:13,14; 4:30; Rom.8:11).

Thus the perishable must be made viable. Living death ($\vartheta\nu\eta\tau\acute{o}\varsigma$ #3914) must become immortal ($\grave{\alpha}\vartheta\alpha\nu\alpha\sigma\acute{\iota}\alpha\nu$ #4254). *Cf.* 2 Cor.5:1-3. The Christian body is now mortal (Rom.6:12) but it is the obligation of the Holy Spirit Who lives within to raise it up (Rom.8:11) and make it immortal. This is the promise of Phil.3:20,21 and 1 John 3:2.

Will the immortal and incorruptible resurrected/raptured body of the Christian look like it was when it was mortal and corruptible? It will be genotypical. If your mother had blue eyes and curly hair and you inherited them from her there is no reason why you should not have blue eyes and curly hair in heaven. That which is genotypical is also phenotypical, for our genetic structure dictates our physical appearance, generally, though it does not prevent our responding to some degree to our environment. If a Christian with a fair skin color happened to have a tan because he had been out in the sun too long at the time of the rapture, there is no reason to suppose that he would have a tan in heaven, but he will look enough like he did on earth that we will recognize him in heaven if we knew him on earth. So the question which is so often asked, "Will we know each other in heaven?" must be answered by saying, "Of course!" We certainly will not know less in heaven than we do now. The kernel of corn which was planted produces another kernel of corn on the new cob that resembles it to a t.

The appearance of the resurrected body is not especially important. Its condition is the glorious feature. If our appearance is different, due to glorification, we shall have an eternity to get acquainted again. If there is no appreciable difference, a prospect that does not particularly thrill some of us (!) we can console ourselves that there will be no more pain and that God will wipe away our tears (Rev.21:4) for "the former things are passed away."

Verse 54 - "So when this corruptible shall have put on incorruption, and this mortal shall have put on immortality, then shall be brought to pass the saying that is written, Death is swallowed up in victory."

ὅταν δὲ τὸ φθαρτὸν τοῦτο ἐνδύσηται ἀφθαρσίαν καὶ τὸ θνητὸν τοῦτο ἐνδύσηται ἀθανασίαν, τότε γενήσεται ὁ λόγος ὁ γεγραμμένος, Κατεπόθη ὁ θάνατος εἰς νῖκος.

"When the perishable puts on the imperishable, and the mortal puts on immortality, then shall come to pass the saying that is written: 'Death is swallowed up in victory.'" . . . RSV

ὅταν (conjunction with the subjunctive in an indefinite temporal clause) 436.
δὲ (continuative conjunction) 11.
τὸ (nom.sing.neut.of the article in agreement with φθαρτὸν) 9.
φθαρτὸν (nom.sing.neut.of φθαρτός, subject of ἐνδύσηται) 3804.
τοῦτο (nom.sing.neut.of οὗτος, in agreement with φθαρτὸν) 93.
ἐνδύσηται (3d.per.sing.aor.mid.subj.of ἐνδύω, indefinite temporal clause) 613.
ἀφθαρσίαν (acc.sing.fem.of ἀφθαρσία, direct object of ἐνδύσηται) 3836.
καὶ (adjunctive conjunction joining temporal clauses) 14.
τὸ (nom.sing.neut.of the article in agreement with θνητὸν) 9.
θνητὸν (nom.sing.neut.of θνητός, subject of ἐνδύσηται) 3914.
τοῦτο (nom.sing.neut.of οὗτος, in agreement with θνητὸν) 93.
ἐνδύσηται (3d.per.sing.aor.mid.subj.of ἐνδύω, indefinite temporal clause) 613.
ἀθανασίαν (acc.sing.fem.of ἀθανασία, direct object of ἐνδύσηται) 4254.
τότε (temporal adverb) 166.
γενήσεται (3d.per.sing.aor.mid.subj.of γίνομαι, potential) 113.
ὁ (nom.sing.masc.of the article in agreement with λόγος) 9.
λόγος (nom.sing.masc.of λόγος, subject of γενήσεται) 510.
ὁ (nom.sing.masc.of the article in agreement with γεγραμμένος) 9.
γεγραμμένος (perf.pass.part.nom.sing.masc.of γράφω, adjectival, emphatic attributive position, ascriptive, in agreement with λόγος) 156.
Κατεπόθη (3d.per.sing.1st.aor.pass.ind.of καταπίνω, constative) 1454.
ὁ (nom.sing.masc.of the article in agreement with θάνατος) 9.
θάνατος (nom.sing.masc.of θάνατος, subject of κατεπόθη) 381.
εἰς (preposition with the accusative, predicate usage) 140.
νῖκος (acc.sing.neut.of νῖκος, adverbial accusative) 990.

Translation - "And when this which is perishable puts on that which is imperishable, and the mortal puts on immortality, then comes to pass the saying which is written,'Death is swallowed down in victory.' "

Comment: The doubt in the ὅταν clause with the subjunctive ἐνδύσηται is not whether or not the resurrection will come, but when it will come. When it does a scripture, Isaiah 25:8, will be fulfilled. Note the potential subjunctive in γενήσεται. It is "widely used in subordinate clauses. These commonly future reference, and are qualified by an element of contingency. All use of the subjunctive in object or conditional clauses are included in this class." (Mantey, *Manual,* 172). *Cf.* 1 Tim.5:21; Mt.17:20; Lk.6:34 for other examples of the potential subjunctive.

φθαρτός (#3804) is destined to be replaced by ἀφθαρσία (#3836) and θνητός by ἀθανασία (#4254). Thus the body of the Christian is brought into conformity with his new nature, acquired at the new birth. This will take place at the resurrection. But resurrection is not possible until death has occurred. Thus death is not a tragedy to the Christian. It is a step toward resurrection. Only thus can we get rid of our old Adamic nature and be make like Him (1 John 3:2).

Verse 55 - "O death, where is thy sting? O grave, where is thy victory?"

ποῦ σου, θάνατε, τὸ νῖκος; ποῦ σου, θάνατε, τὸ κέντρον ;

" 'O death, where is thy victory? O death, where is thy sting?' " . . . RSV

ποῦ (interrogative adverb of place) 142.
σου (gen.sing.masc.of σύ, possession) 104.
θάνατε (voc.sing.masc.of θάνατος, address) 381.
τὸ (nom.sing.neut.of the article in agreement with νῖκος) 9.
νῖκος (nom.sing.neut.of νῖκος, subject of ἐστιν understood) 990.
ποῦ (interrogative adverb of place) 142.
σου (gen.sing.masc.of σύ, possession) 104.
θάνατε (voc.sing.masc.of θάνατος, address) 381.
τὸ (nom.sing.neut.of the article in agreement with κέντρον) 9.
κέντρον (nom.sing.neut.of κέντρον, subject of ἐστιν understood) 3662.

Translation - "Where, death, is your victory? Where, death, is your sting?"

Comment: The quotation is from Hosea 13:14, albeit a loose translation. Death seems cruel and painful, and its victory seems obvious as the disintegrating corpse is committed to the ground, where further chemical disintegration finishes its dissolution. But this is prerequisite to resurrection, for all except those Christians who will live until our Lord returns. Hence death contributes to its own defeat, because the last Adam was not a living soul made out of soil from the earth, but a life-giving Spirit from Heaven.

Christianity is unique in its claim that the body of the saint is destined to be glorified and made like the incarnate body of its Creator (1 John 3:2; Phil.3:20,21).

Verse 56 - "The sting of death is sin; and the strength of sin is the law."

τὸ δὲ κέντρον τοῦ θανάτου ἡ ἁμαρτία, ἡ δὲ δύναμις τῆς ἁμαρτίας ὁ νόμος.

"The sting of death is sin, and the power of sin is the law." . . . RSV

τὸ (nom.sing.neut.of the article in agreement with κέντρον) 9.
δὲ (explanatory conjunction) 11.
κέντρον (nom.sing.neut.of κέντρον, subject of ἐστιν understood) 3662.
τοῦ (gen.sing.masc.of the article in agreement with θανάτου) 9.
θανάτου (gen.sing.masc.of θάνατος, description) 381.
ἡ (nom.sing.masc.of the article in agreement with ἁμαρτία) 9.
ἁμαρτία (nom.sing.fem.of ἁμαρτία, predicate nominative) 111.
ἡ (nom.sing.fem.of the article in agreement with δύναμις) 9.
δὲ (continuative conjunction) 11.
δύναμις (nom.sing.fem.of δύναμις, subject of ἐστιν understood) 687.
τῆς (gen.sing.fem.of the article in agreement with ἁμαρτίας) 9.
ἁμαρτίας (gen.sing.fem.of ἁμαρτία, description) 111.
ὁ (nom.sing.masc.of the article in agreement with νόμος) 9.
νόμος (nom.sing.masc.of νόμος, predicate nominative) 464.

Translation - "Now the sting of death is sin and the power of sin is the law."

Comment: *Cf.* Romans 3:23; 5:12; 6:23. Sin and death are inevitably associated as cause is to result. The power of sin to bring death is God's moral law in the universe that punishes transgression. Transgression of natural law as well as violation of the moral code which God gave to Moses at Sinai has its consequences. But the last Adam can give us victory.

Verse 57 - "But thanks be to God which giveth us the victory through our Lord Jesus Christ."

τῷ δὲ θεῷ χάρις τῷ διδόντι ἡμῖν τὸ νῖκος διὰ τοῦ κυρίου ἡμῶν Ἰησοῦ Χριστοῦ.

"But thanks be to God, who gives us the victory through our Lord Jesus Christ." . . . RSV

τῷ (dat.sing.masc.of the article in agreement with θεῷ) 9.
δὲ (adversative conjunction) 11.
θεῷ (dat.sing.masc.of θεός, indirect object of verb understood) 124.
χάρις (nom.sing.fem.of χάρις, interjectional nominative) 1700.
τῷ (dat.sing.masc.of the article in agreement with διδόντι) 9.
διδόντι (pres.act.part.dat.sing.masc.of δίδωμι, substantival, in apposition) 362.
ἡμῖν (dat.pl.masc.of ἐγώ, indirect object of διδόντι) 123.
τὸ (acc.sing.neut.of the article in agreement with νῖκος) 9.
νῖκος (acc.sing.neut.of νῖκος, direct object of διδόντι) 990.
διὰ (preposition with the ablative of agent) 118.
τοῦ (abl.sing.masc.of the article in agreement with κυρίου) 9.

κυρίου (abl.sing.masc.of κύριος, agent) 97.
ἡμῶν (gen.pl.masc.of ἐγώ, relationship) 123.
Ἰησοῦ (abl.sing.masc.of Ἰησοῦς, apposition) 3.
Χριστοῦ (abl.sing.masc.of Χριστός, apposition) 4.

Translation - "But thanks be to God, the One Who is always giving us the victory through our Lord Jesus Christ."

Comment: Verse 56 if it stood alone would frighten us, but Paul hastens to add the adversative δὲ of verse 57. The law of God empowers sin to bring death to the race, *but* God be thanked. He is always giving (present tense in διδόντι) us victory through His redemptive Agent, our Lord Jesus Christ.

Thus Paul, having begun the chapter with a clear statement of what the gospel of Jesus Christ is (1 Cor.15:3,4) goes on to prove that Jesus actually conquered death and then went on to analyze how Christ's resurrection assures our own to make us wholly like Him (Rom.8:29) in spirit and also in body. The entire chapter has been didactic. Now Paul adds his conclusion in verse 58 - a hortatory appeal for victorious Christian living.

Verse 58 - "Therefore, my beloved brethren, be ye stedfast, unmoveable, always abounding in the work of the Lord, forasmuch as ye know that your labour is not in vain in the Lord."

Ὥστε, ἀδελφοί μου ἀγαπητοί, ἑδραῖοι γίνεσθε, ἀμετακίνητοι, περισσεύοντες ἐν τῷ ἔργῳ τοῦ κυρίου πάντοτε, εἰδότες ὅτι ὁ κόπος ὑμῶν οὐκ ἔστιν κενὸς ἐν κυρίῳ.

"Therefore, my beloved brethren, be steadfast, immovable, always abounding in the work of the Lord, knowing that in the Lord your labor is not in vain." . . .
                                                                                                    RSV

Ὥστε (inferential conjunction) 752.
ἀδελφοί (voc.pl.masc.of ἀδελφός, address) 15.
μου (gen.sing.masc.of ἐγώ, relationship) 123.
ἀγαπητοί (voc.pl.masc.of ἀγαπητός, in agreement with ἀδελφοί) 327.
ἑδραῖοι (nom.pl.masc.of ἑδραῖος, predicate adjective) 4170
γίνεσθε (2d.per.pl.pres.impv.of γίνομαι, entreaty) 113.

#**4255** ἀμετακίνητοι (nom.pl.masc.of ἀμετακίνετος, predicate adjective).

King James Version

unmoveable - 1 Cor.15:58.

Revised Standard Version

immoveable - 1 Cor.15:58.

Meaning: α privative plus μετά (#50) plus κινέω (#1435). *Cf.* μετακινέω (#4605). Hence, not to be moved out of place. Immoveable, steadfast. With reference to

Christian faith and practice - 1 Cor.15:58.

περισσεύοντες (pres.act.part.nom.pl.masc.of περισσεύω, adverbial, manner) 473.

ἐν (preposition with the locative of sphere) 80.

τῷ (loc.sing.neut.of the article in agreement with ἔργῳ) 9.

ἔργῳ (loc.sing.neut.of ἔργον, sphere) 460.

τοῦ (gen.sing.masc.of the article in agreement with κυρίου) 9.

κυρίου (gen.sing.masc.of κύριος, description) 97.

πάντοτε (adverbial) 1567.

εἰδότες (perf.act.part.nom.pl.masc.of ὁράω, adverbial, causal) 144b.

ὅτι (conjunction introducing an object clause in indirect discourse) 211.

ὁ (nom.sing.masc.of the article in agreement with κόπος) 9.

κόπος (nom.sing.masc.of κόπος, subject of ἔστιν) 1565.

ὑμῶν (gen.pl.masc.of σύ, possession) 104.

οὐκ (negative particle with the indicative) 130.

ἔστιν (3d.per.sing.pres.ind.of εἰμί, aoristic) 86.

κενὸς (nom.sing.masc.of κενός, predicate adjective) 1836.

ἐν (preposition with the instrumental of association) 80.

κυρίῳ (instru.sing.masc.of κύριος, association) 97.

Translation - "So, my beloved brethren, you must be steadfast, immovable, abounding in the work of the Lord at all times, because you have learned that your labor is not in vain in the Lord."

Comment: The didactic argument (verses 1-57) culminates in an exhortation to which the argument leads. The imperative γίνεσθε is durative. "Be always steadfast and immovable." Cf.#'s 4170 and 4255. The participle περισσεύοντες is manner, and is really redundant, except that it reinforces the durative force of γίνεσθε. The way to be steadfast in the faith is to be always busy. Doing what? The locative of sphere follows - ἐν τῷ ἔργῳ τοῦ κυρίου. Note the distinction between ἔργῳ and κόπος. The activities of the Lord (ἔργῳ τοῦ κυρίου) are the "good works which He hath before ordained that we should walk in them" (Eph.2:10). The κόπος is the inconvenience (trouble, bother, pain, cost, sacrifice, that which is unpleasant) that accompanies our work (ἔργον) for Him.

The participle εἰδότες is another adverb - this time causal. It is *because* we have discovered in the past, and therefore are aware now (perfect tense in εἰδότες) that the Lord will always reward what we do for Him. The sacrifice which may seem great at the time is worth it, in terms of results achieved. Our painful, laborious, sacrificial work for Him (cf.#1565) is not without its significance (cf.#1836). Why is it significant? Because Jesus died and rose again and what we do for Him, however inconvenient and costly it may be, in the short run, is fruitful and we will be rewarded eternally.

It is worth noting that the New Testament never divorces doctrine from Christian ethics. Paul always follows didactic passages of doctrinal significance with exhortations for holy living. Cf. e.g. Romans 12:1 and that which goes before. Also Gal.5:1; Eph.4:1; Col.3:1. In each of these verses the inferential conjunction οὖν occurs, pointing backward to the doctrine and forward to the practical teaching.

The Contribution for the Saints

(1 Corinthians 16:1-4)

1 Cor.16:1 - "*Now concerning the collection for the saints, as I have given order to the churches of Galatia, even so do ye.*"

Περὶ δὲ τῆς λογείας τῆς εἰς τοὺς ἁγίους, ὥσπερ διέταξα ταῖς ἐκκλησίαις τῆς Γαλατίας, οὕτως καὶ ὑμεῖς ποιήσατε.

"*Now concerning the contribution for the saints: as I directed the churches of Galatia, so you also are to do.*" . . . RSV

Περὶ (preposition with the genitive of reference) 173.
δὲ (explanatory conjunction) 11.
τῆς (gen.sing.fem.of the article in agreement with λογείας) 9.

#4256 λογείας (gen.sing.fem.of λογία, reference).

King James Version

collection - 1 Cor.16:1.
gathering - 1 Cor.16:2.

Revised Standard Version

contribution - 1 Cor.16:1,2.

Meaning: Cf. λέγω (#66) - "to collect." A collection. In 1 Cor.16:1,2, a financial offering for the poor saints in Jerusalem.

τῆς (gen.sing.fem.of the article in agreement with λογείας) 9.
εἰς (preposition with the accusative, purpose) 140.
τοὺς (acc.pl.masc.of the article in agreement with ἁγίους) 9.
ἁγίους (acc.pl.masc.of ἅγιος, purpose) 84.
ὥσπερ (intensive comparative particle) 560.
διέταξα (1st.per.sing.aor.act.ind.of διατάσσω, constative) 904.
ταῖς (dat.pl.fem.of the article in agreement with ἐκκλησίαις) 9.
ἐκκλησίαις (dat.pl.fem.of ἐκκλησία, indirect object of διέταξα) 1204.
τῆς (gen.sing.fem.of the article in agreement with Γαλατίας) 9.

#4257 Γαλατίας (gen.sing.fem.of Γαλατία, description).

King James Version

Galatia - 1 Cor.16:1; Gal.1:2; 2 Tim.4:10; 1 Pet.1:1.

Revised Standard Version

Galatia - 1 Cor.16:1; Gal.1:2; 2 Tim.4:10; 1 Pet.1:1.

Meaning: Gallograecia, a region of Asia Minor, bounded by Paphlagonia, Pontus, Cappadocia, Lycaonia, Phrygia and Bithynia. It took its name from those Gallic tribes that crossed into Asia Minor, B.C. 278 and after roaming about there for a time at length settled down permanently in the above-mentioned region and intermarried with the Greeks. From B.C. 189 on, though subject to the Romans they were governed by their own chiefs, but in B.C. 24 (al.25) their country was formally reduced to a Roman province." (Thayer, 108). - 1 Cor.16:1; Gal.1:2; 2 Tim.4:10; 1 Pet.1:1.

οὕτως (demonstrative adverb) 74.
καὶ (adjunctive conjunction joining substantives) 14.
ὑμεῖς (nom.pl.masc.of σύ, subject of ποιήσατε) 104.
ποιήσατε (2d.per.pl.aor.act.impv.of ποιέω, command) 127.

Translation - "Now with reference to the offering for the saints, precisely as I gave orders to the churches of Galatia, so also should you do."

Comment: Paul devotes chapter 16 to four matters: his instruction with reference to the financial gifts of the Corinthians to the famine-stricken Christians in Palestine (verses 1-4), is followed by a discussion of his travel plans (verses 5-12). He closes the epistle with two verses devoted to admonitions in the spirit of 1 Cor.15:58 and 1 Cor.13 (verses 13-14). The remainder of the epistle is concerned with greetings and the close (verses 15-24).

The εἰς clause with the accusative is purpose. Note the intensified ὥσπερ rather than the less intensive ὡς (#'s 560, 128), followed by οὕτως (#74). What he had told the various churches in Galatian country to do he now spells out to the Corinthians.

Verse 2 - "Upon the first day of the week let every one of you lay by him in store, as God hath prospered him, that there be no gatherings when I come."

κατὰ μίαν σαββάτου ἕκαστος ὑμῖν παρ᾿ ἑαυτῷ τιθέτω θησαυρίζων ὅ τι ἐὰν εὐοδῶται, ἵνα μὴ ὅταν ἔλθω τότε λογεῖαι γίνωνται.

"On the first day of every week, each of you is to put something aside and store it up, as he may prosper, so that contributions need not be made when I come."...
. RSV

κατὰ (preposition with the accusative, distributive) 98.
μίαν (acc.sing.fem.of εἷς, in agreement with ἡμέραν, understood) 469.
σαββάτου (gen.sing.neut.of σάββατον, description) 962.
ἕκαστος (nom.sing.masc.of ἕκαστος, subject of τιθέτω) 1217.
ὑμῶν (gen.pl.masc.of σύ, partitive genitive) 104.
παρ᾿ (preposition with the locative of place) 154.
ἑαυτῷ (loc.sing.masc.of ἑαυτοῦ, place) 288.
τιθέτω (3d.per.sing.pres.act.impv.of τίθημι, command) 455.
θησαυρίζων (pres.act.part.nom.sing.masc.of θησαυρίζω, adverbial, manner) 591.
ὅ (acc.sing.neut.of ὅς, relative pronoun, direct object of εὐοδῶται) 65.
τι (acc.sing.neut.of τις, indefinite pronoun, extent) 486.

ἐὰν (conditional particle with the subjunctive in a third-class condition) 363.
εὐοδῶται (3d.per.sing.pres.pass.subj.of εὐοδόομαι, third-class condition) 3788.
ἵνα (conjunction with the subjunctive in a negative purpose clause) 114.
μὴ (negative particle with the subjunctive in a negative purpose clause) 87.
ὅταν (conjunction with the subjunctive in an indefinite temporal clause) 436.
ἔλθω (1st.per.sing.aor.subj.of ἔρχομαι, indefinite temporal clause) 146.
τότε (temporal adverb) 166.
λογεῖαι (nom.pl.fem.of λογία, subject of γίνωνται) 4256.
γίνωνται (3d.per.pl.pres.subj.of γίνομαι,negative purpose clause) 113.

Translation - "On the first day of the week let each one of you put aside in savings whatever he can afford, so that when I come, at that time no offering will be taken."

Comment: κατὰ with the accusative in a distributive time sense. ἕκαστος - "each individual," followed by the partitive genitive. The participle θησαυρίζων is an adverbial of manner - "in savings."

The Corinthians were to save something if they could after normal consumption needs had been met. ὅ τι ἐὰν εὐοδῶται - "to whatever extent, if any, you are enabled to do so, as a result of your earnings for the week. The ἐὰν clause with the subjunctive expresses some doubt that all will be able to give. "If you prosper, give. Otherwise, not." The negative purpose clause with ἵνα μὴ . . . λογεῖαι γίνωνται tells us why Paul wanted them to lay up their gifts in advance. He did not wish to take an offering when he arrived in Corinth. Rather he hoped that the money would be already collected so that he could account for it and send or take it to Jerusalem where it was needed. Note in the ὅταν ἔλθω clause that he was not sure when he could come to Corinth.

There is nothing here about tithing in the ten percent sense. The saving for the gift was to be contingent upon whatever prosperity might have been enjoyed during the week in question. Note that this was to be a regular thing and it was to take place on Sunday. Note also that every Christian in Corinth was under this obligation.

The tithe, with its demand for ten percent of net gain is a proportionate tax and as such it is regressive. It falls heaviest upon the poor who are least able to pay it. For example, the Christian who nets one thousand dollars per week will pay the tithe of one hundred dollars and have nine hundred dollars remaining for his own needs. The poor man who nets one hundred dollars per week must pay ten and live on ninety. The tithe which Malachi demanded (Mal.3:9,10) was the rule under the ideal theocratic government of Israel. Thus it included the tax which the Jew paid to the king as well as his offering which he was to bring to the priest. This was the total tax which he was expected to pay. In order to have a parallel situation in America the Christian should add what he gives to the Lord in his church the taxes which he pays to the governments, at municipal, state and federal levels. Paul's advice about giving is found in 2 Cor.8:9-14; 9:1-10.

Verse 3 - "And when I come, whomsoever ye shall approve by your letters, them will I send to bring your liberality unto Jerusalem."

ὅταν δὲ παραγένωμαι, οὓς ἐὰν δοκιμάσητε, δι' ἐπιστολῶν τούτους πέμφω ἀπενεγκεῖν τὴν χάριν ὑμῶν εἰς Ἰερουσαλήμ.

"And when I arrive, I will send those whom you accredit by letter to carry your gift to Jerusalem." . . . RSV

ὅταν (conjunction introducing the subjunctive in an indefinite temporal clause) 436.

δὲ (continuative conjunction) 11.

παραγένωμαι (1st.per.sing.aor.mid.subj.of παραγίνομαι, indefinite temporal clause) 139.

οὓς (acc.pl.masc.of ὅς, relative pronoun, direct object of δοκιμάσητε) 65.

ἐὰν (conditional particle with the subjunctive in a third-class condition) 363.

δοκιμάσητε (2d.per.pl.aor.act.subj.of δοκιμάζω, third-class condition) 2493.

δι' (preposition with the ablative of means) 118.

ἐπιστολῶν (abl.pl.fem.of ἐπιστολή, means) 3180.

τούτους (acc.pl.masc.of οὗτος, direct object of πέμφω) 93.

πέμφω (1st.per.sing.fut.act.ind.of πέμπω, predictive) 169.

ἀπενεγκεῖν (2d.aor.act.inf.of ἀποφέρω, purpose) 2583.

τὴν (acc.sing.fem.of the article in agreement with χάριν) 9.

χάριν (acc.sing.fem.of χάρις, direct object of ἀπενεγκεῖν) 1700.

ὑμῶν (gen.pl.masc.of σύ, possession) 104.

εἰς (preposition with the accusative of extent) 140.

Ἰερουσαλήμ (acc.sing.masc.of Ἰερουσαλήμ, extent) 141.

Translation - "And when I arrive, whomever you may authorize with letters of credentials, them I will send to Jerusalem to deliver your gift."

Comment: The doubt in ὅταν . . . παραγένωμαι is not doubt that Paul will visit Corinth but doubt as to the precise time when he will arrive. Note the hypotactic clause οὓς ἐὰν δοκιμάσητε δι' ἐπιστολῶν. Paul did not know whether the Corinthians would be willing to authorize any as messengers to take the money to Jerusalem, nor if they did, who it would be. Hence the third-class condition. δι' ἐπιστολῶν can be joined either to δοκιμάσητε or to πέμφω. If the former he is asking the Corinthian church to name certain persons and certify by written credentials that they have been approved by the church and entrusted with the money. If the latter he is saying that he will send with the messengers, selected by the church, letters commending the messengers to the church authorities in Jerusalem. In either case Paul is following his own advice (Rom.12:17; 1 Cor.9:12). Paul was sensitive to the fact that he had critics in Corinth and he was anxious to avoid all possibility that they might accuse him of stealing the money.

Verse 4 - "And if it be meet that I go also, they shall go with me."

ἐὰν δὲ ἄξιον ᾖ τοῦ κἀμὲ πορεύεσθαι, σὺν ἐμοὶ πορεύσονται.

"If it seem advisable that I should go also, they will accompany me." . . . RSV

ἐὰν (conditional particle with the subjunctive in a third-class condition) 363.
δὲ (continuative conjunction) 11.
ἄξιον (nom.sing.neut.of ἄξιος, predicate adjective) 285.
ᾖ (3d.per.sing.pres.subj.of εἰμί, third-class condition) 86.
τοῦ (gen.sing.neut.of the article in agreement with πορεύεσθαι) 9.
κἀμὲ (acc.sing.masc.of κἀγώ, general reference) 178.
πορεύεσθαι (pres.mid.inf.of πορεύομαι, subject infinitive of ᾖ) 170.
σὺν (preposition with the instrumental of association) 1542.
ἐμοὶ (instru.sing.masc.of ἐμός, association) 1267.
πορεύσονται (3d.per.pl.fut.mid.ind.of πορεύομαι, predictive) 170.

Translation - "And in the event that it seems worthwhile for me to go also, they will go with me."

Comment: Paul is not sure what his plan will be after he visits Corinth. He may or may not decide that a trip from Corinth to Jerusalem, to accompany the messengers whom the church will send with the money, will be worthwhile. If so (third-class condition in ἐὰν . . . ἄξιον ᾖ τοῦ κἀμὲ πορεύεσθαι), the messengers selected and approved by the church will go with Paul.

If Paul should decide to go with the messengers to Jerusalem, why could he not take the money and save the Corinthians a trip? Why did he not suggest this? Because he would be laying himself open to the charge that he would misappropriate the funds. Under his plan the Corinthian messengers would keep the money in their custody. Note the articular infinitive τοῦ πορεύεσθαι as the subject of ᾖ, with ἄξιον as the predicate adjective.

Plans for Travel

(1 Corinthians 16:5-12)

Verse 5 - "Now I will come to you, when I shall pass through Macedonia; for I do pass through Macedonia."

Ἐλεύσομαι δὲ πρὸς ὑμᾶς ὅταν Μακεδονίαν διέλθω, Μακεδονίαν γὰρ διέρχομαι.

"I will visit you after passing through Macedonia, for I intend to pass through Macedonia, . . . " . . . RSV

Ἐλεύσομαι (1st.per.sing.fut.ind.of ἔρχομαι, predictive) 146.
δὲ (explanatory conjunction) 11.
πρὸς (preposition with the accusative of extent) 197.
ὑμᾶς (acc.pl.masc.of σύ, extent) 104.
ὅταν (conjunction introducing the subjunctive in an indefinite temporal clause) 436.

Μακεδονίαν (acc.sing.fem.of Μακεδονία, extent) 3360.
διέλθω (1st.per.sing.aor.subj.of διέρχομαι, indefinite temporal clause) 1017.
Μακεδονίαν (acc.sing.fem.of Μακεδονία, object of διέλθω) 3360.
γὰρ (causal conjunction) 105.
διέρχομαι (1st.per.sing.pres.ind.of διέρχομαι, futuristic) 1017.

Translation - "Now I will come to you when I have passed through Macedonia, because I am going to pass through Macedonia."

Comment: Note the futuristic present in διέρχομαι. Paul's trip when he made it, would take him north from Ephesus (1 Cor.16:8) to Philippi, down south to Berea, Thessalonica and then further to the south to Corinth. *Cf.* Acts 19:21.

Verse 6 - "And it may be that I will abide, yea, and winter with you, that ye may bring me on my journey whithersoever I go."

πρὸς ὑμᾶς δὲ τυχὸν παραμενῶ ἢ καὶ παραχειμάσω, ἵνα ὑμεῖς με προπέμψητε οὗ ἐὰν πορεύωμαι.

"and perhaps I will stay with you or even spend the winter, so that you may speed me on my journey, wherever I go." . . . RSV

πρὸς (preposition with the accusative, extent) 197.
ὑμᾶς (acc.pl.masc.of σύ, extent) 104.
δὲ (continuative conjunction) 11.
τυχὸν (2d.aor.act.part.acc.sing.neut.of τυγχάνω, adverbial, accusative absolute) 2699.

#4258 παραμενῶ (1st.per.sing.fut.act.ind.of παραμένω, predictive).

　　　King James Version

abide - 1 Cor.16:6.
continue - Heb.7:23; James 1:25; Phil.1:25.

　　　Revised Standard Version

stay with - 1 Cor.16:6.
continue - Heb.7:23.
persevere - James 1:25; Phil.1:25.

Meaning: A combination of παρά (#154) and μένω (#864); to remain along the side of; to continue with - in a physical sense - 1 Cor.16:6; Phil.1:25; to continue functioning in the role as a priest, that is, to continue to serve in the temple - Heb.7:23. To continue to hold a given philosophy; opposed to ἀκροατής (#3841) - James 1:25.

ἢ (disjunctive) 465.
καὶ (ascensive conjunction) 14.
παραχειμάσω (1st.per.sing.fut.act.ind.of παραχειμάζω, predictive) 3702.

ἵνα (conjunction with the subjunctive in a purpose clause) 114.

ὑμεῖς (nom.pl.masc.of σύ, subject of προτέμφητε) 104.

μέ (acc.sing.masc.of ἐγώ, direct object of προπέμφητε) 123.

προπέμφητε (2d.per.pl.aor.act.subj.of προπέμπω, purpose) 3335.

οὗ (gen.sing.neut.of ὅς, relative pronoun, place description) 65.

ἐὰν (conditional particle in a third-class condition) 363.

πορεύωμαι (1st.per.sing.pres.mid.subj.of πορεύομαι, third-class condition) 170.

Translation - *"And perhaps I may stay with you or even spend the winter, so that you may send me on wherever I may go."*

Comment: τυχόν, an accusative neuter aorist participle is really an accusative absolute used here adverbially. It expresses manner. καὶ is ascensive. Paul was not certain whether he would stay in Corinth a short time and leave before cold weather, when sea travel on the Mediterranean was hazardous (Acts 27:12), or whether he would spend the winter months there in order that when he did decide to leave, to whatever point he might choose, they might be able to pay his travel expenses. All was very tentative in Paul's plans as ought the plans of all Spirit-led Christians to be (James 4:13-15).

Verse 7 - *"For I will not see you now by the way; but I trust to tarry a while with you, if the Lord permit."*

οὐ θέλω γὰρ ὑμᾶς ἄρτι ἐν παρόδῳ ἰδεῖν, ἐλπίζω γὰρ χρόνον τινὰ ἐπιμεῖναι πρὸς ὑμᾶς ἐὰν ὁ κύριος ἐπιτρέφῃ.

"For I do not want to see you now just in passing; I hope to spend some time with you, if the Lord permits." . . . RSV

οὐ (negative particle with the indicative) 130.

θέλω (1st.per.sing.pres.act.ind.of θέλω, aoristic) 88.

γὰρ (inferential conjunction) 105.

ὑμᾶς (acc.pl.masc.of σύ, direct object of ἰδεῖν) 104.

ἄρτι (temporal adverb) 320.

ἐν (preposition with the locative of time point) 80.

#4259 παρόδῳ (loc.sing.masc.of πάραδος, time point).

King James Version

way - 1 Cor.16:7.

Revised Standard Version

in passing - 1 Cor.16:7.

Meaning: A combination of παρά (#154) and ὁδός (#199). By the way. With the locative of time point - "as I am passing by." Contrasted with χρόνον τινά in 1 Cor.16:7, thus to indicate that ἐν παρόδῳ means a short visit as opposed to some longer period of time.

ἰδεῖν (aor.act.inf.of ὁράω, epexegetical) 144.

ἐλπίζω (1st.per.sing.pres.act.ind.of ἐλπίζω, present progressive retroactive) 991.

γὰρ (causal conjunction) 105.

χρόνον (acc.sing.masc.of χρόνος, time extent) 168.

τινὰ (acc.sing.masc.of τις, indefinite pronoun, in agreement with χρόνον) 486.

ἐπιμεῖναι (aor.act.inf.of ἐπιμένω, epexegetical) 2379.

πρὸς (preposition with the accusative of extent) 197.

ὑμᾶς (acc.pl.masc.of σύ, extent) 104.

ἐὰν (conditional particle with the subjunctive in a third-class condition) 363.

ὁ (nom.sing.masc.of the article in agreement with κύριος) 9.

κύριος (nom.sign.masc.of κύριος, subject of ἐπιτρέφῃ) 97.

ἐπιτρέφῃ (3d.per.sing.aor.act.subj.of ἐπιτρέπω, third-class condition) 747.

Translation - "So I do not want to see you now in a short visit, because I have been hoping to stay with you for some time, if the Lord permit."

Comment: In the light of verses 5 and 6, the first γὰρ is inferential, though the second is causal. Paul wished to forego a short visit - a stop over (ἐν παρόδῳ) which is all that he would have time for had he crossed the Aegean, from Ephesus to Corinth, instead of going north and west into Macedonia. Rather, if he went to Macedonia first, and then went south to Corinth, he hoped to say there a longer time of indefinite duration (χρόνον τινά). ἐλπίζω is the indicative apodosis in the third-class condition. If the Lord permits it (Paul could not be sure) he hoped to follow the plan he has outlined.

He reveals his immediate plans in

Verse 8 - "But I will tarry at Ephesus until Pentecost."

ἐπιμενῶ δὲ ἐν Ἐφέσῳ ἕως τῆς πεντηκοστῆς.

"But I will stay in Ephesus until Pentecost." . . . RSV

ἐπιμενῶ (1st.per.sing.fut.act.ind.of ἐπιμένω, predictive) 2379.

δὲ (adversative conjunction) 11.

ἐν (preposition with the locative of place) 80.

Ἐφέσῳ (loc.sing.masc.of Ἐφεσος, place) 3452.

ἕως (preposition with the genitive of time description) 71.

τῆς (gen.sing.fem.of the article in agreement with πεντηκοστῆς) 9.

πεντηκοστῆς (gen.sing.fem.of πεντεκοστή, time description) 2956.

Translation - "But I will stay in Ephesus until Pentecost."

Comment: ἐπιμενῶ is a futuristic present tense. He means that he is now in Ephesus and will remain there for some time. How long? ἕως with the genitive in a time expression tells us - "until Pentecost." A look at the contrast between verses 7 and 8 tells us something about the leading of the Lord in the Spirit-filled life. In verse 7, Paul could only speculate about his future plans as they were subject to the permissive will of God. He would spend some time with the Corinthians "if the Lord permit." In verse 8 he seems certain about the will of God for him the immediate future. He will remain in Ephesus until Pentecost. He tells us why he is certain of the will of God for the moment in

Verse 9 - "For a great door and effectual is opened unto me, and there are many adversaries."

θύρα γάρ μοι ἀνέῳγεν μεγάλη καὶ ἐνεργής, καὶ ἀντικείμενοι πολλοί.

"for a wide door for effective work has opened to me, and there are many adversaries." . . . RSV

θύρα (nom.sing.fem.of θύρα, subject of ἀνεῳγεν) 571.
γάρ (causal conjunction) 105.
μοι (dat.sing.masc.of ἐγώ, personal advantage) 123.
ἀνέῳγεν (3d.per.sing.2d.perf.act.ind.of ἀνοίγω, intensive) 188.
μεγάλη (nom.sing.fem.of μέγας, in agreement with θύρα) 184.
καὶ (adjunctive conjunction joining adjectives) 14.

#4260 ἐνεργής (nom.sing.fem.of ἐνεργής, in agreement with θύρα).

King James Version

effectual - 1 Cor.16:9; Philemon 6.
powerful - Heb.4:12.

Revised Standard Version

for effective work - 1 Cor.16:9.
promote - Philemon 6.
active - Heb.4:12.

Meaning: Always in the New Testament as a predicate adjective, and always associated with the preaching of the Word of God. The open door, *i.e.* the opportunity to preach the gospel of Christ in Ephesus - 1 Cor.16:9; Philemon's expression of his faith - Philemon 6; the Word of God - Heb.4:12. *Cf.* ἐνέργεια (#4466), ἐνέργημα (#4213) and ἐνεργέω (#1105).

καὶ (adversative conjunction) 14.
ἀντικείμενοι (pres.part.nom.pl.masc.of ἀντίκειμαι, substantival, subject of εἰσίν understood) 2506.
πολλοί (nom.pl.masc.of πολύς, in agreement with ἀντικείμενοι) 228.

Translation - "Because a door stands open to me for great and productive ministry, but there are many who oppose."

Comment: The reason for Paul's decision to stay in Ephesus is an open door of opportunity that offered to him great and effective production in preaching. Thus γάρ is causal. The 2d.perfect ἀνέῳγεν is intransitive and intensive. This open door and the opposition which he faced are described in Acts 19:1-20. Note that the Word of God was "mighty" (Acts 19:20) as #4260 indicates. A research on the opposition to the gospel of Christ is availabe under #2506. Immorality (1 Tim.1:10), bigotry (Luke 13:17), end-time unbelievers (Luke 21:15), Antichrist (2 Thess.2:4) and gainsayers (1 Tim.5:14) all add to the general opposition of Phil.1:28. But the explosive power (Rom.1:16) of the gospel (Heb.4:12) is sufficient to overcome all opposition.

Note that Paul's attitude toward the gospel adversaries differs somewhat from that of modern evangelists. They seek a city which has been previously organized by all the cooperating churches, with the media in full cooperation, before they move in. Paul in Ephesus had none of this. Instead of saying, "There are many adversaries; let us get out of town" he said, "The door is open and the opposition is great, but the gospel is dynamite. I am going to stay until Pentecost."

Verse 10 - "Now if Timotheus come, see that he be with you without fear: for he worketh the work of the Lord, as I also do."

Ἐὰν δὲ ἔλθῃ Τιμόθεος, βλέπετε ἵνα ἀφόβως γένηται πρὸς ὑμᾶς, τὸ γὰρ ἔργον κυρίου ἐργάζεται ὡς κἀγώ.

"When Timothy comes, see that you put him at ease among you, for he is doing the work of the Lord, as I am." . . . RSV

Ἐὰν (conditional particle with the subjunctive in a third-class condition) 363.
δὲ (explanatory conjunction) 11.
ἔλθῃ (3d.per.sing.aor.subj.of ἔρχομαι, third-class condition) 146.
Τιμόθεος (nom.sing.masc.of Τιμόθεος, subject of ἔλθῃ) 3354.
βλέπετε (2d.per.pl.pres.act.impv.of βλέπω, entreaty) 499.
ἵνα (conjunction with the subjunctive in a sub-final clause) 114.
ἀφόβως (adverbial) 1853.
γένηται (3d.per.sing.aor.subj.of γίνομαι, sub-final clause) 113.
πρὸς (preposition with the accusative of extent) 197.
ὑμᾶς (acc.pl.masc.of σύ, extent) 104.
τὸ (acc.sing.neut.of the article in agreement with ἔργον) 9.
γὰρ (causal conjunction) 105.
ἔργον (acc.sing.neut.of ἔργον, direct object of ἐργάζεται) 460.
κυρίου (gen.sing.masc.of κύριος, description) 97.
ἐργάζεται (3d.per.sing.pres.mid.ind.of ἐργάζομαι, present progressive retroactive) 691.
ὡς (comparative particle) 128.
κἀγώ (adjunctive conjunction and first personal pronoun, crasis, subject of verb understood) 178.

Translation - "Now if Timothy comes, see to it that he is at ease during his visit, because he has been doing the work of the Lord as well as I."

Comment: The third-class condition is followed in the apodosis with the imperative. Note the sub-final (purpose and result) ἵνα clause after the imperative rather than a ὅτι object clause. "Take care to act toward Timothy, if he comes, in order (and with the result) that during his visit he will be free from trepidation." The suggestion is not so much a fear of physical violence, but perhaps the embarrassment naturally felt by a young preacher in a sophisticated city and in a church that had a reputation for bigotry. Paul is trying to smooth Timothy's path in Corinth. Thus his plea. "If Timothy comes, respect him for he has been serving the Lord as have I." Note the present progressive retroactive in ἐργάζεται. *Cf.*Acts 19:22.

Verse 11 - "Let no man therefore despise him: but conduct him forth in peace, that he may come unto me: for I look for him with the brethren."

μή τις οὖν αὐτὸν ἐξουθενήσῃ. προπέμψατε δὲ αὐτὸν ἐν εἰρήνῃ, ἵνα ἔλθῃ πρός με, ἐκδέχομαι γὰρ αὐτὸν μετὰ τῶν ἀδελφῶν.

"So let no one despise him. Speed him on his way in peace, that he may return to me; for I am expecting him with the brethren." . . . RSV

μή (negative particle with the subjunctive in a prohibition) 87.
τις (nom.sing.masc.of τις, indefinite pronoun, subject of ἐξουθενήσῃ) 486.
οὖν (inferential conjunction) 68.
αὐτὸν (acc.sing.masc.of αὐτός, direct object of ἐξουθενήσῃ) 16.
ἐξουθενήσῃ (3d.per.sing.1st.aor.act.subj.of ἐξουθενέω, prohibition) 2628.
προπέμψατε (2d.per.pl.aor.act.impv.of προπέμπω, command) 3335.
δὲ (adversative conjunction) 11.
αὐτὸν (acc.sing.masc.of αὐτός, direct object of προπέμψατε) 16.
ἐν (preposition with the locative of accompanying circumstance) 80.
εἰρήνῃ (loc.sing.fem.of εἰρήνη, accompanying circumstance) 865.
ἵνα (conjunction with the subjunctive in a sub-final clause) 114.
ἔλθῃ (3d.per.sing.aor.subj.of ἔρχομαι, sub-final clause) 146.
πρός (preposition with the accusative of extent) 197.
με (acc.sing.masc.of ἐγώ, extent) 123.
ἐκδέχομαι (1st.per.sing.pres.mid.ind.of ἐκδέχομαι, present progressive retroactive) 3398.
γὰρ (causal conjunction) 105.
αὐτὸν (acc.sing.masc.of αὐτός, direct object of ἐκδέχομαι) 16.
μετὰ (preposition with the genitive of accompaniment) 50.
τῶν (gen.pl.masc.of the article in agreement with ἀδελφῶν) 9.
ἀδελφῶν (gen.pl.masc.of ἀδελφός, accompaniment) 15.

Translation - "So do not let anyone look down on him, but send him on his way in peace in order (and with the result) that he may come to me, because I have been waiting for him along with the brethren."

Comment: μή with the aorist subjunctive in prohibitions is common in the New

Testament. *Cf.#87.* Timothy was a young man of God and they were not to disparage him (inferential οὖν). On the contrary they were to take good care of him. If he needed money for passage from Corinth to Ephesus, Paul asks that they supply it. Paul wanted Timothy to join him along with the other brethren before he left Macedonia. The other brethren not mentioned here are named in Acts 20:4. Apparently the Corinthian church treated Timothy with the respect that Paul requested for him. *Cf.* 1 Tim.4:12.

Verse 12 - "As touching our brother Apollos, I greatly desired him to come unto with the brethren; but his will was not at all to come at this time; but he will come when he shall have convenient time."

Περὶ δὲ Ἀπολλῶ τοῦ ἀδελφοῦ, πολλὰ παρεκάλεσα αὐτὸν ἵνα ἔλθῃ πρὸς ὑμᾶς μετὰ τῶν ἀδελφῶν. καὶ πάντως οὐκ ἦν θέλημα ἵνα νῦν ἔλθῃ, ἐλεύσεται δὲ ὅταν εὐκαιρήσῃ.

"As for our brother Apollos, I strongly urged him to visit you with the other brethren, but it was not at all his will to come now. He will come when he has opportunity." . . . RSV

Περὶ (preposition with the genitive of reference) 173.
δὲ (explanatory conjunction) 11.
Ἀπολλῶ (gen.sing.masc.of Ἀπολλῶς, reference) 3454.
τοῦ (gen.sing.masc.of the article in agreement with ἀδελφοῦ) 9.
ἀδελφοῦ (gen.sing.masc.of ἀδελφός, apposition) 15.
πολλὰ (acc.pl.neut.of πολύς, adverbial) 228.
παρεκάλεσα (1st.per.sing.aor.act.ind.of παρακαλέω, constative) 230.
αὐτὸν (acc.sing.masc.of αὐτός, direct object of παρεκάλεσα) 16.
ἵνα (conjunction with the subjunctive, in a purpose clause) 114.
ἔλθῃ (3d.per.sing.aor.subj.of ἔρχομαι, purpose clause) 146.
πρὸς (preposition with the accusative of extent) 197.
ὑμᾶς (acc.pl.masc.of σύ, extent) 104.
μετὰ (preposition with the genitive of accompaniment) 50.
τῶν (gen.pl.masc.of the article in agreement with ἀδελφῶν) 9.
ἀδελφῶν (gen.pl.masc.of ἀδελφός, accompaniment) 15.
καὶ (adversative conjunction) 14.
πάντως (adverbial) 2029.
οὐκ (negative particle with the indicative) 130.
ἦν (3d.per.sing.imp.ind.of εἰμί, progressive duration) 86.
θέλημα (nom.sing.neut.of θέλημα, subject of ἦν) 577.
ἵνα (conjunction with the subjunctive in a purpose clause) 114.
νῦν (temporal adverb) 1497.
ἔλθῃ (3d.per.sing.aor.subj.of ἔρχομαι, purpose clause) 146.
ἐλεύσεται (3d.per.sing.fut.ind.of ἔρχομαι, predictive) 146.
δὲ (adversative conjunction) 11.
ὅταν (conjunction with the subjunctive in an indefinite temporal clause) 436.
εὐκαιρήσῃ (3d.per.sing.aor.act.subj.of εὐκαιρέω, indefinite temporal clause) 2263.

Translation - *"Now with reference to brother Apollos, I have begged him much to come to you with the other brethren, but he has been totally against it at this time, but he will come when the opportunity affords."*

Comment: Paul is protecting himself against the charge that he is jealous of Apollos. *Cf.* 1 Cor.1:11-12; 3:1-8,22. On the contrary he begged Apollos to go with Timothy and Erastus (Acts 19:22) to Corinth. But to no avail. The reason for Apollos' refusal to go to Corinth at that particular time is not known. Perhaps he wished to remain in Ephesus where a great revival was in progress. He was an intellectual (Acts 18:24-28) and he may have been disgusted with the bigoted lack of sophistication so prevalent in the Corinthian church. At any rate Paul could not be accused of seeking to prevent Apollos from visiting Corinth, where he had some devoted followers.

Final Request and Greetings

(1 Corinthians 16:13-24)

Verse 13 - *"Watch ye, stand fast in the faith; quit you like men, be strong."*

Γρηγορεῖτε, στήκετε ἐν τῇ πίστει, ἀνδρίζεσθε, κραταιοῦσθε.

"Be watchful, stand firm in your faith, be courageous, be strong." . . . RSV

Γρηγορεῖτε (2d.per.pl.pres.act.impv.of γρηγορέω, command) 1520.
στήκετε (2d.per.pl.pres.act.impv.of στήκω, command) 1957.
ἐν (preposition with the locative of sphere) 80.
τῇ (loc.sing.fem.of the article in agreement with πίστει) 9.
πίστει (loc.sing.fem.of πίστις, sphere) 728.

#4261 ἀνδρίζεσθε (2d.per.pl.pres.mid.impv.of ἀνδρίζομαι, command).

King James Version

quit you like men - 1 Cor.16:13.

Revised Standard Version

be courageous - 1 Cor.16:13.

Meaning: *Cf.* ἀνήρ (#63). In the middle voice, to make oneself a man. Be manlike; be courageous. With reference to the Corinthian Christian testimony - 1 Cor.16:13.

κραταιοῦσθε (2d.per.pl.pres.mid.impv.of κραταιόω, command) 1861.

Translation - *"Always be alert; stand steadfastly for what you believe; be courageous; be strong."*

Comment: In order to stand fast in the sphere of Christian faith, watchfulness, courage and strength will be needed. Some Christians who do not watch are taken unaware by false teaching. Watchful Christians may know that Satan's attack is coming, but they lack courage to resist him. Some who are alert and courageous have not availed themselves of the strength of our risen Lord and thus try to fight him in their own strength which is never sufficient. The flesh is never profitable and it can never win (John 6:63) but "greater is He that is in you than he that is in the world" (1 John 4:4).

All three - watchfulness, courage and strength are required. But without love even these are not enough.

Verse 14 - "Let all your things be done with charity."

πάντα ὑμῶν ἐν ἀγάπῃ γινέσθω.

"Let all that you do be done in love." . . . RSV

πάντα (acc.pl.neut.of πᾶς, direct object of γινέσθω) 67.
ὑμῶν (gen.pl.masc.of σύ, possession) 104.
ἐν (preposition with the locative of accompanying circumstance) 80.
ἀγάπῃ (loc.sing.fem.of ἀγάπη, accompanying circumstance) 1490.
γινέσθω (3d.per.sing.pres.impv.of γίνομαι, entreaty) 113.

Translation - "Let everything be done with love."

Comment: This is a brief reiteration of Chapter 13. Only that which is done in love edifies the Body of Christ and thus enables the church to carry out the Great Commission.

Verse 15 - "I beseech you, brethren (ye know the house of Stephanas, that it is the firstfruits of Achaia, and that they have addicted themselves to the ministry of the saints,)"

Παρακαλῶ δὲ ὑμᾶς, ἀδελφοί. οἴδατε τὴν οἰκίαν Στεφανᾶ, ὅτι ἐστὶν ἀπαρχὴ τῆς Ἀχαΐας καὶ εἰς διακονίαν τοῖς ἁγίοις ἔταξαν ἑαυτούς,

"Now, brethren, you know that the household of Stephanas were the first converts in Achaia, and they have devoted themselves to the service of the saints;" . . . RSV

Παρακαλῶ (1st.per.sing.pres.act.ind.of παρακαλέω, aoristic) 230.
δὲ (explanatory conjunction) 11.
ὑμᾶς (acc.pl.masc.of σύ, direct object of παρακαλῶ) 104.
ἀδελφοί (voc.pl.masc.of ἀδελφός, address) 15.
οἴδατε (2d.per.pl.perf.act.ind.of ὁράω, intensive) 144b.
τὴν (acc.sing.fem.of the article in agreement with οἰκίαν) 9.
οἰκίαν (acc.sing.fem.of οἰκία, direct object of οἴδατε) 186.
Στεφανᾶ (gen.sing.masc.of Στεφανᾶς, description) 4104.
ὅτι (conjunction introducing an object clause in indirect discourse) 211.
ἐστὶν (3d.per.sing.pres.ind.of εἰμί, static) 86.

ἀπαρχή (nom.sing.fem.of ἀπαρχή, predicate nominative) 3946.
τῆς (gen.sing.fem.of the article in agreement with Ἀχαΐας) 9.
Ἀχαΐας (gen.sing.fem.of Ἀχαΐα, description) 3443.
καὶ (adjunctive conjunction joining verbs in indirect discourse) 14.
εἰς (preposition with the accusative, purpose) 140.
διακονίαν (acc.sing.fem.of διακονία, purpose) 2442.
τοῖς (dat.pl.masc.of ἅγιος, personal advantage) 84.
ἔταξαν (3d.per.pl.aor.act.ind.of τάσσω, culminative) 722.
ἑαυτούς (acc.pl.masc.of ἑαυτοῦ, direct object of ἔταξαν) 288.

Translation - *"Now I encourage you, brethren, (you know of the Stephanas family - that they are the first to be saved in Achaia and that they have devoted themselves to the service of the saints,)"*

Comment: The material οἴδατε . . . ἑαυτούς is parenthetical. Thus verse 16 ἵνα καὶ . . . κ.τ.λ. is joined to παρακαλῶ ὑμᾶς of verse 15. ὅτι in indirect discourse is epexegetical as it introduces the material about the Stephanas family. They were the first converts to Christ from Greece. Second, they had assigned to themselves the task of collecting money for the poor saints in Jerusalem. The predicate use of εἰς διακονίαν is purpose.

Stephanas and his family were among the very few whom Paul personally immersed (1 Cor.1:16).

Having called attention to Stephanas and his family as shining examples of Christian charity (verse 15) Paul goes on to beg the Corinthians to cooperate with Stephanas in his effort to help the famine stricken Christians in Palestine.

Verse 16 - *"That ye submit yourselves unto such, and to every one that helpeth with us, and laboureth."*

ἵνα καὶ ὑμεῖς ὑποτάσσησθε τοῖς τοιούτοις καὶ παντὶ τῷ συνεργοῦντι καὶ κοπιῶντι.

"I urge you to be subject to such men and to every fellow worker and laborer."
                                                             . . . RSV

ἵνα (conjunction introducing the subjunctive in a purpose clause) 114.
καὶ (adjunctive conjunction joining substantives) 14.
ὑμεῖς (nom.pl.masc.of σύ, subject of ὑποτάσσησθε) 104.
ὑποτάσσησθε (2d.per.pl.pres.pass.subj.of ὑποτάσσω, purpose) 1921.
τοῖς (dat.pl.masc.of the article in agreement with τοιούτοις) 9.
τοιούτοις (dat.pl.masc.of τοιοῦτος, personal advantage) 785.
καὶ (adjunctive conjunction joining substantives) 14.
παντὶ (dat.sing.masc.of πᾶς, in agreement with συνεργοῦντι and κοπιῶντι) 67.
τῷ (dat.sing.masc.of the article in agreement with συνεργοῦντι and κοπιῶντι) 9.
συνεργοῦντι (pres.act.part.dat.sing.masc.of συνεργέω, substantival, personal advantage) 2931.

καὶ (adjunctive conjunction joining participles) 14.

κοπιῶντι (pres.act.part.dat.sing.masc.of κοπιόω, substantival, personal advantage) 629

Translation - ". . . that you also cooperate with such and with everyone who is working together and sacrificing."

Comment: The purpose clause is joined to παρακαλῶ δὲ ὑμᾶς, ἀδελφοί of verse 15. Every Corinthian christian is asked to place himself at Stephanas' disposal, to help him in the work which he has undertaken. Stephanas and those who are helping him in this project are described by the two substantival participles συνεργοῦντι καὶ κοπιῶντι - "those who are working together and making sacrifices." A church that works together and suffers together in order to accomplish goals for Christ and others is a church that has neither time, disposition nor strength to quarrel about everything that the Corinthians found to fight about - who is the best preacher? Whose baptism is most valid? Should an adulterer be disciplined? In which court should a lawsuit be tried? Sex, marriage and divorce? Meats offered to idols? Who should wear a hat? Women's rights? Tongues, interpretations, prophets, new revelations? What kind of bodies will we have in heaven? Prayer in public schools?! Should Christians teach creationism in public schools?! Should the government feed the hungry or let them starve?!

If Fundamentalists now would spend their time preaching the gospel of Christ, witnessing to the unsaved and feeding the poor, as Paul asked the Corinthians to help Stephanas in his project there would be no time left for using the police power of the state, which is neutral on religious questions, to force upon the unregenerate those moral standards which are appropriate for Christians. And they would be giving no "great occasion to the enemies of the Lord to blaspheme" (2 Samuel 12:14). Like David, who listened to Nathan, they ought to repent and prayer the prayer of Psalm 51.

Verse 17 - "I am glad of the coming of Stephanas and Fortunatus and Achaicus: for that which was lacking on your part, they have supplied."

χαίρω δὲ ἐπὶ τῇ παρουσίᾳ Στεφανᾶ καὶ Φορτουνάτου καὶ'Ἀχαϊκοῦ, ὅτι τὸ ὑμέτερον ὑστέρμα οὗτοι ἀνεπλήρωσαν.

"I rejoice at the coming of Stephanas and Fortunatus and Achaicus, because they have made up for your absence;" . . . RSV

χαίρω (1st.per.sing.pres.act.ind.of χαίρω, aoristic) 182.
δὲ (explanatory conjunction) 11.
ἐπὶ (preposition with the instrumental of cause) 47.
τῇ (instru.sing.fem.of the article in agreement with παρουσίᾳ) 9.
παρουσίᾳ (instru.sing.fem.of παρουσία, cause) 1482.
Στεφανᾶ (gen.sing.masc.of Στεφανᾶς, description) 4104.
καὶ (adjunctive conjunction joining nouns) 14.

#4262 Φορτουνάτου (gen.sing.masc.of Φορτουνάτος, description).

King James Version

Fortunatus - 1 Cor.16:17.

Revised Standard Version

Fortunatos - 1 Cor.16:17.

Meaning: A Christian of Corinth - 1 Cor.16:17.

καὶ (adjunctive conjunction joining nouns) 14.

#4263 Ἀχαϊκοῦ (gen.sing.masc.of Ἀχαϊκός, description).

King James Version

Achaicus - 1 Cor.16:17.

Revised Standard Version

Achaicus - 1 Cor.16:17.

Meaning: A Corinthian Christian - 1 Cor.16:17.

ὅτι (conjunction introducing a subordinate causal clause) 211.
τὸ (acc.sing.neut.of the article in agreement with ὑστέρημα) 9.
ὑμέτερον (acc.sing.neut.of ὑμέτερος, in agreement with ὑστέρημα) 2127.
ὑστέρημα (acc.sing.neut.of ὑστέρημα, direct object of ἀνεπλήρωσαν) 2707.
οὗτοι (nom.pl.masc.of οὗτος, subject of ἀνεπλήρωσαν) 93.
ἀνεπλήρωσαν (3d.per.pl.aor.act.ind.of ἀναπληρόω, culminative) 1040.

Translation - "Now I am glad that Stephanas, Fortunatos and Achaicus have come, because they have made up your quota which had not been met."

Comment: Two interpretations of what Stephanas *et al* provided are possible. It is possible that ὑστέρημα (#2707) refers to the physical absence of the Corinthians from Paul. Thus Stephanas and his friends came to Ephesus to visit Paul, who was cheered by their presence as though the other Corinthians had also come. But this is a money context. *Cf.*verses 1,2,3,4,15,16. Stephanas was brought into the story as one who had been devoted to the matter of collecting money for the poor saints in Jerusalem. They are admonished to cooperate with him and it is suggested that they should give him money for this noble purpose, even though it requires sacrifice, since Stephanas is also sacrificing.

Now Stephanas and his party have joined Paul in Ephesus and they have brought sufficient money to fill the quota which had been assigned to the Corinthians. It is possible that they arrived during the time that Paul was writing this chapter. Was their arrival in Ephesus timed to come between the writing of the 16th and 17th verses? Did Paul write verses 1-16 before Stephanas arrived with the money? This would explain why he asked them to be faithful in this matter, since before Stephanas and his party arrived Paul did not know that they had already met their quota. Now, with Stephanas and his friends at his door with the remainder of the money, Paul can continue his writing and announce that Stephanas has come and delivered the money and that he is glad.

There is also the possibility that Stephanas, Fortunatos and Achaicus made up the deficit out of their own pockets.

Meyer says, " . . . liguistically both renderings alike may be correct." (Meyer, *2 Corinthians*, 402), though he has opted for the former interpretation.

Verse 18 - "For they have refreshed my spirit and yours: therefore acknowledge ye them that are such."

ἀνέπαυσαν γὰρ τὸ ἐμὸν πνεῦμα καὶ τὸ ὑμῶν. ἐπιγινώσκετε οὖν τοὺς τοιούτους.

"for they refreshed my spirit as well as yours. Give recognition to such men." . .
                                                                        RSV

ἀνέπαυσαν (3d.per.pl.aor.act.ind.of ἀναπαύω, culminative) 955.
γὰρ (inferential conjunction) 105.
τὸ (acc.singneut.of the article in agreement with πνεῦμα) 9.
ἐμὸν (acc.sing.neut.of ἐμός, in agreement with πνεῦμα) 1267.
πνεῦμα (acc.sing.neut.of πνεῦμα, direct object of ἀνέπαυσαν) 83.
καὶ (adjunctive conjunction joining substantives) 14.
τὸ (acc.sing.neut.of the article in agreement with πνεῦμα) 9.
ὑμῶν (gen.pl.masc.of σύ, possession) 104.
ἐπιγινώσκετε (2d.per.pl.pres.act.impv.of ἐπιγινώσκω, command) 675.
οὖν (inferential conjunction) 68.
τοὺς (acc.pl.masc.of the article in agreement with τοιούτους) 9.
τοιούτους (acc.pl.masc.of τοιοῦτος, direct object of ἐπιγινώσκετε) 785.

Translation - "Therefore they relieved my mind and yours. So you should appreciate men like that."

Comment: Note Paul's use in juxtaposition of the possessive pronoun and the genitive - τὸ ἐμὸν πνεῦμα καὶ τὸ ὑμῶν - "My spirit and that of yours." When Stephanas and his companions were in Corinth, busying themselves about collecting money for the poor - a job that the Corinthians should have been engaged in voluntarily (verses 1-4) they relieved the minds of the Corinthians, as they may have said, "We need not do it since Stephanas is doing it." Now that Stephanas has brought the money to Paul in Ephesus, Paul's mind is set at rest and the Corinthians back in Corinth are glad that the quota is met, no thanks perhaps to them. Paul feels that they do not sufficiently recognize (#675) the worth of these men and of others of similar character.

Verse 19 - "The churches of Asia salute you. Aquila and Priscilla salute you much in the Lord, with the church, that is in their house."

Ἀσπάζονται ὑμᾶς αἱ ἐκκλησίαι τῆς Ἀσίας. ἀσπάζεται ὑμᾶς ἐν κυρίῳ πολλὰ

'Ακύλας καί Πρίσκα σὺν τῇ κατ' οἶκον αὐτῶν ἐκκλησίᾳ,

"*The churches of Asia send greetings. Aquila and Prisca together with the church in their house, send you hearty greetings in the Lord.*" . . . RSV

'Ασπάζονται (3d.per.pl.pres.mid.ind.of ἀσπάζομαι, aoristic) 551.
ὑμᾶς (acc.pl.masc.of σύ, direct object of 'Ασπάζονται) 104.
αἱ (nom.pl.fem.of the article in agreement with ἐκκλησίαι) 9.
ἐκκλησίαι (nom.pl.fem.of ἐκκλησία, subject of 'Ασπάζονται) 1204.
τῆς (gen.sing.fem.of the article in agreement with 'Ασίας) 9.
'Ασίας (gen.sing.fem.of 'Ασία, description) 2968.
ἀσπάζεται (3d.per.sing.pres.mid.ind.of ἀσπάζομαι, 551.
ὑμᾶς (acc.pl.masc.of σύ, direct object of ἀσπάζεται) 104.
ἐν (preposition with the instrumental of association) 80.
κυρίῳ (instru.sing.masc.of κύριος, association) 97.
πολλά (acc.pl.neut.of πολύς, adverbial) 228.
'Ακύλας (nom.sing.masc.of 'Ακύλας, subject of ἀσπάζεται) 3429.
καὶ (adjunctive conjunction joining nouns) 14.
Πρίσκα (nom.sing.fem.of Πρίσκα for Πρίσκιλλα, subject of ἀσπάζεται) 3433.
σὺν (preposition with the instrumental of association) 1542.
τῇ (instru.sing.fem.of the article in agreement with ἐκκλησίᾳ) 9.
κατ' (preposition with the accusative, in a local expression, notion of rest) 98.
οἶκον (acc.sing.masc.of οἶκος, local expression) 784.
αὐτῶν (gen.pl.masc.of αὐτός, possession) 16.
ἐκκλησίᾳ (instru.sing.fem.of ἐκκλησία, association) 1204.

Translation - "The churches of Asia send you their greeting. Aquila and Priscilla greet you heartily in the Lord, along with the church in their house."

Comment: Paul was seeking to promote fellowship between the churches in Asia Minor (modern Turkey), east of the Aegean, with those in the area west of the Aegean, in what is now Greece. *Cf.*#'s 3429 and 3433 for an account of these two Christian people.

The preposition κατά (#98) with the accusative, in a local expression, indicates a horizontal "down along" position. *Cf.* Lk.9:6; 10:4; 15:14; Acts 27:5,12; 8:26; Gal.2:11; Lk.8:39; Gal.3:1; Phil.3;14; Acts 15:21a; 17:28. The notion of rest has κατά and the accusative in Acts 2:46; 11;1; Col.4:15; Acts 13:1; 7:28; 18:15.

Verse 20 - "All the brethren greet you. Greet ye one another with an holy kiss."

ἀσπάζονται ὑμᾶς οἱ ἀδελφοὶ πάντες. 'Ασπάσασθε ἀλλήλους ἐν φιλήματι ἁγίῳ.

"*All the brethren send greetings. Greet one another with a holy kiss.*"

ἀσπάζονται (3d.per.pl.pres.mid.ind.of ἀσπάζομαι, aoristic) 551.

ὑμᾶς (acc.pl.masc.of σύ, direct object of ἀσπάζονται) 104.

οἱ (nom.pl.masc.of the article in agreement with ἀδελφοὶ) 9.

ἀδελφοὶ (nom.pl.masc.of ἀδελφός, subject of ἀσπάζονται) 15.

πάντες (nom.pl.masc.of πᾶς, in agreement with ἀδελφοὶ) 67.

ἀσπάσασθε (2d.per.pl.1st.aor.mid.impv.of ἀσπάζομαι, command) 551.

ἀλλήλους (acc.pl.masc.of ἀλλήλων, direct object of ἀσπάσασθε) 1487.

ἐν (preposition with the instrumental of manner) 80.

φιλήματι (instru.sing.neut.of φίλημα, manner) 2175.

ἁγίῳ (instru.sing.neut.of ἅγιος, in agreement with φιλήματι) 84.

Translation - *"All the brethren wish to be remembered to you. Greet one another with a holy kiss."*

Comment: *Cf.* Acts 20:4 for a partial list of the brethren, though Paul included all the Christians in Ephesus, indeed in Asia Minor. The usual apostolic greeting is added.

Verse 21 - *"The salutation of me Paul with mine own hand."*

Ὁ ἀσπασμὸς τῇ ἐμῇ χειρὶ Παύλου.

"I, Paul, write this greeting with my own hand." . . . RSV

Ὁ (nom.sing.masc.of the article in agreement with ἀσπασμὸς) 9.

ἀσπασμὸς (nom.sing.masc.of ἀσπασμός, nominative absolute) 1442.

τῇ (instru.sing.fem.of the article in agreement with χειρὶ) 9.

ἐμῇ (instru.sing.fem.of ἐμός, in agreement with χειρὶ) 1267.

χειρὶ (instru.sing.fem.of χείρ, means) 308.

Παύλου (gen.sing.masc.of Παῦλος, possession) 3284.

Translation - *"The greeting I, Paul, add in my own hand."*

Comment: Apparently an amenuensis wrote the letter at Paul's dictation, but he signed it, to make it official. One wonders what an autograph collector would be willing to pay for the manuscript if it were available? Perhaps it is providential that it is lost. If it were available it is likely that we would rather make it an object of veneration than read it, believe its message and follow its precepts. We can be sure that if it fell into the wrong hands it would be exploited financially.

Verse 22 - *"If any man love not the Lord Jesus Christ, let him be Anathema Maranatha."*

εἴ τις οὐ φιλεῖ τὸν κύριον, ἤτω ἀνάθεμα. Μαρανα θα.

"If any one has no love for the Lord, let him be accursed. Our Lord, come!"
RSV

εἴ (conditional particle in a first-class condition) 337.

τις (nom.sing.masc.of τις, indefinite pronoun, subject of φιλεῖ) 486.

οὐ (negative particle with the indicative) 130.

φιλεῖ (3d.per.sing.pres.act.ind.of φιλέω, first-class condition) 566.
τὸν (acc.sing.masc.of the article in agreement with κύριον) 9.
κύριον (acc.sing.masc.of κύριος, direct object of φιλεῖ) 97.
ἤτω (3d.per.sing.pres.impv.of εἰμί, entreaty) 86.
ἀνάθεμα (nom.sing.neut.of ἀνάθεμα, predicate nominative) 3597.

#4264 Μαρανα θα

King James Version

Maranatha - 1 Cor.16:22.

Revised Standard Version

Our Lord, come - 1 Cor.16:22.

Meaning: A transliteration from two Aramaic words - "Our Lord, come!" or "The Lord will come." Contextual considerations indicate the former in 1 Cor.16:22.

Translation - "Since there are some who do not love the Lord, let them continue under a curse. Our Lord, come."

Comment: The imperative with an imprecation ἤτω ἀνάθεμα takes the place of the classical optative. The first-class condition assumes the truth. There were some in Corinth who did not love the Lord. Paul's theology is indeed divisive. It separates elect from non-elect, believers from unbelievers, saved from lost, children of God from children of the devil. Any blurring of these distinctions destroys Christianity, for it is nothing if it does not do something for the believer that it does not do for the unbeliever. Paul emphasizes this at the close of the epistle - an emphasis that some of the Corinthian Christians needed. The curse pronounced upon the unbeliever is potential, not imposed. The curse will be activated when the Lord comes (2 Thess.1:7-10). This passage, taken alone, will give the wrong impression of the great heart of the Apostle. *Cf.*Romans 9:3; Acts 20:17-27 for the burden which he had for the lost and the prodigious effort he made to tell the good news to everyone.

Verse 23 - "The grace of our Lord Jesus Christ be with you."

ἡ χάρις τοῦ κυρίου Ἰησοῦ μεθ' ὑμῶν.

"The grace of the Lord Jesus be with you." . . . RSV

ἡ (nom.sing.fem.of the article in agreement with χάρις) 9.
χάρις (nom.sing.fem.of χάρις, subject of εἴη understood) 1700.
τοῦ (gen.sing.masc.of the article in agreement with κυρίου) 9.
κυρίου (gen.sing.masc.of κύριος, description) 97.
Ἰησοῦ (gen.sing.masc.of Ἰησοῦς, apposition) 3.
μεθ' (preposition with the genitive, fellowship) 50.
ὑμῶν (gen.pl.masc.of σύ, fellowship) 104.

Translation - "The grace of our Lord Jesus be with you."

Comment: The usual close. But Paul felt impelled to add assurances of his love for those who had come to Christ under his ministry. Perhaps he wished to reassure them especially due to the stern tone, sometimes amounting to asperity, which we find in this epistle.

Verse 24 - "My love be with you all in Christ Jesus. Amen."

ἡ ἀγάπη μου μετὰ πάντων ὑμῶν ἐν Χριστῷ Ἰησοῦ.

"My love be with you all in Christ Jesus. Amen." . . . RSV

ἡ (nom.sing.fem.of the article in agreement with ἀγάπη) 9.
ἀγάπη (nom.sing.fem.of ἀγάπη, subject of εἴη understood) 1490.
μου (gen.sing.masc.of ἐγώ, possession) 123.
μετὰ (preposition with the genitive, fellowship) 50.
πάντων (gen.pl.masc.of πᾶς, fellowship) 67.
ὑμῶν (gen.pl.masc.of σύ, partitive genitive) 104.
ἐν (preposition with the instrumental of association) 80.
Χριστῷ (instru.sing.masc.of Χριστός, association) 4.
Ἰησοῦ (instru.sing.masc.of Ἰησοῦς, apposition) 3.

Translation - "My love be with everyone of you in Christ Jesus."

Comment: Almost as an afterthought since Paul's harsh treatment of the Corinthians in this epistle might possibly have led them to think that he did not love them. But he assures them that he does, not because of their merit, because they were not very lovable people, but because of Christ Jesus.

Paul's Second Epistle to the Corinthians

Salutation

(2 Corinthians 1:1-2)

2 Cor.1:1 - "Paul, an apostle of Jesus Christ by the will of God, and Timothy our brother, unto the church of God which is at Corinth, with all the saints which are in all Achaia."

Παῦλος ἀπόστολος Χριστοῦ Ἰησοῦ διὰ θελήματος θεοῦ, καὶ Τιμόθεος ὁ ἀδελφός, τῇ ἐκκλησίᾳ τοῦ θεοῦ τῇ οὔσῃ ἐν Κορίνθῳ, σὺν τοῖς ἁγίοις πᾶσιν τοῖς οὖσιν ἐν ὅλῃ τῇ Ἀχαΐᾳ.

"PAUL, AN APOSTLE OF CHRIST JESUS by the will of God, and Timothy our brother. To the church of God which is at Corinth, with all the saints who are in the whole of Achaia." . . . RSV

Παῦλος (nom.sing.masc.of Παῦλος, nominative absolute) 3284.

ἀπόστολος (nom.sing.masc.of ἀπόστολος, apposition) 844.

Χριστοῦ (gen.sing.masc.of Χριστός, relationship) 4.

Ἰησοῦ (gen.sing.masc.of Ἰησοῦς, apposition) 3.

διὰ (preposition with the genitive of means) 118.

θελήματος (gen.sing.neut.of θέλημα, means) 577.

θεοῦ (gen.sing.masc.of θεός, description) 124.

καὶ (adjunctive conjunction joining nouns) 14.

Τιμόθεος (nom.sing.masc.of Τιμόθεος, nominative absolute) 3354.

ὁ (nom.sing.masc.of the article in agreement with ἀδελφός) 9.

ἀδελφός (nom.sing.masc.of ἀδελφός, apposition) 15.

τῇ (dat.sing.fem.of the article in agreement with ἐκκλησίᾳ) 9.

ἐκκλησίᾳ (dat.sing.fem.of ἐκκλησίᾳ, indirect object) 1204.

τοῦ (gen.sing.masc.of the article in agreement with θεοῦ) 9.

θεοῦ (gen.sing.masc.of θεός, possession) 124.

τῇ (dat.sing.fem.of the article in agreement with οὔσῃ) 9.

οὔσῃ (pres.part.dat.sing.fem.of εἰμί, adjectival, emphatic attributive position, ascriptive) 86.

ἐν (preposition with the locative of place) 80.

Κορίνθῳ (loc.sing.masc.of Κόρινθος, place) 3428.

σὺν (preposition with the instrumental of association) 1542.

τοῖς (instru.pl.masc.of the article in agreement with ἁγίοις) 9.

ἁγίοις (instru.pl.masc.of ἅγιος, association) 84.

πᾶσιν (instru.pl.masc.of πᾶς, in agreement with ἁγίοις) 67.

τοῖς (instru.pl.masc.of the article in agreement with οὖσιν) 9.

οὖσιν (pres.part.instru.pl.masc.of εἰμί, adjectival, emphatic attributive position, ascriptive) 86.

ἐν (preposition with the locative of place) 80.

ὅλῃ (loc.sing.fem.of ὅλος, in agreement with Ἀχαΐᾳ) 112.

τῇ (loc.sing.fem.of the article in agreement with Ἀχαΐᾳ) 9.

Ἀχαΐᾳ (loc.sing.fem.of Ἀχαΐα, place) 3443.

Translation - "Paul, an Apostle of Christ Jesus by the will of God, and Timothy, the brother, to the church of God in Corinth, with all the saints in all Achaia."

Comment: In his earlier epistle Paul had promised the Corinthians that he would visit them, perhaps to spend the winter of A.D.55 (1 Cor.16:1-9), though he would remain in Ephesus until Pentecost. The letter was carried to Corinth by Titus, whom Paul hoped to meet again in Troas, at which time Titus would report that Paul's first letter had been kindly received, despite the asperity which often characterized it. In this hope Paul was disappointed (2 Cor.2:12-13), and he left Troas and came to Macedonia, where he wrote them again, perhaps in A.D.57.

He had suffered greatly since since his first letter to Corinth (2 Cor.1:8), but God had delivered him from death (2 Cor.1:10).

He had defended his Apostleship in his previous letter (1 Cor.9) and he opens this one by calling himself an Apostle and basing his claim to his apostleship on the will of God.

Verse 2 - "Grace be to you and peace from God our Father, and from the Lord Jesus Christ."

χάρις ὑμῖν καὶ εἰρήνη ἀπὸ θεοῦ πατρὸς ἡμῶν καὶ κυρίου Ἰησοῦ Χριστοῦ.

"Grace to you and peace from God our Father and the Lord Jesus Christ." . . .
                                                                      RSV

χάρις (nom.sing.fem.of χάρις, subject of εἴη, understood) 1700.
ὑμῖν (dat.pl.masc.of σύ, indirect object) 104.
καὶ (adjunctive conjunction joining nouns) 14.
εἰρήνη (nom.sing.fem.of εἰρήνη, subject of εἴη understood) 865.
ἀπὸ (preposition with the ablative of source) 70.
θεοῦ (abl.sing.masc.of θεός, source) 124.
πατρὸς (abl.sing.masc.of πατήρ, apposition) 238.
ἡμῶν (gen.pl.masc.of ἐγώ, relationship) 123.
καὶ (adjunctive conjunction joining nouns) 14.
κυρίου (abl.sing.masc.of κύριος, source) 97.
Ἰησοῦ (abl.sing.masc.of Ἰησοῦς, apposition) 3.
Χριστοῦ (abl.sing.masc.of Χριστός, apposition) 4.

Translation - "Grace unto you and peace from God, our Father and from the Lord Jesus Christ."

Comment: The same salutation was used in his first epistle (1 Cor.1:3).

Paul's Thanksgiving after Affliction

(2 Corinthians 1:3-11)

Verse 3 - "Blessed be God, even the Father of our Lord Jesus Christ, the Father of mercies, and the God of all comfort."

Εὐλογητὸς ὁ θεὸς καὶ πατὴρ τοῦ κυρίου ἡμῶν Ἰησοῦ Χριστοῦ, ὁ πατὴρ τῶν οἰκτιρμῶν καὶ θεὸς πάσης παρακλήσεως,

"Blessed be the God and Father of our Lord Jesus Christ, the Father of mercies and God of all comfort." . . . *RSV*

Εὐλογητὸς (nom.sing.masc.of εὐλογητός, predicate adjective) 1849.
ὁ (nom.sing.masc.of the article in agreement with θεός) 9.
θεὸς (nom.sing.masc.of θεός, subject of ἔστιν understood) 124.
καὶ (adjunctive conjunction joining nouns) 14.
πατὴρ (nom.sing.masc.of πατήρ, subject of ἔστιν understood) 238.
τοῦ (gen.sing.masc.of the article in agreement with κυρίου) 9.
κυρίου (gen.sing.masc.of κύριος, relationship) 97.

ἡμῶν (gen.pl.masc.of ἐγώ, relationship) 123.
Ἰησοῦ (gen.sing.masc.of Ἰησοῦς, apposition) 3.
Χριστοῦ (gen.sing.masc.of Χριστός, apposition) 4.
ὁ (nom.sing.masc.of the article in agreement with πατήρ) 9.
πατήρ (nom.sing.masc.of πατήρ, in apposition with θεὸς) 238.
τῶν (gen.pl.masc.of the article in agreement with οἰκτιρμῶν) 9.
οἰκτιρμῶν (gen.pl.masc.of οἰκτιρμός, description) 4009.
καὶ (adjunctive conjunction joining nouns) 14.
θεὸς (nom.sing.masc.of θεός, appellation) 124.
πάσης (gen.sing.fem.of πᾶς, in agreement with παρακλήσεως) 67.
παρακλήσεως (gen.sing.fem.of παράκλησις, description) 1896.

Translation - *"God, the Father of our Lord Jesus Christ is blessed! He is the Father of mercies and the God of all comfort."*

Comment: Note that the predicate adjective Εὐλογητὸς is emphasized by its position. We may supply either the indicative ἔστιν or the voluntative optative εἴη, depending upon whether we are stating a fact or expressing a wish. If we intend the statement to be a command we would supply the imperative ἔστω - "Let God be proclaimed as blessed." It is Paul's praise to God Who has brought him safely through great trials. Mercy and comfort have God as their source. They are truly causes for praise. *Cf.*#'s 4009 and 1896. The sentence continues in

Verse 4 - *"Who comforteth us in all our tribulation, that we may be able to comfort them which are in any trouble, by the comfort wherewith we ourselves are comforted of God."*

    ὁ παρακαλῶν ἡμᾶς ἐπὶ πάσῃ τῇ θλίψει ἡμῶν, εἰς τὸ δύνασθαι ἡμᾶς παρακαλεῖν τοὺς ἐν πάσῃ θλίψει διὰ τῆς παρακλήσεως ἧς παρακαλούμεθα αὐτοὶ ὑπὸ τοῦ θεοῦ.

    "who comforts us in all our affliction, so that we may be able to comfort those who are in any affliction, with the comfort with which we ourselves are comforted by God." . . . *RSV*

ὁ (nom.sing.masc.of the article in agreement with παρακαλῶν) 9.
παρακαλῶν (pres.act.part.nom.sing.masc.of παρακαλέω, substantival, in apposition) 230.
ἡμᾶς (acc.pl.masc.of ἐγώ, direct object of παρακαλῶν) 123.
ἐπὶ (preposition with the locative, time point) 47.
πάσῃ (loc.sing.fem.of πᾶς, in agreement with θλίψει) 67.
τῇ (loc.sing.fem.of the article in agreement with θλίψει) 9.
θλίψει (loc.sing.fem.of θλίψις, time point) 1046.
ἡμῶν (gen.pl.masc.of ἐγώ, possession) 123.
εἰς (preposition with the accusative, purpose) 140.
τὸ (acc.sing.neut.of the article in agreement with δύνασθαι, articular infinitive of purpose) 9.

δύνασθαι (pres.inf.of δύναμαι, articular infinitive, acc.neut. purpose) 289.

ἡμᾶς (acc.pl.masc.of σύ, direct object of παρακαλεῖν) 123.

παρακαλεῖν (pres.act.inf.of παρακαλέω, epexegetical) 230.

τοὺς (acc.pl.masc.of the article, direct object of παρακαλεῖν) 9.

ἐν (preposition with the locative of accompanying circumstance) 80.

πάσῃ (loc.sing.fem.of πᾶς, in agreement with θλίψει) 67.

θλίψει (loc.sing.fem.of θλίψις, accompanying circumstance) 1046.

διὰ (preposition with the genitive, means) 118.

τῆς (gen.sing.fem.of the article in agreement with παρακλήσεως) 9.

παρακλήσεως (gen.sing.fem.of παράκλησις, means) 1896.

ὅς (gen.sing.fem.of ὅς, relative pronoun, in agreement with παρακλήσεως) 65.

παρακαλούμεθα (1st.per.pl.pres.pass.ind.of παρακαλέω, present iterative retroactive) 230.

αὐτοὶ (nom.pl.masc.of αὐτός, predicate position, intensive) 16.

ὑπὸ (preposition with the ablative of agent) 117.

τοῦ (abl.sing.masc.of the article in agreement with θεοῦ) 9.

θεοῦ (abl.sing.masc.of θεός, agent) 124.

Translation - " . . . the one Who has always comforted us in all our trouble by means of the comfort by which we ourselves have been comforted again and again by God."

Comment: The participial substantive ὁ παρακαλῶν - "the Comforter" is in apposition to ὁ θεὸς of verse 3. Note ἐπί with the time point locative. The infinitive clause is purpose with παρακαλεῖν as epexegetical. One of the gracious purposes of God, of which there are many, is to console (comfort, encourage) His children who are in distress. Why? In order that they in turn can comfort others. How will they comfort others? διὰ τῆς παρακλήσεως. "With comfort." What comfort? ἧς παρακαλούμεθα - "that by which we ourselves are comforted" (intensive αὐτοί, in the predicate position). ἐν πάσῃ θλίψει is a locative of accompanying circumstance. Thus we have the privilege of passing on to others who are in distress the same comfort which we received from God when we were in distress. It is thus a blessing to suffer for Christ, since we are thus in a better position to comfort others. We are able to empathaize and sympathize, and thus offer comfort only if we have known a similar experience and enjoyed the comfort of the Lord. A Christian boy may say to another who has lost his mother, "I know how you feel," but he really does not, however sincere he may be in offering comfort to his friend, unless he has lost his mother.

This is the thought of

Verse 5 - "For as the sufferings of Christ abound in us, so our consolation also aboundeth in Christ."

ὅτι καθὼς περισσεύει τὰ παθήματα τοῦ Χριστοῦ εἰς ἡμᾶς, οὕτως διὰ τοῦ Χριστοῦ περισσεύει καὶ ἡ παράκλησις ἡμῶν.

"For as we share abundantly in Christ's sufferings, so through Christ we share abundantly in comfort too." . . . RSV

ὅτι (conjunction introducing a subordinate causal clause) 211.

καθὼς (compound particle in a comparative clause) 1348.

περισσεύει (3d.per.sing.pres.act.ind.of περισσεύω, present iterative retroactive) 473.

τὰ (nom.pl.neut.of the article in agreement with παθήματα) 9.

παθήματα (nom.pl.neut.of πάθημα, subject of περισσεύει) 3919.

τοῦ (gen.sing.masc.of the article in agreement with Χριστοῦ) 9.

Χριστοῦ (gen.sing.masc.of Χριστός, description) 4.

εἰς (preposition with the accusative, locative usage) 140.

ἡμᾶς (acc.pl.masc.of ἐγώ, locative usage) 123.

οὕτως (demonstrative adverb) 74.

διὰ (preposition with the ablative of agent) 118.

τοῦ (abl.sing.masc.of the article in agreement with Χριστοῦ) 9.

Χριστοῦ (abl.sing.masc.of Χριστός, agent) 4.

περισσεύει (3d.per.sing.pres.act.ind.of περισσεύω, futuristic) 473.

καὶ (adjunctive conjunction joining nouns) 14.

ἡ (nom.sing.fem.of the article in agreement with παράκλησις) 9.

παράκλησις (nom.sing.fem.of παράκλησις, subject of περισσεύει) 1896.

ἡμῶν (gen.pl.masc.of ἐγώ, possession) 123.

Translation - "Because just as the sufferings of Christ have been multiplied in us again and again, in the same way through Christ our comfort will also multiply."

Comment: As Paul lived the Christian life in a world of gainsayers his share of the sufferings of Christ increased with repeated persecutions which had been his lot. This is the retroactive force of the present iterative in περισσεύει in the first clause. (2 Tim.3:12; 1 Pet.4:12,13,14; Mt.5:10-12). In the same way also Paul's ability to comfort others will increase. This is the force of the futuristic present in περισσεύει in the last clause. This would be true, not only because Paul's sufferings would continue until he died, but also because he would have increasing opportunity to comfort others as he continued his ministry, with its contact with the saints, each of whom would need his comfort. Note the καθὼς . . . . οὕτως . . . καὶ sequence - "Just as . . . even so . . . also." Here is a straight line equation with a direct relation between the Christian's sufferings for Christ and his ability to comfort others who are suffering. Paul looks back retroactively to his past experiences of suffering and consolation and he also looks forward futuristically to new opportunities to help others. This is the kind of edification of the Body of Christ that he spoke of in 1 Cor.12-14. And it is motivated by the love (ἀγάπη) of 1 Corinthians 13. This comfort is not of ourselves, but it is διὰ τοῦ Χριστοῦ - "through the agency of Christ." The Christian who is the source of comfort for others in distress is the Christian who has had his share of suffering and hence liberal portions of Christ's comfort for himself. Paul certainly was qualified to speak on the subject of suffering. The Christian who compromises his testimony for Christ in order to avoid suffering knows nothing of this.

A minister was invited to join a hunting party in quest of big game in the Canadian Rockies. He was delighted as he was noted as a successful big game hunter. His wife asked him if he did not fear that he would be persecuted by others in the party when they discovered that he was a Christian. He replied, "They are not going to find out that I am a Christian." (!).

Verse 6 - "And whether we be afflicted, it is for your consolation and salvation, which is effectual in the enduring of the same sufferings which we also suffer; or whether we be comforted, it is for your consolation and salvation."

εἴτε δὲ θλιβόμεθα, ὑπὲρ τῆς ὑμῶν παρακλήσεως καὶ σωτηρίας. εἴτε παρακαλούμεθα, ὑπὲρ τῆς ὑμῶν παρακλήσεως τῆς ἐνεργουμένης ἐν ὑπομονῇ τῶν αὐτῶν παθημάτων ὧν καὶ ἡμεῖς πάσχομεν.

"If we are afflicted, it is for your comfort and salvation; and if we are comforted, it is for your comfort, which you experience when you patiently endure the same sufferings that we suffer." . . . *RSV*

εἴτε (disjunctive) 4016.

δὲ (adversative conjunction) 11.

θλιβόμεθα (1st.per.pl.pres.pass.ind.of θλίβω, aoristic) 667.

ὑπὲρ (preposition with the ablative, "for the sake of") 545.

τῆς (abl.sing.fem.of the article in agreement with παρακλήσεως) 9.

ὑμῶν (gen.pl.masc.of σύ possession) 104.

παρακλήσεως (abl.sing.fem.of παράκλησις, "for the sake of") 1896.

καὶ (adjunctive conjunction joining nouns) 14.

σωτηρίας (abl.sing.fem.of σωτηρία, "for the sake of") 1852.

εἴτε (disjunctive) 4016.

παρακαλούμεθα (1st.per.pl.pres.pass.ind.of παρακαλέω, aoristic) 230.

ὑπὲρ (preposition with the ablative "for the sake of") 545.

τῆς (abl.sing.fem.of the article in agreement with παρακλήσεως) 9.

ὑμῶν (gen.pl.masc.of σύ, possession) 104.

παρακλήσεως (abl.sing.fem.of παράκλησις, "for the sake of") 1896.

τῆς (abl.sing.fem.of the article in agreement with ἐνεργουμένης) 9.

ἐνεργουμένης (pres.pass.part.abl.sing.fem.of ἐνεργέω, adjectival, emphatic attributive position, ascriptive, in agreement with παρακλήσεως) 1105.

ἐν (preposition with the instrumental of means) 80.

ὑπομονῇ (instru.sing.fem.of ὑπομονή, means) 2204.

τῶν (gen.pl.neut.of the article in agreement with παθημάτων) 9.

αὐτῶν (gen.pl.masc.of αὐτός, intensive, attributive position, possession) 16.

παθημάτων (gen.pl.neut.of πάθημα, description) 3919.

ὧν (gen.pl.neut.of ὅς, relative pronoun, in agreement with παθημάτων) 65.

καὶ (adjunctive conjunction joining substantives) 14.

ἡμεῖς (nom.pl.masc.of ἐγώ, subject of πάσχομεν) 123.

πάσχομεν (1st.per.pl.pres.act.ind.of πάσχω, present progressive) 1208.

Translation - "But whether we are being put under pressure, it is for your comfort and salvation, if we are being comforted it is for your comfort which is being generated by means of your enduring the same sufferings which we are suffering."

Comment: Whether Paul was in trouble or being comforted in his trouble, the result was good for the Corinthians. If he endured persecution or physical trial, or both, it was because he was trying to bring comfort to the Corinthian saints and salvation to the lost in the city. In any case Paul was going to have to make the sacrifice. If the saints were comforted and the lost were saved, it would be because Paul travelled about preaching a gospel which was everywhere spoken against. But Paul's comfort was also a comfort to the troubled saints, generated by their own patient submission to the same sufferings which he had endured.

The old expression that "Misery loves company" may have application here. If a Corinthian saint was under pressure to could take comfort in knowing that Paul was also suffering for his testimony for Christ.

Verse 7 - "And our hope of you is steadfast, knowing that as ye are partakers of the sufferings, so shall ye be also of the consolation."

καὶ ἡ ἐλπὶς ἡμῶν βεβαία ὑπὲρ ὑμῶν, εἰδότες ὅτι ὡς κοινωνοί ἐστε τῶν παθημάτων, οὕτως καὶ τῆς παρακλήσεως.

"Our hope for you is unshaken; for we know that as you share in our sufferings, you will also share in our comfort." . . . RSV

καὶ (continuative conjunction) 14.
ἡ (nom.sing.fem.of the article in agreement with ἐλπὶς) 9.
ἐλπὶς (nom.sing.fem.of ἐλπίς, subject of ἐστιν understood) 2994.
ἡμῶν (gen.pl.masc.of ἐγώ, possession) 123.
βεβαία (nom.sing.fem.of βέβαιος, predicate adjective) 3889.
ὑπὲρ (preposition with the ablative "in behalf of") 545.
ὑμῶν (abl.pl.masc.of σύ, "in behalf of") 104.
εἰδότες (perf.act.part.nom.pl.masc.of ὁράω, adverbial, causal) 144b.
ὅτι (conjunction introducing an object clause in indirect discourse) 211.
ὡς (comparative particle) 128.
κοινωνοί (nom.pl.masc.of κοινωνός, predicate nominative) 1470.
ἐστε (2d.per.pl.pres.ind.of εἰμί, present iterative retroactive) 84.
τῶν (gen.pl.neut.of the article in agreement with παθημάτων) 9.
παθημάτων (gen.pl.neut.of πάθημα, description) 3919.
οὕτως (demonstrative adverb) 74.
καὶ (adjunctive conjunction joining nouns) 14.
τῆς (gen.sing.fem.of the article in agreement with παρακλήσεως) 9.
παρακλήσεως (gen.sing.fem.of παράκλησις, description) 1896.

Translation - "And our confidence in you does not waver because we know as you are participants in the sufferings, so also will you be in the comfort."

Comment: The copula is missing in the first clause as has so often been the case in Paul's letters to Corinth. His hope (confidence) that the Corinthians would live victoriously was unshaken. *Cf.#3889.* This is a concession to them, since he had implied on many occasions in his first epistle that they were not genuinely converted. The participle is causal. Paul's faith in them was the result of the fact that he had come to understand (intensive perfect tense in εἰδότες) that (objective ὅτι in indirect discourse), just as the Corinthians had suffered with Paul, so they would share in his comfort.

The suffering of persecution, with the comfort which it brings from God (verses 3,4) is a stabilizing and edifying influence in the life of a true child of God. This is the message of the Book of Job. The fact that the Corinthians were suffering is proof that they were genuine, for the world does not persecute its own. Thus the suffering saint is the refined saint.

There is MSS confusion here due to an oversight caused by homoeoteleuton (different clauses having the same ending).

Verse 8 - "For we would not, brethren, have you ignorant of our trouble which came to us in Asia, that we were pressed out of measure, above strength, insomuch that we despaired even of life."

Οὐ γὰρ θέλομεν ὑμᾶς ἀγνοεῖν, ἀδελφοί, ὑπὲρ τῆς θλίφεως ἡμῶν τῆς γενομένης ἐν τῇ Ἀσίᾳ, ὅτι καθ᾽ ὑπερβολὴν ὑπὲρ δύναμιν ἐβαρήθημεν, ὥστε ἐξαπορηθῆναι ἡμᾶς καὶ τοῦ ζῆν.

"For we do not want you to be ignorant, brethren, of the affliction we experienced in Asia; for we were so utterly, unbearably crushed that we despaired of life itself." . . . RSV

Οὐ (negative particle with the indicative) 130.
γὰρ (inferential conjunction) 105.
θέλομεν (1st.per.pl.pres.act.ind.of θέλω, aoristic) 88.
ὑμᾶς (acc.pl.masc.of σύ, general reference) 104.
ἀγνοεῖν (pres.act.inf.of ἀγνοέω, noun use, object of θέλομεν) 2345.
ἀδελφοί (voc.pl.masc.of ἀδελφός, address) 15.
ὑπὲρ (preposition with the genitive of reference) 545.
τῆς (gen.sing.fem.of the article in agreement with θλίφεως) 9.
θλίφεως (gen.sing.fem.of θλίφις, reference) 1046.
ἡμῶν (gen.pl.masc.of ἐγώ, possession) 123.
τῆς (gen.sing.fem.of the article in agreement with γενομένης) 9.
γενομένης (aor.mid.part.gen.sing.fem.of γίνομαι, adjectival, emphatic attributive position, ascriptive, in agreement with θλίφεως) 113.
ἐν (preposition with the locative of place) 80.
τῇ (loc.sing.fem.of the article in agreement with Ἀσίᾳ) 9.
Ἀσίᾳ (loc.sing.fem.of Ἀσία, place) 2968.
ὅτι (epexegetic conjunction) 211.
καθ᾽ (preposition with the accusative, measure) 98.

ὑπερβολὴν (acc.sing.fem.of ὑπερβολή, measure) 3923.
ὑπὲρ (preposition with the accusative of extent, "more than") 545.
δύναμιν (acc.sing.fem.of δύναμις, extent) 687.
ἐβαρήθημεν (1st.per.pl.1st.aor.pass.ind.of βαρέω, constative) 1589.
ὥστε (conjunction with the infinitive, result) 752.

#4265 ἐξαπορηθῆναι (aor.mid.inf.of ἐξαπορέω, result).

King James Version

despair - 2 Cor.1:8.
in despair - 2 Cor.4:8.

Revised Standard Version

despair - 2 Cor.1:8.
driven to despair - 2 Cor.4:8.

Meaning: A combination of ἐκ (#19) and ἀπορέω (#2254). To be utterly without resources; hopeless; in total despair; to be at a loss. Followed by ascensive καὶ and the articular infinitive - 2 Cor.1:8. In contrast to ἀπορέω in 2 Cor.4:8. *Cf.* comment *en loc.*

ἡμᾶς (acc.pl.masc.of ἐγώ, general reference) 123.
καὶ (ascensive conjunction) 14.
τοῦ (abl.sing.neut.of the article in agreement with ζῆν) 9.
ζῆν (pres.act.inf.of ζάω, separation) 340.

Translation - "Therefore, brethren, I do not want you to be unaware of our difficulties which beset us in Asia — that more than could be measured we were burdened beyond our endurance, with the result that we even gave up hope that we could survive.

Comment: Why should γάρ be inferential here? Because he said in verses 6 and 7 that the Corinthians' knowledge of his troubles helped them to bear their own and to be comforted. Since this is how it reacted upon them, Paul wanted them to know all about it. The ὅτι clause is epexegetical.

Note the result infinitive with ὥστε. Paul suffered so much that he could bear it no longer and even despaired of life itself. The result infinitive ἐξαπορηθῆναι has as its object the infinitive τοῦ ζῆν in the ablative of separation.

Paul apparently had reference to the mob action of the silversmiths in Ephesus (Acts 19:21-41, with particular reference to verse 30). His justification for recounting his difficulties is thus explained as his attempt to let the Corinthians know that all that live godly in Christ Jesus can expect to suffer. Thus they are not surprised but rather comforted in their own sufferings (2 Tim.3:12; 1 Pet.4:12,13; Mt.5:11,12).

Verse 9 - "But we had the sentence of death in ourselves, that we should not trust in ourselves, but in God which raiseth the dead:"

ἀλλὰ αὐτοὶ ἐν ἑαυτοῖς τὸ ἀπόκριμα τοῦ θανάτου ἐσχήκαμεν, ἵνα μὴ
πεποιθότες ὦμεν ἐφ' ἑαυτοῖς ἀλλ' ἐπὶ τῷ θεῷ τῷ ἐγείροντι τοὺς νεκρούς.

*"Why, we felt that we had received the sentence of death; but that was to make
us rely not on ourselves but on God who raises the dead;" . . . RSV*

ἀλλὰ (continuative conjunction) 342.
αὐτοὶ (nom.pl.masc.of αὐτός, subject of ἐσχήκαμεν, intensive) 16.
ἐν (preposition with the locative, with plural pronouns) 80.
ἑαυτοῖς (loc.pl.masc.of ἑαυτός, place) 288.
τὸ (acc.sing.neut.of the article in agreement with ἀπόκριμα) 9.

#4266 ἀπόκριμα (acc.sing.neut.of ἀπόκριμα, direct object of ἐσχήκαμεν).

King James Version

sentence - 2 Cor.1:9.

Revised Standard Version

sentence - 2 Cor.1:9.

Meaning: Cf. ἀποκρίνομαι (#318); ἀπόκρισις (#1919). Hence, an answer - 2
Cor.1:9.

τοῦ (gen.sing.masc.of the article in agreement with θανάτου) 9.
θανάτου (gen.sing.masc.of θάνατος, description) 381.
ἐσχήκαμεν (1st.per.pl.perf.act.ind.of ἔχω, dramatic present perfect) 82.
ἵνα (conjunction with the subjunctive in a negative purpose clause) 114.
μὴ (negative particle with the subjunctive, negative purpose) 87.
πεποιθότες (2d.per.act.part.nom.pl.masc.of πείθω, perfect periphrastic)
1629.
ὦμεν (1st.per.pl.pres.subj.of εἰμί, perfect periphrastic, negative purpose) 86.
ἐφ' (preposition with the locative, basis) 47.
ἑαυτοῖς (loc.pl.masc.of ἑαυτός, basis) 288.
ἀλλ' (alternative conjunction) 342.
ἐπὶ (preposition with the locative, basis) 47.
τῷ (loc.sing.masc.of the article in agreement with θεῷ) 9.
θεῷ (loc.sing.masc.of θεός, basis) 124.
τῷ (loc.sing.masc.of the article in agreement with ἐγείρονται) 9.
ἐγείροντι (pres.act.part.loc.sing.masc.of ἐγείρω, adjectival, emphatic
attributive position, ascriptive, in agreement with θεῷ) 125.
τοὺς (acc.pl.masc.of the article in agreement with νεκρούς) 9.
νεκρούς (acc.pl.masc.of νεκρός, direct object of ἐγείροντι) 749.

*Translation - "In fact we ourselves have had within ourselves the answer to the
death problem, in order that we should not have trusted in ourselves, but in the
God who raises the dead."*

Comment: If we translate ἀπόκριμα τοῦ θανάτου as "the sentence of death," meaning that Paul was certain that he was going to be killed, we have only a repetition of what he has already said in verse 8. But ἀπόκριμα can mean only an answer - that which is given in rebuttal. Paul uses a dramatic present perfect in ἐσχήκαμεν to give special attention to the fact that though he thought that he might die in Ephesus, he also had the answer to the question as to why he felt that way. It was to prevent him from trusting in himself, but rather (alternative ἀλλ') to make him trust in the God of resurrection. This being so, it did not really matter whether they killed him or not, since God is characterized as "the God, the One who customarily raises up the dead." Note the emphatic attributive position of the adjectival participle to define τῷ θεῷ.

We have here in the Dramatic Perfect "what in former classifications of tense usage we have called a special use, but this single indirect application of the root idea of the tense would hardly justify separate classification. It is a rhetorical application of the perfect tense. Since the perfect represents an existing state, it may be used for the purpose of describing a fact in an unusually vivid and realistic way. The historical present and dramatic aorist are also used in a sense similar to this, but for the purpose the perfect is the most forcible of the three. It is like our vernacular expression when we wish to describe vividly the expedition and ease with which one does a thing, "The first thing you know, he has done it." The Greek would just say, πεποίηκε τοῦτο. Like the intensive perfect, the dramatic perfect emphasizes the results of action. In fact, it is a sort of special rhetorical use of the intensive perfect, for its emphasis is upon the existing state. The New Testament writers used this construction quite frequently." (Mantey, *Manual*,204).

Paul understood this when he was in Ephesus and he had never forgotten it. So long as there is a possibility that we can deliver ourselves from whatever danger confronts us, it is natural for us to trust in ourselves and forget about God. When we are at our wits end and death seems certain, we are compelled to trust in God. This was Abraham's experience when he determined to obey God and kill Isaac. He did not try to persuade the Lord to change the order. He looked forward with complete trust that God would raise Isaac from the dead (Gen.22:5 - two will go, two will worship, *two* will return; Heb.11:17-19).

Because Paul was aware of why he knew that he was going to die, he did what God wanted him to do - he trusted in God and the result was that he did not die. This he says in

Verse 10 - "Who delivered us from so great a death, and doth deliver: in whom we trust that he will yet deliver us."

ὃς ἐκ τηλικούτων θανάτων ἐρρύσατο ἡμᾶς καὶ ῥύσεται, εἰς ὃν ἠλπίκαμεν καὶ ἔτι ῥύσεται,

"he delivered us from so deadly a peril, and he will deliver us; on him we have set our hope that he will deliver us again." . . . RSV

ὃς (nom.sing.masc.of ὅς, relative pronoun, subject of ἐρρύσατο) 65.
ἐκ (preposition with the ablative of separation) 19.

#4267 τηλικούτων (abl.pl.masc.of τηλικοῦτους, in agreement with θανάτων).

King James Version

so great - 2 Cor.1:10; Heb.2:3; James 3:4.
so mighty - Rev.16:18.

Revised Standard Version

so deadly - 2 Cor.1:10.
so great - Heb.2:3; James 3:4; Rev.16:18.

Meaning: τηλίκος — "so great" plus οὗτος (#93). Of such great size - James 3:4; of such great intensity - Rev.16:18; of such great importance - Heb.2:3; of such dreadful and destructive character - 2 Cor.1:10.

θανάτων (abl.pl.masc.of θάνατος, separation) 381.
ἐρρύσατο (3d.per.sing.aor.mid.ind.of ῥύω, constative) 584.
ἡμᾶς (acc.pl.masc.of ἐγώ, direct object of ἐρρύσατο) 123.
καὶ (adjunctive conjunction joining verbs) 14.
ῥύσεται (3d.per.sing.fut.mid.ind.of ῥύω, predictive) 584.
εἰς (preposition with the accusative of extent) 140.
ὅν (acc.sing.masc.of ὅς, relative pronoun, extent) 65.
ἠλπίκαμεν (1st.per.pl.perf.act.ind.of ἐλπίζω, present perfect intensive) 991.
καὶ (continuative conjunction) 14.
ἔτι (temporal adverb) 448.
ῥύσεται (3d.per.sing.fut.mid.ind.of ῥύω, predictive) 584.

Translation - "Who delivered us from such great deaths, and He will deliver, in Whom we have been trusting also that He will continue to deliver."

Comment: ὅς has as its antecedent τῷ θεῷ of verse 9. It is nominative because of its use in its own clause. ὅν, with the same antecedent is accusative for the same reason. God saved Paul's life in Ephesus. He will continue to do so. Paul, since that day at least, has always trusted Him to continue to do so.

Some MSS read ῥύεται for the first ῥύσεται. This supports the King James Version. "In view of the following ῥύσεται the words καὶ ῥύσεται strongly supported by p46 Sinaiticus B C P 33 itg vg copsa bo arm *al* seemed to some scribes to be superfluous and were therefore omitted (A D* Ψ itd,81 syrp ethpp): other scribes altered the first ῥύσεται to ῥύεται (Dc Ggr K 614 1739 1881 Byz Lect syrhal) thus producing the sequence of past, present and future." (Metzger, *A Textual Commentary on the Greek New Testament*, 574). It seems more logical to think in terms of the three tenses, but we have no choice but to follow the strongest support in the manuscripts. Paul's point is not disturbed in any case. The lesson which Paul has learned has served him well in the past and he will continue to apply it in the future. He was trusting "the God Who raises the dead" when he wrote 2 Tim.4:6-8.

At the risk of spoiling some good sermon outlines (including one of the favorites of the author) it must be pointed out that the context here speaks of Paul's physical death and not to the spiritual death of the believer. Thus, the Three Deliverances - in the past from the Penalty of Sin, in the present from the Power of Sin and in the future from the Presence of Sin, and the Three Shepherds - Good (John 10:11), Great (Heb.13:20) and Chief (1 Pet.5:4), and the Three Appearings (Heb.9:26,24,28) and the events that suggest this trilogy - Our Lord fed the multitude with the Bread of Life (Mt.14:14-21), He went up into the mountain to pray for them (Mt.14:23) and He came down from the mountain to rescue the disciples from the storm at sea (Mt.14:24-33), although it is a good outline and is amply supported by many other passages of Scripture, is not supported by 2 Cor.1:10. We may keep the outline and use it in a series of sermons, but support it elsewhere and leave 2 Cor.1:10 out of it or be guilty of eisegesis.

Verse 11 - "Ye also helping together by prayer for us, that for the gift bestowed upon us by the means of many persons thanks may be given by many on your behalf."

συνυπουργούντων καὶ ὑμῶν ὑπὲρ ἡμῶν τῇ δεήσει, ἵνα ἐκ πολλῶν προσώπων τὸ εἰς ἡμᾶς χάρισμα διὰ πολλῶν εὐχαριστηθῇ ὑπὲρ ἡμῶν.

"You also must help us by prayer, so that many will give thanks on our behalf for the blessing granted us in answer to many prayers." . . . RSV

#4268 συνυπουργούντων (pres.act.part.gen.pl.masc.of συνυπουργέω, adverbial, temporal, causal).

King James Version

help together - 2 Cor.1:11.

Revised Standard Version

help us - 2 Cor.1:11.

Meaning: A combination of σύν (#1542), ὑπό (#117) and ἔργω - hence, to help together; to assist - 2 Cor.1:11.

καὶ (adjunctive conjunction) 14.
ὑμῶν (gen.pl.masc.of σύ, possession) 104.
ὑπὲρ (preposition with the ablative, "in behalf of") 545.
ἡμῶν (abl.pl.masc.of ἐγώ, "in behalf of") 123.
τῇ (instru.sing.fem.of the article in agreement with δεήσει) 9.
δεήσει (instru.sing.fem.of δέησις, means) 1796.
ἵνα (conjunction with the subjunctive in a purpose clause) 114.
ἐκ (preposition with the ablative of source) 19.
πολλῶν (abl.pl.neut.of πολύς, in agreement with προσώπων) 228.
προσώπων (abl.pl.neut.of πρόσωπον source) 588.
τὸ (nom.sing.neut.of the article in agreement with χάρισμα) 9.

τό (nom.sing.neut.of the article in agreement with χάρισμα) 9.
εἰς (preposition with the accusative of extent) 140.
ἡμᾶς (acc.pl.masc.of ἐγω, extent) 123.
χάρισμα (nom.sing.neut.of χάρισμα, subject of εὐχαριστηθῇ) 3790.
διά (preposition with the ablative of agency) 118.
πολλῶν (abl.pl.masc.of πολύς, agent) 228.
εὐχαριστηθῇ (3d.per.sing.1st.aor.pass.subj.of εὐχριστέω, constative) 1185.
ὑπέρ (preposition with the ablative, "in behalf of") 545.
ἡμῶν (abl.pl.masc.of ἐγώ, "in behalf of") 123.

Translation - ". . . while you are helping me by your prayer so that from many people thanks may be given on our behalf for the gift given to us in answer to many prayers."

Comment: Paul's deliverance from future peril will be in answer to the continuing prayers of the Corinthians. The result will be that many other Christians will be grateful to God that Paul has been spared, in answer to the prayers of the saints in Corinth.

The Postponement of Paul's Visit

(2 Corinthians 1:12 — 2:4)

Verse 12 - "For our rejoicing is this; the testimony of our conscience, that in simplicity and godly sincerity, not with fleshly wisdom, but by the grace of God, we have had our converstion in the world, and more abundantly to you-ward."

Ἡ γὰρ καύχησις ἡμῶν αὕτη ἐστίν, τὸ μαρτύριον τῆς συνειδήσεως ἡμῶν, ὅτι ἐν ἁπλότητι καὶ εἰλικρινείᾳ τοῦ θεοῦ, (καὶ) οὐκ ἐν σοφίᾳ σαρκικῇ ἀλλ' ἐν χάριτι θεοῦ, ἀνεστράφημεν ἐν τῷ κόσμῳ, περισσοτέρως δὲ πρὸς ὑμᾶς.

"For our boast is this, the testimony of our conscience that we have behaved in the world, and still more toward you, with holiness and godly sincereity, not with earthly wisdom but by the grace of God." . . . RSV

Ἡ (nom.sing.fem.of the article in agreement with καύχησις) 9.
γάρ (causal conjunction) 105.
καύχησις (nom.sing.fem.of καύχησις, subject of ἐστίν) 3877.
ἡμῶν (gen.pl.masc.of ἐγω, possession) 123.
αὕτη (nom.sing.fem.of οὗτος, predicate nominative) 98.
ἐστίν (3d.per.sing.pres.ind.of εἰμί, aoristic) 86.
τό (nom.sing.neut.of the article in agreement with μαρτύριον) 9.
μαρτύριον (nom.sing.neut.of μαρτύριον, apposition) 716.
τῆς (gen.sing.fem.of the article in agreement with συνειδήσεως) 9.
συνειδήσεως (gen.sing.fem.of συνείδησις, description) 3590.
ἡμῶν (gen.pl.masc.of ἐγώ, possession) 123.
ὅτι (epexegetical) 211.

ἐν (preposition with the instrumental of manner) 80.
ἁπλότητι (instru.sing.masc.of ἁπλότης, manner) 4018.
καὶ (adjunctive conjunction joining nouns) 14.
εἰλικρινείᾳ (instru.sing.fem.of εἰλικρίνεια, manner) 4138.
τοῦ (abl.sing.masc.of the article in agreement with θεοῦ) 9.
θεοῦ (abl.sing.masc.of θεός, source) 124.
καὶ (adjunctive conjunction joining nouns) 14.
οὐκ (negative particle with the indicative) 130.
ἐν (preposition with the instrumental of manner) 80.
σοφίᾳ (instru.sing.fem.of σοφία, manner) 934.
σαρκικῇ (instru.sing.fem.of σαρκικός in agreement with σοφίᾳ) 4058
ἀλλ' (alternative conjunction) 342.
ἐν (preposition with the instrumental of means) 80.
χάριτι (instru.sing.fem.of χάρις, means) 1700.
θεοῦ (gen.sing.masc.of θεός, description) 124.
ἀνεστράφημεν (1st.per.pl.2d.aor.pass.ind.of ἀναστρέφω, constative) 3061.
ἐν (preposition with the locative of place) 80.
τῷ (loc.sing.masc.of the article in agreement with κόσμῳ) 9.
κόσμῳ (loc.sing.masc.of κόσμος, place) 360.
περισσοτέρως (adverbial) 525.
δὲ (adversative conjunction) 11.
πρὸς (preposition with the accusative of extent) 197.
ὑμᾶς (acc.pl.masc.of σύ, extent) 104.

Translation - *"Because our boast, the testimony of our conscience, is this: that by simplicity and a sincereity born of God and not of human wisdom, but by divine grace, we have conducted ourselves in the world, but especially toward you."*

Comment: αὕτη is deictic, pointing to the ὅτι clause which is objective and epexegetical. τὸ μαρτύριον . . . ἡμῶν is in apposition to καύχησις.

Paul's conscience told him that in all of his relations to the world of unsaved men and women, as well as to Christians, he had gone about preaching the gospel, not with devious methods nor duplicit motives, but with pure motives (simplicity) and with a sincerity that comes from God (#4138). Not with human wisdom had he preached. This part is not quite true, as he resorted to "scholarship" on Mars Hill (Acts 17:22-34) to too great an extent. He adds that his motives and mode of operation was most proper in Corinth. *Cf.* comment on 1 Cor.2:1-5 as related to Acts 18;1. *Cf.*#3877 for the things that Paul most liked to "boast" about. *Cf.*#4018 - "lack of duplicity." *Cf.*#3061 for other uses of ἀναστρέφω in this sense. Note the adverb περισσοτέρως - *Cf.*#525.

Verse 13 - *"For we write none other things unto you than what ye read or acknowledge: and I trust ye shall acknowledge even to the end."*

οὐ γὰρ ἄλλα γράφομεν ὑμῖν ἀλλ' ἢ ἃ ἀναγινώσκετε ἢ ἐπιγινώσκετε, ἐλπίζω δὲ ὅτι ἕως τέλους ἐπιγνώσεσθε,

"For we write you nothing but what you can read and understand; I hope you

will understand fully," . . . RSV

οὐ (negative particle with the indicative) 130.
γὰρ (causal conjunction) 105.
ἀλλὰ (acc.pl.neut.of ἄλλος, direct object of γράφομεν) 198.
γράφομεν (1st.per.pl.pres.act.ind.of γράφω, aoristic) 156.
ὑμῖν (dat.pl.masc.of σύ, indirect object of γράφομεν) 104.
ἀλλ' (adversative conjunction) 342.
ἤ (disjunctive) 465.
ἃ (acc.pl.neut.of ὅς, relative pronoun, direct object of ἀναγινώσκετε) 65.
ἀναγινώσκετε (2d.per.pl.pres.act.ind.of ἀναγινώσκω, customary) 967.
ἤ (disjunctive) 465.
καὶ (adjunctive conjunction joining verbs) 14.
ἐπιγινώσκετε (2d.per.pl.pres.act.ind.of ἐπιγινώσκω, customary) 675.
ἐλπίζω (1st.per.sing.pres.act.ind.of ἐλπίζω, aoristic) 991.
δὲ (continuative conjunction) 11.
ὅτι (conjunction introducing an object clause) 211.
ἕως (preposition with the genitive in a time expression) 71.
τέλους (gen.sing.neut.of τέλος, time description) 881.
ἐπιγνώσεσθε (2d.per.pl.fut.mid.ind.of ἐπιγινώσκω, deliberative) 675.

Translation - "Because we are writing nothing to you except those things which you both read and understand perfectly, and I hope that you will understand unto the end."

Comment: He is restating the fact that his relations with them have always been simplistic (without duplicity). He had no hidden or double meanings in his first epistle. He wrote nothing between the lines, but everything on the line in the Greek that they could understand. He meant everything that he said and only what he said and he hoped that they would read and understand exactly what he wrote. The text does not reveal whether ἕως τέλους means "to the end of the epistle" or "to the second coming." Verse 14 may be a hint that he means the latter.

Verse 14 - "As also ye have acknowledged us in part, that we are your rejoicing, even as ye also are ours, in the day of the Lord Jesus,"

καθὼς καὶ ἐπέγνωτε ἡμᾶς ἀπὸ μέρους, ὅτι καύχημα ὑμῶν ἐσμεν καθάπερ καὶ ὑμεῖς ἡμῶν ἐν τῇ ἡμέρᾳ τοῦ κυρίου Ἰησοῦ.

"as you have understood in part, that you can be proud of us as we can be of you, on the day of the Lord Jesus." . . . RSV

καθὼς (compound comparative particle) 1348.
καὶ (adjunctive conjunction) 14.
ἐπέγνωτε (2d.per.pl.2d.aor.act.ind.of ἐπιγινώσκω, culminative) 675.
ὑμᾶς (acc.pl.masc.of σύ, direct object of ἐπέγνωτε) 104.
ἀπὸ (preposition with the ablative, partitive) 70.

μέρους (abl.pl.neut.of μέρος, partitive) 240.
ὅτι (conjunction introducing an object clause in indirect discourse) 211.
καύχημα (nom.sing.neut.of καύχημα, predicate nominative) 3881.
ὑμῶν (gen.pl.masc.of σύ, possession) 104.
ἐσμεν (1st.per.pl.pres.ind.of εἰμί, editorial, aoristic) 86.
καθάπερ (compound intensive comparative particle) 3883.
καὶ (adjunctive conjunction joining pronouns) 14.
ὑμεῖς (nom.pl.masc.of σύ, subject of εἰσίν, understood) 104.
ἡμῶν (gen.pl.masc.of ἐγώ, possession) 123.
ἐν (preposition with the locative of time point) 80.
τῇ (loc.sing.fem.of the article in agreement with ἡμέρᾳ) 9.
ἡμέρᾳ (loc.sing.fem.of ἡμέρα, time point) 135.
τοῦ (gen.sing.masc.of the article in agreement with κυρίου) 9.
κυρίου (gen.sing.masc.of κύριος, description) 97.
Ἰησοῦ (gen.sing.masc.of Ἰησοῦς, apposition) 3.

Translation - *"As also some of you have come to appreciate that we are your reason to be proud, just as also you will be ours on the day when the Lord Jesus returns."*

Comment: Paul had some loyal friends in Corinth who understood Paul's character and his worth, just as he saw the same qualities in them. At the second coming they would look upon each other as sources of pride and rejoicing.

Verse 15 - *"And in this confidence I was minded to come unto you before, that ye might have a second benefit."*

Καὶ ταύτῃ τῇ πεποιθήσει ἐβουλόμην πρότερον πρὸς ὑμᾶς ἐλθεῖν, ἵνα δευτέραν χάριν σχῆτε,

"Because I was sure of this, I wanted to come to you first, so that you might have a double pleasure;" . . . RSV

καὶ (continuative conjunction) 14.
ταύτῃ (instru.sing.fem.of οὗτος, in agreement with πεποιθήσει) 93.
τῇ (instru.sing.fem.of the article in agreement with πεποιθήσει) 9.

#4269 πεποιθήσει (instru.sing.fem.of πεποίθησις, cause).

King James Version

confidence - 2 Cor.1:15; 8:22; 10:2; Eph.3:12; Phil.3:4.
trust - 2 Cor.3:4.

Revised Standard Version

was sure of - 2 Cor.1:15.
confidence - 2 Cor.8;22; 10:2; Eph.3:12; Phil.3:4; 2 Cor.3:4.

Meaning: Cf. πείθω (#1629). Hence, trust, confidence, reliance. Followed by an infinitive indicating confidence in the wisdom of a proposed policy - 2 Cor.1:15;

followed by διὰ τοῦ Χριστοῦ in 2 Cor.3:4; Eph.3:2; followed by εἰς ὑμᾶς in 2 Cor.8:22; with reference to Paul's confidence in himself - 2 Cor.10:2; followed by ἐνσάρκι in Phil.3:4.

ἐβουλόμην (1st.per.sing.imp.mid.ind.of ἐβουλόμην, voluntative) 953.

πρότερον (acc.sing.neut.of πρότερος, adverbial) 2293.

πρὸς (preposition with the accusative of extent) 197.

ὑμᾶς (acc.pl.masc.of σύ, extent) 104.

ἐλθεῖν (aor.inf.of ἔρχομαι, epexegetical) 146.

ἵνα (conjunction with the subjunctive in a purpose clause) 114.

δευτέραν (acc.sing.fem.of δεύτερος, in agreement with χάριν) 1371.

χάριν (acc.sing.fem.of χάρις, direct object of σχῆτε) 1700.

σχῆτε (2d.per.pl.aor.act.subj.of ἔχω, purpose) 82.

Translation - "*And because of this confidence I had been rather planning before to visit you that you might have a double advantage.*"

Comment: ταύτῃ τῇ πεποιθήσει refers to verse 14. Since Paul believed that, although he had some detractors at Corinth, he also had some loyal Christian friends who believed in him, he had rather hoped previously (πρότερον) to come to Corinth again. His purpose in coming was to give the church the spiritual uplift of his ministry among them. He hoped also that they would have the added blessing of his fellowship, since some of them were proud of him, as he was of them. He said the same thing to the Romans (Rom.1:11,12).

In ἐβουλόμην we have a rare instance of the voluntative imperfect tense. "The want of attainment in the imperfect prepares it to submit quite easily to the expression of a desire or disposition, since the statement of a wish itself implies the lack of realization. There are but a few instances of this usage in the New Testament, but adequate grammatical treatment requires that they be recognized as a distinct class. *Cf.* Acts 25:22; Rom.9:3; Gal.4:20; Philemon 13." (Mantey, *Manual*, 190).

Some MSS read χαράν (joy) instead of χάριν (grace, gift, benefit). In either case the exegesis is not appreciably affected. If Paul be charged with egotism because he believed that his ministry could be beneficial to Corinth, it should be remembered that he was one of the twelve Apostles. Any Christian who intends to teach and preach the Word can say, without egotism, that his ministry will be a blessing, since the source of the blessing is not in the teacher, but in what he teaches.

Verse 16 - "*And to pass by you into Macedonia, and to come again out of Macedonia unto you, and of you to be brought on my way toward Judea.*"

καὶ δι' ὑμῶν διελθεῖν εἰς Μακεδονίαν, καὶ πάλιν ἀπὸ Μακεδονίας ἐλθεῖν πρὸς ὑμᾶς καὶ ὑφ' ὑμῶν προπεμφθῆναι εἰς τὴν Ἰουδαίαν.

"*I wanted to visit you on my way to Macedonia, and to come back to you from Macedonia and have you send me on my way to Judea.*" ... RSV

καὶ (adjunctive conjunction joining infinitives) 14.

δι' (preposition with the genitive, physically "through") 118.
ὑμῶν (gen.pl.masc.of σύ, physical passage) 104.
διελθεῖν (aor.inf.of διέρχομαι, epexegetical) 1017.
εἰς (preposition with the accusative, extent) 140.
Μακεδονίαν (acc.sing.fem.of Μακεδονία, extent) 3360.
καὶ (adjunctive conjunction joining infinitives) 14.
πάλιν (adverbial) 355.
ἀπὸ (preposition with the ablative of separation) 70.
Μακεδονίας (abl.sing.fem.of Μακεδονία, separation) 3360.
ἐλθεῖν (aor.inf.of ἔρχομαι, epexegetical) 146.
πρὸς (preposition with the accusative of extent) 197.
ὑμᾶς (acc.pl.masc.of σύ, extent) 104.
καὶ (adjunctive conjunction joining infinitives) 14.
ὑφ' (preposition with the ablative of agent) 117.
ὑμῶν (abl.pl.masc.of σύ, agent) 104.
προπεμφθῆναι (aor.pass.inf.of προπέμπω, epexegetical) 3335.
εἰς (preposition with the accusative, extent) 140.
τὴν (acc.sing.fem.of the article in agreement with Ἰουδαίαν) 9.
Ἰουδαίαν (acc.sing.fem.of Ἰουδαίας, extent) 134.

Translation - "And to pass through Corinth on my way into Macedonia, and again to come from Macedonia to you and with your help to be sent on to Judea."

Comment: Thus Paul outlined the travel plans which he had hoped to follow. He would sail westward across the Aegean from Ephesus to Corinth and travel by land up north into Macedonia. After his visit there, with the churches in Berea, Thessalonica and Philippi, and any others which may have been established, he planned to return southward to Corinth and pick up travel expenses for the sea voyage to Judea. This conflicts with what he told them in 1 Cor.16:5-8, where he said that he would not stop in Corinth on his way to Macedonia. After all Paul was only human, despite the fact that he tried always to seek the will of God for his ministry. His plans were often set aside (Romans 1:13).

Verse 17 - "When I therefore was thus minded, did I use lightness? Or the things that I purpose, do I purpose according to the flesh, that with me there should be yea, yea and nay, nay?"

τοῦτο οὖν βουλόμενος μήτι ἄρα τῇ ἐλαφρίᾳ ἐχρησάμην; ἢ ἃ βουλεύομαι κατὰ σάρκα βουλεύομαι, ἵνα ᾖ παρ' ἐμοὶ τὸ Ναὶ ναὶ καὶ Οὖ οὖ;

"Was I vacillating when I wanted to do this? Do I make my plans like a worldly man, ready to say Yes and No at once?" . . . RSV

τοῦτο (acc.sing.neut.of οὗτος, direct object of βουλόμενος) 93.
οὖν (inferential conjunction) 68.
βουλόμενος (pres.mid.part.nom.sing.masc.of βούλομαι, adverbial, temporal) 953.

μήτι (negative particle in rhetorical question expecting a negative reply) 676.

ἄρα (illative particle) 995.

τῇ (instru.sing.fem.of the article in agreement with ἐλαφρίᾳ) 9.

#4270 ἐλαφρίᾳ (instru.sing.fem.of ἐλαφρία, manner).

King James Version

lightness - 2 Cor.1:17.

Revised Standard Version

was I vacillating? - 2 Cor.1:17.

Meaning: Cf.ἐλαφρός (#961); ἐλαφρία - "lack of sincerity." Levity, fickleness of purpose. τῇ ἐλαφρίᾳ ἐχρησάμην - "was I joking?" - 2 Cor.1:17.

ἐχρησάμην (1st.per.sing.aor.mid.ind.of χράω, constative) 2447.

ἤ (disjunctive) 465.

ἅ (acc.pl.neut.of ὅς, relative pronoun, direct object of βουλεύομαι) 65.

βουλεύομαι (1st.per.sing.pres.mid.ind.of βουλεύομαι, customary) 90.

κατά (preposition with the accusative, standard) 98.

σάρκα (acc.sing.fem.of σάρξ, standard) 1202.

βουλεύομαι (1st.per.sing.pres.mid.ind.of βουλεύομαι, customary) 90.

ἵνα (conjunction with the subjunctive in a result clause) 114.

ᾖ (3d.per.sing.pres.subj.of εἰμί, result) 86.

παρ' (preposition with the locative, in ethical relations) 154.

ἐμοὶ (loc.sing.masc.of ἐμός, ethical relations) 1267.

τὸ (nom.sing.neut.of the article, joined with Ναὶ ναί) 9.

Ναὶ (particle of affirmation) 524.

ναί (particle of affirmation) 524.

καὶ (adjunctive conjunction) 14.

οὐ (particle of negation) 130.

οὐ (particle of negation) 130.

Translation - "Therefore when I was planning this trip I was not being adroit was I? Or do I that which I plan on the basis of human wisdom, so that my policy is only double talk?"

Comment: τοῦτο βουλόμενος is temporal - "at the time that I was making those plans . . ." He then asks a rhetorical question and he expects a negative reply. "Was I really only being dexterous?" After ἤ, the disjunctive, he offers another explanation. Perhaps what he planned was only the plan of a man who follows only human wisdom? If so the result is (ἵνα ᾖ) that I am being guilty of duplicity. Note the ethical relation idea in παρ' ἐμοὶ - When it comes to me, what policy should I pursue?

To the extent that any Christian makes plans without consulting the Lord, his word may be untrustworthy. James has warned us about that (James 4:13-15). To plan κατὰ σάρκα is to seek to arrange one's affairs with a view to maximizing one's own benefit in the short run. When we turn the schedule for our lives over to the Lord we learn that He has already made the plan that maximizes our benefit in the long run. Paul learned from his experiences to avoid the folly of planning for the future, which he could never know, and the wisdom of allowing the Lord to guide, for He knows the end from the beginning. Happy is the child of God who takes the hands of his own control off his life, because he has "eternity's values in view."

However mistaken Paul may have been in his travel plans, his motives were not self-serving, as he assures them in

Verse 18 - "But as God is true, our word toward you was not yea and nay."

πιστὸς δὲ ὁ θεὸς ὅτι ὁ λόγος ἡμῶν ὁ πρὸς ὑμᾶς οὐκ ἔστιν Ναὶ καὶ Οὔ.

"As surely as God is faithful, our word to you has not been Yes and No.". RSV

πιστὸς (nom.sing.masc.of πιστός, predicate adjective) 1522.
δὲ (adversative conjunction) 11.
ὁ (nom.sing.masc.of the article in agreement with θεὸς) 9.
θεὸς (nom.sing.masc.of θεός, subject of ἔστιν, understood) 124.
ὅτι (conjunction in a declarative clause) 211.
ὁ (nom.sing.masc.of the article in agreement with λόγος) 9.
λόγος (nom.sing.masc.of λόγος, subject of ἔστιν) 510.
ἡμῶν (gen.pl.masc.of ἐγώ, possession) 123.
ὁ (nom.sing.masc.of the article in agreement with λόγος) 9.
πρὸς (preposition with the accusative of extent in a context of speaking) 197.
ὑμᾶς (acc.pl.masc.of σύ extent) 104.
οὐκ (negative particle with the indicative) 130.
ἔστιν (3d.per.sing.pres.ind.of εἰμί, aoristic) 86.
Ναὶ (particle of affirmation) 524.
καὶ (adjunctive conjunction) 14.
οὔ (particle of negation) 130.

Translation - "But as God is faithful I swear that our word to you is not Yes and No."

Comment: The copula is ellided in the first clause of this solemn oath. We may supply ὄμνυμι (#516) before ὅτι. Paul insists that there was no equivocation in his previous statement of his plans, despite the fact that they were not carried out, due to the inexorable progression of events.

Verse 19 - "For the Son of God, Jesus Christ, who was preached among you by us, even by me and Silvanus and Timotheus, was not yea and nay, but in him was yea."

ὁ τοῦ θεοῦ γὰρ υἱὸς Ἰησοῦς Χριστὸς ὁ ἐν ὑμῖν δι' ἡμῶν κηρυχθείς, δι' ἐμοῦ καὶ Σιλουανοῦ καὶ Τιμοθέου, οὐκ ἐγένετο Ναὶ καὶ Οὔ, ἀλλὰ Ναὶ ἐν αὐτῷ γέγονεν.

"For the Son of God, Jesus Christ whom we preached among you, Silvanus

and Timothy and I, was not Yes and No; but in him it is always Yes." . . . RSV

ὁ (nom.sing.masc.of the article in agreement with υἱός) 9.

τοῦ (gen.sing.masc.of the article in agreement with θεοῦ) 9.

θεοῦ (gen.sing.masc.of θεός, relationship) 124.

γάρ (causal conjunction) 105.

υἱός (nom.sing.masc.of υἱός, subject of ἐγένετο) 5.

Ἰησοῦς (nom.sing.masc.of Ἰησοῦς, apposition) 3.

Χριστός (nom.sing.masc.of Χριστός, apposition) 4.

ὁ (nom.sing.masc.of the article in agreement with κηρυχθείς) 9.

ἐν (preposition with the locative with plural pronouns) 80.

ὑμῖν (loc.pl.masc.of σύ, association) 104.

δι' (preposition with the ablative of agent) 118.

ἡμῶν (abl.pl.masc.of ἐγώ, agent) 123.

κηρυχθείς (aor.pass.part.nom.sing.masc.of κηρύσσω, apposition with υἱός) 249.

δι' (preposition with the ablative of agent) 118.

ἐμοῦ (abl.sing.masc.of ἐμός, agent) 1267.

καί (adjunctive conjunction joining nouns) 14.

Σιλουνοῦ (abl.sing.masc.of Σιλουανός, agent) 3345.

καί (adjunctive conjunction joining nouns) 14.

Τιμοθέου (abl.sing.masc.of Τιμόθεος, agent) 3354.

οὐκ (negative particle with the indicative) 130.

ἐγένετο (3d.per.sing.aor.mid.ind.of γίνομαι, constative) 113.

Ναί (particle of affirmation) 524.

καί (adjunctive conjunction) 14.

Οὔ (particle of negation) 130.

ἀλλά (alternative conjunction) 342.

Ναί (particle of affirmation) 524.

ἐν (preposition with the instrumental of association) 80.

αὐτῷ (instru.sing.masc.of αὐτός, association) 16.

γέγονεν (3d.per.sing.2d.perf.ind.of γίνομαι, intensive) 113.

Translation - "Because the Son of God, Jesus Christ, the One Who has been preached among you by us - by Silas and Timothy and I, was not Yes and No; but He has always been Yes."

Comment: The connection between verses 18 and 19, suggested by causal γάρ is that Paul swore on oath by the faithful God (πιστὸς δὲ ὁ θεός) that his letter to them about his travel plans, though wrong, was not deliberately equivocal, and now he says that the Son of God, Who is God's Faithful Witness (Rev.1:5), Whose message he, Silas and Timothy preached, is likewise unequivocal. What Jesus Christ says, man can depend upon. There is no double talk from Him and any double talk from Paul must be charged to the fact that Paul had motivated by the flesh (verse 17) rather than to any deliberate effort on Paul's part to deceive. The message of the gospel of Christ has always been positive. The Lord Jesus says "No" only in the short run so that He can say a bigger "Yes" in the eternal long run.

Verse 20 - "For all the promises of God in him are Yea, and in him Amen, unto the glory of God by us."

ὅσαι γὰρ ἐπαγγελίαι θεοῦ, ἐν αὐτῷ τὸ Ναί. διὸ καὶ δι' αὐτοῦ τὸ 'Αμὴν τῷ θεῷ πρὸς δόξαν δι' ἡμῶν.

"For all the promises of God find their Yes in him. That is why we utter the Amen through him, to the glory of God." . . . RSV

ὅσαι (nom.pl.fem.of ὅσος, in agreement with ἐπαγγελίαι) 660.
γὰρ (inferential conjunction) 105.
ἐπαγγελίαι (nom.pl.fem.of ἐπαγγελία, subject of εἰσιν understood) 2929.
θεοῦ (gen.sing.masc.of θεός, description) 124.
ἐν (preposition with the instrumental of association) 80.
αὐτῷ (instrumental sing.masc.of αὐτός, association) 16.
τό (nom.sing.neut.of the article in agreement with Ναί) 9.
Ναί (particle of affirmation, predicate nominative) 524.
διὸ (inferential conjunction) 1622.
καὶ (continuative conjunction) 14.
δι' (preposition with the ablative of agent) 118.
αὐτοῦ (abl.sing.masc.of αὐτός, agent) 16.
τό (nom.sing.neut.of the article in agreement with 'Αμὴν) 9.
'Αμὴν (nom.sing.neut.of 'Αμὴν, predicate nominative) 466.
τῷ (dat.sing.masc.of the article in agreement with θεῷ) 9.
θεῷ (dat.sing.masc.of θεός, personal advantage) 124.
πρὸς (preposition with the accusative of purpose) 197.
δόξαν (acc.sing.fem.of δόξα, purpose) 361.
δι' (preposition with the ablative of agent) 118.
ἡμῶν (abl.pl.masc.of ἐγώ, agent) 123.

Translation - "So those divine promises that were issued through Him are Yes; thus also through His enabling we say 'Amen' to the glory of God."

Comment: γὰρ now is inferential as it connects the thought of verse 20 to that of verse 19. Jesus Christ, the Son of God and Faithful Witness always tells the truth (John 14:6). Therefore all of the divine promises that are issued in His name are certain to be fulfilled. That indeed includes all of the promises of God, for God does nothing for man apart from the Lord Jesus Christ. But it does not include anything which we, in fleshly wisdom, *assume* to be a promise of God, when in reality it is not. Paul thought that he was planning his itinerary in the will of God in 1 Cor.16:5,6, but he was not. His error was not in his motive, for he insists that he was sincere, but as events were to prove, he was sincerely *mistaken*. Thus the Lord Jesus did not say "Yes" to those plans. On the contrary He vetoed them. If God did everything for us for which we imagine we have His promise, His universe would be *chaos* instead of *cosmos*. But when we claim a promise which in truth has come from God and has been ratified in the person of Jesus Christ, we can say "Amen" and in doing so glorify God. What God does for us is that which He ordained to do before the foundation of the world. And it was ratified in the mediatorial agency of Christ and made legal by His death, burial and resurrection. Thus God is not only the Promiser but He is also the Performer. His word is sure. If Christians could and would always plan their lives in accordance with His will (Eph.2:10) then our word would be as unequivocal as His. But this is far too idealistic. The reality is that we plan κατὰ σάρκα, verse 17- "according to the flesh." In which cases our promise is Ναί, but His is Οὔ. When we lay our plans as Paul did without consulting Him, or after consulting Him, either misunderstand or fail to heed His advice, we make promises, albeit in total sincerity, that deceive our friends. When we follow His plan we rejoice to say "Amen" to whatever happens, even if, in the short run, it looks to us like tragedy. God's short run "tragedies" are long run blessings.

Thus the "bottom line" teaching of this passage is that intelligent Christians will surrender the driver's seat to Christ and allow the nail-pierced hands to rest upon the steering wheel while we take our place in the back seat and **SHUT UP.** A Christian life always guided by the Lord would be a Christian life in which "all things work together for good. . . " (Romans 8:28) and it would be a life always characterized by our saying "Amen" to all of His positive affirmations. In reality it does not work that way, so we should be grateful to Him that He sometimes says "No" and pray that we may yield to Him so completely that He will always be able to say, "Yes."

Verse 21 - "Now He which stablisheth us with you in Christ, and hath anointed us, is God."

ὁ δὲ βεβαιῶν ἡμᾶς σὺν ὑμῖν εἰς Χριστὸν καὶ χρίσας ἡμᾶς θεός.

"But it is God who establishes us with you in Christ, and has commissioned us;" . . . RSV

ὁ (nom.sing.masc.of the article in agreement with βεβαιῶν) 9.

δὲ (explanatory conjunction) 11.

βεβαιῶν (pres.act.part.nom.sing.masc.of βεβαιόω, substantival, subject of ἐστιν understood) 2932.

ἡμᾶς (acc.pl.masc.of ἐγώ, direct object of βεβαιῶν) 123.

σὺν (preposition with the instrumental of association) 1542.

ὑμῖν (instru.sing.masc.of σύ, association) 104.

εἰς (preposition with the accusative, locative, static use) 140.

Χριστὸν (acc.sing.masc.of Χριστός, original static locative use) 4.

καὶ (adjunctive conjunction joining participles) 14.

χρίσας (aor.act.part.nom.sing.masc.of χρίω, substantival, subject of ἐστιν understood) 2021.

ἡμᾶς (acc.pl.masc.of ἐγώ, direct object of χρίσας) 123.

θεός (nom.sing.masc.of θεός, predicate nominative) 124.

Translation - "Now the One Who is keeping us firmly established along with you in Christ and Who has anointed us is God."

Comment: Note the meaning of βεβαιῶν (#2932) and the present progressive action. God is always interested in establishing us firmly in our Christian faith and practice. Since it is God whose word is always Ναί, and can always be trusted, it is comforting to know that He who cannot be equivocal is the One Who is always cementing (making firm, establishing, fixing) us. He is also the One Who has anointed us (aorist tense in the participle χρίσας). The permanence of our relationship to Christ depends upon the credibility of the One who has established us in that relationship. Since God is totally reliable, we are completely safe.

God's further work for us is described in

Verse 22 - "Who hath also sealed us, and given us the earnest of the Spirit in our hearts."

ὁ καὶ σφραγισάμενος ἡμᾶς καὶ δοὺς τὸν ἀρραβῶνα τοῦ πνεύματος ἐν ταῖς καρδίαις ἡμῶν.

"he has put his seal upon us and given us his Spirit in our hearts as a guarantee." . . . RSV

ὁ (nom.sing.masc.of the article in agreement with σφραγισάμενος) 9.
καὶ (adjunctive conjunction joining participles) 14.
σφραγισάμενος (aor.mid.part.nom.sing.masc.of σφραγίζω, substantival, in apposition with θεός) 1686.
ἡμᾶς (acc.pl.masc.of ἐγώ, direct object of σφραγισάμενος) 123.
καὶ (adjunctive conjunction joining participles) 14.
δοὺς (aor.act.part.nom.sing.masc.of δίδωμι, in apposition with θεός) 362.
τὸν (acc.sing.masc.of the article in agreement with ἀρραβῶνα) 9.

#4271 ἀρραβῶνα (acc.sing.masc.of ἀρράβων, direct object of δοὺς).

King James Version

earnest - 2 Cor.1:22; 5:5; Eph.1:14.

Revised Standard Version

guarantee - 2 Cor.1:22; 5:5; Eph.1:14.

Meaning: A word which passed from the Phoenicians to the Greeks and subsequently into Latin. Earnest money; down payment, pledged in advance to assure that the remainder would be paid and the deal consummated. "The meaning of 'earnest money' (*Scottice,* 'arles') is well illustrated in P Par 58₁₂ (ii/BC) (Witkowski 2, p.81), where a woman who was selling a cow received 1000 drachmae a ἀραβῶνα" (Moulton & Milligan, 79). Other examples are numerous. It is reported that taxi drivers in Athens charge the ἀρράβων (a part of the total fee) at the beginning of the cab ride, because tourists have been known to leap from the cab and flee without paying at the terminal point. Associated with the Holy Spirit, at regeneration, Who assures the believer of a bodily resurrection at the second coming of Christ - 2 Cor.1:22; 5:5; Eph.1:14.

τοῦ (gen.sing.neut.of the article in agreement with πνεύματος) 9.
πνεύματος (gen.sing.neut.of πνεῦμα, description) 83.
ἐν (preposition with the locative, place) 80.
ταῖς (loc.pl.fem.of the article in agreement with καρδίαις) 9.
καρδίαις (loc.pl.fem.of καρδία, place) 432.
ἡμῶν (gen.pl.masc.of ἐγώ, possession) 123.

Translation - "Who also has sealed us and has given the guarantee of the Spirit in our hearts."

Comment: Two more substantival participles, σφραγισάμενος and δοὺς are added to χρίσας (verse 21) in apposition to ϑεός. God is described as the One Who has established us, anointed us, sealed us and made His down payment upon us as His guarantee ("earnest money") that He will consummate redemption's plan, which includes the glorification of our mortal bodies. All of this is the work of God Who is not Ναὶ καὶ οὔ, ἀλλὰ Ναί. Some people are so mealy-mouthed that no one knows what they mean by what they say. God is not like that. God does not say "Yes" and "No." He says "Yes" and when He says it He means it and we can depend upon it.

χρίσας may be identical to βαπτίσας (1 Cor.12:13) at regeneration. At that time the believer was sealed as His eternal possession (#1686) and His Spirit began at that time His indwelling in our body, which He considers His temple (1 Cor.6:19,20). He is the "down payment" to guarantee that we are God's property and that the work of redemption will not be finished until even our bodies are made like Christ's resurrection body (Rom.8:11,16; John 14:17).

All of this speaks in no uncertain terms, and it is the ground for the highest possible degree of assurance. When a king causes his steward to put a drop of hot wax upon the seal of a document and then makes the impression of his ring upon the wax, so that when it dries, the document is sealed, he who would break the seal, read the document and interfere with its order would face the combined strength of the military forces at the king's command. Let Satan and his demons take note. God has sealed us, and "all power is given unto Him in heaven and in earth" (Mt.28:18; Eph.1:19-23; 1 John 4:4).

Verse 23 - "Moreover I call God for a record upon my soul, that to spare you I came not as yet to Corinth."

Ἐγὼ δὲ μάρτυρα τὸν ϑεὸν ἐπικαλοῦμαι ἐπὶ τὴν ἐμὴν φυχήν, ὅτι φειδόμενος ὑμῶν οὐκέτι ἦλϑον εἰς Κόρινϑον.

"But I call God to witness against me - it was to spare you that I refrained from coming to Corinth." . . . RSV

Ἐγὼ (nom.sing.masc.of ἐγώ, subject of ἐπικαλοῦμαι) 123.
δὲ (continuative conjunction) 11.
μάρτυρα (acc.sing.masc.of μάρτυς, double accusative) 1263.
τὸν (acc.sing.masc.of the article in agreement with ϑεὸν) 9.
ϑεὸν (acc.sing.masc.of ϑεός, direct object of ἐπικαλοῦμαι) 124.

ἐπικαλοῦμαι (1st.per.sing.pres.mid.ind.of ἐπικαλέω, aoristic) 884.
ἐπὶ (preposition with the accusative, reference) 47.
τὴν (acc.sing.fem.of the article in agreement with ψυχήν) 9.
ἐμὴν (acc.sing.fem.of ἐμός, in agreement with ψυχήν) 1267.
ψυχήν (acc.sing.fem.of ψυχή, reference) 233.
ὅτι (conjunction introducing an object clause) 211.
φειδόμενος (pres.mid.part.nom.sing.masc.of φείδομαι, adverbial, telic) 3533.
ὑμῶν (gen.pl.masc.of σύ, objective genitive) 104.
οὐκέτι (temporal adverb) 1289.
ἦλθον (1st.per.sing.aor.ind.of ἔρχομαι, culminative) 146.
εἰς (preposition with the accusative of extent) 140.
Κόρινθον (acc.sing.masc.of Κόρινθος, extent) 3428.

Translation - "And I now call God as my witness with reference to the integrity of my soul that it is in order to spare you that I have not yet come to Corinth."

Comment: Since verse 18 he has been stressing the integrity of God. Now Paul calls Him to witness "upon my soul." This is an accusative of reference in a metaphorical sense. *Cf.* Lk.1:12,33; 2 Cor.12:9 for similar uses. After μάρτυρα we have an objective ὅτι clause. To witness what? That Paul's decision to postpone his visit to Corinth was for the purpose (telic adverb in φειδόμενος) of sparing the Corinthians the disciplinary measures which he would have imposed upon them had he gone. Lest this should sound as if Paul considered himself a dictator over the Corinthian church in matters of faith and practice, he quickly added his disclaimer in

Verse 24 - "Not for that we have dominion over your faith, but are helpers of your joy: for by faith ye stand."

οὐχ ὅτι κυριεύομεν ὑμῶν τῆς πίστεως, ἀλλὰ συνεργοί ἐσμεν τῆς χαρᾶς ὑμῶν, τῇ γὰρ πίστει ἐστήκατε.

"Not that we lord it over your faith; we work with you for your joy, for you stand firm in your faith." . . . RSV

οὐχ (negative particle with the indicative) 130.
ὅτι (conjunction introducing a subordinate causal clause) 211.
κυριεύομεν (1st.per.pl.pres.act.ind.of κυριεύω, futuristic) 2776.
ὑμῶν (gen.pl.masc.of σύ, possession) 104.
τῆς (gen.sing.fem.of the article in agreement with πίστεως) 9.
πίστεως (gen.sing.fem.of πίστις, objective genitive) 728.
ἀλλὰ (alternative conjunction) 342.
συνεργοί (nom.pl.masc.of συνεργός, predicate nominative) 4066.
ἐσμεν (1st.per.pl.pres.ind.of εἰμί, aoristic) 86.
τῆς (gen.sing.fem.of the article in agreement with χαρᾶς) 9.
χαρᾶς (gen.sing.fem.of χαρά, reference) 183.
ὑμῶν (gen.pl.masc.of σύ, possession) 104.
τῇ (loc.sing.fem.of the article in agreement with πίστει) 9.

γὰρ (causal conjunction) 105.
πίστει (loc.sing.fem.of πίστις, sphere) 728.
ἑστήκατε (2d.per.pl.perf.act.ind.of ἵστημι, intensive) 180.

Translation - *"Not as though we are going to dictate your faith; rather that we are working with you to increase your joy, because you have been standing firm in your faith."*

Comment: ὅτι is causal. Verse 23 might have been construed to mean that Paul's responsibility as an Apostle was to dictate to them what they were to believe and how they were to behave. The passage is strongly anti-clerical. Paul's authority as an Apostle extended to his ability as one with the gift of prophecy (1 Cor.13:8), due to be phased out when the New Testament literature became complete, and who was to write his share of it. Once a member of the Body of Christ has been regenerated, his position in the Body is in no sense inferior to any position of any other member, even to that of one of the twelve Apostles. And so Paul disclaims his authority over the Corinthians. On the contrary his function was only to work with them to enhance their joy in the Lord. Their standing in Christ is distinct from their state (Rom.5:1-5). It is the duty of every member of the Body of Christ to contribute to the edification of every other member, and thus to enhance their joy. Thus the Body is made healthy and kept that way.

The Corinthians had stood since they were saved, by faith (intensive perfect tense in ἑστήκατε). Whether their condition be joyous or sad, backslidden or victorious, based on truth or heresy, their standing was inviolate by faith in Christ. The fact that a Christian believes that which is false detracts from his joy and peace but it does not lessen his relation with Christ. The passage clearly destroys the notion that the salvation of the laity depends upon the whim of the clergy. Here is a death blow to sacerdotalism.

But though Paul is not concerned that the Corinthians will be lost, for all of their aberrations, in opposition to which he wrote much in his first epistle, he is anxious to avoid any loss of their joy. And he feared that had he followed his original travel plan and come to Corinth, he would have been forced to say something, on his arrival that they did not wish to hear. His instruction, had he made the visit which he described in 1 Cor.16:5-7, would have been in the area of their practice, not in the area of their theological position, since he now says that in that sphere they were standing firm.

2 Cor.2:1 - "But I determined this, with myself, that I would not come again to you in heaviness."

ἔκρινα γὰρ ἐμαυτοῦ τοῦτο, τὸ μὴ πάλιν ἐν λύπῃ πρὸς ὑμᾶς ἐλθεῖν.

"For I made up my mind not to make you another painful visit." . . . RSV

ἔκρινα (1st.per.sing.aor.act.ind.of κρίνω, culminative) 531.
γὰρ (inferential conjunction) 105.
ἐμαυτῷ (dat.sing.masc.of ἐμαυτοῦ, personal interest) 723.
τοῦτο (acc.sing.neut.of οὗτος, direct object of ἔκρινα) 93.
τὸ (acc.sing.neut.of the article in agreement with ἐλθεῖν) 9.

μή (negative particle with the infinitive) 87.
πάλιν (adverbial) 355.
ἐν (preposition with the locative, accompanying circumstance) 80.
λύπῃ (loc.sing.fem.of λύπη, accompanying circumstance) 2788.
πρὸς (preposition with the accusative of extent) 197.
ὑμᾶς (acc.pl.masc.of σύ, extent) 104.
ἐλθεῖν (aor.inf.of ἔρχομαι, apposition to τοῦτο) 146.

Translation - "So I made up my mind that I would not make you another painful visit."

Comment: γὰρ is inferential because of the connection between verses 1 and the two preceding verses. Note the infinitive in apposition to τοῦτο. With nouns and pronouns the infinitive is appositional because limitative; with verbs it is epexegetical because explicative by limitation. *Cf.* Rom.14:13; 2 Cor.7:11; Rom.4:13; 1 Thess.4:6,6. What had Paul determined? That he would not again go to Corinth until he could go and avoid any further unpleasantness. He has reference to the censure which he imposed upon them in the first epistle. The fruit of the Holy Spirit is gentleness (Gal.5:22). Love in kind and not easily provoked (1 Cor.13:4,5). The great Apostle tried always to be filled with the Spirit (Eph.5:18b), and he shrank from controversy, especially if other Christians were involved.

Verse 2 - "For if I make you sorry who is he then that maketh me glad, but the same which is made sorry by me?"

εἰ γὰρ ἐγὼ λυπῶ ὑμᾶς, καὶ τίς ὁ εὐφραίνων με εἰ μὴ ὁ λθπούμενος ἐξ ἐμοῦ;

"For if I cause you pain, who is there to make me glad but the one whom I have pained?" . . . RSV

εἰ (conditional particle in a first-class condition) 337.
γὰρ (causal conjunction) 105.
ἐγὼ (nom.sing.masc.of ἐγώ, subject of λυπῶ) 123.
λυπῶ (1st.per.sing.pres.act.ind.of λυπέω, first-class condition) 1113.
ὑμᾶς (acc.pl.masc.of σύ, direct object of λυπῶ) 104.
καὶ (inferential conjunction) 14.
τίς (nom.sing.masc.of τίς, interrogative pronoun, subject of ἐστιν understood) 281.
ὁ (nom.sing.masc.of the article in agreement with εὐφραίνων) 9.
εὐφραίνων (pres.act.part.nom.sing.masc.of εὐφραίνω, substantival, predicate nominative) 2479.
με (acc.sing.masc.of ἐγώ, direct object of εὐφραίνων) 123.
εἰ (conditional particle in an elliptical condition) 337.
μή (negative particle with the participle in an elliptical condition) 87.
ὁ (nom.sing.masc.of the article in agreement with λυπούμενος) 9.
λυπούμενος (pres.pass.part.nom.sing.masc.of λυπέω, substantival, predicate nominative) 1113.

ἐξ (preposition with the ablative of agent) 19.
ἐμοῦ (abl.sing.masc.of ἐμός, agent) 1267.

Translation - "Because if I make you sad who then is going to make me glad except the one who has been saddened by me?"

Comment: The first-class condition assumes that Paul has hurt their feelings . He has said in verse 1 that he will not come again to Corinth until he can come without censure. Now he explains this decision. γάρ is causal - "Because if I sadden you who will gladden me?" There was no one else in Corinth to make Paul glad. Thus if any one made him glad it would have to be the very ones who were made sad by his criticisms. Apparently Paul could find no fellowship with the unsaved (2 Cor.6:14-18). This is a far cry from the modern church member who finds his happiness among the unregenerate. No one in Corinth could interest Paul and make him glad except a happy Christian.

Verse 3 - "And I wrote this same unto you, lest when I came, I should have sorrow from them of whom I ought to rejoice: having confidence in you all, that my joy is the joy of you all."

καὶ ἔγραψα τοῦτο αὐτὸ ἵνα μὴ ἐλθὼν λύπην σχῶ ἀφ' ὧν ἔδει με χαίρειν, πεποιθὼς ἐπὶ πάντας ὑμᾶς ὅτι ἡ ἐμὴ χαρὰ πάντων ὑμῶν ἐστιν.

"And I wrote as I did, so that when I came I might not be pained by those who should have made me rejoice, for I felt sure of all of you, that my joy would be the joy of you all." . . . RSV

καὶ (inferential conjunction) 14.
ἔγραψα (1st.per.sing.aor.act.ind.of γράφω, constative) 156.
τοῦτο (acc.sing.neut.of οὗτος, direct object of ἔγραψω) 93.
αὐτὸ (acc.sing.neut.of αὐτός, intensive, attributive) 16.
ἵνα (conjunction with the subjunctive in a negative purpose clause) 114.
μὴ (negative particle with the subjunctive) 87.
ἐλθὼν (aor.part.nom.sing.masc.of ἔρχομαι, adverbial, temporal) 146.
λύπην (acc.sing.fem.of λύπη, direct object of σχῷ) 2788.
σχῷ (1st.per.sing.aor.act.subj.of ἔχω, negative purpose clause) 82.
ἀφ' (preposition with the ablative of source) 70.
ὧν (abl.pl.masc.of ὅς, relative pronoun, source) 65.
ἔδει (3d.per.sing.imp.ind.of δέω, impersonal) 1207.
με (acc.sing.masc.of ἐγώ, general reference) 123.
χαίρειν (pres.act.inf.of χαίρω, complementary) 182.
πεποιθὼς (2d.per.part.nom.sing.masc.of πείθω, adverbial, causal) 1629.
ἐπὶ (preposition with the accusative, reference) 47.
πάντας (acc.pl.masc.of πᾶς, in agreement with ὑμᾶς) 67.
ὑμᾶς (acc.pl.masc.of σύ, reference) 104.
ὅτι (conjunction introducing an object clause in indirect discourse) 211.
ἡ (nom.sing.fem.of the article in agreement with χαρὰ) 9.
ἐμὴ (nom.sing.fem.of ἐμός, in agreement with χαρὰ) 1267.
χαρὰ (nom.sing.fem.of χαρά, subject of ἐστιν) 183.

πάντων (gen.pl.masc.of πᾶς, in agreement with ὑμῶν) 67.
ὑμῶν (gen.pl.masc.of σύ, possession) 104.
ἐστιν (3d.per.sing.pres.ind.of εἰμί, aoristic) 86.

Translation - *"That is why I have written like this in order that, when I arrive I might not have sorrow from those from whom I ought to derive joy, because I am already convinced with regard to all of you that my joy is the joy of all of you."*

Comment: Paul wrote "the same things" (τοῦτο αὐτό) that he would have said to them if he had visited Corinth. This is a reference to his first epistle to the Corinthians. He hoped that his letter to them would solve their problems. Had it done so, the negative result, introduced by ἵνα μή would have been avoided. That is, that when he came to Corinth he would have found a victorious church rather than one torn in dissension and tainted with heresy. Thus he would not have had sorrow from them. We supply ἀπὸ τούτων before ἀφ' to read ἀπὸ τούτων ἀφ' ὧν - "From those from whom I ought to have joy." ἔδει is a verb of propriety or obligation, in the imperfect tense, indicating that in the present (at the time of writing) it had not yet been met. Paul had not yet been made happy in the knowledge that the Corinthian saints had repented, though having been persuaded, he was confident (2d.perfect participle in πεποιθώς) that what would make him happy would also rejoice the hearts of the Corinthians.

Verse 4 - *"For out of much affliction and anguish of heart I wrote unto you with many tears; not that ye should be grieved, but that ye might know the love which I have more abundantly unto you."*

ἐκ γὰρ πολλῆς θλίφεως καὶ συνοχῆς καρδίας ἔγραφα ὑμῖν διὰ πολλῶν δακρύων, οὐχ ἵνα λυπηθῆτε ἀλλὰ τὴν ἀγάπην ἵνα γνῶτε ἣν ἔχω περισσοτέρως εἰς ὑμᾶς.

"For I wrote you out of much affliction and anguish of heart and with many tears, not to cause you pain but to let you know the abundant love that I have for you." . . . RSV

ἐκ (preposition with the ablative of source) 19.
γὰρ (causal conjunction) 105.
πολλῆς (abl.sing.fem.of πολύς, in agreement with θλίφεως) 228.
θλίφεως (abl.sing.fem.of θλίφις, source) 1046.
καὶ (adjunctive conjunction joining nouns) 14.
συνοχῆς (abl.sing.fem.of συνοχή, source) 2727.
καρδίας (gen.sing.fem.of καρδία, description) 432.
ἔγραφα (1st.per.sing.aor.act.ind.of γράφω, constative) 156.
ὑμῖν (dat.pl.masc.of σύ, indirect object of ἔγραφα) 104.
διὰ (preposition with the genitive - "physically through") 118.
πολλῶν (gen.pl.neut.of πολύς, in agreement with δακρύων) 228.
δακρύων (gen.pl.neut.of δάκρυ, physically through) 2166.
οὐχ (negative particle, with the indicative understood) 130.

ἵνα (conjunction introducing the subjunctive in a purpose clause) 114.

λυπηθῆτε (2d.per.pl.aor.pass.subj.of λυπέω, purpose) 1113.

ἀλλά (alternative conjunction) 342.

τὴν (acc.sing.fem.of the article in agreement with ἀγάπηνν) 9.

ἀγάπην (acc.sing.fem.of ἀγάπη, direct object of γνῶτε) 1490.

ἵνα (conjunction with the subjunctive in a purpose clause) 114.

γνῶτε (2d.per.pl.aor.act.subj.of γινώσκω, purpose) 131.

ἥν (acc.sing.fem.of ὅς, relative pronoun, in agreement with ἀγάπην) 65.

ἔχω (1st.per.sing.pres.act.ind.of ἔχω, aoristic) 82.

περισσοτέρως (comparative of περισσός, adverbial) 525.

εἰς (preposition with the accusative of extent) 140.

ὑμᾶς (acc.pl.masc.of σύ, extent, predicate use) 104.

Translation - *"Because it was with much distress and with a broken heart, as many tears flowed, that I wrote to you, not that you might be burdened but that you might realize the great love which I have for you."*

Comment: The source or cause of his first letter was the great distress which he felt for their unhappy and unhealthy spiritual condition. διὰ πολλῶν δακρύων can be construed here literally - "in between many years." It is a touching picture of Paul as he sat, trying to see the parchment and direct his pen as his eyes were suffused and his cheeks drenched with tears. His motive was not that they should be saddened but that they might come to appreciate the extraordinary love which he felt for them.

Forgiveness for the Offender

(2 Corinthians 2:5-11)

Verse 5 - *"But if any have caused grief, he hath not grieved me, but in part; that I may not overcharge you all."*

Εἰ δέ τις λελύπηκεν, οὐκ ἐμὲ λελύπηκεν, ἀλλὰ ἀπὸ μέρους, ἵνα μὴ ἐπιβαρῶ, πάντας ὑμᾶς.

"But if any one has caused pain, he has caused it not to me, but in some measure - not to put it too severely - to you all." . . . *RSV*

Εἰ (conditional particle in a first-class condition) 337.

δέ (adversative conjunction) 11.

τις (nom.sing.masc.of τις, indefinite pronoun, subject of λελύπηκεν) 486.

λελύπηκεν (3d.per.sing.perf.act.ind.of λυπέω, intensive) 1113.

οὐκ (negative conjunction with the indicative) 130.

ἐμὲ (acc.sing.masc.of ἐμός, direct object of λελύπηκεν) 1267.

λελύπηκεν (3d.per.sing.perf.act.ind.of λυπέω, intensive) 1113.

ἀλλά (adversative conjunction) 342.

ἀπὸ (preposition with the partitive genitive) 70.

μέρους (gen.sing.neut.of μέρος, partitive) 240.
ἵνα (conjunction with the subjunctive in a negative purpose clause) 114.
μή (negative conjunction with the subjunctive) 87.

#4272 ἐπιβαρῶ (1st.per.sing.pres.act.subj.of ἐπιβαρέω, negative purpose).

King James Version

be chargeable to - 2 Thess.3:8.
be chargeable unto - 1 Thess.2:9.
overcharge - 2 Cor.2:5.

Revised Standard Version

put it too severely - 2 Cor.2:5.
be a burden - 1 Thess.2:9; 2 Thess.3:8.

Meaning: A combination of ἐπί (#47) and βαρέομαι (#1589). Hence to be excessively burdensome. With reference to money - 2 Thess.3:8; 1 Thess.2:9. To use language excessively harsh to create unnecessary pain - 2 Cor.2:5.

πάντας (acc.pl.masc.of πᾶς, in agreement with ὑμᾶς) 67.
ὑμᾶς (acc.pl.masc.of σύ, direct object of ἐπιβαρῶ) 104.

Translation - "But if some one has caused grief, he has not grieved me as much as some of you, not to be too hard upon you all."

Comment: The first-class condition has the perfect indicative in both protasis and apodosis. Paul is referring to some one in the church (perhaps the man in 1 Cor.5:1-5, or some other), whose life of inconsistency had caused grief - not to Paul, but to some degree to some in the church. Paul does not wish to give this unfortunate incident a greater status than it merits. He is about to suggest that the man had suffered enough and that he should be forgiven and the incident forgotten, lest Satan use the issue to divide the church further.

Verse 6 - "Sufficient to such a man is this punishment, which was inflicted of many."

ἱκανὸν τῷ τοιούτῳ ἡ ἐπιτιμία αὕτη ἡ ὑπὸ τῶν πλειόνων,

"For such a one this punishment by the majority is enough;" . . . RSV

ἱκανὸν (acc.sing.neut.of ἱκανός, predicate accusative) 304.
τῷ (dat.sing.masc.of the article in agreement with τοιούτῳ) 9.
τοιούτῳ (dat.sing.masc.of τοιοῦτος, personal disadvantage) 785.
ἡ (nom.sing.fem.of the article in agreement with ἐπιτιμία).

#4273 ἐπιτιμία (nom.sing.fem.of ἐπιτιμία, subject of ἐστιν understood).

King James Version

punishment - 2 Cor.2:6.

Revised Standard Version

punishment - 2 Cor.2:6.

Meaning: A combination of ἐπί (#47) and τιμάω (#1142). *Cf.*ἐπιτιμάω (#757). Punishment, meted out on a judicial basis - 2 Cor.2:6.

αὕτη (nom.sing.fem.of οὗτος, in agreement with ἐπιτιμία) 93.
ἡ (nom.sing.fem.of the article in agreement with ἐπιτιμία) 9.
ὑπό (preposition with the ablative of agent) 117.
τῶν (abl.pl.masc.of the article in agreement with πλειόνων) 9.
πλειόνων (abl.pl.masc.of πλείων, agent) 474.

Translation - "Sufficient to such is this punishment at the hands of the majority."

Comment: Note the emphasis of the predicate adjective ἱκανόν. Most of the Corinthian Christians had followed Paul's advice in 1 Cor.5:1-5, and the punishment poured out upon the man Paul now decrees to have been sufficient. When the sinning saint, once disciplined by the church, repents and forsakes his sin, he should then be forgiven.

Verse 7 - "So that contrariwise ye ought rather to forgive him, and comfort him, lest perhaps such a one should be swallowed up with overmuch sorrow."

ὥστε τοὐναντίον μᾶλλον ὑμᾶς χαρίσασθαι καὶ παρακαλέσαι, μὴ πως τῇ περισσοτέρᾳ λύπῃ καταποθῇ ὁ τοιοῦτος.

"so you should rather turn to forgive and comfort him, or he may be overwhelmed by excessive sorrow." . . . RSV

ὥστε (conjunction with the infinitive in a result clause) 752.

#4274 τοὐναντίον (adverbial).

King James Version

contrariwise - 2 Cor.2:6; Gal.2:7; 1 Pet.3:9.

Revised Standard Version

turn - 2 Cor.2:6.
on the contrary - Gal.2:7; 1 Pet.3:9.

Meaning: by crasis - τὸ ἐναντίος (#1128). A neuter adverb - "on the contrary" - 2 Cor.2:6; Gal.2:7; 1 Pet.3:9.

μᾶλλον (adverbial) 619.
ὑμᾶς (acc.pl.masc.of σύ, general reference) 104.
χαρίσασθαι (aor.mid.inf.of χαρίζομαι, result) 2158.
καί (adjunctive conjunction joining infinitives) 14.
παρακαλέσαι (aor.act.inf.of παρακαλέω, result) 230.

μή (negative particle with the subjunctive in a negative purpose clause) 87.

πως (indefinite adverbial in a negative purpose clause) 3700.

τῇ (instru.sing.fem.of the article in agreement with λύπῃ) 9.

περισσοτέρᾳ (instru.sing.fem.of περισσός, comparative, in agreement with λύπῃ) 525.

λύπῃ (instru.sing.fem.of λύπη, cause) 2788.

καταποθῇ (3d.per.sing.aor.pass.subj.of καταπίνω, negative result) 1454.

ὁ (nom.sing.masc.of the article in agreement with τοιοῦτος) 9.

τοιοῦτος (nom.sing.masc.of τοιοῦτος, subject of καταποθῇ) 785.

Translation - "... with the result that you should rather forgive and comfort such a one lest perhaps he be overwhelmed because of such great sorrow."

Comment: The punishment meted out to the man is enough (verse 6). The result (verse 7) is that now an opposite course of action should be pursued (τουναντίον #4274). Forgiveness and comfort should now replace censure. Why? *Cf.* μή πως (#3700) in the sense of "lest" or "for fear that." Otherwise he may be "drowned" (#1454) by floods of sorrow. This is the opposite advice to what Paul told them to do in 1 Cor.5:1-5. The difference is that apparently the man in question repented and forsook his sin.

Verse 8 - "Wherefore I beseech you that ye would confirm your love toward him."

διὸ παρακαλῶ ὑμᾶς κυρῶσαι εἰς αὐτὸν ἀγάπην.

"So I beg you to reaffirm your love for him." . . . *RSV*

διὸ (inferential conjunction) 1622.

παρακαλῶ (1st.per.sing.pres.act.ind.of παρακαλέω, aoristic) 230.

ὑμᾶς (acc.pl.masc.of σύ, general reference) 104.

#4275 κυρῶσαι (aor.act.inf.of κυρόω, direct object of παρακαλῶ).

   King James Version

confirm - 2 Cor.2:8; Gal.3:15.

   Revised Standard Version

reaffirm - 2 Cor.2:8.
ratified - Gal.3:15.

Meaning: Cf. κῦρος - "head." Hence, action from the chief authority or head executive. Hence, to ratify, reaffirm, make further proof of. With reference to the love for a Christian - 2 Cor.2:8; to ratify or notarize a legal agreement - Gal.3:15.

εἰς (preposition with the accusative, metaphorical extent) 140.

αὐτὸν (acc.sing.masc.of αὐτός, metaphorical extent) 16.

ἀγάπην (acc.sing.fem.of ἀγάπη, direct object of κυρῶσαι) 1490.

Translation - "Therefore I beg you to reaffirm to him your love."

Comment: διὸ in inferential. Since the man in question was in danger of becoming totally overwhelmed in his despondency, Paul begs them to reverse the treatment. The fact that he reacted to his exclusion as he did makes it evident that he was truly regenerate, although temporarily disobedient. Had he been unsaved it is not likely that exclusion from the fellowship of the church, with which he had little in common would have devastated him.

The Corinthians had passed the test of obedience and had followed Paul's instructions to the letter, with the result that the sinner had indeed turned from his wickedness. Paul now tells them that it was in order that he might know whether they would still obey the Apostolic order that he had written to them previously about this matter.

Verse 9 - "For to this end also did I write that I might know the proof of you, whether ye be obedient in all things."

εἰς τοῦτο γὰρ καὶ ἔγραφα ἵνα γνῶ τὴν δοκιμὴν ὑμῶν, εἰ εἰς πάντα ὑπήκοοί ἐστε.

"For this is why I wrote, that I might test you and know whether you are obedient in everything." . . . RSV

εἰς (preposition with the accusative, purpose) 140.
γὰρ (causal conjunction) 105.
τοῦτο (acc.sing.neut.of οὗτος, purpose) 93.
καὶ (emphatic conjunction) 14.
ἔγραφα (1st.per.sing.aor.act.ind.of γράφω, constative) 156.
ἵνα (conjunction with the subjunctive in a purpose clause) 114.
γνῶ (1st.per.sing.2d.aor.act.subj.of γινώσκω, purpose) 131.
τὴν (acc.sing.fem.of the article in agreement with δοκιμὴν) 9.
δοκιμὴν (acc.sing.fem.of δοκιμή, direct object of γνῶ) 3897.
ὑμῶν (gen.pl.masc.of σύ, description) 104.
εἰ (conditional particle in indirect question) 337.
εἰς (preposition with the predicate accusative) 140.
πάντα (acc.pl.neut.of πᾶς, accusative of reference) 67.
ὑπήκοοί (nom.pl.masc.of ὑπήκοος, predicate adjective) 3136.
ἐστε (2d.per.pl.pres.ind.of εἰμί, present iterative retroactive) 86.

Translation - "It was for this reason in fact that I wrote you - in order that I might know your fidelity - whether you had been obedient in every thing."

Comment: καὶ here seems to fit into the context best as an emphatic. He had sent his advice in this matter in his previous letter (1 Cor.5:1-5). Now he wants to know the degree of their obedience. Were they obedient in every respect (εἰ πάντα)? εἰ here in indirect question. εἰς τοῦτο in a purpose construction. The ἵνα clause can be construed as epexegesis, explaining τοῦτο. A B (Tertullian) have ἦ for εἰ; 460 1836 and cops_a? have ὡς, while p46 436 2495 omit εἰ. The omission of εἰ is accidental, due to its juxtaposition with εἰς. Metzger explains ῇ which is variously supported as a possible orthographic variant since in later Greek εἰ and ῇ were pronounced alike. The reading of ὡς may have originated through palaeographical confusion (ΥΜΩΕΙΕΙΣ); (Metzger, *A Textual Commentary on the Greek New Testament*, 577).

We must remember that Paul was not universally accepted as an Apostle in Corinth and there was some question in his mind as to whether or not the church would follow his instructions. They not only did, but to a degree that now makes it necessary for him to call upon them to bank the fires of their righteous condemnation against the sinning brother. They now need to know if Paul has forgiven the man.

Verse 10 - "To whom ye forgive any thing, I forgive also; for if I forgave any thing, to whom I forgave it, for your sakes forgave it in the person of Christ."

ᾧ δέ τι χαρίζεσθε, κἀγώ. καὶ γὰρ ἐγὼ ὃ κεχάρισμαι, εἰ τι κεχάρισμαι, δι᾽ ὑμᾶς ἐν προσώπῳ Χριστοῦ,

"Any one whom you forgive, I also forgive. What I have forgiven, if I have forgiven anything, has been for your sake in the presence of Christ." . . . RSV

ᾧ (dat.sing.masc.of ὅς, relative pronoun, personal advantage) 65.

δέ (explanatory conjunction) 11.

τι (acc.sing.neut.of τις, indefinite pronoun, direct object of χαρίζεσθε) 486.

χαρίζεσθε (2d.per.pl.pres.mid.ind.of χαρίζομαι, aoristic) 2158.

κἀγώ (adjunctive conjunction and first personal pronoun, crasis) 178.

καὶ (emphatic conjunction) 14.

γὰρ (inferential conjunction) 105.

ἐγώ (nom.sing.masc.of ἐγώ, subject of κεχάρισμαι) 123.

ὃ (acc.sing.neut.of ὅς, relative pronoun, direct object of κεχάρισμαι) 65.

κεχάρισμαι (1st.per.sing.perf.mid.ind.of χαρίζομαι, intensive) 2158.

εἰ (conditional particle in a first-class condition) 337.

τι (acc.sing.neut.of τις, indefinite pronoun, direct object of κεχάρισμαι) 486.

κεχάρισμαι (1st.per.sing.perf.mid.ind.of χαρίζομαι, intensive, in a first-class condition) 2158.

δι᾽ (preposition with the accusative, cause) 118.

ὑμᾶς (acc.pl.masc.of σύ, cause) 104.

ἐν (preposition with the locative of place, metaphorical) 80.

προσώπῳ (loc.sing.neut.of πρόσωπον, metaphorical place) 588.

Χριστοῦ (gen.sing.masc.of Χριστός, possession) 4.

Translation - "Now for whom you forgive anything, I also forgive; therefore in fact that which I have forgiven, if I have forgiven anything was because of you in the presence of Christ."

Comment: Paul agrees to follow the judgment of the Corinthians with reference to the sinning brother. If he has repented and they have forgiven him, that is good enough for Paul, who was absent and has no way of knowing whether he has repented or not. Thus Paul must depend upon the judgment of the Corinthian church. They were closer to the situation than he. And since both he and they are members of the Body of Christ, their judgment on the matter is as good as his. This is why he says that if he has forgiven anything for anyone he did so "because of you" (δι' ὑμᾶς). Whatever they have done in this matter he has done also.

Here again Paul strikes a blow for local church autonomy and against hierarchical authority.

Cf.#588 for other examples of this construction. The presence of our Lord, as Head over all things to His church (Eph.1:22) wipes out the geographical barriers. The Head of the church presides over all the members of His body, whether they be Apostles or Christians without the gifts of prophecy and knowledge, whether they be in Corinth or Ephesus or Peoria. All forgiveness of sin, whether for saints or sinners, must be granted in contemplation of the finished work of atonement by our Lord. This is true but it is not what Paul means by the phrase ἐν προσώπῳ Χριστοῦ.

The εἰ κεχάρισμαι clause is a first-class condition, with the premise in the protasis assumed true, although it may be false. Paul had no way of knowing whether the Corinthians and he himself had any scriptural authority to forgive the man. The prerequisite was his repentance and the abandonment of his previous life style. *Cf.* 2 Cor.4:6 for ἐν προσώπῳ Χριστοῦ.

In verse 11 Paul tells us why he followed the policy which he described in verse 10.

Verse 11 - "Lest Satan should get an advantage of us: for we are not ignorant of his devices."

ἵνα μὴ πλεονεκτηθῶμεν ὑπὸ τοῦ Σατανᾶ, οὐ γὰρ αὐτοῦ τὰ νοήματα ἀγνοοῦμεν.

"to keep Satan from gaining the advantage over us; for we are not ignorant of his designs." . . . RSV

ἵνα (conjunction with the subjunctive in a negative purpose clause) 114.
μή (negative particle with the subjunctive) 87.

#4276 πλεονεκτηθῶμεν (1st.per.pl.aor.pass.subj.of πλεονεκτέω, negative purpose).

King James Version

defraud - 2 Cor.7:2; 1 Thess.4:6.
get an advantage - 2 Cor.2:11.
make a gain of - 2 Cor.12:17,18.

Revised Standard Version

gain the advantage - 2 Cor.2:11.
take advantage - 2 Cor.7:2; 12:17,18.

wrong (verb) - 1 Thess.4:6.

Meaning: Cf.πλεονάζω (#3907); πλεονέκτης (#4141); πλεονεξία (#2302). To take an advantage; intrans., to have more; followed by an ablative of agent in 2 Cor.2:11; followed by an object accusative in 2 Cor.7:2; 12:17,18 where the context seems to indicate financial exploitation; general exploitation in 1 Thess.4:6.

ὑπὸ (preposition with the ablative of agent) 117.
τοῦ (abl.sing.masc.of the article in agreement with Σατανᾶ) 9.
Σατανᾶ (abl.sing.masc.of Σατανᾶ, agent) 365.
οὐ (negative conjunction with the indicative) 130.
γὰρ (causal conjunction) 105.
αὐτοῦ (gen.sing.masc.of αὐτός, possession) 16.
τὰ (acc.pl.neut.of the article in agreement with νοήματα) 9.

#4277 νοήματα (acc.pl.neut.of νόημα, direct object of ἀγνοοῦμεν).

King James Version

device - 2 Cor.2:11.
mind - 2 Cor.3:14; 4:4; 11:3; Phil.4:7.
thought - 2 Cor.10:5.

Revised Standard Version

designs - 2 Cor.2:11.
mind - 2 Cor.3:14; 4:4; Phil.4:7.
thought - 2 Cor.10:5; 11:3.

Meaning: The vehicle of thought; the mind; the brain - 2 Cor.3:14; 4:4; 11:3; Phil.4:7. The plan or purpose which the mind entertains - 2 Cor.2:11; 10:5.

ἀγνοοῦμεν (1st.per.pl.pres.act.ind.of ἀγνοέω, present progressive retroactive) 2345.

Translation - "Lest we be exploited by Satan, for we have never been unaware of his strategy."

Comment: Paul's policy, described in verse 10, is a means to an end, which follows in the negative purpose clause ἵνα μὴ πλεον . . . Σατανᾶ - "Lest we be exploited by Satan. The man's sin (1 Cor.5:1-5), the church's disciplinary on Paul's previous suggestion, his repentance and their attitude toward it might provide Satan with an opportunity to drive a wedge of disharmony into the fellowship. What if some should agree to forgive the man and forget about it while others did not? And what if they should continue to agitate the question? Love and forgiveness by all should be the order if Satan's strategy of which Paul was not unaware, were to be frustrated.

We can construe ἀγνοοῦμεν as a retroactive present progressive in this case, since Paul with his apostolic discernment had long been aware of the way the enemy operates. Thus our translation.

Paul's Anxiety and Relief

(2 Corinthians 2:12-17)

Verse 12 - "Furthermore, when I came to Troas to preach Christ's gospel, and a door was opened unto me of the Lord,"

Ἐλθὼν δὲ εἰς τὴν Τρῳάδα εἰς τὸ εὐαγγέλιον τοῦ Χριστοῦ, καὶ θύρας μοι ἀνεῳγμένης ἐν κυρίῳ,

"When I came to Troas to preach the gospel of Christ, a door was opened for me in the Lord;" . . . RSV

Ἐλθὼν (aor.part.nom.sing.masc.of ἔρχομαι, adverbial, temporal) 146.

δὲ (continuative conjunction) 11.

εἰς (preposition with the accusative of extent) 140.

τὴν (acc.sing.fem.of the article in agreement with Τρῳάδα) 9.

Τρῳάδα (acc.sing.fem.of Τρῳάς, extent) 3358.

εἰς (preposition with the accusative, purpose) 140.

τὸ (acc.sing.neut.of the article in agreement with εὐαγγέλιον) 9.

εὐαγγέλιον (acc.sing.neut.of εὐαγγέλιον, purpose) 405.

τοῦ (gen.sing.masc.of the article in agreement with Χριστοῦ) 9.

Χριστοῦ (gen.sing.masc.of Χριστός, description) 4.

καὶ (adjunctive conjunction joining participles) 14.

θύρας (gen.sing.fem.of θύρα, genitive absolute) 571.

μοι (dat.sing.masc.of ἐγώ, personal advantage) 123.

ἀνεῳγμένης (perf.pass.part.gen.sing.fem.of ἀνοίγω, intensive, genitive absolute) 188.

ἐν (preposition with the instrumental of means) 80.

κυρίῳ (instru.sing.masc.of κύριος, means) 97.

Translation - "And when I came to Troas to preach the gospel of Christ, a door having been previously opened for me by the Lord, . . . "

Comment: Ἐλθὼν is a temporal adverbial participle. Thus its action is antecedent to that of the main verb, ἔσχηκα in verse 13. It was *after* Paul arrived in Troas that he became worried. εἰς τὸ εὐαγγέλιον is purpose. He went to Troas in order to preach the gospel. The door of opportunity had already been opened for him before he arrived, possibly before he left to go to Troas. Of course in the plan of God, it had been opened since the eternal ages. The θύρας μοι ἀνεῳγμένης clause is a genitive absolute, *i.e.* its thought does nothing to advance the main thought of the sentence. The way to recognize a genitive absolute construction is to remove it from the sentence. If the sentence "bleeds" when the clause is removed, *i.e.* if the thought of the sentence is not complete without it, it is not an absolute construction. If it is an "aside" *i.e.* a comment that contributes nothing to the main thought of the sentence it is absolute.

The main thought of the sentence is that when Paul arrived in Troas he became worried. The fact that the door of opportunity had already been opened for him to preach in Troas has nothing to do with the fact that he was worried. It only explains why he went to Troas. The causal clause in verse 13 tells us why he was worried, and the last clause tells us what he did about it.

Verse 13 - "I had no rest in my spirit, becaue I found not Titus my brother: but taking my leave of them, I went from thence into Macedonia."

οὐκ ἔσχηκα ἄνεσιν τω πνεύματί μου τῷ μὴ εὑρεῖν με Τίτον τὸν ἀδελφόν μου, ἀλλὰ ἀποταξάμενος αὐτοῖς ἐξῆλθον εἰς Μακεδονίαν.

"*but my mind could not rest because I did not find my brother Titus there. So I took leave of them and went on to Macedonia.*" . . . RSV

οὐκ (negative conjunction with the indicative) 130.
ἔσχηκα (1st.per.sing.perf.act.ind.of ἔχω, intensive) 82.
ἄνεσιν (acc.sing.fem.of ἄνεσις, direct object of ἔχηκα) 3628.
τῷ (loc.sing.neut.of the article in agreement with πνεύματι) 9.
πνεύματί (loc.sing.neut.of πνεῦμα, sphere) 83.
μου (gen.sing.masc.of ἐγώ, possession) 123.
τῷ (instru.sing.neut.of the article in agreement with εὑρεῖν) 9.
μὴ (negative conjunction with the infinitive) 87.
εὑρεῖν (aor.act.inf.of εὑρίσκω, cause) 79.
με (acc.sing.mac.of ἐγω, general reference) 123.

#4278 Τίτον (acc.sing.masc.of Τίτος, direct object of εὑρεῖν).

King James Version and Revised Standard Version

Titus - 2 Cor.2:13; 7:6,13,14; 8:6,16,23; 12:18,18; Gal.2:1,3; 2 Tim.4:10; Titus 1:4.

Meaning: Titus, a Gentile Christian. Paul's companion and fellow Christian worker. Not to be confused with Τιτίου Ἰούστου of Acts 18:7 (#3438) - 2 Cor.2:13; 7:6,13,14; 8:6,16,23; 12:18,18; Gal.2:13; 2 Tim.4:10; Titus 1:4.

τὸν (acc.sing.masc.of the article in agreement with ἀδελφόν) 9.
ἀδελφόν (acc.sing.masc.of ἀδελφός, apposition) 15.
μου (gen.sing.masc.of ἐγώ, relationship) 123.
ἀλλὰ (alternative conjunction) 342.
ἀποταξάμενος (aor.mid.part.nom.sing.masc.of ἀποτάσσω, adverbial, temporal) 2281.
αὐτοῖς (instru.pl.masc.of αὐτός, association) 16.
ἐξῆλθον (1st.per.sing.aor.ind.of ἐξέρχομαι, constative) 161.
εἰς (preposition with the accusative of extent) 140.

Μακεδονίαν (acc.sing.fem.of Μακεδονία, extent) 3360.

Translation - "I had been worried because I did not find Titus, my brother, so I left them and went to Macedonia."

Comment: In ἔσχηκα we have a present perfect with preterit punctilian action. Paul did have ἄνεσις for his spirit (*i.e.* he was no longer worried) after Titus came and reported to him that the Corinthians had accepted his first epistle in the spirit in which he had written it. But it was no complete relaxation since he continues in the second epistle to show that he was not certain that the Corinthians were developing spiritually as he wished. Paul had been burdened with the heavy load of anxiety up to the time that Titus arrived, a burden only partially lifted when he came. The articular infinitive τῷ εὑρεῖν is the only instance of the instrumental case in an infinitive indicating cause. He was worried because when he got to Troas, Titus was not there. Paul said good bye (ἀποταξάμενος), left Troas and went to Macedonia.

Verse 14 - "Now thanks be unto God, which always causeth us to triumph in Christ, and maketh manifest the savour of his knowledge by us in every place."

Τῷ δὲ θεῷ χάρις τῷ πάντοτε θριαμβεύοντι ἡμᾶς ἐν τῷ Χριστῷ καὶ τὴν ὀσμὴν τῆς γνώσεως αὐτοῦ φανεροῦντι δι᾽ ἡμῶν ἐν παντὶ τόπῳ.

"But thanks be to God, who in Christ always leads us in triumph, and through us spreads the fragrance of the knowledge of him everywhere." . . . *RSV*

τῷ (dat.sing.masc.of the article in agreement with θεῷ) 9.
δὲ (explanatory conjunction) 11.
θεῷ (dat.sing.masc.of θεός, indirect object) 124.
χάρις (nom.sing.fem.of χάρις, nominative absolute) 1700.
τῷ (dat.sing.masc.of the article in agreement with θριαμβεύοντι) 9.
πάντοτε (temporal adverb) 1567.

#4279 θριαμβεύοντι (pres.act.part.dat.sing.masc.of θριαμβεύω, substantival, in apposition with θεῷ).

King James Version

cause to triumph - 2 Cor.2:14.
triumph over - Col.2:15.

Revised Standard Version

leads us in triumph - 2 Cor.2:14.
triumph over - Col.2:15.

Meaning: Cf. θρίαμβος - a hymn sung in festal parades in honor of Bacchus. Thus in Rome it was a triumphal procession, in celebration of a great victory. Not in this sense in the New Testament, but in a meaning unknown to profane Greek - to cause to triumph. To grant complete success. With reference to the

Christian's victory in Christ - 2 Cor.2:14; of Christ's total victory over ceremonial and ritualistic religion as a means of salvation - Col.2:15.

ἡμᾶς (acc.pl.masc.of ἐγώ, direct object of θριαμβεύοντι) 123.
ἐν (preposition with the instrumental of association) 80.
τῷ (instru.sing.masc.of the article in agreement with Χριστῷ) 9.
Χριστῷ (instru.sing.masc.of Χριστός, association) 4.
καὶ (adjunctive conjunction joining participles) 14.
τὴν (acc.sing.fem.of the article in agreement with ὀσμὴν) 9.
ὀσμὴν (acc.sing.fem.of ὀσμή, direct object of φανεροῦντι) 2750.
τῆς (gen.sing.fem.of the article in agreement with γνώσεως) 9.
γνώσεως (gen.sing.fem.of γνῶσις, description) 1856.
αὐτοῦ (gen.sing.masc.of αὐτός, description) 16.
φανεροῦντι (pres.act.part.dat.sing.masc.of φανερόω, substantival, in apposition to θεῷ) 1960.
δι' (preposition with the ablative of agent) 118.
ἡμῶν (abl.pl.masc.of ἐγώ, agent) 123.
ἐν (preposition with the locative of place) 80.
παντὶ (loc.sing.masc.of πᾶς, in agreement with τόπῳ) 67.
τόπῳ (loc.sing.masc.of τόπος, place) 1019.

Translation - *"But thanks be to God Who always makes us a winner in Christ, and Who reveals the odor of His knowledge through our ministry in every place."*

Comment: Paul is always marching in triumph at the head of God's victory parade (#4279). Only the resurrected Christ goes before him. The participles are in apposition to τῷ θεῷ. God is the One Who makes Paul a winner and Who uses him to spread the odor from the censer, carried in the parade, wherever Paul goes. The odor is the knowledge of Christ. It is pleasing only to the elect as we learn in verses 15 and 16.

The figure is that of the victory parade with Paul carrying the censer from which the odor exudes. Note πάντοτε. Paul was *always* a winner, even though not all who heard him preach were saved. This he explains in the next two verses.

Verse 15 - *"For we are unto God a sweet savour of Christ, in them that are saved, and in them that perish."*

ὅτι Χριστοῦ εὐωδία ἐσμὲν τῷ θεῷ ἐν τοῖς σωζομένοις καὶ ἐν τοῖς ἀπολλυμένοις,

"For we are the aroma of Christ to God among those who are being saved and among those who are perishing," . . . RSV

ὅτι (conjunction introducing a causal clause) 211.
Χριστοῦ (gen.sing.masc.of Χριστός, description) 4.

#4280 εὐωδία (nom.sing.fem.of εὐωδία, predicate nominative).

King James Version

sweet savour - 2 Cor.2:15.
sweet smell - Phil.4:18.
sweet smelling - Eph.5:2.

Revised Standard Version

aroma - 2 Cor.2:15.
fragrant offering - Phil.4:18; Eph.5:2.

Meaning: A combination of εὖ (#1536) and ὄζω - "smell." Hence a sweet odor. Aroma. Something with a pleasing odor. Metaphorically in reference to Christian service as an acceptable offering to God. The gospel which Paul preached - 2 Cor.2:15; the sacrifice of Christ on the cross - Eph.5:2; the Philippian money gift to Paul - Phil.4:18.

ἐσμὲν (1st.per.pl.pres.ind.of εἰμί, aoristic) 86.
τῷ (dat.sing.masc.of the article in agreement with θεῷ) 9.
θεῷ (dat.sing.masc.of θεός, personal advantage) 124.
ἐν (preposition with the locative of sphere) 80.
τοῖς (loc.pl.masc.of the article in agreement with σωζομένοις) 9.
σωζομένοις (pres.pass.part.loc.pl.masc.of σώζω, substantival, sphere) 109.
καὶ (adjunctive conjunction joining participles) 14.
ἐν (preposition with the locative of sphere) 80.
τοῖς (loc.pl.masc.of the article in agreement with ἀπολλυμένοις) 9.

ἀπολλυμένοις (pres.pass.part.loc.pl.masc.of ἀπόλλυμι, substantival, sphere) 208.

Translation - "*Because we exude the fragrance of Christ to God in the case of those who are being saved and in the case of those who perish.*"

Comment: Only with this translation (or another that says essentially the same thing) can we give full credit to πάντοτε in verse 14. If Paul's gospel does not fulfill God's will in the cases of both the saved and the lost, then he does not always win, but wins only when men believe and are saved. This Arminian view implies that the unrepentant and unbelieving sinner who perishes is able to defeat God. On the contrary Paul is always a winner, but his winning is contingent upon his faithful proclamation of the gospel of Christ. If he preaches the gospel faithfully it is effective in fulfilling God's will and thus it is a sweet smell (#4280) to God, whether men are saved as a result of what he preached or lost because what he preached offended them. This he explains more fully in verse 16.

Goodspeed, with whom we seldom quarrel, has gone astray in my opinion, with his translation: "Yes, I am the fragrance of Christ to God, diffused among those who are being saved and those who are perishing alike" (verse 15), to which he adds in verse 16, "to the one, a deathly, deadly odor, to the other a vital, lifegiving one." His 16th verse is correct, but verse 15 seems to say that the "sweet smell" is diffused among the lost, whereas in verse 16 he says that to the lost, the gospel, the message that smells sweet to God, smells like death to the non-elect. Thus we must conclude that the fragrance (εὐωδία) relates, not to the reaction of the people in the audiences to whom Paul preached, but to the reaction of God, Who always monitors which the preacher preaches. For example, it is doubtful that what Paul preached on Mars Hill smelled good to God, whereas his message to the Corinthians was fragrant in the divine nostrils. Paul seems to imply in the last clause of verse 16 that he was not too satisfied with his performance on Mars Hill - a feeling that was the basis of his statement to the Corinthians in his first epistle (1 Cor.2:1-8). *Cf.* comment *en loc.*.

Verse 16 - "To the one we are the savour of death unto death; and to the other the savour of life unto life. And who is sufficient for these things?"

οἷς μὲν ὀσμὴ ἐκ θανάτου εἰς θάνατον, οἷς δὲ ὀσμὴ ἐκ ζωῆς εἰς ζωήν. καὶ πρὸς ταῦτα τίς ἱκανός;

"to one a fragrance from death to death, to the other a fragrance from life to life. Who is sufficient for these things?" . . . RSV

οἷς (dat.pl.masc.of ὅς, relative pronoun, personal disadvantage) 65.
μὲν (correlative particle of affirmation) 300.
ὀσμὴ (nom.sing.fem.of ὀσμή, predicate nominative) 2750.
ἐκ (preposition with the ablative of source) 19.
θανάτου (abl.sing.masc.of θάνατος, source) 381.
εἰς (preposition with the accusative of extent) 140.
θάνατον (acc.sing.masc.of θάνατος, metaphorical extent) 381.
οἷς (dat.pl.masc.of ὅς, relative pronoun, personal advantage) 65.
δὲ (correlative adversative particle) 11.
ὀσμὴ (nom.sing.fem.of ὀσμή, predicate nominative) 2750.
ἐκ (preposition with the ablative of source) 19.
ζωῆς (abl.sing.fem.of ζωή, source) 668.
εἰς (preposition with the accusative of extent) 140.
ζωήν (acc.sing.fem.of ζωή, metaphorical extent) 668.
καὶ (adversative conjunction) 14.
πρὸς (preposition with the accusative, purpose) 197.
ταῦτα (acc.pl.neut.of οὗτος, purpose) 93.
τίς (nom.sing.masc.of τίς, interrogative pronoun, subject of ἐστιν understood) 281.
ἱκανός (nom.sing.masc.of ἱκανός, predicate adjective) 304.

Translation - "To some we smell like an odor arising from death and resulting in death, but to others we are an aroma coming from life and resulting in life. But who is capable of this ministry?"

Comment: The same gospel message gets one reaction from the non-elect and the opposite reaction from the elect. Paul said the same thing in 1 Cor.1:18. The perishing are repelled by the message to which the elect are attracted. The lost say that the gospel stinks like a corpse, because for them Jesus is dead and that it can only lead to death, as though they were alive when they made that observation - a fallacy held widely by the unregenerate.

The gospel of Christ, which smells like death to the lost can only lead to the second death in a lake of fire, if they reject it (Rev.20:14). It is the misconception of the unsaved that they are now alive and that their life will continue unless they give up their "freedom" and become Christians.

But the elect hear the gospel of Christ and react in the opposite manner. To them it smells good. It is an aroma, not a stench. Christ Jesus is forever alive and His resurrection victory means life for all who trust in Him (John 10:9,10).

The same sun that melts wax hardens clay, although this analogy is misleading as are all analogies if we carry them too far. We do not mean that the difference between that which melts and that which is hardened is in the original lump. All in Adam are of the same lump. We are all clay and all would be hardened by the gospel were it not for the convincing work of the Holy Spirit (John 16:7-11) who calls some and not others. Nor is the difference between those who say that the gospel stinks and those who say that it is fragrant in the subjective abilities of either group to evaluate odor. To all of us the gospel of Christ smelled like death when we first heard it. Only as the Holy Spirit overwhelmed us and incorporated us into the Body of Christ did we detect the fragrance of the life of Christ.

As Paul carried on this ministry, which smells like death or life, depending upon who heard it, he was always smelling good to God (verse 15). Thus always he was made triumphant (πάντοτε). It is here that we see the contextual connection between verses 14-17 and that which has gone before, where he was commiserating about his travel plans between Troas and Macedonia and his distress because he could not locate Titus. Wherever Paul went, as he walked through the open doors of opportunity which had been stood ajar for him, he preached the gospel of Christ, whether he found Titus or not, and whether he was sad or glad about the reaction of the Corinthians to his letters. His own personal feelings were not important. The important thing is how his ministry appealed to God. And he gives God thanks that God was always pleased with it - at least if he always preached the gospel.

What qualifications must a preacher have, then, if his ministry is to have the effect which Paul describes? This is the essence of Paul's question in the last sentence of verse 16 and his reply is in

Verse 17 - "For we are not as many which corrupt the word of God: but as of sincerity, but as of God, in the sight of God speak we in Christ."

οὐ γάρ ἐσμεν ὡς οἱ πολλοὶ καπηλεύοντες τὸν λόγον τοῦ θεοῦ, ἀλλ' ὡς ἐξ εἰλικρινείας, ἀλλ' ὡς ἐκ θεοῦ κατέναντι θεοῦ ἐν Χριστῷ λαλοῦμεν.

"For we are not, like so many, peddlers of God's word; but as men of sincerity, as commissioned by God, in the sight of God we speak in Christ." . . . RSV

οὐ (negative particle with the indicative) 130.

γὰρ (inferential conjunction) 105.

ἐσμεν (1st.per.pl.pres.ind.of εἰμί, aoristic) 86.

ὡς (comparative particle) 128.

οἱ (nom.pl.masc.of the article in agreement with καπηλεύοντες) 9.

πολλοὶ (nom.pl.masc.of πολύς, in agreement with καπηλεύοντες) 228.

#4281 καπηλεύοντες (pres.act.part.nom.pl.masc.of καπηλεύω, substantival, subject of εἰσιν understood).

King James Version

corrupt - 2 Cor.2:17.

Revised Standard Version

peddlers - 2 Cor.2:17.

Meaning: Cf. κάπηλος - a petty retailer; a huckster; a peddler; small time merchant who carries his inventory in a pack on his back; travelling medicine man who sells snake oil. Originally the word meant an inn keeper; a bar keeper who serves small drinks for profit. In 2 Cor.2:17 Paul means that he is not selling the word of God for a financial profit. Thus he does not find it necessary to adulterate the product in order to increase sales.

τὸν (acc.sing.masc.of the article in agreement with λόγον) 9.

λόγον (acc.sing.masc.of λόγος, direct object of καπηλεύοντες) 510.

τοῦ (gen.sing.masc.of the article in agreement with θεοῦ) 9.

θεοῦ (gen.sing.masc.of θεός, description) 124.

ἀλλ' (alternative conjunction) 342.

ὡς (comparative particle) 128.

ἐξ (preposition with the ablative of source) 19.

εἰλικρινείας (abl.sing.fem.of εἰλικρινεία, source) 4138.

ἀλλ' (alternative conjunction) 342.

ὡς (comparative particle) 128.

ἐκ (preposition with the ablative of source) 19.

θεοῦ (abl.sing.masc.of θεός, source) 124.

κατέναντι (improper preposition with the genitive of reference) 1342.

θεοῦ (gen.sing.masc.of θεός, reference) 124.

ἐν (preposition with the instrumental of association) 80.

Χριστῷ (instrumental sing.masc.of Χριστός, association) 4.

λαλοῦμεν (1st.per.pl.pres.act.ind.of λαλέω, customary) 815.

Translation - "Therefore we are not peddling the word of God as many do, but we speak from sincere motives, as sent from God with reference to our association with God in Christ."

Comment: A Calvinistic gospel, when preached in a manner consistent with its entire message will have God's intended results. Thus the same message smells like death to some and like life to others. Any sermon that attracts all or repels all is not God's message. Who then preaches this true message? This is the question of verse 16. Paul insists that he does, though he does not say that he has always done so. Perhaps the memory of his failure on Mars Hill was haunting him. But Paul was mature enough to learn from past mistakes. He never again presented the story of the cross "with enticing words of man's wisdom" (1 Cor.2:4). Thus now he says that he has not gone about like a peddler who reduces the price of the product in order to see it accepted in the competitive market of ideas. Unfortunately not all preachers since Paul have followed his policy. It is possible to adulterate the gospel to the point where there is much superficial acceptance and little rejection. Invitations to walk down the aisle at the close of a service which are dripping with maudlin sentimentality tend to attract those with IQ's in direct proportion to their emotional boiling points. Every sinner, however sunken in depravity may wish to see his mother in heaven. Thus the evangelistic huckster gains the attention of the media and his crowds keep pace with the front page coverage in the press.

Not Paul. His motives were born of sincerity. He preached as one sent from God. He was always aware of the fact that God was listening to him (κατέναντι θεοῦ). He was a "labourer together with God" (1 Cor.3:9).

Ministers of the New Covenant

(2 Corinthians 3:1-18)

2 Cor.3:1 - "Do we begin again to commend outselves? Or need we, as some others, epistles of commendation to you, or letters of commendation from you?"

Ἀρχόμεθα πάλιν ἑαυτοὺς συνιστάνειν; ἢ μὴ χρῄζομεν ὥς τινες συστατικῶν ἐπιστολῶν πρὸς ὑμᾶς ἢ ἐξ ὑμῶν;

"Are we beginning to commend ourselves again? Or do we need, as some do, letters of recommendation to you, or from you?" . . . RSV

Ἀρχόμεθα (1st.per.pl.pres.mid.ind.of ἄρχω direct question) 383.
πάλιν (adverbial) 355.
ἑαυτοὺς (acc.pl.masc.of ἑαυτός, direct object of συνιστάνειν) 288.
συνιστάνειν (pres.act.inf.of συνίστημι, complementary) 2328.
ἢ (disjunctive) 465.
μὴ (negative conjunction in rhetorical question which expects a negative reply) 87.
χρῄζομεν (1st.per.pl.pres.act.ind.of χρῄζω, aoristic) 638.
ὥς (comparative particle) 128.
τινες (nom.pl.masc.of τις, indefinite pronoun, subject of verb understood) 486.

#4282 συστατικῶν (gen.pl.fem.of συστατικός, description).

King James Version

of commendation - 2 Cor.3:1.

Revised Standard Version

of recommendation - 2 Cor.3:1.

Meaning: A combination of σύν (#1542) and στατικός, from συνίστημι (#2328). In a genitive of description with ἐπιστολῶν in 2 Cor.3:11 - "letters of recommendation."

ἐπιστολῶν (gen.pl.fem.of ἐπιστολή, objective genitive) 3180.
πρός (preposition with the accusative of extent after a verb of speaking or writing) 197.
ὑμᾶς (acc.pl.masc.of σύ, extent) 104.
ἤ (disjunctive) 465.
ἐξ (preposition with the ablative of source) 19.
ὑμῶν (abl.pl.masc.of σύ, source) 104.

Translation - "Do we begin again to commend ourselves? We do not need, like some, letters of recommendation either to you or from you, do we?"

Comment: These are rhetorical questions. Paul had written much in his first letter defending his status as an Apostle and his ministry as such. Now he asks if it appears that he is repeating himself? The obvious reply to the last question is "No." He certainly needed no letters of recommendation either to or from the Corinthians.

The reason why Paul needs no such letters is found in

Verse 2 - "Ye are our epistles written in our hearts, known and read of all men."

ἡ ἐπιστολὴ ἡμῶν ὑμεῖς ἐστε, ἐγγεγραμμένη ἐν ταῖς καρδίαις ἡμῶν, γινωσκομένη καὶ ἀναγινωσκομένη ὑπὸ πάντων ἀνθρώπων.

"You yourselves are our letter of recommendation, written on your hearts, to be known and read by all men." . . . RSV

ἡ (nom.sing.fem.of the article in agreement with ἐπιστολή) 9.
ἐπιστολή (nom.sing.fem.of ἐπιστολή, predicate nominative) 3180.
ἡμῶν (gen.pl.masc.of σύ, possession, editorial) 123.
ὑμεῖς (nom.pl.masc.of σύ, emphatic, subject of ἐστε) 104.
ἐστε (2d.per.pl.pres.ind.of εἰμί, aoristic) 86.

#4283 ἐγγεγραμμένη (perf.pass.part.nom.sing.fem.of ἐγγράφω, adjectival, predicate position, restrictive in agreement with ἐπιστολή).

King James Version

write in - 2 Cor.3:2,3.

Revised Standard Version

write on - 2 Cor.3:2,3.

Meaning: A combination of ἐν (#80) and γράφω (#156). Hence, to write on or in. To inscribe. Metaphorically in 2 Cor.2:3.

ἐν (preposition with the locative of place) 80.
ταῖς (loc.pl.fem.of the article in agreement with καρδίαις) 9.
καρδίαις (loc.pl.fem.of καρδία, metaphorical place) 432.
ἡμῶν (gen.pl.masc.of ἐγώ, possession, editorial) 123.
γινωσκομένη (pres.pass.part.nom.sing.fem.of γινώσκω, adjectival, predicate position, restrictive, in agreement with ἐπιστολή) 131.
καί (adjunctive conjunction joining participles) 14.
ἀναγινωσκομένη (pres.pass.part.nom.sing.fem.of ἀναγινώσκω, adjectival, predicate position, restrictive, in agreement with ἐπιστολή) 967.
ὑπό (preposition with the ablative of agent) 117.
πάντων (abl.pl.masc.of πᾶς, in agreement with ἀνθρώπων) 67.
ἀνθρώπων (abl.pl.masc.of ἄνθρωπος, agent) 341.

Translation - "You yourselves are our letter, which has been written upon our hearts, and is being known and read by all men."

Comment: ὑμεῖς is emphatic, but ἡ ἐπιστολή ἡμῶν is in a prior position. Note the repetition of ἐν after ἐν in composition. ἐν ταῖς καρδίαις is a metaphorical locative, due to the repetition of the thought in the analogy of verse 3.

Paul had the memory of the great Corinthian revival and the experiences of the Corinthians as they came to Christ forever inscribed in his heart, as he relived the days when he first preached Christ to them. The Corinthian Christian experience was known and evaluated by all classes of men who came and went through the prominent Mediterranean port city. Paul's reputation as an Apostle of Jesus Christ was thoroughly established in the minds of all who had been to Corinth and seen the church there.

Verse 3 - "Forasmuch as ye are manifestly declared to be the epistle of Christ, ministered by us, written not with ink, but with the Spirit of God; not in tables of stone, but in fleshly tables of the heart."

φανερούμενοι ὅτι ἐστὲ ἐπιστολὴ Χριστοῦ διακονηθεῖσα ὑφ᾽ ἡμῶν, ἐγγεγραμμένη οὐ μέλανι ἀλλὰ πνεύματι θεοῦ ζῶντος, οὐκ ἐν πλαξὶν λιθίναις ἀλλ᾽ ἐν πλαξὶν καρδίαις σαρκίναις.

"and you show that you are a letter from Christ delivered by us, written not with ink but with the Spirit of the living God, not on tablets of stone but on tablets of human hearts." . . . RSV

φανερούμενα (pres.pass.part.nom.pl.masc.of φανερόω, adjectival, predicate position, restricive, in agreement with ἐπιστολή) 1960.
ὅτι (declarative) 211.
ἐστε (2d.per.pl.pres.ind.of εἰμί, present periphrastic) 86.
ἐπιστολή (nom.sing.fem.of ἐπιστολή, predicate nominative) 3180.
Χριστοῦ (gen.sing.masc.of Χριστός, description) 4.

διακονηθεῖσα (aor.pass.part.nom.sing.fem.of διακονέω, adjectival, predicate position, restrictive, in agreement with ἐπιστολή) 367.

ὑφ' (preposition with the ablative of agent) 117.

ἡμῶν (abl.pl.masc.of ἐγώ, agent) 123.

ἐγγεγραμμένη (perf.pass.part.nom.sing.fem.of ἐγγράφω, adjectival, predicate position, restrictive, in agreement with ἐπιστολή) 4283.

οὐ (negative particle with the participle) 130.

#4284 μέλανι (instru.sing.neut.of μέλαν, means).

King James Version

ink - 2 Cor.3:3; 2 John 12; 3 John 13.

Revised Standard Version

ink - 2 Cor.3:3; 2 John 12; 3 John 13.

Meaning: Cf. μέλας (#523). Hence, black ink - 2 Cor.3:3; 2 John 12; 3 John 13.

ἀλλά (alternative conjunction) 342.

πνεύματι (instru.sing.neut.of πνεῦμα, means) 83.

θεοῦ (gen.sing.masc.of θεός, description) 124.

ζῶντος (pres.act.part.gen.sing.masc.of ζάω, adjectival, predicate position, restrictive, in agreement with θεοῦ) 340.

οὐκ (negative particle with the participle) 130.

ἐν (preposition with the locative of place) 80.

#4285 πλαξὶν (loc.pl.fem.of πλάξ, place).

King James Version

tables -   2 Cor.3:3a; Heb.9:4.

Revised Standard Version

tablets - 2 Cor.3:3,3.
tables - Heb.9:4.

Meaning: Cf. πλάτος (#4487). A wide flat surface, suitable for writing. Followed by λιθίναις, such as those upon which the Ten Commandments were inscribed - 2 Cor.3:3a; heb.9;4. In a metaphorical sense in 2 Cor.3:3b.

λιθίναις (loc.pl.fem.of λίθινος, in agreement with πλαξὶν) 1969.

ἀλλ' (alternative conjunction) 342.

ἐν (preposition with the locative of place) 80.

πλαξὶν (loc.pl.fem.of πλάξ, place, metaphorical) 4285.

καρδίαις (loc.pl.fem.of καρδία, in agreement with πλαξὶν) 432.

σαρκίναις (loc.pl.fem.of σάρκινος, in agreement with καρδίαις) 3924.

Translation - "You are prominently displayed as a letter from Christ, written by us, not with ink but by the Spirit of the Living God - not on stone tablets, but upon tablets of human hearts."

Comment: Note the personal construction with ὅτι. *Cf.* 1 Cor.15:12; 1 John 2:19.

Paul's letters of recommendation already existed in the regenerated lives of the Corinthian christians. He takes full credit for them. They were produced by the Holy Spirit Who used Paul as His human agent (διακονηθεῖσα ὑφ' ἡμῶν). *Cf.*2 Cor.8:19,20; 1 Pet.1:12; 4:10,11. Having been written in the past, the message was still there (perfect passive participle in ἐγγεγραμμένη) to be read by the great numbers of visitors who had business in Corinth. But they were not written with ink, nor upon stone tablets. It was the work of the Holy Spirit Who wrote on human hearts. Note the οὐ . . . ἀλλά sequences. - "Not . . . but an alternative." God once wrote His law on stone tablets. He accomplished His purpose, but His purpose was not to change the human heart. It was to prove to man that he needed a supernatural change of heart before he could live by the Ten Commandments (Gal.3:19). The divine code of ethics given at Sinai could only point to the divine standard of accomplishment, without which no man can enter the Kingdom of God. It could not enable man to attain that standard. But it could point forward to the Mediator (Gal.3:20). The Mediator came (1 Tim.2:5,6), redeemed the Corinthians, was buried, arose from the dead and went back to heaven. He then sent the Holy Spirit Whose function was to testify about the Mediator, grant repentance and faith and then by regeneration write what God wrote on the tablets which He gave to Moses, upon the hearts of His elect. Since from the heart come the issues of life (Mt.15:19; Mk.7:21), a clean heart is prerequisite to a clean life. And only God can create a clean heart (Psalm 19:14; 51:10). The Holy Spirit of the Living God had done this for the Corinthians. He will also perform this miracle of regeneration for elect Israel when Messiah returns (Jer.24:7; 31:31-33). Christians will testify that the regenerated heart always holds up the same ethical standard for him to follow that was contained in the tablets of stone of the Mosaic code.

Verse 4 - "And such trust have we through Christ to God-ward."

Πεποίθησιν δὲ τοιαύτην ἔχομεν διὰ τοῦ Χριστοῦ πρὸς τὸν θεόν.

"Such is the confidence that we have through Christ toward God." . . . *RSV*

Πεποίθησιν (acc.sing.fem.of πεποίθησις, direct object of ἔχομεν) 4269.
δὲ (continuative conjunction) 11.
τοιαύτην (acc.sing.fem.of τοιοῦτος, in agreement with πεποίθησιν) 785.
ἔχομεν (1st.per.pl.pres.act.ind.of ἔχω, aoristic) 82.
διὰ (preposition with the ablative of agent) 118.
τοῦ (abl.sing.masc.of the article in agreement with Χριστοῦ) 9.
Χριστοῦ (abl.sing.masc.of Χριστός, agent) 4.
πρὸς (preposition with the accusative of extent) 197.
τὸν (acc.sing.masc.of the article in agreement with θεόν) 9.
θεόν (acc.sing.masc.of θεός, extent) 124.

Translation - "And we have that kind of confidence through Christ toward God."

Comment: Thus Paul sums up his reason for not needing written letters of recommendation. The preacher who has been called of God and who is certain that his ministry has been carried on as Paul described his in 2 Cor.2:14-17 is not responsible for the results. He could never produce the results which God produces through him, for they are supernatural. God asks no man to be successful. He does ask His servants to be faithful. Paul had been faithful, and the result was that the Spirit of the Living God had written His moral law upon the hearts of the Corinthians. Once He has begun His work the Holy Spirit is committed to finish it (Phil.1:6). This is assurance unavailable to the Arminian who can never be certain that the supernatural work of God once begun will be carried out. But Paul's theology was never understood nor accepted by Arminius. Paul did not mean that the permanent results of supernatural regeneration in the lives of the saints in Corinth were to be credited to him personally, but rather through his ministry God had done the work. That is why he had confidence in the results, for only God's redemptive and regenerative work is permanent. This is the thought in

Verse 5 - "Not that we are sufficient of ourselves to think anything as of ourselves; but our sufficiency is of God."

οὐχ ὅτι ἀφ' ἑαυτῶν ἱκανοί ἐσμεν λογίσασθαί τι ὡς ἐξ ἑαυτῶν, ἀλλ' ἡ ἱκανότης ἡμῶν ἐκ τοῦ θεοῦ,

"Not that we are sufficient of ourselves to claim anything as coming from us; our sufficiency is from God, . . . " . . . RSV

οὐχ (negative conjunction with the indicative) 130.
ὅτι (declarative) 211.
ἀφ' (preposition with the ablative of source) 70.
ἑαυτῶν (abl.pl.masc.of ἑαυτοῦ, source) 288.
ἱκανοί (nom.pl.masc.of ἱκανός, predicate adjective) 304.
ἐσμεν (1st.per.pl.pres.ind.of εἰμί, aoristic) 86.
λογίσασθαί (aor.mid.inf.of λογίζομαι, complementary) 2611.
τι (acc.sing.neut.of τις, indefinite pronoun, direct object of λογίσασθαί) 486.
ὡς (comparative particle) 128.
ἐξ (preposition with the ablative of source) 19.
ἑαυτῶν (abl.pl.masc.of ἑαυτός, source) 288.
ἀλλ' (alternative conjunction) 342.
ἡ (nom.sing.fem.of the article in agreement with ἱκανότης) 9.

#4286 ἱκανότης (nom.sing.fem.of ἱκανότης, subject of ἐστιν understood).

King James Version

sufficiency - 2 Cor.3:5.

Revised Standard Version

sufficiency - 2 Cor.3:5.

Meaning: Cf. ἱκανός (#304); ἱκανόω (#4287). Hence, competence, ability to do a thing. With reference to Paul's ability to produce genuine regenerative results, which ability he disclaims - 2 Cor.3:5.

ἡμῶν (gen.pl.masc.of ἐγώ, possession) 123.
ἐκ (preposition with the ablative of source) 19.
τοῦ (abl.sing.masc.of the article in agreement with θεοῦ) 9.
θεοῦ (abl.sing.masc.of θεός, source) 124.

Translation - "Not that we suppose that we can do anything with our own resources; on the contrary our competence comes from God."

Comment: Paul denies that the competence of the gospel which began its development and now continues it in the lives of the Corinthians originates with him. He is not saying that he is certain that the Corinthians will continue in the faith because they are *his* converts. His own evaluation of his merits does not justify the opinion that anything good could come from him. He takes no personal credit at all. On the contrary the supernatural competence that produces supernatural results in the believer comes from a supernatural Source.

Had Paul been a "huckster" of the gospel (2 Cor.2:17) who watered down the terms of the gospel to make it more attractive and thus secure a larger number of superficial "converts" he could not have spoken with the confidence which he now displays. When the preacher is more interested in quantity than in quality he robs the gospel of its supernatural character and vitiates its power to change human lives. When the gospel of Christ "smells like life" (2 Cor.2:16) to the elect, and they accept it, the Holy Spirit of the Living God writes divine ethics into regenerated hearts. The preacher's reward for his fidelity is his assurance that those who responded, though perhaps not comprising a great number, are at least genuine. And if they are genuine they will be viable.

When an inebriate staggered up to Dwight L.Moody and said, "Mr. Moody, I am one of your converts," Moody replied, "You must be one of mine. You certainly are not one of the Lord's."

Paul had many converts and they were genuine. The demand for quality does not rule out the possibility of quantity. When the Body of Christ is complete and He returns to glorify us, the number will include all whom He has chosen and redeemed. Not one will be missing. The "mystery" (Eph.3:1-8) will be completed when the "last trump" (1 Cor.15:52) begins to sound (Rev.10:7). If one is interested in numbers it is well to remember that the majority of the human race died in infancy. As for those who are called to salvation after they have reached the age of discretion, it is well to remember that all whom He has foreknown, He has also predestinated, called, justified and glorified (Rom.8:29,30). The little girl in the kindergarten Sunday School class concluded that since that is true it was also true that "If God be for us you are up against it." ! (Rom.8:31).

Verse 6 - "Who also hath made us able ministers of the new testament; not of the letter, but of the spirit: for the letter killeth, but the spirit giveth life."

ὃς καὶ ἱκάνωσεν ἡμᾶς διακόνους καινῆς διαθήκης, οὐ γράμματος ἀλλὰ πνεύματος. τὸ γὰρ γράμμα ἀποκτέννει, τὸ δὲ πνεῦμα ζῳοποιεῖ.

"who has qualified us to be ministers of a new covenant, not in a written code but in the Spirit; for the written code kills, but the Spirit gives life." . . . RSV

ὅς (nom.sing.masc.of ὅς, relative pronoun, subject of ἱκάνωσεν) 65.
καὶ (emphatic conjunction) 14.

#4287 ἱκάνωσεν (3d.per.sing.aor.act.ind.of ἱκανόω, culminative).

King James Version

make able - 2 Cor.3:6.
make meet - Col.1:12.

Revised Standard Version

qualified - 2 Cor.3:6; Col.1:12.

Meaning: Cf. ἱκανός (#304); ἱκανότης (#4286). To make one competent; to make one able to do something. With a double accusative - 2 Cor.3:6; with a single object in Col.1:12.

ἡμᾶς (acc.pl.masc.of ἐγώ, direct object of ἱκάνωσεν) 123.
διακόνους (acc.pl.masc.of διάκονας, direct object of ἱκάνωσεν) 1334.
καινῆς (gen.sing.fem.of καινός, in agreement with διαθήκης) 812.
διαθήκης (gen.sing.fem.of διαθήκη, description) 1575.
οὐ (negative conjunction with the indicative) 130.
γράμματος (gen.sing.neut.of γράμμα, description) 2100.
ἀλλὰ (alternative conjunction) 342.
πνεύματος (gen.sing.neut.of πνεῦμα, description) 83.
τὸ (nom.sing.neut.of the article in agreement with γράμμα) 9.
γράμμα (nom.sing.neut.of γράμμα, subject of ἀποκτέννει) 2100.
ἀποκτέννει (3d.per.sing.pres.act.ind.of ἀποκτείνω, static) 889.
τὸ (nom.sing.neut.of the article in agreement with πνεῦμα) 9.
δὲ (adversative conjunction) 11.
πνεῦμα (nom.sing.neut.of πνεῦμα, subject of ζῳοποιεῖ) 83.
ζῳοποιεῖ (3d.per.sing.pres.act.ind.of ζῳοποιέω, static) 2098.

Translation - "Who has in fact qualified us as ministers of a new covenant, not a written code but of the Spirit; because the written code kills but the Spirit makes alive."

Comment: The antecedent of ὅς is θεοῦ of verse 5. God has made Paul able to preach (culminative aorist in ἱκάνωσεν). Whom God calls He enables. History proves that while God does not rule against formal education as a possible qualification for the ministry of His word, He has not always chosen to call only those with graduate degrees. Saul of Tarsus was highly educated before God called him, and God used Paul's sophistication to His own glory, once Paul had learned to lay it on the altar, but God also called Charles H. Spurgeon and

Dwight L. Moody, neither of whom had more than secondary education at the time that God called them, although both had good minds and both studied diligently. The sovereign God can use anyone who is yielded to His purpose. One evangelist who was mightily used of the Lord to bring thousands to Christ wrote to his mother and asked, "How is your cate?"(*sic*). God even used Balaam's loquacious ass to forbid the insanity of his perverse prophet (2 Pet.2:16; Numbers 22:28).

Note the double accusative in ἡμᾶς διακόνους. Paul was made a deacon, or servant, to administer a new covenant. *Cf.* #1575 for the difference between the covenants of law and grace. The new covenant is not a code of behavior, written down as a guide which forbids this and mandates that, but it is a new way of life. Israel gave slavish obedience to the letter of the law. Her spiritually dead condition testifies that the written code can only kill. Instead of looking forward with eager anticipation to the birth of her Messiah, at a time when Simeon, through the study of the prophecy of Daniel knew that his birth was at hand, her learned Scribes could only answer that if and when He did come He would come to Bethlehem, and then instead of hastening to the City of David to worship Him they continued to display their sanctimonious observance of a code of rules, praying long and loud in the streets, and when He offered Himself to the nation as their Messiah, in keeping with that which was written in their Old Testament prophets, they demanded that the Roman government nail Him to a cross. Thus the written code kills, but the Holy Spirit gave life to some of them. No one was deader than Saul of Tarsus, the bigot who could boast of his religious achievements (Phil.3:4-6) and who witnessed the stoning of a Christian deacon and then determined to kill the rest of the Christians, but the Holy Spirit made him alive. Thus there was no one in Israel who could speak with greater authority from his own experience about the difference between the written code of Sinai and the way of life in Christ which the Holy Spirit generates.

That when Paul wrote τὸ . . . γράμμα ἀποκτέννει, he meant the Mosaic code is evident as we examine verses 7-11 in which he contrasts the two covenants.

Verse 7 - "But if the ministration of death written and engraven in stones, was glorious, so that the children of Israel could not stedfastly behold the face of Moses for the glory of his countenance; which glory was to be done away,"

Εἰ δὲ ἡ διακονία τοῦ θανάτου ἐν γράμμασιν ἐντετυπωμένη λίθοις ἐγενήθη ἐν δόξῃ, ὥστε μὴ δύνασθαι ἀτενίσαι τοὺς υἱοὺς Ἰσραὴλ εἰς τὸ πρόσωπον Μωϋσέως διὰ τὴν δόξαν τοῦ προσώπου αὐτοῦ τὴν καταργουμένην,

"Now if the dispensation of death, carved in letters on stone, came with such splendor that the Israelites could not look at Moses' face because of its brightness, fading as this was, . . . " . . . RSV

Εἰ (conditional particle in a first-class condition) 337.
δὲ (adverstive conjunction) 11.
ἡ (nom.sing.fem.of the article in agreement with διακονία) 9.
διακονία (nom.sing.fem.of διακονία, subject of ἐγενήθη) 2442.

τοῦ (gen.sing.masc.of the article in agreement with θανάτου) 9.
θανάτου (gen.sing.masc.of θάνατος, description) 381.
ἐν (preposition with the instrumental of means) 80.
γράμμασιν (instru.pl.neut.of γράμμα, means) 2100.

#4288 ἐντετυπωμένη (perf.pass.part.nom.sing.fem.of ἐντυπόω, adjectival, predicate position, restrictive, in agreement with διακονία).

King James Version

engrave - 2 Cor.3:7.

Revised Standard Version

carve - 2 Cor.3:7.

Meaning: A combination of ἐν (#80) and τυπόω - "to impress." Hence to make an impression upon. To engrave. To carve. With reference to the Mosaic law written on tablets of stone - 2 Cor.3:7.

λίθοις (loc.pl.masc.of λίθος, place) 290.
ἐγενήθη (3d.per.sing.aor.pass.ind.of γίνομαι, constative, first-class condition) 113.
ἐν (preposition with the instrumental of manner) 80.
δόξῃ (instru.sing.fem.of δόξα, manner) 361.
ὥστε (conjunction with the infinitive, result) 752.
μὴ (negative conjunction with the infinitive) 87.
δύνασθαι (pres.infinitive of δύναμαι, result) 289.
ἀτενίσαι (aor.act.inf.of ἀτενίζω, complementary) 2028.
τοὺς (acc.pl.masc.of the article in agreement with υἱοὺς) 9.
υἱοὺς (acc.pl.masc.of υἱός, general reference) 5.
Ἰσραὴλ (gen.sing.masc.of Ἰσραήλ, description) 165.
εἰς (preposition with the accusative of extent) 140.
τὸ (acc.sing.neut.of the article in agreement with πρόσωπον) 9.
πρόσωπον (acc.sing.neut.of πρόσωπον, extent) 588.
Μωϋσέως (gen.sing.masc.of Μωϋσῆς, possession) 715.
διὰ (preposition with the accusative, cause) 118.
τὴν (acc.sing.fem.of the article in agreement with δόξαν) 9.
δόξαν (acc.sing.fem.of δόξα, cause) 361.
τοῦ (gen.sing.neut.of the article in agreement with προσώπου) 9.
προσώπου (gen.sing.neut.of πρόσωπον, description) 588.
αὐτοῦ (gen.sing.masc.of αὐτός, possession) 16.
τὴν (acc.sing.fem.of the article in agreement with καταργουμένην) 9.
καταργουμένην (pres.pass.part.acc.sing.fem.of καταργέω, adjectival, predicate position, restrictive, in agreement with δόξαν) 2500.

Translation - "But if the administration of death which had been engraved with letters upon stones was so glorious that the sons of Israel were unable to look into the face of Moses, because of the glory of his face, even though the glory is now superseded . . . "

Comment: Verse 7 is the protasis of a first-class condition, with the question of verse 8 serving as the apodosis. Eἰ with the indicative states the condition in the protasis as a fact. And so it was. *Cf.* Exodus 34:29-30. The Ten Commandments and the Mosaic regulations which accompanied them were the ministers of death to the human race. *Cf.* verse 6. But the presentation of the law was accompanied by a great demonstration of God's presence and glory. (Exod.19:10-25). A God Who in grace bears Israel on "eagles' wings" is unapproachable by sinful man under law. The Shekinah glory came down upon the mountain. There were thunders and lightnings, a thick cloud and the sound of a great trumpet. The result of this manifestation of God's glory is set forth in the ὥστε clause. The people were unable to look into the face of Moses because of the glory that shone from it. All of this, and yet the glory with which the covenant of death was administered was due to be superseded by a greater glory (Gal.3:17). The rest of the sentence is in

Verse 8 - "How shall not the ministration of the spirit be rather glorious?"

πῶς οὐχὶ μᾶλλον ἡ διακονία τοῦ πνεύματος ἔσται ἐν δόξῃ;

"will not the dispensation of the Spirit be attended with greater splendor?" . . .
                                                                              RSV

πῶς (interoggative adverb) 627.

οὐχὶ (negative conjunction in rhetorical question expecting a positive reply) 130.

μᾶλλον (adverbial) 619.

ἡ (nom.sing.fem.of the article in agreement with διακονία) 9.

διακονία (nom.sing.fem.of διακονία, subject of ἔσται) 2442.

τοῦ (gen.sing.neut.of the article in agreement with πνεύματος) 9.

πνεύματος (gen.sing.neut.of πνεῦμα, description) 83.

ἔσται (3d.per.sing.fut.ind.of εἰμί, deliberative) 86.

ἐν (preposition with the instrumental of means) 80.

δόξῃ (instru.sing.fem.of δόξα, means) 361.

Translation - "Should not the administration of the Spirit be more glorious?"

Comment: If the death dealing letter of the law (verse 6) was administered under circumstances of glory and splendor described in verse 7, should not the life giving salvation of the Holy Spirit be more glorious? The same thought is expressed again in

Verse 9 - "For if the ministration of condemnation be glory, much more doth the ministration of righteousness exceed in glory."

εἰ γὰρ ἡ διακονία τῆς κατακρίσεως δόξα, πολλῷ μᾶλλον περισσεύει ἡ διακονία τῆς δικαιοσύνης δόξῃ.

"For if there was splendor in the dispensation of condemnation, the dispensation of righteousness must far exceed it in splendor." . . . RSV

εἰ (conditional particle in a first-class condition) 337.
γὰρ (causal conjunction) 105.
τῇ (loc.sing.fem.of the article in agreement with διακονίᾳ) 9.
διακονίᾳ (loc.sing.fem.of διακονία, accompanying circumstance) 2442.
τῆς (gen.sing.fem.of the article in agreement with καρακρίσεως) 9.

#4289 κατακρίσεως (gen.sing.fem.of κατάκρισις, description).

King James Version

condemnation - 2 Cor.3:9.
to condemn - 2 Cor.7:3.

Revised Standard Version

condemnation - 2 Cor.3:9.
to condemn - 2 Cor.7:3.

Meaning: A combination of κατά (#98) and κρίσις (#478). *Cf.* κατακρίνω (#1012). Hence, condemnation. As a descriptive genitive in 2 Cor.3:9; in a purpose phrase with πρός and the accusative in 2 Cor.7:3.

δόξα (nom.sing.fem.of δόξα, subject of ἦν) 361.
πολλῷ (instru.sing.neut.of πολύς, measure) 228.
μᾶλλον (adverbial) 619.
περισσεύει (3d.per.sing.pres.act.ind.of περισσεύω, present progressive retroactive) 473.
ἡ (nom.sing.fem.of the article in agreement with διακονία) 9.
διακονία (nom.sing.fem.of διακονία, subject of περισσεύει) 2442.
τῆς (gen.sing.fem.of the article in agreement with δικαιοσύνης) 9.
δικαιοσύνης (gen.sing.fem.of δικαιοσύνη, description) 322.
δόξῃ (loc.sing.fem.of δόξα, accompanying circumstance) 361.

Translation - "For since there was glory at the administration of condemnation, the administration of righteousness goes far beyond it in glory."

Comment: Another first-class condition. God's law, given at Sinai, even though it was an instrument of condemnation was administered gloriously. The gospel which provides a righteous fulfillment of the law is sure to be more glorious. Some MSS read τῇ διακονίᾳ for ἡ διακονία. "A majority of the Committee, impressed by the weight of the external evidence supporting τῇ διακονίᾳ, was inclined to regard the nominative as due to scribal assimilation to the preceding (and following) διακονία." (Metzger, *A Textual Commentary on the Greek New Testament*, 578).

Thus Paul continues to extol the superiority of his message to that of the law and to explain that this superior gospel is his reason for his confidence in the quality of Christian life in Corinth (verses 4,5).

Verse 10 - "For even that which was made glorious had no glory in this respect, by reason of the glory that excelleth."

καὶ γὰρ οὐ δεδόξασται τὸ δεδοξασμένον ἐν τούτῳ τῷ μέρει εἵνεκεν τῆς ὑπερβαλλούσης δόξης.

"Indeed, in this case, what once had splendor has come to have no splendor at all, because of the splendor that surpasses it." . . . RSV

καὶ (emphatic conjunction) 14.
γὰρ (causal conjunction) 105.
οὐ (negative conjunction with the indicative) 130.
δεδόξασται (3d.per.sing.perf.pass.ind.of δοξάζω, intensive) 461.
τὸ (nom.sing.neut.of the article in agreement with δεδοξασμένον) 9.
δεδοξασμένον (perf.pass.part.nom.sing.neut.of δοξάζω, substantival, subject of δεδόξασται) 461.
ἐν (preposition with the locative of sphere) 80.
τούτῳ (loc.sing.neut.of οὗτος, in agreement with μέρει) 93.
τῷ (loc.sing.neut.of the article in agreement with μέρει) 9.
μέρει (loc.sing.neut.of μέρος, sphere) 240.
εἵνεκεν (improper preposition with the genitive, Ionic form, cause) 435.
τῆς (gen.sing.fem.of the article in agreement with δόξης) 9.

#4290 ὑπερβαλλούσης (pres.act.part.gen.sing.fem.of ὑπερβάλλω, adjectival, attributive position, ascriptive, in agreement with δόξης).

King James Version

exceed - 2 Cor.9:14; Eph.1:19; 2:7.
excel - 2 Cor.3:10.
pass - Eph.3:19.

Revised Standard Version

surpass - 2 Cor.3:10; 9:14; Eph.3:19.
exceed - Eph.1:19; 2:7.

Meaning: A combination of ὑπέρ (#545) and βάλλω (#299). Hence to throw or cast above or beyond; hence, to excel, exceed go further, transcend, surpass. The glory of the grace covenant is greater than that of the law - 2 Cor.3:10. As an adjective meaning "excessive" and defining grace - 2 Cor.9:14; defining power - Eph.1:19; defining the riches of His grace - Eph.2:7; defining knowledge - Eph.3:19.

δόξης (gen.sing.fem.of δόξα, cause) 361.

Translation - "Because in fact that which has been glorified is not now glorified in the sense that there is a transcendant glory."

Comment: Paul now compares the glory that was evident when the covenant of the law was given at Sinai with the greater glory of the gospel of Christ. He concludes that in comparison what happend at Sinai was not really glorious at all. *Cf.*2 Cor9:3 and Col.2:16 for ἐν τῷ μέρει τούτῳ and ἐν μέρει - "in respect to this" as we say "not really." Paul's use of the participles as substantives and adjectives throughout this passage (2 Cor.3:8-11) is rich.

When we compare Sinai with Calvary it is easy to see what Paul means. At Sinai a holy God warned the people to stand back lest they die. At Calvary He died for the people so that they need not die. At Sinai He roared His displeasure. At Calvary He whispered His forgiveness. At Sinai sinners were condemned to die. At Calvary sinners were justified and given eternal life. Holiness and its guard, the righteousness of God, was the theme in the desert as the mountain quaked. Holiness and righteousness combined in the same man - the God-Man at Golgotha and the whole earth quaked. There was love at Sinai but God did not express it. At Calvary He demonstrated that there is no greater love than that one should die for his friends. There was truth and righteousness at Sinai. There was also truth and righteousness at the cross, but they were combined with mercy and peace (Psalm 85:10,11). The glory of the new covenant is so much greater than that of the old that we conclude that the giving of the tablets of stone in the desert was not glorious at all.

Paul says this one more time in

Verse 11 - "For if that which is done away was glorious, much more than which remaineth is glorious."

εἰ γὰρ τὸ καταργούμενον διὰ δόξης, πολλῷ μᾶλλον τὸ μένον ἐν δόξῃ.

"For if what faded away came with splendor, what is permanent must have much more splendor." . . . RSV

εἰ (conditional particle in a first-class condition) 337.

γὰρ (causal conjunction) 105.

τὸ (nom.sing.neut.of the article in agreement with καταργούμενον) 9.

καταργούμενον (pres.pass.part.nom.sing.neut.of καταργέω, substantival, subject of verb understood) 2500.

διὰ (preposition with the genitive, manner) 118.

δόξης (gen.sing.fem.of δόξα, manner) 361.

πολλῷ (instru.sing.neut.of πολύς, measure) 228.

μᾶλλον (adverbial) 619.

τὸ (nom.sing.neut.of the article in agreement with μένον) 9.

μένον (pres.act.part.nom.sing.neut.of μένω, substantival, subject of verb understood) 864.

ἐν (preposition with the locative of accompanying circumstance) 80.

δόξῃ (loc.sing.fem.of δόξα, accompanying circumstance) 361.

Translation - "Because since that which is superseded was surrounded with glory, to a far greater extent, that which remains lives on in glory."

Comment: *Cf.*#2500 for the basic meaning of κατaργέω. It is important to fit this meaning into its context with great care. What has Paul been talking about since the beginning of this chapter? It is not the moral law of God itself, but that law as it was written upon tablets of stone and given to Moses at Sinai. God's moral standards are not *ad hoc*, but their inscription upon stone was. Jesus Christ is the same always (Heb.13:8). The Mosaic code is only the expression of what the Judge of all the earth (Gen.18:25; John 5:22; Acts 17:31) has always known to be morally right and morally wrong. If it had been phased out (superseded, rendered nugatory) there would have been no need for our Lord to fulfill it in His incarnation, for it would already have been made a thing of the past - a long forgotten moral standard that had long since lost its relevance. But Jesus did fulfill it (Mt.5:17), because it was a part of His divine nature and it is the standard by which He will judge the world. The glory of the Kingdom Age, to which every Christian looks forward with such breathless anticipation, could never be without the ethical standard of the code which God gave to Moses.

If then God's law was not phased out, as something that had only temporary value and made way for something better, what was it at Sinai which, despite the glory that surrounded it, was *ad hoc*? It was God's moral law written only upon stone, which was replaced by the same law written now, by the Holy Spirit upon human hearts. It is futile to tell depraved sons and daughters of Adam that what they wish to do and what they are determined to do is wrong and that if they do it they will be judged and lost forever. The warning of the "Thou shalt not" does nothing to deter the sinner. It only tells him that he is a sinner. This he is willing to accept. He may even boast about it and deny moral responsibility for his sins on the ground of environmental determinism. Peer pressure is a powerful force. It is so easy to excuse oneself with the observation that though it may be sin "Every body is doing it."

But it is not futile for the Holy Spirit to write the law of God upon the regenerated heart. In fact that is what regeneration is.

Paul says that though the tablets of stone were scheduled to be set aside, they took their leave "through glory." (διὰ δόξης). There was glory on all sides as that which was *ad hoc* bowed out. But that glory was not to compare with the glory with which the permanent covenant of God's redemptive and regenerative grace lives on. In fact in the comparison there was no splendor at all at Sinai.

Thus in verses 7-11 Paul has given all of the credit for the supernatural results of his gospel in the lives of the Corinthians to the supernatural character of the gospel itself, not to himself as a great preacher (verse 5). A salesman may be less than convincing in his sales speech as he presents the product, but if the product is of the highest quality the customer is going to profit by the purchase. Actually Paul was not the salesman. That function is carried out by the Holy Spirit. Nor could Paul take credit for the quality of the product, but he knew from his own experience on the Damasuc road that it was of the highest quality.

Verse 12 - "Seeing then that we have such hope, we use great plainness of speech."

Ἔχοντες οὖν τοιαύτην ἐλπίδα πολλῇ παρρησίᾳ χρώμεθα.

"Since we have such a hope, we are very bold, . . . " . . . RSV

Ἔχοντες (pres.act.part.nom.pl.masc.of ἔχω, adverbial, causal) 82.
οὖν (inferential conjunction) 68.
τοιαύτην (acc.sing.fem.of τοιοῦτος, in agreement with ἐλπίδα) 785.
ἐλπίδα (acc.sing.fem.of ἐλπίς, direct object of ἔχοντες) 2994.
πολλῇ (instru.sing.fem.of πολύς, in agreementwith παρρησίᾳ) 228.
παρρησίᾳ (instru.sing.fem.of παρρησία, manner) 2319.
χρώμεθα (1st.per.pl.pres.mid.ind.of χράω, customary) 2447.

Translation - "So since we have such hope we always speak with reckless abandon."

Comment: Ἔχοντες is causal and οὖν is inferential. It was because of Paul's great hope that his gospel, due to its supernatural character (verses 7-11), would produce supernatural results in the lives of his converts, that he was emboldened to speak without reservation. It was his custom   (customary present in χρώμεθα) to speak with great frankness (πολλῇ παρρησίᾳ, manner). He needed no letters to commend him. He had the Corinthians. But though their testimony for Christ (or against Paul) was observed by all men (verse 2) how could he be sure that what they displayed to the world would be a recommendation? Might they not reveal the seamy side of their character and embarrass Paul rather than commend him? He was not worried about this (verse 4), not because he was a good preacher (verse 5), but because he had a supernatural message, infinitely superior to the covenant of the law (verses 6-11). With the message of the Holy Spirit which gives life (verse 6) and which is administered in great glory (verses 8-11), which supersedes its predecessor never to be superseded (verse 11), Paul would preach it fully, with no reservations and with great boldness (verse 12).

Paul had no confidence in social reform. That is all that the law of God, written on stone tablets, could ever attempt. But Paul had great confidence in individual regeneration. That is what the Holy Spirit can and does produce. Thus its surpassing and permanent glory. There are those misguided Fundamentalists who would hand down to society from a quaking and smoky Sinai their own list of "Thou shalt nots" and seek the legislative, judicial and police power of the secular state to enforce the ban. To seek to enforce with police power upon the unregenerate the moral standards that the Holy Spirit produces in Christians, is to overlook Paul's thought here

He now says that the law covenant blinded the minds of Israel and made God unapproachable (verses 13-15). In contrast the gospel of the covenant allows man to look at it squarely, see and understand it all. He then adds that the intensity with which we look at God, something that the law would not permit, transfigures us into God's image (verses 16-18). This is the outline of the remainder of the chapter.

Verse 13 - "And not as Moses, which put a vail over his face, that the children of

Israel could not steadfastly look to the end of that which is abolished."

καὶ οὐ καθάπερ Μωϋσῆς ἐτίθει κάλυμμα ἐπὶ τὸ πρόσωπον αὐτοῦ, πρὸς τὸ μὴ ἀτενίσαι τοὺς υἱοὺς Ἰσραὴλ εἰς τὸ τέλος τοῦ καταργουμένου.

"not like Moses, who put a veil over his face so that the Israelites might not see the end of the fading splendor." . . . RSV

καὶ (adversative conjunction) 14.
οὐ (negative conjunction with the indicative understood) 130.
καθάπερ (intensive compound comparative particle) 3883.
Μωϋσῆς (nom.sing.masc.of Μωϋσῆς, subject of ἐτίθει) 715.
ἐτίθει (3d.per.sing.imp.act.ind.of τίθημι, iterative) 455.

#4291 κάλυμμα (acc.sing.neut.of κάλυμμα, direct object of ἐτίθει).

King James Version

veil - 2 Cor.3:13,14,15,16.

Revised Standard Version

veil - 2 Cor.3:13,14,15,16.

Meaning: Cf. καλύπτω (#753). A veil or covering to hinder sight - 2 Cor.3:13. Metaphorically, that which makes intellectual and spiritual perception impossible - 2 Cor.314,15,16.

ἐπὶ (preposition with the accusative of extent) 47.
τὸ (acc.sing.neut.of the article in agreement with πρόσωπον) 9.
πρόσωπον (acc.sing.neut.of πρόσωπον, extent) 588.
αὐτοῦ (gen.sing.masc.of αὐτός, possession) 16.
πρὸς (preposition with the infinitive, purpose) 197.
τὸ (acc.sing.neut.of the article in agreement with ἀτενίσαι) 9.
μὴ (negative conjunction with the infinitive) 87.
ἀτενίσαι (aor.act.inf.of ἀτενίζω, acc.sing.neut., negative purpose) 2028.
τοὺς (acc.pl.masc.of the article in agreement with υἱούς) 9.
υἱοὺς (acc.pl.masc.of υἱός, general reference) 5.
Ἰσραὴλ (gen.sing.masc.of Ἰσραήλ, relationship) 165.
εἰς (preposition with the accusative of extent) 140.
τὸ (acc.sing.neut.of the article in agreement with τέλος) 9.
τέλος (acc.sing.neut.of τέλος, extent) 881.
τοῦ (gen.sing.neut.of the article in agreement with καταργουμένου) 9.
καταργουμένου (pres.pass.part.gen.sing.neut.of καταργέω, substantival, description) 2500.

Translation - "But (Paul) was not like Moses (who) put a veil upon his face, so that the children of Israel could not look at him attentively to understand the end result of that which was in the process of being phased out."

Comment: The contrast is between Paul's open, bold, frank and completely expounded gospel message and that of Moses, who had a veil on his face. God had warned that a sinner under the law before a holy God was not free to be intimate with Him. God cannot call a sinner under the law a friend (John 15:13-15). The warning at Sinai was "keep a safe distance." πρὸς τὸ ἀτενίσαι is one of four subjective purpose articular infinitives with πρός and the accusative in the New Testament. *Cf.* Eph.6:11; 1 Thess.2:9; 2 Thess.3:8; 2 Cor.3:13. MSS D E F G use εἰς instead of πρός in Eph.6:11. The idiom expresses purpose - "to the intent that" *i.e.* to bring about a given result.

The veil indicates a lack of clear vision as opposed to 2 Cor.3:18 where we have an "unveiled face" looking into a mirror. Israel never understood the purpose of God in giving the law on tablets of stone (τὸ τέλος τοῦ καταργουμένου), which tablets were destined to have only an *ad hoc* ministry in the divine economy, to be superseded by a permanent covenant (verse 11, #2500). It was designed to make them realize that they were sinners who needed the "eagles' wings" of God's grace (Exodus 19:4; Gal.3:19). They misunderstood it. They supposed that God was telling them that they could save themselves by keeping its precepts, as though they were able to be as holy as God's standard demands. In their mistaken zeal to keep it they crucified the Son of God. When the veil is removed, we look into the face of the Son of God and, far from crucifying Him, we are transformed into His image (verse 18).

As the phased out glory faded from the face of Moses, one wonders if he continued to wear the veil because his face revealed that he knew that Israel could never keep the law written upon the tablets. As he came down the mountain slope of Sinai he interrupted the party in which the children of Israel were transgressing every precept of the law which he held in his hand - and that after having said, "All that the Lord hath spoken we will do" (Ex. 19:8).

Israel is still blinded by the veil as we learn in

Verse 14 - "But their minds were blinded: for until this day remaineth the same vail untaken away in the reading of the old testament; which vail is done away in Christ."

ἀλλὰ ἐπωρώθη τὰ νοήματα αὐτῶν. ἄχρι γὰρ τῆς σήμερον ἡμέρας τὸ αὐτὸ κάλυμμα ἐπὶ τῇ ἀναγνώσει τῆς παλαιᾶς διαθήκης μένει μὴ ἀνακαλυπτόμενον, ὅτι ἐν Χριστῷ καταργεῖται.

"But their minds were hardened; for to this day, when they read the old covenant, that same veil remains unlifted, because only through Christ is it taken away." . . . RSV

ἀλλὰ (adversative conjunction) 342.
ἐπωρώθη (3d.per.sing.aor.pass.ind.of πωρόω, constative) 2282.
τὰ (nom.pl.neut.of the article in agreement with νοήματα) 9.
νοήματα (nom.pl.neut.of νοῦς, subject of ἐπωρώθη) 2928.
αὐτῶν (gen.pl.masc.of αὐτός, possession) 16.
ἄχρι (preposition with the genitive in a time expression) 1517.

γάρ (inferential conjunction) 105.
τῆς (gen.sing.fem.of the article in agreement with ἡμέρας) 9.
σήμερον (adverbial) 579.
ἡμέρας (gen.sing.fem.of ἡμέρα, time description) 135.
τὸ (nom.sing.neut.of the article in agreement with κάλυμμα) 9.
αὐτὸ (nom.sing.neut.of αὐτός, intensive, in agreement with κάλυμμα) 16.
κάλυμμα (nom.sing.neut.of κάλυμμα, subject of μένει) 4291.
ἐπὶ (preposition with the locative, time point) 47.
τῇ (loc.sing.fem.of the article in agreement with ἀναγνώσει) 9.
ἀναγνώσει (loc.sing.fem.of ἀνάγνωσις, time point) 3290.
τῆς (gen.sing.fem.of the article in agreement with διαθήκης) 9.
παλαιᾶς (gen.sing.fem.of παλαιός, in agreement with διαθήκης) 804.
διαθήκης (gen.sing.fem.of διαθήκη, description) 1575.
μένει (3d.per.sing.pres.act.ind.of μένω, present progressive retroactive) 864.
μὴ (negative conjunction with the participle) 87.

#4292 ἀνακαλυπτόμενον (pres.pass.part.nom.sing.neut.of ἀνακαλύπτω, adjectival, predicate position, in agreement with κάλυμμα).

King James Version

open - 2 Cor.3:18.
untaken away - 2 Cor.3:14.

Revised Standard Version

unveiled - 2 Cor.3:18.
unlifted - 2 Cor.3:14.

Meaning: A combination of ἀνά (#1059) and καλύπτω (#753). Hence, to uncover, unveil. Metaphorically with reference to the powers of spiritual and intellectual perception -2 Cor.3:14,18.

ὅτι (nom.sing.neut.of ὅστις subject of καταργέω) 163.
ἐν (preposition with the instrumental of means) 80.
Χριστῷ (instru.sing.masc.of Χριστός, means) 4.
καταργεῖται (3d.per.sing.pres.pass.ind.of καταργέω, aoristic) 2500.

Translation - "But their minds were made imperceptive; therefore until this very day when the old covenant which is superseded by Christ, is read the same veil remains, not yet removed."

Comment: The verse explains why Israel misunderstands the purpose of the tablets of stone (verse 13). Their minds were made dull. *Cf.#2282* for meaning. The result is set forth in the inferential γάρ clause. Note the emphasis of σήμερον, attributive to ἡμέρας after ἄχρι. Note also the attributive intensive αὐτό. The old covenant is now superseded but Israel is not aware of the fact. τῆς παλαιᾶς διαθήκης is antecedent to ὅτι, the nominative singular of ὅστις, not the causal ὅτι. Thus blinded Israel is putting her trust in an outmoded covenant

of good works which was never intended to be a saving ordinance. The contrast
is between an obscuring veil, connected with the law covenant, which blinds
minds and dulls perception and the open face-to-face view of God's grace.

The thought is repeated in

*Verse 15 - "But even unto this day, when Moses is read, the vail is upon their
heart."*

ἀλλ᾽ ἕως σήμερον ἡνίκα ἂν ἀναγινώσκηται Μωϋσῆς κάλυμμα ἐπὶ τὴν
καρδίαν αὐτῶν κεῖται.

"Yes, to this day whenever Moses is read a veil lies over their minds;" ... RSV

ἀλλ᾽ (adversative conjunction) 342.
ἕως (preposition with the genitive in a time expression) 71.
σήμερον (adverbial) 579.

#**4293** ἡνίκα (temporal adverb).

King James Version

when - 2 Cor.3:15,16.

Revised Standard Version

whenever - 2 Cor.3:15.
when - 2 Cor.3:16.

Meaning: A relative adverb of time. Followed by ἂν and the present subjunctive
in 2 Cor.3:15; by ἐάν and the subjunctive in 2 Cor.3:16.
ἂν (contingent particle in an indefinite temporal clause) 205.
ἀναγινώσκηται (3d.per.sing.pres.subj.pass.of ἀναγιώσκω, in an indefinite
temporal clause) 967.
Μωϋσῆς (nom.sing.masc.of Μωϋσῆς, subject of ἀναγινώσκηται) 715.
κάλυμμα (nom.sing.neut.of κάλυμμα, subject of κεῖται) 4291.
ἐπὶ (preposition with the accusative of extent) 47.
τὴν (acc.sing.fem.of the article in agreement with καρδίαν) 9.
καρδίαν (acc.sing.fem.of καρδία, extent) 432.
αὐτῶν (gen.pl.masc.of αὐτός, possession) 16.
κεῖται (3d.per.sing.pres.pass.ind.of κεῖμαι, present iterative retroactive) 295.

*Translation - "But to this day whenever Moses is read, a veil is laid upon their
heart."*

Comment: The same thought as in verse 14, except that their hearts as well as
their minds are obfuscated when Moses is read to them. ἡνίκα with ἂν and the
subjunctive is indefinite. But this veil can be removed, as we learn in

*Verse 16 - "Nevertheless, when it shall turn to the Lord, the vail shall be taken
away."*

ἡνίκα δὲ ἐὰν ἐπιστρέφῃ πρὸς κύριον, περιαιρεῖται τὸ κάλυμμα.

"but when a man turns to the Lord the veil is removed." . . . RSV

ἡνίκα (temporal adverb with the subjunctive in an indefinite temporal clause) 4293.

δὲ (adversative conjunction) 11.

ἐὰν (conditional particle with the subjunctive in a third-class condition) 363.

ἐπιστρέφῃ (3d.per.sing.aor.act.subj.of ἐπιστρέφω, third-class condition) 866.

πρὸς (preposition with the accusative of extent) 197.

κύριον (acc.sing.masc.of κύριος, extent) 97.

περιαιρεῖται (3d.per.sing.pres.pass.ind.of περιαιρέω, futuristic) 3724.

τὸ (nom.sing.neut.of the article in agreement with κάλυμμα) 9.

κάλυμμα (nom.sing.neut.of κάλυμμα, subject of περιαιρεῖται) 4291.

Translation - *"But whenever he shall turn to the Lord the veil will be removed."*

Comment: Note the change in subject. The subject of verse 15 was κάλυμμα. The context however is clear. It is the blinded sinner, not the veil, who repents (#866). If and when he does (indefinite with ἐὰν and the subjunctive) the veil is taken away. Note περί in composition - "It is lifted up (or taken away) from about the head and heart."

Repentance here involves an awareness that the old covenant is not for salvation purposes but for the purpose of making the sinner aware of the vast gulf that separates him as a sinner from a holy God. To understand this is to turn to Christ and the new covenant. Now (after he turns away from law and human merit to grace and the merit in Christ) he is in touch with the Spirit of life. He thus has freedom (verse 17) and access to God with the result that he can now look at God openly (verse 18) with the supernatural results of transformation.

Verse 17 - "Now the Lord is that Spirit: and where the Spirit of the Lord is, there is liberty."

ὁ δὲ κύριος τὸ πνεῦμά ἐστιν. οὗ δὲ τὸ πνεῦμα κυρίου, ἐλευθερία.

"Now the Lord is the Spirit, and where the Spirit of the Lord is, there is freedom." . . . RSV

ὁ (nom.sing.masc.of the article in agreement with κύριος) 9.

δὲ (explanatory conjunction) 11.

κύριος (nom.sing.masc.of κύριος, subject of ἐστιν) 97.

τὸ (nom.sing.neut.of the article in agreement with πνεῦμά) 9.

πνεῦμά (nom.sing.neut.of πνεῦμα, predicate nominative) 83.

ἐστιν (3d.per.sing.pres.ind.of εἰμί, static) 86.

οὗ (gen.sing.neut.of ὅς, relative pronoun, introducing a relative time clause) 132,65.

δὲ (continuative conjunction) 11.
τὸ (nom.sing.neut.of the article in agreement with πνεῦμα) 9.
πνεῦμα (nom.sing.neut.of πνεῦμα, subject of verb understood) 83.
κυρίου (gen.sing.masc.of κύριος, description) 97.
ἐλευθερία (nom.sing.fem.of ἐλευθερία, subject of ἐστιν understood) 3943.

Translation - "*Now the Lord is the Spirit, and where the Lord's Spirit is, there is liberty.*"

Comment: The verse identifies the Holy Spirit with the Lord and adds that His presence brings liberty. *Cf.* verse 16. To turn to the Lord is to be forever free from the veil which obscures and confuses. It is by the Spirit (John 16:7-14; 1 Cor.12:3) that repentance and faith turns us to the Lord to find this freedom from the confusion which characterizes Israel's blindness. The covenant of the law generates bondage (Gal.4:24,25); the coverant of grace takes away the veil and brings liberty. This is why Jesus said, "Ye shall know the truth and the truth shall make you free" (John 8:32) and then identified Himself with the truth by adding, "If the Son therefore shall make you free you shall be free indeed." (John 8:36; John 14:6).

Now that we are free we are in a position to grow in grace until we become like Him in all respects. This is the thought of the last verse in the chapter.

Verse 18 - "*But we all, with open face beholding as in a glass the glory of the Lord, are changed into the same image from glory to glory, even as by the Spirit of the Lord.*"

ἡμεῖς δὲ πάντες ἀνακεκαλυμμένῳ προσώπῳ τὴν δόξαν κυρίου κατοπτριζόμενοι τὴν αὐτὴν εἰκόνα μεταμορφούμεθα ἀπὸ δόξης εἰς δόξαν, καθάπερ ἀπὸ κυρίου πνεύματος.

"*And we all, with unveiled face, beholding the glory of the Lord, are being changed into his likeness from one degree of glory to another; for this comes from the Lord who is the Spirit.*" . . . RSV

ἡμεῖς (nom.pl.masc.of ἐγώ, subject of μεταμορφούμεθα) 123.
δὲ (continuative conjunction) 11.
πάντες (nom.pl.masc.of πᾶς, in agreement with ἡμεῖς) 67.
ἀνακεκαλυμμένῳ (perf.pass.part.instru.sing.neut.of ἀνακαλύπτω, adjectival, attributive position, ascriptive, in agreement with προσώπῳ) 4292.
προσώπῳ (instru.sing.neut.of πρόσωπον, manner) 588.
τὴν (acc.sing.fem.of the article in agreement with δόξαν) 9.
δόξαν (acc.sing.fem.of δόξα, direct object of κατοπτριζόμεθα) 361.
κυρίου (gen.sing.masc.of κύριος, description) 97.

#4294 κατοπτριζόμενοι (pres.mid.part.nom.pl.masc.of κατοπτρίζω, adverbial, modal).

King James Version

behold as in a glass - 2 Cor.3:18.

Revised Standard Version

beholding - 2 Cor.3:18.

Meaning: Cf. κάτοπτρον - "a mirror." Hence to look at oneself in a mirror. Joined with τὴν δόξαν κυρίου. The Christian, an elect child of God's grace beholds the Lord's glory and the reflection transfigures him - 2 Cor.3:18.

τὴν (acc.sing.fem.of the article in agreement with εἰκόνα) 9.

αὐτὴν (acc.sing.fem.of αὐτός, in agreement with εἰκόνα, intensive) 16.

εἰκόνα (acc.sing.fem.of εἰκων, adverbial accusative) 1421.

μεταμορφούμεθα (1st.per.pl.pres.pass.ind.of μεταμορφόω, aoristic) 1222.

ἀπὸ (preposition with the ablative of source) 70.

δόξης (abl.sing.fem.of δόξα, source) 361.

εἰς (preposition with the accusative of extent) 140.

δόξαν (acc.sing.fem.of δόξα, extent) 361.

καθάπερ (intensive compound comparative particle) 3883.

ἀπὸ (preposition with the ablative of agent) 70.

κυρίου (gen.sing.masc.of κύριος, description) 97.

πνεύματος (abl.sing.neut.of πνεῦμα, agent) 83.

Translation - "And all of us by looking into a mirror with unveiled face at the Lordly glory are being transfigured into the same image from glory to glory even by the Lordly Spirit."

Comment: The participle ἀνακεκαλυμμένῳ is an adjective in the attributive position (before the noun with no intervening article), and is thus ascriptive, modifying face, the instrumental of manner. How do we look into the mirror to see the glory of the Lord? It is with a face that is no longer shrouded with a veil. Now we see clearly. The veil which covers the face of the Hebrew, who is afflicted with partial blindess (Romans 11:25), so that he is unable to appreciate the glory of the new covenant, is taken away when he turns, by the direction of the Holy Spirit to the Lord. Now, as a result of a past completed action, we have vision which is unclouded (perfect participle in ἀνακεκαλυμμένῳ).

How glorious is the glory of the Lord which we now see and which is reflected back to us? It is so much greater than the glory that surrounded Moses as he received the Ten Commandments that the former glory pales into insignificance in the comparison (verse 10). And yet the glory of Sinai was so brilliant that the people dared not look upon it. But now the child of God is privileged to look always at our Lord in all of His glory. Then He was glorious because of His holiness and the majesty of His righteous power. Now, while He still has all of that glory, He also has the greater glory of His love which drove Him to Calvary and the grace that reaches down to save those who failed his holiness test in the foothills of Mount Sinai. His glory in redemption (Rev.5:9,10) is greater than His glory in creation (Rev.4:11).

Israel looked and was confused. They misunderstood the purpose (τέλος, verse 13) of the law covenant. The believer looks and is transfigured. The verb μεταμορφόω (#1222) is translated "transfigured" in Mt.17:2 and Mk.9:2, with reference to Jesus on the Mount of transfiguration and in Rom.12:2 it is translated "transformed." *Cf.* comments *en loc.* Note that the transfiguration of the believer is accomplished by "the renewing of the mind" (Rom.12:2). What happened to Jesus on Mount Horeb happens to use both spiritually (2 Cor.3:18) and intellectually (Rom.12:2). But only if we spend our time in looking at Him (Heb.12:2). Note that the image that is reflected back to us and that transfigures us is "the same image" - τὴν αὐτὴν εἰκόνα. *Cf.* 1 Cor.15:49b; Rom.8:29; Col.3:10. Transformation to the divine image is the essence of salvation. The glory of God is the source (ἀπὸ δόξης) and the end result (εἰς δόξαν). The agent of this divine transformation is the Divine Spirit.

We become like what we look at. *Cf.* Washington Irving, *The Great Stone Face.*

Thus the contrast between the two covenants, law and grace, results in a great contrast of fruits in the lives of the devotees.

To sum up the chapter, it is because of these supernatural results that flow from the gospel of God's grace that Paul had such confidence in the supernatural ethics of the Corinthian saints.

Treasure in Earthen Vessels

(2 Corinthians 4:1-15)

2 Cor.4:1 - "Therefore, seeing we have this ministry, as we have received mercy, we faint not."

Διὰ τοῦτο, ἔχοντες τὴν διακονίαν ταύτην, καθὼς ἠλεήθημεν, οὐκ ἐγκακοῦμεν,

"Therefore, having this ministry by the mercy of God, we do not lose heart."...
RSV

Διὰ (preposition with the accusative of cause) 118.
τοῦτο (acc.sing.neut.of οὗτος, cause) 93.
ἔχοντες (pres.act.part.nom.pl.masc.of ἔχω, adverbial, causal) 82.
τὴν (acc.sing.fem.of the article in agreement with διακονίαν) 9.
διακονίαν (acc.sing.fem.of διακονία, direct object of ἔχοντες) 2442.
ταύτην (acc.sing.fem.of οὗτος, in agreement with διακονίαν) 93.
καθὼς (compound comparative particle) 1348.
ἠλεήθημεν (1st.per.pl.1st.aor.pass.ind.of ἐλεέω,constative) 430.
οὐκ (negative conjunction with the indicative) 130.
ἐγκακοῦμεν (1st.per.pl.pres.act.ind.of ἐγκακέω, aoristic) 2622.

Translation - "It is because of the fact that we have this ministry, just as we have received mercy, so we are not discouraged."

Comment: Διὰ τοῦτο refers to the glorious results of the supernatural gospel set forth in 2 Cor.3:18. Because (διὰ τοῦτο) such results flow from the gospel of Christ, Paul is not discouraged since (causal participle in ἔχοντες) he was called to preach this gospel - a gospel which extended God's mercy to him. The gospel which Paul preached to others had produced the same results in his own life. When a preacher sees the same work of divine grace which was effectual in his own heart, being wrought in the hearts of his converts, he is by no means discouraged. And this confidence in the supernatural power of God's gospel has led Paul to preach it in its fulness with no gimmicks. On the contrary Paul had renounced all of that.

Verse 2 - "But have renounced the hidden things of dishonesty, not walking in craftiness, nor handling the word of God deceitfully; but by manifestation of the truth commending ourselves to every man's conscience in the sight of God."

ἀλλὰ ἀπειπάμεθα τὰ κρυπτὰ τῆς αἰσχύνης, μὴ περιπατοῦντες ἐν πανουργίᾳ μηδὲ δολοῦντες τὸν λόγον τοῦ θεοῦ, ἀλλὰ τῇ φανερώσει τῆς ἀληθείας συνιστάνοντες ἑαυτοὺς πρὸς πᾶσαν συνείδησιν ἀνθρώπων ἐνώπιον τοῦ θεοῦ.

"We have renounced disgraceful, underhanded ways; we refuse to practice cunnng or to tamper with God's word, but by the open statement of truth we would commend ourselves to every man's conscience in the sight of God." . . .
                                                                                          RSV

ἀλλὰ (alternative conjunction) 342.

#4295 ἀπειπάμεθα (1st.per.pl.1st.aor.mid.ind.of ἀπεῖπον, constative).

King James Version

renounce - 2 Cor.4:2.

Revised Standard Version

renounce - 2 Cor.4:2.

Meaning: A combination of ἀπό (#70) and εἶπον (#155). Hence, to renounce; to give up; to abandon. Followed by an accusative of the thing. With reference to Paul's ministry - 2 Cor.4:2.

τὰ (acc.pl.neut.of the article in agreement with κρυπτὰ) 9.
κρυπτὰ (acc.pl.neut.of κρυπτός, direct object of ἀπειπάμεθα) 565.
τῆς (gen.sing.fem.of the article in agreement with αἰσχύνης) 9.
αἰσχύνης (gen.sing.fem.of αἰσχύνη, description) 2523.
μὴ (negative conjunction with the participle) 87.
περιπατοῦντες (pres.act.part.nom.pl.masc.of περιπατέω, adverbial, modal) 384.
ἐν (preposition with the locative of sphere) 80.
πανουργίᾳ (loc.sing.fem.of πανουργία, sphere) 2693.
μηδὲ (negative continuative particle) 612.

#4296 δολοῦντες (pres.act.part.nom.pl.masc.of δολόω, adverbial, modal).

King James Version

handle deceitfully - 2 Cor.4:2.

Revised Standard Version

underhanded ways - 2 Cor.4:2.

Meaning: Cf. δόλος (#1557). Hence, to ensnare; to take with guile; to employ underhanded methods - followed by an accusative, τὸν λόγον τοῦ θεοῦ - 2 Cor.4:2.

τὸν (acc.sing.masc.of the article in agreement with λόγον) 9.
λόγον (acc.sing.masc.of λόγος, direct object of δολοῦντες) 510.
τοῦ (gen.sing.masc.of the article in agreement with θεοῦ) 9.
θεοῦ (gen.sing.masc.of θεός, description) 124.
ἀλλά (alternative conjunction) 342.
τῇ (loc.sing.fem.of the article in agreement with φανερώσει) 9.
φανερώσει (loc.sing.fem.of φανέρωσις, sphere) 4214.
τῆς (gen.sing.fem.of the article in agreement with ἀληθείας) 9.
ἀληθείας (gen.sing.fem.of ἀλήθεια, description) 1416.
συνιστάνοντες (pres.act.part.nom.pl.masc.of συνίστημι, adverbial, modal) 2328.
ἑαυτοὺς (acc.pl.masc.of ἑαυτοῦ, direct object of συνιστάνοντες) 288.
πρὸς (preposition with the accusative of extent, after a verb of speaking or showing) 197.
πᾶσαν (acc.sing.fem.of πᾶς, in agreement with συνείδησιν) 67.
συνείδησιν (acc.sing.fem.of συνείδησις, extent) 3590.
ἀνθρώπων (gen.pl.masc.of ἄνθρωπος, description) 341.
ἐνώπιον (preposition with the genitive, with persons) 1798.
τοῦ (gen.sing.masc.of the article in agreement with θεοῦ) 9.
θεοῦ (gen.sing.masc.of θεός, with persons) 124.

Translation - "But we have repudiated the hidden things of disgrace, never going about our work with various schemes to manipulate, nor handling the Word of God in an underhanded way, but with a clear statement of the truth commending ourselves to every human conscience before God."

Comment: Here is a bold statement of a fearless gospel preacher. By implication Paul here speaks volumes about the preaching methods of demagogues.

ἀλλά is in contrast to οὐκ ἐγκακοῦμεν - "not discouraged ... but" (ἀλλά). We cannot interpret ἀπειπάμεθα here as being a repudiation of a policy which Paul previously followed. He never employed the dishonest methods of preaching which he here described. He attacks these tools of the religious demagogue as something which he never would employ. *Cf.*2 Cor.11:13-15. They are methods of manipulation (#2693). Paul was not a mob psychologist. The evangelist who asks Christians to respond to the invitation call and to come forward as though they were seeking salvation, in order to get a "band wagon" psychology going is a crowd manipulator. The usual justification for this wicked practice is that those who come down the aisle "break the ice," because "monkey see, monkey do"! If it is that cold in the meeting one may as well have the benediction and go home. There was no ice to break in Paul's meetings, but a warm spiritual environment as the Holy Spirit honored the faithful exposition of His word by Paul and convinced the elect to repond to His divine summons. When the Holy Spirit calls the unsaved to salvation they will come forward without recourse to human psychology - indeed they will come despite the dicatates of human psychology.

Paul did not thus handle the Word of God. On the contrary, by revealing all of the truth of the gospel (2 Cor.3:12) he gained the respect of all his listeners, even that of those who rejected his invitation. The meanest sinner in the world secretly admires the candor and courage of the preacher who "tells it like it is," even though he may reject the message. Why then, if Paul's honest, frank and open presentation of the Word of God elicited admiration from all men, did not all of them accept Christ? Paul answers this question in

Verse 3 - "But if our gospel be hid, it is hid to them that are lost."

εἰ δὲ καὶ ἔστιν κεκαλυμμένον τὸ εὐαγγέλιον ἡμῶν, ἐν τοῖς ἀπολλυμένοις ἐστὶν κεκαλυμμένον,

"And even if our gospel is veiled, it is veiled only to those who are perishing." . . RSV

εἰ (conditional particle in a first-class condition) 337.
δὲ (adversative conjunction) 11.
καὶ (emphatic conjunction) 14.
ἔστιν (3d.per.sing.pres.ind.of εἰμί, perfect periphrastic) 86.
κεκαλυμμένον (perf.pass.part.nom.sing.neut.of καλύπτω, perfect periphrastic, in agreement with εὐαγγέλιον, predicate adjective) 753.
τὸ (nom.sing.neut.of the article in agreement with εὐαγγέλιον) 9.
εὐαγγέλιον (nom.sing.neut.of εὐαγγέλιον, subject of ἔστιν) 405.
ἡμῶν (gen.pl.masc.of ἐγώ, possession) 123.
ἐν (preposition with the locative of sphere) 80.
τοῖς (loc.pl.masc.of the article in agreement with ἀπολλυμένοις) 9.
ἀπολλυμένοις (pres.pass.part.loc.pl.masc.of ἀπολλύμι, sphere) 208.
ἐστὶν (3d.per.sing.pres.ind.of εἰμί, perfect periphrastic) 86.
κεκαλυμμένον (perf.pass.part.nom.sing.neut.of καλύπτω, perfect periphrastic, in agreement with εὐαγγέλιον) 753.

Translation - "But since our gospel has in fact been hidden, it is hidden among the lost."

Comment: The first-class condition assumes as true the statement in the protasis. Paul knew, not only from his theology, but also from his experience that not all men respond to the gospel of Christ. The if-clause implies that not all who hear will believe, but Paul did not know who would and who would not. δὲ is adversative and καὶ is emphatic - "But (despite Paul's honest proclamation of the gospel with its commendation to all men," verse 2) it had in fact (emphatic καὶ) been hidden" (perfect tense). In what sphere of the Apostle's ministry was it hidden? Among the perishing ones. *Cf.* 2 Cor.2:15,16; Mt.11:25,26. This is a strong Calvinistic passage. What is the source of this obfuscation?

Verse 4 -"In whom the god of this world hath blinded the minds of them which believe not, lest the light of the glorious gospel of Christ, who is the image of God, should shine unto them."

ἐν οἷς ὁ θεὸς τοῦ αἰῶνος τούτου ἐτύφλωσεν τὰ νοήματα τῶν ἀπίστων εἰς τὸ μὴ αὐγάσαι τὸν φωτισμὸν τοῦ εὐαγγελίου τῆς δόξης τοῦ Χριστοῦ, ὅς ἐστιν εἰκὼν τοῦ θεοῦ.

"In their case the god of this world has blinded the minds of the unbelievers, to keep them from seeing the light of the gospel of Christ, who is the likeness of God." . . . RSV

ἐν (preposition with the locative of sphere) 80.

οἷς (loc.pl.masc.of ὅς, relative pronoun, sphere) 65.

ὁ (nom.sing.masc.of the article in agreement with θεὸς) 9.

θεὸς (nom.sing.masc.of θεός, subject of ἐτύφλωσεν) 124.

τοῦ (gen.sing.neut.of the article in agreement with αἰῶνος) 9.

αἰῶνος (gen.sing.neut.of αἰών, description) 1002.

τούτου (gen.sing.neut.of οὗτος, in agreement with αἰῶνος) 93.

ἐτύφλωσεν (3d.per.sing.aor.act.ind.of τυφλόω, constative) 2709.

τὰ (acc.pl.neut.of the article in agreement with νοήματα) 9.

νοήματα (acc.pl.neut.of νοῦς, direct object of ἐτύφλωσεν) 2928.

τῶν (gen.pl.masc.of the article in agreement with ἀπίστων) 9.

ἀπίστων (gen.pl.masc.of ἄπιστος, possession) 1231.

εἰς (preposition with the accusative infinitive, negative purpose) 140.

τὸ (acc.sing.neut.of the article, in agreement with αὐγάσαι, negative purpose) 9.

μὴ (negative conjunction with the infinitive) 87.

#4297 αὐγάσαι (aor.act.inf.of αὐγάζω, acc.sing.neut. negative purpose).

King James Version

shine - 2 Cor.4:4.

Revised Standard Version

keep from seeing - 2 Cor.4:4.

Meaning: Cf. αὐγή (#3516). To shine upon; to irradiate; to beam upon; enlighten. With reference to the spiritual illumination of regeneration - 2 Cor.4:4.

τὸν (acc.sing.masc.of the article in agreement with φωτισμὸν) 9.

#4298 φωτισμὸν (acc.sing.masc.of φωτισμός, general reference).

King James Version

light - 2 Cor.4:4.
give light - 2 Cor.4:6.

Revised Standard Version

light - 2 Cor.4:4.
give light - 2 Cor.4:6.

Meaning: Cf. φωτίζω (#1697) - the act of giving light. Hence φωτισμός means enlightenment. Followed by a genitive of description in 2 Cor.4:4; in a purpose construction with πρὸς and the accusative in 2 Cor.4:6.

τοῦ (gen.sing.neut.of the article in agreement with εὐαγγελίου) 9.
εὐαγγελίου (gen.sing.neut.of εὐαγγέλιον, description) 405.
τῆς (gen.sing.fem.of the article in agreement with δόξης) 9.
δόξης (gen.sing.fem.of δόξα, description) 361.
τοῦ (gen.sing.masc.of the article in agreement with Χριστοῦ) 9.
Χριστοῦ (gen.sing.masc.of Χριστός, possession) 4.
ὅς (nom.sing.masc.of ὅς, relative pronoun, subject of ἐστιν) 65.
ἐστιν (3d.per.sing.pres.ind.of εἰμί, static) 86.
εἰκὼν (nom.sing.masc.of εἰκών, predicate nominative) 1421.
τοῦ (gen.sing.masc.of the article in agreement with θεοῦ) 9.
θεοῦ (gen.sing.masc.of θεός, description) 124.

Translation - "*Among whom the god of this age has blinded the minds of the unbelievers in order that the light of the good news of the glory of Christ, Who is an image of God should not enlighten them.*"

Comment: The antecedent of οἷς is τοῖς ἀπολλυμένοις of verse 3. The god of this age is Satan (Eph.2:2). Jesus opened eyes and minds. Satan blinds the understanding of the unbelieving. Why? The negative purpose clause tells us. εἰς τὸ μὴν αὐγάσαι - neuter articular infinitive in the accusative case, after εἰς - this is negative purpose. Thus we know Satan's diabolical purpose. He wishes to prevent their illumination. The enlightenment that comes with the good news that Christ is glorious and the Source of glory would regenerate them, just as it did in the case of the elect (2 Cor.3:18) whose enlightenemnt Satan was unable to prevent.

The antecedent of ὅς is Χριστοῦ. The Messiah, the image of God is as glorious as God because He is God and, as such, the source of glory which transfigures the believer (2 Cor.3:18). This is indeed good news. Unfortunately the non-elect never realize it. The spirit who works in the "children of disobedience" prevents it (Eph.2:2). To them the good news smells like death (2 Cor.2:15,16). Thus Paul explains why not all who hear his gospel accept it. *Cf.* John 12:40; 1 John 2:11.

Verse 5 - "For we preach not ourselves, but Christ Jesus the Lord; and ourselves your servants for Jesus' sake."

οὐ γὰρ ἑαυτοὺς κηρύσσομεν ἀλλὰ Ἰησοῦν Χριστὸν κύριον, ἑαυτοὺς δὲ δούλους ὑμῶν διὰ Ἰησοῦν.

"For what we preach is not ourselves, but Jesus Christ as Lord, with ourselves as your servants for Jesus' sake." . . . RSV

οὐ (negative conjunction with the indicative) 130.
γὰρ (inferential conjunction) 105.
ἑαυτοὺς (acc.pl.masc.of ἑαυτοῦ) 288.
κηρύσσομεν (1st.per.pl.pres.act.ind.of κηρύσσω, customary) 249.
ἀλλὰ (alternative conjunction) 342.
Ἰησοῦν (acc.sing.masc.of Ἰησοῦς, direct object of κηρύσσομεν) 3.
Χριστὸν (acc.sing.masc.of Χριστός, apposition) 4.
κύριον (acc.sing.masc.of κύριος, predicate accusative) 97.
ἑαυτοὺς (acc.pl.masc.of ἑαυτοῦ, direct object of κηρύσσομεν) 288.
δὲ (continuative conjunction) 11.
δούλους (acc.pl.masc.of δοῦλος, predicate accusative) 725.
ὑμῶν (gen.pl.masc.of σύ, relationship) 104.
διὰ (preposition with the accusative, cause) 118.
Ἰησοῦν (acc.sing.masc.of Ἰησοῦς, cause) 3.

Translation - "Therefore we are not preaching ourselves but we are preaching Jesus Christ as Lord, while we represent ourselves as your servants because of Jesus."

Comment: The glory of the gospel comes from Christ Who is the image of God. To preach about the goodness or wisdom of the preacher is to rob the gospel of its glory and short-circuit its power to produce supernatural results. Therefore Paul's policy to say nothing about himself when he preached except that he was a bond-slave of the people in his audience. He was willing to take this lowly position because of Jesus Christ (διὰ Ἰησοῦν).

Verse 6 - "For God, who commanded the light to shine out of darkness, hath shined in our hearts, to give the light of the knowledge of the glory of God in the face of Jesus Christ."

ὅτι ὁ θεὸς ὁ εἰπών, Ἐκ σκότους φῶς λάμψει, ὃς ἔλαμψεν ἐν ταῖς καρδίαις ἡμῶν πρὸς φωτισμὸν τῆς γνώσεως τῆς δόξης τοῦ θεοῦ ἐν προσώπῳ Χριστοῦ.

"For it is the God who said, 'Let light shine out of darkness," who has shone in our hearts to give the light of the knowledge of the glory of God in the face of Christ." . . . RSV

ὅτι (causal conjunction) 211.
ὁ (nom.sing.masc.of the article in agreement with θεὸς) 9.

θεὸς (nom.sing.masc.of θεός, subject of ἐστιν understood) 124.

ὁ (nom.sing.masc.of the article in agreement with εἰπών) 9.

εἰπών (aor.part.nom.sing.masc.of εἶπον, substantival, in apposition to θεὸς) 155.

ἐκ (preposition with the ablative of separation) 19.

σκότους (abl.sing.masc.of σκότος, separation) 602.

φῶς (nom.sing.neut.of φῶς, subject of λάμφει) 379.

λάμφει (3d.per.sing.fut.act.ind.of λάμπω, imperative) 458.

ὅς (nom.sing.masc.of ὅς, relative pronoun, predicate nominative) 65.

ἔλαμφεν (3d.per.sing.aor.act.ind.of λάμπω, constative) 379.

ἐν (preposition with the locative of place) 80.

ταῖς (loc.pl.fem.of the article in agreement with καρδίαις) 9.

καρδίαις (loc.pl.fem.of καρδία, place) 432.

ἡμῶν (gen.pl.masc.of ἐγώ, possession) 123.

πρὸς (preposition with the accusative, purpose) 197.

φωτισμὸν (acc.sing.masc.of φωτισμός, purpose) 4298.

τῆς (gen.sing.fem.of the article in agreement with γνώσεως) 9.

γνώσεως (gen.sing.fem.of γνῶσις, description) 1856.

τῆς (gen.sing.fem.of the article in agreement with δόξης) 9.

δόξης (gen.sing.fem.of δόξα, description) 361.

τοῦ (gen.sing.masc.of the article in agreement with θεοῦ) 9.

θεοῦ (gen.sing.masc.of θεός, description) 124.

ἐν (preposition with the instrumental of means) 80.

προσώπῳ (instru.sing.neut.of πρόσωπον, means) 588.

Χριστοῦ (gen.sing.masc.of Χριστός, possession) 4.

Translation - "Because the God who said, 'Light will shine out of darkness" is the One Who has shone in our hearts in order to reveal the knowledge of the glory of God in the face of Christ."

Comment: ὅτι here introduces a paratactic causal clause and is little different from causal γάρ. *Cf.* similar uses of ὅτι in 2 Cor.7:8,14. ὁ εἰπών is in apposition to ὁ θεός. The copula is missing. ἐκ σκότους φῶς λάμφει is a reference to Genesis 1:3. The LXX has Γενηθήτω - the imperative, while Paul has the imperative future. The God Who in creation dispelled darkness and overcame it with light is the same God who illumines the hearts of sinners, elect according to the foreknowledge of God (1 Pet.1:2), with the sunrise illumination of the knowledge of His glory, as it is revealed in the face of Jesus Christ. The disciples saw this glory of God upon the face of Jesus (John 14:5-9).

Unbelievers are blinded by Satan (verse 4) and can never be saved except by the illumining decree of a sovereign God, Who is greater than Satan who blinds his victims (1 John 4:4). Paul's message, because it was full and honest, was humanly acceptable to all (verse 2), but spiritually rejected by unbelievers who were blinded (verse 4). Only those in whose hearts the God of creation gave light were saved (Eph.1:3; Acts 13:48). Thus the glory of God revealed in creation is also revealed in regeneration (John 8:12; 1 John 1:5).

Verse 7 - "But we have this treasure in earthen vessels, that the excellency of the power may be of God, and not of us."

Ἔχομεν δὲ τὸν θησαυρὸν τοῦτον ἐν ὀστρακίνοις σκεύεσειν, ἵνα ἡ ὑπερβολὴν τῆς δυνάμεως ᾖ τοῦ θεοῦ καὶ μὴ ἐξ ἡμῶν.

"But we have this treasure in earthen vessels, to show that the transcendant power belongs to God and not to us." . . . RSV

Ἔχομεν (1st.per.pl.pres.act.ind.of ἔχω, aoristic) 82.
δὲ (adversative conjunction) 11.
τὸν (acc.sing.masc.of the article in agreement with θησαυρὸν) 9.
θησαυρὸν (acc.sing.masc.of θησαυρός, direct object of ἔχομεν) 189.
τοῦτον (acc.sing.masc.of οὗτος, in agreement with θησαυρὸν) 93.
ἐν (preposition with the locative of place) 80.

#4299 ὀστρακίνοις (loc.pl.neut.of ὀστράκινος, in agreement with σκεύεσιν).

King James Version

earthen - 2 Cor.4:7.
of earth - 2 Tim.2:20.

Revised Standard Version

earthen - 2 Cor.4:7.
earthenware - 2 Tim.2:20.

Meaning: Cf.ὄστρακον - "baked clay." As a predicate adjective in 2 Tim.2:20. Metaphorically, with an added implication of frailty - 2 Cor.4:7.

σκεύεσιν (loc.pl.neut.of σκεῦος, place) 997.
ἵνα (conjunction with the subjunctive in a sub-final clause) 114.
ἡ (nom.sing.fem.of the article in agreement with ὑπερβολὴ) 9.
ὑπερβολὴ (nom.sing.fem.of ὑπερβολή, subject of ᾖ) 3923.
τῆς (gen.sing.fem.of the article in agreement with δυνάμεως) 9.
δυνάμεως (gen.sing.fem.of δύναμις, description) 687.
ᾖ (3d.per.sing.pres.subj.of εἰμί, sub-final clause) 86.
τοῦ (abl.sing.masc.of the article in agreement with θεοῦ) 9.
θεοῦ (abl.sing.masc.of θεός, source) 124.
καὶ (adjunctive conjunction joining ablative phrases) 14.
μὴ (negative conjunction with the subjunctive in a sub-final clause) 87.
ἐξ (preposition with the ablative of source) 19.
ἡμῶν (abl.pl.masc.of ἐγώ, source) 123.

Translation - "But we have this treasure in clay pots in order (and with the result) that the superiority of the power may be from God and not from us."

Comment: The superior power of God to enlighten, as opposed to the power of Satan to blind has been noted in 2 Cor.4:6. Lest anyone should attribute this victory of light over darkness to Paul he adds verse 7. It is a repetition of 2 Cor.3:5. *Cf.* also 1 Cor.2:1-5; Zechariah 4:6.

The gospel of Christ indeed is a treasure (#189). That God would disseminate such treasure, with such great power, in frail human bodies, and allow it to be interpreted by frail human minds only proves that the superabundance of power has its source in God and not in human beings. It was God's eternal purpose that it should be so. What He purposes results. Hence the sub-final (purpose/result) clause with ἵνα . . . ᾖ.

Paul devotes the remainder of the chapter to a discussion of his experiences in this earthen vessel.

Verse 8 - "We are troubled on every side, yet not distressed; we are perplexed, but not in despair."

ἐν παντὶ θλιβόμενοι ἀλλ' οὐ στενοχωρούμενοι, ἀπορούμενοι ἀλλ' οὐκ ἐξαπορούμενοι,

"We are afflicted in every way, but not crushed; perplexed, but not driven to despair;" . . . RSV

ἐν (preposition with the locative of sphere) 80.

παντὶ (loc.pl.masc.of πᾶς, sphere) 67.

θλιβόμενοι (pres.pass.part.nom.pl.masc.of θλίβω, present periphrastic, εἰσίν understood) 667.

ἀλλ' (adversative conjunction) 342.

οὐ (negative particle with the indicative understood) 130.

#**4300** στενοχωρούμενοι (pres.pass.part.nom.pl.masc.of στενοχωρέω, present periphrastic, εἰσίν understood).

  King James Version

distress - 2 Cor.4:8.
straiten - 2 Cor.6:12,12.

  Revised Standard Version

crushed - 2 Cor.4:8.
restrict - 2 Cor.6:12,12.

Meaning: Cf. στενοχωρία (#3838), στενός (#661), χωρέω (#1162). Cf. also στενόχωρος equals στενός plus χῶρας - "a space." Hence, "limited space." Hence, to be pressured; to have one's freedom restricted. With reference to Paul's experiences generally - 2 Cor.4:8; of the Corinthians' emotional reaction to Paul's recital of his problems - 2 Cor.6:12,12.

ἀπορούμενοι (pres.pass.part.nom.pl.masc.of ἀπορέομαι, present periphrastic, εἰσίν understood) 2254.

ἀλλ' (adversative conjunction) 342.

οὐκ (negative conjunction with the indicative understood) 130.

ἐξαπορούμενοι (pres.pass.part.nom.pl.masc.of ἐξαπορέομαι, present periphrastic, with εἰσίν understood) 4265.

Translation - "I am always under pressure, but never totally helpless; with no way to procede, I am never without a way out."

Comment: The ἐν παντὶ phrase is a locative of sphere. In every sphere of his activity Paul was under pressure. Note the contrast between #'s 667 and 4300 and between #'s 2254 and 4265. The two sets of words seem to make the passage contradictory. "Pressured but not totally so." "No way forward but not lacking a way out." It is the difference between the human and the divine viewpoint. Humanly speaking Paul was θλιβόμενος and ἀπορούμενος, but with God at his disposal he was never στενοχωρούμενος or ἐξαπορούμενος. Man' extremity is always God's opportunity. These verses serve to remind us that, whatever the superiority of the power of the gospel, we are only earthen vessels. And it is our peril if we forget it.

Verse 9 - "Persecuted, but not forsaken; cast down, but not destroyed."

διωκόμενοι, ἀλλ' οὐκ ἐγκαταλειπόμενοι, καταβαλλόμενοι ἀλλ' οὐκ ἀπολλύμενοι,

"persecuted, but not forsaken; struck down, but not destroyed;" . . . RSV

διωκόμενοι (pres.pass.part.nom.pl.masc.of διώκω, present periphrastic, with εἰσίν understood) 434.

ἀλλ' (adversative conjunction) 342.

οὐκ (negative conjunction with the indicative understood) 130.

ἐγκαταλειπόμενοι (pres.pass.part.nom.pl.masc.of ἐγκαταλείπω, present periphrastic, with εἰσίν understood) 1654.

#4301 καταβαλλόμενοι (pres.pass.part.nom.pl.masc.of καταβάλλω, present periphrastic, with εἰσίν understood).

King James Version

cast down - 2 Cor.4:9,
lay - Heb.6:1.

Revised Standard Version

struck down - 2 Cor.4:9.
lay - Heb.6:1.

Meaning: A combination of κατά (#98) and βάλλω (#299). Hence, to throw, strike or cast down; to overthrow. With reference to Paul's experience - 2 Cor.4:9. In a metaphorical usage to lay a foundation in an architectural sense - Heb.6:1.

ἀλλ' (adversative conjunction) 342.

οὐκ (negative conjunction with the indicative understood) 130.

ἀπολλύμενοι (pres.pass.part.nom.pl.masc.of ἀπόλλυμι, present periphrastic, with εἰσίν understood) 208.

Translation - "Always persecuted but never abandoned (left in the lurch); frequently floored, but never destroyed."

Comment: *Cf.*#434 - "to pursue with a view to murder." In a more general sense, "to persecute." *Cf.*#1654. Christ was abandoned by the Father (Mt.27:46; Mt.15:34) so that Paul might not be abandoned. Nor will God forsake any of His children (Heb.13:5). Though God abandoned Jesus on the cross, He did not forsake His soul in Hades (Acts 2:27,31). Nor will He permanently forsake His covenant people (Rom.9:29).

The picture in verses 8 and 9 is one of constant jeopardy accompanied by constant rescue. Paul was viable, and so are all Christians who are dedicated only to the performance of the will of God (Rom.8:28; Phil.1:6; 2 Tim.4:6,7; Rev.3:2). The "earthen vessel" is the object of the world's attack but also the object of God's protection because of the treasure of the gospel which it contains (verse 7). This is why "all things work together for good . . . " (Romans 8:28).

Verse 10 - "Always bearing about in the body the dying of the Lord Jesus, that the life also of Jesus might be manifest in our body."

πάντοτε τὴν νέκρωσιν τοῦ Ἰησοῦ ἐν τῷ σώματι περιφέροντες, ἵνα ἡ ζωὴ τοῦ Ἰησοῦ ἐν τῷ σώματι ἡμῶν φανερωθῇ.

"always carrying in the body the death of Jesus, so that the life of Jesus may also be manifested in our bodies." . . . RSV

πάντοτε (temporal adverb) 1567.

τὴν (acc.sing.fem.of the article in agreement with νέκρωσιν) 9.

νέκρωσιν (acc.sing.fem.of νέκρωσις, direct object of περιφέροντες) 3893.

τοῦ (gen.sing.masc.of the article in agreement with Ἰησοῦ) 9.

Ἰησοῦ (gen.sing.masc.of Ἰησοῦς, description) 3.

ἐν (preposition with the locative of place) 80.

τῷ (loc.sing.neut.of the article in agreement with σώματι) 9.

σώματι (loc.sing.neut.of σῶμα, place) 507.

περιφέροντες (pres.act.part.nom.pl.masc.of περιφέρω, present periphrastic, with εἰσίν understood) 2286.

ἵνα (conjunction with the subjunctive in a final clause) 114.

καὶ (adjunctive conjunction joining nouns) 14.

ἡ (nom.sing.fem.of the article in agreement with ζωὴ) 9.

ζωὴ (nom.sing.fem.of ζωή, subject of φανερωθῇ) 668.

τοῦ (gen.sing.masc.of the article in agreement with Ἰησοῦ) 9.

Ἰησοῦ (gen.sing.masc.of Ἰησοῦς, description) 3.

ἐν (preposition with the locative of place) 80.

τῷ (loc.sing.neut.of the article in agreement with σώματι) 9.

σώματι (loc.sing.neut.of σῶμα, place) 507.

ἡμῶν (gen.pl.masc.of ἐγώ, possession) 123.

φανερωθῇ (3d.per.sing.1st.aor.pass.subj.of φανερόω, purpose) 1960.

Translation - "Always in my body carrying around the evidence of Jesus' death in order that the evidence of the life of Jesus also may be displayed."

Comment: The literal translation is "Always carrying around the dying of Jesus . . . the life of Jesus." Does Paul mean the scar tissue in his body which bore testimony that just as the world hated and murdered Jesus so they also tried to murder Paul? (John 15:18). The scars of a follower of Christ, if they result from his faithful witness, are evidence that the world hates Christ. But the fact that, despite his scars, Paul was still alive is evidence that just as Christ lives, even though He died on a cross, so permanent death can never be the lot of one of His followers. The Goodspeed translation suggests that Paul carried in his body, not the evidence that Jesus had died, as we suggest, but the possibility that Paul too would be martyred. "never free from the danger of being put to death like Jesus, so that in my body the life of Jesus also may be seen." Verse 11 seems supportive of Goodspeed's interpretation, though neither his nor mine can be derived from a strictly literal rendering of the grammar and syntax of verse 10.

It is often the case that when Paul gets emotional he tends to omit the verb. Note the nine cases of the present periphrastic in verses 8-10, and the omission of εἰσίν in each case. These constructions are decidedly durative. The fact that they are plural may be editorial or Paul may be including those who travelled and witnessed with him.

Verse 11 - "For we which live are alway delivered unto death for Jesus' sake, that the life also of Jesus might be made manifest in our mortal flesh."

ἀεὶ γὰρ ἡμεῖς οἱ ζῶντες εἰς θάνατον παραδιδόμεθα διὰ Ἰησοῦν, ἵνα καὶ ἡ ζωὴ τοῦ Ἰησοῦ φανερωθῇ ἐν τῇ θνητῇ σαρκὶ ἡμῶν.

"For while we live we are always being given up for death for Jesus' sake, so that the life of Jesus may be manifested in our mortal flesh." . . . *RSV*

ἀεὶ (temporal adverb) 3149.

γὰρ (causal conjunction) 105.

ἡμεῖς (nom.pl.masc.of ἐγώ, subject of παραδιδόμεθα) 123.

οἱ (nom.pl.masc.of the article in agreement with ζῶντες) 9.

ζῶντες (pres.act.part.nom.pl.masc.of ζάω, substantival, apposition) 340.

εἰς (preposition with the accusative, purpose) 140.

θάνατον (acc.sing.masc.of θάνατος, purpose) 381.

παραδιδόμεθα (1st.per.pl.pres.pass.ind.of παραδίδωμι, present iterative retroactive) 368.

διὰ (preposition with the accusative, cause) 118.

Ἰησοῦν (acc.sing.masc.of Ἰησοῦς, cause) 3.

ἵνα (conjunction with the subjunctive in a purpose clause) 114.

καὶ (adjunctive conjunction joining nouns) 14.

ἡ (nom.sing.fem.of the article in agreement with ζωή) 9.

ζωή (nom.sing.fem.of ζωή, subject of φανερωθῇ) 668.

τοῦ (gen.sing.masc.of the article in agreement with Ἰησοῦ) 9.

Ἰησοῦ (gen.sing.masc.of Ἰησοῦς, description) 3.

φανερωθῇ (3d.per.sing.1st.aor.pass.subj.of φανερόω, purpose) 1960.

ἐν (preposition with the locative of place) 80.

τῇ (loc.sing.fem.of the article in agreement with σαρκὶ) 9.

θνητῇ (loc.sing.fem.of θνητός, in agreement with σαρκὶ) 3914.

σαρκὶ (loc.sing.fem.of σάρξ, place) 1202.

ἡμῶν (gen.pl.masc.of ἐγώ, possession) 123.

Translation - *"Because we, the living, are always being betrayed unto death because of Jesus, in order also that the life of Jesus might be displayed in our mortal flesh."*

Comment: This is essentially what he said in verse 10. There he said that his body bore evidence of his having been attacked in the past. Now he adds that this is the usual thing. The child of God may be betrayed to death at any time. Why? Because of his organic connection (John 15:18; 17:21) with Jesus and hence with the Godhead. This is the force of διὰ Ἰησοῦν - "because of Jesus."

God has a purpose in the fact that the life of the Christian is so precarious. The ἵνα clause is essentially the same as in verse 10, except that Paul describes his flesh as mortal, *i.e.* subject to death. If Christians do not die in the flesh they can never demonstrate that they will also live in the flesh. The exceptions to this rule, of course, are those who, like Enoch and Elijah, will go to heaven without dying (1 Thess.4:17).

Verse 12 - "So then death worketh in us, but life in you."

ὥστε ὁ θάνατος ἐν ἡμῖν ἐνεργεῖται, ἡ δὲ ζωὴ ἐν ὑμῖν.

"So death is at work in us, but life in you." . . . RSV

ὥστε (conjunction with the indicative, actual result) 752.

ὁ (nom.sing.masc.of the article in agreement with θάνατος) 9.

θάνατος (nom.sing.masc.of θάνατος, subject of ἐνεργεῖται) 381.

ἐν (preposition with the locative of place) 80.

ἡμῖν (loc.pl.masc.of ἐγώ, place) 123.

ἐνεργεῖται (3d.per.sing.pres.mid.ind.of ἐνγεργέω, aoristic) 1105.

ἡ (nom.sing.fem.of the article in agreement with ζωή) 9.

δὲ (adversative conjunction) 11.

ζωὴ (nom.sing.fem.of ζωή, subject of ἐνεργεῖται) 668.

ἐν (preposition with the locative of place) 80.

ὑμῖν (loc.pl.masc.of σύ, place) 104.

Translation - *"The result is that death works its way in us but life in you."*

Comment: ὥστε with the indicative in a result clause is rare in the New Testament. "With the infinitive ὥστε expresses conceived or intended result, but with the indicative (only two occurrences in the New Testament) it expresses actual result. But actual result may also be expressed by the infinitive with ὥστε (Mt.8:24; 12:22; Lk.5:7).(Mantey, *Manual*, 286). If Mantey's count is correct the two occurrences where ὥστε and the indicative mode expressed actual result are John 3:16 and 2 Cor.4:12.

Paul was willing to go about preaching the gospel of Christ and thus making himself constantly liable to a violent death for Jesus' sake, because his gospel brought eternal life to those to whom he preached and who accepted Christ. The physical death principle is contrasted with the spiritual life principle. It is worth a thousand physical deaths if that is the only way that one spiritual life can be assured.

Verse 13 - "We having the same spirit of faith, according as it is written, I believed, and therefore have I spoken; we also believe, and therefore speak."

ἔχοντες δὲ τὸ αὐτὸ πνεῦμα τῆς πίστεως, κατὰ τὸ γεγραμμένον,Ἐπίστευσα, διὸ ἐλάησα, καὶ ἡμεῖς πιστεύομεν, διὸ καὶ λαλοῦμεν,

"Since we have the same spirit of faith as he had who wrote, 'I believed, and so I spoke,' we too believe, and so we speak," . . . RSV

ἔχοντες (pres.act.part.nom.pl.masc.of ἔχω, adverbial, causal) 82.
δὲ (inferential conjunction) 11.
τὸ (acc.sing.neut.of the article in agreement with πνεῦμα) 9.
αὐτὸ (acc.sing.neut.of αὐτός, intensive, in agreement with πνεῦμα) 16.
πνεῦμα (acc.sing.neut.of πνεῦμα, direct object of ἔχοντες) 83.
τῆς (gen.sing.fem.of the article in agreement with πίστεως) 9.
πίστεως (gen.sing.fem.of πίστις, description) 728.
κατὰ (preposition with the accusative, standard) 98.
τὸ (acc.sing.neut.of the article in agreement with γεγραμμένον) 9.
γεγραμμένον (perf.pass.part.acc.sing.neut.of γράφω, substantival, standard) 156.
Ἐπίστευσα (1st.per.sing.aor.act.ind.of πιστεύω, constative) 734.
διὸ (inferential conjunction) 1622.
ἐλάλησα (1st.per.sing.aor.act.ind.of λαλέω, constative) 815.
καὶ (adjunctive conjunction joining pronouns) 14.
ἡμεῖς (nom.pl.masc.of ἐγώ, subject of πιστεύομεν and λαλοῦμεν) 123.
πιστεύομεν (1st.per.pl.pres.act.ind.of πιστεύω, aoristic) 734.
διὸ (inferential conjunction) 1622.
καὶ (adjunctive conjunction joining verbs) 14.
λαλοῦμεν (1st.per.pl.pres.act.ind.of λαλέω, aoristic) 815.

Translation - ". . . because we have the same Spirit of faith, according to that which stands written, 'I believed so I spake.' We also believe so we are speaking."

Comment: The participle ἔχοντες is causal. It explains the principle of verse 12. It was because Paul had the same Spirit of faith, as did David (Psalm 116:10), that his life, characterized as a living death, nevertheless generated life in his converts. It is possible to construe ἔχοντες as joined to πιστεύομεν which translates, "Because we have the same Spirit of faith . . . we believe. . . κ.τ.λ." But that is obvious. Paul was not given to tautology. How else does anyone believe except by faith?!. Thus ἔχοντες is joined not to πιστεύομεν, but to the material in verse 12. The Christian who has the spirit that stems from faith cannot believe something without telling about it. Psalm 116 is the testimony of David after he had been delivered from many trials. *Cf.* Psalm 116:1-9. Paul too believed the gospel that he preached and he could not resist speaking about it, even though to do so invited persecution and possible death.

He was further emboldened to speak because of his faith in the resurrection of Jesus and of all the saints. This he adds in

Verse 14 - "Knowing that he which raised up the Lord Jesus shall raise up us also by Jesus, and shall present us with you."

εἰδότες ὅτι ὁ ἐγείρας τὸν κύριον Ἰησοῦν καὶ ἡμᾶς σὺν Ἰησοῦ ἐγερεῖ καὶ παραστήσει σὺν ὑμῖν.

"knowing that he who raised the Lord Jesus will raise us also with Jesus and bring us with you into his presence." . . . RSV

εἰδότες (perf.part.nom.pl.masc.of ὁράω, adverbial, causal) 144b.
ὅτι (conjunction introducing an object clause in indirect discourse) 211.
ὁ (nom.sing.masc.of the article in agreement with ἐγείρας) 9.
ἐγείρας (aor.act.part.nom.sing.masc.of ἐγείρω, substantival, subject of ἐγερεῖ) 125.
τὸν (acc.sing.masc.of the article in agreement with κύριον) 9.
κύριον (acc.sing.masc.of κύριος, direct object of ἐγείρας) 97.
Ἰησοῦν (acc.sing.masc.of Ἰησοῦς, apposition) 3.
καὶ (adjunctive conjunction joining substantives) 14.
ἡμᾶς (acc.pl.masc.of ἐγώ, direct object of ἐγερεῖ) 123.
σὺν (preposition with the instrumental of accompaniment) 1542.
Ἰησοῦ (instru.sing.masc.of Ἰησοῦς, accompaniment) 3.
ἐγερεῖ (3d.per.sing.fut.act.ind.of ἐγείρω, predictive) 125.
καὶ (continuative conjunction) 14.
παραστήσει (3d.per.sing.fut.act.ind.of παρίστημι, predictive) 1596.
σὺν (preposition with the instrumental of accompaniment) 1542.
ὑμῖν (instru.pl.masc.of σύ, accompaniment) 104.

Translation - "Because we know that the One Who raised up the Lord Jesus also will raise up us with Jesus and He will stand by your side."

Comment: Just as ἔχοντες was causal in verse 13 explaining verse 12, so εἰδότες is causal here, explaining why Paul could not forbear speaking. He was possessed with a supernatural message, a heavenly treasure in an earthen vessel. This message can transform lives. Paul certainly had plenty of evidence for that in the lives of his converts as well as in his own experience. He also believed that his God was a God of resurrection. ὅτι introduces indirect discourse. The participial substantive ὁ ἐγείρας refers to God. He raised up the Lord Jesus. He will also raise up Paul and all the members of His Body at the resurrection/rapture and He will stand by our side. Note the similarity between παραστήσει (#1596) and παρουσία (#1482).   The result of παραστήσει, the verb, is the fact of παρουσία, the noun.   To "stand by one's side" is to "be present at one's side." Our Lord will "stand in that day upon the Mount of Olives" (Zechariah 14:4) and we will stand with Him. Such assurance is sufficient to motivate a preacher to speak, despite the odds against him.

Note that the resurrection of the believer is made contingent upon the resurrection of Jesus, for it is the same God Who raised Jesus from the dead Who will also raise us up.

Variant readings such as τὸν Ἰησοῦν, τὸν κύριον ἡμῶν Ἰησοῦν, τὸν κύριον Ἰησοῦν Χριστόν and τὸν κύριον Ἰησοῦ ἐκ νέκρων are obviously "scribal expansions." (Metzger, *Ibid.*, 579). This "scribal expansion" is a good example of the fact that the copyists knew little or nothing of hermeneutics. Otherwise they would not have felt it necessary to expand the original text. The exegete with normal skill in hermeneutics knows from the context that Jesus is Lord (κύριος), that He is ours (ἡμῶν), that Jesus is the Christ (Χριστός) and that to be raised is to be raised from the dead (ἐκ νεκρῶν). The exegete of the modern world need feel no distress because of variations in the text, as textual criticism has developed to become a very exact science, and there is no doubt that for purposes of interpretation we have a text which reveals to us all that the Holy Spirit wishes us to know at this time. Otherwise His revelation in the Greek New Testament is faulty and cannot stand as the basis for Christian theology. Nothing that the Holy Spirit wishes us to know is clouded by textual variations, once the student remembers 2 Peter 1:20, 2 Timothy 2:15 and other guides to proper hermeneutics.

Verse 15 - "For all things are for your sakes, that the abundant grace might through the thanksgiving of many redound to the glory of God."

τὰ γὰρ πάντα δι' ὑμᾶς, ἵνα ἡ χάρις πλεονάσασα διὰ τῶν πλειόνων τὴν εὐχαριστίαν περισσεύσῃ εἰς τὴν δόξαν τοῦ θεοῦ.

"For it is all for your sake, so that as grace extends to more and more people it may increase thanksgiving, to the glory of God." . . . RSV

τὰ (nom.pl.neut.of the article in agreement with πάντα) 9.
γὰρ (causal conjunction) 105.
πάντα (nom.pl.neut.of πᾶς, subject of ἐστιν understood) 67.
δι' (preposition with the accusative, cause) 118.
ὑμᾶς (acc.pl.masc.of σύ, cause) 104.
ἵνα (conjunction with the subjunctive in a sub-final clause) 114.
ἡ (nom.sing.fem.of the article in agreement with χάρις) 9.
χάρις (nom.sing.fem.of χάρις, subject of περισσεύσῃ) 1700.
πλεονάσασα (aor.act.part.nom.sing.fem.of πλεονάζω, adjectival, predicate position, restrictive, in agreement with χάρις) 3907.
διὰ (preposition with the accusative, cause) 118.

τῶν (gen.pl.masc.of the article in agreement with πλειόνων) 9.

πλειόνων (gen.pl.masc.of πλείων, description) 474.

τὴν (acc.sing.fem.of the article in agreement with εὐχαριστίαν) 9.

εὐχαριστίαν (acc.sing.fem.of εὐχαριστία, cause) 3616.

περισσεύσῃ (3d.per.sing.aor.act.subj.of περισσεύω, purpose) 473.

εἰς (preposition with the accusative of purpose) 140.

τὴν (acc.sing.fem.of the article in agreement with δόξαν) 9.

δόξαν (acc.sing.fem.of δόξα, purpose) 361.

τοῦ (gen.sing.masc.of the article in agreement with θεοῦ) 9.

θεοῦ (gen.sing.masc.of θεός, description) 124.

Translation - *"Because everything (is done) for you, in order that the amplified grace which results from the thanksgiving of many, may rise in a crescendo unto the glory of God."*

Comment: The ultimate purpose in Paul's ministry, as it ought to be in the ministry of all of us, is to promote in ever-increasing crescendo, the constant amplification of the chorus of thanksgiving to God that results from an ever increasing number of saved people. The grace is amplified grace (adjectival participle in πλεονάσασα). Why? Because to it is added the thanksgiving of many more saints who continue to be saved under Paul's ministry. The tide of gratitude ever rises to glorify God. *Cf.* Eph.2:7. The ultimate purpose of God in salvation is His own glory. If some suggest that this divine purpose is essentially selfish and therefore unworthy of God, the reply is that were it not for the eternal, uncreated Creator there would be none to suggest that it is wrong for Him to do what He has chosen to do in order to glorify Himself.

Living by Faith

(2 Corinthians 4:16-5:10)

Verse 16 - *"For which cause we faint not; but though our outward man perish, yet the inward man is renewed day by day."*

Διὸ οὐκ ἐγκακοῦμεν, ἀλλ᾽ εἰ καὶ ὁ ἔξω ἡμῶν ἄνθρωπος διαφθείρεται, ἀλλ᾽ ὁ ἔσω ἡμῶιν ἀνακαινοῦται ἡμέρᾳ καὶ ἡμέρᾳ.

"So we do not lose heart. Though our outer nature is wasting away, our inner nature is being renewed every day." . . . *RSV*

Διὸ (inferential conjunction) 1622.

οὐκ (negative particle with the indicative) 130.

ἐγκακοῦμεν (1st.per.pl.pres.act.ind.of ἐγκακέω, present progressive retroactive) 2622.

ἀλλ᾽ (alternative conjunction) 342.

εἰ (conditional particle in a first-class condition) 337.

καὶ (concessive conjunction) 14.

ὁ (nom.sing.masc.of the article in agreement with ἄνθρωπος) 9.

ἔξω (adjectival adverb) 449.

ἡμῶν (gen.pl.masc.of ἐγώ, possession) 123.

ἄνθρωπος (nom.sing.masc.of ἄνθρωπος, subject of διαφθείρεται) 341.

διαφθείρεται (3d.per.sing.pres.pass.ind.of διαφθείρω, present progressive retroactive) 2485.

ἀλλ' (alternative conjunction) 342.

ὁ (nom.sing.masc.of the article in agreement with ἄνθρωπος, understood) 9.

ἔσω (adjectival adverb) 1601.

ἡμῶν (gen.pl.masc.of ἐγώ, possession) 123.

#4302 ἀνακαινοῦται (3d.per.sing.pres.pass.ind.of ἀνακαινόω, present progressive iterative).

King James Version

renew - 2 Cor.4:16; Col.3:10.

Revised Standard Version

renew - 2 Cor.4:16; Col.3:10.

Meaning: A combination of ἀνά (#1059) and καινός (#812). *Cf.* καινότης (#3910). To make new; to cause to grow. *Cf.* ἀνακαίνωσις (#4013). To rejuvenate. With reference to the spiritual nature, the product of regeneration, - the inner man - 2 Cor.4:16; Col.3:10.

ἡμέρᾳ (loc.sing.fem.of ἡμέρα, time point) 135.

καὶ (adjunctive conjunction joining nouns) 14.

ἡμέρᾳ (loc.sing.fem.of ἡμέρα, time point) 135.

Translation - "*Therefore we have not become discouraged, but though it is true that our physical body has been disintegrating, our inner nature is being made new again and again, day after day.*"

Comment: The translation reflects the retroactive force of the present progressive of ἐγκακοῦμεν and διαφθείρεται and the iterative force of the present progressive in ἀνακαινοῦται. Paul had never lost heart (ἐγκακοῦμεν).It is true of course that with the onset of senility the physical body continues in the process of disintegration. But, though Paul's inner nature, the result of his birth from above (John 3:3,7) was not continuously being renewed, it was being renewed on an iterative basis. The Christian who has learned how to live the victorious life must pray often (in some cases every five minutes) for the refilling of the Holy Spirit, and this experience of dying to the flesh daily (1 Cor.15:31) is a day by day experience. If it were progressive, rather than iterative, the Christian would be without sin at all times. This contradicts 1 John 1:8.

In 2 Cor.4:1 Paul cited the supernatural results of his ministry (2 Cor.3:18) as his reason for high morale. Now he adds that the resurrection hope (verse 14) and the expanding acceptance of his gospel (verse 15) maintains his courage. And this, despite the fact that (concessive καὶ and εἰ in a first-class condition) his physical body was being debilitated under the sledgehammer blows of physical demands made upon him in the ministry. Lack of food and medicine, hazardous travel conditions, not to mention personal danger from persecution and possibile assassination, had taken their toll upon him physically. However his spiritual nature - that new creation which was his in the new birth (2 Cor.5 17) - was as young as ever because it was periodically renewed by the filling of the Holy Spirit day after day.

Note the adverbs ἔξω and ἔσω used like adjectives. Also note the interesting use of the locative of time point in ἡμέρᾳ καὶ ἡμέρᾳ - "on this day and on this day and . . . on this day." The old nature is subject to the law of sin and death (Rom.7:5; 8:7) but the new nature, the inner man, is oriented around the eternal and heavenly point of view. Hence its daily rejuvenation (Lamentations 3:22,23). This is the thought of verses 17 and 18.

Verse 17 - "For our light affliction, which is but for a moment, worketh for us a far more exceeding and eternal weight of glory."

τὸ γὰρ παραυτίκα ἐλαφρὸν τῆς θλίψεως ἡμῶν καθ' ὑπερβολὴν εἰς ὑπερβολὴν αἰώνιον βάρος δόξης κατεργάζεται ἡμῖν.

"For this slight momentary affliction is preparing for us an eternal weight of glory beyond all comparison,. . ." . . . RSV

τὸ (nom.sing.neut.of the article in agreement with ἐλαφρὸν) 9.
γὰρ (causal conjunction) 105.

#4303 παραυτίκα (temporal adverb).

King James Version

but for a moment - 2 Cor.4:17.

Revised Standard Version

momentary - 2 Cor.4:17.

Meaning: A combination of παρά (#154) and αὐτίκα - "forthwith, at once, in a moment." Hence, momentary, temporary. With reference to Paul's afflictions - 2 Cor.4:17.

ἐλαφρὸν (nom.sing.neut.of ἐλαφρός, subject of κατεργάζεται) 961.
τῆς (gen.sing.fem.of the article in agreement with θλίψεως) 9.
θλίψεως (gen.sing.fem.of θλῖψις, description) 1046.
ἡμῶν (gen.pl.masc.of ἐγώ, description) 123.
καθ' (preposition with the accusative of measure) 98.
ὑπερβολὴν (acc.sing.fem.of ὑπερβολή, measure) 3923.
εἰς (preposition with the accusative of extent) 140.
ὑπερβολὴν (acc.sing.fem.of ὑπερβολή, extent) 3923.
αἰώνιον (acc.sing.nom.of αἰώνιος, in agreement with βάρος) 1255.

βάρος (acc.sing.neut.of βάρος, direct object of κατεργάζεται) 1324.

δόξης (gen.sing.fem.of δόξα, description) 361.

κατεργάζεται (3d.per.sing.pres.mid.ind.of κατεργάζομαι, present progressive) 3815.

ἡμῖν (dat.pl.masc.of ἐγώ, personal advantage) 123.

Translation - "Because this temporary insignificant bit of pressure is generating for us an incomparable and eternal burden of glory."

Comment: Three contrasts make Paul's point. θλῖφις is opposed to δόξα. The affliction (pressure, burden, trial) is light. The glory is a weight (βάρος - oppression). The light affliction is temporary (παραυτίκα). The weight of glory is eternal (εἰς ὑπερβολὴν αἰώνιον). Thus, an insignificant burden, which, comparatively speaking, is only for a short time, is contrasted with a glory that will go on forever and will be of such great magnitude (as contrasted with the trifle of the burden) that Paul describes it as a *weight*. The temporary trial generates the eternal reward (Rom.8:18). Thank God, therefore for the trial (James 1:2; Mt.5:11,12; Rom.5:3-5).

A realization of the fact that trouble now generates reward later is enough to change the Christian's attitude toward present trial, and thus renew the inner man every day. Why does Paul view the matter as he does? Because of the causal participle in

Verse 18 - "While we look not at the things which are seen, but at the things which are not seen: for the things which are seen are temporal; but the things which are not seen are eternal."

μὴ σκοπούντων ἡμῶν τὰ βλεπόμενα ἀλλὰ τὰ μὴ βλεπόμενα. τὰ γὰρ βλεπόμενα πρόσκαιρα, τὰ δὲ μὴ βλεπόμενα αἰώνια.

"because we look not to the things that are seen but to the things that are unseen; for the things that are seen are transient, but the things that are unseen are eternal." . . . RSV

μὴ (negative conjunction with the participle) 87.

σκοπούντων (pres.act.part.gen.pl.masc.of σκοπέω, adverbial, causal, genitive absolute) 2460.

ἡμῶν (gen.pl.masc.of ἐγώ, genitive absolute) 123.

τὰ (acc.pl.neut.of the article in agreement with βλεπόμενα) 9.

βλεπόμενα (pres.pass.part.acc.pl.neut.of βλέπω, substantival, direct object of σκοπούντων) 499.

ἀλλὰ (alternative conjunction) 342.

τὰ (acc.pl.neut.of the article in agreement with βλεπόμενα) 9.

μὴ (negative conjunction with the participle) 87.

βλεπόμενα (pres.pass.part.acc.pl.neut.of βλέπω, substantival, direct object of σκοπούντων) 499.

τὰ (nom.pl.neut.of the article in agreement with βλεπόμενα) 9.

γὰρ (causal conjunction) 105.

βλεπόμενα (pres.pass.part.nom.pl.neut.of βλέπω, substantival, subject of εἰσίν) 499.

πρόσκαιρα (nom.pl.neut.of πρόσκαιρος, predicate adjective) 1045.

τὰ (nom.pl.neut.of the article in agreement with βλεπόμενα) 9.

δὲ (adversative conjunction) 11.

μὴ (negative conjunction with the participle) 87.

βλεπόμενα (pres.pass.part.nom.pl.neut.of βλέπω, substantival, subject of εἰσίν understood) 499.

αἰώνια (nom.pl.neut.of αἰών, predicate adjective) 1255.

Translation - *"Because we are not evaluating the visible things, but the invisible; for the visible is temporary but the invisible is eternal."*

Comment: The genitive absolute is causal. Paul was taking the long look. He was looking not at temporary shadows on the wall but eternal realities outside the cave. (Plato, *The Allegory of the Cave,"* The Republic, VII, 514-519). *Cf.*#2460 for meaning - not physical sight, but intellectual contemplation. The empiricist cannot look at the unseen; therefore he is enslaved by the temporary agony, which for him, is all there is. Faith (only the Christian has it) ignores the temporary and visible and bases his philosophy upon the eternal, which, though some day to be visible, is not now in physical view. Thus the Christian is able to escape environmental determinism with its Stoic despair.

Some would have us believe that faith which sees the invisible is not the ground for certitude. And so it is not, when viewed from the empirical viewpoint. But for the Christian "faith is knowledge, and a higher sort of knowledge." (A.H.Strong, *Systematic Theology*, I, 3). It is "certitude with respect to matters in which verification is unattainable." (*Ibid.*). "Tennyson was wrong when he wrote, 'We have but faith; we cannot know: For knowledge is of things we see." . . . "Faith in supersensible realities on the contrary is the highest exercise of reason." (*Ibid.*). Paul had faith, but he had no physical look at the future. But he knew! See the first word in Chapter 5.

2 Cor.5:1 - *"For we know that if our earthly house of this tabernacle were dissolved, we have a building of God, an house not made with hands, eternal in the heavens."*

Οἴδαμεν γὰρ ὅτι ἐὰν ἡ ἐπίγειος ἡμῶν οἰκία τοῦ σκήνους καταλυθῇ, οἰκοδομὴν ἐκ θεοῦ ἔχομεν οἰκίαν ἀχειροποίητον αἰώνιον ἐν τοῖς οὐρανοῖς.

"For we know that if the earthly tent we live in is destroyed, we have a building from God, a house not made with hands, eternal in the heavens." . . . RSV

Οἴδαμεν (1st.per.pl.perf.ind.of ὁράω, intensive) 144b.

γὰρ (causal conjunction) 105.

ὅτι (conjunction introducing an object clause in indirect discourse) 211.

ἐὰν (conditional particle with the subjunctive in a third-class condition) 363.

ἡ (nom.sing.fem.of the article in agreement with οἰκία) 9.

ἐπίγειος (nom.sing.fem.of ἐπίγειος, in agreement with οἰκία) 1988.

ἡμῶν (gen.pl.masc.of ἐγώ, possession) 123.
οἰκία (nom.sing.fem.of οἰκία, subject of καταλυθῇ) 186.
τοῦ (gen.sing.masc.of the article in agreement with σκήνους) 9.

#4304 σκήνους (gen.sing.masc.of σκῆνος, description).

King James Version

tabernacle - 2 Cor.5:1,4.

Revised Standard Version

tent - 2 Cor.5:1,4.

Meaning: Cf. σκηνή (#1224), σκήνωμα (#3145), σκηνόω (#1698), σκηνοπηγία (#2357) and σκηνοποιός (#3436). A temporary dwelling place; tabernacle; tent. Metaphorically with reference to the human body in which the soul and spirit of the Christian lives before the resurrection - 2 Cor.5:1,4.

καταλυθῇ (3d.per.sing.aor.pass.subj.of καταλύω, third-class condition) 463.
οἰκοδομὴν (acc.sing.fem.of οἰκοδομή, direct object of ἔχομεν) 1481.
ἐκ (preposition with the ablative of source) 19.
θεοῦ (abl.sing.masc.of θεός, source) 124.
ἔχομεν (1st.per.pl.pres.act.ind.of ἔχω, futuristic) 82.
οἰκίαν (acc.sing.fem.of οἰκία, in apposition to οἰκοδομὴν) 186.
ἀχειροποίητον (acc.sing.fem.of ἀχειροποίητος, in agreement with οἰκίαν) 2810.
αἰώνιον (acc.sing.fem.of αἰώνιος, in agreement with οἰκίαν) 1255.
ἐν (preposition with the locative of place) 80.
τοῖς (loc.pl.masc.of the article in agreement with οὐρανοῖς) 9.
οὐρανοῖς (loc.pl.masc.of οὐρανός, place where) 254.

Translation - "Because we know that if our earthly house, which is temporary be destroyed, we have a house of divine construction, a house not made with hands, eternal in the heavens."

Comment: γάρ is causal. Paul's contemplation of the eternal, invisible things (2 Cor.4:18) was based upon what he knew by faith. οἴδαμεν, an intensive perfect tense indicates present knowledge (at the time of writing) resulting from a past learning experience. The regeneration experience teaches the Christian much that is ever present knowledge from that point on, upon which to base a Christian philosophy. The world, of course, with its anti-faith, radical empirical philosophy, attacks what the Christian "knows" (the empiricist's quotation marks, not ours) but what we *know* (my emphasis) is the basis for a victorious philosophy of life. Only the Christian who *knows* what the empircists cannot know can be optimistic in this world of wrath and tears. The unregenerate who is optimistic is an intellectual light-weight.

The doubt involved in the third-class condition refers not to the fact that the physical body, prior to glorification, will be destroyed, but to the time when it will be destroyed at death.

Note that the resurrection dwelling place is also a body. οἰκία (#186) is used for our body, both before and after resurrection. The difference is that the former is ἐπίγειος and the latter is ἀχειροποίητος - "not made with hands." The first will be destroyed (καταλύω); the second is eternal and heavenly. *Cf.* 1 Cor.15:42-44. Any attempt to show that the eternal bodies of Christians, because they are *spiritual*, are not *bodies* falls before this passage. Now we have a house (οἰκία) which is a body. Then we will have a house (οἰκία) which is also a body.

The Christian is not happy with his present house, as we learn in

Verse 2 - "For in this we groan, earnestly desiring to be   clothed upon with our house which is from heaven."

καὶ γὰρ ἐν τούτῳ στενάζομεν, τὸ οἰκητήριον ἡμῶν τὸ ἐξ οὐρανοῦ ἐπενδύσασθαι ἐπιποθοῦντες,

"Here indeed we groan, and long to put on our heavenly dwelling, . . . RSV

καὶ (emphatic conjunction) 14.

γὰρ (causal conjunction) 105.

ἐν (preposition with the locative of place) 80.

τούτῳ (loc.sing.neut.of οὗτος, place where) 93.

στενάζομεν (1st.per.pl.pres.act.ind.of στενάζω, present iterative retroactive) 2310.

τὸ (acc.sing.neut.of the article in agreement with οἰκητήριον) 9.

#**4305** οἰκητήριον (acc.sing.neut.of οἰκητήριον, general reference).

King James Version

habitation - Jude 6.
house - 2 Cor.5:2.

Revised Standard Version

dwelling - 2 Cor.5:2; Jude 6.

Meaning: Cf. οἰκητήρ - "dwelling place; habitation." Metaphorically of the resurrection body of the Christian - 2 Cor.5:2. With reference to the proper place of habitation assigned to fallen angels - Jude 6.

ἡμῶν (gen.pl.masc.of ἐγώ, possession) 123.

τὸ (acc.sing.neut.of the article in agreement with οἰκητήριον) 9.

ἐξ (preposition with the ablative of source) 19.

οὐρανοῦ (abl.sing.masc.of οὐρανός, source) 254.

#**4306** ἐπενδύσασθαι (aor.pass.inf.of ἐπενδύομαι, noun use, direct object of ἐπιποθοῦντες) .

King James Version

be clothed upon - 2 Cor.5:2,4.

Revised Standard Version

put upon - 2 Cor.5:2.
clothed - 2 Cor.5:4.

Meaning: A combination of ἐπί (#47), ἐν (#80) and δύω - "to put on, get into, dress." Hence, to dress; in the passive, to be clothed. With reference to the Christian's desire to be "dressed" in his resurrection body - 2 Cor.5:2,4.

ἐπιποθοῦντες (pres.act.part.nom.pl.masc.of ἐπιποθέω, adverbial, causal) 3789.

Translation - "Because in fact in this house we are sighing, because we are greatly longing to be clothed with our house from heaven."

Comment: Emphatic καὶ and causal γὰρ, connect this verse with verse 1. The Christian knows that he is destined to spend eternity in a body incomparably superior to that in which he now lives. Because he knows this (γὰρ) he now in fact (καὶ) is dissatisfied. His disaffection with his present body, with its aches, pains and sins (Rom.7:24,25) stems from his anticipation of a better body. Note the infinitive as the direct object of the participle. *Cf.* Romans 8:23 where Paul expresses the same thought. Christians can never be fully satisfied with the status quo in this age. The one who thinks of heaven only in terms of what we are able to enjoy now has no eternal point of view. Paul was not in this category.

Verse 3 - "If so be that being clothed we shall not be found naked."

εἴ γε καὶ ἐνδυσάμενοι οὐ γυμνοὶ εὑρεθησόμεθα.

"... *so that by putting it on we may not be found naked."* ... *RSV*

εἴ (conditional particle in an elliptical second-class condition) 337.
γε (intensive particle) 2449.
καὶ (emphatic conjunction) 14.
ἐνδυσάμενοι (aor.pass.part.nom.pl.masc.of ἐνδύω, adverbial, temporal) 613.
οὐ (negative conjunction with the indicative) 130.
γυμνοὶ (nom.pl.masc.of γυμνός, predicate adjective) 1548.
εὑρεθησόμεθα (1st.per.pl.fut.pass.ind.of εὑρίσκω, predictive) 79.

Translation - "If in fact after we have been clothed we shall not be found naked."

Comment: The contrary-to-fact element is that once we are clothed with our new bodies at the resurrection we shall not be found to be naked. We cannot be certain about the exact nature of the new body (1 John 3:2) but we are certain that it is superior to the old body. We are also certain that it is physical - the same in identity but superior in condition. To lay down the old in exchange for the new is not to leave the soul (the self-conscious) and the spirit (the intellectual) unclothed. He explains further in

"Verse 4 - "For we that are in this tabernacle do groan, being burdened; not for that we would be unclothed, but clothed upon, that mortality might be swallowed up of life."

καὶ γὰρ οἱ ὄντες ἐν τῷ σκήνει στενάζομεν βαρούμενοι, ἐφ' ᾧ οὐ θέλομεν ἐκδύσασθαι ἀλλ' ἐπενδύσασθαι, ἵνα καταποθῇ τὸ θνητὸν ὑπὸ τῆς ζωῆς.

"For while we are still in this tent, we sigh with anxiety; not that we would be unclothed, but that we would be further clothed, so that what is mortal may be swallowed up by life." . . . RSV

καὶ (emphatic conjunction) 14.

γὰρ (causal conjunction) 105.

οἱ (nom.pl.masc.of the article in agreement with ὄντες) 9.

ὄντες (pres.part.nom.pl.masc.of εἰμί, substantival, subject of στενάζομεν) 86.

ἐν (preposition with the locative of place) 80.

τῷ (loc.sing.masc.of the article in agreement with σκήνει) 9.

σκήνει (loc.sing.masc.of σκῆνος, place) 4304.

στενάζομεν (1st.per.pl.pres.act.ind.of στενάζω, present iterative retroactive) 2310.

βαρούμενοι (pres.pass.part.nom.pl.masc.of βαρέομαι, adverbial, causal) 1589.

ἐφ' (preposition with the instrumental of cause) 47.

ᾧ (instru.sing.neut.of ὅς, cause) 65.

οὐ (negative conjunction with the indicative) 130.

θέλομεν (1st.per.pl.pres.act.ind.of θέλω, aoristic) 88.

ἐκδύσασθαι (aor.pass.inf.of ἐκδύω, epexegetical) 1636.

ἀλλ' (alternative conjunction) 342.

ἐπενδύσασθαι (aor.pass.inf.of ἐπενδύομαι, epexegetical) 4306.

ἵνα (conjunction with the subjunctive, purpose) 114.

καταποθῇ (3d.per.sing.aor.pass.subj.of καταπίνω, purpose) 1454.

τὸ (nom.sing.neut.of the article in agreement with θνητὸν) 9.

θνητὸν (nom.sing.neut.of θνητός, subject of καταποθῇ) 3914.

ὑπὸ (preposition with the ablative of agent) 117.

τῆς (abl.sing.fem.of the article in agreement with ζωῆς) 9.

ζωῆς (abl.sing.fem.of ζωή, agent) 668.

Translation - "Because in fact we in this tabernacle continue to sigh because we have been burdened, not because we wish to be unclothed, but we wish to be better dressed, in order that that which is subject to death may be engulfed by life."

Comment: The participle βαρούμενοι is causal. It is because we have been burdened that we have been sighing. Our dissatisfaction is not that we wish to be disembodied spirits, but rather that we want better bodies than what we have now. The present body is mortal. Let death be swallowed up by life (2 Cor.5:4) and victory (1 Cor.15:54). This dissatisfaction with our mortal bodies - this recognition that the spiritual nature of man is superior to the physical and longs to be free from it, was shown in Romans 7:14-25. Note especially verses 14,23-25. Plato's analogy of the black and white horses indicates that Plato felt the same thing. This is also related to the Freudian difference between ἔρος and θάνατος, -the life wish versus the death wish. Why did Paul feel this way? And why do all Christians share this dissatisfaction with the flesh and the longing for a spiritual body? The answer is in

Verse 5 - "Now he that hath wrought us for the selfsame thing is God, who also hath given unto us the earnest of the Spirit."

ὁ δὲ κατεργασάμενος ἡμᾶς εἰς αὐτὸ τοῦτο θεός, ὁ δοὺς ἡμῖν τὸν ἀρραβῶνα τοῦ πνεύματος.

"He who has prepared us for this very thing is God, who has given us the Spirit as a guarantee." . . . *RSV*

ὁ (nom.sing.masc.of the article in agreement with κατεργασάμενος) 9.

δὲ (explanatory conjunction) 11.

κατεργασάμενος (aor.mid.part.nom.sing.masc.of κατεργάζομαι, substantival, subject of ἐστίν understood) 3815.

ἡμᾶς (acc.pl.masc.of ἐγώ, direct object of κατεργασάμενος) 123.

εἰς (preposition with the accusative of purpose) 140.

αὐτὸ (acc.sing.neut.of αὐτός, intensive) 16.

τοῦτο (acc.sing.neut.of οὗτος, purpose) 93.

θεός (nom.sing.masc.of θεός, predicate nominative) 124.

ὁ (nom.sing.masc.of the article in agreement with δοὺς) 9.

δοὺς (aor.act.part.nom.sing.masc.of δίδωμι, substantival, in apposition with θεός) 362.

ἡμῖν (dat.pl.masc.of ἐγώ, indirect object of δοὺς) 123.

τὸν (acc.sing.masc.of the article in agreement with ἀρραβῶνα) 9.

ἀρραβῶνα (acc.sing.masc.of ἀρραβών, direct object of δοὺς) 4271.

τοῦ (gen.sing.neut.of the article in agreement with πνεύματος) 9.

πνεύματος (gen.sing.neut.of πνεῦμα, designation) 83.

Translation - "Now the one who has prepared us for this same thing is God, Who gave to us the Spirit as a guarantee."

Comment: Who has planted this divine dissatisfaction with the earthly and longing for the heavenly in the heart of the Christian? It is God, Who in regeneration gave us the down payment (earnest money) - the assurance that we are destined for better things. *Cf.*2 Cor.1:22; Eph.1:14; Rom.8:11. ὁ δοὺς is in apposition with ὁ θεός. The "down-payment" is the Holy Spirit, Whose fruit in the life of the believer (Gal.5:22-25) explains his sorrowful dissatisfaction with the flesh. As Augustine said, "Thou hast made us for Thyself, and our hearts are restless until they rest in thee." And we may add, "And so are our bodies."

Verse 6 - "Therefore, we are always confident, knowing that, whilst we are at home in the body, we are absent from the Lord."

Θαρροῦντες οὖν πάντοτε καὶ εἰδότες ὅτι ἐνδημοῦντες ἐν τῷ σώματι ἐκδημοῦμεν ἀπὸ τοῦ κυρίου,

"So we are always of good courage; we know that while we are at home in the body we are away from the Lord, . . . " . . . RSV

#4307 Θαρροῦντες (pres.act.part.nom.pl.masc.of θαρρέω, adverbial, circumstantial).

King James Version

be bold - 2 Cor.10:1,2.
be confident - 2 Cor.5:8.
have confidence - 2 Cor.7:16.
boldly - Heb.13:6.
confident - 2 Cor.5:6.

Revised Standard Version

of good courage - 2 Cor.5:6,8.
have confidence - 2 Cor.7:16.
be bold - 2 Cor.10:1.
show boldness - 2 Cor.10:2.
confidently - Heb.13:6.

Meaning: A later form, from Plato on, for the earlier Ionic and Attic θαρσέω - "to be of good courage." To be hopeful; confident. Followed by ὅτι in 2 Cor.5:6; followed by εἰς and the accusative in 2 Cor.10:1; by ἐν and the locative in 2 Cor.7:16; by ἐπί and the accusative in 2 Cor.10:2; absolutely in 2 Cor.5:8; as a modal participle in Heb.13:6.

οὖν (inferential conjunction) 68.
πάντοτε (temporal adverb) 1567.
καὶ (continuative conjunction) 14.
εἰδότες (aor.act.part.nom.pl.masc.of ὁράω, adverbial, causal) 144b.
ὅτι (conjunction introducing an object clause in indirect discourse) 211.

#4308 ἐνδημοῦντες (pres.act.part.nom.pl.masc.of ἐνδημέω, adverbial, temporal).

King James Version

be at home - 2 Cor.5:6.
be present - 2 Cor.5:8.
present - 2 Cor.5:9.

Revised Standard Version

be at home - 2 Cor.5:6,8,9.

Meaning: A combination of ἐν (#80) and δῆμος (#3264). Hence among his own people; at home; present. Followed by ἐν τῷ σώματι in 2 Cor.5:6; followed by πρὸς τὸν κύριον in 2 Cor.5:8. Absolutely and opposed to ἐκδημοῦντες in 2 Cor.5:9.

ἐν (preposition with the locative of place) 80.
τῷ (loc.sing.neut.of the article in agreement with σώματι) 9.
σώματι (loc.sing.neut.of σῶμα, place) 507.

#4309 ἐκδημοῦμεν (1st.per.pl.pres.act.ind.of ἐκδημέω, aoristic).

King James Version

be absent - 2 Cor.5:6,8.
absent - 2 Cor.5:9.

Revised Standard Version

away - 2 Cor.5:6,8,9.

Meaning: A combination of ἐκ (#19) and δῆμος (#3264). Hence away from the people; absent. Opposed to ἐνδημέω (#4308). Followed by ἀπὸ τοῦ κυρίου in 2 Cor.5:6; by ἐκ τοῦ σώματος in 2 Cor.5:8. Absolutely, opposed to ἐνδημοῦντες in 2 Cor.5:9.

ἀπὸ (preposition with the ablative of separation) 70.
τοῦ (abl.sing.masc.of the article in agreement with κυρίου) 9.
κυρίου (abl.sing.masc.of κύριος, separation) 97.

Translation - "Therefore being always confident because we know that when we are present in the body we are absent from the Lord."

Comment: Paul's confidence is based upon what he knows. Note that his faith is equated with knowledge, not with speculation. The ὅτι clause is indirect discourse. Paul does not mean that he has no fellowship with the Lord during the time that he is still in the body. The Holy Spirit indwells the body of the believer (1 Cor.6:19) and bears His own witness with ours (Rom.8:16). Paul is speaking here of the body, not the new nature which was his with his new birth.

If Paul was to exercise the ministry of the gospel which was committed to him, with its ability to generate supernatural results in the lives of the saints, he was forced to endure the pains of bodily existence on this earth. From a selfish point of view he preferred not to remain in the flesh (Phil.1:22-26), but he realized that his ministry on earth was needed. The point here is that Paul was certain of his alternatives. He could remain upon the earth in a disintegrating body of sinful and pain-ridden flesh or be in the presence of the Lord, temporarily disembodied and thus set free from the body, but, after the resurrection, rejoined to his body, now glorified, to live eternally in a perfect body. The third alterantive, *viz.*

oblivion, Paul did not for one minute consider.

If the question is asked, "How can Paul be sure that the alternative to life on earth is life in heaven?" the answer is in the parenthesis of

Verse 7 - ("For we walk by faith, not by sight.")

διὰ πίστεως γὰρ περιπατοῦμεν οὐ διὰ εἴδους —

"for we walk by faith, not by sight." . . . RSV

διὰ (preposition with the ablative of means) 118.
πίστεως (abl.sing.fem.of πίστις, means) 728.
γὰρ (causal conjunction) 105.
περιπατοῦμεν (1st.per.pl.pres.act.ind.of περιπατέω, aoristic) 384.
οὐ (negative conjunction with the indicative) 130.
διὰ (preposition with the ablative of means) 118.
εἴδους (abl.sing.neut.of εἶδος, means) 1950.

Translation - "Because we walk by faith, not by sight."

Comment: Paul here rejects the empirical world as a guide to ethical policy. His life style was based, not upon what he saw, which would have made him a pessimist, but upon what he believed by faith. This exercise of faith was by divine enabling. He repeats the thought of verse 6 in

Verse 8 - "We are confident, I say, and willing rather to be absent from the body, and to be present with the Lord."

θαρροῦμεν δὲ καὶ εὐδοκοῦμεν μᾶλλον ἐκδημῆσαι ἐκ τοῦ σώματος καὶ ἐνδημῆσαι πρὸς τὸν κύριον.

"We are of good courage, and we would rather be away from the body and at home with the Lord." . . . RSV

θαρροῦμεν (1st.per.pl.pres.act.ind.of θαρρέω, aoristic) 4307.
δὲ (explanatory conjunction) 11.
καὶ (continuative conjunction) 14.
εὐδοκοῦμεν (1st.per.pl.pres.act.ind.of εὐδοκέω, aoristic) 328.
μᾶλλον (adverbial) 619.
ἐκδημῆσαι (aor.act.inf.of ἐκδημέω, epexegetical) 4309.
ἐκ (preposition with the ablative of separation) 19.
τοῦ (abl.sing.neut.of the article in agreement with σώματος) 9.
σώματος (abl.sing.neut.of σῶμα, separation) 507.
καὶ (adjunctive conjunction joining infinitives) 14.
ἐνδημῆσαι (aor.act.inf.of ἐνδημέω, epexegetical) 4308.
πρὸς (preposition with the accusative of extent) 197.
τὸν (acc.sing.masc.of the article in agreement with κύριον) 9.
κύριον (acc.sing.masc.of κύριος, extent) 97.

Translation - "And yet in fact I am confident and would rather be absent from the body and at home with the Lord."

Comment: ϑαρροῦντες is an anacoluthon. Paul leaves the sentence hanging in mid air and then, after the parenthesis of verse 7 he starts over, this time with the indicative ϑαρροῦμεν rather than the participle. The infinitives are epexegetical. Paul is not only confident that he will have a better body in eternity than he has upon earth (verse 5) but he ventures his own personal preference. Better to be dead and free from his Adamic body (Rom.7:25) and present with the Lord, even though in the interim - until the resurrection/rapture - his soul and spirit are without a body. The heresy known as soul sleeping falls before this verse. If in the interim period between physical death and bodily resurrection of the Christian, the soul and spirit (emotional and intellectual functions) are unconscious this passage about desiring the one above the other makes no sense. Paul wishes to be out of the body because when he escapes his "body of death" (Rom.7:25) by physical death, he will be πρὸς τὸν κύριον (2 Cor.5:8). This is the same place where our Lord is - πρὸς τὸν ϑεόν (John 1:1) and πρὸς τὸν πατέρα (1 John 1:2).

The world cannot understand why the Christian does not fear death. The victorious Christian looks forward to it with joy. The world dreads death because for the unsaved it brings to an end the epicurean indulgences for which they lived. The Christian anticipates death with joy for the same reason in reverse, for the Christian deplores what the unsaved sinner enjoys.

Since Paul's future is assured in victory, he now expresses his determination that his present existence, although fraught with pain and a constant struggle with his hated flesh, shall be victorious. This is the thought of verse 9.

It should be apparent that the heresy which is widespread that a "second work of grace" renders the believer free from all temptation, sin and sorrow, coupled with the equally heretical view that physical healing is in the atonement in the same sense in which forgiveness is in the atonement, and therefore that release from sickness and pain is available for the asking, also falls before this passage. If Paul had been living beyond the pale of temptation, sin and physical pain and death, his desire to depart this life for something better would be without point.

Verse 9 - "Wherefore we labor, that, whether present or absent, we may be accepted of him."

διὸ καὶ φιλοτιμούμεϑα, εἴτε ἐνδημοῦντες εἴτε ἐκδημοῦντες, εὐάρεστοι αὐτῷ εἶναι.

"So whether are are at home or away, we make it our aim to please him." . . .
                                                                    RSV

διὸ (inferential conjunction) 1622.
καὶ (adjunctive conjunction joining verbs) 14.
φιλοτιμούμεϑα (1st.per.pl.pres.mid.ind.of φιλοτιμέομαι, present progressive) 4054.
εἴτε (disjunctive) 4016.

ἐνδημοῦντες (pres.act.part.nom.pl.masc.of ἐνδημέω, adverbial, conditional) 4308.

εἴτε (disjunctive) 4016.

ἐκδημοῦντες (pres.act.part.nom.pl.masc.of ἐκδημέω, adverbial, conditional) 4309.

εὐάρεστοι (nom.pl.masc.of εὐάρεστος, predicate adjective) 4010.

αὐτῷ (dat.sing.masc.of αὐτός, personal interest) 16.

εἶναι (pres.inf.of εἰμί, purpose) 86.

Translation - "And so we are aspiring to be acceptable to Him, whether present or absent."

Comment: Paul had no discretion with regard to the time when he might transfer from the body to the Lord. Nor has any Christian. He was certain that such a transition would be made in God's own appointed time, but he did not know the specific time. Meanwhile he was ambitious (#4054) to conduct himself so that (purpose in εἶναι) his life would please the Lord, under whichever condition - be it absent in physical life or present after death. (Phil.1:20-25). Note that Paul had no doubt that when he died he would enter into the Lord's presence. He was certain that he was saved, but he was in doubt as to whether or not, when he stood before the Lord, his service would be acceptable to Christ. Antinomians may be too smug and self-assured. Arminians may be too apprehensive. The latter should put away their fears that they will lose their salvation which Christ purchased and graciously gave to them. The former should begin to be concerned about whether their assurance of salvation, which is proper, has not developed in them a presumptuous attitude toward sin, which is highly improper. Paul was certain of salvation, but he was not certain that the quality of his performance as a servant of Christ measured up to the divine standard.

That the performance of the Christian, from the time when he is saved, until he dies or is raptured, is to be reviewed in clear in

Verse 10 - "For we must all appear before the judgment seat of Christ; that every one may receive the things done in his body, according to that he hath done, whether it be good or bad."

τοὺς γὰρ πάντας ἡμᾶς φανερωθῆναι δεῖ ἔμπροσθεν τοῦ βήματος τοῦ Χριστοῦ, ἵνα κομίσηται ἔκαστος τὰ διὰ τοῦ σώματος πρὸς ἃ ἔπραξεν, εἴτε ἀγαθὸν εἴτε φαῦλον.

"For we must all appear before the judgment seat of Christ, so that each one may receive good or evil, according to what he has done in the body." ... RSV

τοὺς (acc.pl.masc.of the article in agreement with ἡμᾶς) 9.

γὰρ (causal conjunction) 105.

πάντας (acc.pl.masc.of πᾶς, in agreement with ἡμᾶς) 67.

ἡμᾶς (acc.pl.masc.of ἐγώ, general reference) 123.

φανερωθῆναι (1st.aor.pass.inf.of φανερόω, complementary) 1960.

δεῖ (pres.ind.impersonal of δεῖ) 1207.

ἔμπροσθεν (preposition with the genitive of place description) 459.

τοῦ (gen.sing.neut.of the article in agreement with βήματος) 9.

βήματος (gen.sing.neut.of βῆμα, place description) 1628.

τοῦ (gen.sing.masc.of the article in agreement with Χριστοῦ) 9.

Χριστοῦ (gen.sing.masc.of Χριστός, description) 4.

ἵνα (conjunction with the subjunctive, purpose) 114.

κομίσηται (3d.per.sing.aor.mid.subj.of κομίζω, purpose) 1541.

ἕκαστος (nom.sing.masc.of ἕκαστος, subject of κομίσηται) 1217.

τὰ (acc.pl.neut.of the article, direct object of κομίσηται) 9.

διὰ (preposition with the genitive of intermediate means) 118.

τοῦ (gen.sing.neut.of the article in agreement with σώματος) 9.

σώματος (gen.sing.neut.of σῶμα, intermediate means) 507.

πρὸς (preposition with the accusative of reference) 197.

ἃ (acc.pl.neut.of ὅς, relative pronoun, reference) 65.

ἔπραξεν (3d.per.sing.aor.act.ind.of πράσσω, culminative) 1943.

εἴτε (disjunctive) 4016.

ἀγαθὸν (acc.sing.neut.of ἀγαθός, predicate adjective) 547.

εἴτε (disjunctive) 4016.

φαῦλον (acc.sing.neut.of φαῦλος, predicate adjective) 1990.

Translation - "Because all of us must appear before the judgment throne of Christ, in order that each one receive recompense for the things done through the body, in accord with that which he has done, whether good or worthless."

Comment: Here is a universal divine subpoena, issued from the bench of Messiah, the Judge (John 5:22) to every Christian. Note the definite nature of the group served with the summons - τοὺς ... πάντας ἡμᾶς - "the entire body of us." None will escape the subpoena (Rom.14:10). The infinitive φανερωθῆναι completes δεῖ, which indicates a necessity because of God's sovereign decree, as well as to accomplish a definite purpose. *Cf.* #1207. There is no doubt about the Christian's appearance. When will this occur? When Christ, our Life, appears then shall we also appear with Him in glory (Col.3:4a,b). Why? The ἵνα clause follows - "that each one of us (note the individuality of ἕκαστος) may receive whatever is our due, whether good or bad. *Cf.* Eph.6:8; 1 Pet.5:4. The deeds of our present life, in our mortal bodies, will come under the divine scrutiny. Note φαῦλος - "insignificant" or "worthless," and therefore evil.

> *"Teach us the folly of all waste to see."*
>   Will Houghton, So This is Life?"

The issue at this judgment is not salvation. That question was settled in the eternal counsels of God, provided at Calvary and implemented by the Holy Spirit in regeneration. The issue is with regard to what we did with our lives after salvation. (Mt.16:27; Lk.14:12-14; 1 Cor.3:11-15; Rev.11:18). The loss suffered at the judgment seat of Christ is not salvation, for that is secure in Him, but a loss of reward that we might have had, had we been more obedient to the Holy Spirit. Here we pay the opportunity cost of Christian resources wasted in the markets of the world (1 Cor.3:15).

That God is serious about this judgment is clear from verse 11.

The Ministry of Reconciliation

(2 Corinthians 5:11-6:13)

Verse 11 - "Knowing therefore the terror of the Lord we persuade men; but we are made manifest unto God; and I trust also are made manifest in your consciences."

Εἰδότες οὖν τὸν φόβον τοῦ κυρίου ἀνθρώπους πείθομεν, θεῷ δὲ πεφανερώμε-εθα. ἐλπίζω δὲ καὶ ἐν ταῖς συνειδήσεσιν ἡμῶν πεφανερῶσθαι.

"Therefore, knowing the fear of the Lord, we persuade men; but what we are is known to God, and I hope it is known also to your conscience." . . . RSV

Εἰδότες (aor.act.part.nom.pl.masc.of ὁράω, adverbial, causal) 144b.

οὖν (inferential conjunction) 68.

τὸν (acc.sing.masc.of the article in agreement with φόβον) 9.

φόβον (acc.sing.masc.of φόβος, direct object of εἰδότες) 1131.

τοῦ (gen.sing.masc.of the article in agreement with κυρίου) 9.

κυρίου (gen.sing.masc.of κύριος, description) 97.

ἀνθρώπους (acc.pl.masc.of ἄνθρωπος, direct object of πείθομεν) 341.

πείθομεν (1st.per.pl.pres.act.ind.of πείθω, aoristic) 1629.

θεῷ (dat.sing.masc.of θεός, indirect object of πεφανερώμεθα) 124.

δὲ (adversative conjunction) 11.

πεφανερώμεθα (1st.per.pl.perf.pass.ind.of φανερόω, iterative) 1960.

ἐλπίζω (1st.per.sing.pres.act.ind.of ἐλπίζω, aoristic) 991.

δὲ (continuative conjunction) 11.

καὶ (adjunctive conjunction joining substantives) 14.

ἐν (preposition with the locative of place) 80.

ταῖς (loc.pl.fem.of the article in agreement with συνειδήσεσιν) 9.

συνειδήσεσιν (loc.pl.fem.of συνείδησις, sphere) 3590.

ὑμῶν (gen.pl.masc.of σύ, possession) 104.

πεφανερῶσθαι (perf.pass.inf.of φανερόω, epexegetical) 1960.

Translation - "Therefore since we know the fear of the Lord we are persuading men; but we have been fully displayed to God, and I hope also that I am being made manifest in your consciences."

Comment: Coming in the context, as it does, immediately following verse 10, it is easy to see in verse 11 that the persuasion which Paul applies is to the Christian and that the "fear of the Lord" is the displeasure of the Lord toward the Christian who has wasted his opportunities to serve Christ. The "wood, hay and stubble" (1 Cor.3:11-15) will be burned away at the judgment seat of Christ and Paul did persuade the Corinthian saints to live for the Lord and avoid this loss.

But it is also true that Paul was busy persuading the unsaved to come to

Christ. The "fear of the Lord" (τὸν φόβον τοῦ κυρίου) is not the same as "the wrath of God" (ὀργὴ θεοῦ) of Romans 1:18 which is to be poured out upon the unsaved. God has not appointed the saints unto wrath (1 Thess.5:9). The "day of His great wrath" (Rev.6:16) is the day when His saints will be glorified and He will be glorified in them (2 Thess.1:7-10).

Paul adds that it is impossible to hide anything from God. The Judge had been monitoring Paul's experience on a day by day basis. Thus Paul's character was an open book to the Judge (verse 10). He adds that he hopes that the Corinthians also understand his true character.

It is a common error for Christians who are deeply taught in the knowledge of God's grace, to become presumptuous about sin in their lives. Antinomianism suggests that a God of grace will not hold us to strict account. Paul affirms that He will. It is a fearful thing for the Christian to stand before the judgment seat of Christ with a record of lost opportunities to glorify God.

Verse 12 - "For we commend not ourselves again unto you, but give you occasion to glory on our behalf, that ye may have something to answer them which glory in appearance, and not in heart."

οὐ πάλιν ἑαυτοὺς συνιστάνομεν ὑμῖν, ἀλλὰ ἀφορμὴν διδόντες ὑμῖν καυχήματος ὑπὲρ ἡμῶν, ἵνα ἔχητε πρὸς τοὺς ἐν προσώπῳ καυχωμένους καὶ μὴ ἐν καρδίᾳ.

"We are not commending ourselves to you again but giving you cause to be proud of us, so that you may be able to answer those who pride themselves on a man's position and not on his heart." . . . RSV

οὐ (negative conjunction with the indicative) 130.
πάλιν (adverbial) 355.
ἑαυτοὺς (acc.pl.masc.of ἑαυτοῦ, direct object of συνιστάνομεν) 288.
συνιστάνομεν (1st.per.pl.pres.act.ind.of συνιστάων, aoristic) 2328.
ὑμῖν (dat.pl.masc.of σύ, person) 104.
ἀλλὰ (alternative conjunction) 342.
ἀφορμὴν (acc.sing.fem.of ἀφορμή, direct object διδόντες) 3921.
διδόντες (pres.act.part.nom.pl.masc.of δίδωμι, adverbial, telic) 362.
ὑμῖν (dat.pl.masc.of σύ, indirect object of διδόντες) 104.
καυχήματος (gen.sing.neut.of καύχημα, description) 3881.
ὑπὲρ (preposition with the genitive of reference) 545.
ἡμῶν (gen.pl.masc.of ἐγώ, reference) 123.
ἵνα (conjunction with the subjunctive, purpose) 114.
ἔχητε (2d.per.pl.pres.act.subj.of ἔχω, purpose) 82.
πρὸς (preposition with the accusative after a verb of saying, understood) 197.
τοὺς (acc.pl.masc.of the article in agreement with καυχωμένους) 9.
ἐν (preposition with the locative of sphere) 80.
προσώπῳ (loc.sing.neut.of πρόσωπον, sphere) 588.
καυχωμένους (pres.mid.part.acc.pl.masc.of καυχάομαι, substantival, extent after a verb of saying understood) 3847.

καὶ (adversative conjunction) 14.
μὴ (negative conjunction) 87.
ἐν (preposition with the locative of sphere) 80.
καρδίᾳ (loc.sing.fem.of καρδία, sphere) 432.

Translation - "We are not again vindicating ourselves to you, but (we are writing these things) in order to give to you a reason to be proud of us, so that you may have (something to say) to those who take pride in appearance, but not in heart."

Comment: Paul had already argued his case before the Corinthians to show that he was a *bona fide* Apostles with a supernatural message from God that yielded supernatural results in the lives of his converts (1 Cor.9:1-15). It is not now his purpose to cover the ground again. He has another reason for writing as he does. Robertson (*Grammar*, 439) thinks that we must add γράφομεν ταῦτα before διδόντες to avoid anacoluthon. "But we are writing these things to you for the purpose (telic participle in διδόντες) of giving to you a ground (occasion, justification, factual support) for being proud (genitive of description in καυχήματος) with reference to us (genitive of reference in ὑπὲρ ἡμῶν). Why should Paul thus equip the Corinthians with ammunition for such an argument? The ἵνα clause of purpose follows - "In order that you may have (the object is omitted) something to say to those who boast (τοὺς καυχωμένους) about (or take pride in) appearances, though not in a sincere heart attitude.

This really seems a bit unnecessary. Why should Paul or the Corinthians be concerned with the question of proving a point to such insincere critics who are concerned with the superficial, outward evidences of success rather than with the genuine inner spiritual results? In fact Paul himself senses that his thinking may be a bit irrational and confesses as much in

Verse 13 - "For whether we be beside ourselves, it is to God: or whether we be sober, it is for your cause."

εἴτε γὰρ ἐξέστημεν, θεῷ. εἴτε σωφρονοῦμεν, ὑμῖν.

"For if we are beside ourselves, it is for God; if we are in our right mind, it is for you." . . . RSV

εἴτε (disjunctive) 4016.
γὰρ (explanatory conjunction) 105.
ἐξέστημεν (1st.per.pl.2d.aor.ind.of ἐξίστημι, ingressive) 992.
θεῷ (dat.sing.masc.of θεός, personal advantage) 124.
εἴτε (disjunctive) 4016.
σωφρονοῦμεν (1st.per.pl.pres.act.ind.of σωφρονέω, aoristic) 2224.
ὑμῖν (dat.pl.masc.of σύ, personal advantage) 104.

Translation - "Now if we have begun to appear deranged, it is for God's glory, or if I am in my right mind it is for your benefit."

Comment: Whether Paul's behavior be adjudged normal or abnormal, he was to the best of his ability serving God in behalf of the people. He points to his motivation in

Verse 14 - "For the love of Christ constraineth us: because we thus judge, that if one died for all, then were all dead."

ἡ γὰρ ἀγάπη τοῦ Χριστοῦ συνέχει ἡμᾶς, κρίναντας τοῦτο, ὅτι εἷς ὑπὲρ πάντων ἀπέθανεν, ἄρα οἱ πάντες ἀπέθανον.

"For the love of Christ controls us, because we are convinced that one has died for all; therefore all have died." . . . RSV

ἡ (nom.sing.fem.of the article in agreement with ἀγάπη) 9.
γὰρ (causal conjunction) 105.
ἀγάπη (nom.sing.fem.of ἀγάπη, subject of συνέχει) 1490.
τοῦ (gen.sing.masc.of the article in agreement with Χριστοῦ) 9.
Χριστοῦ (gen.sing.masc.of Χριστός, subjective genitive) 4.
συνέχει (3d.per.sing.pres.act.ind.of συνέχω, present iterative retroactive) 414.
ἡμᾶς (acc.pl.masc.of ἐγώ, direct object of συνέχει) 123.
κρίναντας (aor.act.part.acc.pl.masc.of κρίνω, adjectival, predicate position, in agreement with ἡμᾶς, restrictive) 531.
τοῦτο (acc.sing.neut.of οὗτος, direct object of κρίναντας) 93.
ὅτι (epexegetic conjunction) 211.
εἷς (nom.sing.masc.of εἷς, subject of ἀπέθανεν) 469.
ὑπὲρ (preposition with the ablative, "in behalf of") 545.
πάντων (abl.pl.masc.of πᾶς, substitution) 67.
ἀπέθανεν (3d.per.sing.aor.act.ind.of ἀποθνήσκω, constative) 774.
ἄρα (illative particle) 995.
οἱ (nom.pl.masc.of the article in agreement with πάντες) 9.
πάντες (nom.pl.masc.of πᾶς, subject of ἀπέθανον) 67.
ἀπέθανον (3d.per.pl.aor.act.ind.of ἀποθνήσκω, constative) 774.

Translation - "Because the love of Christ (Christ by His love) puts me under obligation, - one who has come to this conclusion, that since one died instead of all, therefore all met death."

Comment: Paul admitted in verse 13 that his life style was likely to be considered irrational by those who did not understand him. Now he tells us why he behaves thus. It is because (causal γὰρ) Christ has put him under great constraint. Χριστοῦ is a subjective genitive, *i.e.* it is the substantive in the genitive case that produces the action of the verb. By His love Christ had put pressure upon Paul. The participle κρίναντας is adjectival, restricting its action to Paul (editorial ἡμᾶς). Paul's theology led him to a certain conclusion. What conclusion? ὅτι thus is epexegetical. It explains what conclusion Paul had reached (*Cf.*2 Cor.1:8,12). The conclusion to which Paul's thought led him is that when Christ died for the elect upon the cross, all those for whom He died, at that time died, in the vicarious sense, in expiation for their sins.

If we push οἱ πάντες to mean the quantitative total of Adam's race, we are driven, either into the camp of the Universalists or into agreement with some watered-down "moral influence" theory of the atonement, which has nothing in it to combat secular humanism.

Paul here enunciates the theory of the atonement later associated with Anselm of Canterbury (1033-1109). Christ, by dying for the elect, actually secured the release from the penalty of death for all for whom He died. If Christ died for the quantitative all then the Universalism that preaches total reconcilation for the entire creation follows. If Universalism is to be avoided an atonement that is qualitatively unlimited must be quantitatively limited. Jacobus Arminius (1560-1609) taught that what Christ did on Calvary he did for all, but that He did not do very much for anyone. The real question is whether Christ made salvation *possible* for all but *certain* for none or *certain* for the elect. Augustine (354-430), Calvin (1509-1564) and the Reformed theologians since teach that Christ secured total release from the penalty of sin for those for whom He died. In our view this is the theology taught by Jesus (John 6:37-39, 44; 17:2,6,9-12,15,20-24) and by Paul (2 Cor.5:14). Its results are recorded by Luke (Acts 13:48).

Those for whom Christ died, died. πάντων does not mean the entire race, but all of the elect. Otherwise we have involved the Holy Spirit in glaring contradictions in the book which He wrote.

It is well to remember that neither Paul nor any other Christian knows who the elect are. We must therefore go to all men announcing to all (Mt.28:18-20) that Christ has paid the total death penalty for some. This is good news. If Christ loved the elect enough to die for them, He puts every elect saint under the pressure (συνέχω, #414) of moral obligation to spend his life witnessing to all men the good news of the gospel of reconciliation. The witness is universal. The results show that to some the good news smells like death but to others it smells like life (2 Cor.2:14-17, upon which *cf.* comment).

2 Cor.5:14 taken by itself, in violation of the principle of 2 Peter 1:20, teaches Universalism, for there is in it nothing of limitation, either in the quantitative or qualitative senses. As we allow the light of other passages which are germane to the point to shine upon and illuminate it, we get limitation upon the work of Christ on the cross. Arminians limit its quality and Calvinists limit its quantity. Qualitative limitation denies the T,the U, the I and the P in the TULIP. Qualitative limitation comports with the TULIP in all of its five points. It is difficult for Arminians to resist the view that man is basicly good and really needs no substitutionary atonement - only a moral push in the right direction. Difficult for some and impossible for those Arminians are think it through.

Calvinists, on the other hand, who think the objective side of the problem through consistently and reach a valid conclusion, sometimes falter on the subjective side and conclude with wicked presumption that since Christ secured salvation for the elect in His death, it is not necessary to carry out the command of our Lord to be "witnesses unto me . . . unto the uttermost part of the earth" (Acts 1:8). This is the view of the "hyper-Calvinist" - a misnomer, since a "hyper-Calvinist" is not a Calvinist at all, since John Calvin did not teach that God would save the elect apart from the preaching of the gospel. The true view is that God has not only ordained the end, but also the means to the end.

Calvinism is the only system that does not involve the Greek New testament in contradition.

There are many passages that clearly contradict both Arminianism and Universalism. There are none that forbid the conclusions of the Reformed theology.

Verse 15 - "And that he died for all, that they which live should not henceforth live unto themselves, but unto him which died for them, and rose again."

καὶ ὑπὲρ πάντων ἀπέθανεν ἵνα οἱ ζῶντες μηκέτι ἑαυτοῖς ζῶσιν ἀλλὰ τῷ ὑπὲρ αὐτῶν ἀποθανόντι καὶ ἐγερθέντι.

"And he died for all, that those who live might live no longer for themselves but for him who for their sake died and was raised." . . . RSV

καὶ (continuative conjunction) 14.

ὑπὲρ (preposition with the ablative "in behalf of") 545.

πάντων (abl.pl.masc.of πᾶς, substitution) 67.

ἀπέθανεν (3d.per.sing.aor.act.ind.of ἀποθνῄσκω, constative) 774.

ἵνα (conjunction with the subjunctive, sub-final) 114.

οἱ (nom.pl.masc.of the article in agreement with ζῶντες) 9.

ζῶντες (pres.act.part.nom.pl.masc.of ζάω, substantival, subject of ζῶσιν) 340.

μηκέτι (temporal adverb) 1368.

ἑαυτοῖς (dat.pl.masc.of ἑαυτοῦ, personal advantage) 288.

ζῶσιν (3d.per.pl.pres.act.subj.of ζάω, sub-final) 340.

ἀλλὰ (alternative conjunction) 342.

τῷ (dat.sing.masc.of the article in agreement with ἀποθανόντι and ἐγερθέντι) 9.

ὑπὲρ (preposition with the ablative, substitution) 545.

αὐτῶν (abl.pl.masc.of αὐτός, substitution) 16.

ἀποθανόντι (pres.act.part.dat.sing.masc.of ἀποθνῄσκω, substantival, personal advantage) 774.

καὶ (adjunctive conjunction joining participles) 14.

ἐγερθέντι (aor.pass.part.dat.sing.masc.of ἐγείρω, substantival, personal advantage) 125.

Translation - "And He died for all in order (and with the result) that the living might no longer live selfishly but for Him Who died for them and was resurrected."

Comment: This is the second part of Paul's theology, the first being the ὅτι clause of verse 14. The objective side is this: One died for all; hence those for whom He died, died when He died. The subjective side follows in verse 15. He died for all with a specific purpose and in contemplation of a specific result. What purpose and what result? The ἵνα clause tells us - "In order (and with the result) that those who will live forever because of His substitutionary death, may not live for their own personal advantage (dative of advantage in ἑαυτοῖς) but for Christ, Who is here designated by the dative participles ἀποθανόντι and ἐγερθέντι.

The ethical demand upon the believer which flows from Calvary is that all who died on the cross in Christ, and who arose from the dead in Him when He arose, shall live for Him Who died for them. There is no place for selfishness. Nothing that the believer does for his own personal advantage (ἑαυτοῖς) is legitimate, if it is not also for the personal advantage of Christ (ἀποθανόντι καὶ ἐγερθέντι). We are δοῦλοι for Christ (Rom.1:1).

Those who criticized Paul's behavior (verse 13) were not justified since he was not living for them or even for himself, but for Christ Who died for him. The eternal life of the believer is possible only because Christ died and rose again. His death was the most selfless act of human history.

Paul's view of the death and resurrection of Jesus revolutionized his social philosophy as he describes it in

Verse 16 - "Wherefore henceforth know we no man after the flesh: yea, though we have known Christ after the flesh, yet now henceforth know we him no more."

Ὥστε ἡμεῖς ἀπὸ τοῦ νῦν οὐδένα οἴδαμεν κατὰ σάρκα. εἰ καὶ ἐγνώκαμεν κατὰ σάρκα Χριστόν, ἀλλὰ νῦν οὐκέτι γινώσκομεν.

"From now on, therefore, we regard no one from a human point of view; even though we once regarded Christ from a human point of view, we regard him thus no longer." . . . RSV

Ὥστε (conjunction with the indicative, actual result) 752.
ἡμεῖς (nom.pl.masc.of ἐγώ, subject of οἴδαμεν) 123.
ἀπὸ (preposition with the ablative of time separation) 70.
τοῦ (abl.sing.neut.of the article, time separation) 9.
νῦν (temporal adverb) 1497.
οὐδένα (acc.sing.masc.of οὐδείς, direct object of οἴδαμεν) 446.
οἴδαμεν (1st.per.pl.perf.act.ind.of ὁράω, intensive, actual result) 144b.
κατὰ (preposition with the accusative, standard) 98.
σάρκα (acc.sing.fem.of σάρξ, standard) 1202.
εἰ (conditional particle in a first-class condition) 337.
καὶ (emphatic conjunction) 14.
ἐγνώκαμεν (1st.per.pl.perf.act.ind.of γινώσκω, first-class condition) 131.
κατὰ (preposition with the accusative, standard) 98.
σάρκα (acc.sing.fem.of σάρξ, standard) 1202.
Χριστόν (acc.sing.masc.of Χριστός, direct object of ἐγνώκαμεν) 4.
ἀλλὰ (adversative conjunction) 342.
νῦν (temporal adverb) 1497.
οὐκέτι (temporal adverb) 1289.
γινώσκομεν (1st.per.pl.pres.act.ind.of γινώσκω, aoristic) 131.

Translation - "The result is that from now on we know nobody from a human point of view, although in fact we have known Christ from that standpoint, but we know Him like this no longer."

Comment: The result of Paul's theology is a social philosophy. No preacher of the gospel who understands the atonement can view any man solely from a human and social point of view. Insofar as we know every person we meet is a potential Christian. The great commission orders us to preach the gospel to all, even though we know that not all will be saved (2 Cor.2:15,16). What we are not told is the personnel of the Body of Christ. It is human folly and wicked presumption to refuse to tell the story of the cross on the ground that those in the audience are non-elect. No one knows that but God. Hence our approach to every man is based upon the assumption that when Christ died, our prospect also died.

William Carey, pastor of a Baptist church in Leicester, England read Cook, *Voyages Around the World,* and became interested in geography. He was also a school teacher and he made a globe of leather and upon it he traced the outlines of the earth for his classes." The thought flashed upon him that four hundred millions of people had never heard of Christ, and that moment, surrounded by a handful of Northamptonshire urchins, the great Baptist missionary enterprise was born. . . . His *Inquiry into the Obligations of Christians to use means for the Conversion of the Heathen* was published in 1792, but found few readers and produced little effect. To most of the Baptists his views were visionary and even wild, in open conflict with God's sovereignty. At a meeting of ministers, where the senior Ryland presided, Carey proposed that at the next meeting they discuss the duty of attempting to spread the Gospel amongst the heathen. Fuller was present, but the audacity of the proposition made him hold his breath, while Ryland,shocked,sprang to his feet and ordered Carey to sit down,saying, "When God pleases to covert the heathen he will do it without your aid or mine.' " But Carey, undaunted, whom Ryland called the "Antinomian Devil" continued to preach the obligations of the great commission to his church, but the message was so revolutionary that his church split. Carey refused to be silent and his efforts brought the organization of the first Baptist Missionary Society on 2 October 1792. "In April, 1793, Cary and Thomas started for India, despite the opposition of the East India Company, the indifference of their own brethren, and the disdain of the public; and did such missionary work there as has not been known since the Apostolic Age." (Thomas Armitage, *History of the Baptists,* 581, 581 *et passim*).

Nineteen years after Carey and Thomas went to India, ". . . Rev. Adoniram Judson . . . with Rev.Luther Rice were appointed by the American Board of Commissioners for Foreign Missions to establish missions in Asia." *(Ibid.,*814). They were pedobaptists. Judson and Rice sailed on different vessels to India. Although they had not discussed their plans before they sailed, each determined to make a fresh study of the mode of baptism. Both men were true Bereans as they searched their Greek New Testaments to determine whether or not the Baptists were correct in insisting that $\beta\alpha\pi\tau\iota\zeta\omega$ (#273) demanded immersion in water. Both reached the conclusion that it did. When Rice and Judson met again in India each was overjoyed to learn that the other had reached the same conclusion and they joined Carey in India, who quite naturally was gratified to meet two former pedobaptists, now ready to join the Baptists.

"Mr. Rice returned to the United States to awaken in the Baptist churches a zeal for the establishment of missions in India. He was heartily welcomed, and measures were adopted for the temporary support of Mr. and Mrs. Judson. Mr. Rice travelled from Boston through the Middle and Southern States, and his addresses kindled a wide-spread enthusiasm, which resulted in the gathering of a convention, composed of thirty-six delegates from eleven States and the District of Columbia, who met in Philadelphia, May 18th, 1814, when a society was formed, called the Baptist General Convention for Foreign Missions. Dr. Furman, of South Carolina, was President of this body, Dr. Baldwin, of Massachusetts, Secretary, and Mr. and Mrs. Judson were adopted as its first missionaries." (*Ibid.*).

Thus American Baptists awoke to the significance of the Great Commission. Five-Point Calvinists before 1814, as they should have been, but with the same presumptuous view of missions that characterized Ryland's outburst in England in 1792, when he told William Carey to sit down, a view to which no Calvinist is entitled, they became Missionary Baptists. The organization formed in Philadelphia in 1814 came to be known as the Triennial Convention, since they determined to meet in plenary sesssion every three years. It was in 1817, chiefly due to the influence of Luther Rice that Isaac McCoy of Charlestown, Indiana, applied for and received an appointment from the Triennial Convention to expand the mission work to include the American Indian. McCoy joined Peck and Welch, who had been appointed previously to work among the Indians in the St. Louis area, who became the first Baptist missionaries to the Indians. After 25 years of faithful ministry to the Indians, in Vincennes and near Rockville, Indiana, at Fort Wayne, at the present sites of Niles and Grand Rapids, Michigan and finally at Westport, Missiouri (Kansas City, Missouri) and Shawnee Mission, Kansas, McCoy organized the American Indian Mission Association, in 1842, which became the nucleus of the Home Mission Board of the Southern Baptist Convention. McCoy died in Louisville in 1846. His last words were, "Tell the brethren never to let the Indian Mission decline." (Randolph O. Yeager, *Indian Enterprises of Isaac McCoy, 1817-1846,* 605), unpublished Ph.D. dissertation, the University of Oklahoma, Norman, 1954).

Unfortunately most American Baptists since 1814, in their zeal for missions, which is proper, and under the influence of secular humanism, as a result of the rise of Darwinism, have abandoned Five Point Calvinism, which is improper and settled for a watered-down one, two, three or four point Calvinism, which is nothing more than Arminianism in respectable Baptist disguise. The usual hackneyed bromide which one hears from the contemporary Baptist is that he is "a Calvinist but not a hyper-Calvinist," by which he means that he wishes to hold fast to the P in the Tulip, but rejects some one or more of the other four points. The truth is that there is no such thing as a "hyper-Calvinist." Those who hold fewer than five of the points represented by the Tulip are not Calvinists at all and have forsaken the theology that all Baptists believed two hundred years ago. The result is the emphasis on "walk down the aisle and sign an application blank" concept of regeneration, a development which has resulted from an overemphasis upon quantity at the expense of quality and which in turn may result in an unregenerate church membership.

Paul adds that once, in his unregenerate days, he viewed Jesus merely as a historic sociological phenomenon like any other man. Now that Paul had met Him on the Damascus road, and had been treated to a special theological education in the third heaven (2 Cor.12:1-4), he views Christ in that light no more. Note that when we change our view of Jesus, we also change our view of society. The Christian who tries to fit into society (Rom.12:1-2) needs a new look at Jesus Christ. Why? Paul tells us in

Verse 17 - "Therefore if any man be in Christ, he is a new creature: old things are passed away; behold, all things are become new."

ὥστε εἴ τις ἐν Χριστῷ, καινὴ κτίσις. τὰ ἀρχαῖα παρῆλθεν, ἰδοὺ γέγονεν καινά.

"Therefore, if any one is in Christ, he is a new creation; the old has passed away, behold, the new has come." . . . RSV

ὥστε (conjunction with the indicative, result) 752.
εἴ (conditional particle in a first-class condition) 337.
τις (nom.sing.masc.of τίς, indefinite pronoun, subject of verb understood) 486.
ἐν (preposition with the instrumental of association) 80.
Χριστῷ (instru.sing.masc.of Χριστός, association) 4.
καινὴ (nom.sing.fem.of καινός, in agreement with κτίσις) 812.
κτίσις (nom.sing.fem.of κρίσις, predicate nominative) 2633.
τὰ (nom.pl.neut.of the article in agreement with ἀρχαῖα) 9.
ἀρχαῖα (nom.pl.neut.of ἀρχαῖος, subject of παρῆλθεν) 475.
παρῆλθεν (3d.per.sing.aor.ind.of παρέρχομαι, culminative) 467.
ἰδοὺ (exclamation) 95.
γέγονεν (3d.per.sing.perf.ind.of γίνομαι, intensive) 113.
καινά (nom.pl.neut.of καινός, subject of γέγονεν) 812.

Translation - "The result is that if any man is associated with Christ, a new creation exists; the old relations have passed by; behold, new relations now exist."

Comment: Whenever any sinner is regenerated and thus finds himself in Christ he undergoes the same change that Saul experienced when he became Paul. The new birth implants a new divine nature (2 Peter 1:4) and the Christian, though physically in the world, and though still unchanged in his physical body, with its fleshly desires, has a new nature, which Paul calls "the inner man" (Eph.3:16). The result of this addition is that he no longer sustains a relationship to the unsaved world that is wholly social. This is because he is now oriented into a new sphere of eternal life. The King James Version "he is a new creature" unfortunately implies that the Adamic nature of the Christian was also changed at regeneration. This mistranslation has contributed to the "second blessing" heresey of the so-called Holiness groups. The child of God is not "a new creature" yet, though he will become such at the rapture/resurrection, but there now resides in the old corrupt Adamic nature "a new creation" which is the "seed of God" (1 John 3:9). New creations by God's redemptive love and grace and regenerative resurrection power can never again sustain the old unregenerate social relations with the world. We are no longer citizens of a democracy but we have our citizenship in heaven (Phil.3:20,21) and are only ambassadors on earth. Our function, as such, is not to meddle in the internal affairs of the world, to which we no longer belong, but to represent the best interests of heaven's court (2 Cor.5:20). Our relation to the unsaved world is expressed in terms of salt and light (Mt.5:13,14). We are the "salt of the earth" which is a figurative way of saying that as long as the saints are here, the world society, from which we have been rescued and of which we are no longer a vital part, cannot disintegrate into the total chaos which will characterize it in hell. To be sure society is getting worse and worse as we approach the end of the age (2 Tim.3:13), but the Holy Spirit, Who indwells the believer (1 Cor.6:19) will not be taken out of the world until He has called the last elect soul for whom Christ died into His Body. And that will not take place until the "days of the voice of the seventh angel when he shall begin to sound" (Rev.10:7). The restraining influence of the Holy Spirit will be "taken out of the way" (ἐκ μέσου; 2 Thess.2:7), but Paul did not write that the Holy Spirit would be taken "out of the earth" (ἐκ τῆς γῆς). The Holy Spirit will be taken out of the earth when the Body of Christ is taken out of the earth at the rapture, which is also said to take place "at the last (seventh) trump" (1 Cor.15:52). This is the same time when the Body of Christ will become complete (Rev.10:7). Thus the believer is the "salt of the earth."

He is also "the light of the world" for the purpose of revealing the truth (1 Pet.2:9; Phil.2:15,16). No permanent compatible relations with the unsaved can be possible (2 Cor.6:14-18). We can never again relate to the unsaved on a human basis (verse 16).

The dedicated Christian must always feel the alienation which separates him from his unsaved colleagues, however gracious and friendly with them he must try to be. After all Christians march to a different drum and we are oriented around opposite poles of power.

A great deal of the loss of spiritual power experienced by the modern church in the world (Rev.3:14-22) is due to her failure to recognize and accept this fact. The Body of Christ is not a leavening influence for good in a corrupt society that is destined for damnation. The Body of Christ is a witness to the redemption in the cross and a heavenly messenger calling the elect who died in Christ to a realization of that glorious fact (Gal.6:15; Col.1:15).

Note that Paul calls the way that he formerly looked at Christ, before he was saved as τὰ ἀρχαῖα which have passed by - "the old fashioned, out-of-date philosophy that has gone by the board." "And yet today there are scholars who are trying to revive the old prejudiced view of Jesus Christ as a mere man, a prophet, to give us a 'reduced Christ.' That was once Paul's view, but it passed by forever for him. It is a false view and leaves us no gospel and no Saviour." (A.T.Robertson, *Word Pictures in the New Testament*, IV, 231,232).

Verse 18 - "And all things are of God, who hath reconciled us to himself by Jesus Christ, and hath given to us the ministry of reconcilation."

τὰ δὲ πάντα ἐκ τοῦ θεοῦ τοῦ καταλλάξαντος ἡμᾶς ἑαυτῷ διὰ Χριστοῦ καὶ δόντος ἡμῖν τὴν διακονίαν τῆς καταλλαγῆς.

"All this is from God, who through Christ reconciled us to himself and gave us the ministry of reconciliation;" . . . RSV

τὰ (nom.pl.neut.of the article in agreement with πάντα) 9.

δὲ (explanatory conjunction) 11.

πάντα (nom.pl.neut.of πᾶς, subject of ἐστίν understood) 67.

ἐκ (preposition with the ablative of source) 19.

τοῦ (abl.sing.masc.of the article in agreement with θεοῦ) 9.

θεοῦ (abl.sing.masc.of θεός, source) 124.

τοῦ (abl.sing.masc.of the article in agreement with καταλλάξαντος) 9.

καταλλάξαντος (aor.act.part.abl.sing.masc.of καταλλάσσω, substantival, in apposition with θεοῦ) 3899.

ἡμᾶς (acc.pl.masc.of ἐγώ, direct object of καταλλάξαντος) 123.

ἑαυτῷ (instru.sing.masc.of ἑαυτοῦ, association) 288.

διὰ (preposition with the ablative of agent) 118.

Χριστοῦ (abl.sing.masc.of Χριστός, agent) 4.

καὶ (adjunctive conjunction joining participles) 14.

δόντος (aor.act.part.abl.sing.masc.of δίδωμι, substantival, in apposition with θεοῦ) 362.

ἡμῖν (dat.pl.masc.of ἐγώ, indirect object of δόντος) 123.

τὴν (acc.sing.fem.of the article in agreement with διακονίαν) 9.

διακονίαν (acc.sing.fem.of διακονία, direct object of δόντος) 2442.

τῆς (gen.sing.fem.of the article in agreement with καταλλαγῆς) 9.

καταλλαγῆς (gen.sing.fem.of καταλλαγή, description) 3900.

Translation - "Now all things originate in God, the One Who has reconciled us to Himself through Christ and Who has given to us the ministry of reconcilation."

Comment: God is the Author and divine Source of all of the supernatural history that flows from an implementation of His plan of salvation - the new man in Christ, the new creation, the passing of the old world order, the regeneration of all things. All of this is God's work, as the ablative of souce ἐκ τοῦ θεοῦ indicates. Two substantival participles in apposition to θεοῦ follow. He is the One Who has reconciled us to Himself and He has given to us the ministry of reconcilation. *Cf.*#'s 3899 and 3900. The student should also look at διαλλάσσομαι (#488), ἀποκαταλλάττω (#4475) and συναλλάσσω (#3125). The point here is the difference between the fact that God has already reconciled us to Himself (τοῦ καταλλάξαντος ἡμᾶς ἑαυτῷ διὰ Χριστοῦ), through the work of Christ on the cross, and the fact that the sinner now needs to be reconciled to God. Reconciliation is a two way street. Since the incarnation and vicarious death of Jesus satisfied the standards of divine justice (Rom.3:25,26; Col.1:20; 1 John 2:2; 4:10) God needs no more reconciliation. What Jesus Christ did for us was upon God's terms and He is satisfied. But the task of reconciling the sinner to God is more difficult, and that task is given to Paul and to us. "God has made possible through Christ our reconciliation to him, but in each case it has to be made effective by the attitude of each individual. The task of winning the unreconciled to God is committed to us. It is a high and holy one, but supremely difficult, because the offending party (the guilty) is the hardest to win over. We must be loyal to God and yet win sinful men to him." (Robertson, *Word Pictures*, 232). As God's ambassadors with the task of winning men to a reconcilation to Him Whose wrath no longer burns against them since it was exhausted upon our substitute at Calvary, we are not authorized to make any deals with the prospect. God indeed is already reconciled, but their reconciliation must come on the terms of the gospel of Christ.

God has exchanged the coin of infinite value, which is the eternal worth of His Son, poured out in death at Calvary, for our lives. We are now worth the same to Him as His Son is. The value of a product to the buyer is measured in direct ratio to the value of the money which he was willing to pay for it. Now from the sinner's point of view, when he is asked to "come and buy wine and milk, without money and without price" (Isa.55:1) he must value the "wine and milk" of salvation enough that he is willing to surrender his will and all future plans for his life. That is the cost which the sinner must pay. (John 7:17).

Paul does not mean that it was his task to convince the sinner to "pay the price" in order to be reconciled to God. His (and ours) is the privilege of witnessing to the good news that God is already reconciled. As we do this faithfully the Holy Spirit is assigned the task of convincing the sinner. This is a supernatural task and calls for powers of persuasion which the witness does not possess. But we have the power to witness. The Holy Spirit takes what we say from the Word and convinces the prospect (John 16:7-11; 1 Cor.12:3b).

This is the only reason why we are still in the world. This is the only proper function for the ambassador for Christ (verse 20). When the ambassador tries to associate with the world κατὰ σάρκα (verse 16) he frustrates the purpose of God.

Paul explains this message of reconciliation further in

Verse 19 - "To wit, that God was in Christ reconciling the world unto himself, not imputing their trespasses unto them; and hath committed to us the word of reconcilation."

ὡς ὅτι θεὸς ἦν ἐν Χριστῷ κόσμον καταλλάσσων ἑαυτῷ, μὴ λογιζόμενος αὐτοῖς τὰ παραπτώματα αὐτῶν, καὶ θέμενος ἐν ἡμῖν τὸν λόγον τῆς καταλλαγῆς.

"that is, God was in Christ reconciling the world to himself, not counting their trespasses against them, and entrusting to us the message of reconciliation." ...
                                                                                    RSV

ὡς (declarative particle with ὅτι) 128.
ὅτι (declarative particle in indirect discourse) 211.
θεὸς (nom.sing.masc.of θεός, subject of ἦν) 124.
ἦν (3d.per.sing.imp.ind.of εἰμί, imperfect periphrastic) 86.
ἐν (preposition with the instrumental of means) 80.
Χριστῷ (instru.sing.masc.of Χριστός, means) 4.

κόσμον (acc.sing.masc.of κόσμος, direct object of καταλλάσσων) 360.

καταλλάσσων (pres.act.part.nom.sing.masc.of καταλλάσσω, imperfect periphrastic) 3899.

ἑαυτῷ (instru.sing.masc.of ἑαυτοῦ, association) 288.

μή (negative conjunction with the participle) 87.

λογιζόμενος (pres.mid.part.nom.sing.masc.of λογίζομαι, adverbial, complementary) 2611.

αὐτοῖς (dat.pl.masc.of αὐτός, indirect object of λογιζόμενος) 16.

τά (acc.pl.neut.of the article in agreement with παραπτώματα) 9.

παραπτώματα (acc.pl.neut.of παράπτωμα, direct object of λογιζόμενος) 585.

αὐτῶν (gen.pl.masc.of αὐτός, possession) 16.

καί (adjunctive conjunction joining participles) 14.

θέμενος (2d.aor.mid.part.nom.sing.masc.of τίθημι, pluperfect periphrastic) 455.

ἐν (preposition with the locative of place, metaphorical) 80.

ἡμῖν (loc.pl.masc.of ἐγώ, metaphorical place) 123.

τόν (acc.sing.masc.of the article in agreement with λόγον) 9.

λόγον (acc.sing.masc.of λόγος, direct object of θέμενος) 510.

τῆς (gen.sing.fem.of the article in agreement with καταλλαγῆς) 9.

καταλλαγῆς (gen.sing.fem.of καταλλαγή, description) 3900.

Translation - "... that God, by means of Christ has been engaged in the process of reconciling a world to Himself, not charging against them their transgressions and He had charged us with the responsibility of preaching the message of reconciliation."

Comment: Blass calls ὡς ὅτι "unclassical" but Robertson (*Grammar*, 1033) says that Paul has κοινή support for the idiom which he repeats in 2 Cor.11:21 and 2 Thess.2:2. It simply means "that." Thus verse 19 explains the phrase τὴν διακονίαν τῆς καταλλαγῆς of verse 18. The imperfect periphrastic ἦν ... καταλλάσσων indicates a process of durative action in time past. The 30 years of the incarnation was a period when God was carrying on a continuous process that culminated at Calvary in the reconciliation of the world to Himself. The work of redemption, once finished (τετέλεσται, John 19:30) allowed God in perfect righteousness to forbear the imputation of our sins to us since He had already imputed them to the Sin Bearer (1 Cor.5:7; 2 Cor.5:21; 1 Peter 2:24; Isaiah 53:5,6).

Paul then alludes to his own call to apostleship. Note the aorist participle, which, joined with ἦν is a pluperfect periphrastic. God had assigned to Paul the task of preaching the message of reconciliation. *Cf.* 1 Cor.12:28 where τίθημι occurs in the same sense of commitment. In obedience to this call Paul assumed the role of a heavenly ambassador and spent the remainder of his life representing his heavenly government in an alien world. Before his regeneration Saul of Tarsus was very much a part of the world. When he was saved he became a part of the "colony of heaven" (Phil.3:20,21).

Verse 20 - "Now then we are ambassadors for Christ, as though God did beseech you by us: we pray you in Christ's stead, be ye reconciled to God."

ὑπὲρ Χριστοῦ οὖν πρεσβεύομεν ὡς τοῦ θεοῦ παρακαλοῦντος δι' ἡμῶν: δεόμεθα ὑπὲρ Χριστοῦ, καταλλάγητε τῷ θεῷ.

"So we are ambassadors for Christ, God making his appeal through us. We beseech you on behalf of Christ, be reconciled to God." . . . RSV

ὑπὲρ (preposition with the ablative, "in behalf of") 545.
Χριστοῦ (abl.sing.masc.of Χριστός, "in behalf of") 4.
οὖν (inferential conjunction) 68.

#4310 πρεσβεύομεν (1st.per.pl.pres.act.ind.of πρεσβεύω, present progressive retroactive).

King James Version

be an ambassador - 2 Cor.5:20; Eph.6:20.

Revised Standard Version

be an ambassador - 2 Cor.5:20; Eph.6:20.

Meaning: Cf. πρεσβεία (#2537); πρεσβυτέριον (#2822); πρεσβύτερος (#1141); πρεσβύτης (#1802); πρεσβῦτις (#4887). One who is old; an old man who is experienced and diplomatic. Hence, an ambassador; a representative - Paul, as an ambassador for Christ - 2 Cor.5:20; Eph.6:20.

ὡς (concessive particle) 128.
τοῦ (gen.sing.masc.of the article in agreement with θεοῦ) 9.
θεοῦ (gen.sing.masc.of θεός, subjective genitive) 124.
παρακαλοῦντος (pres.act.part.gen.sing.masc.of παρακαλέω, adverbial, concessive) 230.
δι' (preposition with the ablative of agent) 118.
ἡμῶν (abl.pl.masc.of ἐγώ, agent) 123.
δεόμεθα (1st.per.pl.pres.mid.ind.of δέομαι, aoristic) 841.
ὑπὲρ (preposition with the ablative "in behalf of") 545.
Χριστοῦ (abl.sing.masc.of Χριστός, "in behalf of") 4.
καταλλάγητε (2d.per.pl.2d.aor.pass.impv.of καταλλάσσω, entreaty) 3899.
τῷ (dat.sing.masc.of the article in agreement with θεῷ) 9.
θεῷ (dat.sing.masc.of θεός, personal advantage) 124.

Translation - "So we are representatives of Christ, as though God were entreating (you) through us, we are begging you in behalf of Christ, be reconciled to God."

Comment: ὡς here is not pretense but concessive, in introduction to the concessive adverbial participle παρακαλοῦντος). "Although God is not personally speaking to you, He is speaking to you through my agency (δι' ἡμῶν), since I am His envoy." The plea is the gospel plea for reconciliation. It is "good news" (#405). It is not directed to God. He needs no further reconciliation since His legal demands were met when Christ died (verse 19). The war between the sinner and God is over, insofar as God is concerned. The basis for peace (judicial absence of war) was established at Calvary. Now God's message to the sinner is the good news that reconcilation is already a potential fact and an appeal to the sinner to recognize the fact and lay down his arms.

How did God effect this reconciliation? The answer is in

Verse 21 - "For he hath made him to be sin for us, who knew no sin; that we might be made the righteousness of God in Him."

τὸν μὴ γνόντα ἁμαρτίαν ὑπὲρ ἡμῶν ἁμαρτίαν ἐποίησεν, ἵνα ἡμεῖς γενώμεθα δικαιοσύνη θεοῦ ἐν αὐτῷ.

"For our sake he made him to be sin who knew no sin, so that in him we might become the righteousness of God."

τὸν (acc.sing.masc.of the article in agreement with γνόντα) 9.

μὴ (negative conjunction with the participle) 87.

γνόντα (2d.aor.act.part.acc.sing.masc.of γινώσκω, substantival, direct object of ἐποίησεν) 131.

ἁμαρτίαν (acc.sing.fem.of ἁμαρτία, direct object of γνόντα) 111.

ὑπὲρ (preposition with the ablative "in our behalf") 545.

ἡμῶν (abl.pl.masc.of ἐγώ, "in our behalf") 123.

ἁμαρτίαν (acc.sing.fem.of ἁμαρτία, direct object of ἐποίησεν) 111.

ἐποίησεν (3d.per.sing.aor.act.ind.of ποιέω, constative) 127.

ἵνα (conjunction with the subjunctive in a sub-final clause) 114.

ἡμεῖς (nom.pl.masc.of ἐγώ, subject of γενώμεθα) 123.

γενώμεθα (1st.per.pl.aor.pass.subj.of γίνομαι, sub-final) 113.

δικαιοσύνη (nom.sing.fem.of δικαιοσύνη, predicate nominative) 322.

θεοῦ (gen.sing.masc.of θεός, description) 124.

ἐν (preposition with the instrumental of association) 80.

αὐτῷ (instru.sing.masc.of αὐτός, association) 16.

Translation - "He made Him Who never knew sin to be sin for us, in order (and with the result) that we might become divine righteousness in association with Him."

Comment: The emphatic point in the verse is the sinlessness of Jesus. τὸν μὴ γνόντα ἁμαρτίαν is the object of ἐποίησεν, but it is in prior position for emphasis. The second ἁμαρτίαν is the direct object of ἐποίησεν. It recalls Isaiah 53:6. The Sinless One was made to be sin? Why? For us (ὑπὲρ ἡμῶν). Whether the ἵνα clause is final or sub-final depends upon the theology of the exegete. Calvinists will call it sub-final (both purpose and result) on the ground that purpose is intended result, and that in God's case, what He intends to do He will do. Thus there is no difference between purpose and result. Arminians are not quite sure that God is big enough to do all that He wishes to do, although some will be reluctant to teach that His Satanic opposition is powerful enough to frustrate Him. Others will insist that God does not lack the power to save but that He has left the issue up to the sinner who may or may not choose to accept salvation even though it is paid for. This stance is based upon the notion that fallen man is nevertheless a "free moral agent" whatever that is supposed to mean! If God's purpose is realized (Calvinists affirming and Arminians declaring that it is the sinner's purpose that counts), then the believer, in association with the Substitute becomes something which he could never become independent of Him, *viz.*, the Divine Righteousness. Note the genitive in θεοῦ without the article which spells description.

Here is the heart of the doctrine of vicarious atonement. We are sinners. Jesus is sinless. He took our sin. We take His righteousness. It was "filthy rags" (Isa.64:6) for Him on the cross, so revolting that His Father could not look upon it. It is fine linen, white and clean (Rev.19:14) for us. *Cf.* Isal.53:5,6; 1 Peter 2:24. The assumption of sin caused His death (2 Cor.5:14; Rom.3:23; 6:23; 2 Sam.7:14). The LXX for 2 Sam.7:14 has καὶ ἐὰν ἔλθῃ ἀδικία αὐτοῦ - "and if unrighteousness come upon him" (a picture of imputation of human sin to Christ) which was in expiation for ours. Thus our debt is paid and we in the exchange are given His righteousness.

Calvinists refuse to limit the *quality* of what Jesus did for us upon the cross. He actually secured our release from the sin penalty and credited His own righteousness to our account. He made salvation *certain* not merely *possible*. Arminians will say that what He did He did for all but that He did not do enough for anyone. For them the salvation equation is the merits of Jesus Christ on the cross *plus* the sinner's merit in his decision to accept the work of Christ. It matters not how the two sides of the equation are weighted. If Jesus did 99.99999999% and we must provide the .00000001%, there will be no salvation without our contribution. Thus the issue is left unresolved. Salvation for the sinner is sure only if Jesus did 100% of that which God required and left nothing for us to do, for nothing is exactly what we are able to do.

Those who limit the atonement neither in *quality* nor in *quantity* must accept Universalism and are faced with the problem of explaining passages that speak of eternal punishment for some.

Since what Paul (and every believer), as Ambassadors of Heaven's Court, have to offer is so wonderful it is important that our offer not be taken lightly. This is the thought of the next verse.

2 Cor.6:1 - "We then, as workers together with him, beseech you also that ye receive not the grace of God in vain."

Συνεργοῦντες δὲ καὶ παρακαλοῦμεν μὴ εἰς κενὸν τὴν χάριν τοῦ θεοῦ δέξασθαι ὑμᾶς —

"Working together with him, then, we entreat you not to accept the grace of God in vain." . . . *RSV*

Συνεργοῦντες (pres.act.part.nom.pl.masc.of συνεργέω, substantival, subject of παρακαλοῦμεν) 2931.

δὲ (inferential conjunction) 11.

καὶ (continuative conjunction) 14.

παρακαλοῦμεν (1st.per.pl.pres.act.ind.of παρακαλέω, aoristic) 230.

μὴ (negative conjunction with the inifnitive) 87.

εἰς (preposition with the adverbial accusative) 140.

κενὸν (acc.sing.neut.of κενός, adverbial accusative) 1836.

τὴν (acc.sing.fem.of the article in agreement with χάριν) 9.

χάριν (acc.sing.fem.of χάρις, direct object of δέξασθαι) 1700.

τοῦ (gen.sing.masc.of the article in agreement with θεοῦ) 9.

θεοῦ (gen.sing.masc.of θεός, description) 124.

δέξασθαι (aor.mid.inf.of δέχομαι, direct object of παρακαλοῦμεν) 867.

ὑμᾶς (acc.pl.masc.of σύ, general reference) 104.

Translation - "And we fellow workers therefore beg you not to receive the grace of God aimlessly."

Comment: δέξασθαι is the object infinitive of παρακαλοῦμεν, with ὑμᾶς as the accusative of general reference. εἰς κενὸν is a predicate use of the adverbial accusative. The supernatural reality of vicarious atonement described in 2 Cor.5:14-21 calls for supernatural results in the lives of those who receive the grace of God. The love of Christ put Paul under pressure, because he understood substitutionary atonement (2 Cor.5:14). Christ also will put pressure on all for whom He died with the manifestation of His love. Paul adds his plea in

Verse 2 - "("For he saith, I have heard thee in a time acceptable, and in the day of salvation have I succoured thee: behold, now is the accepted time; now is the day of salvation.)"

λέγει γάρ, Καιρῷ δεκτῷ ἐπήκουσά σου καὶ ἐν ἡμέρᾳ σωτηρίας ἐβοήθησά σοι. ἰδοὺ νῦν καιρὸς εὐπρόσκεκτος, ἰδοὺ νῦν ἡμέρα σωτηρίας —

"For he says, 'At the acceptable time I have listened to you, and helped you on the day of salvation.' Behold, now is the acceptable time; behold, now is the day of salvation." . . . RSV

λέγει (3d.per.sing.pres.act.ind.of λέγω, historical) 66.

γάρ (causal conjunction) 105.

καιρῷ (loc.sing.masc.of καιρός, time point) 767.

δεκτῷ (loc.sing.masc.of δεκτός, in agreement with καιρῷ) 2026.

#4311 ἐπήκουσά (1st.per.sing.aor.act.ind.of ἐπακούω, constative).

King James Version

hear - 2 Cor.6:2.

Revised Standard Version

listen to - 2 Cor.6:2.

Meaning: A combination of ἐπί (#47) and ἀκούω (#148). Hence, to listen to; give an ear to. LXX in Isa.49:8. Followed by an objective genitive in 2 Cor.6:2.

σοῦ (gen.sing.masc.of σύ, objective genitive) 104.

καὶ (adjunctive conjunction joining verbs) 14.

ἐν (preposition with the locative of time point) 80.

ἡμέρᾳ (loc.sing.fem.of ἡμέρα, time point) 135.

σωτηρίας (gen.sing.fem.of σωτηρία, description) 1852.

ἐβοήθησα (1st.per.sing.aor.act.ind.of βοηθέω, constative) 3716.

σοι (dat.sing.masc.of σύ, personal advantage) 104.

ἰδού (exclamation) 95.

νῦν (temporal adverb) 1497.

καιρὸς (nom.sing.masc.of καιρός, predicate nominative) 767.

εὐπρόσδεκτος (nom.sing.masc.of εὐπρόσδεκτος, in agreement with καιρὸς) 4052.

ἰδού (exclamation) 95.

νῦν (temporal adverb) 1497.

ἡμέρα (nom.sing.fem.of ἡμέρα, predicate nominative) 135.

σωτηρίας (gen.sing.fem.of σωτηρία, description) 1852.

Translation - "Because He said, 'I heard you at the proper time, and in the day of salvation I rescued you.' Look! Now is the accepted time. Look! Now is the day of salvation."

Comment: The quotation is from Isa.49:8. A careful reading of Isaiah's context reveals that God raised up national Israel and in His own good time He will do in and through the nation Israel all that pleases Him. The passage also says that Israel's light (Messiah) will also be "a light to the Gentiles" (Isa.49:6) to bring "salvation unto the end of the earth." God heard Israel's cry and rescued the nation from Egypt and will again rescue Israel from Antichrist and the combined Gentile powers (Zech.14:1-11) at the second coming of Messiah. He does all that He does *on time.* His time.

Now Paul says to the Corinthian gentile saints that "now is God's acceptable time to call out the gentiles - the day of salvation for them. The passage makes clear that God deals with Israel as a nation at one time and with His church at a different time, although there is temporal blending between the time periods, both at the beginning of His program to call out the gentiles and also at the end of this period. The Church, as the Body of Christ began before the close of Daniel's 69th week and it will not be complete until the close of Daniel's 70th week. (Rev.10:7).

The Corinthians who had received the grace of God (verse 1) are admonished not to regard their calling as something to be taken lightly.

Verse 2 is a parenthesis. The syntax of verse 1 connects with that of verse 3.

Verse 3 - "Giving no offence in any thing, that the ministry be not blamed."

μηδεμίαν ἐν μηδενὶ διδόντες προσκοπήν, ἵνα μὴ μωμηθῇ ἡ διάκονία,

"We put no obstacle in any one's way, so that no fault may be found with our ministry." . . . RSV

μηδεμίαν (acc.sing.fem.of μηδείς, in agreement with προσκοπήν) 713.
ἐν (preposition with the locative, accompanying circumstance) 80.
μηδενὶ (loc.sing.neut.of μηδείς, accompanying circumstance) 713.
διδόντες (pres.act.part.nom.pl.masc.of δίδωμι, adverbial, circumstantial) 362.

#4312 προσκοπήν (acc.sing.fem.of προσκοπή, direct object of διδόντες).

King James Version

offence - 2 Cor.6:3.

Revised Standard Version

obstacle - 2 Cor.6:3.

Meaning: A combination of πρός (#197) and κόπτω (#929). *Cf.*προσκόπτω (#352). Hence, something to stumble against; stumbling block. *Cf.*#3974. An occasion for making a valid criticism of someone. With μωμήομαι (#4313) in 2 Cor.6:3.

ἵνα (conjunction with the subjunctive, negative purpose) 114.
μὴ (negative conjunction with the subjunctive) 87.

#4313 μωμηθῇ (3d.per.sing.aor.pass.subj.of μωμάομαι, negative purpose).

King James Version

blame - 2 Cor.6:3; 8:20.

Revised Standard Version

find fault - 2 Cor.6:3.
blame - 2 Cor.8:20.

Meaning: Cf. μῶμος (#5257). Hence, to blame; to find fault; criticize; point to a blemish or imperfection. The unsaved should not be able to make a valid criticism of the gospel ministry - 2 Cor.6:3; 8:20.

ἡ (nom.sing.fem.of the article in agreement with διακονία) 9.
διακονία (nom.sing.fem.of διακονία, subject of μωμηθῇ) 2442.

Translation - "Giving not a single reason for offence in a single circumstance, lest the ministry be blamed."

Comment: Keep in mind that verse 2 is parenthetical. Thus we must take διδόντες in connection with verse 1, where the warning was against receiving the gospel of Christ with insufficient commitment to its ethical standards. Otherwise we are certain to behave in ways that reflect unfavorably on the gospel of Christ. The church age is God's accepted time period to allow the light of Israel also to lighten the Gentiles. How can Christians hinder God's work? By receiving the grace of God for salvation presumptuously. This results in antinomianism (Rom.6:1,2) and its inconsistent living which tends to reduce the impact of the gospel upon the unsaved to a nullity (verse 1). Thus we create a stumbling block and the result is criticism for the ministry of the gospel.

Note the particularity with which we should avoid offence - "Not a single offence on a single occasion." The negative side of the victorious life is given in verse 3. The positive side is given in

Verse 4 - "But in all things approving ourselves as the ministers of God, in much patience, in afflictions, in necessities, in distresses."

ἀλλ' ἐν παντὶ συνιστάνοντες ἑαυτοὺς ὡς θεοῦ διάκονοι, ἐν ὑπομονῇ πολλῇ, ἐν θλίφεσιν, ἐν ἀνάγκαις, ἐν στενοχωρίαις,

". . . but as servants of God we commend ourselves in every way: through great endurance, in afflictions, hardships, calamities, . . . " . . . RSV

ἀλλ' (alternative conjunction) 342.
ἐν (preposition with the locative of accompanying circumstance) 80.
παντὶ (loc.sing.neut.of πᾶς, accompanying circumstance) 67.
συνιστάνοντες (pres.act.part.nom.pl.masc.of συνίστημι, adverbial, modal) 2328.
ἑαυτοὺς (acc.pl.masc.of ἑαυτοῦ, direct object of συνιστάνοντες) 288.
ὡς (comparative particle) 128.
θεοῦ (gen.sing.masc.of θεός, relationship) 124.
διάκονοι (nom.pl.masc.of διάκονος, predicate nominative) 1334.
ἐν (preposition with the instrumental of means) 80.
ὑπομονῇ (instru.sing.fem.of ὑπομονή, means) 2204.
πολλῇ (instru.sing.fem.of πολύς, in agreement with ὑπομονῇ) 228.
ἐν (preposition with the locative, accompanying circumstance) 80.
θλίφεσιν (loc.pl.fem.of θλίφις, accompanying circumstance) 1046.
ἐν (preposition with the locative, accompanying circumstance) 80.
ἀνάγκαις (loc.pl.fem.of ἀνάγκη, accompanying circumstance) 1254.
ἐν (preposition with the locative, accompanying circumstance) 80.
στενοχωρίαις (loc.pl.fem.of στενοχωρία, accompanying circumstance) 3838.

Translation - "But in every situation as ministers of God we commend ourselves, by great patience, in tribulations, in dire need, under great pressure."

Comment: Note that διάκονοι is nominative, while ἑαυτοὺς is accusative. διάκονοι in the comparative clause is the predicate nominative of ἐσμέν which we supply - "We commend ourselves as we are the ministers of God." The locative of accompanying circumstances with ἐν except in ἐν ὑπομονῇ πολλῇ - an instrumental of means. Paul stayed under the load (ὑπομονή, #2204), despite the unfortunate circumstances of his life - persecutions, neccesities, pressures from all sides. The minister of God must behave in such circumstances like Jesus did (1 Pet.2:23). Only the Christian with an eternal point of view could behave in this fashion and still give a rational justification (2 Cor.4:16-18; Rom.8:18). The list of unhappy circumstances continues in

Verse 5 - "In stripes, in imprisonments, in tumults, in labours, in watchings, in fastings;"

ἐν πληγαῖς, ἐν φυλακαῖς, ἐν ἀκαταστασίαις, ἐν κόποις, ἐν ἀγρυπνίαις, ἐν νηστείαις,

"beatings, imprisonments, tumults, labors, watching, hunger;

ἐν (preposition with the locative of accompanying circumstance) 80.
πληγαῖς (loc.pl.fem.of πληγή, accompanying circumstance) 2421.
ἐν (preposition with the locative of accompanying circumstance) 80.
φυλακαῖς (loc.pl.fem.of φυλακή, accompanying circumstance) 494.
ἐν (preposition with the locative of accompanying circumstance) 80.
ἀκαταστασίαις (loc.pl.fem.of ἀκαταστασία, accompanying circumstance) 2718.
ἐν (preposition with the locative of accompanying circumstance) 80.
κόποις (loc.pl.masc.of κόπος, accompanying circumstance) 1565.
ἐν (preposition with the locative of accompanying circumstance) 80.

#4314 ἀγρυπνίαις (loc.pl.fem.of ἀγρυπνία, accompanying circumstance).

King James Version

watching - 2 Cor.6:5; 11:27.

Revised Standard Version

watching - 2 Cor.6:5.
sleepless night - 2 Cor.11:27.

Meaning: Insomnia. Inability to sleep - 2 Cor.6:5; 11:27.

ἐν (preposition with the locative of accompanying circumstance) 80.
νηστείαις (loc.pl.fem.of νηστεία, accompanying circumstance) 1239.

Translation - "when wounded, when in prison, in mob actions, in arduous toil, during sleepless nights, while fasting."

Comment: All of these are the circumstances that accompanied Paul at one time or another, because he was a faithful witness to Christ and to His saving grace. Thus he spells out ἐν παντί (verse 4), during which he seeks to commend himself to the public as befits God's minister. Literal bodily wounds, the result of stoning and whipping (#2421); the Ephesus mob where he almost lost his life (#2718); only here and in 2 Cor.11:27 does he mention his inability to sleep.

Not only in the midst of unfortunate circumstances does he commend himself, but also by certain Christian personal accomplishments and characteristics as in verses 6 and 7.

Verse 6 - "By pureness, by knowledge, by longsuffering, by kindness, by the Holy Ghost, by love unfeigned."

ἐν ἁγνότητι, ἐν γνώσει, ἐν μακροθυμίᾳ, ἐν χρηστότητι, ἐν πνεύματι ἁγίῳ, ἐν ἀγάπῃ ἀνυπκρίτῳ,

"by purity, knowledge, forbearance, kindness, the Holy Spirit, genuine love,.. ." . . . RSV

ἐν (preposition with the instrumental of means) 80.

#4315 ἁγνότητι (instru.sing.masc.of ἁγνότης, means).

King James Version

pureness - 2 Cor.6:6.
(not translated) - 2 Cor.11:3 (mgn.).

Revised Standard Version

purity - 2 Cor.6:6.
pure - 2 Cor.11:3 (mgn.).

Meaning: Cf. ἁγνός (#43330); ἁγνῶς (#4544). Chastity, purity, uprightness of life; with no taint of ethical inconsistency - 2 Cor.6:6; 11:3.

ἐν (preposition with the instrumental of means) 80.
γνώσει (instru.sing.fem.of γνῶσις, means) 1856.
ἐν (preposition with the instrumental of means) 80.
μακροθυμίᾳ (instru.sing.fem.of μακροθυμία, means) 3832.
ἐν (preposition with the instrumental of means) 80.
χρηστότητι (instru.sing.masc.of χρηστότης, means) 3830.
ἐν (preposition with the instrumental of agent) 80.
πνεύματι (instru.sing.neut.of πνεῦμα, agent) 83.
ἁγίῳ (instru.sing.neut.of ἅγιος, in agreement with πνεύματι) 84.
ἐν (preposition with the instrumental of means) 80.
ἀγάπῃ (instru.sing.fem.of ἀγάπη, means) 1490.
ἀνυποκρίτῳ (instru.sing.fem.of ἀνυπόκριτος, in agreement with ἀγάπῃ) 4021.

Translation - "By ethical purity, by knowledge, by forebearance, by kindness, by the Holy Spirit, by genuine love."

Comment: Moral and intellectual qualities are mentioned. Self-control is present in μακροθυμία (#3832). Sincerity is present in ἀνυποκρίτῳ - "non hypocritical" - the kind of love that is shown because one really feels it. Absence of pretense.

Verse 7 - "By the word of truth, by the power of God, by the armour of righteousness on the right hand and on the left."

ἐν λόγῳ ἀληθείας, ἐν δυνάμει θεοῦ. διὰ τῶν ὅπλων τῆς δικαιοσύνης τῶν δεξιῶν καὶ ἀριστερῶν,

"truthful speech, and the power of God; with the weapons of righteousness for the right hand and for the left;" . . . RSV

ἐν (preposition with the instrumental of means) 80.
λόγῳ (instru.sing.masc.of λόγος, means) 510.
ἀληθείας (gen.sing.fem.of ἀλήθεια, description) 1416.
ἐν (preposition with the instrumental of means) 80.
δυνάμει (instru.sing.fem.of δύναμις, means) 687.
θεοῦ (gen.sing.masc.of θεός, description) 124.
διὰ (preposition with the ablative of means) 118.
τῶν (abl.pl.neut.of the article in agreement with ὅπλων) 9.
ὅπλων (abl.pl.neut.of ὅπλον, means) 2804.
τῆς (gen.sing.fem.of the article in agreement with δικαιοσύνης) 9.
δικαιοσύνης (gen.sing.fem.of δικαιοσύνη, description) 322.
τῶν (gen.pl.neut.of the article in agreement with δεξιῶν) 9.
δεξιῶν (gen.pl.neut.of δεξιός, place description) 502.
καὶ (adjunctive conjunction joining nouns) 14.
ἀριστερῶν (gen.pl.neut.of ἀριστερός, place description) 564.

Translation - "By the truth of what I preach, by divine power, by means of the weapons of righteousness on the right hand and the left."

Comment: Note Paul's turn from an instrumental of means in ἐν λόγῳ and ἐν δυνάμει to the ablative of means with διὰ τῶν ὅπλων τῆς δικαιοσύνης. The ablative indicates source as well as means. The positive uprightness of God is a powerful weapon to commend the Christian to the world. *Cf.* Rom.13:12; 6:13b; 2 Cor.10:4. The supernatural characteristics of the Christian repertoire are featured in this verse. Truth, power and righteousness all come from God.

"The sword of the Spirit which is the word of God" is God's weaponry on the right and "the shield of faith wherewith . . . to quench all of the fiery darts of the wicked" is God's defense on the left (Eph.6:16,17).

The list goes on in

Verse 8 - "By honor and dishonor, by evil report and good report; as deceivers, and yet true;"

διὰ δόξης καὶ ἀτιμίας, διὰ δυσφημίας καὶ εὐφημίας. ὡς πλάνοι καὶ ἀληθεῖς,

"in honor and dishonor, in ill repute and good repute. We are treated as imposters, and yet are true;" . . . RSV

διὰ (preposition with the ablative, state) 118.
δόξης (abl.sing.fem.of δόξα, state) 361.
καὶ (adjunctive conjunction joining nouns) 14.
ἀτιμίας (abl.sing.fem.of ἀτιμία, state) 3808.
διὰ (preposition with the ablative, state) 118.

#4316 δυσφημίας (abl.sing.fem.of δυσφημία, state).

King James Version

evil report - 2 Cor.6:8.

Revised Standard Version

ill repute - 2 Cor.6:8.

Meaning: Cf. δυσφημέω (#4128). Defamation of character - 2 Cor.6:8.

καὶ (adjunctive conjunction joining nouns) 14.

#4317 εὐφημίας (abl.sing.fem.of εὐφημία, state).

King James Version

good report - 2 Cor.6:8.

Revised Standard Version

good repute - 2 Cor.6:8.

Meaning: A combination of εὖ (#1536) and φημί (#354). Hence, the result of a good report. Cf. εὔφημος (#4587). 2 Cor.6:8.

ὡς (comparative particle) 128.
πλάνοι (nom.pl.masc.of πλάνος, nominative absolute) 1682.
καὶ (adversative conjunction) 14.
ἀληθεῖς (nom.pl.masc.of ἀληθής, nominative absolute) 1415.

Translation - "*Amid honor and dishonor; when slandered and praised; as deceivers but true.*"

Comment: The explanation of ἐν παντί (verse 4) continues. Christians should labor to approve themselves as ambassadors of God in the world in all sorts of situations. Here Paul adds in periods when we are honored or dishonored; when we are maligned and when we are praised. He had used ἐν and the locative of accompanying circumstance, (verse 4), ἐν with the instrumental of means (vss.6,7) and διὰ with the ablative of state or condition (vss.7,8). Now he employs ὡς and the adversative καὶ (vss.8-10). He was honored by the saints and insulted by the sinners. On a few occasions superstitious people tried to worship him (Acts 14:11-13; 28:6). Both situations are fraught with danger for one who wishes only to glorify Christ. Paul knew how to behave both when under attack and when being unduly praised. "In the Clementines St.Paul is expressly described by his adversaries as πλανός and as disseminating deceit (πλανήν)." (Bernard, as cited in A.T.Robertson, *Word Pictures in the New Testament*, 235).

Verse 9 - *"As unknown, and yet well known; as dying, and, behold, we live; as chastened, and not killed."*

ὡς ἀγνοούμενοι καὶ ἐπιγινωσκόμενοι, ὡς ἀποθνῄσκοντες καὶ ἰδοὺ ζῶμεν, ὡς παιδευόμενοι καὶ μὴ θανατούμενοι,

"as unknown, and yet well known; as dying, and behold we live; as punished, and yet not killed;" . . . RSV

ὡς (comparative particle) 128.

ἀγνοούμενοι (pres.pass.part.nom.pl.masc.of ἀγνοέω, substantival, nominative absolute) 2345.

καὶ (adversative conjunction) 14.

ἐπιγινωσκόμενοι (pres.pass.part.nom.pl.masc.of ἐπιγινώσκω, substantival, nominative absolute) 675.

ὡς (comparative particle) 128.

ἀποθνῄσκοντες (pres.act.part.nom.pl.masc.of ἀποθνῄσκω, substantival, nominative absolute) 774.

καὶ (adversative conjunction) 14.

ἰδοὺ (exclamation) 95.

ζχῶμεν (1st.per.pl.pres.act.ind.of ζάω, aoristic) 340.

ὡς (comparative particle) 128.

παιδευόμενοι (pres.pass.part.nom.pl.masc.of παιδεύω, substantival, nominative absolute) 2838.

καὶ (adversative conjunction) 14.

μὴ (negative conjunction with the participle) 87.

θανατούμενοι (pres.pass.part.nom.pl.masc.of θανατόω, substantival, nominative absolute) 879.

Translation - *"Ignored and yet well known, reported as dying but Look! We are alive. Chastened but not killed."*

Comment: Paul's enemies tried to ignore him as though he were a nonentity - an obscure person without credentials, despite the fact that the Corinthian saints were his credentials (2 Cor.3:2). He was well known by those who really mattered (2 Cor.11:6). If Paul was a nobody who could safely be ignored, why did they try to kill him? Left for dead outside the city of Lystra (Acts 14:19), he revived and returned to the city (verse 20). Chastened often, he always survived. "His whole career is full of paradox" (Robertson, *Ibid.*). In all of this he tried to commend himself to the world as a minister of Christ.

Verse 10 - *"As sorrowful, yet alway rejoicing; as poor, yet making many rich; as having nothing, and yet possessing all things."*

ὡς λυπούμενοι ἀεὶ δὲ χαίροντες, ὡς πτωχοὶ πολλοὺς δὲ πλουτίζοντες, ὡς μηδὲν ἔχοντες καὶ πάντα κατέχοντες.

"as sorrowful, yet always rejoicing; as poor, yet making many rich; as having nothing, and yet possessing everything." . . . RSV

ὡς (comparative particle) 128.

λυπούμενοι (pres.pass.part.nom.pl.masc.of λυπέω, substantival, nominative absolute) 1113.

ἀεὶ (locative adverb, time point) 3149.

δὲ (adversative conjunction) 11.

χαίροντες (pres.act.part.nom.pl.masc.of χαίρω, substantival, nominative absolute) 182.

ὡς (comparative particle) 128.

πτωχοὶ (nom.pl.masc.of πτωχός, predicate adjective) 423.

πολλοὺς (acc.pl.masc.of πολύς, direct object of πλουτίζοντες) 228.

δὲ (adversative conjunction) 11.

πλουτίζοντες (pres.act.part.nom.pl.masc.of πλουτίζω, substantival, nominative absolute) 4100.

ὡς (comparative particle) 128.

μηδὲν (acc.sing.neut.of μηδείς, direct object of ἔχοντες) 713.

ἔχοντες (pres.act.part.nom.pl.masc.of ἔχω, substantival, nominative absolute) 82.

καὶ (concessive conjunction) 14.

πάντα (acc.pl.neut.of πᾶς, direct object of κατέχοντες) 67.

κατέχοντες (pres.act.part.nom.pl.masc.of κατέχω, substantival, nominative absolute) 2071.

Translation - "*As those overcome with sorrow, yet always rejoicing; as poor, but enriching many; as having nothing but in complete possession of everything.*"

Comment: Note the perfective force in κατά in κατέχοντες. The opposing emotions are characteristic of the victorious Christian. Sorrowful in the short run, yet rejoicing because of the eternal verities of the Christian long run. Sorrowful for the lost condition of sinners, yet happy in the joy of salvation. Stricken with poverty in an economic sense, yet, through his ministry, enriching his converts with spiritual riches. Possessing nothing in this world but an heir to all (Rom.8:17; 1 Cor.3:21-23). Paul knew how to commend himself as a Christian in poverty and wealth (Phil.4:12).

Verses 4-10 contain some of the most inspired writing of all Paul's God-breathed literature. The point is that everything else pales into insignificance in comparison with the problem the Christian faces in being a good representative of Jesus Christ, since this is the acceptable time when God is busy saving Gentiles (2 Cor.6:1-3). All else - whether we are beaten, imprisoned, caught up in riots, burdened with odious tasks, sleepless, hungry, dishonored, slandered, ignored, sorrowful and poor, is nothing compared with the fact that we display purity, knowledge, longsuffering, kindness, love, truth, God's power and faith. A

Christian who establishes a record of service for Christ like that indicates that truly he has "set (his) affection on things above, not on things on the earth" (Col.3:2). He has served with "eternity's values in view."

Verse 11 - "O ye Corinthians, our mouth is open unto you, our heart is enlarged."

Τὸ στόμα ἡμῶν ἀνέῳγεν πρὸς ὑμᾶς, Κορίνθιοι, ἡ καρδία ἡμῶν πεπλάτυνται.

"Our mouth is open to you, Corinthians; our heart is wide." . . . RSV

Τὸ (nom.sing.neut.of the article in agreement with στόμα) 9.
στόμα (nom.sing.neut.of στόμα, subject of ἀνέῳγεν) 344.
ἡμῶν (gen.pl.masc.of ἐγώ, possession) 123.
ἀνέῳγεν (3d.per.sing.2d.per.ind.of ἀνοίγω, intensive) 188.
πρὸς (preposition with the accusative, after a verb of speaking) 197.
ὑμᾶς (acc.pl.masc.of σύ, extent after a verb of speaking) 104.
Κορίνθιοι (voc.pl.masc.of Κορίνθιος, address) 3441.
ἡ (nom.sing.fem.of the article in agreement with καρδία) 9.
καρδία (nom.sing.fem.of καρδία, subject of πεπλάτυνται) 432.
ἡμῶν (gen.pl.masc.of ἐγώ, possession) 123.
πεπλάτυνται (3d.per.sing.perf.pass.ind.of πλατύνω, intensive) 1436.

Translation - "We are telling you everything, Corinthians. Our heart has been bursting."

Comment: The KJV translation is literal. ἀνέῳγεν is an intensive present perfect - almost purely durative. Paul is stressing the fact that he has never stopped appealing to the men of Corinth to live lives consistent with their Christian profession. In the past he has told them all that was in his heart and he will continue to do so. Then he emphasizes the intensity of his feeling toward them and his concern that they heed his message.

Verse 12 - "Ye are not straitened in us, but ye are straitened in your own bowels."

οὐ στενοχωρεῖσθε ἐν ἡμῖν, στενοχωρεῖσθε δὲ ἐν τοῖς σπλάγχνοις ὑμῶν.

"You are not restricted by us, but you are restricted in your own affections." . . . RSV

οὐ (negative conjunction with the indicative) 130.
στενοχωρεῖσθε (2d.per.pl.pres.pass.ind.of στενοχωρέω, aoristic) 4300.
ἐν (preposition with the instrumental of means) 80.
ἡμῖν (instrumental pl.masc.of ἐγώ, means) 123.
στενοχωρεῖσθε (2d.per.pl.pres.pass.ind.of στενοχωρέω, aoristic) 4300.
δὲ (adversative conjunction) 11.
ἐν (preposition with the instrumental of means) 80.
τοῖς (instru.pl.neut.of the article in agreement with σπλάγχνοις) 9.
σπλάγχνοις (instru.pl.neut.of σπλάγχνα, means) 1857.
ὑμῶν (gen.pl.masc.of σύ, possession) 104.

Translation - "You are not being put under pressure by us, but you are being constrained by your own feelings."

Comment: Paul seeks to show the Corinthians the true source of their affections for him and of their feeling of moral obligation to live victorious lives for Christ. He is putting pressure upon them but it is not a pressure that they could not and would not resist if they were not also placed under moral obligation by their own feelings. They knew in their own hearts what Paul was telling them and they were sure that he was right. *Cf.* James 5:11 where we have πολύσπλαγχνός (#5163) and 1 Pet.3:8 where we have εὔσπλαγχνοι (#4506).

Verse 13 - "Now for a recompence in the same (I speak as unto my children) be ye also enlarged."

τὴν δὲ αὐτὴν ἀντιμισθίαν, ὡς τέκνοις λέγω, πλατύνθητε καὶ ὑμεῖς.

"In return — I speak as to children — widen your hearts also." . . . *RSV*

τὴν (acc.sing.fem.of the article in agreement with ἀντιμισθίαν) 9.
δὲ (explanatory conjunction) 11.
αὐτὴν (acc.sing.fem.of αὐτός, in agreement with ἀντιμισθίαν, intensive) 16.
ἀντιμισθίαν (acc.sing.fem.of ἀντιμισθία, adverbial accusative) 3816.
ὡς (comparative particle) 128.
τέκνοις (dat.pl.masc.of τέκνον, indirect object of λέγω) 229.
λέγω (1st.per.sing.pres.act.ind.of λέγω, aoristic) 66.
πλατύνθητε (2d.per.pl.aor.pass.impv.of πλατύνω, entreaty) 1436.
καὶ (adjunctive conjunction joining substantives) 14.
ὑμεῖς (nom.pl.masc.of σύ, emphatic, subject of πλατύνθητε) 104.

Translation - "Now (I am speaking to you as my children) reward me in the same way by opening your hearts."

Comment: In exchange for Paul's heart, bursting with love for them, he pleads that they will reciprocate by pouring out their love for him. They can best show that love for him by living lives of separation from antiChristian forces. This is the final thought of the chapter in verses 14-18.

The Temple of the Living God

(2 Corinthians 6:14-7:1)

Verse 14 - "Be ye not unequally yoked together with unbelievers: for what fellowship hath righteousness with unrighteousness? And what communion hath light with darkness?"

Μὴ γίνεσθε ἑτεροζυγοῦντες ἀπίστοις, τίς γὰρ μετοχὴ δικαιοσύνῃ καὶ ἀνομίᾳ; ἢ τίς κοινωνία φωτὶ πρὸς σκότος;

"Do not be mismated with unbelievers. For what partnership have righteousness and iniquity? Or what fellowship has light with darkness?" . . .
RSV

Μή (negative conjunction with the imperative) 87.

γίνεσθε (2d.per.pl.pres.mid.impv.of γίνομαι, prohibition, present periphrastic) 113.

#4318 ἑτεροζυγοῦντες (pres.act.part.nom.pl.masc.of ἑτεροζυγέω, present periphrastic).

King James Version

be unequally yoked together with - 2 Cor.6:14.

Revised Standard Version

mismated - 2 Cor.6:14.

Meaning: A combination of ἕτερος (#605) and ζυγέω - "to march in line." *Cf.* ἑτερόζυγος in Lev.19:19, where crossbreeding of livestock is forbidden. With reference to Christians and their social and marriage relationships with unbelievers - 2 Cor.6:14.

ἀπίστοις (instrumental pl.masc.of ἄπιστος, association) 1231.
τίς (nom.sing.fem.of τίς, interrogative pronoun, in agreement with μετοχή) 281.

#4319 μετοχή (nom.sing.fem.of μετοχή, subject of γίνεται understood).

King James Version

fellowship - 2 Cor.6:14.

Revised Standard Version

partnership - 2 Cor.6:14.

Meaning: Cf. μέτοχος (#2050); μετέχω (#4176). Hence, mutual possession; sharing; partnership; fellowship. With reference to the lack of fellowship between δικαιοσύνη and ἀνομίᾳ - 2 Cor.6:14.

δικαιοσύνη (instru.sing.fem.of δικαιοσύνη, association) 322.
καί (adjunctive conjunction joining nouns) 14.
ἀνομίᾳ (instru.sing.fem.of ἀνομία, association) 692.
ἤ (disjunctive) 465.
τίς (nom.sing.fem.of τίς, interrogative pronoun, in agreement with κοινωνία) 281.
κοινωνία (nom.sing.fem.of κοινωνία, subject of γίνεται understood) 3001.
φωτί (instru.sing.neut.of φῶς, association) 379.
πρός (preposition with the accusative, extent) 197.

σκότος (acc.sing.neut.of σκότος, extent, metaphorical) 602.

Translation - "Put an end to your mismatch with unbelievers. What do righteousness and lawlessness have in common? Or what common benefit can exist between light and darkness?"

Comment: The present periphrastic with the imperative is rare in the New Testament. *Cf.* Mt.5:25; Lk.19:17; Eph.5:5. The present tense indicates that already the Corinthians were associated with unbelievers, and Paul orders them to sever the connection forthwith. - "Do not continue to be yoked together. . . "
The word is used in Lev.19:19 (LXX) to forbid crossbreeding of animals. The two rhetorical questions make the point. What do δικ. and άνομ have in common? δικαιοσύνη (#322) speaks of that which is legal; άνομία (#692) of that which is against the law. The setting into which each is oriented is totally opposed to that of the other. They strive for opposing goals and are motivated by opposing forces. δικαιοσύνη means order; άνομία results in chaos. Similarly there is no advantage either to light (φωτί) or darkness (σκότος) in their association. The light will not be harmed (John 1:5) and the darkness will be destroyed.

The New Testament bifurcation between opposites is clear from this passage. Relativism objects to clear-cut distinction between righteousness and lawnessness or between light and darkness, because of its inability clearly to define the one or the other. Thus the plea is for compromise - perhaps in the Hegelian sense. That it is sometimes difficult for us to tell the difference, due to human frailty, the lack of data and in the absence of an eternal point of view, can be admitted, but that a difference does in fact exist cannot be doubted by the Bible believer. God knows that a difference exists and He knows what it is.

Perhaps some separatist groups have gone too far in drawing distinctions, but the societal groups who insist upon including everything within a given fellowship are in clear opposition to Paul's directive here. Certainly Trinitarian and Unitarian theology, Theism, Deism and Atheism, secular humanism with its naturalism and Christianity with its supernaturalism - these are opposing concepts. We must be tolerant for temperance is one of the fruits of the Holy Spirit (Gal.5:23) but we must guard against the tolerance which becomes acceptance of Satan's error. Light has nothing to gain from association with its enemy, darkness (John 1:5). The student should study all the references under #'s 322, 692, 379 and 602 to realize how diametrically opposed these concepts are.

The rhetorical questions, making the same point, go on in verses 15 and 16.

Verse 15 - "And what concord hath Christ with Belial? Or what part hath he that believeth with an infidel?"

τίς δὲ συμφώνησις Χριστοῦ πρὸς Βελιάρ, ἢ τίς μερὶς πιστῷ μετὰ ἀπίστου;

"What accord has Christ with Belial? Or what has a believer in common with an unbeliever?" . . . RSV

τίς (nom.sing.fem.of τίς, interrogative pronoun, in agreement with συμφώνησις) 281.

δέ (continuative conjunction) 11.

#**4320** συμφώνησις (nom.sing.fem.of συμφώνησις, subject of verb understood).

King James Version

concord - 2 Cor.6:15.

Revised Standard Version

accord - 2 Cor.6:15.

Meaning: A combination of σύν (#1542) and φώνησις - "sounding, speaking, calling." *Cf.* φωνή (#222); φωνέω (#1338); συμφωνέω (#1265); συνφωνία (#2557); σύμφωνος (#4153). Hence, agreement, harmony - 2 Cor.6:15.

Χριστοῦ (gen.sing.masc.of Χριστός, possession) 4.
πρός (preposition with the accusative of extent, metaphorical) 197.

#**4321** Βελιάρ (acc.sing.masc.of Βελιάρ, metaphorical extent).

King James Version

Belial - 2 Cor.6:15.

Revised Standard Version

Belial - 2 Cor.6:15.

Meaning: The name of Satan in 2 Cor.6:15. Lord of the forest and desert. *Cf.* Isa.13:21; Mt.12:43.

ἤ (disjunctive) 465.
τίς (nom.sing.fem.of τίς, interrogative pronoun, in agreement with μερίς) 281.
μερίς (nom.sing.fem.of μερίς, subject of verb understood) 2445.
πιστῷ (dat.sing.masc.of πιστός, personal advantage) 1522.
μετά (preposition with the genitive, fellowship) 50.
ἀπίστου (gen.sing.masc.of ἄπιστος, fellowship) 1231.

Translation - "And what harmony exists between Messiah and Beliar? Or what part has a believer with an unbeliever?"

Comment: Since Messiah and Satan are the poles apart, the latter devoted to the task of pulling down the Former, Who is destined to cast the latter into Hell, it is manifestly impossible for the Christian believer in Messiah to have anything in common with an unbeliever whose mind is blinded by Beliar (2 Cor.4:4). The talk shows and round table discussion groups in which Christians and unbelievers seek common ground are exercises in futility, if the discussion goes beyond the weather forecast or the question as to who will win the World Series. It is here that the Christian parts company with the Hegelian dialectic. The

Christian thesis can never achieve synthesis with the unchristian antithesis. The Hegelian method is useful in seeking superficial accommodations in controversies that are not trenchant and therefore do not distinguish themselves in the cogent. Christians and unbelievers who build superstructural edifices of thought upon foundations of epistemology and metaphysics will come to agreement only at the expense of consistency of one side or the other and in most cases on the side of both.

Herbert Spencer's monumental *Social Statics* began with chapters on *Religion and Science, Ultimate Religious Ideas* and *Ultimate Scientific Ideas.* These are the first three chapters of Volume 1 which he called *The Unknowable.* Spencer accepted without question the Darwinian hypothesis and sought to bring all other "truth" into conformity with it. Thus we have the "Social Darwinism" with its *laissez faire* "get the government off our backs" philosophy that natural law demands that only the fit survive or deserve to survive. Thus antitrust laws like the Sherman, Clayton and Federal Trade Commission acts are mistakes, since the giant corporations should be rewarded for their size and allowed to control the market, with administered prices, even if this means the bankruptcies of small business and the end of free enterprise in a capitalist system. The Darwinian assumption is that natural law has shown that man is an evolving and therefore a rising creature and thus that every generation of survivors is better than the generation which is bested in the struggle for survival.

It is impossible for the logical mind to accommodate this line of thought with Christianity with its basic premise that man is a fallen, not a rising creature and its promise that despite the fall of man "the meek shall inherit the earth" and that the "peacemakers" not the warmongers "shall be called the children of God." Meekness ultimately shall prevail because Jesus in His incarnation was "meek and lowly of heart" for the suffering of death, but that after his resurrection "all power" which He will not hesitate to employ in the establishment of elemental justice has been "given unto Him in heaven and on earth" and He will use this power to establish a kingdom of righteousness which will never be destroyed.

Thus Darwinism and Christianity are as far apart as "righteousness and lawlessness," "light and darkness," "Christ and Beliar" and "he that believeth with an infidel." Christians who speak of theistic evolution indicate that they do not grasp the essence, either of evolution or Christianity, and they pay the price of being relegated to the level of intellectual mediocrity, just as Herbert Spencer was. Only in America was he "wined and dined." Oxford and Cambridge in his own native Great Britain withheld the praises which were heaped upon Spencer at Delmonico's at the end of his visit in America, as the master of ceremonies said that Spencer was the greatest mind of the century and expressed the hope that although they would never see each other again on earth they "would meet again in heaven"! We are not told how Spencer reacted to this prospect that he would spend eternity in heaven with an American preacher, but if his colleagues in Oxford and Cambridge had been offered the same hope it is likely that they would have chosen rather to spend eternity in a different climate. For Spencer had been sententious enough to write that ". . . the poverty of the incapable, the distresses that come upon the imprudent, the starvation of the idle, and those shoulderings aside of the weak by the strong, which leave so many 'in shallows and in miseries,' are the decrees of a large, farseeing benevolence. . . . It seems hard that widows and orphans should be left to struggle for life or death. Nevertheless, when regarded not separately, but in connection with the interests of universal humanity, these harsh fatalities are seen to be full of the highest beneficence. . . . " (Herbert Spencer, *Social Statics*, as cited in Stow Persons, *American Minds, A History of Ideas*, 226). This is Social Darwinism at its plainest and worst. It is in line with William Graham Sumner's remark that if a man cannot make his way in this world, it is his right to "make his way out of it." It is for the Fundamentalists in America who are famous for their opposition to Darwinism to explain why they engage in an all-out effort to deliver the Christian vote to the political party that promises to adjust fiscal policy in favor of the rich and powerful at the expense of the poor and helpless. It is probable that their intellectual level is on a par with that of the New York city preacher at Delmonico's who said goodbye to Herbert Spencer with the hope that they would "meet in heaven"! What agreement indeed, hath the temple of God with idols?" This is Paul's question in

Verse 16 - "And what agreement hath the temple of God with idols? For ye are the temple of the living God: as God hath said, I will dwell in them and walk in them; and I will be their God, and they shall be my people."

τίς δὲ συγκατάθεσις ναῷ θεοῦ μετὰ εἰδώλων; ἡμεῖς γὰρ ναὸς θεοῦ ἐσμεν ζῶντος. καθὼς εἶπεν ὁ θεὸς ὅτι, Ἐνοικήσω ἐν αὐτοῖς καὶ ἐμπεριπατήσω, καὶ ἔσομαι αὐτῶν θεός, καὶ αὐτοὶ ἔσονταί μου λαός.

"What agreement has the temple of God with idols? For we are the temple of the living God; as God said, 'I will live in them and move among them, and I will be their God, and they shall be my people.' " . . . RSV

τίς (nom.sing.fem.of τίς, interrogative pronoun, in agreement with συγκατάθεσις) 281.

δὲ (continuative conjunction) 11.

#4322 συγκατάθεσις (nom.sing.fem.of συγκατάθεσις, subject of the verb understood, in rhetorical question).

King James Version

agreement - 2 Cor.6:16.

Revised Standard Version

agreement - 2 Cor.6:16.

Meaning: A combination of σύν (#1542), κατά (#98) and τίθημι (#455). *Cf.* συγκατατίθεμαι (#2877). The result of placing (joint deposit) of votes which are thus expressed as being in agreement. Hence, agreement, approval, assent - 2 Cor.6:16.

ναῷ (dat.sing.masc.of ναός, personal advantage) 1447.

θεοῦ (gen.sing.masc.of θεός, description) 124.

μετά (preposition with the genitive, fellowship) 50.

εἰδώλων (gen.pl.neut.of εἴδωλον, fellowship) 3138.

ἡμεῖς (nom.pl.masc.of ἐγώ, subject of ἐσμεν) 123.

γάρ (causal conjunction) 105.

ναός (nom.sing.masc.of ναός, predicate nominative) 1447.

θεοῦ (gen.sing.masc.of θεός, description) 124.

ἐσμεν (1st.per.pl.pres.ind.of εἰμί, aoristic) 86.

ζῶντος (pres.act.part.gen.sing.masc.of ζάω, adjectival, predicate position, restrictive) 340.

καθώς (adverbial) 1348.

εἶπεν (3d.per.sing.aor.act.ind.of εἶπον, constative) 155.

ὁ (nom.sing.masc.of the article in agreement with θεός) 9.

θεός (nom.sing.masc.of θεός, subject of εἶπεν) 124.

ὅτι (recitative) 211.

Ἐνοικήσω (1st.per.sing.fut.act.ind.of ἐνοικέω, predictive) 3932.

ἐν (preposition with the locative of place) 80.

αὐτοῖς (loc.pl.masc.of αὐτός, place/association) 16.

καί (adjunctive conjunction joining verbs) 14.

#**4323** ἐμπεριπατήσω (1st.per.sing.fut.act.ind.of ἐμπεριπατέω, predictive).

King James Version

walk in - 2 Cor.6:16.

Revised Standard Version

move among - 2 Cor.6:16.

Meaning: A combination of ἐν (#80) and περιπατέω (#384). Hence, to walk around in the midst of; to walk among - with reference to God's fellowship with the saints - 2 Cor.6:16.

καί (adjunctive conjunction) 14.

ἔσομαι (1st.per.sing.fut.ind.of εἰμί, predictive) 86.

αὐτῶν (gen.pl.masc.of αὐτός, relationship) 16.

θεός (nom.sing.masc.of θεός, predicate nominative) 124.

καί (continuative conjunction) 14.

αὐτοί (nom.pl.masc.of αὐτός, subject of ἔσονταί) 16.

ἔσονταί (3d.per.pl.fut.ind.of εἰμί, predictive) 86.

μου (gen.sing.masc.of ἐγώ, relationship) 123.

λαός (nom.sing.masc.of λαός, predicate nominative) 110.

Translation - *"And what agreement does a divine temple enjoy with idols? Because we are each a temple of a living God, just as God said, 'I will dwell with them and move about among them; and I will be their God, and they will be my people."*

Comment: Another rhetorical question with an obvious reply. God cannot and will not make a deal with an idol. First, because it is far beneath His dignity, like a Ph.D. arguing with a low-grade moron or a line backer arguing with Casper Milquetoast. Unrelenting warfare exists between the living God and idolatry (Ex.20:1-6). There is no doubt that this warfare will result in the total destruction of the idols. What possible need has God for them? What possible advantage can He gain from their association? What have they to teach Him?

Now Paul reminds us that the body of every Christian is God's temple. He said this also in his first epistle to the Corinthians (1 Cor.3:16,17,17; 6:19). Note ἡμεῖς (plural) as subject with ἐσμεν (plural), but ναός, the singulate predicate nominative. Each Christian is *a temple* of God, the Living One. This fact of the mystical union of God and Christ in the believer (John 17:21) is alluded to in many scriptures *Cf.* Lev.26:12; Jer.32:38; Ezek.37:27; Isa.52:11; Ezek.20:34,41; Rev.18:4. The Living God is in us - closer than hands and feet and the air we breathe. He walks with us and among other Christians with whom we walk. Where we go, He goes. He is our God and we are His people. Our eternal destiny is tied up with Him. He is our Saviour and Lord, but He is also the unrelenting Judge of unbelievers and their lawlessness (verse 14), darkness (verse 14), Beliar and his infidels (verse 15) and with idols (verse 16).

It has often been remarked that Satan's programs could not long exist but for the financial and moral support given to them by God's people who ought to know better. If Christians would cease giving aid and comfort and financial support to the enemy, any one of the Devil's programs (drugs, liquor, illicit sex, gambling, etc.) would be forced to compete with the others for the consumption spending power of the Devil's children. When an unbeliever spends his money on drugs, he has none left for liquor. Thus, were it not for the Christian's money spent in the liquor market, that market would decline. And so with all of the others. A little more than 50% of the population of the United States are members of some kind of Christian church, though it is perhaps naive to suppose that every church member is a regenerate member of the Body of Christ. It would be interesting to discover what would happen in the sin markets of America if every church member complied with Paul's suggestion in verse 17.

The enervating effect of compromise with the world upon the spiritual impact of the Christian witness dishonors God, Who lives within us. The conclusion of the argument, based upon these rhetorical questions of verses 14-16 is the imperative of verse 17 and the promise of verse 18.

Verse 17 - "Wherefore come out from among them, and be ye separate, saith the Lord, and touch not the unclean thing; and I will receive you."

διὸ ἐξέλθατε ἐκ μέσου αὐτῶν καὶ ἀφορίσθητε, λέγει κύριος, καὶ ἀκαθάρτου μὴ ἅπτεσθε. καγὼ εἰσδέξομαι ὑμᾶς,

"Therefore come out from them, and be separate from them, says the Lord, and touch nothing unclean; then I will welcome you, . . . " . . . RSV

διὸ (inferential particle) 1622.

ἐξέλθατε (2d.per.pl.aor.impv.of ἐξέρχομαι, command) 161.

ἐκ (preposition with the ablative of separation) 19.

μέσου (abl.sing.masc.of μέσος, separation) 873.

αὐτῶν (gen.pl.masc.of αὐτός, description) 16.

καὶ (adjunctive conjunction joining verbs) 14.

ἀφορίσθητε (2d.per.pl.aor.mid.impv.of ἀφορίζω, command) 1093.

λέγει (3d.per.sing.pres.act.ind.of λέγω, historical) 66.

κύριος (nom.sing.masc.of κύριος, subject of λέγει) 97.

καὶ (adjunctive conjunction joining verbs) 14.

ἀκαθάρτου (gen.sing.neut.of ἀκάθαρτος, objective genitive) 843.

μὴ (negative conjunction with the imperative) 87.

ἅπτεσθε (2d.per.pl.pres.mid.impv.of ἅπτω, command) 711.

κἀγὼ (continuative conjunction and first personal pronoun, crasis) 178.

#4324 εἰσδέξομαι (1st.per.sing.fut.mid.ind.of εἰσδέχομαι, predictive).

King James Version

receive - 2 Cor.6:17.

Revised Standard Version

welcome - 2 Cor.6:17.

Meaning: A combination of εἰς (#140) and δέχομαι (#867). Hence, to receive; to welcome - 2 Cor.6:17.

ὑμᾶς (acc.pl.masc.of σύ, direct object of εἰσδέξομαι) 104.

Translation - "So come out from among them and separate yourselves once for all, said the Lord, and stop touching that which is unclean and I will welcome you."

Comment: The imperatives ἐξέλθατε and ἀφορίσθητε are aorist while ἅπτεσθε is present tense. God is demanding a "once for all" separation from and ban upon any further association with the unclean. He assumes that they are guilty - "Stop touching" ("do not go on touching") the unclean." *Cf.* Isa.52:11.

Separatist Christian groups point to this passage as scriptural warrant for their voluntary exodus from alleged apostate church bodies. In order to determine whether or not 2 Cor.6:17 supports their view we must identify the antecedent of αὐτῶν and the identity of ἀκαθάρτου. Who or what is ἀκαθάρτου and whom did Paul mean by αὐτῶν? It seems clear that the antecedents of αὐτῶν are ἀπίστοις, ἀνομίᾳ and σκότος of verse 14, βελιάρ and ἀπίστου of verse 15 and εἰδώλων of verse 16. Unbelievers, lawlessness, darkness, Satan, infidels and idols are clearly off limits to Christians. Where were these to be found in Corinth? Chiefly in the idol temples and the Christians were forbidden to frequent them. But if also in the church in individual cases, the remedy was not that the majority should withdraw from the heretical minority, but that the former should discipline and dismiss the latter. The Corinthian saints were told to boycott the temple of the pagan idol which was dedicated to heresy, lawlessness, darkness, unbelief, Satan and his program, but they were told, not in this passage, but in 1 Cor.5:4,5, to discipline and dismiss from their fellowship the evil doer.

All forms of the so-called "Modernism" by which should be meant unitarian theology, with its denial of Christ's deity, virgin birth, vicarious death, bodily resurrection, etc., etc. and other apostate denials of the Christian faith must be forsaken for the same reason that Paul told the Corinthians to boycott the pagan temple and its program. Paul was not speaking to them about unbelievers in the church. He was speaking to them about their associations with pagans in the temple of pagan worship.

Had the Christian churches, through the ages disciplined heretics, schismatics and other unworthy Christians and, in the event that they did not respond to treatment with repentance, dismissed them from the fellowship, the present need for minority groups of believers to withdraw from larger apostate bodies would never have arisen. In the 1930's several large denominational bodies were thought by some to be securely held in the control of apostates. Thus it was thought that there was nothing for Christians to do but secede. These people who severed their connections with those whom they called heretics pointed to 2 Cor.6:17 for justification for their action. For them the large church bodies had become what to the Corinthian Christians was a pagan temple. Whether their action was necessary in order to preserve the purity of the Christian theology as revealed in the New Testament is a question which may not be settled satisfactorily until we get to heaven. There is no doubt that these small seceder groups have themselves given aid and comfort to doctrines which are not scriptural.

It should be pointed out that minor differences of opinion among brethren who otherwise are in agreement upon the foundational facts of Christian orthodoxy, should not be grounds for disfellowship. A failure to distinguish between focal and peripheral differences has resulted in turning Christians with grounds for separation because of heresy in focal areas into bigots with only unchristian intolerance for minor, albeit honest differences of opinion with reference to peripheral truth. A church body that splits over a piano only to see the split splinter over a tuning fork (!) is an example of bigotry. Whether what is served at the Lord's table is wine or grape juice is not grounds for separation, in the opinion of most sophisticated Christians. But the question is more serious when a Christian is asked to fellowship, in terms of personal presence, service and financial support with a group who rejects, out of hand, the deity of Jesus Christ. Just how we separate focal from peripheral truth is a question to be decided by each individual. Personally I had rather fellowship a Trinitarian, Calvinistic, Redemptionist who is also a pedo-baptist than a Baptist who denies the deity of Jesus Christ. Minor eschatological differences of opinion have been the source of much unchristian intolerant bigotry. It would seem that all who can agree upon Peter's confession of Mt.16:16 should be able to fellowship in an ecumenical structure, while worshipping in their own church groups on a more strictly defined basis. He who says with Peter, "Thou art the Christ, the Son of the Living God," is my brother, whether he agrees with me on the peripheral issues or not.

The rest of God's promise to the obedient Christian is in

Verse 18 - "And will be a Father unto you, and ye shall be my sons and daughters, saith the Lord Almighty."

καὶ ἔσομαι ὑμῖν εἰς πατέρα, καὶ ὑμεῖς ἔσεσθέ μοι εἰς υἱοὺς καὶ θυγατέρας, λέγει κύριος παντοκράτωρ.

". . . and I will be a father to you, and you shall be my sons and daughters, says the Lord Almighty." . . . RSV

καὶ (adjunctive conjunction joining verbs) 14.
ἔσομαι (1st.per.sing.fut.ind.of εἰμί, predictive) 86.
ὑμῖν (dat.pl.masc.of σύ, personal advantage) 104.
εἰς (preposition with the accusative, predicate use) 140.
πατέρα (acc.sing.masc.of πατήρ, predicate accusative) 238.
καὶ (continuative conjunction) 14.
ὑμεῖς (nom.pl.masc.of σύ, subject of ἔσεσθε, emphatic) 104.
ἔσεσθέ (2d.per.pl.fut.ind.of εἰμί, predictive) 86.
μοι (dat.sing.masc.of ἐγώ, personal advantage) 123.
εἰς (preposition with the accusative, predicate use) 140.
υἱοὺς (acc.pl.masc.of υἱός, predicate accusative) 5.
καὶ (adjunctive conjunction joining nouns) 14.
θυγατέρας (acc.pl.fem.of θυγάτηρ, predicate accusative) 817.
λέγει (3d.per.sing.pres.act.ind.of λέγω, historical) 66.
κύριος (nom.sing.masc.of κύριος, subject of λέγει) 97.

#4325 παντοκράτωρ (nom.sing.masc.of παντοκράτωρ, apposition).

King James Version

Almighty - 2 Cor.6:18; Rev.1:8; 4:8; 11:17; 15:3; 16:7,14; 19:15; 21:22.
Omnipotent - Rev.19:6.

Revised Standard Version

Almighty - 2 Cor.6:18; Rev.1:8; 4:8; 11:17; 15:3; 16:7,14; 19:6,15; 21:22.

Meaning: A combination of πᾶς (#67) and κρατέω (#828). The One Who controls and rules over all. Almighty. Omnipotent. In apposition with Κύριος often. Only in 2 Cor.6:18 outside of the Revelation.

Translation - "And I will be to you a Father, and you will be to me sons and daughters, said the Lord Almighty."

Comment: Note εἰς and the accusative in a predicate use instead of the predicate nominative. *Cf.* #140. *Cf.* Robertson, *Grammar*, 457,458; 595. The idiom is "formed on a Hebrew model though it is not un-Greek." Those with whom the

Sovereign Lord wishes to be identified as a Father and whom He thus claims as sons and daughters can never be denied participation in the Body of Christ, nor denied the advantage of our personal fellowship even though for disciplinary purposes they have been excluded from the fellowship of the local church. The Corinthians did not boycott the man of 1 Cor.5:1-5 after they had excluded him from membership in the church. Had they done so, it is not likely that he would have been restored to their fellowship (2 Cor.2:1-7). The practice which some groups call "Shunning" is a cruel social discrimination against the backslider who has been dismissed from the church. If one practices sin without repentance and resists all efforts of the church to lead him back to obedience he should be dismissed, after the prescribed procedure has been followed (Mt.18:15-17), but he should not be shunned. Whom the Father has not forsaken should never be forsaken by the Father's sons and daughters.

Some separatist groups have gone far beyond this and have withdrawn from associations in which God's sons and daughters were still to be found. If God calls another Christian His son or His daughter I cannot exclude him from my fellowship however we might disagree with reference to peripheral matters of faith and practice. God, of course is not the Father of those who reject His Son.

The careful distinctions which must be drawn between focal and peripheral theology and between personal and church fellowship are necessary if we are to avoid the confusion and bitterness which now prevails in the Body of Christ.

2 Cor.7:1 - "Having therefore these promises, dearly beloved, let us cleanse ourselves from all filthiness of the flesh and spirit, perfecting holiness in the fear of God."

ταύταις οὖν ἔχοντες τὰς ἐπαγγελίας, ἀγαπητοί, καθαρίσωμεν ἑαυτοὺς ἀπὸ παντὸς μολυσμοῦ σαρκὸς καὶ πνεύματος, ἐπιτελοῦντες ἁγιωσύνην ἐν φόβῳ θεοῦ.

"Since we have these promises, beloved, let us cleanse ourselves from every defilement of body and spirit, and make holiness perfect in the fear of God." ...
                                                                                    RSV

ταύτας (acc.pl.fem.of οὗτος, in agreement with ἐπαγγελίας) 93.
οὖν (inferential conjunction) 68.
ἔχοντες (pres.act.part.nom.pl.masc.of ἔχω, adverbial, causal) 82.
τὰς (acc.pl.fem.of the article in agreement with ἐπαγγελίας) 9.
ἐπαγγελίας (acc.pl.fem.of ἐπαγγελία, direct object of ἔχοντες) 2929.
ἀγαπητοί (voc.pl.masc.of ἀγαπητός, address) 327.
καθαρίσωμεν (1st.per.pl.aor.act.subj.of καθαρίζω, hortatory) 709.
ἑαυτοὺς (acc.pl.masc.of ἑαυτός, direct object of καθαρίσωμεν) 288.
ἀπὸ (preposition with the ablative of separation) 70.
παντὸς (abl.sing.masc.of πᾶς, in agreement with μολυσμοῦ) 67.

#4326 μολυσμοῦ (abl.sing.masc.of μολυσμός, separation).

King James Version

filthiness - 2 Cor.7:1.

Revised Standard Version

defilement - 2 Cor.7:1.

Meaning: Cf. μολύνω (#4171); an action by which a thing is defiled. Followed by a genitive of description in 2 Cor.7:1.

σαρκὸς (gen.sing.fem.of σάρξ, description) 1202.
καὶ (adjunctive conjunction joining nouns) 14.
πνεύματος (gen.sing.neut.of πνεῦμα, description) 83.
ἐπιτελοῦντες (pres.act.part.nom.pl.masc.of ἐπιτελέω, adverbial, telic) 4059.
ἁγιωσύνην (acc.sing.fem.of ἁγιωσύνη, direct object of ἐπιτελοῦντες) 3784.
ἐν (preposition with the instrumental of cause) 80.
φόβῳ (instru.sing.masc.of φόβος, cause) 1131.
θεοῦ (gen.sing.masc.of θεός, description) 124.

Translation - "So, since we have these promises, beloved, let us begin to cleanse ourselves of all defilement of flesh and spirit, in order to perfect holiness out of reverence for God."

Comment: ταύτας is anaphoric, referring to verses 16-18 of Chapter 6. οὖν is inferential. ἔχοντες is cause. It is because we have the promises of the preceding verses that Paul exhorts us (hortatory subjunctive) to cleanse ourselves. Note that the defilement is both fleshly and spiritual (intellectual, psychological). Sins of the flesh are not the only sins that militate against the Christian's fellowship with God. *Cf.* Gal.5:19-21; Mk.7:21-23. In both these lists both mind and body are defiled. *Cf.* also Romans 1:29-32.

The realization of the truth contained in God's promise, *viz.* that we are His sons and daughters and that He wants to enjoy close fellowship with us should be sufficient motivation for our efforts to complete the *gestalt* (pattern) of holiness. Note ἐπιτελοῦντες, the telic adverbial participle. If we do not rid ourselves of the defilements of flesh and mind we shall never be able to complete the sanctification process (perfect holiness). This is a goal for every Christian, albeit not to be realized fully until glorification. That we shall not be like Him totally until we see Him as He is (1 John 3:1-3) is no reason for us not to try to achieve the goal. Every Christian who has this hope makes the effort and every effort results in some progress. *Cf.* Mt.5:48. The Heavenly Father is perfect. Thus we reverence Him. He is *our* Father. The relationship is personal and suggests the closest of human ties and it is much to be desired. Thus the Christian ethic is the perfection of holiness. And this requires separation from the enemy as Paul had suggested in 2 Cor.6:14-18.

A prominent reason why Christians are involved with the enemy in close friendly relationships is their lack of appreciation of the fact that the divine power of God, with which they are associated in Christ, is in unremitting combat with the forces of evil with which they are allied in social relationships on earth. These evil forces are destined for total destruction. Why should a child of God cooperate with and give aid and comfort to the mortal enemies of his Heavenly Father? The demands of ἁγιωσύνη (#3784) require the Christian to "die daily" (1 Cor.15:31), to "reckon (ourselves) to be dead indeed unto sin, but alive unto God through Jesus Christ our Lord" (Romans 6:11) and to "pray without ceasing" (1 Thess.5:17) for the fulness of the Holy Spirit (Luke 11:11-13). It means completion of the will of God for us (Phil.1:6).

A popular slogan for Christians who understand this says

> *Be patient! God is not through with me yet.*

Paul's Joy at the Church's Repentance

(2 Corinthians 7:2-16)

Verse 2 - "Receive us; we have wronged no man, we have corrupted no man, we have defrauded no man."

Χωρήσατε ἡμᾶς. οὐδένα ἠδικήσαμεν, οὐδένα ἐφθείραμεν, οὐδένα ἐπλεονεκτήσαμεν.

"Open your hearts to us; we have wronged no one, we have corrupted no one, we have taken advantage of no one." . . . RSV

Χωρήσατε (2d.per.pl.aor.act.impv.of χωρέω, entreaty) 1162.

ἡμᾶς (acc.pl.masc.of ἐγώ, direct object of χωρήσατε) 123.

οὐδένα (acc.sing.masc.of οὐδείς, direct object of ἠδικήσαμεν) 446.

ἠδικήσαμεν (1st.per.pl.aor.act.ind.of ἀδικέω, culminative) 1327.

οὐδένα (acc.sing.masc.of οὐδείς, direct object of ἐφθείραμεν) 446.

ἐφθείραμεν (1st.per.pl.1st.aor.act.ind.of φθείρω, culminative) 4119.

οὐδένα (acc.sing.masc.of οὐδείς, direct object of ἐπλεονεκτήσαμεν) 446.

ἐπλεονεκτήσαμεν (1st.per.pl.aor.act.ind.of πλεονεκτέω, culminative) 4276.

Translation - "Make room for us; we have been unjust to no one; we have corrupted no one; we have cheated no one."

Comment: *Cf.* #'s 1162, 1327, 4119 and 4276 for the basic meaning of the words. Paul pleads for acceptance from the Corinthians and defends his past behavior. Note the culminative aorists. Nothing evil has resulted from Paul's treatment of the Corinthians. That he means "Make room for us in your hearts" is clear from the emotional tone of

Verse 3 - "I speak not this to condemn you; for I have said before, that ye are in our hearts to die and live with you."

πρὸς κατάκρισιν οὐ λέγω, προείρηκα γὰρ ὅτι ἐν ταῖς καρδίαις ἡμῶν ἐστε εἰς τὸ συναποθανεῖν καὶ συζῆν.

"I do not say this to condemn you, for I said before that you are in our hearts, to die together and to live together." . . . RSV

πρὸς (preposition with the accusative, purpose) 197.

κατάκρισιν (acc.sing.fem.of κατάκρισις, purpose) 4289.

οὐ (negative conjunction with the indicative) 130.

λέγω (1st.per.sing.pres.act.ind.of λέγω, aoristic) 66.

προείρηκα (1st.per.sing.perf.act.ind.of προεῖπον, dramatic) 1501.

γὰρ (causal conjunction) 105.

ὅτι (conjunction introducing an object clause in indirect discourse) 211.

ἐν (preposition with the locative, place, metaphorical) 80.

ταῖς (loc.pl.fem.of the article in agreement with καρδίαις) 9.

καρδίαις (loc.pl.fem.of καρδία, metaphorical place) 432.

ἡμῶν (gen.pl.masc.of ἐγώ, possession) 123.

ἐστε (2d.per.pl.pres.ind.of εἰμί, present retroactive) 86.

εἰς (preposition with the accusative, purpose) 140.

τὸ (acc.sing.neut.of the article, in agreement with συναποθανεῖν) 9.

συναποθανεῖν (aor.act.inf.of συναποθνήσκω, articular infinitive of purpose) 2769.

καὶ (adjunctive conjunction joining infinitives) 14.

συζῆν (pres.act.inf.of συζάω, purpose) 3912.

Translation - "I am not saying this in order to condemn you, for I have said before that you have a place in our hearts so that we may die with you and always live."

Comment: The emotional outburst of verse 2 calls for explanation - even apology. He says that he does not mean to imply that they would not receive him in their hearts, nor that they were in fact accusing him of harming anyone. Now he assures them that he still feels the same as he did when he said previously (2 Cor.6:11,12) that (indirect discourse with ὅτι) they had such a place of devotion in his heart that he hoped both to die with them and then live with them forever (purpose with εἰς and the articular infinitives). Note only one death (aorist in συναποθανεῖν) but continuous life (present tense in συζῆν).

Verse 4 - "Great is my boldness of speech toward you, great is my glorying of you: I am filled with comfort, I am exceedingly joyful in all our tribulation."

πολλή μοι παρρησία πρὸς ὑμᾶς, πολλή μοι καύχησις ὑπὲρ ὑμῶν. πεπλήρωμαι τῇ παρακλήσει, ὑπερπερισσεύομαι τῇ χαρᾷ ἐπὶ πάσῃ τῇ θλίψει ἡμῶν.

"I have great confidence in you; I have great pride in you; I am filled with comfort. With all our affliction, I am overjoyed." . . . RSV

πολλή (nom.sing.fem.of πολύς, predicate adjective) 228.

μοι (dat.sing.masc.of ἐγώ, possession) 123.

παρρησία (nom.sing.fem.of παρρησία, subject of ἐστίν understood) 2319.

πρὸς (preposition with the accusative of extent, after a verb of speaking) 197.
ὑμᾶς (acc.pl.masc.of σύ, extent after a verb of speaking) 104.
πολλή (nom.sing.fem.of πολύς, predicate adjective) 228.
μοι (dat.sing.masc.of ἐγώ, possession) 123.
καύχησις (nom.sing.fem.of καύχησις, subject of ἐστίν understood) 3877.
ὑπὲρ (preposition with the genitive of reference) 545.
ὑμῶν (gen.pl.masc.of σύ, reference) 104.
πεπλήρωμαι (1st.per.sing.perf.pass.ind.of πληρόω, intensive) 115.
τῇ (instru.sing.fem.of the article in agreement with παρακλήσει) 9.
παρακλήσει (instru.sing.fem.of παράκλησις, manner) 1896.
ὑπερπερισσεύομαι (1st.per.sing.pres.mid.ind. of ὑπερπερισσεύω, aoristic) 3908.
τῇ (instru.sing.fem.of the article in agreement with χαρᾷ) 9.
χαρᾷ (instru.sing.fem.of χαρά, manner) 183.
ἐπὶ (preposition with the locative of accompanying circumstance) 47.
πάσῃ (loc.sing.fem.of πᾶς, in agreement with θλίφει) 67.
τῇ (loc.sing.fem.of the article in agreement with θλίφει) 9.
θλίφει (loc.sing.fem.of θλίφις, accompanying circumstance) 1046.
ἡμῶν (gen.pl.masc.of ἐγώ, possession) 123.

Translation - "My boldness toward you is great; I am very proud of you; I am filled with consolation; I am overflowing with joy in the midst of all our tribulation."

Comment: μοι is a dative of possession. Paul's lack of restraint results from his pride in the Corinthians and his complete comfort and overflowing joy, despite his trouble. *Cf.* Mt.5:10-12; 1 Pet.4:12-14; James 1:2.

Having mentioned his troubles he goes further to describe them in

Verse 5 - "For, when we were come into Macedonia, our flesh had no rest, but we were troubled on every side; without were fightings, within were fears."

Καὶ γὰρ ἐλθόντων ἡμῶν εἰς Μακεδονίαν οὐδεμίαν ἔσχηκεν ἄνεσιν ἡ σάρξ ἡμῶν, ἀλλ' ἐν παντὶ θλιβόμενοι — ἔξωθεν μάχαι, ἔσωθεν φόβοι.

"For even when we came into Macedonia, our bodies had no rest but we were afflicted at every turn — fighting without and fear within." . . . RSV

Καὶ (emphatic conjunction) 14.
γὰρ (causal conjunction) 105.
ἐλθόντων (aor.act.part.gen.pl.masc.of ἔρχομαι, genitive absolute, culminative) 146.
ἡμῶν (gen.pl.masc.of ἐγώ, genitive absolute) 123.
εἰς (preposition with the accusative of extent) 140.
Μακεδονίαν (acc.sing.fem.of Μακεδονία, extent) 3360.
οὐδεμίαν (acc.sing.fem.of οὐδείς, in agreement with ἄνεσιν) 446.
ἔσχηκεν (3d.per.sing.perf.ind.of ἔχω, intensive) 82.
ἄνεσιν (acc.sing.fem.of ἄνεσις, direct object of ἔσχηκεν) 3628.

ἡ (nom.sing.fem.of the article in agreement with σάρξ) 9.
σάρξ (nom.sing.fem.of σάρξ, subject of ἔσχηκεν) 1202.
ἡμῶν (gen.pl.masc.of ἐγώ, possession) 123.
ἀλλ' (alternative conjunction) 342.
ἐν (preposition with the locative of accompanying circumstance) 80.
παντὶ (loc.sing.neut.of πᾶς, accompanying circumstance) 67.
θλιβόμενοι (pres.pass.part.nom.pl.masc.of θλίβω, adverbial, causal) 667.
ἔξωθεν (preposition with the ablative) 1455.

#4327 μάχαι (nom.pl.fem.of μάχη, subject of verb understood).

King James Version

fighting - 2 Cor.7:5; Jam.4:1.
strife - 2 Tim.2:23.
striving - Titus 3:9.

Revised Standard Version

fighting - 2 Cor.7:5; Jam.4:1.
quarrels - 2 Tim.2:23; Titus 3:9.

Meaning: Cf. μάχαιρα (#896); μάχομαι (#2291). Hence, fight, combat, controversy, in some cases physical - 2 Cor.7:5; Jam.4:1; of an intellectual, theoretical nature - 2 Tim.2:23; Titus 3:9.

ἔσωθεν (adverbial) 672.
φόβοι (nom.pl.masc.of φόβος, subject of verb understood) 1131.

Translation - "Because as a matter of fact, after we came to Macedonia our flesh had not a single moment of relaxation, but, under pressure in all circumstances, we were beset by external conflicts and internal fears."

Comment: καὶ is emphatic and γὰρ is causal. ἐλθόντων ἡμῶν is a genitive absolute in the aorist tense, indicating antecedent time to that of the main verb, the present perfect ἔσχηκεν. After Paul got to Macedonia he was in constant tumult. There was not a moment of rest. This, of course, is hyperbole. Otherwise Paul could not have survived. Read the story of Paul's difficulties in Acts 16-17. But Paul was not left without relief as we learn in

Verse 6 - "Nevertheless God, that comforteth those that are cast down, comforted us by the coming of Titus."

ἀλλ' ὁ παρακαλῶν τοὺς ταπεινοὺς παρεκάλεσεν ἡμᾶς ὁ θεός, ἐν τῇ παρουσίᾳ Τίτου.

"But God, who comforts the downcast, comforted us by the coming of Titus, . . ." . . . RSV

ἀλλ' (adversative conjunction) 342.
ὁ (nom.sing.masc.of the article in agreement with παρακαλῶν) 9.

παρακαλῶν (pres.act.part.nom.sing.masc.of παρακαλέω, substantival, subject of παρεκάλεσεν) 230.

τοὺς (acc.pl.masc.of the article in agreement with ταπεινοὺς) 9.

ταπεινοὺς (acc.pl.masc.of ταπεινός, direct object of παρεκάλεσεν) 957.

παρεκάλεσεν (3d.per.sing.aor.act.ind.of παρακαλέω, constative) 230.

ἡμᾶς (acc.pl.masc.of ἐγώ, direct object of παρεκάλεσεν) 123.

ὁ (nom.sing.masc.of the article in agreement with θεὸς) 9.

θεὸς (nom.sing.masc.of θεός, apposition) 124.

ἐν (preposition with the instrumental of means) 80.

τῇ (instru.sing.fem.of the article in agreement with παρουσίᾳ) 9.

παρουσίᾳ (instru.sing.fem.of παρουσία, means) 1482.

Τίτου (gen.sing.masc.of Τίτος, description) 4278.

Translation - *"But the One Who comforts those who are discouraged is God Who comforted us by the coming of Titus."*

Comment: The presence of the articles, both with παρακαλῶν and θεὸς, and the accusative cases, both of ταπεινοὺς and ἡμᾶς, make it difficult to say which is subject of the verb and which is in apposition. "The Comforter" and "God" refer to the same person and "the discouraged" and "us" also refers to Paul and his friends. The fact that God is the Comforter is emphasized. As such He comforted Paul. How? By the arrival of Titus from Corinth with his report about how the Corinthians reacted to Paul's first epistle. Thus Paul was greatly relieved since he had feared that they would react the wrong way. *Cf.*2 Cor.2:13.

This point Paul develops in the remainder of the chapter.

Verse 7 - *"And not by his coming only, but by the consolation wherewith he was comforted in you, when he told us your earnest desire, your mourning, your fervent mind toward me; so that I rejoiced the more."*

οὐ μόνον δὲ ἐν τῇ παρουσίᾳ αὐτοῦ ἀλλὰ καὶ ἐν τῇ παρακλήσει ᾗ παρεκλήθη ἐφ' ὑμῖν, ἀναγγέλλων ἡμῖν τὴν ὑμῶν ἐπιπόθησιν, τὸν ὑμῶν ὀδυρμόν, τὸν ὑμῶν ζῆλον ὑπὲρ ἐμοῦ, ὥστε με μᾶλλον χαρῆναι.

"and not only by his coming but also by the comfort with which he was comforted in you, as he told us of your longing, your mourning, your zeal for me, so that I rejoiced still more." . . . RSV

οὐ (negative conjunction with the indicative) 130.

μόνον (acc.sing.neut.of μόνος, adverbial) 339.

δὲ (continuative conjunction) 11.

ἐν (preposition with the instrumental of means) 80.

τῇ (instru.sing.fem.of the article in agreement with παρουσίᾳ) 9.

παρουσίᾳ (instru.sing.fem.of παρουσία, means) 1482.

αὐτοῦ (gen.sing.masc.of αὐτός, description) 16.

ἀλλὰ (adversative conjunction) 342.

καὶ (adjunctive conjunction joining prepositional phrases) 14.

ἐν (preposition with the instrumental of means) 80.

τῇ (instru.sing.fem.of the article in agreement with παρακλήσει) 9.
παρακλήσει (instru.sing.fem.of παράκλησις, means) 1896.
ᾗ (instru.sing.fem.of ὅς, relative pronoun, means) 65.
παρεκλήθη (3d.per.sing.aor.pass.ind.of παρακαλέω, constative) 230.
ἐφ' (preposition with the instrumental of agent) 47.
ὑμῖν (instru.pl.masc.of σύ, agent) 104.
ἀναγέλλων (pres.act.part.nom.sing.masc.of ἀναγγέλλω, adverbial, temporal) 2012.
ἡμῖν (dat.pl.masc.of ἐγώ, indirect object of ἀναγέλλων) 123.
τήν (acc.sing.fem.of the article in agreement with ἐπιπόθησιν) 9.
ὑμῶν (gen.pl.masc.of σύ, description) 104.

#**4328** ἐπιπόθησιν (acc.sing.fem.of ἐπιπόθησις, direct object of ἀναγγέλλων).

King James Version

earnest desire - 2 Cor.7:7.
vehement desire - 2 Cor.7:11.

Revised Standard Version

longing - 2 Cor.7:7,11.

Meaning: A combination of ἐπί (#47) and πόθησις - "desire." *Cf.* ἐπιποθέω (#3789); ἐπιπόθητος (#4579) and ἐπιποθία (#4056). ἐπί heightens the intensity of the desire. Hence, great desire; longing; intense yearning. With reference to the desire of the Corinthians to live consistent Christian lives - 2 Cor.7:7,11.

τόν (acc.sing.masc.of the article in agreement with ὀδυρμόν) 9.
ὑμῶν (gen.pl.masc.of σύ, description) 104.
ὀδυρμόν (acc.sing.masc.of ὀδυρμός, direct object of ἀναγγέλλων) 227.
τόν (acc.sing.masc.of the article in agreement with ζῆλον) 9.
ὑμῶν (gen.pl.masc.of σύ, description) 104.
ζῆλον (acc.sing.masc.of ζῆλος, direct object of ἀναγγέλλων) 1985.
ὑπέρ (preposition with the genitive of reference) 545.
ἐμοῦ (gen.sing.msc.of ἐμός, reference) 1267.
ὥστε (conjunction introducing the infinitive in a consecutive clause) 752.
με (acc.sing.masc.of ἐγώ, general reference) 123.
μᾶλλον (adverbial) 619.
χαρῆναι (2d.aor.pass.inf.of χαίρω, consecutive) 182.

Translation - "And not only by his coming but also by the encouragement by which he was comforted by you, when he described to us your intense desire, your mourning, your concern for us, with the result that I was made even happier.

Comment: Thus Paul explains the source of his worry of verses 5 and 6. In addition to the persecution which he suffered from the unsaved world, he was uncertain that the Corinthians had reacted to his strong censure contained in the former epistle as he had hoped they would. Titus' report reassured him on the point. Note that Titus also experienced another wave of consolation as he reported to Paul how the Corinthians had reacted to Paul's first epistle. One can imagine the scene as Titus and Paul rejoiced together during Titus' recital. ὥστε and the 2d.aorist infinitive speaks of result. Titus' coming was cause for rejoicing, for Paul had been worried about him personally, but the good news that Titus brought from Corinth was cause for even greater (μᾶλλον) rejoicing.

Paul continues to discuss the content of his former epistle and their reaction to it throughout the rest of the chapter.

Verse 8 - *"For though I made you sorry with a letter, I do not repent, though I did repent. For I perceive that the same epistle hath made you sorry, though it were but for a season."*

ὅτι εἰ καὶ ἐλύπησα ὑμᾶς ἐν τῇ ἐπιστολῇ, οὐ μεταμέλομαι εἰ καὶ μετεμελόμην (βλέπω ὅτι ἡ ἐπιστολὴ ἐκείνη εἰ καὶ πρὸς ὥραν ἐλύπησεν ὑμᾶς),

"For even if I made you sorry with my letter, I do not regret it (though I did regret it), for I see that that letter grieved you, though only for a while."... RSV

ὅτι (conjunction introducing a subordinate causal clause) 211.
εἰ (conditional particle in a first-class condition) 337.
καὶ (emphatic conjunction) 14.
ἐλύπησα (1st.per.sing.aor.act.ind.of λυπέω, first-class condition) 1113.
ὑμᾶς (acc.pl.masc.of σύ, direct object of ἐλύπησα) 104.
ἐν (preposition with the instrumental of means) 80.
τῇ (instru.sing.fem.of the article in agreement with ἐπιστολῇ) 9.
ἐπιστολῇ (instru.sing.fem.of ἐπιστολή, means) 3180.
οὐ (negative conjunction with the indicative) 130.
μεταμέλομαι (1st.per.sing.pres.mid.ind.of μεταμέλομαι, aoristic) 1371.
εἰ (conditional particle in a concessive clause) 337.
καὶ (emphatic conjunction in a concessive clause) 14.
μετεμελόμην (1st.per.sing.imp.mid.ind.of μεταμέλομαι, progressive description, in a concessive clause) 1371.
βλέπω (1st.per.sing.pres.act.ind.of βλέπω, aoristic) 499.
ὅτι (conjunction introducing an object clause in indirect discourse) 211.
ἡ (nom.sing.fem.of the article in agreement with ἐπιστολή) 9.
ἐπιστολὴ (nom.sing.fem.of ἐπιστολή, subject of ἐλύπησεν) 3180.
ἐκείνη (nom.sing.fem.of ἐκεῖνος, in agreement with ἐπιστολή) 246.
εἰ (conditional particle in a concessive clause) 337.
καὶ (emphatic conjunction) 14.
πρὸς (preposition with the accusative, time extent) 197.
ὥραν (acc.sing.fem.of ὥρα, time extent) 735.
ἐλύπησεν (3d.per.sing.aor.act.ind.of λυπέω, constative) 1113.
ὑμᾶς (acc.pl.masc.of σύ, direct object of ἐλύπησεν) 104.

Translation - "Because if in fact I made you sorry by the epistle, I am not sorry, (although as a matter of fact I was sorry for a while). I see that that letter made you sad if only for a short time."

Comment: εἰ καὶ with the indicative forms a logical concessive clause. "The concession is assumed to be a fact." (Mantey, *Manual*, 292). "I rejoiced (verse 7) despite the fact that I know that my letter hurt your feelings. I did not regret sending it because I see that the same letter made you sad for a short time." Paul did admit however that he had some second thoughts about the wisdom of being so harsh with them in his first epistle. Note the imperfect progressive description in μετεμελόμην. The word is the emotional reaction to repentance, which is the intellectual "change of the mind" (#251). These two words (#'s 251 and 1371) should not be confused. However Paul may have felt he hastens to add that all is well that ends well.

Verse 9 - "Now I rejoice, not that ye were made sorry, but that ye sorrowed to repentance: for ye were made sorry after a godly manner, that ye might receive damage by us in nothing."

νῦν χαίρω, οὐχ ὅτι ἐλυπήθητε,   ἀλλ' ὅτι ἐλυπήθητε εἰς μετάνοιαν. ἐλυπήθητε γὰρ κατὰ θεόν, ἵνα ἐν μηδενὶ ζημιωθῆτε ἐξ ἡμῶν.

"As it is, I rejoice, not because you were grieved, but because you were grieved into repenting; for you felt a godly grief, so that you suffered no loss through us."
                                                                    . . . RSV

νῦν (temporal adverb) 1497.
χαίρω (1st.per.sing.pres.act.ind.of χαίρω, progressive description) 182.
οὐχ (negative conjunction with the indicative) 130.
ὅτι (conjunction introducing a subordinate causal clause) 211.
ἐλυπήθητε (2d.per.pl.aor.pass.ind.of λυπέω, ingressive) 1113.
ἀλλ' (alternative conjunction) 342.
ὅτι (conjunction introducing a subordinate causal clause) 211.
ἐλυπήθητε (2d.per.pl.aor.pass.ind.of λυπέω, constative) 1113.
εἰς (preposition with the accusative, result) 140.
μετάνοιαν (acc.sing.fem.of μετάνοια, result) 286.
ἐλυπήθητε (2d.per.pl.aor.pass.ind.of λυπέω, constative) 1113.
γὰρ (causal conjunction) 105.
κατὰ (preposition with the accusative, standard) 98.
θεόν (acc.sing.masc.of θεός, standard) 124.
ἵνα (conjunction with the subjunctive in a consecutive clause) 114.
ἐν (preposition with the locative of accompanying circumstance) 80.
μηδενὶ (loc.sing.neut.of μηδείς, accompanying circumstance) 713.
ζημιωθῆτε (2d.per.pl.1st.aor.pass.subj.of ζημιόω, consecutive) 1215.
ἐξ (preposition with the ablative of source) 19.
ἡμῶν (abl.pl.masc.of ἐγώ, source) 123.

Translation - "Now I am rejoicing, not because you were made sorry, but because your sorrow led to repentance; because you were made sad before God with the result that you were not damaged by me in any way."

Comment: The end result was that Paul's sharp rebukes in his first epistle had the desired effect. The sorrow that they felt because of his rebuke resulted in repentance. In no way were they spiritually damaged because of Paul. The first ἐλυπήθητε is ingressive, *i.e.* the emphasis is upon the beginning of the action.

Titus' visit ". . . was the occasion of the noble outburst in 2:12 to 6:10. . . . Note the sharp difference here between 'sorrow' (λύπη) which is merely another form of μεταμέλομαι (regret, remorse) and 'repentance' (μετάνοια) or change of mind and life. It is a linguistic and theological tragedy that we have to go on using 'repentance' for μετάνοια. But observe that the 'sorrow' has led to 'repentance' and was not itself the repentance." (Robertson, *Word Pictures in the New Testament*, IV, 240). Robertson goes on to say, "Purpose clause with ἵνα and first aorist passive subjunctive of ζημιόω, old verb to suffer damage." *(Ibid.).* But later *(Robertson, Grammar*, 997, 998) he wrote, "It is debatable whether ἵνα has the ecbatic use in the N.T. There is in itself no reason why it should not have it, since undoubtedly it was so used in the later Greek (Jannaris, *History of Greek Grammar*, 455, as cited in Robertson, *Grammar*, 997). It occurs also in modern Greek, ...There is not space to follow the long debate in the grammars and commentaries on this subject. Kuhner (Kuhner-Blass, *Ausfuhrliche Grammatik d. griech. Sprache,* para 555, 2, Anm.3, as cited in *Ibid.)* held that ἵνα had the ecbatic sense, but Thayer (*Lexicon*, 304, as cited in *Ibid.*) boldly accepts the verdict of Fritzsche and Winer who ('have clearly shown that in all the passages adduced from the N.T. to prove the usage the telic (or final) force prevails.' W.F.Moulton (*Winer-Moulton*, 421, as cited in *Ibid.*) agreed with Winer as against Fritzsche in the admission of the sub-final use of ἵνα, but he balked at the consecutive idea. 'But it does not follow that the weakened ἵνα is generally equivalent to ὥστε: this use of ἵνα is rather, as we can still perceive in most cases, an extension of *eo consilio ut.*' Yes, in most cases, beyond a doubt. I once had just this feeling and stood against (*Short Grammar of the Greek New Testament*, 153, 155) the admission of the consecutive force of ἵνα. J.H. Moulton (*Prolegomena*, 206, as cited in *Ibid.*) confesses to a similar development of opinion on this subject. He had once (*Introduction to New Testament Greek*, 217, as cited in *Ibid.*) committed himself against the ecbatic ἵνα, but now he confesses himself 'troubled with unsettling doubts.' He boldly advocates the freedom of commentators to interpret ἵνα as the context demands (final, sub-final, consecutive)." (Robertson, *Grammar*, 997,998).

It is heartening to note the willingness of the scholars to announce their change of mind. Fifty years ago, as a beginner, I followed, with the slavish obedience which I felt necessary at that time, the writings of the scholars. Since then I have found a few contexts in which ἵνα with the subjunctive seems to indicate result, rather than purpose or the sub-final mixture of purpose and result. Such a passage is 2 Cor.7:9.

The student who wishes to check the references cited *supra* will note that Robertson's citation to his *Short Grammar*, was to an early edition. In his tenth edition, published in 1933, he takes the same position as he took one year later in the last edition of his *The Greek New Testament in the Light of Historical Research*, which I cite as *Grammar* in *The Renaissance New Testament*. In his last edition of the *Short Grammar*, he says, "The use of ἵνα has been sharply disputed, but gradually modern grammarians have come to admit the actual ecbatic use of ἵνα in the New Testament like the Latin *ut* and as is certainly true in modern Greek." (*A New Short Grammar of the Greek Testament*, X, 346).

"Grammarians have been reluctant to admit (the ecbatic) use for ἵνα. But J.H.Moulton and A.T.Robertson, who at first stood against admitting the consecutive force of ἵνα, came to do so later (R.997)." (Mantey, *Manual*, 286). "Again we find ἵνα used in result clauses, when it is translatable *so that*, but this usage is rare and it is a late Koine development (*cf.* Jn.9:2, "Rabbi, who sinned, this man or his parents, *so that* he was born blind?" Rev.3:9, "Behold I will make them ἵνα ἥξουσιν καὶ προσκυνήσουσιν ἐνώπιον τῶν ποδῶν σου, *so that they will come and worship before thy feet* (see also Gal.5:17; 1 Jn.1:9; Rev.9:20). We agree with Abbott-Smith's statement in his *Lexicon:* "In late writers, ecbatic denoting result - ὥστε, *that, so that:* Rom.11:11; 1 Cor.7:29; 1 Ths.5:4; al.; so with the formula referring to the fulfillment of prophecy, ἵνα πληρωθῇ; Mt.1:22; 2:14; 4:14; Jn.13:8; al." (*Ibid.*, 249).

The student who possesses the spirit of the Bereans (Acts 17:11,12) will examine these contexts and make up his own mind. A check of the passages cited by Robertson and Mantey in the *Renaissance New Testament* will reveal that I have not always so understood this possible use of ἵνα and the subjunctive. The day has not yet come when any scholar, however erudite and well experienced, will write the definitive grammar of the Greek New Testament. In some contexts the final (purpose); sub-final (purpose/result) and ecbatic (result) ideas are not necessarily in conflict.

Verse 10 - "For godly sorrow worketh repentance to salvation not to be repented of; but the sorrow of the world worketh death."

ἡ γὰρ κατὰ θεὸν λύπη μετάνοιαν εἰς σωτηρίαν ἀμεταμέλητον ἐργάζεται. ἡ δὲ τοῦ κόσμου λύπη θάνατον κατεργάζεται.

"For godly grief produces a repentance that leads to salvation and brings no regret, but worldly grief produces death." . . . RSV

ἡ (nom.sing.fem.of the article in agreement with λύπη) 9.
γὰρ (causal conjunction) 105.
κατὰ (preposition with the accusative, standard) 98.
θεὸν (acc.sing.masc.of θεός, standard) 124.
λύπη (nom.sing.fem.of λύπη, subject of ἐργάζεται) 2788.
μετάνοιαν (acc.sing.fem.of μετάνοια, direct object of ἐργάζεται) 286.
εἰς (preposition with the accusative, purpose) 140.
σωτηρίαν (acc.sing.fem.of σωτηρία, purpose) 1852.
ἀμεταμέλητον (acc.sing.fem.of ἀμεταμέλητος, in agreement with σωτηρίαν) 4002.
ἐργάζεται (3d.per.sing.pres.mid.ind.of ἐργάζομαι, customary) 691.

ἡ (nom.sing.fem.of the article in agreement with λύπη) 9.

δὲ (adversative conjunction) 11.

τοῦ (gen.sing.masc.of the article in agreement with κόσμου) 9.

κόσμου (gen.sing.masc.of κόσμος, description) 360.

λύπη (nom.sing.fem.of λύπη, subject of κατεργάζεται) 2788.

θάνατον (acc.sing.masc.of θάνατος, direct object of κατεργάζεται) 381.

κατεργάζεται (3d.per.sing.pres.mid.ind.of κατεργάζομαι, customary) 3815.

Translation - "Because sorrow of the godly sort generates repentance unto salvation, for which we need never to be sorry, but the sorrow of the world produces death."

Comment: Note εἰς σωτηρίαν here in a reference to the rescue of the backslidden saint from the results of his defeated life, rather than from the eternal penalty for sin. In the judicial sense the Corinthians already had salvation. They needed however to be rescued from the results of the wasted lives they would have lived had they not repented. Note κατὰ θεὸν again here as in verse 9 - "sorrow in relation to God and such as meets His standards." See the same idea in 2 Cor.1:12a where we have τοῦ θεοῦ in the descriptive genitive usage. κόσμος here in the evil sense. *Cf.*#360. The Christ rejecting κόσμος produces a sorrow that ends in death. No Christian need feel obligated to be sorry for the remorse which he feels because of his sin, if that remorse leads him to repentance and the salvage of the remainder of his life, which otherwise would have remained blighted. David's greatest service for God came after he prayed the prayer of Psalm 51.

Verse 11 - "For behold the selfsame thing, that ye sorrowed after a godly sort, what carefulness it wrought in you; yea, what clearing of yourselves, yea, what indignation, yea, what fear, yea, which vehement desire, yea, what zeal, yea, what revenge! In all things ye have approved yourselves to be clear in this matter."

ἰδοὺ γὰρ αὐτὸ τοῦτο τὸ κατὰ θεὸν λυπηθῆναι πόσην κατειργάσατο ὑμῖν σπουδήν, ἀλλὰ ἀπολογίαν, ἀλλὰ ἀγανάκτησιν, ἀλλὰ φόβον, ἀλλὰ ἐπιπόθησιν, ἀλλὰ ζῆλον, ἀλλὰ ἐκδίκησιν. ἐν παντὶ συνεστήσατε ἑαυτοὺς ἁγνοὺς εἶναι τῷ πράγματι.

"For see what earnestness this godly grief has produced in you, what eagerness to clear yourselves, what indignation, what alarm, what longing, what zeal, what punishment! At every point you have proved yourselves guiltless in the matter." .

. . RSV

ἰδοὺ (exclamation) 95.

γὰρ (causal conjunction) 105.

αὐτὸ (nom.sing.neut.of αὐτός, in agreement with λυπηθῆναι, intensive) 16.

τοῦτο (nom.sing.neut.of οὗτος, in agreement with λυπηθῆναι) 93.

τὸ (nom.sing.neut.of the article in agreement with λυπηθῆναι) 9.

κατὰ (preposition with the accusative, standard) 98.

θεὸν (acc.sing.masc.of θεός, standard) 124.

λυπηθῆναι (aor.pass.inf.of λυπέω, noun use, nom.sing.neut., subject of κατειργάσατο) 1113.

πόσην (acc.sing.fem.of πόσος, in agreement with σπουδήν) 603.

κατειργάσατο (3d.per.sing.1st.aor.mid.ind.of κατεργάζομαι, culminative) 3815.

ὑμῖν (dat.pl.masc.of σύ, personal advantage) 104.

σπουδήν (acc.sing.fem.of σπουδή, direct object of κατειργάσατο) 1819.

ἀλλὰ (confirmatory conjunction) 342.

ἀπολογίαν (acc.sing.fem.of ἀπολογία, direct object of κατειργάσατο) 3573.

ἀλλὰ (confirmatory conjunction) 342.

#4329 ἀγανάκτησιν (acc.sing.fem.of ἀγανάκτησις, direct object of κατειργάσατο).

King James Version

indignation - 2 Cor.7:11.

Revised Standard Version

indignation - 2 Cor.7:11.

Meaning: indignation - 2 Cor.7:11. P Grenf. II 82 17b (c.A.D. 400) μεταγνῶναι ἔχετε ὥστε καὶ ἀγανακτήσεως δοκαστηκῆς πειραθῆναι, where certain offenders are threatened with legal proceedings and penalties, if they disregard the writers' demand. (Moulton & Milligan, *The Vocabulary of the Greek New Testament*, 1). The Corinthians reacted to Paul's first epistle as those who had been unjustly accused - 2 Cor.7:11.

ἀλλὰ (confirmatory conjunction) 342.

φόβον (acc.sing.masc.of φόβος, direct object of κατειργάσατο) 1131.

ἀλλὰ (confirmatory conjunction) 342.

ἐπιπόθησιν (acc.sing.fem.of ἐπιπόθησις, direct object of κατειργάσατο) 4328.

ἀλλὰ (confirmatory conjunction) 342.

ζῆλον (acc.sing.masc.of ζῆλος, direct object of κατειργάσατο) 1985.

ἀλλὰ (confirmatory conjunction) 342.

ἐκδίκησιν (acc.sing.fem.of ἐκδίκησις, direct object of κατειργάσατο) 2625.

ἐν (preposition with the locative of accompanying circumstance) 80.

παντὶ (loc.sing.neut.of πᾶς, accompanying circumstance) 67.

συνεστήσατε (2d.per.pl.aor.mid.ind.of συνίστημι, culminative) 2328.

ἑαυτοὺς (acc.pl.masc.of ἑαυτοῦ, direct object of συνεστήσατε) 288.

#4330 ἀγνοὺς (acc.pl.masc.of ἀγνός, predicate adjective).

King James Version

chaste - 2 Cor.11:2; Titus 2:5; 1 Peter 3:2.

clear - 2 Cor.7:11.
pure - Phil.4:8; 1 Tim.5:22; James 3:17; 1 John 3:3.

Revised Standard Version

pure - 2 Cor.11:2; Phil.4:8; 1 Tim.5:22; James 3:17; 1 John 3:3.
chaste - Titus 2:5; 1 Peter 3:2.

Meaning: Pure, with special reference to sexual morality (metaphorical) in 2 Cor.11:2; Titus 2:5. Generally without guilt, immaculate, free from fault - 2 Cor.7:11; Phil.4:8; 1 Tim.5:22; James 3:17; 1 John 3:3; 1 Peter 3:2.

εἶναι (pres.inf.of εἰμί, apposition) 86.
τῷ (loc.sing.neut.of the article in agreement with πράγματι) 9.
πράγματι (loc.sing.neut.of πρᾶγμα, sphere) 1266.

Translation - "For look at the results - your godly sorrow - what diligence it generated in you! What explanation! What righteous indignation! What fear! What great desire! What zeal! What vengeance! In every circumstance you have shown yourselves to be guiltless in this matter."

Comment: Note the exclamatory use of πόσην. ἀλλά is confirmatory. Paul seems delighted, amazed and thoroughly convinced. He is satisfied with the response of the Corinthians to his rebukes in his first epistle. They had been shocked that he should scold them and with utmost diligence (#1819), indignation (#4329), fear (#1131), earnest desire (#4328), zeal (#1985) and revenge (#2625) they presented to Titus their explanation (#3573) and convinced him and Paul that in all of the matters involved in his rebuke they had conducted themselves as Christians. That they loved and respected Paul seems clear. Otherwise they would not have been so aroused by his allegations. If they had despised him they would not have taken steps to clear themselves.

Verse 12 - "Wherefore, though I wrote unto you, I did it not for his cause that had done the wrong, nor for his cause that suffered wrong, but that our care for you in the sight of God might appear unto you."

ἄρα εἰ καὶ ἔγραφα ὑμῖν, οὐχ ἕνεκεν τοῦ ἀδικήσαντος, οὐδὲ ἕνεκεν τοῦ ἀδικηθέντος, ἀλλ' ἕνεκεν τοῦ φανερωθῆναι τὴν σπουδὴν ὑμῶν τὴν ὑπὲρ ἡμῶν πρὸς ὑμᾶς ἐνώπιον τοῦ θεοῦ.

"So although I wrote to you, it was not on account of the one who did the wrong, nor on account of the one who suffered the wrong, but in order that your zeal for us might be revealed to you in the sight of God." . . . RSV

ἄρα (illative particle) 995.
εἰ (concessive particle) 337.
καὶ (concessive conjunction) 14.
ἔγραφα (1st.per.sing.aor.act.ind.of γράφω, constative) 156.
ὑμῖν (dat.pl.masc.of σύ, indirect object of ἔγραφα) 104.

οὐχ (negative conjunction with the indicative) 130.

ἕνεκεν (preposition with the genitive, "for the sake of") 435.

τοῦ (gen.sing.masc.of the article in agreement with ἀδικήσαντος) 9.

ἀδικήσαντος (1st.aor.act.part.gen.sing.masc.of ἀδικέω, substantival, "for the sake of") 1327.

οὐδὲ (disjunctive) 452.

ἕνεκεν (preposition with the genitive, "for the sake of") 435.

τοῦ (gen.sing.masc.of the article in agreement with ἀδικηθέντος) 9.

ἀδικηθέντος (1st.aor.pass.part.gen.sing.masc.of ἀδικέω, "for the sake of") 1327.

ἀλλ' (alternative conjunction) 342.

ἕνεκεν (preposition with the genitive, purpose) 435.

τοῦ (gen.sing.neut.of the article in agreement with φανερωθῆναι) 9.

φανερωθῆναι (1st.aor.pass.inf.of φανερόω, purpose) 1960.

τὴν (acc.sing.fem.of the article in agreement with σπουδὴν) 9.

σπουδὴν (acc.sing.fem.of σπουδή, general reference) 1819.

ὑμῶν (gen.pl.masc.of σύ, description) 104.

τὴν (acc.sing.fem.of the article in agreement with σπουδὴν, emphatic attributive position) 9.

ὑπὲρ (preposition with the ablative, "in your behalf") 545.

ἡμῶν (abl.pl.masc.of ἐγώ, "in your behalf") 123.

πρὸς (preposition with the accusative, metaphorical extent) 197.

ὑμᾶς (acc.pl.masc.of σύ, metaphorical extent) 104.

ἐνώπιον (preposition with the genitive of place description) 1798.

τοῦ (gen.sing.masc.of the article in agreement with θεοῦ) 9.

θεοῦ (gen.sing.masc.of θεός, place description) 124.

Translation - "Therefore, although I wrote to you, I did it not because of the wrong doer nor because of the one who suffered wrong, but in order to make clear to you your care for us before God."

Comment: Paul is saying that his letter of rebuke was written for the purpose of making the Corinthians realize their concern for their standing with Paul in God's sight. A secondary purpose may have been to help the wrong doer and his victim. His purpose was realized. The Corinthians repented and vehemently defended themselves to Paul. Thus they proved to themselves, as well as to Paul that they held him in the highest esteem as God's apostle. Note εἰ καί again in a concessive sense. *Cf.*#337. Note the infinitive with τοῦ ιν α φιναλ σενσε.

Verse 13 - "Therefore we were comforted in your comfort: yea, and exceedingly the more joyed we for the joy of Titus, because his spirit was refreshed by you all."

διὰ τοῦτο παρακεκλήμεθα. Ἐπὶ δὲ τῇ παρακλήσει ἡμῶν περισσοτέρως μᾶλλον ἐχάρημεν ἐπὶ τῇ χαρᾷ Τίτου, ὅτι ἀναπέπαυται τὸ πνεῦμα αὐτοῦ ἀπὸ πάντων ὑμῶν.

"Therefore we are comforted. And besides our own comfort we rejoiced still more at the joy of Titus, because his mind has been set at rest by you all." . . . RSV

διὰ (preposition with the accusative, cause) 118.

τοῦτο (acc.sing.neut.of οὗτος, cause) 93.

παρακεκλήμεθα (1st.per.pl.perf.pass.ind.of παρακαλέω, intensive) 230.

Ἐπὶ (preposition with the instrumental of means) 47.

δὲ (continuative conjunction) 11.

τῇ (instru.sing.fem.of the article in agreement with παρακλήσει) 9.

παρακλήσει (instru.sing.fem.of παράκλησις, means) 1896.

ἡμῶν (gen.pl.masc.of ἐγώ, description) 123.

περισσοτέρως (adverbial) 1630.

μᾶλλον (adverbial) 619.

ἐχάρημεν (1st.per.pl.2d.aor.pass.ind.of χαίρω, culminative) 182.

ἐπὶ (preposition with the instrumental, cause) 47.

τῇ (instru.sing.fem.of the article in agreement with χαρᾷ) 9.

χαρᾷ (instru.sing.fem.of χάά, cause) 183.

Τίτου (gen.sing.masc.of Τίτος, possession) 4278.

ὅτι (conjunction introducing a subordinate causal clause) 211.

ἀναπέπαυται (3d.per.sing.perf.pass.ind.of ἀναπαύω, intensive) 955.

τὸ (nom.sing.neut.of the article in agreement with πνεῦμα) 9.

πνεῦμα (nom.sing.neut.of πνεῦμα, subject of ἀναπέπαυται) 83.

αὐτοῦ (gen.sing.masc.of αὐτός, possession) 16.

ἀπὸ (preposition with the ablative of agent) 70.

πάντων (abl.pl.masc.of πᾶς, in agreement with ὑμῶν) 67.

ὑμῶν (abl.pl.masc.of σύ, agent) 104.

Translation - "This is why we have been comforted, and because of our encouragement we rejoiced even more because of Titus' joy, because his spirit was refreshed by all of you."

Comment: Note the double comparative περισσοτέρως μᾶλλον which is pleonastic. διὰ τοῦτο in a causal sense. Note the various ways in which cause is expressed in the verse. Paul drew comfort from the fact that he knew that his letter had proved to the Corinthians his love for them (verse 12) and also their love for him. Also that Titus had been comforted and refreshed spiritually by his visit in Corinth. He now adds in verse 14 that his evaluation of the Corinthians which he had given to Titus before Titus' visit had been proved accurate.

Verse 14 - "For if I have boasted anything to him of you, I am not ashamed, but as we spake all things to you, even so our boasting, which I made before Titus is found a truth."

ὅτι εἴ τι αὐτῷ ὑπὲρ ὑμῶν κεκαύχημαι οὐ καρησχύνθην, ἀλλ' ὡς πάντα ἐν ἀληθείᾳ ἐλαλήσαμεν ὑμῖν, οὕτως καὶ ἡ καύχησις ἡμῶν ἡ ἐπὶ Τίτου ἀλήθεια ἐγενήθη.

"For if I have expressed to him some pride in you, I was not put to shame; but

just as everything we said to you was true, so our boasting before Titus has proved true." . . . RSV

ὅτι (causal conjunction) 211.

εἰ (conditional particle in a first-class condition) 337.

τι (acc.sing.neut.of τις, indefinite pronoun, direct object of κεκαύχημαι) 486.

αὐτῷ (dat.sing.masc.of αὐτός, indirect object of κεκαύχημαι) 16.

ὑπὲρ (preposition with the genitive of reference) 545.

ὑμῶν (gen.pl.masc.of σύ, reference) 104.

κεκαύχημαι (1st.per.sing.perf.mid.ind.of καυχάομαι, first-class condition) 3847.

οὐ (negative conjunction with the indicative) 130.

κατῃσχύνθην (1st.per.sing.1st.aor.pass.ind.of καταισχύνω, first-class condition, culminative) 2505.

ἀλλ' (alterantive conjunction) 342.

ὡς (comparative particle) 128.

πάντα (acc.pl.neut.of πᾶς, direct object of ἐλαλήσαμεν) 67.

ἐν (preposition with the locative, pregnant construction) 80.

ἀληθείᾳ (loc.sing.fem.of ἀλήθεια, pregnant construction) 1416.

ἐλαλήσαμεν (1st.per.pl.aor.act.ind.of λαλέω, constative) 815.

ὑμῖν (dat.pl.masc.of σύ, indirect object of ἐλαλήσαμεν) 104.

οὕτως (comparative adverb) 74.

καὶ (adjunctive conjunction joining nouns) 14.

ἡ (nom.sing.fem.of the article in agreement with καύχησις) 9.

καύχησις (nom.sing.fem.of καύχησις, subject of ἐγενήθη) 3877.

ἡμῶν (gen.pl.masc.of ἐγώ, possession) 123.

ἡ (nom.sing.fem.of the article in agreement with ἀλήθεια) 9.

ἐπὶ (preposition with the genitive of place description) 47.

Τίτου (gen.sing.masc.of Τίτος, "in the presence of") 4278.

ἀλήθεια (nom.sing.fem.of ἀλήθεια, predicate nominative) 1416.

ἐγενήθη (3d.per.sing.aor.ind.of γίνομαι, constative) 113.

Translation - *"Because since I have been boasting to him about you, I was not embarrassed; on the contrary as I told everything to you truthfully, so also my boast to Titus has been vindicated."*

Comment: εἰ and the indicative κεκαύχημαι indicates a first-class condition. Paul had indeed boasted to Titus about what wonderful Christians the Corinthians were. But after Titus had gone to Corinth and returned to Paul, he was not embarrassed by the fact. εἰ can be taken as concessive here - "Although he had boasted . . . he was not ashamed." ἀλλά is strongly adversative - "On the contrary" what he had said to Titus about the Corinthians was just as true as what he had told the Corinthians when he preached the gospel to them. Note the sequence ὡς . . . οὕτως καὶ - "as . . . so also."

Verse 15 - "And his inward affection is more abundant toward you, whilst he remembereth the obedience of you all, how with fear and trembling ye received him."

καὶ τὰ σπλάγχνα αὐτοῦ περισσοτέρως εἰς ὑμᾶς ἐστιν ἀναμιμνησκομένου
τὴν πάντων ὑμῶν ὑπακοήν, ὡς μετὰ φόβου καὶ τρόμου ἐδέξασθε αὐτόν.

*"And his heart goes out all the more to you, as he remembers the obedience of
you all, and the fear and trembling with which you received him." . . . RSV*

καὶ (continuative conjunction) 14.

τὰ (nom.pl.neut.of the article in agreement with σπλάγχνα) 9.

σπλάγχνα (nom.pl.neut.of σπλάγχνα, subject of ἐστιν) 1857.

αὐτοῦ (gen.sing.masc.of αὐτός, possession) 16.

περισσοτέρως (adverbial) 1630.

εἰς (preposition with the accusative of extent, metaphorical) 140.

ὑμᾶς (acc.pl.masc.of σύ, metaphorical extent) 104.

ἐστιν (3d.per.sing.pres.ind.of εἰμί, aoristic) 86.

ἀναμιμνησκομένου (pres.mid.part.gen.sing.masc.of ἀναμιμνήσκω adverbial, causal) 2681.

τὴν (acc.sing.fem.of the article in agreement with ὑπακοήν) 9.

πάντων (gen.pl.masc.of πᾶς in agreement with ὑμῶν) 67.

ὑμῶν (gen.pl.masc.of σύ, description) 104.

ὑπακοήν (acc.sing.fem.of ὑπακοή, direct object of ἀναμιμνησκμένου) 3785.

ὡς (temporal particle) 128.

μετὰ (preposition with the genitive, metaphorical accompaniment) 50.

φόβου (gen.sing.masc.of φόβος, accompaniment) 1131.

καὶ (adjunctive conjunction joining nouns) 14.

τρόμου (gen.sing.masc.of τρόμος, accompaniment) 2889.

ἐδέξασθε (2d.per.pl.aor.mid.ind.of δέχομαι, constative) 867.

αὐτόν (acc.sing.masc.of αὐτός, direct object of ἐδέξασθε) 16.

Translation - *"And his feelings of affection toward you are much greater as he
remembers the obedience of all of you as with fear and trembling you received
him."*

Comment: εἰς ὑμᾶς - accusative of extent in a metaphorical sense. Titus' heart
went out to the Corinthians as (and because) he remembered their attitude
toward him during his visit in Corinth.

Verse 16 - *"I rejoice therefore, that I have confidence in you in all things."*

χαίρω ὅτι ἐν παντὶ θαρρῶ ἐν ὑμῖν.

"I rejoice, because I have perfect confidence in you." . . . RSV

χαίρω (1st.per.sing.pres.act.ind.of χαίρω, aoristic) 182.

ὅτι (conjunction introducing an object clause) 211.

ἐν (preposition with the locative of sphere) 80.

παντὶ (loc.sing.neut.of πᾶς, sphere) 67.

θαρρῶ (1st.per.sing.pres.act.ind.of θαρρέω, aoristic) 4307.

ἐν (preposition with the instrumental of cause) 80.

ὑμῖν (instru.pl.masc.of σύ, cause) 104.

Translation - "I am glad that I have confidence in you in all circumstances."

Comment: ἐν παντί - accompanying circumstance - in every situation, Paul had confidence in them because of what he thought he knew about their character as a result of their Christian experience.

The seventh chapter reveals the love which Paul felt for the Corinthians and the insecurity that he felt because of his sharp criticisms in his first epistle. He appears almost frantic in his fear that their reaction to his thrusts would be negative, and his relief was great when Titus returned and relieved his mind.

In chapter eight he takes up the question of the gift for the poor saints in Judea.

Liberal Giving
(2 Corinthians 8:1-15)

2 Corinthians 8:1 - "Moreover, brethren, we do you to wit of the grace of God bestowed on the churches of Macedonia."

Γνωρίζομεν δὲ ὑμῖν, ἀδελφοί, τὴν χάριν τοῦ θεοῦ τὴν δεδομένην ἐν ταῖς ἐκκλησίαις τῆς Μακεδονίας,

"We want you to know, brethren, about the grace of God which has been shown in the churches of Macedonia," . . . RSV

Γνωρίζομεν (1st.per.pl.pres.act.ind.of γνωρίζω, aoristic) 1882.
δὲ (explanatory conjunction) 11.
ὑμῖν (dat.pl.masc.of σύ, indirect object of Γνωρίζομεν) 104.
ἀδελφοί (voc.pl.masc.of ἀδελφός, address) 15.
τὴν (acc.sing.fem.of the article in agreement with χάριν) 9.
χάριν (acc.sing.fem.of χάρις, direct object of γνωρίζομεν) 1700.
τοῦ (gen.sing.masc.of the article in agreement with θεοῦ) 9.
θεοῦ (gen.sing.masc.of θεός, description) 124.
τὴν (acc.sing.fem.of the article in agreement with δεδομένην) 9.
δεδομένην (perf.pass.part.acc.sing.fem.of δίδωμι, adjectival, predicate position, restrictive, in agreement with χάριν) 362.
ἐν (preposition with the locative, with plural nouns) 80.
ταῖς (loc.pl.fem.of the article in agreement with ἐκκλησίαις) 9.
ἐκκλησίαις (loc.pl.fem.of ἐκκλησία, place where) 1204.
τῆς (gen.sing.fem.of the article in agreement with Μακεδονίας) 9.
Μακεδονίας (gen.sing.fem.of Μακεδονία, ·description) 3360.

Translation - "Now, brethren, let me tell you about the grace of God given among the churches of Macedonia."

Comment: δὲ is either explanatory or adversative. The adversative idea can be seen if we note the preceding verse (7:16) in which he speaks of his confidence in them ἐν παντί ("in all things"), yet feels it necessary now to give them an eloquent account of the generosity of other churches with reference to giving.

The thought may be, "I have confidence in you but (adversative δέ) I want to stimulate your generosity by showing what the Macedonians, who are poor, gave to the relief fund." It seems to be a pressure tactic (*cf.* verse 7). Paul seems to be trying to provoke the Corinthians to emulation.

Whether adversative or explanatory, δέ introduces a new subject. God's favor has been poured out upon the Macedonians. Note that the desire to make a sacrificial gift is a gift from God. Note the perfect tense in δεδομένην, the restrictive adjectival participle which modifies χάριν. Paul is speaking only of the gift of God which was given (past tense) and is therefore now being enjoyed by the Christians in Macedonian country - Philippi, Thessalonica and Berea. Note ἐν with the locative with plural nouns. The gift of giving was distributed *among* the churches *to* individuals. Churches do not give money. Christians in the churches do. ὅτι which follows in verse 2 is epexegetical.

Verse 2 - "How that in a great trial of affliction the abundance of their joy and their deep poverty abounded unto the riches of their liberality.

ὅτι ἐν πολλῇ δοκιμῇ θλίψεως ἡ περισσεία τῆς χαρᾶς αὐτῶν καὶ ἡ κατὰ βάθους πτωχεία αὐτῶν ἐπερίσσευσεν εἰς τὸ πλοῦτον τῆς ἁπλότητος αὐτῶν.

"for in a severe test of affliction, their abundance of joy and their extreme poverty have overflowed in a wealth of liberality on their part." . . . RSV

ὅτι (epexegetical conjunction) 211.
ἐν (preposition with the locative of accompanying circumstance) 80.
πολλῇ (loc.sing.fem.of πολύς, in agreement with δοκιμῇ) 228.
δοκιμῇ (loc.sing.fem.of δοκιμή, accompanying circumstance) 3897.
θλίψεως (abl.sing.fem.of θλῖψις, source) 1046.
ἡ (nom.sing.fem.of the article in agreement with περισσεία) 9.
περισσεία (nom.sing.fem.of περισσεία, subject of ἐπερίσσευσεν) 3904.
τῆς (gen.sing.fem.of the article in agreement with χαρᾶς) 9.
χαρᾶς (gen.sing.fem.of χαρά, description) 183.
αὐτῶν (gen.pl.masc.of αὐτός, possession) 16.
καὶ (adjunctive conjunction joining nouns) 14.
ἡ (nom.sing.fem.of the article in agreement with πτωχεία) 9.
κατὰ (preposition with the adverbial genitive, time) 98.
βάθους (gen.sing.neut.of βάθος, adverbial, "throughout the time of") 1031.

#4331 πτωχεία (nom.sing.fem.of πτωχεία, subject of ἐπερίσσευσεν).

King James Version

poverty - 2 Cor.8:2,9; Rev.2:9.

Revised Standard Version

poverty - 2 Cor.8:2,9; Rev.2:9.

Meaning: Cf. πτωχεύω (#4335); πτωχός (#423). Poverty. In the New Testament, as opposed to πλούσιος in a financial sense - 2 Cor.8:2,9; Rev.2:9. Modified in 2 Cor.8:2 by κατὰ βάθους - "down to the depths" poverty, *i.e.* in extreme poverty.

αὐτῶν (gen.pl.masc.of αὐτός, possession) 16.
ἐπερίσσευσεν (3d.per.sing.aor.act.ind.of περισσεύω, constative) 473.
εἰς (preposition with the accusative, predicate usage) 140.
τὸ (acc.sing.neut.of the article in agreement with πλοῦτος) 9.
πλοῦτος (acc.sing.neut.of πλοῦτος, predicate use) 1050.
τῆς (gen.sing.fem.of the article in agreement with ἀπλότητος) 9.
ἀπλότητος (gen.sing.fem.of ἀπλότης, description) 4018.
αὐτῶν (gen.pl.masc.of αὐτός, possession) 16.

Translation - "How that in a severe test growing out of the pressure of tribulation, the overflow of their joy, coupled with their extreme poverty, has overflowed unto their sincere generosity."

Comment: ὅτι is epexegetical in explanation of τὴν χάριν τοῦ θεοῦ of verse 1. What a gift God gave to them! First the circumstances: a great test growing out of the pressure that they felt, due to tribulation. When a Christian is persecuted for his faith he finds himself under pressure (θλῖψις, #1046). This pressure - the dilemma of not knowing what to do, was very great (πολλῇ). Into this situation we introduce two seemingly contradictory ingredients: they had overflowing joy and poverty that extended down to the very depths (κατὰ βάθους) of subsistence living. This must mean that these Christians had scarcely enough to eat and were short of the simplest necessities of life. Out of this mixture (great joy and dire poverty), mixed together under circumstances of tribulation and its pressures, came a product - a tremendous manifestation of sincere, unpretentious giving (Note the meaning of ἀπλότητος #4018). Christians who give money for pretense never give their last dime, when they have not enough to eat. To give under these circumstances demonstrates great sincerity. Note that two of the three ingredients in this amazing spiritual chemistry, tribulation and poverty, are the product of the world of sin, while the other, overflowing joy, is the fruit of the Spirit (Gal.5:22). There are few verses of scripture that refute Marxian dialectical materialism as does this one. When a man under the pressures of tribulation and persecution for his faith and plagued with the extreme poverty that scarcely provides a subsistence standard of living is nevertheless so overwhelmed with joy that with complete lack of pretense he gives his last dollar or dime, it is difficult to understand how that the means of production of commodities explains all superstructural social, psychological and religious valunes! Marx must show that those Macedonian Christians had a financial axe to grind! He must show that their purpose in making these temporary financial sacrifices was some hidden scheme by which they expected to recoup their losses and make a profit. The Marxians have little difficulty in showing that the typical electronic religious huckster who buys time on the television channels has a financial goal in mind. Note how the sermon or "healing service" is suddenly interrupted by a plea for money and the offer of a free book, which may have cost a dollar, in exchange for a letter of request and an offering of ten dollars! Thus the religious racketeer exploits the gospel of Christ while the enemies of our Lord watch their performance, analyze their motives and reach their desired conclusions. In objectivity and fairness it must be added that there are Christian radio and television projects carried on by producers and broadcast by station managers that demand sacrifices similar to those which the Macedonians made when they gave their love gifts of money to feed the starving Hebrew Christians in Judea.

What was the result of this spiritual chemistry in Philippi, Thessalonica and Berea?

Verse 3 - "For to their power I bear record, yea, and beyond their power they were willing of themselves."

ὅτι κατὰ δύναμιν, μαρτυρῶ, καὶ παρὰ δύναμιν, αὐθαίρετοι

"For they gave according to their means, as I can testify, and beyond their means, of their own free will, . . . " . . . RSV

ὅτι (epexegetical conjunction) 211.
κατὰ (preposition with the accusative, limitation) 98.
δύναμιν (acc.sing.fem.of δύναμις, limitation) 687.
μαρτυρῶ (1st.per.sing.pres.act.ind.of μαρτυρέω, aoristic) 1471.
καὶ (ascensive conjunction) 14.
παρὰ (preposition with the accusative, limitation) 154.
δύναμιν (acc.sing.fem.of δύναμις, limitation) 687.

#**4332** αὐθαίρετοι (nom.pl.masc.of αὐθαίρετος, predicate adjective).

King James Version

of one's own accord - 2 Cor.8:17.
willing of one's self - 2 Cor.8:3.

Revised Standard Version

of their own free will - 2 Cor.8:3.
of his own accord - 2 Cor.8:17.

Meaning: Cf. αὐθάδης (#4878), αὐτός (#16) and αἱρέομαι (#4546). Hence, self chosen; with reference to a decision arrived at without outside motivation. The Macedonian Christians gave their money - 2 Cor.8:3. With reference to Titus' decision to visit Corinth - 2 Cor.8:17.

Translation - "That to the full extent of their ability, I tell you that even beyond their ability, they made a voluntary choice."

Comment: ὅτι again is explanatory. κατὰ δύναμιν "to the fullest extent of their ability" which means that they were giving all they had. They were even (ascensive καὶ) willing to give more than that (παρὰ with the accusative of limitation, cf.#154). Thus they were sorry because they were unable to give more.

Verse 4 indicates that they wanted to give more than Paul thought they ought to give.

Verse 4 - "Praying us with much intreaty that we would receive the gift; and take upon us the fellowship of the ministering to the saints."

μετὰ πολλῆς παρακλήσεως δεόμενοι ὑμῶν τὴν χάριν καὶ τὴν κοινωνίαν τῆς διακονίας τῆς εἰς τοὺς ἁγίους —

"begging us earnestly for the favor of taking part in the relief of the saints —".

. . RSV

μετὰ (preposition with the genitive, time description) 50.

πολλῆς (gen.sing.fem.of πολύς, in agreement with παρακλήσεως) 228.

παρακλήσεως (gen.sing.fem.of παράκλησις, time description) 1896.

δεόμενοι (pres.mid.part.nom.pl.masc.of δέομαι, adverbial, temporal) 841.

ἡμῶν (gen.pl.masc.of ἐγώ, objective genitive) 123.

τὴν (acc.sing.fem.of the article in agreement with χάριν) 9.

χάριν (acc.sing.fem.of χάρις, direct object of δέχεσθαι understood) 1700.

καὶ (adjunctive conjunction joining nouns) 14.

τὴν (acc.sing.fem.of the article in agreement with κοινωνίαν) 9.

κοινωνίαν (acc.sing.fem.of κοινωνία, direct object of δέχεσθαι understood) 3001.

τῆς (gen.sing.fem.of the article in agreement with διακονίας) 9.

διακονίας (gen.sing.fem.of διακονία, description) 2442.

τῆς (gen.sing.fem.of the article in agreement with διακονίας) 9.

εἰς (preposition with the accusative, purpose) 140.

τοὺς (acc.pl.masc.of the article in agreement with ἁγίους) 9.

ἁγίους (acc.pl.masc.of ἅγιος, purpose) 84.

Translation - "With much pleading, begging us to take the gift and the privilege of delivering it to the saints."

Comment: Paul's syntax here is astray. There is no verb. The last verb, except the parenthetical μαρτυρῶ in verse 3, is ἐπερίσσευσεν of verse 2, which has its adjunct in the predicate use of the εἰς τὸ πλοῦτος. . . αὐτῶν phrase. δεόμενοι,the temporal participle is joined to no main verb. "With great pleading (earnest entreaty)" they begged Paul to take the gift and deliver it to Jerusalem. Note that the object infinitive δέχεσθαι must also be supplied. They wanted Paul to take the gift of money and assume the responsibility of delivering it to the saints in Jerusalem. Note εἰς τοὺς ἁγίους as a prepositional phrase, used like an adjective in the emphatic attributive position to modify διακονίας.

It appears that Paul was reluctant to take the money because he realized the extent of their own personal sacrifice in giving it. Only under great pressure (πολλῆς παρακλήσεως) did he agree to take it and carry it to Judea.

A pastor of a rural church in a poverty-stricken area once told the author that he was afraid to ask his people for increased giving because of their willingness to comply with money which he knew that they could not afford to give.

Apparently generosity is the fruit of poverty, not affluence. Another factor must be present. The giver must first of all give himself to the Lord. *Cf.* Rom.15:26; 2 Cor.9:1; Acts 11:29.

Verse 5 - *"And this they did, not as we hoped, but first gave their own selves to the Lord, and unto us by the will of God."*

καὶ οὐ καθὼς ἠλπίσαμεν ἀλλ᾽ ἑαυτοὺς ἔδωκαν πρῶτον τῷ κυρίῳ καὶ ἡμῖν διὰ θελήματος θεοῦ,

"and this, not as we expected, but first they gave themselves to the Lord and to us by the will of God." . . . RSV

καὶ (continuative conjunction) 14.
οὐ (negative conjunction with the indicative) 130.
καθὼς (comparative adverb) 1348.
ἠλπίσαμεν (1st.per.pl.aor.act.ind.of ἐλπίζω, constative) 991.
ἀλλ᾽ (alternative conjunction) 342.
ἑαυτοὺς (acc.pl.masc.of ἑαυτός, direct object of ἔδωκαν) 288.
ἔδωκαν (3d.per.pl.1st.aor.act.ind.of δίδωμι, constative) 362.
πρῶτον (acc.sing.neut.of πρῶτος, adverbial) 487.
τῷ (dat.sing.masc.of the article in agreement with κυρίῳ) 9.
κυρίῳ (dat.sing.masc.of κύριος,indirect object of ἔδωκαν) 97.
καὶ (adjunctive conjunction joining substantives) 14.
ἡμῖν (dat.pl.masc.of ἐγώ, indirect object ofd ἔδωκαν) 123.
διὰ (preposition with the ablative of means) 118.
θελήματος (abl.sing.neut.of θέλημα, means) 577.
θεοῦ (gen.sing.masc.of θεός, possession) 124.

Translation - *". . . and not merely as we hoped, but they gave themselves first to the Lord and to us by the divine will."*

Comment: We have οὐ with the indicative in a subordinate comparative clause. In such a construction "the negative comes outside in the principal sentence, since comparison is usually made with a positive note." (Robertson, *Grammar*, 1159). The thought is that the Macedonians had exceeded Paul's expectations. It was not as he had hoped; it was better. He had hoped for their money. They gave that, but they first gave themselves to the Lord and to Paul in a spiritual devotion - something that Paul had not expected.

Only as a Christian gives himself to Christ can he give his money without pretense as they did (verse 2). Once the believer belongs wholly to Christ, everything he has also belongs to Christ.

The heart of the stewardship message is not to be found in the asking and giving of money or other valuable assets, but in the recognition that the believer himself is "not (his) own, but is bought with a price" (1 Cor.6:19,20). This means that before he can glorify God with his money he must glorify God with his own body, which is the temple of the Holy Spirit. This means the dedication of all talent, time and money. Only thus do we present our bodies "holy, acceptable unto God, which is our reasonable service" (Rom.12:1).

Verse 6 - "Insomuch that we desired Titus, that as he had begun, so he would also finish in you the same grace also."

εἰς τὸ παρακαλέσαι ἡμᾶς Τίτον ἵνα καθὼς προενήρξατο οὕτως καὶ ἐπιτελέσῃ εἰς ὑμᾶς καὶ χάριν ταύτην.

"Accordingly we have urged Titus that as he had already made a beginning, he should also complete among you this gracious work." . . . RSV

εἰς (preposition with the articular infinitive, result) 140.
τὸ (acc.sing.neut.of the article, in agreement with παρακαλέσαι) 9.
παρακαλέσαι (aor.act.inf.of παρακαλέω, result) 230.
ἡμᾶς (acc.pl.masc.of ἐγώ, general reference) 123.
Τίτον (acc.sing.masc.of Τίτος, direct object of παρακαλέσαι) 4278.
ἵνα (conjunction with the subjunctive in a purpose clause) 114.
καθὼς (comparative adverb) 1348.

#4333 προενήρξατο (3d.per.sing.aor.mid.ind.of προενάρχομαι, ingressive).

King James Version

begin - 2 Cor.8:6.
begin before - 2 Cor.8:10.

Revised Standard Version

made a beginning - 2 Cor.8:6.
begin - 2 Cor.8:10.

Meaning: A combination of πρό (#442), ἐν (#80) and ἄρχομαι (#383). Hence, to be the first one to make a beginning; to begin before others. Titus began his ministry of strengthening the Corinthians by visiting them - 2 Cor.8:6. The Corinthians began the collection for the poor saints in Jerusalem a year before Paul's second letter to them - 2 Cor.8:10.

οὕτως (demonstrative adverb) 74.
καὶ (adjunctive conjunction, joining verbs) 14.
ἐπιτελέσῃ (3d.per.sing.1st.aor.act.subj.of ἐπιτελέω, purpose) 4059.
εἰς (preposition with the accusative, static use) 140.
ὑμᾶς (acc.pl.masc.of σύ, static use) 104.
καὶ (adjunctive conjunction joining substantives) 14.
τὴν (acc.sing.fem.of the article in agreement with χάριν) 9.
χάριν (acc.sing.fem.of χάρις, direct object of ἐπιτελέσῃ) 1700.
ταύτην (acc.sing.fem.of οὗτος, in agreement with χάριν) 93.

Translation - "With the result that we asked Titus that, just as he had made preliminary arrangements, so also he would also complete among you this gracious ministry."

Comment: εἰς with the articular infinitive with τὸ as a consecutive construction is rare but not unknown in the Greek New Testament. Mantey suggests others in Rom.1:20; Phil.1:10; Heb.11:3 and James 1:19 (*Manual*, 286).

The Macedonians had responded to the offering so graciously, even exceeding Paul's expectations, with the result that Paul was encouraged to suggest to Titus, in order that (purpose with ἵνα . . . ἐπιτελέσῃ) he might finish among the Corinthians what he had already begun - *viz.* an offering from them. This indicates that Titus had been in Corinth a year before (verse 10). Note the καθὼς . . . οὕτως καὶ sequence - "Just as . . . even so also."

Verse 7 - *"Therefore, as ye abound in everything, in faith, and utterance, and knowledge, and in all diligence, and in your love to us, see that ye abound in this grace also."*

ἀλλ᾿ ὥσπερ ἐν παντὶ περισσεύετε, πίστει καὶ λόγῳ καὶ γνώσει καὶ πάσῃ σπουδῇ καὶ τῇ ἐξ ἡμῶν ἐν ὑμῖν ἀγάπῃ, ἵνα καὶ ἐν ταύτῃ τῇ χάριτι περισσεύητε.

"Now as you excel in everything — in faith, in utterance, in knowledge, in all earnestness, and in your love for us — see that you excel in this gracious work also." . . . RSV

ἀλλ᾿ (confirmatory conjunction) 342.
ὥσπερ (intensive comparative particle) 560.
ἐν (preposition with the locative of sphere) 80.
παντὶ (loc.sing.neut.of πᾶς, sphere, with nouns) 67.
περισσεύετε (2d.per.pl.pres.act.ind.of περισσεύω, present progressive) 473.
πίστει (loc.sing.fem.of πίστις, sphere with nouns) 728.
καὶ (adjunctive conjunction joining nouns) 14.
λόγῳ (loc.sing.masc.of λόγος, sphere, with nouns) 510.
καὶ (adjunctive conjunction joining nouns) 14.
γνώσει (loc.sing.fem.of γνῶσις, sphere with nouns) 1856.
καὶ (adjunctive conjunction joining nouns) 14.
πάσῃ (loc.sing.fem.of πᾶς, in agreement with σπουδῇ) 67.
σπουδῇ (loc.sing.fem.of σπουδή, sphere with nouns) 1819.
καὶ (adjunctive conjunction joining nouns) 14.
ἐξ (preposition with the ablative of source) 19.
ἡμῶν (abl.pl.masc.of ἐγώ, source) 123.
ἐν (preposition with the locative with plural pronouns) 80.
ὑμῖν (loc.pl.masc.of σύ, place) 104.
ἀγάπῃ (loc.sing.fem.of ἀγάπη, sphere, with nouns) 1490.
ἵνα (conjunction introducing an elliptical imperative) 114.
καὶ (adjunctive conjunction joining verbs) 14.
ἐν (preposition with the locative of sphere with nouns) 80.
ταύτῃ (loc.sing.fem.of οὗτος, in agreement with χάριτι) 93.
τῇ (loc.sing.fem.of the article in agreement with χάριτι) 9.
χάριτι (loc.sing.fem.of χάρις, sphere, with nouns) 1700.
περισσεύητε (2d.per.pl.pres.act.subj.of περισσεύω, elliptical imperative) 473.

Translation - "*But just as you are doing so well in every area - in the sphere of faith and communication and knowledge and in all diligence and in the love from us to you, see that you also abound in this gift.*"

Comment: *Cf.* comment on verse 1. Paul is employing psychology. He had great confidence in them (2 Cor.7:16) but he wanted them to know what was being done in Philippi, Thessalonica and Berea, (2 Cor.8:1-6) with the added thought that such talented saints as they were in every area - faith, communication, knowledge, diligence and love - should also be expert givers also. Note the intensive ὥσπερ (#560). The ἵνα clause with the subjunctive represents "An innovation in Hellenistic" Greek. "ἵνα c.subj.in commands, which takes the place of the classic ὅπως c.fut.indic." (Moulton, *Prologomena*, 178, as cited in Robertson, *Grammar*, 994).   Robertson adds, "Moulton cites a moderate number of examples of this abrupt use of ἵνα in the paryri. . . . There is a doubtful ex. of this sense of ἵνα in Soph.,*Oed.C.*155, though ὅπως was so used. It appears in Arrian and Epictetus. In the modern Greek the νά clause sometimes "approaches the nature of a principal sentence." (Thumb, *Handbook*, 198). But this elliptical imperative is undoubted in the N.T. Cf. Mk.5:23, ἵνα ἐλθὼν ἐπιθῇς. So also Mt.20:32; 1 Cor.7:23; 2 Cor.8:7; Eph.4:29; 5:33." (Robertson, *Grammar*, 994).

Verse 8 - "*I speak not by commandment, but by occasion of the forwardness of others, and to prove the sincerity of your love.*"

Οὐ κατ᾽ ἐπιταγὴν λέγω, ἀλλὰ διὰ τῆς ἑτέρων σπουδῆς καὶ τὸ τῆς ὑμετέρας ἀγάπης γνήσιον δοκιμάζων.

"*I say this not as a command, but to prove by the earnestness of others that your love also in genuine.*" . . . RSV

οὐ (negative conjunction with the indicative) 130.
κατ᾽ (preposition with the accusative, aim) 98.
ἐπιταγὴν (acc.sing.fem.of ἐπιταγή, aim or tendency) 4099.
λέγω (1st.per.sing.pres.act.ind.of λέγω, aoristic) 66.
ἀλλὰ (alternative conjunction) 342.
διὰ (preposition with the genitive of reference) 118.
τῆς (gen.sing.fem.of the article in agreement with σπουδῆς) 9.
ἑτέρων (gen.pl.masc.of ἕτερος, possession) 605.
σπουδῆς (gen.sing.fem.of σπουδή, adverbial, reference) 1819.
καὶ (adjunctive conjunction joining verbs) 14.
τὸ (acc.sing.neut.of the article in agreement with γνήσιον) 9.
τῆς (gen.sing.fem.of the article in agreement with ἀγάπης) 9.
ὑμετέρας (gen.sing.fem.of ὑμέτερας, possession) 2127.
ἀγάπης (gen.sing.fem.of ἀγάπη, adverbial, reference) 1490.

#4334 γνήσιον (acc.sing.neut.of γνήσιος, direct object of δοκιμάζων).

King James Version

own - 1 Tim.1:2; Titus 1:4.
true - Phil.4:3.
sincerity - 2 Cor.8:8.

Revised Standard Version

genuine - 2 Cor.8:8.
true - Phil.4:3; 1 Tim.1:12; Titus 1:4.

Meaning: by syncope from γενήσιος from γίνομαι (#113). *cf.* γέννησις (#73). Legitimately born; not spurious; genuine; true. With a genitive of description in 2 Cor.8:8 with reference to the love of the Corinthians. As an adjective in the attributive position - a true yokefellow - Phil.4:3; true son - 1 Tim.1:12; Titus 1:4.

δοκιμάζων (pres.act.part.nom.sing.masc.of δοκιμάζω, adverbial, telic) 2493.

Translation - "I am not speaking with a view to command you, but with reference to the diligence of others and for the purpose of proving that your love is a result of a supernatural birth."

Comment: κατὰ with the accusative can indicate aim, purpose or tendency. Paul did not wish his remarks to be interpreted as an order. Why then? He was speaking with reference to the zeal of the Macedonians and for the purpose (δοκιμάζων) of putting to a test the love of the Corinthians for Christ. Would they give their money as the Macedonians had given, without pretense (verse 2)? If their love was the genuine fruit of the Holy Spirit as a result of their new birth (#4334) they would give as had the Macedonians. Regenerated love can only repond to the love of Christ without pretense. This is the thought in

Verse 9 - "For ye know the grace of our Lord Jesus Christ, that, though He was rich, yet for your sakes He became poor; that ye through His poverty might be rich."

γινώσκετε γὰρ τὴν χάριν τοῦ κυρίου ἡμῶν Ἰησοῦ Χριστοῦ, ὅτι δι' ὑμᾶς ἐπτώχευσεν πλούσιος ὤν, ἵνα ὑμεῖς τῇ ἐκείνου πτωχείᾳ πλουτήσητε.

"For you know the grace of our Lord Jesus Christ, that though he was rich, yet for your sake he became poor, so that by his poverty you might become rich."
                                                                    . . . *RSV*

γινώσκετε (2d.per.pl.pres.act.ind.of γινώσκω, aoristic) 131.
γὰρ (causal conjunction) 105.
τὴν (acc.sing.fem.of the article in agreement with χάριν) 9.
χάριν (acc.sing.fem.of χάρις, direct object of γινώσκετε) 1700.
τοῦ (gen.sing.masc.of the article in agreement with κυρίου) 9.
κυρίου (gen.sing.masc.of κύριος, possession) 97.
ἡμῶν (gen.pl.masc.of ἐγώ, relationship) 123.
Ἰησοῦ (gen.sing.masc.of Ἰησοῦς, apposition) 3.

Χριστοῦ (gen.sing.masc.of Χριστός, apposition) 4.
ὅτι (epexegetical conjunction) 211.
δι' (preposition with the accusative, cause) 118.
ὑμᾶς (acc.pl.masc.of σύ, cause) 104.

#4335 ἐπτώχευσεν (3d.per.sing.aor.act.ind.of πτωχεύω, ingressive).

King James Version

became poor - 2 Cor.8:9.

Revised Standard Version

became poor - 2 Cor.8:9.

Meaning: Cf. πτωχεία (#4331); πτωχός (#423). In classical Greek, to be a beggar; to beg. In 2 Cor.8:9, to be poor. *Cf.*ἐκένωσεν of Phil.2:7, of the poverty of Messiah in His incarnation to which Paul alludes.

πλούσιος (nom.sing.masc.of πλούσιος, predicate adjective) 1306.
ὤν (pres.part.nom.sing.masc.of εἰμί, adverbial, concessive) 86.
ἵνα (conjunction introducing the subjunctive in a purpose clause) 114.
ὑμεῖς (nom.pl.masc.of σύ, subject of πλουτήσητε) 104.
τῇ (instru.sing.fem.of the article in agreement with πτωχείᾳ) 9.
ἐκείνου (gen.sing.masc.of ἐκεῖνος, possession, deictic) 246.
πτωχείᾳ (instru.sing.fem.of πτωχεία, cause) 4331.
πλουτήσητε (2d.per.pl.aor.subj.of πλουτέω, ingressive) 1834.

Translation - "Because you are aware of the grace of our Lord Jesus Christ - that although He was rich, yet, because of you He became poor in order that through the poverty of that one you might become rich."

Comment: γὰρ is causal. Paul is testing the quality of their love by telling them about the performance of the Macedonians, because (γὰρ) he knows that they know about the incarnation and its significance. ὅτι is epexegetical. δι' ὑμᾶς - because (δια with the accusative) of the Corinthians and their fallen and unhappy state, He, the Plutocrat of Glory (John 1:1-3; Col.1:14-19) became poor (ingressive aorist in ἐπτώχευσεν). Why? The ἵνα clause denotes purpose. The divine purpose in the incarnation was that the poverty-stricken Corinthians might become rich (ingressive aorist in πλουτήσητε). And how was this brought about? Because of the poverty on the cross of "that man." Note the deictic use of ἐκείνου. Note the contrast between the emphatic ὑμεῖς and deictic ἐκείνου, which refers to Christ. If Christ, the Plutocrat (Col.1:19; 2:3) was stricken with poverty (Mt.8:20) because His divine love was supernaturally genuine (Gal.2:20), in order that through His sacrifice the Corinthians might be enriched (1 Cor.3:21-23), an acid test of the quality of their Christian love (2 Cor.8:8) would be revealed by their response to Paul's appeal for help for the starving Judean Christians. The proof of divine love is seen when we trade our riches for someone's poverty, in order to make them rich. This is the pattern that Jesus set on the cross.

Verse 10 - "And herein I give my advice: for this is expedient for you, who have begun before, not only to do, but also to be forward a year ago."

καὶ γνώμην ἐν τούτῳ δίδωμι. τοῦτο γὰρ ὑμῖν συμφέρει, οἵτινες οὐ μόνον τὸ ποιῆσαι ἀλλὰ καὶ τὸ θέλειν προενήρξασθε ἀπὸ πέρυσι.

"And in this matter I give my advice: it is best for you now to complete what a year ago you began not only to do but to desire," . . . RSV

καὶ (inferential conjunction) 14.
γνώμην (acc.sing.fem.of γνώμη, direct object of δίδωμι) 3499.
ἐν (preposition with the locative of sphere) 80.
τούτῳ (loc.sing.neut.of οὗτος, sphere, substantives) 93.
δίδωμι (1st.per.sing.pres.act.ind.of δίδωμι, aoristic) 362.
τοῦτο (nom.sing.neut.of οὗτος, subject of συμφέρει) 93.
γὰρ (causal conjunction) 105.
ὑμῖν (dat.pl.masc.of σύ, personal interest) 104.
συμφέρει (3d.per.sing.pres.act.ind.of συμφέρω, static) 505.
οἵτινες (nom.pl.masc.of ὅστις, definite relative pronoun, subject of προενήρξασθε) 163.
οὐ (negative conjunction with the indicative) 130.
μόνον (acc.sing.neut.of μόνος, adverbial) 339.
τὸ (acc.sing.neut.of the article in agreement with ποιῆσαι) 9.
ποιῆσαι (aor.act.inf.of ποιέω, object infinitive of προενήρξασθε) 127.
ἀλλὰ (alternative conjunction) 342.
καὶ (adjunctive conjunction joining infinitives) 14.
τὸ (acc.sing.neut.of the article in agreement with θέλειν) 9.
θέλειν (pres.act.inf.of θέλω, object infinitive of προενήρξασθε) 88.
προενήρξασθε (2d.per.pl.aor.mid.ind.of προενάρχομαι, ingressive) 4333.
ἀπὸ (preposition with an adverb of time separation) 70.

#**4336** πέρυσι (adverbial).

King James Version

a year ago - 2 Cor.8:10; 9:2.

Revised Standard Version

a year ago - 2 Cor.8:10.
since last year - 2 Cor.9:2.

Meaning: Cf. πέρας (#1016). Last year; the year just past. With ἀπὸ - "during the past year" - 2 Cor.8:10; 9:2.

Translation - "So I am giving my opinion about this, since this is the best plan for you - those of you who began not only to carry out the plan but also have continued to want it for the past year."

Comment: Paul has made his point and the Corinthians are on the spot. So Paul feels it proper to venture his opinion, because of the points that he has made previously. He was bold because such an approach was the best way to deal with the Corinthians. Some had already begun the year before (ἀπὸ πέρυσι) not only to set the plan in motion but had, since that time, continued to hope for its success. The infinitives are objects of the verb.

Verse 11 - "Now therefore perform the doing of it; that as there was a readiness to will so there may be a performance also out of that which ye have."

νυνὶ δὲ καὶ τὸ ποιῆσαι ἐπιτελέσατε, ὅπως καθάπερ ἡ προθυμία τοῦ θέλειν οὕτως καὶ τὸ ἐπιτελέσαι ἐκ τοῦ ἔχειν.

"so that your readiness in desiring it may be matched by your completing it out of what you have." . . . *RSV*

νυνὶ (adverbial) 1497.
δὲ (continuative conjunction) 11.
καὶ (inferential conjunction) 14.
τὸ (acc.sing.neut.of the article in agreement with ποιῆσαι) 9.
ποιῆσαι (aor.act.inf.of ποιέω, object infintive of ἐπιτελέσατε) 127.
ἐπιτελέσατε (2d.per.pl.aor.act.impv.of ἐπιτελέω, command) 4059.
ὅπως (conjunction introducing the subjunctive, understood, purpose) 177.
καθάπερ (intensive comparative compound) 3883.
ἡ (nom.sing.fem.of the article in agreement with προθυμία) 9.
προθυμία (nom.sing.fem.of προθυμία, subject of ἦ understood) 3395.
τοῦ (gen.sing.neut.of the article in agreement with θέλειν) 9.
θέλειν (pres.act.inf.of θέλω, gen. sing.neut. adnominal) 88.
οὕτως (demonstrative adverb) 74.
καὶ (adjunctive conjunction joining infinitives) 14.
τὸ (acc.sing.neut.of the article in agreement with ἐπιτελέσαι) 9.
ἐπιτελέσαι (aor.act.inf.of ἐπιτελέω, adnominal) 4059.
ἐκ (preposition with the ablative of source) 19.
τοῦ (abl.sing.neut.of the article in agreement with ἔχειν) 9.
ἔχειν (pres.act.inf.of ἔχω, noun use, source) 82.

Translation - "And now therefore finish the execution of the plan, so that just as there was an enthusiastic desire, so also there will be an implementation of it out of what you have."

Comment: Paul now asks that the program begun the year before to collect money may now to implemented. The purpose clause tells us why he wanted this. He wanted the actual giving of the money to match in enthusiasm the zeal with which they planned to give it. He seems to be afraid that their interest in the plan had waned. τοῦ θέλειν is adnominal. *Cf.* Rom.15:23; 1 Cor.9:10; 16:14; Phil.3:21 for others with τοῦ, while ἐκ τοῦ ἔχειν is an ablative of source. They were told to give what they could, even if it was not very much.

Verse 12 - "For if there be first a willing mind, it is accepted according to that a man hath, and not according to that he hath not."

εἰ γὰρ ἡ προθυμία πρόκειται, καθὸ ἐὰν ἔχῃ εὐπρόσδεκτος, οὐ καθὸ οὐκ ἔχει.

"For if the readiness is there, it is acceptable according to what a man has, not according to what he has not." . . . RSV

εἰ (conditional particle in a first-class condition) 337.
γὰρ (causal conjunction) 105.
ἡ (nom.sing.fem.of the article in agreement with προθυμία) 9.
προθυμία (nom.sing.fem.of προθυμία, subject of πρόκειται) 3395.

#4337 πρόκειται (3d.per.sing.pres.mid.ind.of πρόκειμαι, first-class condition).

King James Version

be first - 2 Cor.8:12.
be set before - Heb.6:18; 12:1,2.
be set forth - Jude 7.

Revised Standard Version

is there - 2 Cor.8:12.
set before - Heb.6:18; 12:1,2.
serve - Jude 7.

Meaning: A combination of πρό (#442) and κεῖμαι (#295). In classical Greek, to lie or be placed before or in front of. To be present first of all, in a chronological sense in 2 Cor.8:12; to be destined for future realization - the hope of salvation - Heb.6;18; for future accomplishment - the Christian race - Heb.12:1; the joy in Jesus' future (after the cross) - Heb.12:2. Established in the past as an example - set forth - of Sodom and Gomorrah, as examples - Jude 7.

καθὸ (comparative adverb) 3947.
ἐὰν (conditional particle in an elliptical third-class condition) 363.
ἔχῃ (3d.per.sing.pres.act.subj.of ἔχω, elliptical third-class condition) 82.
εὐπρόσκεκτος (nom.sing.masc.of εὐπρόσδεκτος, predicate adjective) 4052.
οὐ (negative conjunction with the indicative) 130.
καθὸ (comparative adverb) 3947.
οὐκ (negative conjunction with the indicative) 130.
ἔχει (3d.per.sing.pres.act.ind.of ἔχω, aoristic) 82.

Translation - "For if the willingness to give is there first, according to whatever he may have, it is accepted: not in accord with what he does not have."

Comment: εἰ and the first-class condition assumes that the giver is willing to give. If he is, what he gives is acceptable on the basis of whatever he has; it is not judged on the basis of what he has not. Note the distinction between the subjunctive ἔχῃ and the indicative ἔχει. Paul was not sure how much wealth any given Corinthian had. The Lord bases his acceptability of every gift upon the degree of willingness displayed by the giver, not upon the size of the gift. The question for the rich man then becomes how much he is willing to give. The plutocrat with assets of one million dollars is certainly willing to give one hundred. He would scarcely miss it. What percentage of his total wealth can he give willingly? Fifty percent? Ninety percent? All of it? If he is a good steward he is willing to give it all since the essence of stewardship is that the child of God owns nothing, but is appointed by the Lord as steward over that which belongs to God. Thus the millionaire who gives much, but with a grudging spirit is less acceptable to the Lord than the pauper who gladly gives all that he has. It is probably easier for the pauper to give all with gladness than for the wealthy man, due to the fact that the difference between the pauper's standard of living before and after he gave his gift is not great, whereas the millionaire who, before the gift lived in the lap of luxury must live like a pauper if he gives it all. This is why Jesus said that it is harder for the rich to enter into the kingdom than for the poor.

Verse 13 - "For I mean not that other men be eased, and ye be burdened."

οὐ γὰρ ἵνα ἄλλοις ἄνεσις, ὑμῖν θλῖψις, ἀλλ' ἐξ ἰσότητος.

"I do not mean that others should be eased and you burdened, . . ." . . . RSV

οὐ (negative conjunction with the indicative understood) 130.
γὰρ (causal conjunction) 105.
ἵνα (conjunction introducing an elliptical purpose clause) 114.
ἄλλοις (dat.pl.masc.of ἄλλος, personal advantage) 198.
ἄνεσις (nom.sing.fem.of ἄνεσις, subject of ᾖ understood) 3628.
ὑμῖν (dat.pl.masc.of σύ, personal disadvantage) 104.
θλῖψις (nom.sing.fem.of θλῖψις, subject of ᾖ understood) 1046.

Translation - "Not that I want relief for others and a burden for you."

Comment: We must supply ᾖ after ἵνα. Paul's purpose is not that relief from the burden of giving should be provided for others, while the Corinthians are asked to bear it. It is more difficult to give much willingly than little. And yet it is the willingness to give that makes the gift acceptable.

This passage is enough to destroy the dogma that a proportionate levy of ten per cent (commonly called the tithe) is levied by the New Testament upon every saint. Proportionate taxation is regressive, *i.e.* it imposes a burden upon the poor and is no burden at all to the rich. The tithe principle taxes the Christian who makes $1000 per week in the amount of $100. It imposes a tax of $10 upon the Christian who makes $100 per week. The former has $900 of disposable income; the latter has $90. This does not provide an equalization of the burden, since disposable income after the tithe is paid, not the tithe itself, is the measure of the standard of living. It is not likely that one can find a diaconate made up of wealthy men who oppose tithing, since this principle places upon the vast majority of the congregation in the average church the burden of financing the program, while the wealthy minority escapes relatively unscathed. Paul is teaching a progressive concept of giving, not a proportional concept.

Verse 14 - *"But by an equality, that now at this time your abundance may be a supply for their want, that their abundance also may be a supply for your want: that there may be equality."*

ἐν τῷ νῦν καιρῷ τὸ ὑμῶν περίσσευμα εἰς τὸ ἐκείνων ὑστέρημα, ἵνα καὶ τὸ ἐκείνων περίσσευμα γένηται εἰς τὸ ὑμῶν ὑστέρημα, ὅπως γένηται ἰσότης.

"but that as a matter of equality your abundance at the present time should supply their want, so that their abundance may supply your want, that there may be equality." . . . RSV

ἀλλ' (adversative conjunction) 342.
ἐξ (preposition with the ablative of source) 19.

#4338 ἰσότητος (abl.sing.fem.of ἰσότης, source).

King James Version

equality - 2 Cor.8:14,14.
that which is equal - Col.4:1.

Revised Standard Version

a matter of equality - 2 Cor.8:14,14.
fairly - Col.4:1.

*Meaning: Cf.*ἴσος (#1323). Equality; equal treatment. In the burden of financial giving to the work of the Lord - 2 Cor.8:14,14; with reference to the treatment of servants, used with τὸ δίκαιον - Col.4:1.

ἐν (preposition with the locative of time point) 80.
τῷ (loc.sing.masc.of the article in agreement with καιρῷ) 9.
νῦν (adverbial) 1497.
καιρῷ (loc.sing.masc.of καιρός, time point) 767.
τὸ (nom.sing.neut.of the article in agreement with περίσσευμα) 9.
ὑμῶν (gen.pl.masc.of σύ, possession) 104.
περίσσευμα (nom.sing.neut.of περίσσευμα, subject of ῇ understood) 1003.
εἰς (preposition with the accusative, purpose) 140.
τὸ (acc.sing.neut.of the article in agreement with ὑστέρημα) 9.
ἐκείνων (gen.pl.masc.of ἐκεῖνος, possession) 246.
ὑστέρημα (acc.sing.neut.of ὑστέρημα, purpose) 2707.
ἵνα (conjunction with the subjunctive in a purpose clause) 114.
καὶ (adjunctive conjunction joining clauses) 14.
τὸ (nom.sing.neut.of the article in agreement with περίσσευμα) 9.
ἐκείνων (gen.pl.masc.of ἐκεῖνος, possession) 246.
περίσευμα (nom.sing.neut.of περίσευμα, subject of γένηται) 1003.
γένηται (3d.per.sing.aor.subj.of γίνομαι, purpose) 113.
εἰς (preposition with the accusative, predicate accusative) 140.
τὸ (acc.sing.neut.of the article in agreement with ὑστέρημα) 9.

ὑμῶν (gen.pl.masc.of σύ, possession) 104.
ὑστέρημα (acc.sing.neut.of ὑστέρημα, predicate accusative) 2707.
ὅπως (conjunction with the subjunctive, purpose) 177.
γένηται (3d.per.sing.aor.subj.of γίνομαι, purpose) 113.
ἰσότης (nom.sing.fem.of ἰσότης, subject of γένηται) 4338.

Translation - ". . . but on a principle of equality. This time your abundance compensates for their lack, in order also that their abundance may provide for your lack, in order that there may be equality."

Comment: ἀλλ', which in the Greek text is a part of verse 13 is in response to the first clause of the verse. Paul is not suggesting that the Corinthians should always bear the burden while others are excused. On the contrary (ἀλλά) he is seeking to establish a principle of equality. Under such a principle those blessed with abundance, as the Christians in Corinth apparently were, would give enough to compensate for the lack of giving from others in financial straits, as the Macedonian Christians were. At some later time this situation would likely be reversed, with the result that an equality of burden would be maintained.

As has already been pointed out, this is a progressive taxation, not proportionate and it militates against the iron-clad principle of the tithe, which works against equality. Paul's teaching here is only a part of the New Testament message on stewardship. The deeper truth is that the total net worth of every Christian belongs to God and that he should manage God's wealth wisely and keep only enough for himself to maintain his position as a good steward.

The equality principle is now illustrated by a quotation from Exodus 16:18.

Verse 15 - "As it is written, He that had gathered much had nothing over; and he that had gathered little had no lack."

καθὼς γέγραπται, Ὁ τὸ πολὺ οὐκ ἐπλεόνασεν, καὶ ὁ τὸ ὀλίγον οὐκ ἠλαττόνησεν.

"As it is written, 'He who gathered much had nothing over, and he who gathered little had no lack.' " . . . RSV

καθὼς (comparative adverb) 1348.
γέγραπται (3d.per.sing.perf.pass.ind.of γράφω, intensive) 156.
Ὁ (nom.sing.masc.of the article, subject the participial substantive understood) 9.
τὸ (acc.sing.neut.of the article in agreement with πολὺ) 9.
πολὺ (acc.sing.neut.of πολύς, direct object of verb understood) 228.
οὐκ (negative conjunction with the indicative) 130.
ἐπλεόνασεν (3d.per.sing.aor.act.ind.of πλεονάζω, constative) 3907.
καὶ (continuative conjunction) 14.
ὁ (nom.sing.masc.of the article, subject of the verb understood) 9.
τὸ (acc.sing.neut.of the article in agreement with ὀλίγον) 9.
ὀλίγον (acc.sing.neut.of ὀλίγος, direct object of verb understood) 669.
οὐκ (negative conjunction with the indicative) 130.

#4339 ἠλαττόνησεν (3d.per.sing.aor.act.ind.of ἐλαττονέω, constative).

King James Version

have lack - 2 Cor.8:15.

Revised Standard Version

have lack - 2 Cor.8:15.

Meaning: Cf. ἐλάσσων (#1977); ἐλαττόω (#1995). Not found in profane Greek. To have less; to be inferior. With reference to the Jews who gathered little manna in the desert as used illustratively in 2 Cor.8:15.

Translation - "As it is written, 'The one having much did not have too much, and the one having little did not have too little.' "

Comment: The usual idom καθὼς γέγραπται - "it stands written" as the perfect tense indicates the present condition as a result of completed past action. The quotation is from Exodus 16:18, where the LXX has οὐκ ἐπλεόνασεν ὁ τὸ πολύ, καὶ ὁ τὸ ἔλαττον οὐκ ἠλαττόνησεν, with reference to Israel gathering manna in the desert. The rule was that the man should gather one omer "by the poll" (*i.e.* per capita) for his family. A man with a large family gathered more than a man with a small family, with the result that everyone had the same amount of manna - one omer. Here is distribution on the principle "to each according to his need." Hoarding was forbidden. It was also impractical since the good was non-durable (Exodus 16:19-21). Hoarding became practical when wealth in goods came to be transferred to wealth in money which is durable and of constant value in periods of stable prices. It became *practical* for the rich to hoard, but it never became *ethical.* The speculative motive for holding money is hardly a Christian ethic.

Titus and His Companions

(2 Corinthians 8:16-24)

Verse 16 - "But thanks be to God, which put the same earnest care into the heart of Titus for you."

Χάρις δὲ τῷ θεῷ τῷ δόντι τὴν αὐτὴν σπουδὴν ὑπὲρ ὑμῶν ἐν τῇ καρδίᾳ Τίτου,

"But thanks be to God who puts the same earnest care for you into the heart of Titus." . . . RSV

Χάρις (nom.sing.fem.of χάρις, independent nominative) 1700.
δὲ (explanatory conjunction) 11.
τῷ (dat.sing.masc.of the article in agreement with θεῷ) 9.
θεῷ (dat.sing.masc.of θεός,indirect object of verb understood) 124.
τῷ (dat.sing.masc.of the article in agreement with δόντι) 9.
δόντι (2d.aor.act.part.dat.sing.masc.of δίδωμι, adjectival, attributive position, ascriptive) 362.

τὴν (acc.sing.fem.of the article in agreement with σπουδὴν) 9.
αὐτὴν (acc.sing.fem.of αὐτός, emphatic, in agreement with σπουδὴν) 16.
σπουδὴν (acc.sing.fem.of σπουδή, direct object of δόντι) 1819.
ὑπέρ (preposition with the ablative, "in behalf of") 545.
ὑμῶν (abl.pl.masc.of σύ, "in behalf of") 104.
ἐν (preposition with the locative of palce) 80.
τῇ (loc.sing.fem.of the article in agreement with καρδίᾳ) 9.
καρδίᾳ (loc.sing.fem.of καρδία, place) 432.
Τίτου (gen.sing.masc.of Τίτος, possession) 4278.

Translation - *"Now thanks be to God who generated in the heart of Titus the same concern for you."*

Comment: We must supply ἔστω in the first clause. Note the participial adjective, modifying θεῷ, in the emphatic attributive position. He is the God who put into the heart of Titus a concern for the Corinthians.

Because Titus now felt a newly generated interest in the Corinthians he voluntarily made plans to visit them.

Verse 17 - *"For indeed he accepted the exhortation; but being more forward, of his own accord he went unto you."*

ὅτι τὴν μὲν παράκλησιν ἐδέξατο, σπουδαιότερος δὲ ὑπάρχων αὐθαίρετος ἐξῆλθεν πρὸς ὑμᾶς.

"For he not only accepted our appeal, but being himself very earnest he is going to you of his own accord." . . . *RSV*

ὅτι (epexegetical conjunction) 211.
τὴν (acc.sing.fem.of the article in agreement with παράκλησιν) 9.
μὲν (particle of affirmation) 300.
παράκλησιν (acc.sing.fem.of παράκλησις, direct object of ἐδέξατο) 1896.
ἐδέξατο (3d.per.sing.aor.mid.ind.of δέχομαι, constative) 867.

#4340 σπουδαιότερος (nom.sing.masc.comp.of σπουδαῖος, predicate adjective).

King James Version

diligent - 2 Cor.8:22,22.
forward - 2 Cor.8:17.

Revised Standard Version

very earnest - 2 Cor.8:17.
earnest - 2 Cor.8:22,22.

Meaning: Cf. σπουδαίως (#2150); σπουδάζω (#4423); σπουδή (#1819). Hence, active, earnest, zealous, diligent, eager to serve. With reference to Titus' attitude toward the Corinthians - 2 Cor.8:17; with reference to Luke - 2 Cor.8:22,22.

δὲ (adversative conjunction) 11.
ὑπάρχων (pres.part.nom.sing.masc.of ὑπάρχω, adverbial, causal) 1303.
αὐθαίρετος (nom.sing.masc.of αὐθαίρετος, predicate adjective) 4332.
ἐξῆλθεν (3d.per.sing.aor.ind.of ἐξέρχομαι, constative) 161.
πρὸς (preposition with the accusative of extent) 197.
ὑμᾶς (acc.pl.masc.of σύ, extent) 104.

Translation - *"Thus in fact he accepted our suggestion, but because he was so eager of his own accord he visited you."*

Comment: ὅτι is epexegetical as Paul procedes to show the results in Titus' decision of God's work in his heart (verse 16). The μὲν . . . δὲ sequence can be translated as though μὲν were concessive. "Though on the one hand Titus accepted our suggestion for him to visit you, on the other hand (δὲ) because he was so eager (causal participle in ὑπάρχων) he came to you of his own accord." Titus needed no urging from Paul. His decision to visit Corinth resulted from verse 16.

Verse 18 - *"And we have sent with him the brother, whose praise is in the gospel throughout all the churches."*

συνεπέμφαμεν δὲ μετ᾽ αὐτοῦ τὸν ἀδελφὸν οὗ ὁ ἔπαινος ἐν τῷ εὐαγγελίῳ διὰ πασῶν τῶν ἐκκλησιῶν . . .

"With him we are sending the brother who is famous among all the churches for his preaching of the gospel; " . . . *RSV*

#4341 συνεπέμφαμεν (1st.per.pl.aor.act.ind.of συμπέμπω, culminative).

King James Version

send with - 2 Cor.8:18,22.

Revised Standard Version

sent with - 2 Cor.8:18,22.

Meaning: A combination of σύν (#1542) and πέμπω (#169). Hence, to send with. To dispatch upon a journey with a companion. Silas was sent along with Titus to Corinth - 2 Cor.8:18,22.

δὲ (continuative conjunction) 11.
μετ᾽ (preposition with the genitive of accompaniment) 50.
αὐτοῦ (gen.sing.masc.of αὐτός, accompaniment) 16.
τὸν (acc.sing.masc.of the article in agreement with ἀδελφὸν) 9.
ἀδελφὸν (acc.sing.masc.of ἀδελφός, direct object of συνεπέμφαμεν) 15.
οὗ (gen.sing.masc.of ὅς, relative pronoun, possession) 65.
ὁ (nom.sing.masc.of the article in agreement with ἔπαινος) 9.
ἔπαινος (nom.sing.masc.of ἔπαινος, subject of ἐστίν understood) 3853.
ἐν (preposition with the locative of sphere, with nouns) 80.

τῷ (loc.sing.neut.of the article in agreement with εὐαγγελίῳ) 9.
εὐαγγελίῳ (loc.sing.neut.of εὐαγγέλιον, sphere, nouns) 405.
διὰ (preposition with the genitive, place description) 118.
πασῶν (gen.pl.fem.of πᾶς, in agreement with ἐκκλησιῶν) 67.
τῶν (gen.pl.fem.of the article in agreement with ἐκκλησιῶν) 9.
ἐκκλησιων (gen.pl.fem.of ἐκκλησία, place description) 1204.

Translation - *"And we sent with him our brother whose fame as a gospel preacher has gone throughout all of the churches."*

Comment: Verse 19 hints that the man of verse 18 is Silas. Another man went with Titus (verse 22). Robertson thinks that the man of verse 18 is Luke and that the other man (verse 22) "may have been Tychicus or Apollos, but we do not know." (*Word Pictures in the New Testament*, IV, 245, 246).

Verse 19 - "And not that only but who was also chosen of the churches to travel with us with this grace, which is administered by us to the glory of the same Lord, and declaration of your ready mind."

— οὐ μόνον δὲ ἀλλὰ καὶ χειροτονηθεὶς ὑπὸ τῶν ἐκκλησιῶν συνέκδημος ἡμῶν σὺν τῇ χάριτι ταύτῃ τῇ διακονουμένῃ ὑφ' ἡμῶν πρὸς τὴν (αὐτοῦ) τοῦ κυρίου δόξαν καὶ προθυμίαν ἡμῶν —

"and not only that, but he has been appointed by the churches to travel with us in this gracious work which we are carrying on, for the glory of the Lord and to show our good will." . . . RSV

οὐ (negative conjunction with the indicative) 130.
μόνον (acc.sing.neut.of μόνος, adverbial) 339.
δὲ (adversative conjunction) 11.
καὶ (adjunctive conjunction, anacoluthon) 14.
χειροτονηθεὶς (aor.pass.part.nom.sing.masc.of χειροτονέω, anacoluthon) 3332.
ὑπὸ (preposition with the ablative of agent) 117.
τῶν (abl.pl.fem.of the article in agreement with ἐκκλησιῶν) 9.
ἐκκλησιῶν (abl.pl.fem.of ἐκκλησία, agent) 1204.
συνέκδημος (nom.sing.masc.of συνέκδημοσ, apposition) 3486.
ἡμῶν (gen.pl.masc.of ἐγώ, relationship) 123.
σὺν (preposition with the dative of reference) 1542.
τῇ (dat.sing.fem.of the article in agreement with χάριτι) 9.
χάριτι (dat.sing.fem.of χάρις, reference) 1700.
ταύτῃ (dat.sing.fem.of οὗτος, in agreement with χάριτι) 93.
τῇ (dat.sing.fem.of the article in agreeement with διακονουμένῃ) 9.
διακονουμένῃ (pres.pass.part.dat.sing.fem.of διακονώ, adjectival, emphatic attributive position, in agreement with χάριτι) 367.
ὑφ' (preposition with the ablative of agent) 117.
ἡμῶν (abl.pl.masc.of ἐγώ, agent) 123.
πρὸς (preposition with the accusative, purpose) 197.

τὴν (acc.sing.fem.of the article in agreement with δόξαν) 9.

(αὐτοῦ) (gen.sing.masc.of αὐτός, emphatic) 16.

τοῦ (gen.sing.masc.of the article in agreement with κυρίου) 9.

κυρίου (gen.sing.masc.of κύριος, possession) 97.

δόξαν (acc.sing.fem.of δόξα, purpose) 361.

καὶ (adjunctive conjunction joining nouns) 14.

προθυμίαν (acc.sing.fem.of προθυμία, purpose) 3395.

ἡμῶν (gen.pl.masc.of ἐγώ, possession) 123.

Translation - *"Not only so but also he was chosen by the churches as a travelling companion with us, in connection with this ministry of grace carried on by us to the glory of the same Lord and to show our eagerness to do it."*

Comment: Verse 19 is a parenthesis. The main sentence begins with συνεπέμψαμεν and continues, after verse 19 with στελλόμενοι of verse 20. Even so the aorist participle χειροτονηθεὶς is anacoluthon, since the proper form would be the aorist passive indicative ἐχειροτονήθη, and so we have translated. In any case Paul's point is clear. He introduced Titus' travel companions of verse 18. Now he adds, parenthetically, that the man is not only well thought of throughout all the churches (verse 18b) but also he was ordained (#3332) by the church and commissioned to travel with Paul (#3486), in connection with the special ministry of funding a relief program for the famine-stricken saints in Judea. Paul has two purposes for this work, and he lists them in the proper order: (a) πρὸς τὴν (αὐτοῦ) τοῦ κυρίου δόξαν - "for the purpose of glorifying the same Lord" and (b) προθυμίαν ἡμῶν - "to demonstrate our own eagerness to do this charitable work."

The presence of the anacoluthon here illustrates the willingness of the Holy Spirit, Who inspired the writing of the text, not in a dictation but in a superintendence sense, to allow the writer to blunder grammatically and syntactically, so long as He knew that the exegete would not be misled in the interpretation. There is no doubt about what Paul intended to say. The context guards his precise thought. Thus we have plenary (complete) divine inspiration, though it is not inerrant from a syntactical point of view. Fundamentalists who insist that there are no errors in the Word of God, as they insist that every word written is there by the dictation of the Holy Spirit are accusing Him of ignorance of Greek grammar. No harm is done to evangelical thought when we face the fact that though there are errors in the text, they do not diminish the power of the text to transmit to the scientific exegete the total truth(s) of what the Holy Spirit intended to say. Fundamentalists on the other hand are vulnerable to attack by unbelievers (modernists, deists, agnostics, atheists, existentialists) who find it easy to point to minor errors in the text. The attack of the unbelievers is based upon plain fact, but it does not threaten the position of evangelicals, although it destroys the position of the Fundamentalists. We do great disservice to the cause of Christ when we insist upon preaching that which is untrue. The evangelical view on the other hand recognizes the same mystery in the incarnation of the written Word of God as we contemplate in the birth of the living Word of God. In each there is a mystifying merge of the human and the divine. Just as the human characteristics, transmitted by genetics, of the virgin Mary are noted in the humanity of Jesus, (with the sole exception of an inducement to evil), so also the literary, grammatical and syntactical characteristics of the human authors of the New Testament are noted in the literature which they produced. "Great is the mystery of godliness. He was manifested in the flesh" (1 Tim.3:16, upon which *cf.* comment). He was manifested in a more complete revelation in the Greek New Testament. When the human and the divine merge to produce a flawed image of the divine, because of the human element, we have no revelation. When they merge as they do both in Jesus and the New Testament to produce a flawless image of the divine we have a total (plenary) revelation of all that God wants us to know at this time. This is to the glory of our matchless Lord. Fundamentalists should repent of their sin of referring to evangelicals who reject their dictation theory as quasi-modernists. They ought also to become Bereans on this issue.

Verse 20 - "Avoiding this, that no man should blame us in this abundance which is administered by us."

στελλόμενοι τοῦτο μή τις ἡμᾶς μωμήσηται ἐν τῇ ἁδρότητι ταύτῃ τῇ διακονουμένῃ ὑφ' ἡμῶν.

"We intend that no one should blame us about this liberal gift which we are administering," . . . RSV

#4342 στελλόμενοι (pres.mid.part.nom.pl.masc.of στέλλω, adverbial, circumstantial).

King James Version

avoid - 2 Cor.8:20.
withdraw one's self - 2 Thess.3:6.

Revised Standard Version

intend - 2 Cor.8:20.
keep away from - 2 Thess.3:6.

Meaning: Cf. στήλη - "a block, buttress or other preventive device." Hence, to take care, provide a safeguard, take preventive measures, guard against. Followed by an epexegetical negative purpose clause in 2 Cor.8:20. Followed by ἀπό and the ablative of separation in 2 Thess.3:6.

τοῦτο (acc.sing.neut.of οὗτος, direct object of στελλόμενοι) 93.
μή (negative conjunction with the subjunctive) 87.
τις (nom.sing.masc.of τις, indefinite pronoun, subject of μωμήσηται) 486.
ἡμᾶς (acc.pl.masc.of ἐγώ, direct object of μωμήσηται) 123.
μωμήσηται (3d.per.sing.1st.aor.mid.subj.of μωμάομαι, negative purpose) 4313.

ἐν (preposition with the locative of sphere, nouns) 80.
τῇ (loc.sing.fem.of the article in agreement with ἁδρότητι) 9.

#4343 ἁδρότητι (loc.sing.fem.of ἁδρότης, sphere, nouns).

King James Version

abundance - 2 Cor.8:20.

Revised Standard Version

liberal gift - 2 Cor.8:20.

Meaning: Cf. ἁδρός - "thick, stout, full grown, strong, abundant. Hence, abundance. With reference to the gift of money for the poor saints in Judea - 2 Cor.8:20.

ταύτῃ (loc.sing.fem.of οὗτος, in agreement with διακονουμένῃ) 93.
τῇ (loc.sing.fem.of the article in agreement with διακονουμένῃ) 9.
διακονουμένῃ (pres.pass.part.loc.sing.fem.of διακονέω, adjectival, emphatic attributive position, in agreement with ἁδρότητι) 367.
ὑφ' (preposition with the ablative of agent) 117.
ἡμῶν (abl.pl.masc.of ἐγώ, agent) 123.

Translation - "Taking care to avoid this - that no man should accuse us of misappropriating this large sum of money which we have collected."

Comment: στελλόμενοι, the circumstantial participle continues the sentence in verse 13, following the parenthesis of verse 19. Paul sent Titus and his companions to Corinth to promote the collection for the poor saints in Judea, but not without taking steps to forestall (#4342) any possible attack upon their honesty in handling the money. We need to supply ἵνα before μή for the negative clause of purpose which is epexegetical, in explanation of τοῦτο. "In order that no man sustain a just accusation against us (#4313) in the sphere of activity of the collection of the money (locative of sphere in τῇ ἁδρότητι ταύτῃ τῇ διακονουμένῃ) which is being administered by us."

This practice of providing for evidence of honesty in matters of handling the Lord's money is often passed over in the churches because no one wishes to imply that the church officials are dishonest. The treasurer himself should ask the church to audit his books occasionally. Such an audit should be conducted without prejudice to the outgoing treasurer, when he leaves the office. This implies nothing about his honesty or the lack of it. It only obeys the principle of 2 Cor.8:20,21. *Cf.* Romans 12:17b.

Verse 21 - "Providing for honest things, not only in the sight of the Lord, but also in the sight of men."

προνοοῦμεν γὰρ καλὰ οὐ μόνον ἐνώπιον κυρίου ἀλλὰ καὶ ἐνώπιον ἀνθρώπων.

"for we aim at what is honorable not only in the Lord's sight but also in the sight of men." . . . RSV

προνοοῦμεν (1st.per.pl.pres.act.ind.of προνοέω, aoristic) 4029.
γὰρ (causal conjunction) 104.
καλὰ (acc.pl.neut.of καλός, direct object of προνοοῦμεν) 296.
οὐ (negative conjunction with the indicative) 130.
μόνον (acc.sing.neut.of μόνος, adverbial) 339.
ἐνώπιον (preposition with the genitive of place description) 1798.
κυρίου (gen.sing.masc.of κύριος, place description) 97.
ἀλλὰ (alternative conjunction) 342.
καὶ (adjunctive conjunction joining prepositional phrases) 14.
ἐνώπιον (preposition with the genitive of place description) 1798.
ἀνθρώπων (gen.pl.masc.of ἄνθρωπος, place description) 341.

Translation - "Because we plan ahead for honesty, not only before the Lord but also before men."

Comment: γὰρ is causal as Paul explains his precaution of verse 20. He would avoid criticism because (γὰρ) he was planning ahead (#4029). καλὰ, the object of προοῦμεν here means "honest dealing" in the collection, transmission and delivery of the money. Paul wanted both the Lord and all men involved to have all possible evidence that his motives were pure.

He now mentions another brother who has been sent along with Titus and his party in

Verse 22 - "And we have sent with them our brother, whom we have oftentimes proved diligent in many things, but now much more diligent, upon the great confidence which I have in you."

συνεπέμφαμεν δὲ αὐτοῖς τὸν ἀδελφὸν ἡμῶν ὃν ἐδοκιμάσαμεν ἐν πολλοῖς πολλάκις σπουδαῖον ὄντα, νυνὶ δὲ πολὺ σπουδαιότερον πεποιθήσει πολλῇ τῇ εἰς ὑμᾶς.

"And with them we are sending our brother whom we have often tested and found earnest in many matters, but who is now more earnest than ever because of his great confidence in you." . . . RSV

συνεπέμφαμεν (1st.per.pl.aor.act.ind.of συμπέμπω, epistolary) 4341.
δὲ (continuative conjunction) 11.
αὐτοῖς (instru.pl.masc.of αὐτός, association) 16.
τὸν (acc.sing.masc.of the article in agreement with ἀδελφὸν) 9.
ἀδελφὸν (acc.sing.masc.of ἀδελφός, direct object of συνεπέμφαμεν) 15.
ἡμῶν (gen.pl.masc.of ἐγώ, relationship) 123.
ὃν (acc.sing.masc.of ὅς, relative pronoun, direct object of ἐδοκιμάσαμεν) 65.
ἐδοκιμάσαμεν (1st.per.pl.aor.act.ind.of δοκιμάζω, culminative) 2493.
ἐν (preposition with the locative of sphere, nouns) 80.
πολλοῖς (loc.pl.neut.of πολύς, sphere, nouns) 228.
πολλάκις (adverbial) 1230.

σπουδαῖον (acc.sing.neut.of σπουδαῖος, predicate adjective) 4340.
ὄντα (pres.part.acc.sing.masc.of εἰμί, indirect discourse) 86.
νυνὶ (temporal adverb) 1497.
δὲ (continuative conjunction) 11.
πολὺ (acc.sing.neut.of πολύς, adverbial) 228.
σπουδαιότερον (acc.sing.neut.comp.of σπουδαῖος, predicate adjective) 4340.
πεποιθήσει (instru.sing.fem.of πεποίθησις, cause) 4269.
πολλῇ (instru.sing.fem.of πολύς, in agreement with πεποιθήσει) 228.
τῇ (instru.sing.fem.of the article in agreement with πεποιθήσει) 9.
εἰς (preposition with the accusative, predicate usage) 140.
ὑμᾶς (acc.pl.masc.of σύ, predicate usage) 104.

Translation - *"And we have sent with them our brother, whom we have often proved diligent with reference to many things; and now he is much more diligent because of his great confidence in you."*

Comment: What Paul had said of Titus (vss.16,17) he now says of the other brother who accompanied Titus. Both men were eager to visit Corinth because they had faith that the Corinthians would respond generously to the need. Luke or Tychicus or Apollos or whoever it was had been found to be diligent on many occasions (πολλάκις) with respect to many matters (ἐν πολλοῖς). Note the participle ὄντα in indirect discourse after ἐδοκιμάσαμεν. In Romans 1:28 it is followed by the infinitive. πολὺ in the accusative, used adverbially.

Verse 23 - *"Whether any do enquire of Titus, he is my partner and fellowhelper concerning you: or our brother be enquired of, they are the messengers of the churches, and the glory of Christ."*

εἴτε ὑπὲρ Τίτου, κοινωνὸς ἐμὸς καὶ εἰς ὑμᾶς συνεργός. εἴτε ἀδελφοὶ ἡμῶν, ἀπόστολοι ἐκκλησιῶν, δόξα Χριστοῦ.

"As for Titus, he is my partner and fellow worker in your service; and as for our brethren, they are the messengers of the churches, the glory of Christ." ... *RSV*

εἴτε (disjunctive) 4016.
ὑπὲρ (preposition with the genitive of reference) 545.
Τίτου (gen.sing.masc.of Τίτος, reference) 4278.
κοινωνὸς (nom.sing.masc.of κοινωνός, predicate nominative) 1470.
ἐμὸς (nom.sing.masc.of ἐμός, in agreement with κοινωνὸς) 1267.
καὶ (adjunctive conjunction joining nouns) 14.
εἰς (preposition with the accusative, predicate usage) 140.
ὑμᾶς (acc.pl.masc.of σύ, predicate usage) 104.
συνεργός (nom.sing.masc.of συνεργός, predicate nominative) 4066.
εἴτε (disjunctive) 4016.
ἀδελφοὶ (nom.pl.masc.of ἀδελφός, predicate nominative) 15.
ἡμῶν (gen.pl.masc.of ἐγώ, relationship) 123.
ἀπόστολοι (nom.pl.masc.of ἀπόστολος, predicate nominative) 844.
ἐκκλησιῶν (gen.pl.fem.of ἐκκλησία, relationship) 1204.

δόξα (nom.sing.fem.of δόξα, predicate nominative) 361.
Χριστοῦ (gen.sing.masc.of Χριστός, description) 4.

Translation - *"If there is a question about Titus, he is my partner and fellow worker for you; as for our brethren, they are messengers of churches and a credit to Christ."*

Comment: There are no copulas. The predicate nominatives do not require them. Paul was anxious that the Corinthians understand that everyone in the visiting party was a duly authorized and qualified person. The phrase ἀπόστολοι ἐκκλησιῶν would seem to indicate that these men had been officially commissioned by their respective churches to travel with Paul and carry on the work of the Lord. There were no "independent" preachers, who went forth on their own initiative, carried on their work without supervision and were responsible for their conduct to no one in the history of the early churches.

Verse 24 - *"Wherefore shew ye to them, and before the churches, the proof of your love, and of our boasting on your behalf."*

τὴν οὖν ἔνδειξιν τῆς ἀγάπης ὑμῶν καὶ ἡμῶν καυχήσεως ὑπὲρ ὑμῶν εἰς αὐτοὺς ἐνδεικνύμενοι εἰς πρόσωπον τῶν ἐκκλησιῶν.

"So give proof, before the churches, of your love and of our boasting about you to these men." . . . *RSV*

τὴν (acc.sing.fem.of the article in agreement with ἔνδειξιν) 9.
οὖν (inferential conjunction) 68.
ἔνδειξιν (acc.sing.fem.of ἔνδειξις, direct object of ἐνδεικνύμενοι) 3874.
τῆς (gen.sing.fem.of the article in agreement with ἀγάπης) 9.
ἀγάπης (gen.sing.fem.of ἀγάπη, description) 1490.
ὑμῶν (gen.pl.masc.of σύ, possession) 104.
καὶ (adjunctive conjunction joining nouns) 14.
ἡμῶν (gen.pl.masc.of ἐγώ, possession) 123.
καυχήσεως (gen.sing.fem.of καύχησις, description) 3877.
ὑπὲρ (gen.pl.masc.of σύ, adverbial genitive, reference) 104.
ὑμῶν (gen.pl.masc.of σύ, adverbial genitive, reference) 104.
εἰς (preposition with the accusative of extent, metaphorical) 140.
αὐτοὺς (acc.pl.masc.of αὐτός, extent) 16.
ἐνδεικνύμενοι (pres.mid.part.nom.pl.masc.of ἐνδείκνυμαι, adjectival, predicate position, restrictive, in agreement with ἀπόστολοι) 3842.
εἰς (preposition with the accusative of extent, metaphorical) 140.
πρόσωπον (acc.sing.neut.of πρόσωπον, metaphorical extent) 588.
τῶν (gen.pl.fem.of the article in agreement with ἐκκλησιῶν) 9.
ἐκκλησιῶν (gen.pl.fem.of ἐκκλησία, place description) 1204.

Translation - *"who then are demonstrating the evidence of your love and the grounds for our boasting to them about you to the churches."*

Comment: Sinaiticus and C read ἐνδείξασθε, the imperative rather than the participle ἐνδεικνύμενοι - a reading that supports the KJV, RSV, Goodspeed, Williams *et al.* Though it is true that the participle is sometimes used as an imperative (*Cf.* 1 Pet.3:1; Mk.5:23; Rom.12:9; 1 Pet.2:18), the context here permits ἐνδεικνύμενοι as a restrictive adjective modifying ἀπόστολοι, verse 23. Whether the sentence of verse 23 ends with δόξα Χριστοῦ is a matter of editing. "Only a few examples of (the imperatival participle) however, occur in the New Testament. Some have regarded it as a Hebraism, but its use in the papyri contradicts this view." (Moulton, *Prolegomena to the Grammar of New Testament Greek*, 180,222, as cited in Mantey, *Manual*, 229). "Adjectives are also sometimes used in what appears to be an imperative construction, but doubtless in these cases the imperative of the verb *to be* is understood. In this construction it is important that the student bear in mind that the participle 'is not technically either indicative, subjunctive, optative of imperative (non-modal) like the infinitive, though it was sometimes drawn out into the modal sphere.' " (Robertson, *Grammar*, 946, as cited in *Ibid.)*

The different uses of the participle are sometimes difficult to distinguish, as, for instance, the attributive and substantive uses, or those of time, cause and manner. The distinctions may at first seem to the student to be arbitrary in some instances, but a close examination will reveal that the differences, even when remote, are real." (*Ibid.*).

Whether Paul is here admonishing the Corinthians to repond to the love offering for the poor Judean Christians in order to prove something or saying that Titus and his friends would present the proof of their faithfulness to the churches, the result is the same.

The Offering for the Saints

(2 Corinthians 9:1-15)

2 Corinthians 9:1 - "For as touching the ministering to the saints, it is superfluous for me to write to you."

Περὶ μὲν γὰρ τῆς διακονίας τῆς εἰς τοὺς ἁγίους περισσόν μοί ἐστιν τὸ γράφειν ὑμῖν,

"Now it is superfluous for me to write to you about the offering for the saints,"
                                                                    . . . RSV

Περὶ (preposition with the adverbial genitive of reference with nouns) 173.

μὲν (particle of affirmation) 300.

γὰρ (inferential conjunction) 105.

τῆς (gen.sing.fem.of the article in agreement with διακονίας) 9.

διακονίας (gen.sing.fem.of διακονία, adverbial genitive of reference with nouns) 2442.

τῇ (gen.sing.fem.of the article in agreement with διακονίας) 9.

εἰς (preposition with the accusative, metaphorical extent) 140.

τοὺς (acc.pl.masc.of the article in agreement with ἁγίους) 9.

ἁγίους (acc.pl.masc.of ἅγιος, metaphorical extent) 84.
περισσόν (nom.sing.neut.of περισσός, predicate adjective) 525.
μοί (dat.sing.masc.of ἐγώ, personal interest) 123.
ἐστιν (3d.per.sing.pres.ind.of εἰμί, aoristic) 86.
τὸ (nom.sing.neut.of the article in agreement with γράφειν) 9.
γράφειν (pres.act.inf.of γράφω, noun use, subject of ἐστιν) 156.
ὑμῖν (dat.pl.masc.of σύ, indirect object of γράφειν) 104.

Translation - "Therefore in so far as I am concerned it is not necessary for me to write to you about the offering for the saints."

Comment: μὲν intensifies the point. Paul has been telling them of his confidence in their generosity. Why say any more about it? Note the adverbial genitive of reference with the noun. Note the repetition of τῆς with the prepositional phrase εἰς τοὺς ἁγίους, used like an adjective in the emphatic attributive position - "the offering, the for the saints offering." τὸ γράφειν is the subject of ἐστιν.

Having said that no more need be said Paul continues to talk about it in

Verse 2 - "For I know the forwardness of your mind, for which I boast of you to them of Macedonia, that Achaia was ready a year ago; and your zeal hath provoked very many."

οἶδα γὰρ τὴν προθυμίαν ὑμῶν ἣν ὑπὲρ ὑμῶν καυχῶμαι Μακεδόσιν ὅτι Ἀχαΐα παρεσκεύασται ἀπὸ πέρυσι, καὶ τὸ ὑμῶν ζῆλος ἠρέθισεν τοὺς πλείονας.

"for I know your readiness, of which I boast about you to the people of Macedonia, saying that Achaia has been ready since last year; and your zeal has stirred up most of them.". . . RSV

οἶδα (1st.per.sing.perf.act.ind.of ὁράω, intensive) 144b.
γὰρ (causal conjunction) 105.
τὴν (acc.sing.fem.of the article in agreement with προθυμίαν) 9.
προθυμίαν (acc.sing.fem.of προθυμία, direct object of οἶδα) 3395.
ὑμῶν (gen.pl.masc.of σύ, possession) 104.
ἣν (acc.sing.fem.of ὅς, relative pronoun, direct object of καυχῶμαι) 65.
ὑπὲρ (preposition with the adverbial genitive of reference, with pronouns) 545.
ὑμῶν (gen.pl.masc.of σύ, reference) 104.
καυχῶμαι (1st.per.sing.pres.act.ind.of καυχάομαι, present iterative retroactive) 3847.
Μακεδόσιν (dat.pl.masc.of Μακεδών, indirect object of καυχῶμαι) 3359.
ὅτι (conjunction introducing an object clause in indirect discourse) 211.
Ἀχαΐα (nom.sing.fem.of Ἀχαΐα, subject of παρεσκεύασται) 3443.
παρεσκεύασται (3d.per.sing.perf.pass.ind.of παρασκευάζω, iterative) 3217.
ἀπὸ (preposition with the ablative, time separation) 70.
πέρυσι (temporal adverb) 4336.
καὶ (continuative conjunction) 14.
τὸ (nom.sing.neut.of the article in agreement with ζῆλος) 9.

ὑμῶν (gen.pl.masc.of σύ, possession) 104.

ζῆλος (nom.sing.neut.of ζῆλος, subject of ἠρέθισεν) 1985.

#4344 ἠρέθισεν (3d.per.sing.1st.aor.act.ind.of ἐρεθίζω, constative).

King James Version

provoke - 2 Cor.9:2; Col.3:21.

Revised Standard Version

stir up - 2 Cor.9:2.
provoke - Col.3:21.

Meaning: Cf. ἐρέθω - "to excite." Hence, to stir up; excite; stimulate to action. With reference to the reaction of the Macedonians to Corinthian generosity - 2 Cor.9:2. Followed by a negative purpose clause in Col.3:21.

τοὺς (acc.pl.masc.of the article in agreement with πλείονας) 9.
πλείονας (acc.pl.masc.of πλείων, direct object of ἠρέθισεν) 474.

Translation - "Because I have known of your eagerness of which I boasted about you to the Macedonians that Achaia has been ready for the past year; and your zeal provoked the most of them to emulation."

Comment: Paul's previous awareness of the fact that the Corinthians were willing to give provided him with a boast to the Macedonians, to whom he said that the Greeks had been ready to give a year ago. As a result, his report of Grecian zeal had provided a stimulus for most of the Maceodnians. Note the article with πλείονας.

Paul had been playing a psychological game, playing off one group against another. His boast about the Corinthians could backfire if they did not perform as he expected.

Verse 3 - "Yet have I sent the brethren, lest our boasting of you should be in vain in this behalf; that, as I said, ye may be ready."

ἔπεμφα δὲ τοὺς ἀδελφούς, ἵνα μὴ τὸ καύχημα ἡμῶν τὸ ὑπὲρ ὑμῶν κενωθῇ ἐν τῷ μέρει τούτῳ, ἵνα καθὼς ἔλεγον παρεσκευασμένοι ἦτε,

"But I am sending the brethren so that our boasting about you may not prove vain in this case, so that you may be ready, as I said you would be;" . . . RSV

ἔπεμφα (1st.per.sing.aor.act.ind.of πέμπω, epistolary) 169.
δὲ (adversative conjunction) 11.
τοὺς (acc.pl.masc.of the article in agreement with ἀδελφούς) 9.
ἀδελφούς (acc.pl.masc.of ἀδελφός, direct object of ἔπεμφα) 15.
ἵνα (conjunction with the subjunctive in a negative purpose clause) 114.
μὴ (negative conjunction with the subjunctive) 87.
τὸ (nom.sing.neut.of the article in agreement with καυχήμα) 9.

καύχημα (nom.sing.neut.of καύχημα, subject of κενωθῇ) 3881.

ἡμῶν (gen.pl.masc.of ἐγώ, possession) 123.

τὸ (nom.sing.neut.of the article in agreement with καύχημα) 9.

ὑπὲρ (preposition with the adverbial genitive, reference, with pronouns) 545.

ὑμῶν (gen.pl.masc.of σύ, reference) 104.

κενωθῇ (3d.per.sing.1st.aor.pass.subj.of κενόω, negative purpose) 3888.

ἐν (preposition with the locative of sphere with nouns) 80.

τῷ (loc.sing.neut.of the article in agreement with μέρει) 9.

μέρει (loc.sing.neut.of μέρος, sphere, with nouns) 240.

τούτῳ (loc.sing.neut.of οὗτος, in agreement with μέρει) 93.

ἵνα (conjunction with the subjunctive in a purpose clause) 114.

καθὼς (comparative adverb) 1348.

ἔλεγον (1st.per.sing.imp.act.ind.of λέγω, progressive duration) 66.

παρεσκευασμένοι (perf.mid.part.nom.pl.masc.of παρασκευάζω, periphrastic pluperfect) 3217.

ἦτε (2d.per.pl.imp.subj.of εἰμί, periphrastic pluperfect, purpose) 86.

Translation - "But I have sent the brethren, lest our boasting about you in this matter be in vain, so that just as I had been saying, you may have prepared yourselves."

Comment: Paul is moving to assure a result which he had predicted. He had told the Macedonians that the Corinthians were eager to give and had been ready to do so for the past year. If, as a result of Corinthian carelessness or unconcern, they were not, then Paul's boast would be proved idle. This he moves to prevent by sending Timothy and his party to Corinth. *Cf.* 2 Cor.3:10 and Col.2:16 for μέρος (#240) in this same sense. Paul had said much about the Corinthians of which this was only a part. He labors the point further in

Verse 4 - "Lest haply if they of Macedonia come with me, and find you unprepared, we (that we say not, ye) should be ashamed in this same confident boasting."

μή πως ἐὰν ἔλθωσιν σὺν ἐμοὶ Μακεδόνες καὶ εὕρωσιν ὑμᾶς ἀπαρασκευάστους καταισχυνθῶμεν ἡμεῖς, ἵνα μὴ λέγω ὑμεῖς, ἐν τῇ ὑποστάσει ταύτῃ.

"lest if some Macedonians come with me and find that you are not ready, we be humiliated — to say nothing of you — for being so confident." . . . RSV

μή (negative conjunction with the subjunctive) 87.

πως (enclitic particle) 3700.

ἐὰν (conditional particle in a third-class condition) 363.

ἔλθωσιν (3d.per.pl.aor.subj.of ἔρχομαι, third-class condition) 146.

σὺν (preposition with the instrumental, association) 1542.

ἐμοὶ (instru.sing.masc.of ἐμός, association) 1267.

Μακεδόνες (nom.pl.masc.of Μακεδών, subject of ἔλθωσιν and εὕρωσιν) 3359.

καὶ (adjunctive conjunction joining verbs) 14.

εὕρωσιν (3d.per.pl.aor.act.subj.of εὑρίσκω, third-class condition) 79.
ὑμᾶς (acc.pl.masc.of σύ, direct object of εὕρωσιν) 104.

#4345 ἀπαρασκευάστους (acc.pl.masc.of ἀπαρασκεύαστος, predicate adjective).

King James Version

unprepared - 2 Cor.9:4.

Revised Standard Version

not ready - 2 Cor.9:4.

Meaning: α privative plus παρά (#154) plus σκευαστός - "prepared." *Cf.* παρασκευάζω (#3217). Hence, unprepared. To give a gift for poor relief - 2 Cor.9:4.

καταισχυνθῶμεν (1st.per.pl.aor.pass.subj.of καταισχύνω, negative purpose) 2505.
ἡμεῖς (nom.pl.masc.of ἐγώ, subject of καταισχυνθῶμεν) 123.
ἵνα (conjunction in a paraleipsis) 114.
μὴ (negative conjunction with the subjunctive understood) 87.
λέγω (1st.per.sing.pres.act.ind.of λέγω, aoristic) 66.
ὑμεῖς (nom.pl.masc.of σύ, subject of verb understood) 104.
τῇ (dat.sing.fem.of the article in agreement with ὑποστάσει) 9.

#4346 ὑποστάσει (dat.sing.fem.of ὑπόστασις, reference).

King James Version

confidence - 2 Cor.11:17; Heb.3:14.
person - Heb.1:3.
substance - Heb.11:1.
confident - 2 Cor.9:4.

Revised Standard Version

confident - 2 Cor.9:4.
boastful confidence - 2 Cor.11:17.
nature - Heb.1:3.
confidence - Heb.3:14.
assurance - Heb.11:1.

Meaning: A combination of ὑπό (#117) and ἵστημι (#180). *Cf.* ὑφίστημι - "to give substance to," "support," "guarantee." Hence, that which has real substance; substantial quality; real objective existence; that which results in confidence and certitude. Moulton and Milligan cite a number of contexts and conclude, "These varied uses are at first sight somewhat perplexing, but in all cases, there is the same central idea of something that *underlies* visible conditions and guarantees a future possession. And as this is the essential meaning in Heb.11:1, we venture to suggest the translation, "Faith is the *title deed* of things hoped for." In Heb.1:3, on the other hand, the notion of *underlying* is applied in a different way. The history of the theological term 'substance' is discussed by T.B.Strong in JFB, ii (1901), p.224*ff.* and in iii (1902), p.22*ff."* (Moulton & Milligan, 660). In 2 Cor.9:4; 11:17 the "substance" underlying the word is Paul's own confident boast that the Corinthians would give their money (2 Cor.9:4) and that he was God's apostle (2 Cor.11:17). In Heb.3:14 it refers to Christian faith.

ταύτῃ (dat.sing.fem.of οὗτος, in agreement with ὑποστάσει) 93.

Translation - "Lest perhaps if the Macedonians came with me and found you unprepared, we, not to mention you, would be embarrassed with reference to this guarantee."

Comment: The postive purpose clause in verse 3 - ἵνα καθὼς ἔλεγον παρεσκευασμένοι ἦτε is followed by the negative with μή πως . . . καταισχυνθῶμεν - "lest we be embarrassed." If the Corinthians persist in their year-long willingness to give there is no problem. If not, should the Macedonians, who had been led to believe that the missionary offering in Corinth would be generous, accompany Paul to Corinth and find them unprepared to contribute, Paul would be humiliated, not to mention the Corinthians themselves. ἵνα μὴ λέγω ὑμεῖς is paraleipsis. He could have said μὴ ποτε καταισχυνθῆτε - "lest you be embarrassed." In reference to what? - ἐν τῇ ὑποστάσει ταύτῃ - "in reference to this confident guarantee," which Paul had given the Macedonians. It was to prevent such an embarrassing development that Paul had sent Titus and his friends to Corinth to prepare them for the offering.

It can scarce be denied that Paul is employing fleshly psychology on the Corinthians. Instead of appealing to their love for the Lord and for the starving saints in Judea, he is appealing to a baser motive - their fear of being found unwilling to do what any Christian should be willing to do. If Paul had been as certain that the zeal of the Corinthians to help in this project, which was cordial a year before, was still cordial, he would not have found it necessary to send Titus to check on it.

Verse 5 - "Therefore I thought it necessary to exhort the brethren, that they would go before unto you, and make up beforehand, your bounty, whereof we had notice before, that the same might be ready, as a matter of bounty, and not as of covetousness."

ἀναγκαῖον οὖν ἡγησάμην παρακαλέσαι τοὺς ἀδελφοὺς ἵνα προέλθωσιν εἰς ὑμᾶς καὶ προκαταρτίσωσιν τὴν προεπηγγελμένην εὐλογίαν ὑμῶν, ταύτην ἑτοίμην εἶναι οὕτως ὡς εὐλογίαν καὶ μὴ ὡς πλεονεξίαν.

"So I thought it necessary to urge the brethren to go on to you before me, and arrange in advance for this gift you have promised, so that it may be ready not as an exaction but as a willing gift." . . . RSV

ἀναγκαῖον (acc.sing.neut.of ἀναγκαῖος, predicate adjective) 3225.
οὖν (inferential conjunction) 68.
ἡγησάμην (1st.per.pl.aor.mid.ind.of ἡγέομαι, constative) 162.
παρακαλέσαι (aor.act.inf.of παρακαλέω, complementary) 230.
τοὺς (acc.pl.masc.of the article in agreement with ἀδελφοὺς) 9.
ἀδελφοὺς (acc.pl.masc.of ἀδελφός, direct object of παρακαλέσαι) 15.
ἵνα (conjunction with the subjunctive in a double purpose clause) 114.
προέλθωσιν (3d.per.pl.aor.subj.of προέρχομαι, purpose) 1587.
εἰς (preposition with the accusative of extent) 140.
ὑμᾶς (acc.pl.masc.of σύ, extent) 104.
καὶ (adjunctive conjunction joining verbs) 14.

#4347 προκαταρτίσωσιν (3d.per.pl.aor.act.subj.of προκαταρτίζω, purpose).

King James Version

make up beforehand - 2 Cor.9:5.

Revised Standard Version

arrange in advance - 2 Cor.9:5.

Meaning: A combination of πρό (#442) and καταρτίζω (#401); hence, to attend to, perfect, make complete arrangements in advance. With reference to the Corinthian missionary offering - 2 Cor.9:5.

τὴν (acc.sing.fem.of the article in agreement with εὐλογίαν) 9.
προεπηγγελμένην (perf.pass.part.acc.sing.fem.of προεπαγγέλλω, adjectival, ascriptive, in agreement with εὐλογίαν) 3783.
εὐλογίαν (acc.sing.fem.of εὐλογία, direct object of προκαταρτίσωσιν) 4060.
ὑμῶν (gen.pl.masc.of σύ, possession) 104.
ταύτην (acc.sing.fem.of οὗτος, general reference) 93.
ἑτοίμην (acc.sing.fem.of ἕτοιμος, predicate adjective) 1399.
εἶναι (pres.inf.of εἰμί, purpose) 86.
οὕτως (comparative adverb) 74.
ὡς (comparative particle) 128.
εὐλογίαν (acc.sing.fem.of εὐλογία, predicate accusative) 4060.
καὶ (adjunctive conjunction joining comparative clauses) 14.
μὴ (negative conjunction with the subjunctive understood) 87.
ὡς (comparative particle) 128.
πλεονεξίαν (acc.sing.fem.of πλεονεξία, predicate accusative) 2302.

Translation - "Therefore we considered it necessary to request the brethren to visit you before I come and collect ahead of time your previously pledged gift so that this gift might be made ready as a willing gift and not as something extorted from you."

Comment: In view of Paul's fear that he and the Corinthians might be embarrassed (verse 4) he felt it necessary to send Titus and his party to Corinth before he came. When they arrived they were to collect the money pledged the year before by the Corinthians. The purpose clause therefore has two subjunctives - προέλθωσιν and προκαταρτίσωσιν - "They should go ahead and make the collection before . . . ." The infinitive εἶναι is also purpose. He explains why he had chosen to follow this precautionary course - so that the Corinthian gift of money, already collected before Paul arrived, might appear to be a gift out of their love rather than an assessment extorted by Paul upon his arrival.

Some may read into this the notion that Paul was manipulating the situation in an attempt to deceive the Macedonians. If he really trusted the Corinthians as much as he said he did, the plans which he has just outlined would not be necessary.

He finishes the chapter with material which is of loftier spiritual content than that which has gone before.

Verse 6 - "But this I say, He which soweth sparingly shall reap also sparingly; and he which soweth bountifully shall reap also bountifully."

Τοῦτο δέ, ὁ σπείρων φειδομένως φειδομένως καὶ θερίσει, καὶ ὁ σπείρων ἐπ' εὐλογίαις ἐπ' εὐλογίαις καὶ θερίσει.

"This point is this: he who sows sparingly will also reap sparingly, and he who sows bountifully will also reap bountifully." . . . RSV

Τοῦτο (nom.sing.neut.of οὗτος, nominative absolute) 93.
δέ (explanatory conjunction) 11.
ὁ (nom.sing.masc.of the article in agreement with σπείρων) 9.
σπείρων (pres.act.part.nom.sing.masc.of σπείρω, substantival, subject of θερίσει) 616.

#4348 φειδομένως (adverbial).

King James Version

sparingly - 2 Cor.9:6,6.

Revised Standard Version

sparingly - 2 Cor.9:6,6.

Meaning: Cf. φείομαι (#3533). *Hence, an adverb -* sparingly - 2 Cor.9:6,6.

φειδομένως (adverbial) 4348.
καὶ (emphatic conjunction) 14.
θερίσει (3d.per.sing.fut.act.ind.of θερίζω, predictive) 617.
καὶ (adversative conjunction) 14.
ὁ (nom.sing.masc.of the article in agreement with σπείρων) 9.
σπείρων (pres.act.part.nom.sing.masc.of σπείρω, substantival, subject of θερίσει) 616.
ἐπ' (preposition with the locative of accompanying circumstance) 47.

εὐλογίαις (loc.pl.fem.of εὐλογία, accompanying circumstance) 4060.
ἐπ' (preposition with the locative of accompanying circumstance) 47.
εὐλογίαις (loc.pl.fem.of εὐλογία, accompanying circumstance) 4060.
καὶ (emphatic conjunction) 14.
θερίσει (3d.per.sing.fut.act.ind.of θερίζω, predictive) 617.

Translation - "Now remember this! the one who sows sparingly shall in fact reap sparingly, but the one who sows with a song of praise will in fact reap with a song of praise."

Comment: Ellipsis with τοῦτο δέ. Paul wishes to lay down a principle by which the Corinthians would be guided. ἐπ' εὐλογίαις is a locative of accompanying circumstance or an instrumental of manner. The gift which is accompanied by a joyous expression of praise (not with a groan of resignation) will be returned the same way.

In the remainder of the chapter Paul plumbs the depths of the scripture teaching about stewardship. The faithful steward is not the one who gives a great deal of money but the one who recognizes that all that he has, in terms of talent, time, strength and opportunity belongs to the Lord and that the Lord will hold him responsible, not only for how much money he gives but also how much of himself he gives. The Christian who realizes this is as joyous when he gives only a little money as when he gives much, so long as what he gives is all that he has to give. He is happy because he knows that God will not allow His faithful steward to suffer for his basic needs. The faithful steward is not necessarily concerned with his *wants* which may rest upon a higher financial status than his *needs*. God has not promised to give His children everything which they may want, but He has promised to give us all that we need (Phil.4:19). Thus the faithful steward gives joyously and with an open testimony of praise to God for the opportunity.

Verse 7 - "Every man according as he purposeth in his heart, so let him give; not grudgingly, or of necessity: for God loveth a cheerful giver."

ἕκαστος καθὼς προῄρηται τῇ καρδίᾳ, μὴ ἐκ λύπης ἢ ἐξ ἀνάγκης, ἱλαρὸν γὰρ δότην ἀγαπᾷ ὁ θεός.

"Each one must do as he has made up his mind, not reluctantly or under compulsion, for God lives a cheerful giver." . . . RSV

ἕκαστος (nom.sing.masc.of ἕκαστος, subject of προῄρηται) 1217.
καθὼς (comparative adverb) 1348.

#4349 προῄρται (3d.per.sing.perf.mid.ind.of προαιρέομαι, intensive).

King James Version

purpose - 2 Cor.9:7.

Revised Standard Version

make up his mind - 2 Cor.9:7.

Meaning: A combination of πρό (#442) and αἱρέω - "to bring." In the middle voice, to bring forward from one's self. To purpose; to decide for one's self. Followed by τῇ καρδίᾳ in 2 Cor.9:7. Thus to make up one's mind by consulting his heart.

τῇ (instrumental sing.fem.of the article in agreement with καρδίᾳ) 9.
καρδίᾳ (instru.sing.fem.of καρδία, means) 432.
μή (negative conjunction with a prohibition understood) 87.
ἐκ (preposition with the ablative of source) 19.
λύπης (abl.sing.fem.of λύπη, source) 2788.
ἤ (disjunctive) 465.
ἐκ (preposition with the ablative of source) 19.
ἀνάγκης (abl.sing.fem.of ἀνάγκη, source) 1254.

#4350 ἱλαρὸν (acc.sing.masc.of ἱλαρός, in agreement with δότην).

King James Version

cheerful - 2 Cor.9:7.

Revised Standard Version

cheerful - 2 Cor.9:7.

Meaning: Cf. ἱλαρότης (#4020), ἵλαος - "propitious." Cheerful, joyous, prompt. Hilarious. Opposed to λύπη (#2788) and ἀνάγκη (#1254). 2 Cor.9:7.

γάρ (causal conjunction) 105.

#4351 δότην (acc.sing.masc.of δότης, direct object of ἀγαπᾷ).

King James Version

giver - 2 Cor.9:7.

Revised Standard Version

giver - 2 Cor.9:7.

Meaning: Cf. δίδωμι (#362). The more usual substantive is δοτήρ - a giver. 2 Cor.9:7.

ἀγαπᾷ (3d.per.sing.pres.act.ind.of ἀγαπάω, static) 540.
ὁ (nom.sing.masc.of the article in agreement with θεός) 9.
θεός (nom.sing.masc.of θεός, subject of ἀγαπᾷ) 124.

Translation - "*Let everyone give as he has been guided by his heart, not in sorrow, nor out of coercion, because God loves a hilarious giver.*"

Comment: We supply δότω, the aorist imperative. προῄρται (perfect middle). The heart must decide. The intellect may dictate a gift that the emotion would reject as too great a sacrifice. In such a case, let the heart rule. The gift out of sadness or compulsion is not good. God does not need the money. We cannot enrich Him with our paltry sums, but we can glorify Him with our willingness to give all that we have to Him on the proposition that if we do He will not allow us to suffer want. It takes great faith in God's promise for us to give hilariously. It is important that we honor God with our attitude toward giving, since God is the source of all that is good. Anyone who understands the principle of verse 8 will be a hilarious giver.

Verse 8 - "And God is able to make all grace abound toward you; that ye, always having all sufficiency in all things, may abound to every good work."

δυνατεῖ δὲ ὁ θεὸς πᾶσαν χάριν περισσεῦσαι εἰς ὑμᾶς, ἵνα ἐν παντὶ πάντοτε πᾶσαν αὐτάρκειαν ἔχοντες περισσεύητε εἰς πᾶν ἔργον ἀγαθόν.

"And God is able to provide you with every blessing in abundance, so that you may always have enough of everything and may provide in abundance for every good work." . . . RSV

δυνατεῖ (3d.per.sing.pres.ind.of δυνατέω, static) 4041.
δὲ (continuative conjunction) 11.
ὁ (nom.sing.masc.of the article in agreement with θεὸς) 9.
θεὸς (nom.sing.masc.of θεός, subject of δυνατεῖ) 124.
πᾶσαν (acc.sing.fem.of πᾶς, in agreement with χάριν) 67.
χάριν (acc.sing.fem.of χάρις, direct object of περισσεῦσαι) 1700
περισσεῦσαι (aor.act.inf.of περισσεύω, complementary) 473.
εἰς (preposition with the accusative, extent) 140.
ὑμᾶς (acc.pl.masc.of σύ, extent) 104.
ἵνα (conjunction with the subjunctive in a sub-final clause) 114.
ἐν (preposition with the locative of sphere with substantives) 80.
παντὶ (loc.sing.neut.of πᾶς, sphere, with a substantive) 67.
πάντοτε (adverbial) 1567.
πᾶσαν (acc.sing.fem.of πᾶς, in agreement with αὐτάρκειαν) 67.

#4352 αὐτάρκειαν (acc.sing.fem.of αὐτάρκεια, direct object of ἔχοντες).

King James Version

contentment - 1 Tim.6:6.
sufficiency - 2 Cor.9:8.

Revised Standard Version

enough - 2 Cor.9:8.
contentment - 1 Tim.6:6.

Meaning: Cf. αὐτάρκης (#4592). A condition of total self sufficiency. No help needed. A total self rule - Cf. αὐτός (#16) and ἀρχέω (#1534). With reference to physical necessities - 2 Cor.9:8; in a psychological sense - 1 Tim.6:6.

ἔχοντες (pres.act.part.nom.pl.masc.of ἔχω, adverbial, causal) 82.
περισσεύητε (2d.per.pl.pres.act.subj.of περισσεύω, sub-final) 473.
εἰς (preposition with the accusative, purpose) 140.
πᾶν (acc.sing.neut.of πᾶς, in agreement with ἔργον) 67.
ἔργον (acc.sing.neut.of ἔργον, purpose) 460.
ἀγαθόν (acc.sing.neut.of ἀγαθός, in agreement with ἔργον) 547.

Translation - "And God is able to oversupply every grace for you in order (and with the result) that, because you always have total self-sufficiency in every circumstance, you may abound in every good work."

Comment: The superlatives abound - ἐν παντὶ, πάντοτε, πᾶσαν. — every gift, every situation, at all times, total self-sufficiency, every good work. God's oversupply of grace contributes to our oversupply of Christian service in every good activity. We need never fear that we will lack the resources to do all that He has marked out for us to do (Eph.2:10, where we have ἐπὶ ἔργοις ἀγαθοῖς οἷς προητοίμασεν ὁ θεὸς ἵνα ἐν αὐτοῖς περιπατήσωμεν). Since this is true why should any Christian sow sparingly, as though he feels that he must withhold some of his resources in order to have enough to do what God has marked out for him to do?! God gives His grace to us for a purpose. The ἵνα clause, which is sub-final (both purpose and result) follows. "That we may abound." Where? In every situation (ἐν παντὶ). When? Always (πάντοτε). How? With complete self-sufficiency (πᾶσαν αὐτάρκειαν). Such a Christian is completely independent of the world. Doing what? Executing every good work (πᾶν ἔργον ἀγαθόν). περισσεῦσαι completes δυνατεῖ. ἔχοντες is the causal participle. A similar thought is found in Phil.4:19. *Cf.* also 1 Cor.3:21-23.

The total competence of the Christian to perform every good work which God has assigned for him to do is a thrilling thought (Phil.1:6; Eph.2:10; 2 Tim.4:6-8; Rev.3:2). His success depends in no way upon cooperation with the world. Autarchy (#4352) in a political and economic sense is the ability of a nation state to survive in total independence of other nation states. Hitler boasted that Germany could be autarkic. He was wrong, as *ersatz* products produced in Germany revealed during the period that she was isolated from the rest of the world. The United States, the most richly endowed nation state in the world cannot be autarkic. We lack tin and molybdenum disulfide among other needed chemicals. The Christian in the world whose only real concern is that he do the will of God has autarkic viability. He needs no one nor anything but God. Of course if he feels that he must drive to his preaching appointment in a chrome plated Cadilac he may be forced to depend upon the unsaved world for that, since such luxury comes under the heading of *wants* not *needs*.

Paul supports his promise of verse 8 with the quotation of verse 9.

"The use of this word (αὐτάρκεια) shows Paul's acquaintance with Stoicism. Paul takes this word of Greek philosophy and applies it to the Christian view of life as independent of circumstances. But he does not accept the view of the Cynics in the avoidance of society." (A.T.Robertson, *Word Pictures in the New Testament*, IV, 248, 249).

Verse 9 - "As it is written, He hath dispersed abroad; he hath given to the poor;

his righteousness remaineth forever."

καθὼς γέγραπται, Ἐσκόρπισεν, ἔδωκεν τοῖς πένησιν, ἡ δικαιοσύνη αὐτοῦ μένει εἰς τὸν αἰῶνα.

"As it is written, 'He scatters abroad, he gives to the poor; his righteousness endures forever.' " . . . RSV

καθὼς (comparative adverb) 1348.

γέγραπται (3d.per.sing.perf.pass.ind.of γράφω, intensive) 156.

ἐσκόρπισεν (3d.per.sing.aor.act.ind.of δκορπίζω, culminative) 1000.

ἔδωκεν (3d.per.sing.aor.act.ind.of δίδωμι, culminative) 362.

τοῖς (dat.pl.masc.of the article in agreement with πένησιν) 9.

#4353 πένησιν (dat.pl.masc.of πένης, indirect object of ἔδωκεν).

> King James Version

poor - 2 Cor.9:9.

> Revised Standard Version

poor - 2 Cor.9:9.

Meaning: Cf. πένομαι - "to work for a living." *Cf.* also πεινάω (#335). *Cf.* the Latin *penuria.* One suffering penury. Financial lack - 2 Cor.9:9.

ἡ (nom.sing.fem.of the article in agreement with δικαιοσύνη) 9.

δικαιοσύνη (nom.sing.fem.of δικαιοσύνη, subject of μένει) 322.

αὐτοῦ (gen.sing.masc.of αὐτός, possession) 16.

μένει (3d.per.sing.pres.act.ind.of μένω, futuristic) 864.

εἰς (preposition with the accusative, time extent) 140.

τὸν (acc.sing.masc.of the article in agreement with αἰῶνα) 9.

αἰῶνα (acc.sing.masc.of αἰών, time extent) 1002.

Translation - "As it stands written, 'He has scattered; He has given to the poor; His righteousness will remain forever.' "

Comment: The quotation is from Psalm 112:9, which includes in its context God's judgment upon the wicked as well as blessing for the righteous. *Cf.* Psalm 112:8,10. ἐσκόρπισεν then can refer to the scattering or disintegration of the fortunes of the wicked (#1000). Or it can refer to a wide dispersal of blessings in a redistribution of the wealth. Perhaps it means both. He takes from the rich and scatters the wealth among the poor in the sense of Luke 1:51-53, where we have another form of the word in διασκόρπισεν (#1538). Keep in mind that Paul is quoting the passage to support his argument that a Christian cannot outgive God. The sparse sower is in contrast to the generous sower (verses 6-8). Since ἔδωκεν τοῖς πένησιν clearly refers to gifts to the poor, ἐσκόρπισεν must refer to God's judgment upon the wicked. Otherwise the writer is repeating himself. God's righteousness is a two-edged sword. It judges the wicked, rewards the righteous and redistributes the wealth on an equitable basis. Since it is δικαιοσύνη it abides forever. Only δικαιοσύνη is viable.

Verse 10 - "Now he that ministereth seed to the sower both minister bread for your food, and multiply your seed sown, and increase the fruits of your righteousness."

ὁ δὲ ἐπιχορηγῶν σπέρμα τῷ σπείροντι καὶ ἄρτον εἰς βρῶσιν χορηγήσει καὶ πληθυνεῖ τὸν σπόρον ὑμῶν καὶ αὐξήσει τὰ γενήματα τῆς δικαιοσύνης ὑμῶν.

"He who supplies seed to the sower and bread for food will supply and multiply your resources and increase the harvest of your righteousness."... RSV

ὁ (nom.sing.masc.of the article in agreement with ἐπιχορηγῶν) 9.
δὲ (continuative conjunction) 11.

#4354 ἐπιχορηγῶν (pres.act.part.nom.sing.masc.of ἐπιχορηγέω, substantival, subject of χορηγήσει, πληθυνεῖ and αὐξήσει).

King James Version

add - 2 Peter 1:5.
minister to - 2 Cor.9:10; Gal.3:5.
minister unto - 2 Peter 1:11.
have nourishment ministered - Col.2:19.

Revised Standard Version

supply - 2 Cor.9:10; Gal.3:5.
nourished - Col.2:19.
supplement - 2 Peter 1:5.
richly provide - 2 Peter 1:11.

Meaning: A combination of ἐπί (#47) and χορηγέω (#4355). Hence, to supply, furnish or present to; to supplement. To give seed to a sower and bread for food - 2 Cor.9:10; to give the Holy Spirit - Gal.3:5; of the supply of nourishment to the body, in a metaphorical reference to the sustaining power of Christ over His body, the church - Col.2:19; with reference to the supplemental additions of various Christian virtues to faith - 2 Peter 1:5; with reference to the presentation to the victorious believer of an entrance into God's kingdom - 2 Peter 1:11. Thus ἐπιχορηγέω means to make something available.

σπέρμα (acc.sing.neut.of σπέρμα, direct object of ἐπιχορηγῶν) 1056.
τῷ (dat.sing.masc.of the article in agreement with σπείροντι) 9.
σπείροντι (pres.act.part.dat.sing.masc.of σπείρω, substantival, indirect object of ἐπιχορηγῶν) 616.
καὶ (adjunctive conjunction joining nouns) 14.
ἄρτον (acc.sing.masc.of ἄρτος, direct object of ἐπιχορηγῶν) 338.

εἰς (preposition with the accusative, purpose) 140.
βρῶσιν (acc.sing.fem.of βρῶσις, purpose) 594.

#4355 χορηγήσει (3d.per.sing.fut.act.ind.of χορηγέω, predictive).

King James Version

give - 1 Peter 4:11.
minister - 2 Cor.9:10.

Revised Standard Version

supply - 1 Peter 4:11; 2 Cor.9:10.

Meaning: Cf. χορηγός - "the leader of a chorus," from χορός - "a dancing chorus line" and ἄγω (#876). Hence χορηγέω - "to produce." To lead in the production of a dance routine. The word came to mean the production or supply of anything. Followed by τὸν σπόρον (#2189) in 2 Cor.9:10. With ἰσχυς (#2419) in 1 Peter 4:11.

καὶ (adjunctive conjunction joining verbs) 14.
πληθυνεῖ (3d.per.sing.fut.act.ind.of πληθύνω, predictive) 1488.
τὸν (acc.sing.masc.of the article in agreement with σπόρον) 9.
σπόρον (acc.sing.masc.of σπόρος, direct object of χορηγήσει and πληθυνεῖ) 2189.
ὑμῶν (gen.pl.masc.of σύ, possession) 104.
καὶ (adjunctive conjunction joining verbs) 14.
αὐξήσει (3d.per.sing.fut.act.ind.of αὐξάνω, predictive) 628.
τὰ (acc.pl.neut.of the article in agreement with γενήματα) 9.
γενήματα (acc.pl.neut.of γέννημα, direct object of αὐξήσει) 279.
τῆς (gen.sing.fem.of the article in agreement with δικαιοσύνης) 9.
δικαιοσύνης (gen.sing.fem.of δικαιοσύνη, description) 322.
ὑμῶν (gen.pl.masc.of σύ, possession) 104.

Translation - "And he who provides seed for the sower and bread to eat will produce and multiply your seed and he will increase the fruits of your righteousness."

Comment: Here is a giant promise that we cannot outgive God. He is the great Overproducer (#4354). *Cf.* Eph.3:20. The farmer sows the grain, and the harvest is more than sufficient to replace the seed and thus it yields a *net produit*. Francois Quesnay, the court physician for Louis XV and father of Physiocracy understood this and built a school of economic thought upon it. But there is little record that either Quesnay or his disciples, the Physiocrats, gave the Lord any special credit for it. Rather most of them looked upon it as a deistic interpretation of natural law. Indeed it is a natural law, but Christ,the Creator, ordained in creation that it should be so.

The sower who has a *net produit* in seed will naturally have bread to eat. *Cf.* Isa.55:8-11. εἰς βρῶσιν is purpose. The principle of overproduction in ἐπιχορηγῶν (#4355) is established in the physical world of agriculture, horticulture and animal husbandry. A grain of wheat grows a stalk of wheat which produces another grain for seed plus many more for food. An apple tree grows apples, each with many seeds, each of which is capable of producing another apple tree. Moreover the apple tree lives on to produce many more crops. When a cow has a calf we have the calf but we also still have the cow to produce another calf. This is what Quesnay meant by *net produit*.

Paul now makes a spiritual application of these matters. Though σπέρμα (#1056) normally means semen, in the places listed under #1056, including 2 Cor.9:10, the context demands botanical seed such as corn or wheat. Here the context seems to demand spiritual fruitage.

The three verbs, χορηγέω (#4355), πληθύνω (#1488) and αὐξάνω (#628) find their objects in the seed of the gospel sown by the Christian (τὸν σπόρον ὑμῶν) and the results of our righteousness. Our Lord produces and multiplies the seed. He augments the fruits of our righteous acts. Note that the gospel seed is produced by God, not by the preacher. The seed that the preacher produces does not multiply! God must be ὁ χορηγῶν if multiplication of result (πληθύνω) is to occur.

It is tragic to observe the sterility and consequent lack of harvest of the sermon based upon "seed" *produced*, not by God but by the human wisdom and knowledge of an improperly (if not diabolically) inflated pulpiteer. But righteousness (ablative singular in δικαιοσύνης) is the source of results (γενήματα, #279), which are subject to amplication and multiplication (αὐξάνω, #628). A chain reaction of the gospel power, released by nuclear fission follows (2 Tim.2:2). Thus it is easy to understand why we have in verse 9 ἡ δικαιοσύνη αὐτοῦ μένει εἰς τὸν αἰῶνα. Only God's righteousness is viable and its viability is seen when, under the direction of the Holy Spirit and in keeping with scholarly exegesis of His revealed Word, the righteous act of one member of the Body of Christ results in *net produit* which in turn multiplies to a greater harvest. The multiplier concept of John Maynard Keynes (*The General Theory of Employment, Interest and Money*), which dictates that economic productivity grows as the reciprocal of the marginal propensity to consume. If on balance the American consumer spends three-fourths of his marginal income and saves only one-fourth, every dollar which he spends will generate four dollars of new national income. Thus we are able to measure the volume of new investment, which is the dynamic of a capitalist system and thus forecast the rate of growth. This tool in the hands of economists who understand it can be used to stimulate production of goods and services, reduce unemployment and promote growth without inflation. One wonders if Lord Keynes got his idea from Paul in 2 Corinthians 9 who was using the argument to stimulate Christian generosity (verses 6-8). Verse 10 expounds more carefully what Paul said in verse 8. The results follow in

Verse 11 - "Being enriched in everything to all bountifulness, which causeth through us thanksgiving unto God."

ἐν παντὶ πλουτιζόμενοι εἰς πᾶσαν ἁπλότητα, ἥτις κατεργάζεται δι' ἡμῶν
εὐχαριστίαν τῷ θεῷ —

*"You will be enriched in every way for great generosity, which through us will
produce thanksgiving to God;" . . . RSV*

ἐν (preposition with the locative of sphere) 80.

παντὶ (loc.sing.neut.of πᾶς, sphere) 67.

πλουτιζόμενοι (present passive participle, nominative plural masculine of
πλουτίζω, anacoluthon) 4100.

εἰς (preposition with the accusative, adverbial accusative) 140.

πᾶσαν (acc.sing.masc.of πᾶς, in agreement with ἁπλότητα) 67.

ἁπλότητα (acc.sing.masc.of ἁπλότης, adverbial accusative) 4018.

ἥτις (nom.sing.fem.of ὅστις, relative pronoun, subject of κατεργάζεται) 163.

κατεργάζεται (3d.per.sing.pres.mid.ind.of κατεργάζομαι, customary) 3815.

δι' (preposition with the ablative of agent) 118.

ἡμῶν (abl.pl.masc.of ἐγώ, agent) 123.

εὐχαριστίαν (acc.sing.fem.of εὐχαριστία, direct object of κατεργάζεται)
3616.

τῷ (dat.sing.masc.of the article in agreement with θεῷ) 9.

θεῷ (dat.sing.masc.of θεός, personal advantage) 124.

*Translation - ". . . you being enriched in every way so that you will give with
complete liberality, which through our ministry generates thanksgiving to God."*

Comment: In his high emotional state in 2 Corinthians Paul is careless with his
participles. πλουτιζόμενοι is anacoluthon. It does not belong to ὁ ἐπιχορηγῶν
of verse 10. The participle is plural number and passive voice. There is nothing in
the context to which it can apply except the Corinthians. They are the ones who
will be enriched and the result will be total liberality the next time they have a
chance to give their money. It is not God who is enriched, for no one can enrich
God. It is God Who is enriching the Corinthians. What God does (verse 10)
results in the spiritual enrichment of the saints (verse 11). They are enriched in
every sphere of life (ἐν παντὶ), and the result is their total sincerity and
unpretentious generosity (εἰς πᾶσαν ἁπλότητα #4018).

Spiritual revival always results in a greater degree of generosity among
Christians, who then give their money (and everything else they possess), not for
pretense, but in sincere love for God.

The antecedent of ἥτις is δικαιοσύνης, the only feminine substantive in the
context. It is their righteousness, with its increased fruitage, manifested in their
sincere liberality that generates thanksgiving to God. From whom does this
burst of gratitude come? From the poor saints in Judea. When? When Paul
delivers the money. Thus δι' ἡμῶν is an ablative of agency. Thus God is the
source of Corinthian righteousness, which generates the fruits of sincere
liberality in giving, which (when Paul and his friends have delivered the money
to the saints in Judea) generates thanksgiving to God from those who receive it.
Paul repeats the thought in

Verse 12 - "For the administration of this service not only supplieth the want of the saints, but is abundant also by many thanksgivings unto God."

ὅτι ἡ διακονία τῆς λειτουργίας ταύτης οὐ μόνον ἐστὶν προσαναπληροῦσα τὰ ὑστερήματα τῶν ἁγίων, ἀλλὰ καὶ περισσεύουσα διὰ πολλῶν εὐχαριστιῶν τῷ θεῷ —

"for the rendering of this service not only supplies the wants of the saints but also overflows in many thanksgivings to God." . . . RSV

ὅτι (conjunction introducing a subordinate causal clause) 211.

ἡ (nom.sing.fem.of the article in agreement with διακονία) 9.

διακονία (nom.sing.fem.of διακονία, subject of ἐστὶν) 2442.

τῆ (gen.sing.fem.of the article in agreement with λειτουργίας) 9.

λειτουργίας (gen.sing.fem.of λειτουργία, description) 1807.

ταύτης (gen.sing.fem.of οὗτος, in agreement with λειτουργίας) 93.

οὐ (negative conjunction with the indicative) 130.

μόνον (acc.sing.neut.of μόνος, adverbial) 339.

ἐστὶν (3d.per.sing.pres.ind.of εἰμί, present periphrastic) 86.

#4356 προσαναπληροῦσα (pres.act.part.nom.sing.fem.of προσαναπληρόω, present periphrastic).

King James Version

supply - 2 Cor.9:12; 11:9.

Revised Standard Version

supply - 2 Cor.9:12; 11:9.

Meaning: A combination of πρός (#197), ἀνά (#1059) and πληρόω (#115). Hence, to fill (πληρόω) up (ἀνά) by supplementing (πρός). To supply that which is lacking. With reference to the financial needs of the Judean Christians - 2 Cor.9:12; to Paul's need - 2 Cor.11:9.

τὰ (acc.pl.neut.of the article in agreement with ὑστερήματα) 9.

ὑστερήματα (acc.pl.neut.of ὑστέρημα, direct object of προσαναπληροῦσα) 2707.

τῶν (gen.pl.masc.of the article in agreement with ἁγίων) 9.

ἁγίων (gen.pl.masc.of ἅγιος, description) 84.

ἀλλὰ (alternative conjunction) 342.

καὶ (adjunctive conjunction joining participles) 14.

περισσεύουσα (pres.act.part.nom.sing.fem.of περισσεύω, present periphrastic) 473.

διὰ (preposition with the ablative of agent) 118.

πολλῶν (abl.pl.masc.of πολύς, in agreement with εὐχαριστιῶν) 228.

εὐχαριστιῶν (pres.act.part.abl.pl.masc.of εὐχαριστέω, substantival, agent) 1185.

τῷ (dat.sing.masc.of the article in agreement with θεῷ) 9.
θεῷ (dat.sing.masc.of θεός, indirect object of εὐχαριστιῶν) 124.

Translation - "Because the performance of this service is not only fully supplementing the deficit of the saints but also it always abounds through the gratitude of many to God."

Comment: Verse 12 is parenthetical, as verse 13 is joined grammatically to verse 11. The righteousness of the saints in Corinth generates thanksgiving to God by the saints in Jerusalem (verse 11). Why? The ὅτι clause of verse 12 follows. We have a double present periphrastic with ἐστὶν joined both to προσαναπληροῦσα and περισσεύουσα. Paul's project of raising money for poor relief yields two results: (a) it makes up the financial deficit of the poor, which is its local primary function, but (b) it also results in an overflow of praise to God of those who are grateful. (διὰ πολλῶν εὐχαριστιῶν). Thus Paul shows why the last clause of verse 11 is true.

Verse 13 - "Whiles by the experiemnt of this ministration they glorified God for your professed subjection unto the gospel of Christ, and for your liberal distribution unto them, and unto all men."

διὰ τῆς δοκιμῆς τῆς διακονίας ταύτης δοξάζοντες τὸν θεὸν ἐπὶ τῇ ὑποταγῇ τῆς ὁμολογίας ὑμῶν εἰς τὸ εὐαγγέλιον τοῦ Χριστοῦ καὶ ἁπλότητι τῆς κοινωνίας εἰς αὐτοὺς καὶ εἰς πάντας.

"Under the test of this service, you will glorify God by your obedience in acknowledging the gospel of Christ, and by the generosity of your contribution for them and for all others;" . . . RSV

διὰ (preposition with the genitive of means) 118.
τῆς (gen.sing.fem.of the article in agreement with δοκιμῆς) 9.
δοκιμῆς (gen.sing.fem.of δοκιμή, means) 3897.
τῆς (abl.sing.fem.of the article in agreement with διακονίας) 9.
διακονίας (abl.sing.fem.of διακονία, source) 2442.
ταύτης (abl.sing.fem.of οὗτος, in agreement with διακονίας) 93.
δοξάζοντες (pres.act.part.nom.pl.masc.of δοξάζω, anacoluthon) 461.
τὸν (acc.sing.masc.of the article in agreement with θεὸν) 9.
θεὸν (acc.sing.masc.of θεός, direct object of δοξάζοντες) 124.
ἐπὶ (preposition with the instrumental of cause) 47.
τῇ (instru.sing.fem.of the article in agreement with ὑποταγῇ) 9.

#4357 ὑποταγῇ (instru.sing.fem.of ὑποταγή, cause).

King James Version

subjection - 2 Cor.9:13; Gal.2:5; 1 Tim.2:11; 3:4.

Revised Standard Version

obedience - 2 Cor.9:13.
submission - Gal.2:5.
submissiveness - 1 Tim.2:11.
submissive - 1 Tim.3:4.

Meaning: A combination of ὑπό (#117) and τάσσω (#722). *Cf.* also ὑποτάσσω (#1921). Hence a willingness to be appointed to a place (τάσσω) beneath (ὑπό) another. Hence, submission; obedience; subjection. To the claims of the gospel of Christ - 2 Cor.9:13. With reference to Paul reaction to false teaching - Gal.2:5; with reference to the relation of women to men - 1 Tim.2:11; of children to parents - 1 Tim.3:4.

τῇ (gen.sing.fem.of the article in agreement with ὁμολογίας) 9.

#4358 ὁμολογίας (gen.sing.fem.of ὁμολογία, description).

King James Version

confession - 1 Tim.6:12,13.
profession - Heb.3:1; 4:14; 10:23.
professed - 2 Cor.9:13.

Revised Standard Version

acknowledging - 2 Cor.9:13.
confession - Heb.3:1; 4:14; 10:23; 1 Tim.6:12,13.

Meaning: Cf. ὁμολογέω (#688); ὁμολογουμένως (#4743). A confession or profession of faith. Subjectively - Heb.3:1; objectively - that which one confesses - 1 Tim.6:12,13; Heb.4:14; 10:23; 2 Cor.9:13.

ὑμῶν (gen.pl.masc.of σύ, possession) 104.
εἰς (preposition with the predicate accusative) 140.
τό (acc.sing.neut.of the article in agreement with εὐαγγέλιον) 9.
εὐαγγέλιον (acc.sing.neut.of εὐαγγέλιον, predicate usage) 405.
τοῦ (gen.sing.masc.of the article in agreement with Χριστοῦ) 9.
Χριστοῦ (gen.sing.masc.of Χριστός, description) 4.
καὶ (adjunctive conjunction joining causal clauses) 14.
ἁπλότητι (instru.sing.masc.of ἁπότης, cause) 4018.
τῆς (gen.sing.fem.of the article in agreement with κοινωνίας) 9.
κοινωνίας (gen.sing.fem.of κοινωνία, description) 3002.
εἰς (preposition with the accusative of extent) 140.
αὐτοὺς (acc.pl.masc.of αὐτός, extent) 16.
καὶ (adjunctive conjunction joining substantives) 14.
εἰς (preposition with the accusative of extent) 140.
πάντας (acc.pl.masc.of πᾶς, extent) 67.

Translation - "By the evidence which this ministry provided they will be glorifying God because of the submission of your confession to the gospel of

Christ and the generosity of the sharing with them and with all."

Comment: Why would the recipients of the money thank God? They would glorify God with their thanks when they saw how the Corinthian Christians passed the test. This opportunity to give provided the Corinthians with the chance to prove the sincerity of their Christian confession. The submission of the will to the moral commitments of the gospel of Christ which they professed to believe was coupled with the sincere liberality with which they shared their wealth, not only with the Judean saints who needed it especially at that time, but also with all others who might need it.

Verse 14 - "And by their prayer for you, which long after you for the exceeding grace of God in you."

καὶ αὐτῶν δεήσει ὑπὲρ ὑμῶν ἐπιποθούντων ὑμᾶς διὰ τὴν ὑπερβάλλουσαν χάριν τοῦ θεοῦ ἐφ' ὑμῖν.

"while they long for you and pray for you, because of the surpassing grace of God in you." . . . RSV

καὶ (adjunctive conjunction joining substantives) 14.
αὐτῶν (gen.pl.masc.of αὐτός, genitive absolute) 16.
δεήσει (instru.sing.fem.of δέησις, means) 1796.
ὑπὲρ (preposition with the genitive "in behalf of") 545.
ὑμῶν (gen.pl.masc.of σύ, "in behalf of") 104.
ἐπιποθούντων (pres.act.part.gen.pl.masc.of ἐπιποθέω, genitive absolute) 3789.
ὑμᾶς (acc.pl.masc.of σύ, direct object of ἐπιποθούντων) 104.
διὰ (preposition with the accusative, cause) 118.
τὴν (acc.sing.fem.of the article in agreement with χάριν) 9.
ὑπερβάλλουσαν (pres.act.part.acc.sing.fem.of ὑπερβάλλω, adjectival, ascriptive, in agreement with χάριν) 4290.
χάριν (acc.sing.fem.of χάρις, cause) 1700.
τοῦ (gen.sing.masc.of the article in agreement with θεοῦ) 9.
θεοῦ (gen.sing.masc.of θεός, description) 124.
ἐφ' (preposition with the locative, metaphorical place) 47.
ὑμῖν (loc.pl.masc.of σύ, metaphorical place) 104.

Translation - ". . . and their prayer for you as they long for you because of the superabundant grace of God in you."

Comment: The thanks to God and the glory to His name which arose from the hearts of the Judean Christians was because of the Corinthians ὑποταγη (verse13), their ἁπλότητι (verse 13) and it results in the prayer of the Judean saints for the Corinthians (verse 14).Note the genitive absolute. As they prayed the Judean Christians were longing to see the Corinthians. Why? διὰ with the accusative is causal. Because of God's grace upon the Corinthians as manifested by the superabundance of their love gifts of money. Thus God is the source of the entire sequence of cause and result developments. *Cf.* verses 8,10,11,14. All of this was made possible by the incarnation.

Note how the supernatural ethics of Christianity as made effective by the filling of the Holy Spirit obliterated the lines of racial prejudice between the Hebrew Christians of Judea and the Gentile Christians of Corinth. The Corinthians gave their money to the Hebrew Christians and the Hebrews loved them for it, prayed for them and longed to see them. Thus the middle wall of partition was broken down (Eph.2:14).

God's gift of salvation to the saints and the blessings which flow from it are possible only because of the gift of His Son.

Verse 15 - "Thanks be unto God for His unspeakable gift."

χάρις τῷ θεῷ ἐπὶ τῇ ἀνεκδιηγήτῳ αὐτοῦ δωρεᾷ.

"Thanks be to God for his inexpressible gift!" . . . RSV

χάρις (nom.sing.fem.of χάρις, nominative absolute) 1700.
τῷ (dat.sing.masc.of the article in agreement with θεῷ) 9.
θεῷ (dat.sing.masc.of θεός, personal advantage) 124.
ἐπὶ (preposition with the instrumental of cause) 47.
τῇ (instru.sing.fem.of the article in agreement with δωρεᾷ) 9.

#4359 ἀνεκδιηγήτῳ (instru.sing.fem.of ἀνεκδιήγητος, in agreement with δωρεᾷ).

King James Version

unspeakable - 2 Cor.9:15.

Revised Standard Version

inexpressible - 2 Cor.9:15.

Meaning: α privative plus ἐκδιηγέομαι - hence, of such great worth as to beggar description. *Cf.* ἐκ (#19) and διηγέομαι (#2225). Indescribable - With δωρεᾷ, the gift of God in 2 Cor.9:15.

αὐτοῦ (gen.sing.masc.of αὐτός, description) 16.
δωρεᾷ (instru.sing.fem.of δωρεά, cause) 2004.

Translation - "Thanks be to God because of His indescribable gift."

Comment: God's gift of love to the world (John 3:16; Rom.5:8; Gal.2:20) is the incarnate Christ. His incarnation is the only logical basis for the kind of sharing which Paul was urging upon the Corinthians in behalf of the suffering saints in Judea. Apart from the gift of God's love the world is a jungle committed to the survival of the fittest philosophy of the Social Darwinists. If evolution as taught by Darwin is true, then there is no gospel of love, nor any reason for the grace of sharing and a man is a fool to give what he needs to others.

Paul Defends His Ministry

(2 Corinthians 10:1-18)

2 Cor.10:1 - *"Now I Paul myself beseech you by the meekness and gentleness of Christ, who in presence am base among you, but being absent am bold toward you."*

Αὐτὸς δὲ ἐγὼ Παῦλος παρακαλῶ ὑμᾶς διὰ τῆς πραΰτητος καὶ ἐπιεικείας τοῦ Χριστοῦ, ὃς κατὰ πρόσωπον μὲν ταπεινὸς ἐν ὑμῖν, ἀπὼν δὲ θαρρῶ εἰς ὑμᾶς

"I, Paul, myself entreat you, by the meekness and gentleness of Christ — I who am humble when face to face with you, but bold to you when I am away!—"...
RSV

Αὐτὸς (nom.sing.masc.of αὐτός, in agreement with Παῦλος, intensive) 16.
δὲ (explanatory conjunction) 11.
ἐγὼ (nom.sing.masc.of ἐγώ, subject of παρακαλῶ) 123.
Παῦλος (nom.sing.masc.of Παῦλος, apposition) 3284.
παρακαλῶ (1st.per.sing.pres.act.ind.of παρακαλέω, aoristic) 230.
ὑμᾶς (acc.pl.masc.of σύ, direct object of παρακαλῶ) 104.
διὰ (preposition with the genitive of means) 118.
τῆς (gen.sing.fem.of the article in agreement with πραΰτητος) 9.
πραΰτητος (gen.sing.fem.of πραΰτης, means) 4133.
καὶ (adjunctive conjunction joining nouns) 14.
ἐπιεικείας (gen.sing.fem.of ἐπιείκεια, means) 3619.
τοῦ (abl.sing.masc.of the article in agreement with Χριστοῦ) 9.
Χριστοῦ (abl.sing.masc.of Χριστός, source) 4.
ὃς (nom.sing.masc.of ὅς, relative pronoun, subject of εἰμί, understood) 65.
κατὰ (preposition with the accusative, standard) 98.
πρόσωπον (acc.sing.neut.of πρόσωπον, standard) 588.
μὲν (particle of affirmation) 300.
ταπεινὸς (nom.sing.masc.of ταπεινὸς, predicate adjective) 957.
ἐν (preposition with the locative, with plural pronouns) 80.
ὑμῖν (loc.pl.masc.of σύ, place) 104.
ἀπὼν (pres.part.nom.sing.masc.of ἄπειμι, adverbial, temporal) 4134.
δὲ (adversative conjunction) 11.
θαρρῶ (1st.per.sing.pres.act.ind.of θαρρέω, aoristic) 4307.
εἰς (preposition with the predicate accusative) 140.
ὑμᾶς (acc.pl.masc.of σύ, predicate accusative) 104.

Translation - *"Now I, Paul, myself am appealing to you by the meekness and gentleness that has its source in Christ, who, when I am with you, am unimposing but when absent bold toward you! —"*

Comment: Note the intensive αὐτός with ἐγώ, which is emphatic, with Παῦλος in apposition. His appeal is on the basis of the meekness and gentleness which have their source in Christ. The relative clause with ὅς is in apposition to Παῦλος. This is the Paul who, in their presence is humble, but who, when absent, is very bold. κατὰ πρόσωπον contrasts with ἀπών. Cf. #98 for other examples of κατὰ πρόσωπον. ταπεινός contrasts with θαρρῶ.

This is the beginning of the third part of the epistle. Paul ". . . vigorously defends himself against the accusations of the stubborn minority of Judaizers in Corinth." He appeals to the meekness and gentleness of Christ. "This appeal shows (Plummer) that Paul had spoken to the Corinthians about the character of Christ. Jesus claimed meekness for himself (Matt.11:29) and felicitated the meek (Matt.5:5) and he exemplified it abundantly (Luke 23:34). See on Matt.5:15 and 1 Cor.4:21 for this great word that has worn thin with us. Plutarch combines πραΰτης with ἐπιεικία as Paul does here. Matthew Arnold suggested "sweet reasonableness" for ἐπιεικεία in Plato, Aristotle, Plutarch. It is in the N.T. only here and Acts 24:4 (τὸ ἐπιεκὲς in Phil.4:5). In Greek Ethics the equitable man was called ἐπιεικές, a man who does not press for the last farthing of his rights (Bernard). . . . Socrates and Aristotle used it (ταπεινός) for littleness of soul. Probably Paul here is quoting one of the sneers of his traducers in Corinth about his humble conduct while with them (1 Cor.2:23; 2 Cor.7:16) and his boldness (ἀπών θαρρῶ when away (1 Cor.7:16). 'It was easy to satirize and misrepresent a depression of spirits, a humility of demeanour, which were either the direct results of some bodily affliction, or which the consciousness of this affliction had rendered habitual.' (Farrar). The words stung Paul to the quick." (A.T.Robertson, *Word Pictures in the New Testament*, IV, 251).

Verse 2 - "But I beseech you, that I may not be bold when I am present with that confidence, wherewith I think to be bold against some, which think of us as if we walked according to the flesh."

δέομαι δὲ τὸ μὴ παρὼν θαρρῆσαι τῇ πεποιθήσει ᾗ λογίζομαι τολμῆσαι ἐπί τινας τοὺς λογιζομένους ἡμᾶς ὡς κατὰ σάρκα περιπατοῦντας.

"I beg of you that when I am present I may not have to show boldness with such confidence as I count on showing against some who suspect us of acting in worldly fashion." . . . RSV

δέομαι (1st.per.sing.pres.mid.ind.of δέομαι, aoristic) 841.

δὲ (adversative conjunction) 11.

τὸ (acc.sing.neut.of the article in agreement with θαρρῆσαι) 9.

μὴ (negative conjunction with the infinitive) 87.

παρὼν (pres.part.nom.sing.masc.of πάρειμι, adverbial, temporal) 1592.

θαρρῆσαι (aor.act.inf.of θαρρέω, direct object of δέομαι) 4307.

τῇ (instru.sing.fem.of the article in agreement with πεποιθήσει) 9.

πεποιθήσει (instru.sing.fem.of πεποίθησις, means) 4269.

ᾗ (instru.sing.fem.of ὅς, relative pronoun, in agreement with πεποιθήσει) 65.

λογίζομαι (1st.per.sing.pres.mid.ind.of λογίζομαι, aorist) 2611.

τολμῆσαι (aor.act.inf.of τολμάω, direct object of λογίζομαι) 1430.

ἐπὶ (preposition with the accusative, hostility) 47.

τινας (acc.pl.masc.of τις, indefinite pronoun in agreement with λογιζομένους) 486.

τοὺς (acc.pl.masc.of the article in agreement with λογιζομένους) 9.

λογιζομένους (pres.mid.part.acc.pl.masc.of λογίζομαι, substantival, hostility) 2611.

ἡμᾶς (acc.pl.masc.of ἐγώ, direct object of λογιζομένους) 123.

ὡς (comparative particle) 128.

κατὰ (preposition with the accusative, standard) 98.

σάρκα (acc.sing.fem.of σάρξ, standard) 1202.

περιπατοῦντας (pres.act.part.acc.pl.masc.of περιπατέω, substantival, in apposition with ἡμᾶς) 384.

Translation - *"But I pray that when I arrive I may not be bold, with the confidence with which I am planning to rebuke those who think of us as behaving as though we were unsaved."*

Comment: Paul was doubting the degree of his self-control when he arrived in Corinth. His reputation, as it had been portrayed by his traducers, was that he could be very stern when he was absent and could only write letters, but that when he was in Corinth he lacked the moral courage to rebuke his enemies. But (adversative δὲ) he is now praying to God? For what? μὴ θαρρῆσαι is the object infinitive of δέομαι - "that I may not be bold." When? παρὼν is the adverbial temporal participle - "when I am present in Corinth." If he is bold when he gets to Corinth, how will he display his courage? With boldness (τῇ πεποιθήσει). What boldness? The relative clause defines τῇ πεποιθήσει. It will be boldness which Paul was planning to use. τολμῆσαι is the object infinitive of λογίζομαι. Against whom will Paul employ this bold approach? ἐπὶ τινας τοὺς λογιζαμένους. Against some (indefinite pronoun) who have a certain attitude toward Paul. What attitude? What were they thinking about him? λογιζομένους has a double object. They regarded Paul (ἡμᾶς) as though (ὡς) he was one who conducted himself κατὰ σάρκα - "according to his own unregenerate fleshly motivations" - either as an unsaved man or as a carnal Christian. These were the Corinthians who suspected Paul of unworthy motives. He was planning to rebuke them sternly when he arrived, but he was praying that this boldness which he would display against his critics would not be necessary, nor that it would be displayed against his friends.

The "strange fire" (Leviticus 10:1) of the attempt to employ human psychology to secure decisions for Christ and the gospel is evident in many modern preachers who substitute the methods of the public relations expert for the dependence for results upon the Holy Spirit. Even those who have a sound, scriptural gospel to present, are often guilty of "walking according to the flesh" as Paul's enemies accused him of doing.

While it is true that we are "in the flesh" and will remain so until glorification (1 John 3:2; 1 Cor.15:51-54; 1 Thess.4:13-18), it does not follow that we must carry on our warfare for the Lord with the tools of human motivation. This is the thought in

Verse 3 - "For though we walk in the flesh, we do not war after the flesh."

ἐν σαρκὶ γὰρ περιπατοῦντες οὐ κατὰ σάρκα στρατευόμεθα —

"For though we live in the world we are not carrying on a worldly war," . . .
RSV

ἐν (preposition with the locative of sphere, with nouns) 80.

σαρκὶ (loc.sing.fem.of σάρξ, sphere with nouns) 1202.

γὰρ (causal conjunction) 105.

περιπατοῦντες (pres.act.part.nom.pl.masc.of περιπατέω, adverbial, concessive) 384.

οὐ (negative conjunction with the indicative) 130.

κατὰ (preposition with the accusative, standard) 98.

σάρκα (acc.sing.fem.of σάρξ, standard) 1202.

στρατευόμεθα (1st.per.pl.pres.mid.ind.of στρατευόμεθα, static) 1944.

Translation - "Because, although we are working in the human sphere we are not waging war by human methods."

Comment: γὰρ is causal. Paul hopes that he will deal with his critics in a manner that becomes a Christian since human methods are not to be applied in the Lord's work, despite the fact that he was still operating in the human sphere. The participle is concessive. *Cf.* 1 Tim.1:18.

In fact if Paul fought his enemies in Corinth on their terms he would be proving their charge against him. To fight the devil with the devil's weapons and tactics, even though one is fighting on the devil's turf is to demonstrate that in reality you are on the devil's side.

The passage is a blow to the Arminian method of evangelism that seeks by methods of human psychology to appeal to the reason of the unregenerate instead of depending upon the convicting ministry of the Holy Spirit. Only He can convince (John 16:7-11; 1 Cor.12:3). It is difficult to imagine Paul inviting to the platform in an evangelistic meeting a Christian athlete, a saved Hollywood celebrity or a Grand Ole Opry hillbilly as a means of helping to elicit a response from the audience. Such methods are categorized here as κατὰ σάρκα. This is not to say that famous people should not tell what Christ has done for them but their testimonies should not relate to athletic, forensic or musical (!) ability. What makes such people so special, if the evangelist is not depending more upon Dale Carnegie than upon the Holy Spirit? Why not advertize a Christian housewife or a Christian factory worker? One evangelist formerly advertized himself as a "coverted scamp." Are not we all? A cowboy evangelist was known to ask his audience to look down the barrel of his silver-plated "hog laig."

Paul used no such methods as we learn in verses 4 and 5.

Verse 4 - ("For the weapons of our warfare are not carnal, but mighty through God to the pulling down of strong holds.")

τὰ γὰρ ὅπλα τῆς στρατείας ἡμῶν οὐ σαρκικὰ ἀλλὰ δυνατὰ τῷ θεῷ πρὸς καθαίρεσιν ὀχυρωμάτων — λογισμοὺς καθαιροῦντες

"For the weapons of our warfare are not worldly but have divine power to destroy strongholds." . . . RSV

τὰ (nom.pl.neut.of the article in agreement with ὅπλα) 9.
ὅπλα (nom.pl.neut.of ὅπλον, subject of ἐστί understood) 2804.
τῆς (gen.sing.fem.of the article in agreement with στρατείας) 9.

#4360 στρατείας (gen.sing.fem.of στρατεία, description).

King James Version

warfare - 2 Cor.10:4; 1 Tim.1:18.

Revised Standard Version

warfare - 2 Cor.10:4; 1 Tim.1:18.

Meaning: Cf. στρατηγός (#2754), στρατεύμα (#1404), στρατεύω (#1944), στρατιά (#1880), στρατατιώτης (#724), στρατολογέω (#4816) and στρατόπεδον (#2724). Hence, warfare. With reference to spiritual warfare - 2 Cor.10:4; 1 Tim.1:18.

ἡμῶν (gen.pl.masc.of ἐγώ, possession) 123.
οὐ (negative conjunction with the indicative) 130.
σαρκικὰ (acc.pl.neut.of σαρκικός, predicate adjective) 4058.
ἀλλὰ (alternative conjunction) 342.
δυνατὰ (acc.pl.neut.of δυνατός, predicate adjective) 1311.
τῷ (dat.sing.masc.of the article in agreement with θεῷ) 9.
θεῷ (dat.sing.masc.of θεός, personal advantage) 124.
πρὸς (preposition with the accusative, purpose) 197.

#4361 καθαίρεσιν (acc.sing.fem.of καθαίρεσις, purpose).

King James Version

destruction - 2 Cor.10:8; 13:10.
pulling down - 2 Cor.10:4.

Revised Standard Version

destroying - 2 Cor.10:8.
tearing down - 2 Cor.13:10.
destroy - 2 Cor.10:4.

Meaning: Cf. καθαιρέω (#1831) and καθαίρω (#2786). Destruction, demolition, pulling down - followed by a genitive of description in 2 Cor.10:4, where the reference is to the edification or destruction of the quality of the Christian life. So also in 2 Cor.13:10.

#4362 ὀχυρωμάτων (gen.pl.masc.of ὀχύρωμα, description).

King James Version

stronghold - 2 Cor.10:14.

Revised Standard Version

stronghold - 2 Cor.10:4.

Meaning: Cf. ὀχυρόω - "to fortify," "make strong". Hence, a stronghold, fort, bastion, bulwark. Metaphorically, of intellectual strongholds in disputation employed by evil - 2 Cor.10:4.

λογισμοὺς (acc.pl.masc.of λογισμός, direct object of καθαιροῦντες) 3845.
καθαιροῦντες (pres.act.part.nom.pl.masc.of καθαιρέω, adverbial, circumstantial) 1831.

Translation - "Because the weapons of our warfare are not human, but they are powerful, as we fight for God to destroy fortifications - - - refuting logical arguments."

Comment: The sphere is human, but the warfare is not against flesh and blood (Eph.6:12). It is against Satan and his forces. Hence the weapons are not human. Christians do not fight with guns, tanks, missiles and long-range bombers. That is why the Christian's weaponry cannot fail. On the contrary (ἀλλὰ) they are δυνατά (#1311). Note the contrast between σαρκικά and δυνατά. We fight for God's benefit (τῷ θεῷ). It is His fight, and He is solely responsible for the outcome. We are only His troops in the field. τῷ θεῷ can also be taken as agency. πρὸς with the accusative is purpose. The objective is the total destruction of the Satanic pill boxes - Biological and Social Darwinism, Secular Humanism, Radical Existentialism, Deism, Agnosticism,Atheism, Environmental Determinism, *et al.*

The KJV translates λογισμοὺς καθαιροῦντες in verse 5. Paul's weapons are intellectual - able to destroy arguments, either by pointing out their lack of logic or by challenging the assumptions upon which the arguments depend (#3845). Here is support for Apologetics and Christian Evidences. The Christian need never fear the philosophical or scientific attacks of Satan. His divine weaponry is more than adequate to demolish Satan's intellectual house of cards. But Christian evidences are to be used only after sinners have become saints. They have no place in evangelism. *Cf.*1 Cor.2:1-5 and comment.

Note the nature of Paul's spiritual arsenal - Rom.13:12 - ὅπλα τοῦ φωτός;. ὅπλα δικαιοσύνης - Rom.6:13b. *Cf.* also 2 Cor.6:7. Light and righteousness are God's powerful weapons. Knowledge and justice will ultimately prevail. It is a pity to see the feeble misdirected efforts of the modern church as she tries to outguess and out entertain the world - fields in which she is obviously inferior, and turns her back upon the all powerful weapons of heaven's light and justice.

Verse 5 - "Casting down imaginations, and every high thing that exalteth itself against the knowledge of God, and bringing into captivity every thought to the obedience of Christ."

καὶ πᾶν ὕφωμα ἐπαιρόμενον κατὰ τῆς γνώσεως τοῦ θεοῦ, καὶ αἰχμαλωτίζοντες πᾶν νόημα εἰς τὴν ὑπακοὴν τοῦ Χριστοῦ.

*"We destroy arguments and every proud obstacle to the knowledge of God,
and take every thought captive to obey Christ." . . . RSV*

καὶ (adjunctive conjunction) 14.

πᾶν (acc.sing.neut.of πᾶς, in agreement with ὕφωμα) 67.

ὕφωμα (acc.sing.neut.of ὕφωμα, direct object of καθαιροῦντες) 3955.

ἐπαιρόμενον (pres.pass.part.acc.sing.neut.of ἐπαίρω, adjectival, predicate
position, restrictive in agreement with ὑπφωμα) 1227.

κατὰ (preposition with the genitive, hostility) 98.

τῆς (gen.sing.fem.of the article in agreement with γνώσεως) 9.

γνώσεως (gen.sing.fem.of γνῶσις, hostility) 1856.

τοῦ (abl.sing.masc.of the article in agreement with θεοῦ) 9.

θεοῦ (abl.sing.masc.of θεός, source) 124.

καὶ (adjunctive conjunction joining participles) 14.

αἰχμαλωτίζοντες (pres.act.part.nom.pl.masc.of αἰχμαλωτίζω, adverbial,
circumstantial) 2726.

πᾶν (acc.sing.neut.of πᾶς, in agreement with νόημα) 67.

νόημα (acc.sing.neut.of νόημα, direct object of αἰχμαλωτίζοντες) 4277.

εἰς (preposition with the accusative of extent, metaphorical) 140.

τὴν (acc.sing.fem.of the article in agreement with ὑπακοὴν) 9.

ὑπακοὴν (acc.sing.fem.of ὑπακοή, metaphorical extent) 3785.

τοῦ (gen.sing.masc.of the article in agreement with Χριστοῦ) 9.

Χριστοῦ (gen.sing.masc.of Χριστός, objective genitive) 4.

*Translation - ". . . and every lofty obstacle that is being exhalted against the
knowledge from God, and bringing every concept into captivity unto the
obedience to Christ."*

Comment: The arrogance of unbelief is in view here. The Christian's fight for
God is an attack upon the fortifications of Satan (ὀχυρωμάτων, verse 4). This
fight involves two actions, represented by the two circumstantial participles,
καθαιροῦντες and αἰχμαλωτίζοντες. We demolish hell's arguments and bring
every thought into conformity with the will of Christ. The arguments which we
refute are those which are raised up against the knowledge of God. The thoughts
which we bring under control are our own. Every thought (idea, concept, mental
construct, theory) is made obedient to Christ. This is the logical result that we
should expect if we refute all of the arguments of Satan who is a liar and the
father of lies (John 8:44). There is no truth in him - only lies. To refute his
arguments which otherwise would lead us to accept his lies, is to leave standing
and untouched in the attack, only the truth. Thus with nothing but true mental
constructs left standing after the battle we are in fellowship with Him in Whom
are hid all of the treasures of wisdom and knowledge (Col.2:3; 1 Cor.2:10).

When we hear, as we often do, that a Christian "lost his faith at the university"
it only means that some misguided saint abandoned a holistic gestalt, based

upon faith, for a barren because incomplete empiricism. Secular universities do not teach what they know about God. They only teach that they know nothing about God. They do not deny that God may be known by those who wish to transcend the scientific method and become like trusting children (Mt.11:25; 18:3). Satan fears the holistic analysis because he knows that his own system has neither consistency, coherence nor correspondance to reality. An application of the laws of logic, in the hands of one who understands and knows how to use them, pokes holes in the arguments of unbelief and reduces the devil's attack to impotence and frustration. This is why the more advanced infidels teach that there is no gestalt and that life is a series of random sensations, derived from environmental stimuli, and that the impressions of the moment bear no cause/result relationship to any other, be it in the past or in the future.

The way to cast down this type of arrogant atheism and blatant materialism is to challenge it to live a life consistent with its philosophy. Few are willing to accept such a challenge because life on this planet lived in ethical accord with existentialism would bring what is left of civilization to a sudden end. Atheists try to have it both ways. They want God's morals, for everyone else but themselves, in a Godless society. If they deny that they favor the morals of the Ten Commandments, it is interesting to reflect upon what they would do if one pointed a gun at them and asked their permission to be free from the one that says, "Thou shalt do no murder." The moral leper generally hopes that his wife will remain by the fireside with his children, faithful to her marriage vows. The thief expects others to keep their hands off his property. The liar who is in court on a charge of which he is innocent hopes that the defene witnesses who can establish his alibi will tell the truth.

Verse 6 - "And having in a readiness to revenge all disobedience, when your obedience is fulfilled."

καὶ ἐν ἑτοίμῳ ἔχοντες ἐκδικῆσαι πᾶσαν παρακοήν, ὅταν πληρωθῇ ὑμῶν ἡ ὑπακοή.

"being ready to punish every disobedience, when your obedience is complete." . . . RSV

καὶ (adjunctive conjunction joining participles) 14.

ἐν (preposition with the locative of accompanying circumstance) 80.

ἑτοίμῳ (loc.sing.masc.of ἕτοιμος, accompanying circumstance) 1399.

ἔχοντες (pres.act.part.nom.pl.masc.of ἔχω, adverbial, circumstantial) 82.

ἐκδικῆσαι (aor.act.inf.of ἐκδικέω, epexegetical) 2623.

πᾶσαν (acc.sing.fem.of πᾶς, in agreement with παρακοήν) 67.

παρακοήν (acc.sing.fem.of παρακοή, direct object of ἐκδικῆσαι) 3905.

ὅταν (conjunction with the subjunctive in an indefinite temporal clause) 436.

πληρωθῇ (3d.per.sing.aor.pass.subj.of πληρόω, indefinite temporal clause) 115.

ὑμῶν (gen.pl.masc.of σύ, possession) 104.

ἡ (nom.sing.fem.of the article in agreement with ὑπακοή) 9.

ὑπακοή (nom.sing.fem.of ὑπακοή, subject of πληρωθῇ) 3785.

Translation - *"And having a willingness to punish all disobedience, when you have been fully obedient."*

Comment: This is the last clause of a long sentence which began in verse 4. Paul's weapons are supernaturally effective (verse 4). He used them to refute antiChristian arguments, humble sophisticated critics, subordinate every thought to Christ (verse 5) and he was ready to discipline any Christian who was disobedient and without repentance. In the meantime he was careful to see that his own record of obedience to the ethical demands of the gospel of Christ was clear. He expected the Corinthian church to exercise her authority in these matters.

Verse 7 - *"Do ye look on things after the outward appearance? If any man trust to himself that he is Christ's, let him of himself think this again, that, as he is Christ's, even so are we Christ's."*

Τὰ κατὰ πρόσωπον βλέπετε. εἴ τις πέποιθεν ἑαυτῷ Χριστοῦ εἶναι, τοῦτο λογιζέσθω πάλιν ἐφ' ἑαυτοῦ ὅτι καθὼς αὐτὸς Χριστοῦ οὕτως καὶ ἡμεῖς.

"Look at what is before your eyes. If any one is confident that he is Christ's, let him remind himself that as he is Christ's, so are we." . . . RSV

Τὰ (acc.pl.neut.of the article, direct object of βλέπετε) 9.

κατὰ (preposition with the accusative, standard) 98.

πρόσωπον (acc.sing.neut.of πρόσωπον, standard) 588.

βλέπετε (2d.per.pl.pres.act.impv.of βλέπω, direct question) 499.

εἰ (conditional particle in a first-class condition) 337.

τις (nom.sing.masc.of τις, indefinite pronoun, subject of πέποιθεν) 486.

πέποιθεν (3d.per.sing.2d.perf.act.ind.of πείθω, intensive, first-class condition) 1629.

ἑαυτῷ (dat.sing.masc.of ἑαυτός, reference) 288.

Χριστοῦ (gen.sing.masc.of Χριστός, relationship) 4.

εἶναι (pres.inf.of εἰμί, complementary) 86.

τοῦτο (acc.sing.neut.of οὗτος, direct object of λογιζέσθω) 93.

λογιζέσθω (3d.per.sing.pres.mid.impv.of λογίζομαι, command) 2611.

πάλιν (adverbial) 355.

ἐφ' (preposition with the adverbial genitive, reference with pronouns) 47.

ἑαυτοῦ (gen.sing.masc.of ἑαυτός, reference) 288.

ὅτι (conjunction introducing an object clause in indirect discourse) 211.

καθὼς (comparative adverb) 1348.

αὐτὸς (nom.sing.masc.of αὐτός, subject of ἐστιν understood) 16.

Χριστοῦ (gen.sing.masc.of Χριστός, relationship) 4.

οὕτως (comparative adverb) 74.

καὶ (adjunctive conjunction joining pronouns) 14.

ἡμεῖς (nom.pl.masc.of ἐγώ, subject of εἰσί understood) 123.

Translation - *"Do you look at things in terms of external appearances? If any one has been persuaded with reference to himself that he is Christ's, let him take this into consideration with reference to himself, that just as he belongs to Christ so also do we."*

Comment: Some of the Corinthians apparently were being influenced by the social and political movements in the church. Some of Paul's enemies were impressive. There was external grounds for their prestige. Paul attacks this. The question as to who belongs to Christ and who does not is an internal matter - not capable of being judged by men. Paul was Christ's man as much as others who made the same profession. ἡμεῖς is literary plural.

Verse 8 - "For though I should boast somewhat more of our authority, which the Lord hath given us for edification, and not for your destruction, I should not be ashamed."

ἐάν (τε) γὰρ περισσότερόν τι καυχήσωμαι περὶ τῆς ἐξουσίας ἡμῶν, ἧς ἔδωκεν ὁ κύριος εἰς οἰκοδομὴν καὶ οὐκ εἰς καθαίρεσιν ὑμῶν, οὐκ αἰσχυνθήσομαι.

"For even if I boast a little too much of our authority, which the Lord gave for building you up and not for destroying you, I shall not be put to shame."... RSV

ἐάν (conditional particle if a concessive third-class condition) 363.
(τε) (correlative particle) 1408.
γὰρ (causal conjunction) 105.
περισσότερόν (acc.sing.neut.comp.of περισσός, in agreement with τι) 525.
τι (acc.sing.neut.of τις, indefinite pronoun, direct object of καυχήσωμαι) 486.
καυχήσωμαι (1st.per.sing.aor.mid.subj.of καυχάομαι, concessive third-class condition) 3847.
περὶ (preposition with the adverbial genitive, reference) 173.
τῆς (gen.sing.fem.of the article in agreement with ἐξουσίας) 9.
ἐξουσίας (gen.sing.fem.of ἐξουσία, reference) 707.
ἡμῶν (gen.pl.masc.of ἐγώ, possession) 123.
ἧς (gen.sing.fem.of ὅς, relative pronoun, objective genitive) 65.
ἔδωκεν (3d.per.sing.aor.act.ind.of δίδωμι, culminative) 362.
ὁ (nom.sing.masc.of the article in agreement with κύριος) 9.
κύριος (nom.sing.masc.of κύριος, subject of ἔδωκεν) 97.
εἰς (preposition with the accusative, purpose) 140.
οἰκοδομὴν (acc.sing.fem.of οἰκοδομή, purpose) 1481.
καὶ (adjunctive conjunction joining prepositional phrases) 14.
οὐκ (negative conjunction with the indicative) 130.
εἰς (preposition with the accusative, purpose) 140.
καθαίρεσιν (acc.sing.fem.of καθείρεσις, purpose) 4361.
ὑμῶν (gen.pl.masc.of σύ, description) 104.
οὐκ (negative conjunction with the indicative) 130.
αἰσχυνθήσομαι (1st.per.sing.fut.pass.ind.of αἰσχύνομαι, predictive) 2563.

Translation - "Because even if I should in fact boast a little too much about our authority which the Lord has given for constructive, though not for destructive criticism, I am not going to be ashamed."

Comment: Paul is denying that he is afraid to be bold with his critics when he sees them in person. The third-class condition is concessive. He is assuming that it is going to be necessary for him to boast about the apostolic authority which the Lord had given to him and to the other apostles. ἡμῶν here is not a literary, as it was in verse 7. The apostles were given authority over the churches in matters of faith and practice. Otherwise there could have been no New Testament literature written nor any New Testament churches established and nurtured in the early years of their development. This was generally understood among the early Christians, and Paul thought perhaps that any further discussion of it would be looked upon as an unnecessary boast. Why continue to boast about a point that everyone admits is true? But there were traducers in the Corinthian church who needed to be put in their place. So even though Paul might find it necessary to remind the church that he was one of the twelve apostles, by virtue of the divine appointment by Christ, the Head over all things to His church (Eph.1:22,23), he did not intend to be embarrassed by his boasting, since it would be necessary to deal with the problem of insubordination among the Judaizers in Corinth who were destroying the unity of the Body of Christ.

The authority which Christ gave to Paul and to the other apostles was not to be used to tear down the churches, but to edify them. Why then be ashamed of it or be afraid to assert and use it?

Church bodies since have forgotten that the pastor, if he has been placed in his position by Christ, the Head of the church, is locally the head of the church and that his word is to be obeyed (Heb.13:17). The pastor, as the under Shepherd is responsible at the judgment seat of Christ for the performance of his flock. Since he is going to be held accountable it is necessary for him to be given full authority for policy making. No one in government accepts responsibility without authority. Yet he is not to use his authority unwisely, as a dictator who lords it over God's people (1 Pet.5:1-3).

Verse 9 - "That I may not seem as if I would terrify you by letters."

ἵνα μὴ δόξω ὡς ἂν ἐκφοβεῖν ὑμᾶς διὰ τῶν ἐπιστολῶν.

"I would not seem to be frightening you with letters." . . . RSV

ἵνα (conjunction with the subjunctive, negative purpose) 114.
μὴ (negative conjunction with the subjunctive) 87.
δόξω (1st.per.sing.aor.act.subj.of δοκέω, negative purpose) 287.
ὡς (comparative particle) 128.
ἂν (comparative particle with ὡς) 205.

#4363 ἐκφοβεῖν (pres.act.inf.of ἐκφοβέω, epexegetical).

King James Version

terrify - 2 Cor.10:9.

Revised Standard Version

to be frightening - 2 Cor.10:9.

Meaning: A combination of ἐκ (#19) and φοβέομαι (#101). *Cf.* ἔκφοβος (#2323). Hence to frighten out (ἐκ) of one's wits; to terrify; cause violent fright - 2 Cor.10:9. To cause one to fear - ἐκ is causative in composition.

ὑμᾶς (acc.pl.masc.of σύ, direct object of ἐκφοβεῖν) 104.
διὰ (preposition with the genitive of means) 118.
τῶν (gen.pl.fem.of the article in agreement with ἐπιστολῶν) 9.
ἐπιστολῶν (gen.pl.fem.of ἐπιστολή, means) 3180.

Translation - "I do not wish to appear to frighten you with the letters."

Comment: The classic idiom ὡς ἄν with the infinitive is found only here in the New Testament. Robertson says, "Even here it is not a clear case since ἐκφοβεῖν depends on δόξω and ὡσ ἄν comes in as a parenthetical clause, 'as if' ('as it were')" (Robertson, *Grammar*, 1095). "This use of ὡς ἄν with the infinitive is seen in the papyri" (Moulton, *Prolegomena*, 167, as cited in Robertson, *Word Pictures in the New Testament*, IV, 254) and it is not ἄν in the apodosis" (*Ibid., cf. Grammar*, 974).

Paul's statement of verse 8 explains verse 9. He assured them that he was Christ's (verse 7) and was fully conscious of his God-given apostolic authority which he would not hesitate to use since it would result, not in their destruction but in their edification. That was why he was not ashamed to use his authority if it became necessary. But he did not wish to appear as one who wished to frighten them with his letters. Note that ἐπιστολῶν is plural. Some have wondered if there was a third epistle to the Corinthians which has been lost.

In the next two verses Paul further replies to his critics.

Verse 10 - "For his letters say they are weighty and powerful, but his bodily presence is weak, and his speech contemptible."

ὅτι, Αἱ ἐπιστολαὶ μὲν, φησίν, βαρεῖαι καὶ ἰσχυραί, ἡ δὲ παρουσία τοῦ σώματος ἀσθενὴς καὶ ὁ λόγος ἐξουθενημένος.

"For they say, 'His letters are weighty and strong, but his bodily presence is weak, and his speech of no account." . . . *RSV*

ὅτι (causal conjunction) 211.
Αἱ (nom.pl.fem.of the article in agreement with ἐπιστολαὶ) 9.
ἐπιστολαὶ (nom.pl.fem.of ἐπιστολή, subject of εἰσίν understood) 3180.
μὲν (particle of affirmation) 300.
φησίν (3d.per.pl.pres.act.ind.of φημί, present iterative retroactive) 354.
βαρεῖαι (nom.pl.fem.of βαρύς, predicate adjective, in agreement with ἐπιστολαί) 1432.
καὶ (adjunctive conjunction joining adjectives) 14.
ἰσχυραί (nom.pl.fem.of ἰσχυρός, predicate adjective, in agreement with ἐπιστολαί) 303.

ἥ (nom.sing.fem.of the article in agreement with παρουσία) 9.

δέ (adversative conjunction) 11.

παρουσία (nom.sing.fem.of παρουσία, subject of ἐστί understood) 1482.

τοῦ (gen.sing.neut.of the article in agreement with σώματος) 9.

σώματος (gen.sing.neut.of σῶμα, description) 507.

ἀσθενής (nom.sing.fem.of ἀσθενής, predicate adjective in agreement with παρουσία) 1551.

καί (continuative conjunction) 14.

ὁ (nom.sing.masc.of the article in agreement with λόγος) 9.

λόγος (nom.sing.masc.of λόγος, subject of ἐστίν understood) 510.

ἐξουθενημένος (pres.mid.part.nom.sing.masc.of ἐξουθενέω, adjectival, predicate adjective in agreement with λόγος) 2628.

Translation - *"Because 'His letters in fact,' he says, 'are ponderous and powerful, but his bodily presence is weak and his speech is despicable.' "*

Comment: Paul's fear that his letters might frighten the Corinthians (verse 9) was based on a commonly reported rumor which had been circulated by one man (singular number in φησίν). Paul's critic had repeated this criticism again and again in the past and was still saying it (present iterative retroactive). ὅτι therefore is not recitative, but causal, as it ties the thought of verse 10 to that of verse 9. The charge was that Paul's letters were ponderous (heavy, burdensome, difficult and of great impact), that is, highly critical and with a great show of logic, but (note the μέν . . . δέ sequence) his bodily presence weak and his speaking style disgusting (revolting, repulsive, contemptible).

Most exegetes will agree that Paul's letters to the Corinthians are much more ponderous (βαρεῖαι, #1432) than his letters to the other churches, though the Corinthian critic had no way to make a comparison, since it is not likely that he had seen any other than the one directed to Corinth. If he had seen Paul's letters to the Thessalonians which were written possibly three or four years before, or if he could have seen the letters to the Philippians, Ephesians and Colossians which were written later, he would have seen that there was perhaps a special reason why Paul wrote to the Corinthians in a different vein that to the other churches. They did not have the problems that the Corinthians had.

Due to the high emotional content of Paul's letters to Corinth his Greek grammar and syntax is much less precise and polished. The modern translator can understand the reaction to the rhetoric of the reader in the first century. Jesus' words are spirit and life (John 6:63). Paul's were ponderous and powerful.

The reference to Paul's bodily presence is an unkind cut which one would expect from a critic who had no desire to be fair. "It seems clear that Paul did not have a commanding appearance like that of Barnabas (Acts 14:12). He had some physical defect of the eyes (Gal.4:14) and a thorn in the flesh (2 Cor.12:27). In the second century *Acts of Paul and Thecla* he is pictured as small, short, bow-legged, with eye-brows knit together, and an aquiline nose. A forgery of the fourth century in the name of Lucian describes Paul as 'the bald-headed, hook-nosed Galilean.' " (Robertson, *Word Pictures in the New Testament*, IV, 254).

Some of "his accusers sneered at his personal appearance as 'weak' (ἀσθενής) . . . . The Corinthians . . . cared more for the brilliant eloquence of Apollos and did not find Paul a trained rhetorician (1 Cor.1:17; 2:1,4; 2 Cor.11:6). He made different impressions on different people. 'Seldom has any one been at once so ardently hated and so passionately loved as St. Paul' (Adolph Deissmann, *St. Paul*, 70, as cited in *Ibid.*) . . . . 'At one time he seemed like a man, and at another he seemed like an angel.' (*Acts of Paul and Thecla*). He spoke like a god at Lystra (Acts 14:8-12), but Eutchus went to sleep on him (Acts 20:9). Evidently Paul winced under this biting criticism of his looks and speech." (*Ibid.*).

Criticism of his personal appearance was unfair. No one can help how he looks. Criticism of his rhetoric was also unfair. Paul chose to speak to the Corinthians as he did, in order to be more effective in his evangelistic preaching (1 Cor.2:1-5). His Corinthian critic who wanted him to speak like Demosthenes should have heard him on Mars Hill (Acts 17:22-31).

If his critic in Corinth wanted Paul to speak and act in Corinth as he wrote in his epistles, that was what he was going to get.

Verse 11 - "Let such an one think this, that, such as we are in word by letters when we are absent, such will we be also in deed when we are present."

τοῦτο λογιζέσθω ὁ τοιοῦτος, ὅτι οἷοί ἐσμεν τῷ λόγῳ δι' ἐπιστολῶν ἀπόντες, τοιοῦτοι καὶ παρόντες τῷ ἔργῳ.

"Let such people understand that what we say by letter when absent, we do when present." . . . RSV

τοῦτο (acc.sing.neut.of οὗτος, direct object of λογιζέσθω) 93.

λογιζέσθω (3d.per.sing.pres.mid.impv.of λογίζομαι, command) 2611.

ὁ (nom.sing.masc.of the article in agreement with τοιοῦτος) 9.

τοιοῦτος (nom.sing.masc.of τοιοῦτος, subject of λογιζέσθω) 785.

ὅτι (conjunction introducing an object clause in indirect discourse) 211.

οἷοί (nom.pl.masc.of ὅσος, correlative qualitative pronoun, subject of ἐσμεν) 660.

ἐσμεν (1st.per.pl.pres.ind.of εἰμί, aoristic) 86.

τῷ (loc.sing.masc.of the article in agreement with λόγῳ) 9.

λόγῳ (loc.sing.masc.of λόγος, sphere with nouns) 510.

δι' (preposition with the adverbial genitive, place) 118.

ἐπιστολῶν (gen.pl.fem.of ἐπιστολή, adverbial, place) 3180.

ἀπόντες (pres.part.nom.pl.masc.of ἄπειμι, adverbial, temporal) 4134.

τοιοῦτοι (nom.pl.masc.of τοιοῦτος, demonstrative correlative, antecedent to οἷοί) 785.

καὶ (adjunctive conjunction joining nouns) 14.

παρόντες (pres.part.nom.pl.masc.of πάρειμι, adverbial, temporal) 1592.

τῷ (loc.sing.neut.of the article in agreement with ἔργῳ) 9.

ἔργῳ (loc.sing.neut.of ἔργον, sphere, with nouns) 460.

Translation - "Let that person think about this - that as we are in the sphere of written discourse when we are absent, so also when we are present are we going to be in the sphere of deeds."

Comment: τοιοῦτοι is antecedent to οἷοί, the predicate adjective. The verb in the last clause is missing, but Paul is clear. Paul promises to translate the words in his epistles into actions when he gets to Corinth. This contradicts the false rumor of verse 10. Note the adverbial temporal participles - "when I am absent . . . when I am present." It is the same Paul in terms of his apostolic authority which he has by divine appointment (verse 8), whether he is present or absent, whether his medium is the written word or the execution of a policy.

Verse 12 - "For we dare not make ourselves of the number, or compare ourselves with some that commend themselves: but they measuring themselves by themselves, and comparing themselves among themselves, are not wise."

Οὐ γὰρ τολμῶμεν ἐγκρῖναι ἢ συγκρῖναι ἑαυτούς τισιν τῶν ἑαυτοὺς συνιστανόντων. ἀλλὰ αὐτοὶ ἐν ἑαυτοῖς ἑαυτοὺς μετροῦντες καὶ συγκρίνοντες ἑαυτοὺς ἑαυτοῖς οὐ συνιᾶσιν.

"Not that we venture to class or compare ourselves with some of those who commend themselves. But when they measure themselves by one another, and compare themselves with one another, they are without understanding."

Οὐ (negative conjunction with the indicative) 130.
γὰρ (inferential conjunction) 105.
τολμῶμεν (1st.per.pl.pres.act.ind.of τολμάω, aoristic) 1430.

#4364 ἐγκρῖναι (1st.aor.act.inf.of ἐγκρίνω, complementary).

King James Version

make of the number - 2 Cor.10:12.

Revised Standard Version

class - 2 Cor.10:12.

Meaning: A combination of ἐν (#80) and κρίνω (#531). Hence, to be reckoned or counted among; to be identified with; to put oneself in a class with - followed by the accusative in 2 Cor.10:12.

ἢ (disjunctive) 465.
συγκρῖναι (1st.aor.act.inf.of συγκρίνω, complementary) 4111.
ἑαυτούς (acc.pl.masc.of ἑαυτός, direct object of ἐγκρῖναι and συγκρῖναι) 288.
τισιν (instru.pl.masc.of τις, indefinite pronoun, association) 486.
τῶν (gen.pl.masc.of the article in agreement with συνιστανόντων) 9.
ἑαυτοὺς (acc.pl.masc.of ἑαυτός, direct object of συνιστανόντων) 288.
συνιστανόντων (pres.act.part.gen.pl.masc.of συνίστημι, substantival, partitive) 2328.

ἀλλὰ (adversative conjunction) 342.
αὐτοὶ (nom.pl.masc.of αὐτός, subject of συνιᾶσιν) 16.
ἐν (preposition with the instrumental of association) 80.
ἑαυτοῖς (instru.pl.masc.of ἑαυτός, association) 288.
ἑαυτοὺς (acc.pl.masc.of ἑαυτός, direct object of μετροῦντες) 288.
μετροῦντες (pres.act.part.nom.pl.masc.of μετρέω, adverbial, causal) 644.
καὶ (adjunctive conjunction joining participles) 14.
συγκρίνοντες (pres.act.part.nom.pl.masc.of συγκρίνω, adverbial, causal) 4111.
ἑαυτοὺς (acc.pl.masc.of ἑαυτός, direct object of συγκρίνοντες) 288.
ἑαυτοῖς (instru.pl.masc.of ἑαυτός, association) 288.
οὐ (negative conjunction with the indicative) 130.
συνιᾶσιν (3d.per.pl.pres.act.ind.of συνίημι, aoristic) 1039.

Translation - "Therefore we do not dare to identify ourselves with some of those who justify themselves; on the contrary these because they measure themselves by themselves and compare themselves with themselves are not very smart."

Comment: γὰρ is inferential. Paul had a commission from heaven as an apostle. His critics had none. Thus he had no desire to identify himself with them. Indeed it would have been unwise for him to have done so. The infinitives are complementary. He wanted to disassociate himself from those in the Corinthian church whom he accuses of commending themselves to the public, particularly to the other Christians. They are the gospel hucksters such as he described in 2 Cor.2:17. Why were they so inconsistent? Because in the process of justifying themselves they had no point of reference - no bench mark outside of themselves. They measured themselves by themselves. They compared themselves to themselves. That is why they were unwise (causal participles in μετροῦντες and συγκρίνοντες). Their philosophy would not hold together. It failed the epistemological test of coherence. Thus Paul strongly attacked the existentialism which has become prevalent in the late 20th century. Because it disclaims all causal connection with both past and future and knows only the immediate present it has no basis for comparison to apply by which to judge its actions or thoughts. If we know only by sense perception, and there is no memory, we cannot know the past. Nor can we know the future until it produces the stimulii which is our only ground of knowledge. Thus we have no standard of excellence to which we can adhere and by comparison with which we can judge the present. The conclusion is that there is no true or false, no good and evil, no right and wrong. To say, "This is good" is to raise the question which cannot be answered - "Compared to what?" We can only compare the present with itself. Similarly we cannot say, "This is bad, true, false, right, wrong, moral, immoral, beautiful, ugly." The shoppers' guide in the mall shows a criss-cross with an arrow and the statement, "You are here." But this would make no sense to the confused shopper if it did not indicate the point in relation to all other points in the mall. An athlete sets a new world's record in some event, only if we are able to compare his performance with all other similar performances of the past. Take away the bench mark, the basis for comparison and there is no way to tell where we are now or how to evaluate the experience of the present moment.

The ship was ploughing her way through the North Atlantic, halfway between New York and Southampton. I was in the Captain's cabin watching the pilot and the navigator. I asked, "Where are we now?" The Captain nodded to the seaman who was standing before his charts. He consulted his navigation instruments, drew intersecting lines on the map and pointed to the intersection. I asked. "If I were in a small boat at this precise point, would I be able to look about me and see this ship?" The Captain said, "Of course." He explained that the margin of error was less than three miles, a distance from which one could easily see on a clear day and on a quiet sea. The seaman had defined the position, but he did it in relation to the fixed position of the stars. Paul's critics who compared themselves only with themselves were like the sea captain who navigated from a lantern hanging in the rigging or like the man who believes that he can reach his home by following his nose. These men were fools, probably because they wished to be knaves. A foolish knave who does not wish to be criticized for his perfidy will reject all divine standards of truth and morality. Paul's critics were working behind his back in Corinth, bent upon destroying his influence with the Corinthian church in order that they might bring it under their own control. Their tribe has increased in modern philosophy. Such men are not approved (δόκιμος), as Paul says in 2 Cor.10:18.

Paul now says that he will evaluate his own performance and the degree of his authority only by the standard which God had given to him.

Verse 13 - "But we will not boast of things without our measure, but according to the measure of the rule which God hath distributed to us, as a measure to reach even unto you."

ἡμεῖς δὲ οὐκ εἰς τὰ ἄμετρα καυχησόμεθα, ἀλλὰ κατὰ τὸ μέτρον τοῦ κανόνος οὗ ἐμέρισεν ἡμῖν ὁ θεὸς μέτρου, ἐφικέσθαι ἄχρι καὶ ὑμῶν.

"But we will not boast beyond limit, but will keep to the limits God has apportioned us, to reach even to you." . . . RSV

ἡμεῖς (nom.pl.masc.of ἐγώ, subject of καυχησόμεθα) 123.
δὲ (adversative conjunction) 11.
οὐκ (negative conjunction with the indicative) 130.
εἰς (preposition with the accusative of limitation) 140.
τὰ (acc.pl.neut.of the article in agreement with ἄμετρα) 9.

#4365 ἄμετρα (acc.pl.neut.of ἄμετρος, adverbial accusative).

King James Version

things without measure - 2 Cor.10:13,15.

Revised Standard Version

beyond limit - 2 Cor.10:13,15.

Meaning: A combination of α privative and μέτρον (#643). Hence, without measure; immense; infinitive. With reference to the exaggerated measurement of immediate evaluation - 2 Cor.10:13,15.

καυχησόμεθα (1st.per.pl.fut.mid.ind.of καυχάομαι, predictive) 3847.
ἀλλὰ (alternative conjunction) 342.
κατὰ (preposition with the accusative, standard) 98.
τὸ (acc.sing.neut.of the article in agreement with μέτρον) 9.
μέτρον (acc.sing.neut.of μέτρον, standard) 643.
τοῦ (gen.sing.masc.of the article in agreement with κανόνος) 9.

#4366 κανόνος (gen.sing.masc.of κανών, description).

King James Version

line - 2 Cor.10:16.
rule - 2 Cor.10:13,15; Gal.6:16; Phil.3:16 (mgn.)

Revised Standard Version

not trans. - 2 Cor.10:13.
field - 2 Cor.10:15,16.
rule - Gal.6:16.

Meaning: Cf. κάννα - "reed" for measurement purposes. ". . . a rod or straight piece of rounded wood to which any thing is fastened to keep it straight; used for various purposes; a measuring rod, rule; a carpenter's line or measuring tape; the measure of a leap, as in the Olympic games; accordingly in the N.T., a definitely bounded or fixed space within the limits of which one's power or influence is confined; the province assigned one; one's sphere of activity - 2 Cor.10:13,15,16. Metaph. any rule or standard; a principle or law of investigating, judging, living, acting - Gal.6:16." (Thayer, 324).

οὗ (gen.sing.masc.of ὅς, relative pronoun, in agreement with κανόνος) 65.
ἐμέρισεν (3d.per.sing.aor.act.ind.of μερίζω, culminative) 993.
ἡμῖν (dat.pl.masc.of ἐγώ, personal advantage) 123.
ὁ (nom.sing.masc.of the article in agreement with θεὸς) 9.
θεὸς (nom.sing.masc.of θεός, subject of ἐμέρισεν) 124.
μέτρου (gen.sing.neut.of μέτρον, means) 643.

#4367 ἐφικέσθαι (2d.aor.mid.inf.of ἐφικνέομαι, purpose).

King James Version

reach unto - 2 Cor.10:13,14.

Revised Standard Version

reach unto you - 2 Cor.10:13,14.

Meaning: A combination of ἐπί (#47) and ἱκνέομαι - ἵκω - "to come." Hence, to come to. Followed by ἄχρι καὶ ὑμῶν in 2 Cor.10:13; followed by εἰς ὑμᾶς in 2 Cor.10:14, in the sense of "apply to you."

ἄχρι (preposition with the genitive of reference, with persons) 1517.
καὶ (adjunctive conjunction) 14.
ὑμῶν (gen.pl.masc.of σύ, adverbial genitive, reference) 104.

Translation - "But we shall not go to extremes with our boasting, but rather in keeping with the measure of the field of activity God has assigned to us, a field which applies also unto you."

Comment: Paul's promise not to boast about τὰ ἄμετρα - "into the unmeasured things" - is a sardonic criticism of his critics with their "no limits" basis for evaluation. Paul's philosophy included a belief in limits and in the existence of a God Who sets limits and establishes bounds of activity and canons of behavior. Each member of the Body of Christ has his own limits which are assigned to him (Eph.2:10). Paul was certain that God had assigned to him a definite field of activity (2 Tim.4:7,8). He was anxious to do all, but only all of that which had been given for him to do. To seek to transcend the boundaries of the divine assignment is presumption. Thus he would boast only up to the extent of the canon, which (οὗ) God marked out for him. Note that Paul repeats the substantive μέτρου in case agreement with οὗ. God's assignment of place and purpose was designed to reach (purpose) even to each Corinthian Christian. The bounds marked out for Paul, within which he was to work, included Corinth. He is saying that he had been "called" to minister to the Corinthian church, and he suggests by inference that his critics (verse 12) are "out of bounds." Any one who denies the existence of a divine canon of ethics in the universe is out of bounds.

Paul wanted to do all that God had planned for him to do, but he did not wish to presume to transcend the bounds of his field of activity. This he says in

Verse 14 - "For we stretch not ourselves beyond our measure, as though we reached not unto you: for we are come as far as to you also in preaching the gospel of Christ."

οὐ γὰρ ὡς μὴ ἐφικνούμενοι εἰς ὑμᾶς ὑπερεκτείνομεν ἑαυτούς, ἄχρι γὰρ καὶ ὑμῶν ἐφθάσαμεν ἐν τῷ εὐαγγελίῳ τοῦ Χριστοῦ.

"For we are not overextending ourselves, as though we did not reach you; we were the first to come all the way to you with the gospel of Christ." . . . RSV

οὐ (negative conjunction with the indicative) 130.
γὰρ (causal conjunction) 105.
ὡς (particle introducing a concessive clause) 128.
μὴ (negative conjunction with the participle) 87.
ἐφικνούμενοι (pres.mid.part.nom.pl.masc.of ἐφικνέομαι, adverbial, concessive) 4367.
εἰς (preposition with the accusative of extent) 140.

ὑμᾶς (acc.pl.masc.of σύ, extent) 104.

#4368 ὑπερεκτείνομεν (1st.per.pl.pres.act.ind.of ὑπερεκτείνω, futuristic).

King James Version

stretch beyond one's measure - 2 Cor.10:14.

Revised Standard Version

overextend - 2 Cor.10:14

Meaning: A combination of ὑπέρ (#545) and ἐκτείνω (#710). Hence, to reach too far; outreach; overextend; go beyond assigned boundaries. With reference to going to a field of gospel ministry to which one is not assigned - 2 Cor.10:14.

ἑαυτούς (acc.pl.masc.of ἑαυτός, direct object of ὑπερεκτείνομεν) 288.
ἄχρι (temporal conjunction) 1517.
γὰρ (causal conjunction) 105.
καὶ (emphatic conjunction) 14.
ὑμῶν (gen.pl.masc.of σύ, adverbial, place) 104.
ἐφθάσαμεν (1st.per.pl.aor.act.ind.of φθάνω, constative) 996.
ἐν (preposition with the locative of sphere) 80.
τῷ (loc.sing.neut.of the article in agreement with εὐαγγελίῳ) 9.
εὐαγγελίῳ (loc.sing.neut.of εὐαγγέλιον, sphere) 405.
τοῦ (gen.sing.masc.of the article in agreement with Χριστοῦ) 9.
Χριστοῦ (gen.sing.masc.of Χριστός, description) 4.

Translation - "Because we are not stepping beyond the limits of our assignment, as though we will not be coming to you, because we came to you before in the capacity of a minister of the gospel of Christ."

Comment: Paul hastens to add that though he does not intend to enter fields of Christian activity not assigned to him by the Lord, this does not mean that he will not come to Corinth again. Indeed he had already come to Corinth to work in the sphere of activity connected with the gospel of Christ. *Cf.* ἐφθάσαμεν (#996) for meaning.

Verse 15 - "Not boasting of things, without our measure, that is, of other men's labours, but having hope, when your faith is increased, that we shall be enlarged by you according to our rule abundantly."

οὐκ εἰς τὰ ἄμετρα καυχώμενοι ἐν ἀλλοτρίοις κόποις, ἐλπίδα δὲ ἔχοντες αὐξανομένης τῆς πίστεως ὑμῶν ἐν ὑμῖν μεγαλυνθῆναι κατὰ τὸν κανόνα ἡμῶν εἰς περισσείαν,

"We do not boast beyond limit, in other men's labors; but our hope is that as your faith increases, our field among you may be greatly enlarged." . . . RSV

οὐκ (negative conjunction with the indicative) 130.

εἰς (preposition with the accusative of limitation) 140.

τὰ (acc.pl.neut.of the article in agreement with ἄμετρα) 9.

ἄμετρα (acc.pl.neut.of ἄμετρος, adverbial accusative) 4365.

καυχώμενοι (pres.mid.part.nom.pl.masc.of καυχάομαι, adverbial, complementary) 3847.

ἐν (preposition with the locative of sphere, with nouns) 80.

ἀλλοτρίοις (loc.pl.masc.of ἀλλότριος, in agreement with κόποις) 1244.

κόποις (loc.pl.masc.of κόπος, sphere, nouns) 1565.

ἐλπίδα (acc.sing.fem.of ἐλπίς, direct object of ἔχοντες) 2994.

δὲ (adversative conjunction) 11.

ἔχοντες (pres.act.part.nom.pl.masc.of ἔχω, adverbial, causal) 82.

αὐξανομένης (present passive participle, genitive singular feminine of αὐξάνω, genitive absolute) 628.

τῆς (gen.sing.masc.ot the article in agreement with πίστεως) 9.

πίστεως (gen.sing.fem.of πίστις, genitive absolute) 728.

ὑμῶν (gen.pl.masc.of σύ, possession) 104.

ἐν (preposition with the instrumental of agent) 80.

ὑμῖν (instru.pl.masc.of σύ, agent) 104.

μεγαλυνθῆναι (aor.pass.inf.of μεγαλύνω, complementary) 1438.

κατὰ (preposition with the accusative, standard) 98.

τὸν (acc.sing.masc.of the article in agreement with κανόνα) 9.

κανόνα (acc.sing.masc.of κανών, standard) 4366.

ἡμῶν (gen.pl.masc.of ἐγώ, possession) 123.

εἰς (preposition with the accusative, predicate usage) 140.

περισσείαν (acc.sing.fem.of περισσεία, adverbial accusative in the predicate) 3904.

Translation - ". . . not boasting beyond measure with reference to the labors of others, but having hope that, as your faith is increased, we may be enriched by you abundantly, in keeping with our appointed bounds."

Comment: The verse continues the sentence beginning with ἄχρι γὰρ καὶ κ.τ.λ. in verse 14. Paul first came to Corinth. How? He was not boasting unduly about the labors of others (complementary participle in καυχώμενοι). What then? "But (adversative δὲ to go with οὐκ) having hope." Hope for what? The infinitive μεγαλυνθῆναι is epexegetical. Paul hoped to be financially enabled by the Corinthians (ἐν ὑμῖν) so that he could preach in other fields (verse 16). He wanted only that ministry which God had assigned to him (κατὰ τὸν κανόνα). He understood the folly that is involved when God's servants stray beyond the parameters established by the divine plan, and he did not wish to go where God had not directed him. He hoped that the financial assistance would be abundant (εἰς περισσείαν). The genitive absolute αὐξανομένης τῆς πίστεως ὑμῶν in the present tense indicates that Paul could expect his hope to be realized only when and because their faith grew.

As Paul preached and the Corinthians accepted Christ and began to grow in grace, they would make it possible for him to extend his ministry within eternally prescribed limits. When Christians, with misguided zeal, enter into fields of Christian acivity not assigned to them, however legitimate under other circumstances they might be, they forfeit the blessing of God, Who has promised to support us only when we are doing the work according to His rule (κανών # 4366) for our lives. The long sentence continues in

Verse 16 - ". . . to preach the gospel in the regions beyond you and not to boast in another man's line of things made ready to our hand."

εἰς τὰ ὑπερέκεινα ὑμῶν εὐαγγελίσασθαι, οὐκ ἐν ἀλλοτρίῳ κανόνι εἰς τὰ ἕτοιμα καυχήσασθαι.

" . . . so that we may preach the gospel in lands beyond you, without boasting of work already done in another's field." . . . RSV

εἰς (preposition with the infinitive, purpose) 140.
τὰ (acc.pl.neut.of the article, direct object of εὐαγγελίσασθαι) 9.

#4369 ὑπερέκεινα (acc.pl.neut.of ὑπερέκεινα, in agreement with τὰ).

King James Version

beyond - 2 Cor.10:16.

Revised Standard Version

beyond - 2 Cor.10:16.

Meaning: A combination of ὑπέρ (#545) and ἐκεῖνος (#246). **Beyond a given** place. Followed by an ablative of separation in 2 Cor.10:16.

ὑμῶν (abl.pl.masc.of σύ, separation) 104.
εὐαγγελίσασθαι (aor.mid.inf.of εὐαγγελίζομαι, purpose) 909.
οὐκ (negative conjunction with the indicative understood) 130.
ἐν (preposition with the locative of place) 80.
ἀλλοτρίῳ (loc.sing.masc.of ἀλλότριος, in agreement with κανόνι) 1244.
κανόνι (loc.sing.masc.of κανών, place) 4366.
εἰς (preposition with the infinitive, purpose) 140.
τὰ (acc.pl.neut.of the article in agreement with ἕτοιμα) 9.
ἕτοιμα (acc.pl.neut.of ἕτοιμος, purpose) 1399.
καυχήσασθαι (aor.mid.inf.of καυχάομαι, purpose) 3847.

Translation - "In order that the areas beyond you may be evangelized, not to boast of things already prepared in another man's territory."

Comment: Why does Paul want the enrichment to which he refers in verse 15? In order that other territories may be evangelized (τὰ). Where? Beyond the confines of Corinth (ὑπερέκεινα ὑμῶν). Only in unevangelized fields could Paul accomplish things for the Lord without seeming to take advantage of the work already done by some previous preacher. It was this that Paul's critics were doing in Corinth.

Verse 17 - "But he that glorieth, let him glory in the Lord."

Ὁ δὲ καυχώμενος ἐν κυρίῳ καυχάσθω.

" 'Let him who boasts, boast of the Lord.' " . . . RSV

Ὁ (nom.sing.masc.of the article in agreement with καυχώμενος) 9.

δὲ (adversative conjunction) 11.

καυχώμενος (pres.mid.part.nom.sing.masc.of καυχάομαι, substantival, subject of καυχάσθω) 3847.

ἐν (preposition with the locative of sphere, with nouns) 80.

κυρίῳ (loc.sing.masc.of κύριος, sphere, with nouns) 97.

καυχάσθω (3d.per.sing.aor.mid.impv.of καυχάομαι, command) 3847.

Translation - "But let the boaster boast in the Lord."

Comment: Wherever Paul went, the Lord got the credit for what was done. Who we are, to what ministry we are called, where we go and the good works which are accomplished are all parts of the foreordained plan of the divine architect of history. We glorify Him only when we fulfill His perfect plan for our lives (Eph.2:10). How often we have seen preachers reaping the fruits of the gospel efforts of those who occupied the field before them. Too often they forget to give credit to Whom it is due - to the Lord Who planned it all (1 Cor.3:5-10). Paul's admonition here is a rebuke to his critics. The quotation is an adaptation of Jeremiah 9:24.

Verse 18 - "For not he that commendeth himself is approved but whom the Lord commendeth."

οὐ γὰρ ὁ ἑαυτὸν συνιστάνων ἐκεῖνός ἐστιν δόκιμος, ἀλλὰ ὃν ὁ κύριος συνίστησιν.

"For it is not the man who commends himself that is accepted, but the man whom the Lord commends." . . . RSV

οὐ (negative conjunction with the indicative) 130.

γὰρ (causal conjunction) 105.

ὁ (nom.sing.masc.of the article in agreement with συνιστάνων) 9.

ἑαυτὸν (acc.sing.masc.of ἑαυτός, direct object of συνιστάνων) 288.

συνιστάνων (pres.act.part.nom.sing.masc.of συνίστημι, substantival, subject of ἐστιν) 2328.

ἐκεῖνος (nom.sing.masc.of ἐκεῖνος, anaphoric, in agreement with συνιστάνων) 246.

ἐστιν (3d.per.sing.pres.ind.of εἰμί, customary) 86.

δόκιμος (nom.sing.masc.of δόκιμος, predicate adjective) 4042.

ἀλλὰ (alternative conjunction) 342.

ὃν (acc.sing.masc.of ὅς, relative pronoun, direct object of συνίστησιν) 65.

ὁ (nom.sing.masc.of the article in agreement with κύριος) 9.

κύριος (nom.sing.masc.of κύριος, subject of συνίστησιν) 97.

συνίστησιν (3d.per.sing.pres.act.ind.of συνίστημι, static) 2328.

Translation - "Because the one who commends himself is not approved, but the one whom the Lord commends."

Comment: ἐκεῖνος ia anaphoric, as it points back in reference to ὁ συνιστάνων. Any preacher can boast about himself. This does not prove that he has gained approval from the Lord. Only God can put the final stamp of approval upon a preacher whom He has called. To be truly called of God to preach does not guarantee divine approval. Paul feared that he would end his days in the ministry in disgrace (1 Cor.9:27). He was unduly alarmed (2 Tim.4:6-8), but perhaps the reason why he succeeded and gained his "crown of righteousness" was that he never once assumed that he would be approved. The field which received the rain, yet grows only thorns and briars is disapproved (Heb.6:8, where the word ἀδόκιμος occurs), but not lost eternally (1 Cor.3:15).

Paul continues in chapter 11 to compare himself and his ministry with that of the false apostles.

Paul and the False Apostles

(2 Corinthians 11:1-15)

2 Cor.11:1 - "Would to God ye could bear with me a little in my folly: and indeed bear with me."

Ὄφελον ἀνείχεσθέ μου μικρόν τι ἀφροσύνης. ἀλλὰ καὶ ἀνέχεσθέ μου,

"I wish you would bear with me in a little foolishness. Do bear with me!" ...
                                                                    RSV

Ὄφελον (interjection) 4123.
ἀνείχεσθε (2d.per.pl.imp.mid.ind.of ἀνέχομαι, voluntative) 1234.
μου (abl.sing.masc.of ἐγώ, source) 123.
μικρόν (acc.sing.neut.of μικρός, time extent, adverbial) 901.
τι (acc.sing.neut.of τις, indefinite pronoun, in agreement with μικρόν) 486.
ἀφροσύνης (gen.sing.fem.of ἀφροσύνη, objective genitive) 2305.
ἀλλὰ (confirmatory conjunction) 342.
καὶ (emphatic conjunction) 14.
ἀνέχεσθέ (2d.per.pl.pres.mid.ind.of ἀνέχομαι, present progressive, retroactive) 1234.
μου (gen.sing.masc.of ἐγώ, objective genitive) 123.

Translation - "I could wish that for a little while you would tolerate some foolishness from me. As a matter of fact you have been putting up with me."

Comment: Wishes about the present are obviously exercises in futility. ὄφελον with the imperfect is used for wishes about the present (Robertson, *Grammar*, 886). μου is an ablative of source. Paul is saying, "The nonesense you are about to hear is coming from me, but I want you to listen to it." ἀλλὰ is confirmatory nor adversative, while καὶ is emphatic. Paul is being ironic. Having wished that they would listen, he now observes that they are listening to him whether they wish it or not! He tells them why he wants them to indulge him in

Verse 2 - "For I am jealous over you with godly jealousy: for I have espoused you to one husband, that I may present you as a chaste virgin to Christ."

ζηλῶ γὰρ ὑμᾶς θεοῦ ζήλῳ, ἡρμοσάμην γὰρ ὑμᾶς ἑνὶ ἀνδρὶ παρθένον ἁγνὴν παραστῆναι τῷ Χριστῷ.

"I feel a divine jealousy for you, for I betrothed you to Christ to present you as a pure bride to her one husband." . . . RSV

ζηλῶ (1st.per.sing.pres.act.ind.of ζηλόω, aoristic) 3105.
γὰρ (causal conjunction) 105.
ὑμᾶς (acc.pl.masc.of σύ, object of ζηλῶ) 104.
θεοῦ (gen.sing.masc.of θεός, definition) 124.
ζήλῳ (instru.sing.masc.of ζῆλος, means) 1985.

#4370 ἡρμοσάμην (1st.per.sing.aor.mid.ind.of ἁρμάζομαι, culminative).

King James Version

espouse - 1 Cor.11:2.

Revised Standard Version

betroth - 2 Cor.11:2.

Meaning: Cf. ἁρμός (#4943). Hence, in Homer, any joining as carpenters do. To join two people in engagement vows. In the middle voice, to secure for oneself a favorable response to a marriage proposal. Metaphorically, of Paul's ministry by which the Corinthians became romantically involved as members of the Body of Christ - 2 Cor.11:2.

γὰρ (causal conjunction) 105.
ὑμᾶς (acc.pl.masc.of σύ, direct object of ἡρμοσάμην) 104.
ἑνὶ (instru.sing.masc.of εἷς, in agreement with ἀνδρὶ) 469.
ἀνδρὶ (instru.sing.masc.of ἀνήρ, association) 63.
παρθένον (acc.sing.masc.of παρθένος, direct object of παραστῆσαι) 120.
ἁγνὴν (acc.sing.fem.of ἁγνός, in agreeement with παρθένον) 4330.
παραστῆσαι (aor.act.inf.of παρίστημι, purpose) 1596.
τῷ (dat.sing.masc.of the article in agreement with Χριστῷ) 9.
Χριστῷ (dat.sing.masc.of Χριστός, indirect object of παραστῆσαι) 4.

Translation - "For I am jealous of you with a divine jealousy, because I have espoused you to one man, in order to present an unsullied virgin to Christ."

Comment: γὰρ is causal. Paul is about to open his heart to them because he is jealous. But it is not on account of his own personal relationship with the

Corinthians. His jealousy was for the Lord. It was his fear that the lack of amicable relations between him and his critics and those in the church whom they may have been influencing indicated their rejection of the gospel of Christ. They were in danger of being led astray by false teachers. Thus Paul wanted them to listen only to him and to others in his party whom he endorsed. He was the "one man" to whom they were "joined" so that he could teach them the truth in order that (παραστῆσαι) he might present them to Christ at the marriage supper of the Lamb (Rev.19:7; Mt.25:1-13) as a "chaste virgin", *i.e.* unsullied by false teaching and impure living.

Paul, whose preaching launched them upon the path of Christian theology felt an obligation to see them through to the end of their course of Christian service. In order to do this, he felt that they should listen only to him and to others who taught what he taught. Paul is not saying that he is the bridegroom in this analogy. He is rather the Bridegroom's agent, sent to secure the marriage contract and lead the virgin bride safely to the maggiage feast. The text does not say that the Corinthians were engaged to Christ. It says that Paul had joined (#4370) to himself so that he could bring them in virgin purity to the Bridegroom. Chapters 11 and 12 are devoted to proving that Paul is the "one man" to whom they are joined.

Verse 3 - "But I fear, lest by any means, as the serpent beguiled Eve through his subtilty, so your minds should be corrupted from the simplicity that is in Christ."

φοβοῦμαι δὲ μή πως, ὡς ὁ ὄφις ἐξηπάτησεν Εὔαν ἐν τῇ πανουργίᾳ αὐτοῦ, φθαρῇ τὰ νοήματα ὑμῶν ἀπὸ τῆς ἁπλότητος (καὶ τῆς ἁγνότητος) τῆς εἰς τὸν Χριστόν.

"But I am afraid that as the serpent deceived Eve by his cunning, your thoughts will be led astray from a sincere and pure devotion to Christ."... RSV

φοβοῦμαι (1st.per.sing.pres.mid.ind.of φοβέομαι, aoristic) 101.

δὲ (adversative conjunction) 11.

μὴ (negative conjunction with the subjunctive) 87.

πως (contingent particle) 3700.

ὡς (particle introducing a comparative clause) 128.

ὁ (nom.sing.masc.of the article in agreement with ὄφις) 9.

ὄφις (nom.sing.masc.of ὄφις, subject of ἐξηπάτησεν) 658.

ἐξηπάτησεν (3d.per.sing.aor.act.ind.of ἐξηπατάω, constative) 3922.

#4371 Εὔαν (acc.sing.fem.of Εὔα, direct object of ἐξηπάτησεν).

King James Version

Eve - 2 Cor.11:3; 2 Tim.2:13.

Revised Standard Version

Eve - 2 Cor.11:3; 1 Tim.2:13.

Meaning: Eve, the first woman - 2 Cor.11:3; 1 Tim.2:13.

ἐν (preposition with the instrumental of means) 80.
τῇ (instru.sing.fem.of the article in agreement with πανουργίᾳ) 9.
πανουργίᾳ (instru.sing.fem.of πανουργία, means) 2693.
αὐτοῦ (gen.sing.masc.of αὐτός, possession) 16.
φθαρῇ (3d.per.sing.2d.aor.pass.subj.of φθείρω, negative result) 4119.
τὰ (nom.pl.neut.of the article in agreement with νοήματα) 9.
νοήματα (nom.pl.neut.of νόημα, subject of φθαρῇ) 4277.
ὑμῶν (gen.pl.masc.of σύ, possession) 104.
ἀπὸ (preposition with the ablative of separation) 70.
τῆς (abl.sing.fem.of the article in agreement with ἁπλότητος) 9.
ἁπλότητος (abl.sing.fem.of ἁπλότης, separation) 4018.
καὶ (adjunctive conjunction joining nouns) 14.
τῆς (abl.sing.fem.of the article in agreement with ἁγνότητος) 9.
ἁγνότητος (abl.sing.fem.of ἁγνότης, separation) 4315.
τῆς (abl.sing.fem.of the article in agreement with ἁγνότητος) 9.
εἰς (preposition with the accusative, original static use) 140.
τὸν (acc.sing.masc.of the article in agreement with Χριστόν) 9.
Χριστόν (acc.sing.masc.of Χριστός, original static use, place where) 4.

Translation - "But I fear that, just as the serpent deceived Eve with his crafty intrigue your minds will be perverted from the sincere simplicity and the purity which is in Christ."

Comment: Paul now explains the grounds for his jealous concern of verse 2. He is afraid that false teachers will corrupt the Corinthian church. His fears militate against his hopes. μή πως (the same as μήποτε) with the aorist subjunctive in a negative result clause. *Cf.* 1 Cor.8:9; 2 Cor.12:20. Note the comparative clause ὡς . . . αὐτοῦ. The fear is that their minds will be perverted (corrupted, sullied) away from (ἀπὸ and the ablative) the simplicity (sincerity) (#4018) and purity (#4315) which is in Christ. Note how Paul further defines the nouns with the article and the prepositional phrase (τῆς εἰς τὸν Χριστόν).

Satan (John 8:44) has always been a deceiver. Paul recognizes that he is still busy (Rev.16:18; 1 Cor.3:18; 2 Thess.2:3). He will be especially busy at the end of the age, as he will realize that he has only a short time to press his fight against God. His method is the manipulation of everything within his power. Note the other uses of πανουργία (#2693) - always in an evil sense in the New Testament. The truth of the gospel of Christ is simple, sincere, non-devious and pure. One must be adroit to deny it.

The human intellect, under the manipulative guidance of Satan (2 Cor.4:4) can devise many devious theories to deny the gospel of Christ. Christian faith is simple - capable of being understood by little children (Mt.18:3), babes (Mt.11:25,26) and fools (1 Cor.3:18). We should beware of the evil, Christ rejecting intellectual who has taken too many philosophy courses! One of Satan's tricks is to plant the idea that πανουργία is really his tool - that if the prospect will look at the entire picture in the scenario he will be forced to reject

Christian truth. But πανουργία is not Satan's tool. He is not God and thus he is incapable of manipulating everything. He cannot provide a complete gestalt. Holism belongs only to God. Only He can put the entire universal puzzle together to reveal its marvelous coherence, consistency and correspondance to that which is real. Satan's deception lies in the fact that his victim falsely assumes that his milieu is the total situation - that every phase of the problem is in view. Hence situation ethics. The hellish ploy is that "Since everything is as I see it, the situation demands this attitude and action." But not everything is as we see it in any human situation. An understanding of all of the laws of God transcends our ability to fathom them, and yet they are readily applied.

Eve was led to believe that God had told her only a part of the story and that He did so in order to keep her in bondage. The devil's first approach was not openly to say that God had lied. Rather he implied that God had forbidden the woman to eat of any tree in the garden. The truth was that God had told her to eat of them all, except one. She was deceived (1 Tim.2:13). She fell into the trap and accused God of saying something that He did not say. He did not tell her that she might not "touch" the forbidden fruit - only that she might not eat it. Sinners are led astray by Satan not only when they refuse to believe what the Word of God says, but also when they accuse it of saying more than it has said. The Christian apologist is not called upon to defend God for saying that which He did not say. Having added to God's word, Eve was then in position to hear Satan boldly call God a liar - "Ye shall not surely die," after which he told her why God had said that she would. God did not want her to be like Him - knowing good and evil. The truth is that God not only wants man to know the difference between good and evil, but He wants man to choose the good and reject the evil. It is Satan's dupes today who tell us that there is no real difference between good and evil.

Satan's final assault upon Eve was his appeal to the "lust of the flesh, the lust of the eye and the pride of life" (1 John 2:15-17). The fruit of the tree was "good to eat" ("the lust of the flesh"), it was "pleasant to the eye" ("the lust of the eye") and it was "a tree to be desired to make one wise" ("the pride of life.")

Satan has never found it necessary to alter his approach to his victims. What worked in the Garden of Eden works very well still.

Since for the existentialist the entire pattern of reality is only that which is, in an empirical and sensory sense, he seems to be in control of everything and hence concludes to behave in keeping with his "sovereign" choice - only to discover too late that his immediate "everything" was only a small part of God's everything.

The false teachers whom Paul is attacking and against whom he is warning the Corinthians are described in more detail in

Verse 4 - "For if he that cometh preacheth another Jesus, whom we have not preached, or if ye receive another spirit, which ye have not received or another gospel, which ye have not accepted, ye might well bear with him."

εἰ μέν γὰρ ὁ ἐρχόμενος ἄλλον Ἰησοῦν κηρύσσει ὃν οὐκ ἐκηρύξαμεν, ἢ πνεῦμα ἕτερον λαμβάνετε ὃ οὐκ ἐλάβετε, ἢ εὐαγγέλιον ἕτερον ὃ οὐκ ἐδέξασθε, καλῶς ἀνέχεσθε.

*"For if some one comes and preaches another Jesus than the one we preached,
or if you receive a different spirit from the one you received, or if you accept a
different gospel from the one you accepted, you submit to it readily enough."*...
RSV

εἰ (conditional particle in a first-class condition) 337.

μὲν (particle of affirmation) 300.

γὰρ (causal conjunction) 105.

ὁ (nom.sing.masc.of the article in agreement with ἐρχόμενος) 9.

ἄλλον (acc.sing.masc.of ἄλλος, in agreement with Ἰησοῦν) 198.

Ἰησοῦν (acc.sing.masc.of Ἰησοῦς, direct object of κηρύσσει) 3.

κηρύσσει (3d.per.sing.pres.act.ind.of κηρύσσει, first -class condition) 249.

ὅν (acc.sing.masc.of ὅς, relative pronoun, direct object of ἐκηρύξαμεν) 65.

οὐκ (negative conjunction with the indicative) 130.

ἐκηρύξαμεν (1st.per.pl.aor.act.ind.of κηρύσσω, constative) 249.

ἤ (disjunctive) 465.

πνεῦμα (acc.sing.neut.of πνεῦμα, direct object of λαμβάνετε) 83.

ἕτερον (acc.sing.neut.of ἕτερος, in agreement with πνεῦμα) 605.

λαμβάνετε (2d.per.pl.pres.act.ind.of λαμβάνω, first-class condition) 533.

ὅ (acc.sing.neut.of ὅς, relative pronoun, direct object of ἐλάβετε) 65.

οὐκ (negative conjunction with the indicative) 130.

ἐλάβετε (2d.per.pl.aor.act.ind.of λαμβάνω, constative) 533.

ἤ (disjunctive) 465.

εὐαγγέλιον (acc.sing.neut.of εὐαγγέλιον, subject of δέχεσθε, understood)
405.

ἕτερον (acc.sing.neut.of ἕτερος, in agreement with εὐαγγέλιον) 605.

ὅ (acc.sing.neut.of ὅς, relative pronoun, direct object of ἐδέξασθε) 65.

οὐκ (negative conjunction with the indicative) 130.

ἐδέξασθε (2d.per.pl.aor.mid.ind.of δέχομαι, constative) 867.

καλῶς (adverbial) 977.

ἀνέχεσθε (2d.per.pl.pres.mid.ind.of ἀνέχομαι, present progressive
retroactive) 1234.

*Translation - "Because, as a matter of fact, if someone comes and preaches
another Jesus whom we did not preach, or you receive another spirit whom you
had not previously received or another gospel which you had not previously
accepted, you put up with it beautifully!"*

Comment: Here is the evidence that Paul's jealousy and fear was justified. He
cites past experience when the Corinthians had shown entirely too much tolerant
hospitality for false teachers. A preacher came and preached a substitute Jesus -
not the one whom Paul had previously presented. They received a different
spirit and a different gospel from those they had received originally. Thus they
now had a totally different religious philosophy - an inferior Jesus; a different
spirit and a different gospel story. Paul then adds sarcastically that on those
occasions they were entirely too tolerant of the fale teacher. They were flirting
dangerously with an illegitimate suitor after they had been betrothed to Christ.

Paul felt that there was no doubt about it. He put the accusation as a first-class condition with the assumption that the premise in the protasis was true. His task is to show that he is God's apostle and that the other teachers are false prophets.

Verse 5 - "For I suppose I was not a whit behind the very chiefest apostles."

λογίζομαι γὰρ μηδὲν ὑστερηκέναι τῶν ὑπερλίαν ἀποστόλων.

"I think that I am not in the least inferior to these superlative apostles." . . .
                                                                    RSV

λογίζομαι (1st.per.sing.pres.mid.ind.of λογίζομαι, aoristic) 2611.
γὰρ (explanatory conjunction) 105.
μηδὲν (acc.sing.neut.of μηδείς, extent) 713.
ὑστερηκέναι (perf.inf.of ὑστερέω, object infinitive of λογίζομαι) 1302.
τῶν (abl.pl.masc.of the article in agreement with ἀποστόλων) 9.

#4372 ὑπερλίαν (adverbial).

King James Version

very chiefest - 2 Cor.11:5; 12:11.

Revised Standard Version

superlative - 2 Cor.11:5; 12:11.

Meaning: A combination of ὑπέρ (#545) and λίαν (#214). Hence, exceeding the excessive; greater than the greatest; above   (ὑπέρ) the highest. In a sarcastic reference to the false teachers in Corinth - 2 Cor.11:5; 12:11.

ἀποστόλων (abl.pl.masc.of ἀπόστολος, comparison) 844.

Translation - "Now I believe that I am not to the slightest degree inferior to those superlative apostles!"

Comment: Here is Paul's sarcasm at its best. There was no false modesty about him because he knew that he had his commission from God, and he knew that his theology was from the divine Source (2 Cor.12:1-4).

In reference to false apostles he speaks with a sense of confirmed superiority. In reference to the other Apostles whom Jesus had chosen as He did Paul, he speaks with utmost modesty (1 Cor.15:9). He is the least of the true Apostles, but eminently superior to the self-appointed apostles.

Note that the infinitive ὑστερηκέναι, the object of λογίζομαι, is in the perfect tense. - "I have always been and now am not in the least subordinate to . . . " your highly touted Corinthian preachers.

Paul's intolerance with reference to false teachers dare not be construed as justification for our intolerance to other preachers who differ with us on peripheral theological points, but share with us an appreciation of the focal theology of the Christian faith. The false teachers in Corinth were destructive to the very foundation, hence to the superstructure of the Christian faith.

Verse 6 - "But though I be rude in speech, yet not in knowledge; but we have been throughly made manifest among you in all things."

εἰ δὲ καὶ ἰδιώτης τῷ λόγῳ, ἀλλ' οὐ τῇ γνώσει, ἀλλ' ἐν παντὶ φανερώσαντες ἐν πᾶσιν εἰς ὑμᾶς.

"Even if I am unskilled in speaking, I am not in knowledge; in every way we have made this plain to you in all things." . . . *RSV*

εἰ (conditional particle in a first-class condition) 337.
δὲ (adversative conjunction) 11.
καὶ (concessive conjunction) 14.
ἰδιώτης (nom.sing.masc.of ἰδιώτης, predicate adjective) 3032.
τῷ (loc.sing.masc.of the article in agreement with λόγῳ) 9.
λόγῳ (loc.sing.masc.of λόγος, sphere) 510.
ἀλλ' (adversative conjunction) 342.
οὐ (negative conjunction with the indicative) 130.
τῇ (loc.sing.fem.of the article in agreement with γνώσει) 9.
γνώσει (loc.sing.fem.of γνῶσις, sphere) 1856.
ἀλλ' (adversative conjunction) 342.
ἐν (preposition with the instrumental, means) 80.
παντὶ (instru.sing.neut.of πᾶς, means) 67.
φανερώσαντες (aor.act.part.nom.pl.masc.of φανερόω, adverbial) 1960.
ἐν (preposition with the locative with plural substantives) 80.
πᾶσιν (loc.pl.neut.of πᾶς, place) 67.
εἰς (preposition with the accusative, metaphorical extent) 140.
ὑμᾶς (acc.pl.masc.of σύ, metaphorical extent) 104.

Translation - "But although I am not a professional orator, yet I am not an amateur in knowledge, but I have always made that perfectly clear as I dealt with you."

Comment: "The Greeks regarded a man as ἰδιώτης who just attended to his own affairs (τὰ ἴδια) and took no part in public life. Paul admits that he is not a professional orator (*cf.*10:10), but denies that he is unskilled in knowledge (ἀλλ' οὐ τῇ γνώσει). . . " (Robertson, *Word Pictures in the New Testament*, IV, 258). Though Paul was not a professional orator he was a good public speaker as his experience on Mars Hill reveals (Acts 17). He chose to abandon oratory when he came to Corinth (1 Cor.2:1-5) and he told them why he chose to speak plainly because of the danger that the gospel, in terms of Greek classical sophistication, produces, not true saving faith, but a false and superficial faith which depends upon human wisdom. By choice he was not a strong orator in Corinth, but he never disclaimed superior knowledge. On the contrary *Cf.* Col.2:3; 1 Cor.2:6,20; 2 Cor.12:1-5; Eph.3:1-5.

He next suggests that perhaps he would have had more prestige in Corinth if he had come to the city and refused to speak until his agent had negotiated a contract with the local promoters which spelled out clearly the financial arrangements.

Verse 7 - "Have I committed an offence in abasing myself that ye might be exalted, because I have preached to you the gospel freely?"

Ἡ ἁμαρτίαν ἐποίησα ἐμαυτὸν ταπεινῶν ἵνα ὑμεῖς ὑφωθῆτε, ὅτι δωρεὰν τὸ τοῦ θεοῦ εὐαγγέλιον εὐηγγελισάμην ὑμῖν;

"Did I commit a sin in abasing myself so that you might be exalted, because I preached God's gospel without cost to you?" . . . RSV

Ἡ (for τὴν, acc.sing.fem.of the article in agreement with ἁμαρτίαν) 9.
ἁμαρτίαν (acc.sing.fem.of ἁμαρτία, direct object of ἐποίησα) 111.
ἐποίησα (1st.per.sing.aor.act.ind.of ποιέω, constative) 127.
ἐμαυτὸν (acc.sing.masc.of ἐμαυτός, direct object of ταπεινῶν) 723.
ταπεινῶν (pres.act.part.nom.sing.masc.of ταπεινόω, adverbial, modal) 1248.
ἵνα (conjunction with the subjunctive in a purpose clause) 114.
ὑμεῖς (nom.pl.masc.of σύ, subject of ὑφωθῆτε) 104.
ὑφωθῆτε (2d.per.pl.aor.pass.subj.of ὑφόω, purpose) 946.
ὅτι (conjunction introducing a subordinate causal clause) 211.
δωρεὰν (adverbial accusative) 858.
τὸ (acc.sing.neut.of the article in agreement with εὐαγγέλιον) 9.
τοῦ (gen.sing.masc.of the article in agreement with θεοῦ) 9.
θεοῦ (gen.sing.masc.of θεός, description) 124.
εὐαγγέλιον (acc.sing.neut.of εὐαγγέλιον, direct object of εὐηγγελλισάμην) 405.
εὐηγγελλισάμην (1st.per.sing.aor.mid.ind.of εὐαγγελίζομαι, constative) 909.
ὑμῖν (dat.pl.masc.of σύ, indirect object of εὐηγγελλισάμην) 104.

Translation - "Did I commit a sin by degrading myself in order that you might be uplifted, because I preached the gospel of God to you without an honorarium?"

Comment: The touch of sarcasm lingers. He could have asked, "Would you have more respect for me if I had come to Corinth and refused to preach without a financial guarantee?" Evidently the false teachers in Corinth had enhanced their prestige by charging for their services. Paul now suggests (!?) that perhaps he sinned in not doing so. Note that his debasement resulted in their exaltation.

He came to Corinth, preached on the streets, in the synagogues and in their homes. He made his home with fellow tent makers (Acts 18:2) and in the home of Justus (Acts 18:7). He made tents to pay his expenses. The Corinthians heard and were exalted. They found Christ and their permanent place in the Body of Christ. But they gave Paul nothing. Now apparently some were using these evidences of Paul's sincerity against him to show that he did not have sufficient prestige to demand money. They may have also suggested that, although Paul preached and accepted no money, he promoted the scheme to help the famine stricken saints in Judea and intended to embezzle the money.

It is well known on the modern lecture circuit that the speakers who demand the $10,000 per lecture fees, are in greatest demand. Conversely those who are willing to speak for nothing are in scant demand except by the Rotary Club.

Verse 8 - "*I robbed other churches, taking wages from them, to do you service.*"

ἄλλας ἐκκλησίας ἐσύλησα λαβὼν ὀφώνιον πρὸς τὴν ὑμῶν διακονίαν,

"*I robbed other churches by accepting support from them in order to serve you.*" . . . *RSV*

ἄλλας (acc.pl.fem.of ἄλλος, in agreement with ἐκκλησίας) 198.
ἐκκλησίας (acc.pl.fem.of ἐκκλησία, direct object of ἐσύλησα) 1204.

#4373 ἐσύλησα (1st.per.sing.aor.act.ind.of συλάω, constative).

King James Version

rob - 2 Cor.11:8.

Revised Standard Version

rob - 2 Cor.11:8.

Meaning: to rob; despoil. In exaggeration, with reference to Paul's accepting money from a church - 2 Cor.11:8.

λαβὼν (aor.act.part.nom.sing.masc.of λαμβάνω, adverbial, modal) 533.
ὀφώνιον (acc.sing.neut.of ὀφώνιον, direct object of λαβὼν) 1947.
πρὸς (preposition with the accusative, purpose) 197.
τὴν (acc.sing.fem.of the article in agreement with διακονίαν) 9.
ὑμῶν (gen.pl.masc.of σύ, description) 104.
διακονίαν (acc.sing.fem.of διακονία, purpose) 2442.

Translation - "*I robbed other churches by taking my living from them in order to work for you.*"

Comment: This is another emotional exaggeration. συλάω (#4373) is a strong word. It meant to rob a slain foe of his weapons on a battlefield. Paul received money gifts from other churches which he used to supplement his own earnings as a tent maker to pay his way in order that (purpose phrase in πρὸς with the accusative) he could preach to the Corinthians without charge. The other churches willingly gave him more than their share. But he did not rob them.
　He continues to boast about it in

Verse 9 - "*And when I was present with you and wanted, I was chargeable to no man: for that which was lacking to me, the brethren which came from Macedonia supplied: and in all things I have kept myself from being burdensome unto you, and so will I keep myself.*"

καὶ παρὼν πρὸς ὑμᾶς καὶ ὑστερηθεὶς οὐ κατενάρκησα οὐθενός. τὸ γὰρ ὑστέρημά μου προσανεπλήρωσαν οἱ ἀδελφοὶ ἐλθόντες ἀπὸ Μακεδονίας. καὶ ἐν παντὶ ἀβαρῆ ἐμαυτὸν ὑμῖν ἐτήρησα καὶ τηρήσω.

"*And when I was with you and was in want, I did not burden any one, for my needs were supplied by the brethren who came from Macedonia. So I refrained and will refrain from burdening you in any way."*

καὶ (continuative conjunction) 14.
παρὼν (pres.part.nom.sing.masc.of παρειμί, adverbial, temporal) 1592.
πρὸς (preposition with the accusative of extent) 197.
ὑμᾶς (acc.pl.masc.of σύ, extent) 104.
καὶ (adjunctive conjunction joining participles) 14.
ὑστερηθεὶς (aor.pass.part.nom.sing.masc.of ὑστερέρω, adverbial, temporal) 1302.
οὐ (negative conjunction with the indicative) 130.

#4374 κατενάρκησα (1st.per.sing.aor.act.ind.of καταναρκάω, ingressive).

　　King James Version

be burdensome to - 2 Cor.12:13,14.
be chargeable to - 2 Cor.11:9.

　　Revised Standard Version

be a burden - 2 Cor.11:9; 12:13,14.

Meaning: A combination of κατά (#98) and ναρκάω - "to grow stiff or numb," "to generate or bring about numbness or deadness," "to benumb." In the New Testament to become a financial burden to another. With reference to Paul and his financial relations with the Corinthians - 2 Cor.11:9; 12:13,14.

οὐθενός (gen.sing.masc.of οὐδείς, objective genitive) 446.
τὸ (acc.sing.neut.of the article in agreement with ὑστέρημά) 9.
γὰρ (causal conjunction) 105.
ὑστέρημά (acc.sing.neut.of ὑστέρμα, direct object of προσανεπλήρωσαν) 2767.
μου (gen.sing.masc.of ἐγώ, possession) 123.
προσανεπλήρωσαν (3d.per.pl.aor.act.ind.of προσαναπληρόω, constative) 4356.
οἱ (nom.pl.masc.of the article in agreement with ἀδελφοὶ) 9.
ἀδελφοὶ (nom.pl.masc.of ἀδελφός, subject of προσανεπλήρωσαν) 15.
ἐλθόντες (aor.part.nom.pl.masc.of ἔρχομαι, adverbial, temporal) 146.
ἀπὸ (preposition with the ablative of source) 70.
Μακεδονίας (abl.sing.fem.of Μακεδονία, source) 3360.
καὶ (continuative conjunction) 14.
ἐν (preposition with the locative of sphere, with substantives) 80.
παντὶ (loc.sing.neut.of πᾶς, sphere) 67.

#4375 ἀβαρῆ (acc.sing.masc.of ἀβαρής, predicate adjective).

　　King James Version

from being burdensome - 2 Cor.11:9.

Revised Standard Version

from burdening - 2 Cor.11:9.

Meaning: α privative plus βάρος (#1324). Hence, not burdensome. In a financial sense, with relation to Paul and the Corinthians - 2 Cor.11:9.

ἐμαυτὸν (acc.sing.masc.of ἐμαυτός, direct object of ἐτήρησα) 723.
ὑμῖν (dat.pl.masc.of σύ, personal interest) 104.
ἐτήρησα (1st.per.sing.aor.act.ind.of τηρέω, constative) 1297.
καὶ (adjunctive conjunction joining verbs) 14.
τηρήσω (1st.per.sing.fut.act.ind.of τηρέω, predictive) 1297.

Translation - "And when I was with you and ran into debt I did not become a burden to any one; when the brethren came from Macedonia they made up the deficit for me, and in every way I have kept and will continue to keep myself from being a burden to you."

Comment: παρὼν is a temporal participle in the present tense indicating simultaneous action with that of the main verb κατενάρκησα. Paul burdened none of the Corinthians with his financial problems. Note the double negative οὐ . . . οὐθενός, which in Greek strengthens the negative force. How was Paul able to be independent of help from the local brethren? His Christian friends from Macedonia came with gifts of money. He adds that just as in the past, so also in the future, he would be dependent upon none of the Corinthians for his physical needs. He adds that there is not a single exception to this rule.

Verse 10 - "As the truth of Christ is in me, no man shall stop me of this boasting in the regions of Achaia."

ἔστιν ἀλήθεια Χριστοῦ ἐν ἐμοὶ ὅτι ἡ καύχησις αὕτη οὐ φραγήσεται εἰς ἐμὲ ἐν τοῖς κλίμασιν τῆς Ἀχαΐας.

"As the truth of Christ is in me, this boast of mine shall not be silenced in the regions of Achaia." . . . RSV

ἔστιν (3d.per.sing.pres.ind.of εἰμί, aoristic) 86.
ἀλήθεια (nom.sing.fem.of ἀλήθεια, subject of ἔστιν) 1416.
Χριστοῦ (gen.sing.masc.of Χριστός, definition) 4.
ἐν (preposition with the locative of place) 80.
ἐμοὶ (loc.sing.masc.of ἐμός, place) 1267.
ὅτι (declarative conjunction) 211.
ἡ (nom.sing.fem.of the article in agreement with καύχησις) 9.
καύχησις (nom.sing.fem.of καύχησις, subject of φραγήσεται) 3877.
αὕτη (nom.sing.fem.of οὗτος, in agreement with καύχησις) 93.
οὐ (negative conjunction with the indicative) 130.
φραγήσεται (3d.per.sing.2d.fur.pass.ind.of φράσσω, predictive) 3870.

εἰς (preposition with the accusative, static use) 140.

ἐμὲ (acc.sing.masc.of ἐμός, static use) 1267.

ἐν (preposition with the locative of place) 80.

τοῖς (loc.pl.neut.of the article in agreement with κλίμασιν) 9.

κλίμασιν (loc.pl.neut.of κλίμα, place) 4055.

τῆς (gen.sing.fem.of the article in agreement with Ἀχαΐας) 9.

Ἀχαΐας (gen.sing.fem.of Ἀχαΐα, description) 3443.

Translation - "I swear by the truth of Christ in me that this boast shall never be silenced in me throughout the regions of Greece."

Comment: ὅτι in the declaration of an oath is also found in Gal.1:20; 2 Cor.1:18,23; Rev.10:6; Rom.14:11. Paul was certain that no one in Grecian territory could be found who could shut his mouth (γραγήσεται #3870) in this boast which he made in verse 9. His policy in regard to money would always be applied in Greece as it had been in the past.

And yet he did not want the Corinthians to think that he adopted this policy because he did not love them.

Verse 11 - "Wherefore? Because I love you not? God knoweth."

διὰ τί; ὅτι οὐκ ἀγαπῶ ὑμᾶς; ὁ θεὸς οἶδεν.

"And why? Because I do not love you? God knows I do!" . . . RSV

διὰ (preposition with the accusative, cause, in direct question) 118.

τί (acc.sing.neut.of τίς, interrogative pronoun, cause, in direct question) 281.

ὅτι (causal conjunction) 211.

οὐκ (negative conjunction with the indicative) 130.

ἀγαπῶ (1st.per.sing.pres.act.ind.of ἀγαπάω, aoristic) 540.

ὑμᾶς (acc.pl.masc.of σύ, direct object of ἀγαπῶ) 104.

ὁ (nom.sing.masc.of the article in agreement with θεὸς) 9.

θεὸς (nom.sing.masc.of θεός, subject of οἶδεν) 124.

οἶδεν (3d.per.sing.perf.ind.of ὁράω, intensive) 144b.

Translation - "Why? Because I do not love you? God knows."

Comment: Cf.#'s 118 and 281 for διὰ τί in a causal idiom. The ὅτι causal clause is a question. Was it because Paul did not love the Corinthians that he insisted on taking no money from them? If so, what should be said about the other churches from whom he did take money? Paul gives no answer to the riddle. He only says that God knows. God knows what? That he does or does not love the Corintians? The text is silent. Moffatt, Goodspeed, Montgomery, Weymouth and the RSV translate, "God knows that I do." They are probably correct but the text does not say so here. However Paul says in other places that he loves the Corinthians. He gives another reason for his policy in

Verse 12 - "But what I do that will I do, that I may cut off occasion from them which desire occasion; that wherein they glory, they may be found even as we."

Ὁ δὲ ποιῶ καὶ ποιήσω, ἵνα ἐκκόψω τὴν ἀφορμὴν τῶν θελόντων ἀφορμήν, ἵνα ἐν ᾧ καυχῶνται εὑρεθῶσιν καθὼς καὶ ἡμεῖς.

"*And what I do I will continue to do, in order to undermine the claim of those who would like to claim that in their boasted mission they work on the same terms as we do.*" . . . *RSV*

Ὁ (acc.sing.neut.of ὅς, relative pronoun, direct object of ποιῶ and ποιήσω) 65.

δὲ (adversative conjunction) 11.

ποιῶ (1st.per.sing.pres.act.ind.of ποιέω, present progressive retroactive) 127.

καὶ (adjunctive conjunction joining verbs) 14.

ποιήσω (1st.per.sing.fut.act.ind.of ποιέω, predictive) 127.

ἵνα (conjunction with the subjunctive in a purpose clause) 114.

ἐκκόψω (1st.per.sing.aor.act.subj.of ἐκκόπτω, purpose) 297.

τὴν (acc.sing.fem.of the article in agreement with ἀφορμήν) 9.

ἀφορμὴν (acc.sing.fem.of ἀφορμή, direct object of ἐκκόψω) 3921.

τῶν (abl.pl.masc.of the article in agreement with θελόντων) 9.

θελόντων (pres.act.part.abl.pl.masc.of θέλω, substantival, separation) 88.

ἀφορμήν (acc.sing.fem.of ἀφορμή, direct object of θελόντων) 3921.

ἵνα (conjunction with the subjunctive in a purpose clause) 114.

ἐν (preposition with the locative, occasion) 80.

ᾧ (loc.sing.neut.of ὅς, relative pronoun, occasion) 65.

καυχῶνται (3d.per.pl.pres.ind.of καυχάομαι, aoristic) 3847.

εὑρεθῶσιν (3d.per.pl.1st.aor.pass.subj.of εὑρίσκω, purpose) 79.

καθὼς (compound comparative particle) 1348.

καὶ (adjunctive conjunction joining pronouns) 14.

ἡμεῖς (nom.pl.masc.of ἐγώ, subject of εἰσίν understood) 123.

Translation - "*But I will continue to do that which I have done in the past and am now doing, in order that I may destroy the argument of those who are looking for evidence, so that when they boast they may be found to work on the same terms as I do.*"

Comment: The false teachers in Corinth who were perverting the theology of the saints, were arguing that they worked in the gospel ministry on the same grounds, and with the same authority as did Paul. Paul now says that if they wish to make such a claim, let them also adopt his financial policy. Thus he will continue the same policy which he now has and has had in the past (present progressive retroactive in ποιῶ). There will be no future financial rewards for preaching in Corinth. His purpose was that by so doing he was taking away from the false teachers, who desired evidence that they were also apostles who worked (καθὼς καὶ ἡμεῖς) as Paul did, the evidence that they desired. "If they are preaching with a commission from the Lord, as I am, and, if their methods are like mine, as they say, then let them follow my example with regard to money."

Paul felt certain that his strategy would succeed since no false prophet is willing to preach without remuneration.

Verse 13 - "For such are false apostles, deceitful workers, transforming themselves into the apostles of Christ."

οἱ γὰρ τοιοῦτοι ψευδαπόστολοι, ἐργάται δόλιοι, μετασχηματιζόμενοι εἰς ἀποστόλους Χριστοῦ.

"For such men are false apostles, deceitful workers, disguising themselves as apostles of Christ." . . . RSV

οἱ (nom.pl.masc.of the article in agreement with τοιοῦτοι) 9.

γὰρ (causal conjunction) 105.

τοιοῦτοι (nom.pl.masc.of τοιοῦτος, subject of εἰσίν understood) 785.

#4376 ψευδαπόστολοι (nom.pl.masc.of ψευδαπόστολος, predicate nominative).

King James Version

false apostle - 2 Cor.11:13.

Revised Standard Version

false apostle - 2 Cor.11:13.

Meaning: A combination of ψεύδομαι (#439) and ἀπόστολοι (#849). Hence, a false apostle. A preacher who laid claim to commissions, as having been sent to preach, though the claims were false. - 2 Cor.11:13. *Cf.* also #'s 3096, 1499, ψευδοδιδάσκαλος (#5243), ψευδολόγος (#4745), 1602, 1299, 1169, 670, ψευδώνυμος (#4800), 2388, 3856, 2389.

ἐργάται (nom.pl.masc.of ἐργάτης, predicate nominative) 840.

#4377 δόλιοι (nom.pl.masc.of δόλιος, in agreement with ἐργάται).

King James Version

deceitful - 1 Cor.11:13.

Revised Standard Version

deceitful - 2 Cor.11:13.

Meaning: Cf. δολιόω (#3863), δολόω (#4296). Hence, deceitful. From δέλω - "to catch with a bait." With reference to the false preachers in Corinth - 2 Cor.11:13.

μετασχηματιζόμενοι (pres.mid.part.nom.pl.masc.of μετασχηματίζω, substantival, apposition) 4121.

εἰς (preposition with the predicate accusative) 140.

ἀποστόλους (acc.pl.masc.of ἀπόστολος, predicate accusative) 844.

Χριστοῦ (abl.sing.masc.of Χριστός, source) 4.

Translation - "Because such people are false apostles, deceitful workers who disguise themselves as apostles from Christ."

Comment: Note the copula ellided after τοιοῦτοι. ἐργάται δόλιοι - "confidence men." They were masquerading as apostles with a commission from the Messiah. Paul is unmasking them. He is saying the same thing about these hypocrites that the Marxians say about all preachers. Take away their financial gain. Challenge them to preach for no pay and pay their own expenses in the bargain by their own toil and see how long they preach! The difference is that there are many true God-called preachers who would pass this acid test as Paul did. Indeed there are some who are passing this test every day.

This masquerade is an old trick of Satan who has perfected it with much success as we learn in

Verse 14 - "And no marvel; for Satan himself is transformed into an angel of light."

καὶ οὐ θαῦμα, αὐτὸς γὰρ ὁ Σατανᾶς μετασχηματίζεται εἰς ἄγγελον φωτός.

"And no wonder, for even Satan disguises himself as an angel of light." . . .
RSV

καὶ (emphatic conjunction) 14.
οὐ (negative conjunction with the indicative) 130.

#4378 θαῦμα (nom.sing.neut.of θαῦμα, predicate nominative).

    King James Version

marvel - 2 Cor.11:14.
admiration - Rev.17:6.

    Revised Standard Version

wonder - 2 Cor.11:14.
marvel - Rev.17:6.

Meaning: Cf. θαυμάσιος (#1360), θαυμαστός (#1391), θαυμάζω (#726). A wonderful thing; something unusual; awe inspiring - in litotes - 2 Cor.11:14; the psychological reaction to θαῦμα - Rev.17:6.

αὐτὸς (nom.sing.masc.of αὐτός, intensive, in agreement with Σατανᾶς) 16.
γὰρ (causal conjunction) 105.
ὁ (nom.sing.masc.of the article in agreement with Σατανᾶς) 9.
Σατανᾶς (nom.sing.masc.of Σατανᾶς, subject of μετασχηματίζεται) 365.
μετασχηματίζεται (3d.per.sing.pres.mid.ind.of μετασχηματίζω, aoristic) 4120.
εἰς (preposition with the predicate accusative) 140.
ἄγγελον (acc.sing.masc.of ἄγγελος, predicate accusative) 96.
φωτός (gen.sing.neut.of φῶς, description) 379.

Translation - "Indeed it is no wonder; because Satan himself is masquerading as an angel of light."

Comment: καὶ is emphatic. Satan's *modus operandi* is one of masquerade. He has always played the role of the enlightenment. This was his approach to Eve in the Garden of Eden (Gen.3:1-7). *Cf.* all references to spiritual darkness under #'s 378 and 602 for Satan's true role in the kingdom of darkness. Only by disguising himself (μετασχηματιζόμενοι #4120) can he appear to be a light bearer. As father is, so also the progeny (John 8:44). Satan's preachers also disguise themselves to deceive the unwary.

In the 18th century the revolt against the Reformed Theology of the Reformation, in terms of the Physiocracy of Francois Quesnay, the empiricism of John Locke, David Hume and George Berkeley, the moral philosophy of Adam Smith in England and the Encyclopedists of the French Revolution, all of which anticipated the evolution of Charles Darwin, has been called the Age of Reason in England, the *Aufklarung* in Germany and the *siecle d' lumiere* in France. "Woe unto them that call evil good; that put darkness for light, and light for darkness. . . " (Isaiah 5:20). When Satan, the "prince of the power of the air" (Eph.2:2) whom Martin Luther "the prince of darkness" (*A Mighty Fortress is our God*) wishes to be most effective he poses as a preacher of the gospel.

Verse 15 - "Therefore it is no great thing if his ministers also be transformed as the ministers of righteousness; whose end shall be according to their works."

οὐ μέγα οὖν εἰ καὶ οἱ διάκονοι αὐτοῦ μετασχηματίζονται ὡς διάκονοι δικαιοσύνης, ὧν τὸ τέλος ἔσται κατὰ τὰ ἔργα αὐτῶν.

"So it is not strange if his servants also disguise themselves as servants of righteousness. Their end will correspond to their deeds." . . . RSV

οὐ (negative conjunction with the indicative) 130.
μέγα (nom.sing.neut.of μέγας, predicate nominative) 184.
οὖν (inferential conjunction) 68.
εἰ (conditional particle in a first-class condition) 337.
καὶ (adjunctive conjunction joining nouns) 14.
οἱ (nom.pl.masc.of the article in agreement with διάκονοι) 9.
διάκονοι (nom.pl.masc.of διάκονος, subject of μετασχηματίζονται) 1334.
αὐτοῦ (gen.sing.masc.of αὐτός, relationship) 16.
μετασχηματίζονται (3d.per.pl.pres.mid.ind.of μετασχηματίζω, first-class condition) 4121.
ὡς (comparative particle) 128.
διάκονοι (nom.pl.masc.of διάκονος, predicate nominative) 1334.
δικαιοσύνης (gen.sing.fem.of δικαιοσύνη, description) 322.
ὧν (gen.pl.masc.of ὅς, relative pronoun, possession) 65.
τὸ (nom.sing.neut.of the article in agreement with τέλος) 9.
τέλος (nom.sing.neut.of τέλος, subject of ἔσται) 881.
ἔσται (3d.per.sing.fut.ind.of εἰμί, predictive) 86.
κατὰ (preposition with the accusative, standard) 98.
τὰ (acc.pl.neut.of the article in agreement with ἔργα) 9.

ἔργα (acc.pl.neut.of ἔργον, standard) 460.
αὐτῶν (gen.pl.masc.of αὐτός, possession) 16.

Translation - *"So it is not unusual that his servants also are masquerading as though they were ministers of righteousness, the destiny of whom will be in keeping with their deeds."*

Comment: οὖν is inferential. The truth of verse 15 follows from that of verse 14. οὐ μέγα - "no big deal" as we say in modern parlance. It should not surprize us. As a matter of fact Satan's *modus operandi* is implemented in his servants (John 8:44).

Qualis pater talis filius

"Such a father, such a son."
William Camden, Remains Concerning Britain, 1605.

"Diogenes struck the father when the son swore."
Robert Burton, *The Anatomy of Melancholy*, III, 1621.

Shakespeare has Sandys say to Anne Bullen

"If I chance to talk a little wild, forgive me; I had it from my father."

Anne asks,

"Was he mad, sir?"

To which Sandys replies,

"O, very mad, exceeding mad . . . "
King Henry VIII, iv, 31-34

εἰ and the indicative μετασχηματίζονται is a first-class condition. "Since Satan's deacons are masquerading" this fact is οὐ μέγα - "nothing strange." The false preachers always behave as though they were architects of righteousness. Modernists in the 20th century are prophets of social, political and economic justice. There is nothing wrong with that. The social gospel preaches righteousness, and Fundamentalists would be better advised to learn something about the Social Sciences so that they also might preach the social gospel. The poison in the Modernist approach is found in their mistaken notion about the source of this practical righteousness in society. Christ is the Source of the behavior that fulfills His law (Mt.5:17), and there is total social gospel righteousness in His law, handed down to Moses and expounded in full in Deuteronomy and in the Sermon on the Mount (Matthew 5-7). This righteousness is worked out through His redemption on the cross and victory over the grave, and through personal regeneration in individual lives of those who have been saved by His grace through faith. Calvinists (and others of trinitarian/redemptionist views) preach the social gospel also, but as a *fruit* of salvation, not as the *root*. Total social righteousness must await the Kingdom

Age when the Messiah, on the throne of His father David (Luke 1:32; 2 Sam.7:12,13) will reign over His kingdom in which "the earth shall be full of the knowledge of the Lord, as the waters cover the sea" (Isaiah 11:9). But this age of universal obedience to the will of God will be made possible, not by sociological osmosis and cultural evolution, but by the supernatural regeneration and glorification of the elect of God and the personal return of the King.

Christians should seek the fullness of the Holy Spirit so that their lives will manifest the righteousness of Christ in society at large, but it is naive and unscriptural to believe that the church in this age will establish righteousness. There can be no kingdom with the King. The social reformer in the pulpit who has rejected Calvinism, with its emphasis on the completion of the Body of Christ, through evangelism, is the one whom Paul describes. Such a speaker is a dangerous demagogue because he is very much in favor of what he calls "righteousness" but he means the righteousness which society can evolve without the help of "the Sun of righteousness (who will) arise with healing in his wings." (Malachi 4:2). The untaught public, who knows little about the Biblical interpretation of history will find it difficult to fault one who appears to be a preacher of righteousness. But his father is Satan, his method is Satan's method and his destiny, like that of his father will be κατὰ τὰ ἔργα αὐτοῦ. Cf. Mk.3:26; Rom.6:21; Phil.3:19.

Paul's Sufferings as an Apostle

(2 Corinthians 11:16-33)

Verse 16 - "I say again, Let no man think me a fool; if otherwise, yet, as a fool receive me, that I may boast myself a little."

Πάλιν λέγω, μή τίς με δόξη ἄφρονα εἶναι. εἰ δὲ μήγε, κἄν ὡς ἄφρονα δέξασθέ με, ἵνα κἀγὼ μικρόν τι καυχήσωμαι.

"I repeat, let no one think me foolish; but even if you do, accept me as a fool, so that I too may boast a little." . . . RSV

Πάλιν (adverbial) 355.

λέγω (1st.per.sing.pres.act.ind.of λέγω, aoristic) 66.

μή (negative conjunction with the subjunctive in a prohibition) 87.

τίς (nom.sing.masc.of τις, indefinite pronoun, subject of δόξη) 486.

με (acc.sing.masc.of ἐγώ, general reference) 123.

δόξη (3d.per.sing.aor.act.subj.of δοκέω, prohibition) 287.

ἄφρονα (acc.sing.masc.of ἄφρων, predicate accusative) 2462.

εἶναι (pres.inf.of εἰμί, object of δόξη) 86.

εἰ (conditional particle in an elliptical first-class condition) 337.

δὲ (adversative conjunction) 11.

μήγε (conditional negative compound) 557.

κἄν (conditional particle) 1370.

ὡς (comparative particle) 128.

ἄφρονα (acc.sing.masc.of ἄφρων, predicate adjective) 2462.

δέξασθέ (2d.per.pl.aor.mid.impv.of δέχομαι, entreaty) 867.

με (acc.sing.masc.of ἐγώ, direct object of δέξασθέ) 123.

ἵνα (conjunction with the subjunctive, purpose) 114.

κἀγώ (adjunctive conjunction and first personal pronoun, crasis) 178.

μικρόν (acc.sing.neut.of μικρός, in agreement with τι) 901.

τι (acc.sing.neut.of τις, indefinite pronoun, extent) 486.

καυχήσωμαι (1st.per.sing.aor.mid.subj.of καυχάομαι, purpose) 3847.

Translation - "I say again, let no man entertain the thought that I am a fool, but if anyone does, receive me, if only as a fool, in order that I also may boast about myself a little."

Comment: The aorist subjunctive in the prohibition μή τίς με δόξῃ ἄφρονα εἶναι, of course forbids a future action and is therefore ingressive. Hence the translation or "Let no man begin to think that I am a fool." A prohibition of an action already taking place is expressed by the present imperative.

No one in Corinth thought Paul was a fool. He had said this before in 2 Cor.11:1. εἶνα is the object infinitive of δόξῃ. εἰ δὲ μήγε - "but if you do" followed by the crasis form κἄν (καί #14 and ἄν #205), means "if only as a fool receive me." Why should they? In order (ἵνα . . . καυχήσωμαι, purpose) that I, like the others (adjunctive καί in κἀγώ) may boast a little about myself. *Cf.* μικρόν τι also in 2 Cor.11:1.

Paul had previously challenged his enemies to follow his example and preach without pay - a challenge that he did not expect them to accept. Now, though he feels like a fool in doing so, he is going to follow their example, and boast about himself as they were so fond of doing. But he felt it necessry, first of all, to apologize to the Corinthians for what follows, *viz.* an eloquent and dramatic list of achievements designed to show that Paul was in a class by himself, vastly superior to his critics and competitors.

In verse 17 he carefully disclaims divine inspiration for what he is about to say. It should be apparent that when a man talks like a fool, Almighty God should not be held responsible.

Verse 17 - "That which I speak, I speak it not after the Lord, but as it were foolishly, in this confidence of boasting."

ὃ λαλῶ οὐ κατὰ κύριον λαλῶ, ἀλλ' ὡς ἐν ἀφροσύνῃ ἐν ταύτῃ τῇ ὑποστάσει τῆς καυχήσεως.

("What I am saying I say not with the Lord's authority but as a fool, in this boastful confidence;" . . . RSV

ὃ (acc.sing.neut.of ὅς relative pronoun, direct object of λαλῶ) 65.

λαλῶ (1st.per.sing.pres.act.ind.of λαλέω, futuristic) 815.

οὐ (negative conjunction with the indicative) 130.

κατὰ (preposition with the accusative, standard) 98.

κύριον (acc.sing.masc.of κύριος, standard) 97.

λαλῶ (1st.per.sing.pres.act.ind.of λαλέω futuristic) 815.

ἀλλ' (adversative conjunction) 342.

ὡς (comparative particle) 128.

ἐν (preposition with the instrumental of manner) 80.

ἀφροσύν (instru.sing.fem.of ἀφροσύνη, manner) 2305.

ἐν (preposition with the locative of sphere) 80.

ταύτῃ (loc.sing.fem.of οὗτος, in agreement with ὑποστάσει) 93.

τῇ (loc.sing.fem.of the article in agreement with ὑποστάσει) 9.

ὑποστάσει (loc.sing.fem.of ὑπόστασις, sphere) 4346.

τῆς (gen.sing.fem.of the article in agreement with καυχήσεως) 9.

καυχήσεως (gen.sing.fem.of καύχησις, description) 3877.

Translation - "I am not going to say what I am about to say at the direction of the Lord, but in foolishness (when I speak of) this evidence of my boasting.

Comment: That Paul should disclaim divine inspiration on occasion implies at least that at other times, when there is no disclaimer, he does indeed speak at the direction of the Holy Spirit (2 Tim.3:16,17). Paul does not wish the Lord to be held accountable for the foolish manner in which he is about to present the evidence (ὑπόστασις #4346) that he is superior to his critics in Corinth. He feels that the evidence cannot be gainsaid. But he wishes his readers to understand that in this recital of his accomplishments and experiences, he is taking full responsibility. He is stepping outside the sphere of divine inspiration. He did this also in 1 Cor.7:6,12. Paul feels it necessary to allow the record to be revealed.

Others have. Why not he?

Verse 18 - "Seeing that many glory after the flesh, I will glory also."

ἐπεὶ πολλοὶ καυχῶνται κατὰ σάρκα, κἀγὼ καυχήσομαι.

". . . since many boast of worldly things, I too will boast.)" . . . RSV

ἐπεὶ (subordinating conjunction introducing a causal clause) 1281.

πολλοὶ (nom.pl.masc.of πολύς, subject of καυχῶνται) 228.

καυχῶνται (3d.per.pl.pres.mid.ind.of καυχάομαι, present progressive iterative) 3847.

κατὰ (preposition with the accusative, standard) 98.

σάρκα (acc.sing.fem.of σάρξ, standard) 1202.

κἀγὼ (adjunctive conjunction and first personal pronoun, crasis) 178.

καυχήσομαι (1st.per.sing.fut.mid.ind.of καυχάομαι, predictive) 3847.

Translation - "In view of the fact that many boast from time to time with fleshly egotism, I also will boast."

Comment: κατὰ σάρκα here is in contrast to κατὰ πνεῦμα ἅγιον. The false apostles who boasted frequently (iterative present tense) of their superiority as qualified preachers were certainly not being motivated by the Spirit of God.

It was sinful human pride, pure and simple. Paul is speaking like a lawyer. The opposition had "opened the door" by listing their assets. This permitted Paul to do the same. He did not say that this approach was ethical or dignified. He only said that it was logical.

Verse 19 - "For ye suffer fools gladly, seeing ye yourselves are wise."

ἡδέως γὰρ ἀνέχεσθε τῶν ἀφρόνων φρόνιμοι ὄντες.

"For you gladly bear with fools, being wise yourselves!" . . . RSV

ἡδέως (adverbial) 2255.
γὰρ (causal conjunction) 105.
ἀνέχεσθε (2d.per.pl.pres.ind.of ἀνέχομαι, present progressive iterative) 1234.
τῶν (gen.pl.masc.of the article in agreement with ἀφρόνων) 9.
ἀφρόνων (gen.pl.masc.of ἄφρων, objective genitive) 2462.
φρόνιμοι (nom.pl.masc.of φρόνιμος, predicate adjective) 693.
ὄντες (pres.part.nom.pl.masc.of εἰμί, adverbial, causal) 86.

Translation - "Because you put up with fools gladly, since you are wise!"

Comment: ὄντες is causal, as Paul dips his pen deeply in sarcasm. It takes a fool to enjoy what another fool is saying. Paul is saying that if they were really wise, they would not be enamoured of the teachings of the false apostles. He seems also to say, "Since you superior Corinthians are so happy to hear a fool boast, I will afford you the added pleasure of listening to me as I boast like a fool." The adverb ἡδέως is irony, like καλῶς in 2 Cor.11:4 and Mark 7:9.

Paul continues his sarcasm in

Verse 20 - "For you suffer, if a man bring you into bondage, if a man devour you, if a man take of you, if a man exalt himself, if a man smite you on the face."

ἀνέχεσθε γὰρ εἴ τις ὑμᾶς καταδουλοῖ, εἴ τις κατεσθίει, εἴ τις λαμβάνει, εἴ τις ἐπαίρεται, εἴ τις εἰς πρόσωπον ὑμᾶς δέρει.

"For you bear it if a man makes slaves of you, or preys upon you, or takes advantage of you, or puts on airs, or strikes you in the face." . . . RSV

ἀνέχεσθε (2d.per.pl.pres.mid.ind.of ἀνέχομαι, customary) 1234.
γὰρ (causal conjunction) 105.
εἴ (conditional particle in a first-class condition) 337.
τις (nom.sing.masc.of τις, indefinite pronoun, subject of καταδουλοῖ) 486.
ὑμᾶς (acc.pl.masc.of σύ, direct object of καταδουλοῖ) 104.

#4379 καταδουλοῖ (3d.per.sing.pres.act.ind.of καταδουλόω, first-class condition).

    King James Version

    bring into bondage - 2 Cor.11:20; Gal.2:4.

Revised Standard Version

make slaves of you - 2 Cor.11:20.
bring into bondage - Gal.2:4.

Meaning: A combination of κατά (#98) and δουλόω (#3103). To bring down into slavery; to reduce one to the status of a slave; to enslave. With reference to the intellectual, institutional and financial slavery imposed upon the Corinthians by false apostles - 2 Cor.11:20; upon the Galatians - Gal.2:4.

εἴ (conditional particle in a first-class condition) 337.

τις (nom.sing.masc.of τις, indefinite pronoun, subject of κατεσθίει) 486.

κατεσθίει (3d.per.sing.pres.act.ind.of κατεσθίω, first-class condition) 1028.

εἴ (conditional particle in a first-class condition) 337.

τις (nom.sing.masc.of τις, indefinite pronoun, subject of λαμβάνει) 486.

λαμβάνει (3d.per.sing.pres.act.ind.of λαμβάνω, first-class condition) 533.

εἴ (conditional particle in a first-class condition) 337.

τις (nom.sing.masc.of τις, indefinite pronoun, subject of ἐπαίρεται) 486.

ἐπίρεται (3d.per.sing.pres.mid.ind.of ἐπαιρέω, first-class condition) 1227.

εἴ (conditional particle in a first-class condition) 337.

τις (nom.sing.masc.of τις, indefinite pronoun, subject of δέρει) 486.

εἰς (preposition with the adverbial accusative) 140.

πρόσωπον (acc.sing.neut.of πρόσωπον, adverbial accusative) 588.

ὑμᾶς (acc.pl.masc.of σύ, direct object of δέρει) 104.

δέρει (3d.per.sing.pres.act.ind.of δέρω, first-class condition) 1383.

Translation - "Because if anyone enslaves you, if anyone devours you, if anyone exploits you, if anyone lords it over you, if anyone slaps you in the face, you tolerate it."

Comment: We have a first-class condition with the apodosis coming ahead of five protases. The false teachers were being tyranical, they were impoverishing the Corinthians; they were exploiting them; they were being arrogant and insulting.

Plummer translates, "You tolerate tyranny, extortion, craftiness, arrogance, violence and insult." (as cited in Robertson, *Word Pictures in the New Testament*, IV, 260). Thus Paul's sarcasm continues. It is as if he is saying, "How do you like the treatment you are getting from the false teachers? Have you had enough? Apparently you enjoy being enslaved, impoverished, exploited, insulted and even slapped in the face." The last clause is probably exaggeration, as Paul tries to awaken the Corinthians to the situation under which they were suffering. Note the impetuosity of Paul's emotion as he repeats εἴ. *Cf.* 1 Tim.5:10.

Verse 21 - "I speak as concerning reproach, as though we had been weak. Howbeit whereinsoever any is bold (I speak foolishly) I am bold also."

κατὰ ἀτιμίαν λέγω, ὡς ὅτι ἡμεῖς ἠσθενήκαμεν. ἐν ᾧ δ' ἄν τις τολμᾷ, ἐν ἀφροσύνῃ λέγω, τολμῶ κἀγώ.

"To my shame, I must say, we were too weak for that! But whatever any one dares to boast of — I am speaking as a fool — I also dare to boast of that." ...

κατά (preposition with the accusative, periphrasis for the genitive of reference) 98.

ἀτιμίαν (acc.sing.fem.of ἀτιμία, reference) 3808.

λέγω (1st.per.sing.pres.act.ind.of λέγω, aoristic) 66.

ὡς (concessive particle) 128.

ὅτι (concessive conjunction) 211.

ἡμεῖς (nom.pl.masc.of ἐγώ, subject of ἠσθενήκαμεν) 123.

ἠσθενήκαμεν (1st.per.pl.perf.act.ind.of ἀσθενέω, consummative) 857.

ἐν (preposition with the locative of sphere) 80.

ᾧ (loc.sing.neut.of ὅς, relative pronoun, sphere) 65.

δ' (adversative conjunction) 11.

ἄν (contingent particle) 205.

τις (nom.sing.masc.of τις, indefinite pronoun, subject of τολμᾷ) 486.

τολμᾷ (3d.per.sing.pres.act.subj.of τολμάω, third-class condition) 1430.

ἐν (preposition with the instrumental of manner) 80.

ἀφροσύνῃ (instru.sing.fem.of ἀφροσύνη, manner) 2305.

λέγω (1st.per.sing.pres.act.ind.of λέγω, futuristic) 66.

τολμῶ (1st.per.sing.pres.act.ind.of τολμάω, futuristic) 1430.

κἀγώ (adjunctive conjunction and first personal pronoun, crasis) 178.

Translation - *"I am embarrassed to say that I have been timid, but if any one is going to be bold — I am going to speak like a fool - I am going to be bold also."*

Comment: κατά ἀτιμίαν is a periphrasis for the genitive of reference. *Cf.* 2 Cor.5:19; 11:21; 2 Thess.2:2 for ὡς ὅτι for "that" - which either ὡς or ὅτι carries alone. It is unclassical, but it appears in the κοινή. "It is like the Latin *quasi* in the Vulgate." (Robertson, *Grammar*, 1033). It introduces indirect discourse.

In his previous visits to Corinth Paul had been timid (1 Cor.2:1-5), but that was a matter of deliberate policy, in reaction to his failure on Mars Hill (Acts 17-18). Apparently the Corinthians reacted more favourably to the flamboyant braggadocia of Paul's critics than to his humble self-effacement. But the Holy Spirit reacted favourably to Paul's style as the great success of his revival in Corinth will attest. Now Paul announces that if his critics are going to play that game he too will play the same game, although he admits that when he says this he is talking like a fool.

He is willing to match his record against theirs as he does throughout the remainder of this chapter and verses 1-13 of chapter twelve.

Verse 22 - *"Are they Hebrews? So am I. Are they Israelites? So am I. Are they the seed of Abraham? So am I."*

Ἑβραῖοί εἰσιν; κἀγώ. Ἰσραηλῖταί εἰσιν; κἀγώ. στέρμα Ἀβραάμ εἰσιν; κἀγώ.

"Are they Hebrews? So am I. Are they Israelites? So am I. Are they

descendants of Abraham? So am I." . . . RSV

Ἑβραῖοί (nom.pl.masc.of Ἑβραῖος, predicate nominative) 3078.
εἰσιν (3d.per.pl.pres.ind.of εἰμί, direct question) 86.
κἀγώ (adjunctive conjunction and first personal pronoun, crasis) 178.
Ἰσραηλῖταί (nom.pl.masc.of Ἰσραηλείτης, predicate nominative) 1967.
εἰσιν (3d.per.pl.pres.ind.of εἰμί, direct question) 86.
κἀγώ (adjunctive conjunction and first personal pronoun, crasis) 178.
σπέρμα (nom.sing.neut.of σπέρμα, predicate nominative) 1056.
Ἀβραάμ (gen.sing.masc.of Ἀβραάμ, definition) 7.
εἰσιν (3d.per.pl.pres.ind.of εἰμί, direct question) 86.
κἀγώ (adjunctive conjunction and first personal pronoun, crasis) 178.

Translation - "Are they Hebrews? I too. Are they Israelites? I too. Are they the children of Abraham? So am I."

Comment: Here begins one of Paul's most eloquent passages. It is significant that when he is at his most dynamic oratorical best, he disclaims the worth of what he is saying by referring to it as foolishness. 2 Cor.11:1,16,21,23; 12:11. Paul's ethnic background as a Hebrew, an Israelite and as a descendant of Abraham, with all the advantages that such might entail, is equal to that of his competitors in Corinth .

Verse 23 - "Are they ministers of Christ? (I speak as a fool). I am more; in labours, more abundant, in stripes above measure, in prisons more frequent, in deaths oft."

διάκονοι Χριστοῦ εἰσιν; παραφρονῶν λαλῶ, ὑπὲρ ἐγώ. ἐν κόποις περισσοτέρως, ἐν φυλακαῖς περισσοτέρως, ἐν πληγαῖς ὑπερβαλλόντως, ἐν θανάτος πολλάκις.

"Are they servants of Christ? I am a better one - I am talking like a madman - with far greater labors, far more imprisonments, with countless beatings, and often near death." . . . RSV

διάκονοι (nom.pl.masc.of διάκονος, predicate nominative) 1334.
Χριστοῦ (gen.sing.masc.of Χριστός, relationship) 4.
εἰσιν (3d.per.pl.pres.ind.of εἰμί, direct question) 86.

#4380 παραφρονῶν (pres.act.part.nom.sing.masc.of παραφρονέω, adverbial, modal).

King James Version

be as a fool - 2 Cor.11:23.

Revised Standard Version

like a mad man - 2 Cor.11:23.

Meaning: A combination of παρά (#154) and φρονέω (#1212). *Cf.* also φρήν (#4235). Hence, to be beside (παρά) one's self. To be out of your mind. Irrational - 2 Cor.11:23.

λαλῶ (1st.per.sing.pres.act.ind.of λαλέω, aoristic) 815.
ὑπὲρ (preposition, used adverbially) 545.
ἐγώ (nom.sing.masc.of ἐγώ, subject of εἰμί understood) 123.
ἐν (preposition with the locative, accompanying circumstance) 80.
κόποις (loc.pl.masc.of κόπος, accompanying circumstance) 1565.
περισσοτέρως (adverbial) 1630.
ἐν (preposition with the locative of place) 80.
φυλακαῖς (loc.pl.fem.of φυλακή, place) 494.
περισσοτέρως (adverbial) 1630.
ἐν (preposition with the locative, accompanying circumstance) 80.
πληγαῖς (loc.pl.fem.of πληγή, accompanying circumstance) 2421.

#4381 ὑπερβαλλόντως (adverbial).

King James Version

above measure - 2 Cor.11:23.

Revised Standard Version

countless - 2 Cor.11:23.

Meaning: An adverb of measure from the participle of ὑπερβάλλω (#4290). Innumberable; countless. With πληγαῖς in 2 Cor.11:23.

ἐν (preposition with the locative, accompanying circumstance) 80.
θανάτοις (loc.pl.masc.of θάνατος, accompanying circumstance) 381.
πολλάκις (adverbial) 1230.

Translation - "Are they servants of Christ? — I am speaking like a fool — I am a better one. In toils more abundant; in jails more often; I have more wounds than I can count; I have been near death often."

Comment: Janneris (*History of Greek Grammar*, 366, as citied in Robertson, *Grammar*, 629) calls ὑπὲρ ἐγώ a "monstrous construction" because it uses a preposition like an adverb, which is a little intemperate on Janneris' part, since prepositions are evolved from adverbs. Homer did not use ὑπέρ as an adverb, but Euripides did in *Medea*, 627. Paul's meaning is clear enough. He was a far better servant of Christ than his critics, because they were not servants of Christ at all. What a bit of egotism! It is scant wonder that he adds, parenthetically, "I am out of my mind!" Note the modal participle. *Cf.* Cor.15:10. πληγαῖς - not the occasions upon which he was beaten but the wounds received on those occasions.

Verse 24 - "Of the Jews five times received I forty stripes save one."

ὑπὸ Ἰουδαίων πεντάκις τεσσαράκοντα παρὰ μίαν ἔλαβον,

"Five times I have received at the hands of the Jews the forty lashes less one." .
. . RSV

ὑπό (preposition with the ablative of agent) 117.
Ἰουδαίων (abl.pl.masc.of Ἰουδαῖος, agent) 143.

#4382 πεντάκις (numeral).

King James Version

five times - 2 Cor.11:24.

Revised Standard Version

five times - 2 Cor.11:24.

Meaning: Cf. πέντε (#1119). Five times - 2 Cor.11:24.

τεσσαράκοντα (acc.pl.neut.of τεσσαράκοντα, numeral) 333.
παρά (preposition with the accusative, measure) 154.
μίαν (acc.sing.fem.of εἶς, measure) 469.
ἔλαβον (1st.per.sing.aor.act.ind.of λαμβάνω, constative) 533.

Translation - "From Jews, on five occasions, I took the forty minus one."

Comment: The τεσσαράκοντα παρά μίαν is a reference to Deut.25:3. In order to avoid forty-one lashes, the result of a miscount and punishment beyond the extent of the law, the Jews had a practice of giving only thirty-nine lashes. Thus the "forty minus one." This treatment was administered in court in the presence of the judge. It grew out of legal controversy. The defendant, if proved guilty of the allegation, was adjudged as "the wicked man." (Deut.25:1-3). Bengal says that it was administered by thirteen strokes with a treble lash. Jameson, Faucett & Brown observe *(en loc)* that this minute agreement with Jewish legal procedure is one that could not have likely been possbile had an imposter written this passage. (*Cf.* Josephus, *Ant.* IV, 8, 1, 21).
There is nothing either in the Acts or the other Epistles about these floggings.

Verse 25 - "Thrice was I beaten with rods, once was I stoned, thrice I suffered shipwreck, a night and a day I have been in the deep."

τρὶς ἐραβδίσθην, ἅπαξ ἐλιθάσθην, τρὶς ἐναυάγησα, νυχθήμερον ἐν τῷ βυθῷ πεποίηκα.

"Three times I have been beaten with rods; once I was stoned. Three times I have been shipwrecked; a night and a day I have been adrift at sea;" . . . RSV

τρὶς (adverbial) 1582.
ἐραβδίσθην (1st.per.sing.aor.pass.ind.of ῥαβδίζω, constative) 3374.

#4383 ἅπαξ (adverbial).

King James Version

once - 2 Cor.11:25; Phil.4:16; 1 Thess.2:18; Heb.6:4; 9:7,26,27,28; 10:2 12:26,27; 1 Pet.3:18; Jude 3,5.

Revised Standard Version

once - 2 Cor.11:25; Phil.4:16; Heb.6:4; 9:7,27,28; 10:2; 12:26,27.
again - 1 Thess.2:18.
once for all - Heb.9:26; 1 Pet.3:18; Jude 3,5.

Meaning: Once, one time - Univ. 2 Cor.11:25; Heb.9:26,27,28; Jude 5; with ἔτι - Heb.12:26,27; followed by τοῦ ἐνιαυτοῦ in Heb.9:7. Meaning once, so well done as to be permanent in effect, never needing repetition - once for all - Heb.6:4; 10:2; 1 Pet.3:18; Jude 3. καὶ ἅπαξ καὶ δίς - "once and again" hence "twice" in 1 Thess.2:18; Phil.4:16. In Nehemiah 13:20, however, and in 1 Maccab.3:30, ἅπαξ καὶ δίς as opposed to καὶ ἅπαξ καὶ δίς means "several times" or "repeatedly."

ἐλιθάσθην (1st.per.sing.aor.pass.ind.of λιθάζω, constative) 2377.
τρὶς (adverbial) 1582.

#4384 ἐναυάγησα (1st.per.sing.aor.act.ind.of ναυαγέω, constative).

King James Version

make shipwreck - 1 Tim.1:19.
suffer shipwreck - 2 Cor.11:25.

Revised Standard Version

shipwrecked - 2 Cor.11:25.
make shipwreck - 1 Tim.1:19.

Meaning: Cf. ναυαγός - "shipwrecked" from ναῦς (#3745) and ἄγνυμι - "to break." To experience shipwreck. Properly, of Paul's experience in Acts 27:41 - 2 Cor.11:25. Figuratively, to destroy the faith - 1 Tim.1:19.

#4385 νυχθήμερον (temporal adverb).

King James Version

a night and a day - 2 Cor.11:25.

Revised Standard Version

a night and a day - 2 Cor.11:25.

Meaning: νύξ (#209) plus ἡμέρα (#135). Hence, a night and a day; a full 24 hours - 2 Cor.11:25.

ἐν (preposition with the locative of place) 80.
τῷ (loc.sing.masc.of the article in agreement with βυθῷ) 9.

#4386 βυθῷ (loc.sing.masc.of βυθός, place).

King James Version

deep - 2 Cor.11:25.

Revised Standard Version

adrift at sea - 2 Cor.11:25.

Meaning: Cf. βνϑίζω (#2051). The bottom of a ditch or trench. The depth of the sea; the deep sea - 2 Cor.11:25.

πεποίηκα (1st.per.sing.perf.act.ind.of ποιέω, dramatic) 127.

Translation - "Three times I was beaten with rods; once I was stoned; three times I was shipwrecked; I spent a night and a day adrift at sea."

Comment: These aorists are constative. That is they "contemplate the action in its entirety." The constative aorist "takes an occurrence and, regardless of its extent of duration, gathers it into a single whole." (Mantey, *Manual*, 196). The dramatic historical perfect πεποίηκα presents a past event as though present for vivid effect. *Cf.* Acts 14:19; 16:22. Luke does not record in Acts all of the experiences to which Paul alludes here.

Verse 26 - "In journeyings often, in perils of waters, in perils of robbers, in perils of mine own countrymen, in perils by the heathen, in perils in the city, in perils in the wilderness, in perils in the sea, in perils among false brethren."

όδοιπορίαις πολλάκις, κινδύνοις ποταμῶν, κινδύνοις λῃστῶν, κινδύνοις ἐξ γένους, κινδύνοις ἐξ ἐθνῶν, κινδύνοις ἐν πόλει, κινδύνοις ἐν ἐρημίᾳ, κινδύνοις ἐν θαλάσσῃ, κινδύνοις ἐν φευδαδέλφοις,

"on frequent journeys, in dangers from rivers, danger from robbers, danger from my own people, danger from Gentiles, danger in the city, danger in the wilderness, danger at sea, danger from false brethren;" . . . RSV

όδοιπορίαις (loc.pl.fem.of όδοιπορία, accompanying circumstance) 2002.
πολλάκις (adverbial) 1230.
κινδύνοις (loc.pl.masc.of κίνδυνος, accompanying circumstance) 3952.
ποταμῶν (gen.pl.masc.of ποταμός, description) 274.
κινδύνοις (loc.pl.masc.of κίνδυνος, accompanying circumstance) 3952.
λῃστῶν (gen.pl.masc.of λῃστής, description) 1359.
κινδύνοις (loc.pl.masc.of κίνδυνος, accompanying circumstance) 3952.
ἐκ (preposition with the ablative of source) 19.
γένους (abl.sing.masc.of γένος, source) 1090.
κινδύνοις (loc.pl.masc.of κίνδυνος, accompanying circumstance) 3952.
ἐξ (preposition with the ablative of source) 19.
ἐθνῶν (abl.pl.neut.of ἔθνος, source) 376.
κινδύνοις (loc.pl.masc.of κίνδυνος, accompanying circumstance) 3952.

ἐν (preposition with the locative of place) 80.
πόλει (loc.sing.fem.of πόλις, place) 243.
κινδύνοις (loc.pl.masc.of κίνδυνος, accompanying circumstance) 3952.
ἐν (preposition with the locative of place) 80.
ἐρημίᾳ (loc.sing.fem.of ἐρημία, place) 1182.
κινδύνοις (loc.pl.masc.of κίνδυνοις, accompanying circumstance) 3952.
ἐν (preposition with the locative of place) 80.
θαλάσσῃ (loc.sing.fem.of θάλασσα, place) 374.
κινδύνοις (loc.sing.fem.of κίνδυνος, accompanying circumstance) 3952.
ἐν (preposition with the locative with plural nouns, association) 80.

#4387 ψευδαδέλφοις (loc.pl.masc.of ψευδάδελφος, assocation).

King James Version

false brethren - 2 Cor.11:26; Gal.2:4.

Revised Standard Version

false brethren - 2 Cor.11:26; Gal.2:4.

Meaning: A combination of ψεύδομαι (#439) and ἀδελφός (#15). Hence, false brethren. In a spiritual sense - 2 Cor.11:26; Gal.2:4.

Translation - "Often on journeys, dangers in rivers, dangers among robbers, dangers from my own nation, dangers from Gentiles, dangers in the city, dangers in the wilderness, dangers at sea, dangers among false brethren."

Comment: There is little need for comment. Paul hastens breathlessly on - *Cf.* Acts 9:23; 14:5.

Verse 27 - "In weariness and painfulness, in watchings often, in hunger and thirst, in fastings often, in cold and nakedness."

κόπῳ καὶ μόχθῳ, ἐν ἀγρυπνίαις πολλάκις, ἐν λιμῷ καὶ δίψει, ἐν νηστείαις πολλάκις, ἐν ψύχει καὶ γυμνότητι.

"in toil and hardship, through many a sleepless night, in hunger and thirst, often without food, in cold and exposure." . . . *RSV*

κόπῳ (loc.sing.masc.of κόπος, accompanying circumstance) 1565.
καὶ (adjunctive conjunction joining nouns) 14.

#4388 μόχθῳ (loc.sing.masc.of μόχθος, accompanying circumstance).

King James Version

painfulness - 2 Cor.11:27.
travail - 1 Thess.2:9; 2 Thess.3:8.

Revised Standard Version

hardship - 2 Cor.11:27.
toil - 1 Thess.2:9.
labor - 2 Thess.3:8.

Meaning: difficult labor; toil; travail. Differs from κόπος (#1565) in that κόπος means the fatigue that results from hard work. μόχθος refers to the hardship itself. In the New Testament πόνος (#4643) simply means "pain" though in classical Greek πόνος means "effort" - the required force in order to do work. Note κόπος and μόχθος used together in 2 Cor.11:27; 1 Thess.2:9; 2 Thess.3:8.

ἐν (preposition with the locative, accompanying circumstance) 80.
ἀγρυπνίαις (loc.pl.fem.of ἀγρυπνία, accompanying circumstance) 4314.
πολλάκις (adverbial) 1230.
ἐν (preposition with the locative, accompanying circumstance) 80.
λιμῷ (loc.sing.masc.of λιμός, accompanying circumstance) 1485.
καὶ (adjunctive conjunction joining nouns) 14.

#4389 δίψει (loc.sing.masc.of δίψος, accompanying circumstance).

King James Version

thirst - 2 Cor.11:27.

Revised Standard Version

thirst - 2 Cor.11:27.

Meaning: Cf. διψάω (#427). Thirst - 2 Cor.11:27.

ἐν (preposition with the locative, accompanying circumstance) 80.
νηστείαις (loc.pl.fem.of νηστεία, accompanying circumstance) 1239.
πολλάκις (adverbial) 1230.
ἐν (preposition with the locative of accompanying circumstance) 80.
ψύχει (loc.sing.neut.of ψύχος, accompanying circumstance) 2821.
καὶ (adjunctive conjunction joining nouns) 14.
γυμνότητι (loc.sing.masc.of γυμνότης, accompanying circumstance) 3951.

Translation - "In fatigue and hard work, during many sleepless nights, in hunger and thirst, during many fasts, in cold and exposure."

Comment: In Romans 8:35 Paul says that for all of these hardships (he mentions λιμός and γυμνότης) they cannot separate him from the love of Christ. Neither the hardships of physical work (μόχθος), the fatigue which it brings (κόπος), the insomnia (ἀγρυπνία) when he was too tired to sleep, the lack of food and water, his frequent enforced fasting, because he had nothing to eat nor the exposure to the cold, when he was only scantily clad could deter him from his Christ appointed commission to preach the gospel.

Could the false apostles in Corinth match this record?

In addition to the physical hardships which he has mentioned, he adds a psychological burden which he always carried in

Verse 28 - "Beside those things that are without, that which cometh upon me daily, the care of all the churches."

χωρὶς τῶν παρεκτὸς ἡ ἐπίστασίς μοι ἡ καθ' ἡμέραν, ἡ μέριμνα πασῶν τῶν ἐκκλησιῶν.

"And, apart from other things there is the daily pressure upon me of my anxiety for all the churches." . . . RSV

χωρὶς (preposition with the ablative of separation) 1077.
τῶν (abl.pl.neut.of the article, separation) 9.
παρεκτὸς (adverb treated as a substantive) 509.
ἡ (nom.sing.fem.of the article in agreement with ἐπίστασίς) 9.
ἐπίστασίς (nom.sing.fem.of ἐπίστασις, nominative absolute) 3624.
μοι (dat.sing.masc.of ἐγώ, personal disadvantage) 123.
ἡ (nom.sing.fem.of the article in agreement with ἐπίστασίς) 9.
καθ' (preposition with the accusative in a time expression) 98.
ἡμέραν (acc.sing.fem.of ἡμέρα, time expression) 135.
ἡ (nom.sing.fem.of the article in agreement with μέριμνα) 9.
μέριμνα (nom.sing.fem.of μέριμνα, nominative absolute) 1048.
πασῶν (gen.pl.fem.of πᾶς, in agreement with ἐκκλησιῶν) 67.
τῶν (gen.pl.fem.of the article in agreement with ἐκκλησιῶν) 9.
ἐκκλησιῶν (gen.pl.fem.of ἐκκλησία, description) 1204.

Translation - "Aside from the external problems, the situation that arises every day to demand my attention, the frustrations of all the churches."

Comment: παρεκτός, an adverb, used here like a substantive with the ablative article τῶν after χωρίς - in addition to all of the problems previously listed (vss.23-27) there was another. ἡ ἐπίστασίς μοι cannot refer to τῶν παρεκτὸς, since it is singular. It is joined rather to ἡ μέριμνα. The anxiety which Paul felt for all of the churches was his daily burden (καθ' ἡμέραν). Cf.#1048 for meaning. The anxieties, worries and frustrations of feeling a spiritual responsibility for the development of the churches which he had founded constituted a great drain on Paul psychologically as his physical hardships did upon his body.

All conscientious pastors know how Paul felt, but only to a small degree, unless, like him they are burdened, not only for the flock of God over which they are appointed, but also for all of the other churches. Paul's situation was different. It was through his ministry that the churches in Asia Minor, Macedonia and Greece had been established. The members of these churches were in most cases his own personal converts, brought to Christ as a direct result of his ministry. In the first century there was a shortage of pastors. Many of the churches perhaps were without pastoral leadership. Thus Paul had the burden upon himself. There was another problem. The literature of the New Testament was not yet complete and the local churches were not equipped as were the later churches to counter the legalistic and Gnostic heresies, to mention only two, which beset the first century Christians. His defence against the Judaizers, his exposition of justification by faith, contained chiefly in Romans, Galatians, had not yet been written.

His Christology which stood against the Gnostic perversion, found in Philippians, Philemon, Colossians and Ephesians, and First and Second Timothy and Titus which dealt with ecclesiastic problems had also not yet been written. Nor did the churches have the Gospel of John.

Verse 29 - "Who is weak, and I am not weak? Who is offended, and I burn not?"

τίς ἀσθενεῖ καὶ οὐκ ἀσθενῶ; τίς σκανδαλίζεται, καὶ οὐκ ἐγὼ πυροῦμαι;

"Who is weak, and I am not weak? Who is made to fall, and I am not indignant?" . . . RSV

τίς (nom.sing.masc.of τίς, interrogative pronoun, in rhetorical question) 281.
ἀσθενεῖ (3d.per.sing.pres.act.ind.of ἀσθενέω, rhetorical question) 857.
καὶ (adversative conjunction) 14.
οὐκ (negative conjunction with the indicative) 130.
ἀσθενῶ (1st.per.sing.pres.act.ind.of ἀσθενέω, aoristic) 857.
τίς (nom.sing.masc.of τίς, interrogative pronoun, in rhetorical question) 281.
σκανδαλίζεται (3d.per.sing.pres.pass.ind.of σκανδαλίζω, aoristic, in rhetorical question) 503.
καὶ (adversative conjunction) 14.
οὐκ (negative conjunction with the indicative) 130.
ἐγώ (nom.sing.masc.of ἐγώ, subject of πυροῦμαι, emphatic) 123.
πυροῦμαι (1st.per.sing.pres.pass.ind.of πυρόω, aoristic, in rhetorical question) 4158.

Translation - "Who is weak, but I am not weak? Who is offended but I am not indignant?"

Comment: These are rhetorical questions, designed to show that Paul's concern for the churches was greater than that of the false teachers, who, he charged were interested only in exploiting them. The care of the churches was felt so strongly by Paul that he dares to ask for an instance when he did not empathize with anyone in their weaknesses, debilitations and offenses. When one was sick, Paul felt it also; when one was offended, Paul felt indignation on their behalf. This is the experience of one whose connection as a member of the Body of Christ is so vital and intimate with that of the other members that he feels their feelings along with them.

Paul dares to imply that the false teachers who were criticizing him and trying to undermine his influence in Corinth did not share his concern for their problems.

Verse 30 - "If I must needs glory, I will glory of the things which concern mine infirmities."

Εἰ καυχᾶσθαι δεῖ, τὰ τῆς ἀσθενείας μου καυχήσομαι.

"If I must boast, I will boast of the things that show my weakness." . . . RSV

Εἰ (conditional particle in a first-class condition) 337.

καυχᾶσθαι (aor.mid.inf.of καυχάομαι, complementary) 3847.

δεῖ (3d.per.sing.pres.ind.of δεῖ, impersonal, first-class condition) 1207.

τὰ (acc.pl.neut.of the article, general reference) 9.

τῆς (gen.sing.fem.of the article in agreement with ἀσθενείας) 9.

ἀσθενείας (gen.sing.fem. of ἀσθένεια, description) 740.

μου (gen.sing.masc.of ἐγώ, possession) 123.

καυχήσομαι (1st.per.sing.fut.mid.ind.of καυχάομαι, predictive, first-class condition) 3847.

Translation - *"Since I must boast, I will boast about my weaknesses!"*

Comment: Here is another touch of sarcasm. Paul's enemies boasted much about their superiority over him - in terms of sophistication, language skills, personal appearance, charm *ad nauseam*. Paul, with tongue in cheek says that since they were boasting he felt it necessary to boast also. But he intends to surpass them in this contest (!) even though he dislikes doing so. The necessity laid upon him (Εἰ with δεῖ in a first-class condition) is in the nature of the case. It has been forced upon him. But if he must boast why not point out, not his strong points, as his enemies did in their own boast, but his weaknesses? Thus he has just treated them to a long and eloquent recital of his sufferings and personal sacrifices as a preacher. But what he has just written pales into insignificance in comparison to what he is about to tell them in verses 32 and 33. As a matter of fact the story is so ridiculous and incredible and so much in the nature of comic opera that he feels it necessary to call God to witness that it is true.

Verse 31 - *"The God and Father of our Lord Jesus Christ, which is blessed forevermore, knoweth that I lie not."*

ὁ θεὸς καὶ πατὴρ τοῦ κυρίου Ἰησοῦ οἶδεν, ὁ ὢν εὐλογητὸς εἰς τοὺς αἰῶνας, ὅτι οὐ ψεύδομαι.

"The God and Father of the Lord Jesus, he who is blessed for ever, knows that I do not lie." . . . RSV

ὁ (nom.sing.masc.of the article in agreement with θεὸς) 9.

θεὸς (nom.sing.masc.of θεός, subject of οἶδεν) 124.

καὶ (adjunctive conjunction joining nouns) 14.

πατὴρ (nom.sing.masc.of πατήρ, subject of οἶδεν) 238.

τοῦ (gen.sing.masc.of the article in agreement with κυρίου) 9.

κυρίου (gen.sing.masc.of κύριος, relationship) 97.

Ἰησοῦ (gen.sing.masc.of Ἰησοῦς, apposition) 3.

οἶδεν (3d.per.sing.perf.ind.of ὁράω, intensive) 144b.

ὁ (nom.sing.masc.of the article in agreement with ὢν) 9.

ὤν (pres.part.nom.sing.masc.of εἰμί, substantival, apposition) 86.

εὐλογητὸς (nom.sing.masc.of εὐλογητός, predicate adjective) 1849.

εἰς (preposition with the accusative of time extent) 140.

τοὺς (acc.pl.masc.of the article in agreement with αἰῶνας) 9.

αἰῶνας (acc.pl.masc.of αἰών, time extent) 1002.

ὅτι (conjunction introducing a subordinate clause in indirect discourse) 211.

οὐ (negative conjunction with the indicative) 130.

ψεύδομαι (1st.per.sing.pres.mid.ind.of ψεύδομαι, indirect discourse, aoristic) 439.

Translation - "The God and Father of the Lord Jesus Who is blessed eternally knows that I am not lying."

Comment: In addition to the account of his sufferings of the past, Paul is about to tell them a story that sounds so incredible that he feels he must call God to witness that he is telling the truth. Luke has already told us the story in Acts 9:23-25.

Verse 32 - "In Damascus the governor under Aretas the king kept the city of the Damascenes with a garrison, desirous to apprehend me."

ἐν Δαμασκῷ ὁ ἐθνάρχης Ἀρέτα τοῦ βασιλέως ἐφρούρει τὴν πόλιν Δαμασκηνῶν πιάσαι με,

"At Damascus, the governor under King Aretas guarded the city of Damascus in order to seize me,. . ." . . . RSV

ἐν (preposition with the locative of place) 80.

Δαμασκῷ (loc.sing.masc.of Δαμασκός, place) 3181.

ὁ (nom.sing.masc.of the article in agreement with ἐθνάρκης) 9.

#**4390** ἐθνάρκης (nom.sing.masc.of ἐθνάρκης, subject of ἐφρούρει).

King James Version

governor - 2 Cor.11:32.

Revised Standard Version

governor - 2 Cor.11:32.

Meaning: A combination of ἔθνος (#376) and ἄρχω (#383). Hence the founder of a nation. A ruler or administrator over a people, though without final authority. With reference to Ἀρέτα in Damascus - 2 Cor.11:32.

#**4391** Ἀρέτα (gen.sing.masc.of Ἀρέτας, relationship).

King James Version

Aretas - 2 Cor.11:32.

Revised Standard Version

Aretas - 2 Cor.11:32.

Meaning: King of Damascus, whose ethnarch tried to arrest Paul - 2 Cor.11:32.

τοῦ (gen.sing.masc.of the article in agreement with βασιλέως) 9.
βασιλέως (gen.sing.masc.of βασιλεύς, apposition) 31.

#4392 ἐφρούρει (3d.per.sing.imp.act.ind.of φρουρέω, progressive description).

King James Version

keep - Gal.3:23; Phil.4:7; 1 Pet.1:5.
keep with a garrison - 2 Cor.11:32.

Revised Standard Version

guard - 2 Cor.11:32; 1 Pet.1:5.
confined - Gal.3:23.
keep - Phil.4:7.

Meaning: Cf. φρουρός - "water" "guard" and this contracted from προορός, from προοράω (#2993). To guard or protect by surrounding with a military guard around a city. To seal off a city with a cordon of men. With reference to the attempt in Damascus to arrest Paul - 2 Cor.11:32. Metaphorically, the legalist is kept under the rule of law before faith comes to save him - Gal.3:23. God's peace will keep the Christian's heart and mind - Phil.4:7. Believers are kept secure by God's power through faith unto salvation - 1 Pet.1:5.

τὴν (acc.sing.fem.of the article in agreement with πόλιν) 9.
πόλιν (acc.sing.fem.of πόλις, direct object of ἐφρούρει) 243.

#4393 Δαμασκηνῶν (gen.pl.masc.of Δαμασκηνός, description).

King James Version

Damascenes - 2 Cor.11:32.

Revised Standard Version

Damascus - 2 Cor.11:32.

Meaning: Of or pertaining to Damascus - 2 Cor.11:32.

πιάσαι (aor.act.inf.of πιάζω, purpose) 2371.
με (acc.sing.masc.of ἐγώ, direct object of πιάσαι) 123.

Translation - "In Damascus the mayor under Aretas, the king, was maintaining a military guard around the city gates in an attempt to arrest me."

Comment: Some MSS read θέλων πιάσαι or θέλων με πιάσαι or πιάσαι με θέλων. We do not need θέλων since the aorist infinitive πιάσαι following ἐφρούει clearly indicates purpose.

This incredible story goes on in

Verse 33 - *"And through a window in a basket was I let down by the wall, and escaped his hands."*

καὶ διὰ θυρίδος ἐν σαργάνῃ ἐχαλάσθην διὰ τοῦ τείχους καὶ ἐξέφυγον τὰς χεῖρας αὐτοῦ.

"but I was let down in a basket through a window in the wall, and escaped his hands." . . . RSV

καὶ (adversative conjunction) 14.
διὰ (preposition with the genitive, physically through) 118.
θυρίδος (gen.sing.fem.of θυρίς, physically through) 3512.
ἐν (preposition with the locative of place) 80.

#4394 σαργάνῃ (loc.sing.fem.of σαργάνη, place).

King James Version

basket - 2 Cor.11:33.

Revised Standard Version

basket - 2 Cor.11:33.

Meaning: A braided rope, or a basket made of braided ropes; a hamper. There are numerous references in the κοινή to support the latter idea. Therefore we translate "in a basket" (locative of place) rather than "by a rope" (instrumental of means) - 2 Cor.11:33. *Cf.* σπυρίς (#1186), the word which Luke uses in Acts 9:25 to describe the event.

ἐχαλάσθην (1st.per.sing.aor.pass.ind.of χαλάω, constative) 2045.
διὰ (preposition with the genitive of place description) 118.
τοῦ (gen.sing.neut.of the article in agreement with τείχους) 9.
τείχους (gen.sing.neut.of τεῖχος, place description) 3196.
καὶ (adjunctive conjunction joining verbs) 14.
ἐξέφυγον (1st.per.sing.aor.act.ind.of ἐκφεύγω, constative) 2740.
τὰς (acc.sing.fem.of the article in agreement with χεῖρας) 9.
χεῖρας (acc.pl.fem.of χείρ, direct object of ἐξέφυγον) 308.
αὐτοῦ (gen.sing.masc.of αὐτός, possession) 16.

Translation - *"But through a window in a basket I was lowered by the wall, and I fled from his clutches."*

Comment: Note διὰ with the genitive, meaning "through" in a physical sense. Paul passed down the wall through a window.

If Paul had been concerned about his dignity and prestige, as these issues were being raised by his critics in Corinth he certainly would not have told this story, or if he had he would have told it with some embarrassment. But he includes the story in his "boast"! His sarcasm is evident. When we contrast the noble bearing of the sophisticated Hellenistic Jews in Corinth, with their Grecian appearances, the classical tone of their discourse and their urbane manner with the ludicrous picture of a little hook-nosed, baldheaded, weak-eyed Jew fleeing down a city wall in a basket from the authorities, we begin to appreciate the grim humor which Paul is employing here. One can scarcely imagine his enemies in Corinth fleeing from the police, or indeed doing anything to make such flight necessary. The false apostles who were annoying the Corinthians had never been forced to resort to such unusual expedients in order to escape from the Jewish Establishment.

Hodge says, "This passage (vss.27-33) makes even the most laborious of the modern ministers of Christ hide their faces in shame. What have they ever done or suffered to compare with what the apostle did? It is a consolation to know that Paul is now as preeminent in glory as he was here in suffering." (Meyer, *2 Corinthians,* 668).

Now that Paul has pictured himself in the ludicrous position of a common criminal going over the wall to escape arrest, he goes to the other extreme and presents the evidence for his claim to the highest possible position of authority in the early church. He who fled over a wall from the Jewish authorities, was let down in a basket, faced the darkness and ran for his life, was also caught up to the third heavens, where he had his own private theological education at the feet of his ascended Lord.

Visions and Revelations

(2 Corinthians 12:1-10)

2 Corinthians 12:1 - "It is not expedient for me doubtless to glory. I will come to visions and revelations of the Lord."

Καυχᾶσθαι δεῖ οὐ συμφέρον μέν, ἐλεύσομαι δὲ εἰς ὀπτασίας καὶ ἀποκαλύψεις κυρίου.

"I must boast; there is nothing to be gained by it but I will go on to visions and revelations of the Lord." . . . RSV

Καυχᾶσθαι (aor.mid.inf.of καυχάομαι, complementary) 3847.
δεῖ (3d.per.sing.pres.ind.impersonal of δεῖ, aoristic) 1207.
οὐ (negative conjunction with the indicative understood) 130.
συμφέρον (pres.part.nom.sing.neut.of συμφέρω, present periphrastic, concessive) 505.
μέν (particle of affirmation) 300.
ἐλεύσομαι (1st.per.sing.fut.ind.of ἔρχομαι, predictive) 146.
δὲ (adversative conjunction) 11.
εἰς (preposition with the accusative of extent, metaphorical) 140.
ὀπτασίας (acc.pl.fem.of ὀπτασία, metaphorical extent) 1804.
καὶ (adjunctive conjunction joining nouns) 14.

ἀποκαλύφεις (acc.pl.fem.of ἀποκαλύφις, metaphorical extent) 1902.
κυρίου (abl.sing.masc.of κύριος, source) 97.

Translation - "I must boast, despite the fact that it is not profitable; but I will procede to visions and revelations from the Lord."

Comment: The infinitive καυχᾶσθαι completes δεῖ. μὲν can be taken as concessive - "despite the fact that it does no good." This explains why Paul suddenly stopped his boasting about his sacrifices (2 Cor.11:30) and came to a sounder and more convincing evidence of his superior authority as an Apostle. What he is about to relate (vss.2-4) is the greatest evidence that Jesus actually chose him and not Matthias (Acts 1:15-26) or some other to replace the apostate Judas Iscariot. There was no doubt that the other eleven Apostles had been chosen by Jesus from a larger group of disciples, all of whom had known Jesus personally (Luke 6:13-16). Saul of Tarsus was the only exception, if indeed he was the exception. He now procedes to say that he too saw Jesus, received his commission to preach and his theology from the Lord. Indeed he had an experience that none of the other Apostles had. He went to theological seminary in Paradise, the third heaven, where Jesus sat at the right hand of God.

Verse 2 - "I knew a man in Christ above fourteen years ago, (whether in the body, I cannot tell; or whether out of the body, I cannot tell: God knoweth:) such an one caught up to the third heaven."

οἶδα ἄνθρωπον ἐν Χριστῷ πρὸ ἐτῶν δεκατεσσάρων — εἴτε ἐν σώματι οὐκ οἶδα, εἴτε ἐκτὸς τοῦ σώματος οὐκ οἶδα, ὁ θεὸς οἶδεν — ἁρπαγέντα τὸν τοιοῦτον ἕως τρίτου οὐρανοῦ.

"I know a man in Christ who fourteen years ago was caught up to the third heaven — whether in the body or out of the body I do not know, God knows."...
                                                                        RSV

οἶδα (1st.per.sing.perf.ind.of ὁράω, intensive) 144b.
ἄνθρωπον (acc.sing.masc.of ἄνθρωπος, direct object of οἶδα) 341.
ἐν (preposition with the instrumental of association) 80.
Χριστῷ (instru.sing.masc.of Χριστός, association) 4.
πρὸ (preposition with the ablative of comparison) 442.
ἐτῶν (abl.pl.neut.of ἔτος, comparison) 821.
δεκατεσσάρων (abl.pl.neut.of δεκατέσσαρες, in agreement with ἐτῶν) 72.
εἴτε (compound disjunctive) 4016.
ἐν (preposition with the locative of place) 80.
σώματι (loc.sing.neut.of σῶμα, place) 507.
οὐκ (negative conjunction with the indicative) 130.
οἶδα (1st.per.sing.perf.ind.of ὁράω, intensive) 144b.
εἴτε (compound disjunctive) 4016.
ἐκτὸς (preposition with the ablative of separation) 1461.
τοῦ (abl.sing.neut.of the article in agreement with σώματος) 9.
σώματος (abl.sing.neut.of σῶμα, separation) 507.

οὐκ (negative conjunction with the indicative) 130.
οἶδα (1st.per.sing.perf.ind.of ὁράω, intensive) 144b.
ὁ (nom.sing.masc.of the article in agreement with θεὸς) 9.
θεὸς (nom.sing.masc.of θεός, subject of οἶδεν) 124.
οἶδεν (3d.per.sing.perf.ind.of ὁράω, intensive) 144b.
ἁρπαγέντα (2d.aor.pass.part.acc.sing.masc.of ἁρπάζω, adjectival, predicate position, restrictive, in agreement with τοιοῦτον) 920.
τὸν (acc.sing.masc.of the article in agreement with τοιοῦτον) 9.
τοιοῦτον (acc.sing.masc.of τοιοῦτος, apposition) 785.
ἕως (preposition with the genitive of place description) 71.
τρίτου (gen.sing.masc.of τρίτος, in agreement with οὐρανοῦ) 1209.
οὐρανοῦ (gen.sing.masc.of οὐρανός place description) 254.

Translation - "I knew a man in Christ more than fourteen years ago, whether in or out of the body, I do not know — God knows — who was caught up unto the third heaven."

Comment: The usual perfect tense in οἶδα and οἶδεν - "having understood in the past I (He) now know (knows)..." ἐν Χριστῷ - associated with Christ in mystic union. πρό - in excess of 14 years, or before 14 years ago. The participle ἁρπαγέντα is adjectival, restricted (predicate position) to either ἄνθρωπον or τὸν τοιοῦτον. This man was raptured! And he was the only one in the context of Paul's thought. How far? ἕως τρίτου οὐρανοῦ. Cf.#254 where spatially speaking three heavens are distinguished: (1) atmosphere; (2) stellar, and (3) God's heaven. This man (Paul is talking about himself) was caught up to the throne of God (Rev.4:1-2), where Jesus Christ sits at God's right hand (Psalm 110:1; Heb.1:3; Col.3:1).

Thus Paul also met Jesus personally, as did the other Apostles. His Damascus road encounter (Acts 9:3-6) was not a session for theological training - a school in which the other Apostles were enrolled for three years - but Paul got his theology from the Lord Jesus as much as they, as we see in verses 3 and 4.

Verse 3 - "And I knew such a man, (whether in the body or out of the body, I cannot tell; God knoweth;)"

καὶ οἶδα τὸν τοιοῦτον ἄνθρωπον — εἴτε ἐν σώματι εἴτε χωρὶς τοῦ σώματος οὐκ οἶδα, ὁ θεὸς οἶδεν —

"And I know that this man was caught up into Paradise — whether in the body or out of the body I do not know, God knows — " . . . RSV

καὶ (continuative conjunction) 14.
οἶδα (1st.per.sing.perf.ind.of ὁράω, intensive) 144b.
τὸν (acc.sing.masc.of the article in agreement with ἄνθρωπον) 9.
τοιοῦτον (acc.sing.masc.of τοιοῦτος, in agreement with ἄνθρωπον) 785.
ἄνθρωπον (acc.sing.masc.of ἄνθρωπος, direct object of οἶδα) 341.
εἴτε (compound disjunctive) 4016.
ἐν (preposition with the locative of place) 80.

σώματι (loc.sing.neut.of σῶμα, place) 507.
εἴτε (compound disjunctive) 4016.
χωρὶς (preposition with the ablative of separation) 1077.
τοῦ (abl.sing.neut.of the article in agreement with σώματος) 9.
σώματος (abl.sing.neut.of σῶμα, separation) 507.
οὐκ (negative conjunction with the indicative) 130.
οἶδα (1st.per.sing.perf.ind.of ὁράω, intensive) 144b.
ὁ (nom.sing.masc.of the article in agreement with θεός) 9.
θεὸς (nom.sing.masc.of θεός, subject of οἶδεν) 124.
οἶδεν (3d.per.sing.perf.ind.of ὁράω, intensive) 144b.

Translation - "And I know this man, whether in or apart from the body, I do not know although God knows. . . . "

Comment: Note the change from ἐκτός to χωρὶς with the ablative of separation. It is interesting that though Paul was not certain about his physical experience, he was very sure about his intellectual experience. He is certain about what he learned at the right hand of God. He is not sure that he was there in the flesh. Did his physical body participate in this rapture? When the mind is engrossed in learning new truth, the body is of little importance. Thus we see Paul's agreement with Plato that the physical real and the intellectual ideal are not necessarily the same. It is possible for the mind to learn as it encounters concepts, and remembers what it learns, whether dependent or independent of the body. The flesh sees only the shadows on the wall. The spirit of man goes outside the cave and understands reality.

The Apostle John later had the same experience (Rev.4-5). And at the second coming of our Lord every member of the Body of Christ will have this experience (1 Thess.4:13-18).

Verse 4 - "How that he was caught up into paradise, and heard unspeakable words, which it is not lawful for a man to utter."

ὅτι ἡρπάγη εἰς τὸν παράδεισον καὶ ἤκουσεν ἄρρητα ῥήματα ἃ οὐκ ἐξὸν ἀνθρώπῳ λαλῆσαι.

"and he heard things that cannot be told, which man may not utter." . . . RSV

ὅτι (conjunction introducing an object clause in indirect discourse) 211.
ἡρπάγη (3d.per.sing.2d.aor.pass.ind.of ἁρπάζω, constative) 920.
εἰς (preposition with the accusative of extent) 140.
τὸν (acc.sing.masc.of the article in agreement with παράδεισον) 9.
παράδεισον (acc.sing.masc.of παράδεισος, extent) 2857.
καὶ (adjunctive conjunction joining verbs) 14.
ἤκουσεν (3d.per.sing.aor.act.ind.of ἀκούω, constative) 148.

#4395 ἄρρητα (acc.pl.neut.of ἄρρητος, in agreement with ῥήματα).

King James Version

unspeakable - 2 Cor.12:4.

Revised Standard Version

that cannot be told - 2 Cor.12:4.

Meaning: ἀρ privative plus ῥητος from ῥέω (#116). Hence, hitherto unspoken or unexpressed. New words - 2 Cor.12:4.

ῥήματα (acc.pl.neut.of ῥῆμα, direct object of ἤκουσεν) 343.
ἃ (acc.pl.neut.of ὅς, relative pronoun, general reference) 65.
οὐκ (negative conjunction with the indicative) 130.
ἐξὸν (pres.part.nom.sing.neut.of ἔξεστι, adjectival, predicate position, restrictive, in agreement with ῥήματα) 966.
ἀνθρώπῳ (dat.sing.masc.of ἄνθρωπος, reference) 341.
λαλῆσαι (aor.act.inf.of λαλέω, epexegetical) 815.

Translation - ". . . that he was raptured into Paradise and he heard words not before spoken which a mere man would not be at liberty to divulge."

Comment: ὅτι introduces the clause in indirect discourse which is the object of οἶδα of verse 3. - "I know . . . that he was caught up. . . κ.τ.λ." The parenthesis about what God knows is concerned with whether Paul was in or out of the body. That is of little importance to Paul. What is important is that he went to heaven and learned the theology which he was to preach.

Note that Paul is repeating what he said in verse 2 except that now he substitutes παράδεισον for τρίτου οὐρανοῦ, thus indicating that these terms refer to the same place. *Cf.* our comment on #2857. *Cf.* Rev.2:7.

Paul, caught up to the throne of God, heard the things that thoroughly established his divinely commissioned authority as Christ's 12th Apostle. He alludes to this experience indirectly in Gal.1:11,12,16,17. The result of this heavenly course in theology was that Paul knew as much theology as the other Apostles (Gal.2:1-10) and had the additional revelation that the Body of Christ was also to include the elect from among the Gentiles. Jesus had hinted at this great truth before, but no one understood it clearly until our Lord gave it to Paul in Paradise. This is the "mystery" of Ephesians 3:1-7.

The phrase ἃ οὐκ ἐξὸν ἀνθρώπῳ λαλῆσαι does not mean that Jesus and Paul spoke in "tongues" (!) during their heavenly conversation; nor does it mean that Paul was forbidden to repeat what he heard. The quality of what he heard was so supernal as to rule out the hypothesis that it came only from a human source. Only the resurrected Lord (Ps.2:7,8; 110:1,4) could have said what Paul heard and was told to preach.

Paul here scores heavily against his enemies in Corinth. Not one of them could boast of this experience, nor could they have known that the divine plan of salvation was to include the uncircumcised Gentiles.

Verse 5 - "Of such an one will I glory: yet of myself I will not glory, but in mine infirmities."

ὑπὲρ τοῦ τοιούτου καυχήσομαι, ὑπὲρ δὲ ἐμαυτοῦ οὐ καυχήσομαι εἰ μὴ ἐν ταῖς ἀσθενείαις (μου).

"On behalf of this man I will boast, but on my own behalf I will not boast, except of my weaknesses." . . . RSV

ὑπὲρ (preposition with the genitive of reference) 545.

τοῦ (gen.sing.masc.of the article in agreement with τοιούτου) 9.

τοιούτου (gen.sing.masc.of τοιοῦτος, reference) 785.

καυχήσομαι (1st.per.sing.fut.mid.ind.of καυχάομαι, predictive) 3847.

ὑπὲρ (preposition with the genitive of reference) 545.

δὲ (adversative conjunction) 11.

ἐμαυτοῦ (gen.sing.masc.of ἐμαυτός, reference) 723.

οὐ (negative conjunction with the indicative) 130.

καυχήσομαι (1st.per.sing.fut.mid.ind.of καυχάομαι, predictive) 3847.

εἰ (conditional particle in an elliptical first-class condition) 337.

μὴ (negative conjunction in an elliptical first-class condition) 87.

ἐν (preposition with the locative of sphere) 80.

ταῖς (loc.pl.fem.of the article in agreement with ἀσθενείαις) 9.

ἀσθενείαις (loc.pl.fem.of ἀσθένεια, sphere) 740.

(μου) (gen.sing.masc.of ἐγώ, possession) 123.

Translation - "I will boast about this man, but I will not boast about myself, except about my ill health."

Comment: The statement sounds inconsistent, since the man who was raptured to heaven was Paul himself (verse 7). He means that he can glory in his experience at God's heavenly throne because he did nothing to deserve it or to bring it about. It was totally the result of the grace of the sovereign God and in keeping with His plan, and thus could be the ground for Paul's rejoicing. Paul, the man, had nothing to do with it except to be the recipient of the blessings and advantages which flowed from it.

On the other hand, Paul's sufferings because of his tragic experiences were something about which he had earned the right to boast. He was happy to have suffered from them since they provided the basis for the excessive grace required to endure them (vss.7-10).

Some current teachers who call themselves charismatics have destroyed this great body of truth which concerns itself with the gifts of the Holy Spirit to the Church, by carrying it to unscriptural and fanatical extremes. They insist that the victorious Christian who by faith appropriates the fulness of the blessing of the resurrected Christ to himself will never suffer. Thus what Paul here calls ἀσθένειαι (#740) in his life is evidence that he was a backslider, and according to their Arminian sotieriology in danger of ultimate damnation. These fanatics have no place in their thought for what other better taught theologians call the ministry of suffering. Could it be that their good health of which they boast *ad infinitum, ad nauseam* results, not from their sanctification, but from the fact that they are not sufficiently intelligent to require the humbling experiences which Paul had? When Paul prayed for healing he was refused and he was told that God's grace would be enough. If it is never God's will for His children to suffer then we must either conclude that Paul was not a Christian or that he was hopelessly backslidden.

Verse 6 - "For though I would desire to glory, I shall not be a fool: for I will say the truth: but now I forbear, lest any man should think of me above that which he seeth me to be, or that he heareth of me."

ἐὰν γὰρ θελήσω καυχήσασθαι, οὐκ ἔσομαι ἄφρων, ἀλήθειαν γὰρ ἐρῶ, φείδομαι δέ, μή τις εἰς ἐμὲ λογίσηται ὑπὲρ ὃ βλέπει με ἢ ἀκούει (τι) ἐξ ἐμοῦ

"Though if I wish to boast, I shall not be a fool, for I shall be speaking the truth. But I refrain from it, so that no one may think more of me than he sees in me or hears from me." . . . RSV

ἐὰν (conditional particle in a third-class condition) 363.
γὰρ (inferential conjunction) 105.
θελήσω (1st.per.sing.1st.aor.act.subj.of θέλω, third-class condition) 88.
καυχήσασθαι (aor.mid.inf.of καυχάομαι, complementary) 3847.
οὐκ (negative conjunction with the indicative) 130.
ἔσομαι (1st.per.sing.fut.mid.ind.of εἰμί, predictive, third-class condition) 86.
ἄφρων (nom.sing.masc.of ἄφρων, predicate nominative) 2462.
ἀλήθειαν (acc.sing.fem.of ἀλήθεια, direct object of ἐρῶ) 1416.
ἐρῶ (1st.per.sing.fut.ind.of εἴρω, predictive) 155.
φείδομαι (1st.per.sing.pres.mid.ind.of φείδομαι, aoristic) 3533.
δέ (adversative conjunction) 11.
μή (negative conjunction with the subjunctive) 87.
τις (nom.sing.masc.of τις, subject of λογίσηται) 486.
εἰς (preposition with the accusative, reference) 140.
ἐμὲ (acc.sing.masc.of ἐμός, reference) 1267.
λογίσηται (3d.per.sing.aor.mid.subj.of λογίζομαι, negative purpose) 2611.
ὑπὲρ (preposition with the accusative of extent, above/beyond/more than) 545.
ὃ (acc.sing.neut.of ὅς, relative pronoun, extent after ὑπὲρ) 65.
βλέπει (3d.per.sing.pres.act.ind.of βλέπω, present progressive) 499.
με (acc.sing.masc.of ἐγώ, direct object of βλέπει) 123.
ἢ (disjunctive) 465.
ἀκούει (3d.per.sing.pres.act.ind.of ἀκούω, present progressive) 148.
(τι) (acc.sing.neut.of τις, direct object of ἀκούει) 486.
ἐξ (preposition with the ablative of source) 19.
ἐμοῦ (abl.sing.masc.of ἐγώ, source) 1267.

Translation - "So if I want to boast I will not be acting like a fool, because I will be telling the truth; but I am going to desist lest anyone should evaluate me more highly than what he sees in me or that which he hears from me."

Comment: Paul has just said that any boasting which he may do in the future will be about his experiences described in 2 Cor.11:23-33, not those described in

2 Cor.12:1-4. Now he adds that if he did decide to boast about his infirmities and misfortunes, since what he said, if he said it (ἐὰν ... θελήσω καυχήσασθαι, a third-class condition) would be only the truth, he would not be talking like a fool. Even if he described more completely his rapture experience (2 Cor.12:1-4) it would not be the mouthings of a fool, but the truthful statement of an honest man. However he determined not to boast, either now or in the future. Why not? Because (negative purpose in μή ... λογίσηται) if he did someone might derive a higher opinion of him than the facts which he observed in Paul or heard from his lips might warrant.

Paul here recognizes the fact that as long as he is in the flesh, however much he may have suffered for Christ in the past, or however great may have been the exaltation of previous spiritual experiences, his future deeds and/or words might be such as to create disillusionment in the empirical observer. Unfortunately, the loftiest heights of previous spiritual experiences are not sufficient to prevent our subsequent fall into the most depraved depths of thought, word and deed. This will always be true as long as the child of God is living in this age before the glorification of the rapture.

Paul had no desire to create a false impression in the minds of his critics that he considered himself a sinless saint. Those who profess too much along the lines of sinless perfection become stumbling blocks to thoughtful unregenerates when the latter see the former "sanctified saints" stagger from the saloon.

Paul expressed this same concern when he said that he kept himself in training, as a disciplined athlete, because he feared that after he had won others to Christ with his preaching, he himself might become disapproved (ἀδόκιμος; 1 Cor.9:27). The Pentecostal who can boast only of two blessings - once when he was saved and the other when he was made incapable of committing sin - may be forced by his own experiences to admit that his theology was incorrect.

God was determined to see to it that Paul would never achieve this degree of hubris which results in later descent to the nadir of self-esteem. To occupy the zenith of spiritual experience, unmindful of this principle is to experience sudden, swift and uncontrolled descent to the nadir of disgrace. Our Lord's gracious safeguard against this tragedy in Paul's experience is described in

Verse 7 - "And lest I should be exalted above measure through the abundance of the revelations, there was given to me a thorn in the flesh, the messenger of Satan to buffet me, lest I should be exalted above measure."

καὶ τῇ ὑπερβολῇ τῶν ἀποκαλύψεων, διό, ἵνα μὴ ὑπεραίρωμαι, ἐδόθη μοι σκόλοφ τῇ σαρκί, ἄγγελος Σατανᾶ, ἵνα με κολαφίξῃ, ἵνα μὴ ὑπεραίρωμαι.

"And to keep me from being too elated by the abundance of revelations, a thorn was given me in the flesh, a messenger of Satan, to harass me, to keep me from being too elated."

καὶ (continuative conjunction) 14.
τῇ (instru.sing.fem.of the article in agreement with ὑπερβολῇ) 9.
ὑπερβολῇ (instru.sing.fem.of ὑπερβολή, cause) 3923.
τῶν (gen.pl.fem.of the article in agreement with ἀποκαλύψεων) 9.

ἀποκαλύφεων (gen.pl.fem.of ἀποκάλυφις, description) 1902.
διό (inferential conjunction) 1622.
ἵνα (conjunction with the subjunctive in a negative purpose clause) 114.
μή (negative conjunction with the subjunctive) 87.

#4396 ὑπεραίρωμαι (1st.per.sing.pres.pass.subj.of ὑπεραίρω, negative purpose).

King James Version

be exalted above measure - 2 Cor.12:7,7.
exalt one's self - 2 Thess.2:4.

Revised Standard Version

too elated - 2 Cor.12:7,7.
exalt one's self - 2 Thess.2:4.

Meaning: A combination of ὑπέρ (#545) and αἴρω (#350). Hence, to lift up; exalt. In the passive, absolutely in 2 Cor.12:7,a,b; in the middle voice with reference to Antichrist in an evil sense, followed by ἐπὶ πάντα λεγόμενον θεὸν ἢ σεβάσμα - 2 Thess.2:4.

ἐδόθη (3d.per.sing.aor.pass.ind.of δίδωμι, constative) 362.
μοι (dat.sing.masc.of ἐγώ, indirect object of ἐδόθη) 123.

#4397 σκόλοφ (nom.sing.masc.of σκόλοφ, subject of ἐδόθη).

King James Version

thorn - 2 Cor.12:7.

Revised Standard Version

thorn - 2 Cor.12:7.

Meaning: a sharp piece of wood or stick; a pole or stake; splinter, such as would cause pain if it penetrated the flesh. Followed by τῇ σαρκί in a metaphorical reference to some bodily ailment which Paul was called to endure - 2 Cor.12:7.

τῇ (loc.sing.fem.of the article in agreement with σαρκί) 9.
σαρκί (loc.sing.fem.of σάρξ, place) 1202.
ἄγγελος (nom.sing.masc.of ἄγγελος, apposition) 96.
Σατανᾶ (abl.sing.masc.of Σατανᾶ, source) 365.
ἵνα (conjunction with the subjunctive in a purpose clause) 114.
με (acc.sing.masc.of ἐγώ, direct object of κολαφίζῃ) 123.
κολαφίζῃ (3d.per.sing.pres.act.subj.of κολαφίζω, purpose) 1607.
ἵνα (conjunction with the subjunctive, negative purpose) 114.
μή (negative conjunction with the subjunctive) 87.
ὑπεραίρωμαι (1st.per.sing.pres.pass.subj.of ὑπεραίρω, negative purpose) 4396.

Translation - "And therefore, because of the great number of the revelations, lest I become too elated, a thorn in the flesh was given to me, a messenger from Satan, in order continually to attack me, lest I become too much elated."

Comment: Many MSS omit διό and the United Bible Societies' Committee has included it only with a D degree of confidence. Metzger explains in part, "Although διό is absent from such important witnesses as p46 D Ψ 88 614, the Committee preferred to retain the word in the text as the more difficult reading, attested, as it is, by Alexandrian and other witnesses (Sinaiticus A B G 33 81 1739 it_g Euthalius). The excision of the conjunction seems to have occurred when copyists mistakenly began a new sentence with καὶ τῇ ὑπερβολῇ τῶν ἀποκαλύφεων, instead of taking these words with the preceding sentence." (*A Textual Commentary on the Greek New Testament*, 585). The punctuation of the UBSC text puts καὶ τῇ . . . ἀποκαλύφεων in the sentence of verse 6, thus to read, "lest anyone should regard me higher . . . κ.τ.λ. in fact because of the abundance of the revelations." This is arbitrary and it seems awkward. It seems smoother to read, "And therefore (διό) because κ.τ.λ. . . . " as we have translated. It must be recalled that the original documents had no punctuation marks, nor even space between words. The subject of the new sentence is σκόλοφ - "And a thorn in the flesh was given to me, therefore, because of . . . κ.τ.λ." Why? Lest Paul become conceited. ἄγγελος is in apposition to σκόλοφ. Why the thorn in the flesh? ἵνα με κολαφίζῃ - "in order to continue to harass me." Why? Again he repeats the negative purpose clause with ἵνα μὴ ὑπεραίρωμαι. The reason for this illness is emphasized. It was because Paul had been abundantly informed (2 Cor.12:1-4) and there was danger that he would become conceited. The warning occurs twice.

Once again as in verse 6, Paul recognizes that high spiritual heights do not guarantee against fleshly attitudes and deeds. Indeed they may contribute to them. Witness the moral lapses to which we may succumb after high spiritual experiences.

It is interesting that God permitted this severe physical treatment for Paul, in order to keep him humble, and permitted Satan to send his messenger to impose the illness. It is the story of Job over again (Job 1:12; 2:6). God permits the treatment for His own good reasons, but it is Satan who comes "to steal, to kill and to destroy" (John 10:10).

Note that Paul's pain of physical suffering was better than the sin of egotism in an otherwise highly honored Christian. Had Paul been allowed to react like a human being to his heavenly experience, God could never have used him as He did and the rapture to the throne of God would have yielded no positive results. God's strength in evangelistic results as Paul was used to establish the Gentile churches was perfected only in Paul's pain.

Paul did not learn this lesson readily as we learn in

Verse 8 - "For this thing I besought the Lord thrice, that it might depart from me."

ὑπὲρ τούτου τρὶς τὸν κύριον παρεκάλεσα ἵνα ἀποστῇ ἀπ᾽ ἐμοῦ.

"Three times I besought the Lord about this, that it should leave me;"... RSV

ὑπέρ (preposition with the genitive of reference) 545.

τούτου (gen.sing.neut.of οὗτος, reference) 93.

τρὶς (adverbial) 1582.

τὸν (acc.sing.masc.of the article in agreement with κύριον) 9.

κύριον (acc.sing.masc.of κύριος, direct object of παρεκάλεσα) 97.

παρεκάλεσα (1st.per.sing.aor.act.ind.of παρακαλέω, constative) 230.

ἵνα (conjunction with the subjunctive, purpose) 114.

ἀποστῇ (3d.per.sing.2d.aor.act.subj.of ἀφίστημι, purpose) 1912.

ἀπ' (preposition with the ablative of separation) 70.

ἐμοῦ (abl.sing.masc.of ἐμός, separation) 1267.

Translation - "Three times I asked the Lord about this - that it might go away."

Comment: ὑπὲρ τούτου - a genitive of reference. The ἵνα clause tells us what Paul prayed. That "divine healing" the highly touted function of certain so-called charismatics is not an objective fruit of Christ's atonement, which must forthwith be granted to the believer, on the same basis as salvation, as some preach is clear from this passage. Paul was sick. He prayed three times that he might be healed. He was never healed.

There is, to be sure, the gift of healing, which the Holy Spirit in His divine wisdom has given to some of the saints. It is solely His prerogative to give this gift or to give another, although He has given some one of the gifts, at least, to every member of the Body of Christ (1 Cor.12:4-11). There is no Christian who has no gift. It is the function of every believer to find out what his gift is and then to use it under the direction of Christ, Who is the Head of the Body (Eph.1:22,23). But those to whom He has given the gift of healing are not always able to heal. It is the prayer of faith that saves the sick (James 5:14,15). If God does not choose to heal the sick, for reasons that are sufficient unto Himself, the healer cannot pray the prayer of faith. Thus not everyone who is sick is healed. Otherwise the entire teaching of Scripture about the purpose of suffering is negated. If it were true that the "healers" always heal God could never terminate the tour of duty for His children and take them home to heaven. "Precious in the sight of the Lord is the death of His saints" (Psalm 116:12) and He will not be forbidden to take His own children home to heaven by some television huckster who perhaps thinks more highly of himself than he ought to think (Rom.12:3).

Paul insisted, but God said no, and He gave His reasons, which Paul came to understand.

Verse 9 - "And he said unto me, My grace is sufficient for thee: for my strength is made perfect in weakness. Most gladly therefore will I rather glory in my infirmities, that the power of Christ may rest upon me."

καὶ εἴρηκέν μοι,'Ἀρκεῖ σοι ἡ χάρις μου. ἡ γὰρ δύναμις ἐν ἀσθενείᾳ τελεῖται. ἥδιστα οὖν μᾶλλον καυχήσομαι ἐν ταῖς ἀσθενείαις μου, ἵνα ἐπισκηνώσῃ ἐπ' ἐμὲ ἡ δύναμις τοῦ Χριστοῦ.

"But he said to me, 'My grace is sufficient for you, for my power is made perfect in weakness.' I will all the more gladly boast of my weaknesses, that the power of Christ may rest upon me." . . . RSV

καὶ (adversative conjunction) 14.
εἴρηκέν (3d.per.sing.perf.act.ind.of εἴρω consummative) 155.
μοι (dat.sing.masc.of ἐγώ, indirect object of εἴρηκεν) 123.
Ἀρκεῖ (3d.per.sing.pres.ind.of ἀρκέω, static) 1534.
σοι (dat.sing.masc.of σύ, personal advantage) 104.
ἡ (nom.sing.fem.of the article in agreement with χάρις) 9.
χάρις (nom.sing.fem.of χάρις, subject of ἀρκεῖ) 1700.
μου (gen.sing.masc.of ἐγώ, possession) 123.
ἡ (nom.sing.fem.of the article in agreement with δύναμις) 9.
γὰρ (causal conjunction) 105.
δύναμις (nom.sing.fem.of δύναμις, subject of τελεῖται) 687.
ἐν (preposition with the locative of accompanying circumstance) 80.
ἀσθενείᾳ (loc.sing.fem.of ἀσθένεια, accompanying circumstance) 740.
τελεῖται (3d.per.sing.pres.pass.ind.of τελειόω, static) 1914.

#4398 ἥδιστα (adverbial).

King James Version

more gladly - 2 Cor.12:9.
very gladly - 2 Cor.12:15.

Revised Standard Version

most gladly - 2 Cor.12:9.
most gladly - 2 Cor.12:15.

Meaning: neuter plural of the superlative ἥδιστος. *Cf.* ἡδύς - "glad." ἡδέως (#2255). Hence, with greatest delight. With reference to Paul's reaction to his suffering - 2 Cor.12:9; with reference to his service to the Corinthian church without pay - 2 Cor.12:15.

οὖν (inferential conjunction) 68.
μᾶλλον (adverbial) 619.
καυχήσομαι (1st.per.sing.fut.mid.ind.of καυχάομαι, predictive) 3847.
ἐν (preposition with the locative of accompanying circumstance) 80.
ταῖς (loc.pl.fem.of the article in agreement with ἀσθενείαις) 9.
ἀσθενείαις (loc.pl.fem.of ἀσθένεια, accompanying circumstance) 740.
μου (gen.sing.masc.of ἐγώ, possession) 123.
ἵνα (conjunction with the subjunctive in a purpose clause) 114.

#4399 ἐπισκηνώσῃ (3d.per.sing.pres.act.subj.of ἐπισκηνόω, purpose).

King James Version

rest upon - 2 Cor.12:9.

Revised Standard Version

rest upon - 2 Cor.12:9.

Meaning: A combination of ἐπί (#47) and σκηνόω (#1698). Hence to pitch a tent upon. To descend upon (ἐπί); metaphorically of the power of God resting upon Paul - 2 Cor.12:9.

ἐπ' (preposition with the accusative of extent) 47.
ἐμὲ (acc.sing.masc.of ἐμός, extent) 1267.
ἡ (nom.sing.fem.of the article in agreement with δύναμις) 9.
δύναμις (nom.sing.fem.of δύναμις, subject of ἐπισκήνωση) 687.
τοῦ (gen.sing.masc.of the article in agreement with Χριστοῦ) 9.
Χριστοῦ (gen.sing.masc.of Χριστός, possession) 4.

Translation - "But he has said to me, 'My grace is always sufficient for you because strength is perfected in weakness.' Therefore it is with delight that I will boast rather in the midst of my infirmities, so that the power of Christ may always be resting upon me."

Comment: καί is adversative. Paul prayed for relief but (καί) God had other plans. We have in εἴρηκέν a good example of the consummative perfect. "Here it is not an existing state, but a consummated process which is presented. However, we are not to suppose that the existing result is entirely out of sight, for 'the writer had in mind both the past act and the present result.' (Burton, *Moods and Tenses*, 38, as cited in Mantey, *Manual*, 202,203). Otherwise he would have used the aorist, which in the culminative sense denotes completed action without reference to existing results." (*Ibid.*) Paul indeed remembered what God said to him, but he is pointing backward to the reply which God gave to him when he prayed.

God's grace always suffices - something that Paul came to understand with reference to himself, his ministry and his suffering. "Thus power is in the process of being perfected when weakness is present" (Zech.4:6).

Now that Paul understands this principle οὖν is inferential. So he is most happy to glory under what previously to him were unfortunate circumstances. Formerly he prayed for release from that which is now the reason for his gladness, but only because thus can the purpose of God for his suffering be realized. This purpose follows in the ἵνα ἐπισκήνωση clause. μᾶλλον points to his change of attitude. Rather than praying against his infirmity, now he is boasting about it.

Verse 10 - "Therefore I take pleasure in infirmities, in reproaches, in necessities, in persecutions, in distresses for Christ's sake: for when I am weak, then am I strong."

διὸ εὐδοκῶ ἐν ἀσθενείαις, ἐν ὕβρεσιν, ἐν ἀνάγκαις, ἐν διωγμοῖς καὶ στενοχωρίαις, ὑπὲρ Χριστοῦ. ὅταν γὰρ ἀσθενῶ, τότε δυνατός εἰμι.

"For the sake of Christ, then, I am content with weakness, insults, hardships, persecutions, and calamities; for when I am weak, then I am strong." . . . RSV

διὸ (inferential conjunction) 1622.

εὐδοκῶ (1st.per.sing.pres.act.ind.of εὐδοκέω, present progressive) 328.

ἐν (preposition with the locative of accompanying circumstance) 80.

ἀσθενείαις (loc.pl.fem.of ἀσθένεια, accompanying circumstance) 740.

ἐν (preposition with the locative of accompanying circumstance) 80.

ὕβρεσιν (loc.sing.fem.of ὕβρις, accompanying circumstance) 3693.

ἐν (preposition with the locative of accompanying circumstance) 80.

ἀνάγκαις (loc.pl.fem.of ἀνάγκη, accompanying circumstance) 1254.

ἐν (preposition with the locative of accompanying circumstance) 80.

διωγμοῖς (loc.pl.masc.of διωγμός, accompanying circumstance) 1047.

καὶ (adjunctive conjunction joining nouns) 14.

στενοχωρίαις (loc.pl.fem.of στενοχωρία, accompanying circumstance) 3838.

ὑπὲρ (preposition with the genitive, "in behalf of") 545.

Χριστοῦ (gen.sing.masc.of Χριστός, "in behalf of") 4.

ὅταν (conjunction with the subjunctive in an indefinite temporal clause) 436.

γὰρ (causal conjunction) 105.

ἀσθενῶ (1st.per.sing.pres.act.subj.of ἀσθενέω, indefinite temporal clause) 857.

τότε (temporal adverb) 166.

δυνατός (nom.sing.masc.of δυνατός, predicate adjective) 1311.

εἰμι (1st.per.sing.pres.ind.of εἰμί, aoristic) 86.

Translation - "Therefore I consider myself fortunate under circumstances of infirmity, insult, necessity, persecution and outside pressures, in the cause of Christ, because when I am weak then I am strong."

Comment: This is the logical conclusion of the text beginning with verse 5. The Christian should rejoice in the midst and because of what, as an unregenerate, he would regard as misfortune. This principle applies of course only if he suffers as a result of his witness for Christ. Paul is not saying that difficulties which are experienced as a result of sin or stupidity in the life of the believer are a source of spiritual strength. *Cf.* James 1:2; Mt.5:11,12; 1 Pet.4:12,13; Rom.5:3-6.

The element of doubt in the ὅταν indefiite temporal clause relates to whether or not Paul will always remain in this happy condition of weakness (!) in which he is strong in God's power. If he should backslide and think himself sufficient to the task of serving Christ, he would lose God's power.

If it is never God's will to permit Satan to send his "messenger" (ἄγγελος) to attack the Christian, the conclusion is that God is unable to prevent that which otherwise He would forbid - else neither Paul nor any others who suffer are Christians. Otherwise the "faith healers" are wrong when they say that healing is in the atonement in the same sense in which salvation is.

Paul's Concern for the Corinthian Church

(2 Corinthians 12:11-21)

Verse 11 - "I am become a fool in glorying: ye have compelled me: for I ought to have been commended of you: for in nothing am I behind the very chiefest apostles, though I be nothing."

Γέγονα ἄφρων. ὑμεῖς με ἠναγκάσατε. ἐγὼ γὰρ ὤφειλον ὑφ' ὑμῶν συνίστασθαι. οὐδὲν γὰρ ὑστέρησα τῶν ὑπερλίαν ἀποστόλων, εἰ καὶ οὐδέν εἰμι.

"I have been a fool! You forced me to it, for I ought to have been commended by you. For I am not at all inferior to these superlative apostles, even though I am nothing." . . . RSV

Γέγονα (1st.per.sing.perf.ind.of γίνομαι, intensive) 113.
ἄφρων (nom.sing.masc.of ἄφρων, predicate nominative) 2462.
ὑμεῖς (nom.pl.masc.of σύ, subject of ἠναγκάσατε) 104.
με (acc.sing.masc.of ἐγώ, direct object of ἠναγκάσατε) 123.
ἠναγκάσατε (2d.per.pl.aor.act.ind.of ἀναγκάζω, constative) 1126.
ἐγὼ (nom.sing.masc.of ἐγώ, subject of ὤφειλον) 123.
γὰρ (causal conjunction) 105.
ὤφειλον (1st.per.sing.imp.ind.of ὀφείλω, voluntative) 1277.
ὑφ' (preposition with the ablative, agent) 117.
ὑμῶν (abl.pl.masc.of σύ, agent) 104.
συνίστασθαι (aor.pass.inf.of συνίστημι, complementary) 2328.
οὐδὲν (acc.sing.neut.of οὐδείς, quasi-cognate accusative) 446.
γὰρ (causal conjunction) 105.
ὑστέρησα (1st.per.sing.aor.act.ind.of ὑστερέω, culminative) 1302.
τῶν (abl.pl.masc.of the article in agreement with ἀποστόλων) 9.
ὑπερλίαν (adverbial) 4372.
ἀποστόλων (abl.pl.masc.of ἀπόστολος, comparison) 844.
εἰ (concessive particle) 337.
καὶ (emphatic conjunction) 14.
οὐδέν (acc.sing.neut.of οὐδείς, quasi-cognate accusative) 448.
εἰμι (1st.per.sing.pres.ind.of εἰμί, aoristic) 86.

Translation - "I have made a fool out of myself. You forced me to do it, because I should have been commended by you. Because I am not to the slightest degree inferior to the superlative apostles, even though in fact I am nothing."

Comment: Paul gets sarcastic again about the "superlative" apostoles in Corinth. He is clear that he does not mean the true Apostles of Christ (1 Cor.15:9). He blames the Corinthians for the fact that he was forced to boast of his achievements. If they had been giving him the recognition that he deserved it would not have been necessary. ὤφειλον here with the voluntative imperfect in a hypotactic clause expressing a wish. "The want of attainment in the imperfect prepares it to submit quite easily to the expression of a desire or disposition, since the statement of a wish itself implies the lack of realization." (Mantey, *Manual*, 190). This use of the imperfect is not often found in the New Testament. *Cf.* Acts 25:22; Rom.9:3; Gal.4:20; Philemon 13. It is possible that some of the Corinthian Christians had been praising Paul's critics, whom he calls false apostles. Why should they not have been fair to him in their evaluation? Therefore he felt compelled to add that he was inferior to those whom he sarcastically calls "superlative apostles" in no way, despite the fact that (concessive εἰ) he was in fact (emphatic καὶ) nothing at all. Even if he was nothing he deserved as much praise as his enemies, which implies that they were nothing. But Paul admits that in order to point this out he had to make a fool of himself. The Cognate Accusative "may be either that of inner content, ἐχάρησαν χαράν (Mt.2:10), objective result ἁμαρτάνοντα ἁμαρτίαν (1 John 5:16), φυλάσσοντες φυλακάς· (Lu.2:8), or even a kindred word in idea but a different root, as δαρήσεται ὀλίγας πληγάς, Lu.12:48). Considerable freedom must thus be given the term "cognate" as to both form and idea.... Some *neuter adjectives* are used to express this accusative, but far less frequently than in the ancient Greek." (Robertson, *Grammar,* 477, 478). Thus we have the cognate accusative in οὐδὲν here in 2 Cor.12:11.

Verse 12 - "Truly the signs of an apostle were wrought among you in all patience, in signs, and wonders, and mighty deeds."

τὰ μὲν σημεῖα τοῦ ἀποστόλου κατειργάσθη ἐν ὑμῖν ἐν πάσῃ ὑπομονῇ, σημείοις τε καὶ τέρασιν καί δυνάμεσιν.

"The signs of a true apostle were performed among you in all patience, with signs and wonders and mighty works." . . . RSV

τὰ (nom.pl.neut.of the article in agreement with σημεῖα) 9.

μὲν (particle of affirmation) 300.

σημεῖα (nom.pl.neut.of σημεῖον, subject of κατειράσθη) 1005.

τοῦ (gen.sing.masc.of the article in agreement with ἀποστόλου) 9.

ἀποστόλου (gen.sing.masc.of ἀπόστολος, description) 844.

κατειργάσθη (3d.per.sing.imp.pass.ind.of κατεργάζομαι, iterative) 3815.

ἐν (preposition with the locative with plural pronouns) 80.

ὑμῖν (loc.pl.masc.of σύ, place) 104.

ἐν (preposition with the instrumental of manner) 80.

πάσῃ (instru.sing.fem.of πᾶς, in agreement with ὑπομονῇ) 67.

ὑπομονῇ (instru.sing.fem.of ὑπομονή, manner) 2204.

σημείοις (instru.pl.neut.of σημεῖον, means) 1005.

τε (correlative particle) 1408.

καὶ (adjunctive conjunction joining nouns) 14.

τέρασιν (instru.pl.neut.of τέρας, means) 1500.

καὶ (adjunctive conjunction joining nouns) 14.

δυνάμεσιν (instru.pl.fem.of δύναμις, means) 687.

Translation - *"Indeed the evidences of my apostleship were given to you again and again, with all patience, both in signs and wonders and works of power."*

Comment: μὲν here without δὲ is emphatically affirmative. Note the iterative imperfect in κατειργάσθη. Thus our translation. Day after day and time after time Paul and the other true Apostles had demonstrated with empirical evidence that they were truly commissioned by Christ. That they were always patient about it, may suggest that the Corinthians had never been totally free from skepticism and had asked for more signs and wonders - repeated requests with which Paul always patiently complied. Signs, wonders, mighty deeds - incapable of reproduction by human power alone. The suggestion is that the false apostles who were seeking to brainwash the Corinthians had been able to reproduce none of these signs. Paul is asking that the Corinthians look at the record.

There is indirect evidence here that the so-called "sign gifts" which modern "charismatics" profess to have and display in public meetings and on television, are spurious. The "signs" did not follow anyone except the twelve Apostles, the uninspired addition to the Gospel of Mark (Mk.16:9-20) to the contrary notwithstanding. To point out to the Pentecostalists that the last twelve verses of the Gospel of Mark are not a part of the original inspired text, is to make application for one's place in the pot of boiling oil reserved for heretics. Nevertheless the best scholarship in the field of textual criticism has ruled against the longer Markan ending. If, in fact, Mark 16:9-20 is a part of what the Holy Spirit gave to the early churches, we must concede to the baptismal regenerationists their point (Mk.16:16), and we must demonstrate our immunity to deadly poisons and join the snake-handlers. Indeed if the signs of Paul's apostleship which he demonstrated in Corinth "follow" then the test of apostleship is not theology but the evidence of the modern religious charlatan, sleight-of-hand magician and religious quack. Pharaoh's court magicians reproduced some of the miracles of Moses and Aaron, but they were not able to command the waters of the Red Sea. Paul's point is that the Corinthians should accept his ministry as an Apostle of Christ and reject that of his false accusers, because his ministry was attested by the "signs, wonders and mighty works" whereas that of his critics was not.

The Corinthians saw as many signs, wonders and mighty works as any of the other churches which Paul established. They were different from the others, only in that Paul refused to accept their money in return for his ministry. This is his thought in

Verse 13 - *"For what is it wherein you were inferior to other churches, except it be that I myself was not burdensome to you? Forgive me this wrong."*

τί γάρ ἐστιν ὃ ἡσσώθητε ὑπὲρ τὰς λοιπὰς ἐκκλησίας, εἰ μὴ ὅτι αὐτὸς ἐγὼ οὐ κατενάρκησα ὑμῶν; χαρίσασθέ μοι τὴν ἀδικίαν ταύτην.

"For in what were you less favored than the rest of the churches, except that I

myself did not burden you? Forgive me this wrong!" . . . *RSV*

τί (nom.sing.neut.of τίς, interrogative pronoun, predicate nominative) 281.
γάρ (inferential conjunction) 105.
ἐστιν (3d.per.sing.pres.ind.of εἰμί, aoristic) 86.
ὅ (acc.sing.neut.of ὅς, anaphoric cognate) 65.

#4400 ἡσσώθητε (2d.per.pl.1st.aor.pass.ind.of ἡττάομαι, direct question).

King James Version

be inferior - 2 Cor.12:13.
be overcome - 2 Pet.2:19,20.

Revised Standard Version

less favored - 2 Cor.12:13.
overcome - 2 Pet.2:19.
overpower - 2 Pet.2:20.

Meaning: Cf. ἥττων (#4208). Hence, to be made inferior; to be placed in an inferior position; to be defeated, overcome, worsted. Followed by ὑπέρ and the accusative of extent in 2 Cor.12:13; to be overpowered by a temptation or false teaching - 2 Pet.2:19; by the world - 2 Pet.2:20.

ὑπέρ (preposition with the accusative, comparative extent, after a verb) 545.
τὰς (acc.pl.fem.of the article in agreement with ἐκκλησίας) 9.
λοιπάς (acc.pl.fem.of λοιπός, in agreement with ἐκκλησίας) 1402.
ἐκκλησίας (acc.pl.fem.of ἐκκλησία, extent) 1204.
εἰ (conditional particle in an elliptical condition) 337.
μὴ (negative conjunction in an elliptical condition) 87.
ὅτι (objective conjunction) 211.
αὐτὸς (nom.sing.masc.of αὐτός, intensive, predicate position) 16.
ἐγώ (nom.sing.masc.of ἐγώ, subject of κατενάρκησα) 123.
οὐ (negative conjunction with the indicative) 130.
κατενάρκησα (1st.per.sing.aor.act.ind.of καταναρκάω, constative) 4374.
ὑμῶν (gen.pl.masc.of σύ, objective genitive) 104.
χαρίσασθέ (2d.per.pl.aor.mid.impv.of χαρίζομαι, entreaty) 2158.
μοι (dat.sing.masc.of ἐγώ, indirect object of χαρίσασθέ) 123.
τὴν (acc.sing.fem.of the article in agreement with ἀδικίαν) 9.
ἀδικίαν (acc.sing.fem.of ἀδικία, direct object of χαρίσασθέ) 2367.
ταύτην (acc.sing.fem.of οὗτος, in agreement with ἀδικίαν) 93.

Translation - "*So how were you treated worse than the other churches, except that I myself did not take your money? Forgive me for this injustice!*"

Comment: ὅ, the accusative of the relative pronoun follows the neuter interrogative pronoun in the nominative. It is anaphoric, calling attention to τί. "What is it?" "What is what?" - "That in which you have been slighted." Note ὑπέρ with the accusative of extent in a comparison - "To what extent more than the other churches were you made inferior?" Intensive αὐτός, may hint that other preachers whom Paul sent to Corinth - Peter, Apollos, Timothy *et al* had taken money for their services, although Paul did not. "I did not work against you by burdening you with demands for your money." This Paul did in the other churches. His plea for forgiveness for what he calls his injustice (ἀδικίαν) is, of course, sarcasm. If he had asked them for money he would have provided his enemies in Corinth with an ostensible ground for criticism .

He planned to visit Corinth again, for the third time, and he will follow the same financial policy as before.

Verse 14 - "Behold, the third time I am ready to come to you: and I will not be burdensome to you; for the children ought not to lay up for the parents, but the parents for the children."

Ἰδοὺ τρίτον τοῦτο ἑτοίμως ἔχω ἐλθεῖν πρὸς ὑμᾶς, καὶ οὐ καταναρκήσω. οὐ γὰρ ζητῶ τὰ ὑμῶν ἀλλὰ ὑμᾶς, οὐ γὰρ ὀφείλει τὰ τέκνα τοῖς γονεῦσιν θησαυρίζειν, ἀλλὰ οἱ γονεῖς τοῖς τέκνοις.

"Here for the third time I am ready to come to you. And I will not be a burden, for I seek not what is yours but you; for children ought not to lay up for their parents, but parents for their children." . . . RSV

Ἰδοὺ (exclamation) 95.

τρίτον (acc.sing.neut.of τρίτος, cognate accusative) 1209.

τοῦτο (acc.sing.neut.of οὗτος, in agreement with τρίτον) 93.

ἑτοίμως (adverbial) 3551.

ἔχω (1st.per.sing.pres.act.ind.of ἔχω, aoristic) 82.

ἐλθεῖν (aor.inf.of ἔρχομαι,complementary) 146.

πρὸς (preposition with the accusative of extent) 197.

ὑμᾶς (acc.pl.masc.of σύ, extent) 104.

καὶ (adversative conjunction) 14.

οὐ (negative conjunction with the indicative) 130.

καταναρκήσω (1st.per.sing.fut.act.ind.of καταναρκάω, predictive) 4374.

οὐ (negative conjunction with the indicative) 130.

γὰρ (causal conjunction) 105.

ζητῶ (1st.per.sing.pres.act.ind.of ζητέω, aoristic) 207.

τὰ (acc.pl.neut.of the article, direct object of ζητῶ) 9.

ὑμῶν (gen.pl.masc.of σύ, possession) 104.

ἀλλὰ (alternative conjunction) 342.

ὑμᾶς (acc.pl.masc.of σύ, direct object of ζητῶ) 104.

οὐ (negative conjunction with the indicative) 130.

γὰρ (causal conjunction) 105.

ὀφείλει (3d.per.sing.pres.ind.of ὀφείλω, customary) 1277.

τὰ (nom.pl.neut.of the article in agreement with τέκνα) 9.

τέκνα (nom.pl.neut.of τέκνον, subject of ὀφείλει) 229.

τοῖς (dat.pl.masc.of the article in agreement with γονεῦσιν) 9.

γονεῦσιν (dat.pl.masc.of γονεύς, personal advantage) 878.
θησαυρίζειν (pres.act.inf.of θησαυρίζω, complementary) 591.
ἀλλὰ (alternative conjunction) 342.
οἱ (nom.pl.masc.of the article in agreement with γονεῖς) 9.
γονεῖς (nom.pl.masc.of γονεύς, subject of ὀφείλει) 878.
τοῖς (dat.pl.neut.of the article in agreement with τέκνοις) 9.
τέκνοις (dat.pl.neut.of τέκνον, personal advantage) 229.

*Translation - "Look! This is the third time that I have got ready to come to you;
but I will not be a burden to you, because I am not seeking yours, but you. Indeed
the children ought not provide for the financial security of the parents, but the
parents for the children."*

Comment: Paul's plan to visit Corinth a third time and to go on to Spain did not
materialize, as he ended his ministry in martyrdom in Rome. *Cf.#*'s 82 and 3551
(the adverb always with ἔχω) - "I have ready plans. . . " The complementary
infinitive ἐλθεῖν describes Paul's plan. καὶ is adversative. He had been saying a
great deal to them about money. Lest they interpret his plan to come to them
again as a means to take their money, he denies it. It is as though he is saying,
"Do not worry. When I come again to Corinth I am not going to ask for money."
He wanted their lives in total dedication to Christ, not their money. He lays
down a principle which does not deny Exodus 20:12, since Paul is speaking not
of biological but of spiritual children. A Chistian need not provide for the
financial security of the preacher who led him to Christ, but the preacher should
provide for the spiritual welfare of his converts. 2 Cor.11:9,10.

*Verse 15 - "And I will very gladly spend and be spent for you: though the more
abundantly I love you, the less I am loved."*

ἐγὼ δὲ ἥδιστα δαπανήσω καὶ ἐκδαπανηθήσομαι ὑπὲρ τῶν ψυχῶν ὑμῶν. εἰ
περισσοτέρως ὑμᾶς ἀγαπῶ, ἦσσον ἀγαπῶμαι;

*"I will most gladly spend and be spent for your souls. If I love you the more,
am I to be loved the less?" . . . RSV*

ἐγὼ (nom.sing.masc.of ἐγώ, subject of δαπανήσω and ἐκδαπανηθήσομαι,
emphatic) 123.
δὲ (adversative conjunction) 11.
ἥδιστα (adverbial) 4398.
δαπανήσω (1st.per.sing.fut.act.ind.of δαπανάω, predictive) 2238.
καὶ (adjunctive conjunction joining verbs) 14.

#**4401** ἐκδαπανηθήσομαι (1st.per.sing.fut.pass.ind.of ἐκδαπανάομαι,
predictive).

King James Version

be spent - 2 Cor.12:15.

Revised Standard Version

be spent - 2 Cor.12:15.

Meaning: A combination of ἐκ (#19) and δαπανάω (#2238). To exhaust by spending everything one has. In a physical, mental and social as well as in a financial sense - ἐκ is perfective - 2 Cor.12:15.

ὑπὲρ (preposition with the genitive "in behalf of") 545.
τῶν (gen.pl.fem.of the article in agreement with φυχῶν) 9.
φυχῶν (gen.pl.fem.of φυχή, "in behalf of") 233.
ὑμῶν (gen.pl.masc.of σύ, possession) 104.
εἰ (conditional particle in a first-class condition) 337.
περισσοτέρως (adverbial, comparative of περισσῶς) 1630.
ὑμᾶς (acc.pl.masc.of σύ, direct object of ἀγαπῶ) 104.
ἀγαπῶ (1st.per.sing.pres.act.ind.of ἀγαπάω, first-class condition) 540.
ἧσσον (acc.sing.neut.of ἧττων, adverbial) 4208.
ἀγαπῶμαι (1st.per.sing.pres.pass.ind.of ἀγαπάω, first-class condition) 540.

Translation - "But I will gladly spend and be spent for the sake of your souls. If I love you intensely will you love me less?"

Comment: ἐγώ is emphatic, since it is implicit in both the verbs of which it is subject. Note the perfect force of ἐκ in composition. Paul was willing to spend all of his money in service for the Corinthians and, in addition, he would serve them until all that he had in every way - financially, physically, psychologically and socially had been poured out in their behalf. His question sounds a little petulant as if he was suffering from a attack of self-pity. He seems to be accusing them, by implication, of failing to recognize his love for them and to take steps to requite this love.

Verse 16 - "But be it so, I did not burden you: nevertheless, being crafty, I caught you with guile."

ἔστω δέ, ἐγώ οὐ κατεβάρησα ὑμᾶς. ἀλλὰ ὑπάρχων πανοῦργος δόλῳ ὑμᾶς ἔλαβον.

"But granting that I myself did not burden you, I was crafty, you say, and got the better of you by guile." . . . RSV

ἔστω (3d.per.sing.pres.impv.of εἰμί, permission) 86.
δέ (adversative conjunction) 11.
ἐγώ (nom.sing.masc.of ἐγώ, subject of κατεβάρησα) 123.
οὐ (negative conjunction with the indicative) 130.

#4402 κατεβάρησα (1st.per.sing.aor.act.ind.of καταβαρέω, constative).

King James Version

burden - 2 Cor.12:16.

Revised Standard Version

burden - 2 Cor. 12:16.

Meaning: A combination of κατά (#98) and βαρέω (#1589). Hence, to press down; to burden; in a financial sense - 2 Cor. 12:16.

ὑμᾶς (acc.pl.masc.of σύ, direct object of κατεβάρησα) 104.
ἀλλά (adversative conjunction) 342.
ὑπάρχων (pres.part.nom.sing.masc.of ὑπάρχω, adverbial, causal) 1303.

#4403 πανοῦργος (nom.sing.masc.of πανοῦργος, predicate adjective).

King James Version

crafty - 2 Cor. 12:16.

Revised Standard Version

crafty - 2 Cor. 12:16.

Meaning: A combination of πᾶς (#67) and ἐργάζομαι (#691). *Cf.* πανουργία (#2693). Hence, crafty. The ability to manipulate every factor in a situation to bring about a desired result. Never in an evil sense in the New Testament. Of Paul's strategy in dealing with the church at Corinth - 2 Cor. 12:16.

δόλῳ (instru.sing.masc.of δόλος, means) 1557.
ὑμᾶς (acc.pl.masc.of σύ, direct object of ἔλαβον) 104.
ἔλαβον (1st.per.sing.aor.act.ind.of λαμβάνω, constative) 533.

Translation - "But be that as it may, I did not burden you down, but because I was crafty I took you by deception."

Comment: The subject of ἔστω is the previous sentence of verse 15. The question as to whether Paul was properly appreciated by the Corinthians is not important. Paul waves aside any further comment on the subject - "Let it pass." "Forget it." "However that may be."

The important thing is that Paul's policy of paying his own expenses was such a manifestation of his sincerity that the Corinthians were impressed to the point that they listened to his gospel preaching and accepted Christ. Paul calls it deception or a trick, as though it had been unethical. It was only good public relations. The gospel appeal of most electronic evangelists on radio and television is short circuited by their ceaseless appeals for money. The least they could do to allay suspicion that they are insincere is to submit to an audit by an accountant with a reputation for objectivity and reveal the true state of their affairs. This should be done an a regular schedule. No one doubts that television and radio time is very expensive, but only the naive will believe that they are not personally interested in the outcome. Those religious hucksters who do "provide things honest in the sight of all men" (Rom. 12:17) will not consider this an affront. Others should.

Paul was being as wise as a serpent and as harmless as a dove (Mt. 10:16). If his policy had been unethical he would have been in a position to exploit them. This he challenges them to prove in

Verse 17 - "Did I make a gain of you by any of them whom I sent unto you?"

μή τινα ὧν ἀπέσταλκα πρὸς ὑμᾶς, δι' αὐτοῦ ἐπλεονέκτησα ὑμᾶς;

"Did I take advantage of you through any of those whom I sent to you?" . . .
RSV

μή (negative conjunction in a rhetorical question expecting a negative reply) 87.
τινα (acc.pl.neut.of τις, indefinite pronoun, direct object of ἀπέσταλκα) 486.
ὧν (gen.pl.masc.of ὅς, partitive genitive) 65.
ἀπέσταλκα (1st.per.sing.perf.act.ind.of ἀποστέλλω, consummative) 215.
πρὸς (preposition with the accusative of extent) 197.
ὑμᾶς (acc.pl.masc.of σύ, extent) 104.
δι' (preposition with the genitive, agent) 118.
αὐτοῦ (gen.sing.masc.of αὐτός, agent) 16.
ἐπλεονέκτησα (1st.per.sing.aor.act.ind.of πλεονεκτέω, culminative) 4276.
ὑμᾶς (acc.pl.masc.of σύ, direct object of ἐπλεονέκτησα) 104.

Translation - "I did not exploit you through any one of those whom I have sent to you, did I?"

Comment: If this rhetorical question could honestly have been answered in the affirmative, then Paul had been unethically crafty with them. His approach had always been that he was not in Corinth for financial gain. He had played the game so well that the Corinthians, convinced of the purity of his motives, had accepted his gospel and had been saved. Thus Paul gained his end, *viz.* their salvation. But did he have an ultimate motive of getting their money? If so his guile was real and dishonest. Hence his challenge. He had sent his representatives to Corinth again and agin (broken continuity in the present perfect in ἀπέσταλκα). This is the iterative intensive perfect. Did any of those whom he sent (τινα ὧν) act as Paul's agent (δι' αὐτοῦ) to exploit the Corinthians? τινα is anacoluthon. μή with the indicative indicates a question that expects a negative reply.

He pursues his point with more specifics in

Verse 18 - "I desired Titus, and with him I sent a brother. Did Titus make a gain of you? Walked we not in the same spirit? Walked we not in the same steps?"

παρεκάλεσα Τίτον καὶ συναπέστειλα τὸν ἀδελφόν. μήτι ἐπλεονέκτησεν ὑμᾶς Τίτος; οὐ τῷ αὐτῷ πνεύματι περιεπατήσαμεν; οὐ τοῖς αὐτοῖς ἴχνεσιν;

"I urged Titus to go, and sent the brother with him. Did Titus take advantage of you? Did we not act in the same spirit? Did we not take the same steps?" . . .
RSV

παρεκάλησα (1st.per.sing.aor.act.ind.of παρακαλέω, constative) 230.

Τίτον (acc.sing.masc.of Τίτος, direct object of παρεκάλησα) 4278.
καὶ (adjunctive conjunction joining verbs) 14.

#**4404** συναπέστειλα (1st.per.sing.aor.act.ind.of συναποστέλλω, constative).

King James Version

send with - 2 Cor.12:18.

Revised Standard Version

send with - 2 Cor.12:18.

Meaning: A combination of σύν (#1542), ἀπό (#70) and στέλλω (# 4342). *Cf.* also ἀποστέλλω (#215). Hence, to send along with; to send one as a companion to another - 2 Cor.12:18.

τὸν (acc.sing.masc.of the article in agreement with ἀδελφόν) 9.
ἀδελφόν (acc.sing.masc.of ἀδελφός, direct object of συναπέστειλα) 15.
μήτι (negative compound particle in a rhetorical question expecting a negative reply) 676.
ἐπλεονέκτησεν (3d.per.sing.aor.act.ind.of πλεονεκτέω, culminative) 4276.
ὑμᾶς (acc.pl.masc.of σύ, direct object of ἐπλεονέκτησεν) 104.
Τίτος (nom.sing.masc.of Τίτος, subject of ἐπλεονέκτησεν) 4278.
οὐ (negative conjunction in rhetorical question expecting a positive reply) 130.
τῷ (instru.sing.neut.of the article in agreement with πνεύματι) 9.
αὐτῷ (instru.sing.neut.of αὐτός, in agreement with πνεύματι, intensive) 16.
πνεύματι (instru.sing.neut.of πνεῦμα, manner) 83.
περιπατήσαμεν (1st.per.pl.aor.act.ind.of περιπατέω, constative) 384.
οὐ (negative conjunction in rhetorical question expecting a postive reply) 130.
τοῖς (instru.pl.masc.of the article in agreement with ἴχνεσιν) 9.
αὐτοῖς (instru.pl.masc.of αὐτός, in agreement with ἴχνεσιν, intensive) 16.
ἴχνεσιν (instru.pl.masc.of ἴχνος, means) 3887.

Translation - "*I implored Titus and I sent the brother with him. Titus did not exploit you did he? Did we not conduct ourselves in the same spirit? In the same steps?*"

Comment: The first rhetorical question demands "No" for an answer - the other two a positive reply. Titus and Luke (or whoever the other brother was) conducted themselves in Corinth as Paul's agents, exactly as he did and as he still would had he gone again to Corinth in person. There was no exploitation of Corinthian money. Thus Paul supports his question of verse 17.

Verse 19 - "*Again, think ye that we excuse ourselves unto you? We speak before God in Christ: but we do all things, dearly beloved, for your edifying.*"

Πάλαι δοκεῖτε ὅτι ὑμῖν ἀπολογούμεθα; κατέναντι θεοῦ ἐν Χριστῷ λαλοῦμεν. τὰ δὲ πάντα, ἀγαπητοί, ὑπὲρ τῆς ὑμῶν οἰκοδομῆς.

"*Have you been thinking all along that we have been defending ourselves before you? It is in the sight of God that we have been speaking in Christ, and all for your upbuilding, beloved."* . . . *RSV*

Πάλαι (adverbial) 941.
δοκεῖτε (2d.per.pl.pres.act.ind.of δοκέω, progressive present retroactive) 287.
ὅτι (conjunction introducing an object clause in indirect discourse) 211.
ὑμῖν (dat.pl.masc.of σύ, indirect object of ἀπολογούμεθα) 104.
ἀπολογούμεθα (1st.per.pl.pres.mid.ind.of ἀπολογέομαι, presen progressive retroactive) 2476.
κατέναντι (improper preposition with the genitive of place description) 1342.
θεοῦ (gen.sing.masc.of θεός, place description) 124.
ἐν (preposition with the instrumental of association) 80.
Χριστῷ (instru.sing.masc.of Χριστός, association) 4.
λαλοῦμεν (1st.per.pl.pres.act.ind.of λαλέω, present progressive) 815.
τὰ (acc.pl.neut.of the article in agreement with πάντα) 9.
δὲ (continuative conjunction) 11.
πάντα (acc.pl.neut.of πᾶς, direct object of λαλοῦμεν) 67.
ἀγαπητοί (voc.pl.masc.of ἀγαπητός, address) 327.
ὑπὲρ (preposition with the genitive "in behalf of") 545.
τῆς (gen.sing.fem.of the article in agreement with οἰκοδομῆς) 9.
ὑμῶν (gen.pl.masc.of σύ, possession) 104.
οἰκοδομῆς (gen.sing.fem.of οἰκοδομή, "in behalf of") 1481.

Translation - *"Have you been thinking all the while that we are apologizing to you? We are saying all of this in God's presence in Christ for your edification, beloved."*

Comment: δοκεῖτε is retroactive with its durative action joined to πάλαι. "Have you been, and are you still thinking . . . κ.τ.λ." Paul had not been defending himself. Everything he had said was for the purpose of their spiritual edification. If he had been concerned only to improve his own personal relationship with them, he would never have written the next verse.

Verse 20 - *"For I fear, lest, when I come, I shall not find you such as I would, and that I shall be found unto you such as ye would not: lest, there be debates, envyings, wraths, strifes, backbitings, whisperings, swellings, tumults."*

φοβοῦμαι γὰρ μή πως ἐλθὼν οὐχ οἵους θέλω εὕρω ὑμᾶς, καγὼ εὑρεθῶ ὑμῖν οἷον οὐ θέλετε, μή πως ἔρις, ζῆλος, θυμοί, ἐριθείαι, καταλαλιαί, ψιθυρισμοί, φυσιώσεις, ἀκαταστασίαι.

"For I fear that perhaps I may come and find you not what I wish, and that you may find me not what you wish; that perhaps there may be quarreling, jealousy, anger, selfishness, slander, gossip, conceit and disorder." . . . *RSV*

φοβοῦμαι (1st.per.sing.pres.ind.of φοβέομαι, aoristic) 101.
γὰρ (causal conjunction) 105.
μή (negative conjunction with the subjunctive, in a sub-final clause) 87.

πως (particle with μή and the subjunctive in a sub-final clause) 3700.
ἐλθών (aor.part.nom.sing.masc.of ἔρχομαι, adverbial, temporal) 146.
οὐχ (negative conjunction with the indicative) 130.
οἵους (acc.pl.masc.of οἷος, direct object of θέλω) 1496.
θέλω (1st.per.sing.pres.act.ind.of θέλω, futuristic) 88.
εὕρω (1st.per.sing.2d.aor.act.subj.of εὑρίσκω, sub-final clause) 79.
ὑμᾶς (acc.pl.masc.of σύ, direct object of εὕρω) 104.
κἀγώ (continuative conjunction and first personal pronoun, crasis) 178.
εὑρεθῶ (1st.per.sing.pres.pass.subj.of εὑρίσκω, sub-final clause) 79.
ὑμῖν (instrumental pl.masc.of σύ, means) 104.
οἷον (acc.sing.neut., cognate accusative of οἷος) 1496.
οὐ (negative conjunction with the indicative) 130.
θέλετε (2d.per.pl.pres.act.ind.of θέλω, futuristic) 88.
μή (negative conjunction with the subjunctive understood in a sub-final clause) 87.
πως (particle with μή in a sub-final clause) 3700.

ἔρις (nom.sing.fem.of ἔρις, subject of verb understood, and so with all following substantives) 3819.
ζῆλος (nom.sing.masc.of ζῆλος) 1985.
θυμοί (nom.pl.masc.of θυμός) 2034.
ἐριθεῖαι (nom.pl.fem.of ἐριθεία) 3837.

#4405 καταλαλιαί (nom.pl.fem.of καταλαλία).

King James Version

backbiting - 2 Cor.12:20.
evil speaking - 1 Pet.2:1.

Revised Standard Version

slander - 2 Cor.12:20; 1 Pet.2:1.

Meaning: Cf.κατάλαλος (#3822). A combination of κατά (#98) and λαλία (#1611). Evil speaking; slander; backbiting; unkind criticism. A Corinthian sin - 2 Cor.12:20; a hindrance to spiritual growth - 1 Pet.2:1.

#4406 ψιθυρισμοί (nom.pl.masc.of ψιθυρισμός).

King James Version

whispering - 2 Cor.12:20.

Revised Standard Version

gossip - 2 Cor.12:20.

Meaning: Cf. ψιθυριστής (#3821); ψιθυρίζω - " to whisper into the ear." Secret gossip - 2 Cor.12:20.

#4407 φυσιώσεις (nom.pl.fem.of φυσίωσις).

King James Version

swelling - 2 Cor.12:20.

Revised Standard Version

conceit - 2 Cor.12:20.

Meaning: Cf. φυσιόω (#4122). The result of one's ego being puffed up. Conceit - 2 Cor.12:20.

ἀκαταστασίαι (nom.pl.fem.of ἀκαταστασία) 2718.

Translation - "Because I am afraid that perhaps when I come I will not find you in a condition such as I wish, and I will be found by you in a mood such as you do not wish; lest, perhaps I find brawls, jealousy, passionate hatred, unfair rivalry, slanders, gossip, conceit, disorders."

Comment: With φοβοῦμαι, a verb of fearing the negative with the subjunctive is μή πως (same as μήποτε). The negative οὐχ is joined to θέλω. This is a classic idiom with a verb of fearing.

Paul dislikes the stern treatment he is giving the Corinthians, and uses this method, not to defend himself but to help them (verse 19). He fears that such stern treatment will still be needed when he visits Corinth again. This third visit did not materialize however. The clause is negative sub-final. He does not wish to find them (οὐχ οἵους θέλω) as he fears he will and he does not wish them to find him such as they dislike (οὐ θέλετε). After μή πως there is ellision of the verb in the subjunctive. He fears that he will find all of these unchristian characteristics which he lists. Study the words to determine exact meanings. Note that they fall within the range of sins of attitude rather   than sins of the body.

Verse 21 - "And lest, when I come again, my God will humble me among you, and that I shall bewail many which have sinned already, and have not repented of the uncleanness and fornication and lasciviousness which they have committed."

μή πάλιν ἐλθόντος μου ταπεινώσῃ με ὁ θεός μου πρὸς ὑμᾶς, καὶ πενθήσω πολλοὺς τῶν προημαρτηκότων καὶ μὴ μετανοησάντων ἐπὶ τῇ ἀκαθαρσίᾳ καὶ πορνείᾳ καὶ ἀσελγείᾳ ᾗ ἔπραξαν.

"I fear that when I come again my God may humble me before you, and I may have to mourn over many of those who sinned before and have not repented of the impurity, immorality, and licentiousness which they have practiced." . . . RSV

μή (negative conjunction with the subjuntive, after a verb of fearing) 87.
πάλιν (adverbial) 355.
ἐλθόντος (aor.part.gen.sing.masc.of ἔρχομαι, genitive absolute) 146.

μου (gen.sing.masc.of ἐγώ, genitive absolute) 123.

ταπεινώσῃ (3d.per.sing.aor.act.subj.of ταπεινόω, negative sub-final clause) 1248.

με (acc.sing.masc.of ἐγώ, direct object of ταπεινώσῃ) 123.

ὁ (nom.sing.masc.of the article in agreement with θεός) 9.

θεός (nom.sing.masc.of θεός, subject of ταπεινώσῃ) 124.

μου (gen.sing.masc.of ἐγώ, relationship) 123.

πρὸς (preposition with the accusative, cause) 197.

ὑμᾶς (acc.pl.masc.of σύ, cause) 104.

καὶ (continuative conjunction) 14.

πενθήσω (1st.per.sing.1st.aor.act.subj.of πενθέω, sub-final) 424.

πολλοὺς (acc.pl.masc.of πολύς, direct object of πενθήσω) 228.

τῶν (gen.pl.masc.of the article in agreement with προημαρτηκότων) 9.

#4408 προημαρτηκότων (perf.act.part.gen.pl.masc.of προμαρτάνω, partitive genitive).

King James Version

sin already - 2 Cor.12:21.
sin heretofore - 2 Cor.13:2.

Revised Standard Version

sin before - 2 Cor.12:21; 13:2.

Meaning: A combination of πρό (#442) and ἁμαρτάνω (#1260). To sin previously; to sin before - 2 Cor.12:21; 13:2.

καὶ (adjunctive conjunction joining participles) 14.

μὴ (negative conjunction with the participle) 87.

μετανοησάντων (aor.act.part.gen.pl.masc.of μετανοέω, partitive genitive) 251.

ἐπὶ (preposition with the instrumental of cause) 47.

τῇ (instru.sing.fem.of the article in agreement with ἀκαθαρσίᾳ) 9.

ἀκαθαρσίᾳ (instru.sing.fem.of ἀκαθαρσία, cause) 1467.

καὶ (adjunctive conjunction joining nouns) 14.

πορνείᾳ (instru.sing.fem.of πορνεία, cause) 511.

καὶ (adjunctive conjunction joining nouns) 14.

ἀσελγείᾳ (instru.sing.fem.of ἀσέλγεια, cause) 2303.

ᾗ (instru.sing.fem.of ὅς, in agreement with antecedents) 65.

ἔπραξαν (3d.per.pl.aor.act.ind.of πράσσω, culminative) 1943.

Translation - "Also lest that after I have arrived my God will humiliate me because of you and I shall weep over many of those who have been sinning but did not once repent of the uncleanness and fornication and immorality in which they have indulged."

Comment: The verse continues the sentence begun with φοβοῦμαι in verse 20.

Paul fears for those conditions described in verse 20 and also (πάλιν) that after he has arrived (genitive absolute in ἐλθόντος μου) God will bring him low in humiliation. It is always humiliating to a preacher when he sees his converts living in defeat. πρὸς ὑμᾶς can mean cause. Cf.#197. πενθέω takes the accusative - "mourn over." Note πολλοὺς with the two partitive genitives. The distinction in the tense of the genitive participles is to be noted. They had always been sinning before Paul's planned arrival (perfect tense in προημαρτηκότων) but they did not once repent (aorist tense in μετανοησάντων). ἐπὶ with the instrumental of cause. Note the attraction of the relative pronoun ᾗ to its antecedents.

Thus the same Paul who is bold and terrifying in his letters, while he entreats his beloved converts to live for Christ (2 Cor.10:10) warns that if he visits Corinth again they will find him just as bold when he is present.

Final Warnings and Greetings

(2 Corinthians 13:1-13)

2 Cor.13:1 - "This is the third time I am coming to you. In the mouth of two or three witnesses shall every word be established."

Τρίτον τοῦτο ἔρχομαι πρὸς ὑμᾶς. ἐπὶ στόματος δύο μαρτύρων καὶ τριῶν σταθήσεται πᾶν ῥῆμα.

"This is the third time I am coming to you. Any charge must be sustained by the evidence of two or three witnesses." . . . RSV

Τρίτον (acc.sing.neut.of τρίτος, cognate accusative) 1209.
τοῦτο (nom.sing.neut.of οὗτος, subject of verb understood) 93.
ἔρχομαι (1st.per.sing.pres.mid.ind.of ἔρχομαι, futuristic) 146.
πρὸς (preposition with the accusative of extent) 197.
ὑμᾶς (acc.pl.masc.of σύ, extent) 104.
ἐπὶ (preposition with the genitive, basis) 47.
στόματος (gen.sing.neut.of στόμα, basis) 344.
δύο (numeral) 385.
μαρτύρων (gen.pl.masc.of μάρτυς, possession) 1263.
καὶ (adjunctive conjunction joining numerals) 14.
τριῶν (gen.pl.masc.of τρεῖς, in agreement with μαρτύρων) 1010.
σταθήσεται (3d.per.sing.fut.pass.ind.of ἵστημι, imperative) 180.
πᾶν (nom.sing.neut.of πᾶς, in agreement with ῥῆμα) 67.
ῥῆμα (nom.sing.neut.of ῥῆμα, subject of σταθήσεται) 343.

Translation - "This is now the third time that I will be coming to you. On the basis of the testimony of two or three witnesses every word will be established."

Comment: Τρίτον τοῦτο - in this cognate accusative construction the pronoun occurs without a substantive. He had suggested in 2 Cor.12:20 that they were gossiping and slandering each other, so he warns them in advance not to accuse each other to him unless they could substantiate their allegations with concurring testimony. *Cf.* Deut.19:15; Mt.18:15; 1 Tim.5:19; 2 Cor.12:14. Church discipline properly administered rests solidly upon this principle. But, though Paul would not credit unsupported slander, he would deal sternly with those who had sinned. This he says in

Verse 2 - "I told you before, and foretell you, as if I were present, the second time, and being absent now I write to them which heretofore have sinned, and to all other, that, if I came again, I will not spare."

προείρηκα καὶ προλέγω ὡς παρὼν τὸ δεύτερον καὶ ἀπὼν νῦν τοῖς προημαρτηκόσιν καὶ τοῖς λοιποῖς πᾶσιν, ὅτι ἐὰν ἔλθω εἰς τὸ πάλιν οὐ φείσομαι,

" *I warned those who sinned before and all the others, and I warn them now while absent, as I did when present on my second visit, that if I come again I will not spare them —* " . . . RSV

#**4409** προείρηκα (1st.per.sing.perf.act.ind. of προλέγω, consummative).

King James Version

foretell - 2 Cor.13:2
tell before - Gal.5:21; 1 Thess.3:4; 2 Cor.13:2.
spoken before - Jude 17; 2 Pet.3:2.

Revised Standard Version

warn - 2 Cor.13:2,2; Gal.5:21.
tell beforehand - 1 Thess.3:4.
prediction - 2 Pet.3:2; Jude 17.

Meaning: A combination of πρό (#442) and λέγω (#66). Hence, to tell before the time; foretell; predict. To warn - 2 Cor.13:2,2; Gal.5:21; 1 Thess.3:4. Followed by ὅτι and indirect discourse in 1 Thess.3:4; Gal.5:21; 2 Cor.13:2,2. With an objective genitive in Jude 17; 2 Peter. 3:2.

καὶ (adjunctive conjunction joining verbs) 14.
προλέγω (1st.per.sing.pres.act.ind. of προλέγω, aoristic) 4409.
ὡς (particle in a temporal clause with the temporal participle) 128.
παρὼν (pres.part.nom.sing.masc. of πάρειμι, adverbial, temporal) 1592.
τὸ (acc.sing.neut. of the article in agreement with δεύτερον) 9.
δεύτερον (acc.sing.neut. of δεύτερος, cognate accusative) 1371.
καὶ (concessive conjunction) 14.
ἀπὼν (pres.part.nom.sing.masc. of ἄπειμι, adverbial, temporal) 4134.
νῦν (temporal adverb) 1497.
τοῖς (dat.pl.masc. of the article in agreement with προημαρτηκόσιν) 9.
προημαρτηκόσιν (perf.act.part.dat.pl.masc. of προαμαρτάνω, substantival, indirect object of προλέγω) 4408.
καὶ (adjunctive conjunction joining substantives) 14.

τοῖς (dat.pl.masc.of the article in agreement with λοιποῖς) 9.

λοιποῖς (dat.pl.masc.of λοιπός, indirect object of προλέγω) 1402.

πᾶσιν (dat.pl.masc.of πᾶς, in agreement with λοιποῖς) 67.

ὅτι (conjunction introducing an object clause in indirect discourse) 211.

ἐὰν (conditional particle in a third-class condition) 363.

ἔλθω (1st.per.sing.aor.mid.subj.of ἔρχομαι, third-class condition) 146.

εἰς (preposition with the accusative of extent) 140.

τὸ (acc.sing.neut.of the article, extent) 9.

πάλιν (adverbial) 355.

οὐ (negative conjunction with the indicative) 130.

φείσομαι (1st.per.sing.fut.mid.ind.of φείδομαι, predictive, third-class condition) 3533.

Translation - *"I have told you before and I am warning you as I did when I was with you the second time, though I am absent now - to those who have been sinning persistently and to all the rest, that if I come to you again I will not spare you."*

Comment: ὡς παρὼν τὸ δεύτερον belongs to προλέγω - "I give warning as I did when I was with you (παρὼν) the second time (τὸ δεύτερον), although (concessive καὶ) I am absent now ... κ.τ.λ." τοῖς προημαρτηκόσιν is the indirect object of προλέγω.

Paul is warning the unrepentant sinners, who, though Christians, have persisted in their wrong doing (2 Cor.12:21), and he is extending his warning to all the rest (τοῖς λοιποῖς πᾶσιν). ὅτι introduces indirect discourse. The third-class condition follows - If he comes again to Corinth (and he never did) he will not hesitate to judge sternly those whose misdeeds have been established in the mouths of the witnesses. Paul has been postponing this trip to Corinth (2 Cor.1:23) because he dreaded the task of disciplining the Corinthians who needed it, if he came. But now he warns that if he comes, although he dislikes disciplinary action, he will not shrink from it.

Verse 3 - *"Since ye seek a proof of Christ speaking in me, which to you-ward is not weak, but is mighty in you."*

ἐπεὶ δοκιμὴν ζητεῖτε τοῦ ἐν ἐμοὶ λαλοῦντος Χριστοῦ. ὃς εἰς ὑμᾶς οὐκ ἀσθενεῖ ἀλλὰ δυνατεῖ ἐν ὑμῖν.

"since you desire proof that Christ is speaking in me. He is not weak in dealing with you, but is powerful in you." . . . *RSV*

ἐπεὶ (subordinating conjunction introducing a causal clause) 1281.

δοκιμὴν (acc.sing.fem.of δοκιμή, direct object of ζητεῖτε) 3897.

ζητεῖτε (2d.per.pl.pres.act.ind.of ζητέω, present progressive durative, retroactive) 207.

τοῦ (gen.sing.masc.of the article in agreement with Χριστοῦ) 9.

ἐν (preposition with the locative of place) 80.

ἐμοὶ (loc.sing.masc.of ἐμός, place) 1267.

λαλοῦντος (pres.act.part.gen.sing.masc.of λαλέω, adjectival, ascriptive, in agreement with Χριστοῦ) 815.

Χριστοῦ (gen.sing.masc.of Χριστός, description) 4.

ὅς (nom.sing.masc.of ὅς, subject of ἀσθενεῖ) 65.

εἰς (preposition with the accusative, predicate usage) 140.

ὑμᾶς (acc.pl.masc.of σύ, predicate usage) 104.

οὐκ (negative conjunction with the indicative) 130.

ἀσθενεῖ (3d.per.sing.pres.act.ind.of ἀσθενέω, aoristic) 857.

ἀλλὰ (alternative conjunction) 342.

δυνατεῖ (3d.per.sing.pres.act.ind.of δυνατέω, aoristic) 4041.

ἐν (preposition with the locative with plural pronouns) 80.

ὑμῖν (loc.pl.masc.of σύ, metaphorical place) 104.

Translation - " . . . *since you are seeking evidence that Christ is speaking in me. He is not weak toward you but He is powerful in you."*

Comment: The ἐπεί clause is joined to the last clause of verse 2 - οὐ φείσομαι - "I will not spare you since you are seeking evidence that Christ speaks through me." Paul is saying that since they want evidence they were going to get it, if he ever got back to Corinth. What further need had the Corinthians for proof of the genuineness of Paul's ministry than the mighty deeds which Christ had already wrought in Corinth when Paul was there?

Verse 4 - *"For though he was crucified through weakness, yet he liveth by the power of God. For we also are weak in him, but we shall live with him by the power of God toward you."*

καὶ γὰρ ἐσταυρώθη ἐξ ἀσθενείας, ἀλλὰ ζῇ ἐκ δυνάμεως θεοῦ. καὶ γὰρ ἡμεῖς ἀσθενοῦμεν ἐν αὐτῷ, ἀλλὰ ζήσομεν σὺν αὐτῷ ἐκ δυνάμεως θεοῦ εἰς ὑμᾶς.

"For he was crucified in weakness, but lives by the power of God. For we are weak in him, but in dealing with you we shall live with him by the power of God."
                                                                        . . . *RSV*

καὶ (concessive conjunction) 14.

γὰρ (causal conjunction) 105.

ἐσταυρώθη (3d.per.sing.aor.pass.ind.of σταυρόω, constative) 1328.

ἐξ (preposition with the ablative, cause) 19.

ἀσθενείας (abl.sing.fem.of ἀσθένεια, cause) 740.

ἀλλὰ (adversative conjunction) 342.

ζῇ (3d.per.sing.pres.act.ind.of ζάω, aoristic) 340.

ἐκ (preposition with the ablative, cause) 19.

δυνάμεως (abl.sing.fem.of δύναμις, cause) 687.

θεοῦ (gen.sing.masc.of θεός, definition) 124.

καὶ (concessive conjunction) 14.

γὰρ (inferential conjunction) 105.

ἡμεῖς (nom.pl.masc.of ἐγώ, subject of ἀσθενοῦμεν) 123.

ἀσθενοῦμεν (1st.per.pl.pres.act.ind.of ἀσθενέω, aoristic) 857.

ἐν (preposition with the instrumental of association) 80.
αὐτῷ (instru.sing.masc.of αὐτός, association) 16.
ἀλλά (adversative conjunction) 342.
ζήσομεν (1st.per.pl.fut.act.ind.of ζάω, predictive) 340.
σὺν (preposition with the instrumental of association) 1542.
αὐτῷ (instru.sing.masc.of αὐτός, association) 16.
ἐκ (preposition with the ablative, cause) 19.
δυνάμεως (abl.sing.fem.of δύναμις, cause) 687.
θεοῦ (gen.sing.masc.of θεός, definition) 124.
εἰς (preposition with the accusative, predicate usage) 140.
ὑμᾶς (acc.pl.masc.of σύ, predicate usage) 104.

Translation - *"Because although He was crucified in weakness He lives because of divine power; so, though we share His weakness we shall live with Him because of the divine power as we deal with you."*

Comment: ἐκ with the ablative indicates cause. The weakness of Christ in incarnation (Phil.2:6-8) resulted in His crucifixion, but it was followed by resurrection. In the same way the believer shares in the weakness of the incarnation, but, as did Christ, so we too have a resurrection life in the future. Paul's resurrection power in Christ will be manifest to the Corinthians if and when he visits them again.

In view of the prospect of another visit and the possibility that some unpleasantness may take place, Paul urges the Corinthians to indulge in some serious introspection in

Verse 5 - *"Examine yourselves, whether ye be in the faith: prove your own selves. Know ye not your own selves, how that Jesus Christ is in you, except ye be reprobates?"*

Ἑαυτοὺς πειράζετε εἰ ἐστὲ ἐν τῇ πίστει, ἑαυτοὺς δοκιμάζετε. ἢ οὐκ ἐπιγινώσκετε ἑαυτοὺς ὅτι Χριστὸς Ἰησοῦς ἐν ὑμῖν; εἰ μήτι ἀδόκιμοί ἐστε.

"Examine yourselves, to see whether you are holding to your faith. Test yourselves. Do you not realize that Jesus Christ is in you? — unless indeed you fail to meet the test!" . . . RSV

Ἑαυτοὺς (acc.pl.masc.of ἑαυτός, direct object of πειράζετε) 288.
πειράζετε (2d.per.pl.pres.act.impv.of πειράζω, entreaty) 330.
εἰ (conditional particle in an elliptical condition) 337.
ἐστὲ (2d.per.pl.pres.ind.of εἰμί, elliptical condition) 86.
ἐν (preposition with the locative of sphere) 80.
τῇ (loc.sing.fem.of the article in agreement with πίστει) 9.
πίστει (loc.sing.fem.of πίστις, sphere) 728.
ἑαυτοὺς (acc.pl.masc.of ἑαυτός, direct object of δοκιμάζετε) 288.
δοκιμάζετε (2d.per.pl.pres.act.impv.of δοκιμάζω, entreaty) 2493.
ἢ (disjunctive) 465.
οὐκ (negative conjunction with the indicative in rhetorical question) 130.
ἐπιγινώσκετε (2d.per.pl.pres.act.ind.of ἐπιγινώσκω, rhetorical question) 675.

ἑαυτοὺς (acc.pl.masc.of ἑαυτός, direct object of ἐπιγινώσκετε) 288.

ὅτι (conjunction introducing an object clause in indirect discourse) 211.

Χριστὸς (nom.sing.masc.of Χριστός, subject of ἐστίν understood) 4.

Ἰησοῦς (nom.sing.masc.of Ἰησοῦς, apposition) 3.

ἐν (preposition with the locative with plural pronouns) 80.

ὑμῖν (loc.pl.masc.of σύ, association) 104.

εἰ (conditional particle in indirect question) 337.

μήτι (negative conjunction in indirect question) 676.

ἀδόκιμοί (nom.pl.masc.of ἀδόκιμος, predicate adjective) 3818.

ἐστε (2d.per.pl.pres.ind.of εἰμί, indirect question) 86.

Translation - "Put yourselves to the test to determine whether or not you are in the faith; examine yourselves critically; or do you yourselves not understand that Christ Jesus is in you, unless you fail the test."

Comment: Note ἑαυτοὺς in emphasis. Having told them that he was coming to Corinth again to put them to a test, he now suggests that they should test themselves. πειράζετε (#330) - "put yourself to a test." In industry we call this quality control. The way to tell that a tire will run 50,000 miles or that a light bulb will burn 1000 hours is to test it. Some professed believers have been good Christians only under controlled ideal conditions. δοκιμάζετε (#2493) - "make a critical examination." The Christian must be objective about himself. Then comes the rhetorical question and the added indirect question. "You do realize, do you not, that Christ Jesus associates Himself with you." Of course, if they failed the test they would not realize the presence of Jesus in their lives.

Christ dwells in many who are so backslidden (ἀδόκιμος #3818) that they do not realize it. *Cf.* 1 Cor.11:28. Note εἰ ἐστε in indirect question.

The Antinomian tends to discourage self-examination. He has every reason to doubt that he truly lives within the sphere of saving faith (Rom.6:1-2). Arminians, at the other extreme, often miss the glorious fact of an indwelling Christ, even though their lives do not always measure up to a rigid holiness test. Self-examination should always be conducted in the light of Gal.5:16-26 and Rom.7:14-25.

Verse 6 - "But I trust that ye shall know that we are not reprobates."

ἐλπίζω δὲ ὅτι γνώσεσθε ὅτι ἡμεῖς οὐκ ἐσμὲν ἀδόκιμοι.

"I hope you will find that we have not failed." . . . RSV

ἐλπίζω (1st.per.sing.pres.act.ind.of ἐλπίζω, aoristic) 991.

δὲ (continuative conjunction) 11.

ὅτι (conjunction introducing an object clause in indirect discourse) 211.

γνώσεσθε (2d.per.pl.fut.mid.ind.of γινώσκω, indirect discourse) 131.

ὅτι (conjunction introducing an object clause in indirect discourse) 211.

ἡμεῖς (nom.pl.masc.of ἐγώ, subject of ἐσμὲν)

οὐκ (negative conjunction with the indicative) 130.

ἐσμὲν (1st.per.pl.pres.ind.of εἰμί, aoristic) 86.

ἀδόκιμοι (nom.pl.masc.of ἀδόκιμος, predicate adjective) 3818.

Translation - *"And I hope that you will know that we are not disapproved."*

Comment: Paul once expressed fear that he would not pass the test (1 Cor.9:27). In order to pass it he ran a good race (1 Cor.9:24-27). He describes this race, in part, in 2 Cor.11:23-33. If any man ever passed the severe test of an obstacles course, Paul did. He now hopes that the Corinthians will be perceptive enough to recognize the fact.

Verse 7 - *"Now I pray to God that ye do no evil; not that we should appear approved, but that ye should do that which is honest, though we be as reprobates."*

εὐχόμεθα δὲ πρὸς τὸν θεὸν μὴ ποιῆσαι ὑμᾶς κακὸν μηδέν, οὐχ ἵνα ὑμεῖς δόκιμοι φανῶμεν, ἀλλ᾽ ἵνα ὑμεῖς τὸ καλὸν ποιῆτε, ἡμεῖς δὲ ὡς ἀδόκιμοι ὦμεν.

"But we pray God that you may not do wrong — not that we may appear to have met the test, but that you may do what is right, though we may seem to have failed." . . . *RSV*

εὐχόμεθα (1st.per.pl.pres.mid.ind.of εὔχομαι, aoristic) 3670
δὲ (explanatory conjunction) 11.
πρὸς (preposition with the accusative of extent after a verb of speaking) 197.
τὸν (acc.sing.masc.of the article in agreement with θεὸν) 9.
θεὸν (acc.sing.masc.of θεός, extent after a verb of speaking) 124.
μὴ (negative conjunction with the infinitive, negative purpose) 87.
ποιῆσαι (aor.act.inf.of ποιέω, negative purpose) 127.
ὑμᾶς (acc.pl.masc.of σύ, general reference) 104.
κακὸν (acc.sing.neut.of κακός, direct object of ποιῆσαι) 1388.
μηδέν (acc.sing.neut.of μηδείς, in agreement with κακὸν) 713.
οὐχ (negative conjunction with the indicative) 130.
ἵνα (conjunction with the subjunctive, in a purpose clause) 114.
ἡμεῖς (nom.pl.masc.of ἐγώ, subject of φανῶμεν) 123.
δόκιμοι (nom.pl.masc.of δόκιμος, predicate adjective) 4042.
φανῶμεν (1st.per.pl.aor.act.subj.of φαίνω, purpose) 100.
ἀλλ᾽ (alternative conjunction) 342.
ἵνα (conjunction with the subjunctive in a purpose clause) 114.
ὑμεῖς (nom.pl.masc.of σύ, subject of ποιῆτε) 104.
τὸ (acc.sing.neut.of the article in agreement with καλὸν) 9.
καλὸν (acc.sing.neut.of καλός, direct object of ποιῆτε) 296.
ποιῆτε (2d.per.pl.pres.act.subj.of ποιέω, purpose) 127.
ἡμεῖς (nom.pl.masc.of ἐγώ, subject of ὦμεν) 123.
δὲ (concessive conjunction) 11.
ὡς (comparative particle) 128.
ἀδόκιμοι (nom.pl.masc.of ἀδόκιμος, predicate adjective) 3818.
ὦμεν (1st.per.pl.pres.subj.of εἰμί, purpose) 86.

Translation - *"Now I am praying to God that you do not one evil deed, not in order that we may appear in a favorable light, but in order that you may be doing the proper thing, though we may appear to have failed."*

Comment: δὲ is explanatory. Paul has been urging Christian perfection upon the Corinthians. He now adds that he is praying to God for them, to that same end. Note the intensifying force of the double negative in μή . . . μηδέν - "that you not do not one evil thing." Bad English! Forceful Greek. οὐχ belongs with the indicative εὐχόμεθα - "We are praying οὐχ ἵνα . . . ἀλλ' ἵνα . . . " "Not that . . . but that. . . ." Paul's purpose in prayer is not that his own record as an Apostle might be demonstrated as a good one. His purpose is not selfish. What then? "But that ye may do the noble thing." He wanted this result even though he might be revealed in a bad light. The subjunctive in ὦμεν indicates that, though such might be the result, it was not likely. What Paul means is that he is putting their victorious Christian living ahead of his own record as a successful Apostle. Otherwise he is guilty of improper motives.

Doing the wrong thing is not only evil; it is stupid. It is stupid because it is evil and evil because it is stupid. The truth cannot be resisted. Therefore nothing is to be gained by resisting it. This is the thought in

Verse 8 - *"For we can do nothing against the truth, but for the truth."*

οὐ γὰρ δυνάμεθά τι κατὰ τῆς ἀληθείας, ἀλλὰ ὑπὲρ τῆς ἀληθείας.

"For we cannot do anything against the truth, but only for the truth." . . . RSV

οὐ (negative conjunction with the indicative) 130.

γὰρ (causal conjunction) 105.

δυνάμεθά (1st.per.pl.pres.mid.ind.of δύναμαι, static) 289.

τι (acc.sing.neut.of τις, indefinite pronoun, direct object of δυνάμεθά) 486.

κατὰ (preposition with the genitive, hostility) 98.

τῆς (gen.sing.fem.of the article in agreement with ἀληθείας) 9.

ἀληθείας (gen.sing.fem.of ἀλήθεια, hostility) 1416.

ἀλλὰ (alternative conjunction)

ὑπὲρ (preposition with the genitive "in behalf of") 545.

τῆς (gen.sing.fem.of the article in agreement with ἀληθείας) 9.

ἀληθείας (gen.sing.fem.of ἀλήθεια, "in behalf of") 1416 .

Translation - *"Because we are powerless to oppose the truth; we can only work in its behalf."*

Comment: All thoughts and deeds, whether those of Paul or the Corinthians, whether of saints or sinners, may as well be pure, since all impure motives against the truth are doomed to fail. It is impossible for anyone to oppose the truth successfully. Opposition to the truth is an exercise in futility. It is only when we work in behalf of the truth that we are ultimately effective. This is a strong statement about the sovereignty of God and the inviolability of His counsel. What a pity that all men and fallen angels do not recognize this fact. All efforts to deceive and to work against reality are doomed before they begin. The problem is to separate the truth (ἀλήθεια) from its opposite (ψεῦδος #2388). For the Christian, the Word of God, historically interpreted, is the authoritative answer. Those who are not Christians must use the alternative empirical method of test. Existentialists even reject this since for them nothing in the universe is related to anything else. If this were true, then nothing could be learned from experience. Experience in God's universe of law ultimately leads to the same conclusions which are stated in the Word of God. God can never allow His universe to operate in a fashion other than that set forth in His Word.

Those who are not known for their sophistication, but who have the faith of the little child settle for the moral standards of the Bible. One may not know why it is wrong to kill or steal or commit adultery but God says that it is. Therefore the transgressor cannot win in the long run. He is ineffective in opposing the truth.

Verse 9 - *"For we are glad when we are weak, and ye are strong; and this also, even your perfection."*

χαίρομεν γὰρ ὅταν ἡμεῖς ἀσθενῶμεν, ὑμεῖς δὲ δυνατοὶ ἦτε. τοῦτο καὶ εὐχόμεθα, τὴν ὑμῶν κατάρτισιν.

"For we are glad when we are weak and you are strong. What we pray for is your improvement." . . . RSV

χαίρομεν (1st.per.pl.pres.act.ind.of χαίρω, aoristic) 182.

γὰρ (inferential conjunction) 105.

ὅταν (conjunction with the subjunctive in an indefinite temporal clause) 436.

ἡμεῖς (nom.pl.masc.of ἐγώ, subject of ἀσθενῶμεν) 123.

ἀσθενῶμεν (1st.per.pl.pres.act.subj.of ἀσθενέω, indefinite temporal clause) 857.

ὑμεῖς (nom.pl.masc.of σύ, subject of ἦτε) 104.

δὲ (adversative conjunction) 11.

δυνατοὶ (nom.pl.masc.of δυνατός, predicate adjective) 1311.

ἦτε (2d.per.pl.pres.subj.of εἰμί, indefinite temporal clause) 86.

τοῦτο (acc.sing.neut.of οὗτος, direct object of εὐχόμεθα) 93.

καὶ (continuative conjunction) 14.

εὐχόμεθα (1st.per.pl.pres.mid.ind.of εὔχομαι, present progressive duration) 3670.

τὴν (acc.sing.fem.of the article in agreement with κατάρτισιν) 9.

ὑμῶν (gen.pl.masc.of σύ, possession) 104.

#4410 κατάρτισιν (acc.sing.fem.of κατάρτισις, apposition).

King James Version

perfection - 2 Cor.13:9.

Revised Standard Version

improvement - 2 Cor.13:9.

Meaning: Cf. καταρτίζω (#401). Hence, a strengthening; a disciplinary program leading to total coordination; achievement of holism in the Christian life - 2 Cor.13:9.

Translation - "So we are happy when we are weak but you are strong; and this we pray for — your maturity."

Comment: Again, as in verse 7, Paul says that the result is what counts. Whether Paul is approved (verse 7) or strong or weak (verse 9) is not important. The goal is the nobility and spiritual maturity of the Corinthian christians. Note the hypotactic construction with ὅταν and the two subjunctives ἀσθνεῶμεν and ἦτε.. Paul has not said that his weakness must always result in their strength, but that if that is what it takes to achieve his goal, he will rejoice.

Verse 10 - "Therefore I write these things being absent, lest being present I should use sharpness, according to the power which the Lord hath given me to edification, and not to destruction."

διὰ τοῦτο ταῦτα ἀπὼν γράφω, ἵνα παρὼν μὴ ἀποτόμως χρήσωμαι κατὰ τὴν ἐξουσίαν ἣν ὁ κύριος ἔδωκέν μοι, εἰς οἰκοδομὴν καὶ οὐκ εἰς καθαίρεσιν.

"I write this while I am away from you, in order that when I come I may not have to be severe in my use of the authority which the Lord has given me for building up and not for tearing down." . . . RSV

διὰ (preposition with the accusative, cause) 118.
τοῦτο (acc.sing.neut.of οὗτος, cause) 93.
ταῦτα (acc.pl.neut.of οὗτος, direct object of γράφω) 93.
ἀπὼν (pres.part.nom.sing.masc.of ἄπειμι, adverbial, temporal) 4134.
γράφω (1st.per.sing.pres.act.ind.of γράφω, aoristic) 156.
ἵνα (conjunction with the subjunctive in a negative purpose clause) 114.
παρὼν (pres.part.nom.sing.masc.of πάρειμι, adverbial, temporal) 1592.
μὴ (negative conjunction with the subjunctive) 87.

#4411 ἀποτόμως (adverbial).

King James Version

sharply - Titus 1:13.
sharpness - 2 Cor.13:10.

Revised Standard Version

severe - 2 Cor.13:10.
sharply - Titus 1:13.

Meaning: Cf. ἀποτομία (#4000). With asperity; with sharp rebuke and/or retort - 2 Cor.13:10; Titus 1:13.

χρήσωμαι (1st.per.sing.aor.mid.subj.of χράω, negative purpose) 2447.
κατὰ (preposition with the accusative, standard) 98.

τὴν (acc.sing.fem.of the article in agreement with ἐξουσίαν) 9.

ἐξουσίαν (acc.sing.fem.of ἐξουσία, standard) 707.

ἣν (acc.sing.fem.of ὅς, relative pronoun, direct object of ἔδωκεν) 65.

ὁ (nom.sing.masc.of the article in agreement with κύριος) 9.

κύριος (nom.sing.masc.of κύριος, subject of ἔδωκεν) 97.

ἔδωκέν (3d.per.sing.aor.act.ind.of δίδωμι, constative) 362.

μοι (dat.sing.masc.of ἐγώ, indirect object of ἔδωκεν) 123.

εἰς (preposition with the accusative, purpose) 140.

οἰκοδομὴν (acc.sing.fem.of οἰκοδομή, purpose) 1481.

καὶ (adversative conjunction) 14.

οὐκ (negative conjunction with the indicative) 130.

εἰς (preposition with the accusative, purpose) 140.

καθαίρεσιν (acc.sing.fem.of καθαίρεσις, purpose) 4361.

Translation - *"This is why I am writing these things while I am absent — in order that when I come I may not speak with asperity, as the Lord has given me authority to do for purposes of edification but not for destruction."*

Comment: διὰ τοῦτο in a causal sense. The ἵνα clause is in apposition with τοῦτο. "This is why." Why? "In order that . . . κ.τ.λ." (ἵνα). The participles are temporal - "When I am absent . . . when I am present."

Paul at the time of writing this did not know that he would never again visit Corinth. He planned to use the authority which the Lord had given to him when he arrived in Corinth. Such authority was never given for the purpose of tearing something down, but for building something up. That was why he did not wish to use it sharply when he got to Corinth. And that was why he was writing as he did. He hoped that a strong letter of rebuke, with admonition to repent, which arrived before Paul did, would result in repentance among the Corinthians and thus obviate the necessity and save the embarrassment of a stern sermon.

Verse 11 - *"Finally, brethren, farewell. Be perfect; be of good comfort, be of one mind, live in peace; and the God of love and peace shall be with you."*

Λοιπόν, ἀδελφοί, χαίρετε, καταρτίζεσθε, παρακαλεῖσθε, τὸ αὐτὸ φρονεῖτε, εἰρηνεύετε, καὶ ὁ θεὸς τῆς ἀγάπης καὶ εἰρήνης ἔσται μεθ᾽ ὑμῶν.

"Finally, brethren, farewell. Mend your ways, heed my appeal, agree with one another, live in peace, and the God of love and peace will be with you." . . . RSV

Λοιπόν (acc.sing.neut.of λοιπός, adverbial) 1402.

ἀδελφοί (voc.pl.masc.of ἀδελφός, address) 15.

χαίρετε (2d.per.pl.pres.act.impv.of χαίρω, command) 182.

καταρτίζεσθε (2d.per.pl.pres.mid.impv.of καταρτίζομαι, command) 401.

παρακαλεῖσθε (2d.per.pl.pres.mid.impv.of παρακαλέω, command) 230.

τὸ (acc.sing.neut.of the article in agreement with αὐτὸ) 9.

αὐτὸ (acc.sing.neut.of αὐτός, direct object of φρονεῖτε) 16.

φρονεῖτε (2d.per.pl.pres.act.impv.of φρονέω, command) 1212.

εἰρηνεύετε (2d.per.pl.pres.act.impv.of εἰρηνεύω, command) 2356.

καὶ (continuative conjunction) 14.

ὁ (nom.sing.masc.of the article in agreement with θεὸς) 9.

θεὸς (nom.sing.masc.of θεός, subject of ἔσται) 124.

τῆς (gen.sing.fem.of the article in agreement with ἀγάπης) 9.

ἀγάπης (gen.sing.fem.of ἀγάπη, description) 1490.

καὶ (adjunctive conjunction joining nouns) 14.

εἰρήνης (gen.sing.fem.of εἰρήνη, description) 865.

ἔσται (3d.per.sing.fut.ind.of εἰμί, predictive) 86.

μεθ' (preposition with the genitive of accompaniment) 50.

ὑμῶν (gen.pl.masc.of σύ, accompaniment) 104.

Translation - *"To conclude, brethren, stay happy, grow up, take comfort, think alike, be at peace and the God of love and peace will be with you."*

Comment: The infinitive χαίρειν in Acts 15:23; 23:26 is an absolute epistolary infinitive meaning "Greetings" or "Best regards." Here we have χαίρετε, the imperative. Hence our translation. It is of a piece with the other imperatives. The need for χαίρετε must have been felt keenly since Paul has been very censorious - "Cheer up!" "Always be happy." *Cf.#401* for meaning.

Note that spiritual maturity (καταρτίζεσθε) is linked with psychological factors - cheer up, comfort each other, think alive, be at peace. The God Who is the source of love and peace is promised as their constant companion if they comply with Paul's suggestions.

Verse 12 - *"Greet one another with a holy kiss."*

ἀσπάσασθε ἀλλήλους ἐν ἁγίῳ φιλήματι.

"Greet one another with a holy kiss." . . . *RSV*

ἀσπάσασθε (2d.per.pl.aor.mid.impv.of ἀσπάζομαι, entreaty) 551.

ἀλλήλους (acc.pl.masc.of ἀλλήλων, direct object of ἀσπάσασθε) 1487.

ἐν (preposition with the instrumental of manner) 80.

ἁγίῳ (instru.sing.neut.of ἅγιος, in agreement with φιλήματι) 84.

φιλήματι (instru.sing.neut.of φίλημα, manner) 2175.

Translation - *"Greet one another with a holy kiss."*

Comment: The KJV division of verses here does not follow the verse division of the Greek manuscripts.

A Church of the Brethren lay minister once said at the close of a foot-washing ceremony, a part of which involved the kiss, that it was difficult not to love with pure Christian love someone who had just washed his feet and then kissed him on the cheek! This practice is a far cry from the sensitivity sessions recently in vogue, where it can be doubted that the kisses and other bodily contacts contribute to spiritual maturity.

Verse 13 - *"All the saints salute you."*

ἀσπάζονται ὑμᾶς οἱ ἅγιοι πάντες.

"*All the saints greet you.*" . . . RSV

ἀσπάζονται (3d.per.pl.pres.mid.ind.of ἀσπάζομαι, aoristic) 551.
ὑμᾶς (acc.pl.masc.of σύ, direct object of ἀσπάζονται) 104.
οἱ (nom.pl.masc.of the article in agreement with ἅγιοι) 9.
ἅγιοι (nom.pl.masc.of ἅγιος, subject of ἀσπάζονται) 84.
πάντες (nom.pl.masc.of πᾶς, in agreement with ἅγιοι) 67.

Translation - "*All the saints send their regards.*"

Comment: ἀσπάζω (#551) is often used in this epistolary manner.

Verse 14 - "*The grace of the Lord Jesus Christ,and the love of God, and the communion of the Holy Ghost, be with you all. Amen.*"

Ἡ χάρις τοῦ κυρίου Ἰησοῦ Χριστοῦ καὶ ἡ ἀγάπη τοῦ θεοῦ καὶ ἡ κοινωνία τοῦ ἁγίου πνεύματος μετὰ πάντων ὑμῶν.

"*The grace of the Lord Jesus Christ and the love of God and the fellowship of the Holy Spirit be with you all.*" . . . RSV

Ἡ (nom.sing.fem.of the article in agreement with χάρις) 9.
χάρις (nom.sing.fem.of χάρις, subject of ἔστω understood) 1700.
τοῦ (abl.sing.masc.of the article in agreement with κυρίου) 9.
κυρίου (abl.sing.masc.of κύριος, source) 97.
Ἰησοῦ (abl.sing.masc.of Ἰησοῦς, apposition) 3.
Χριστοῦ (abl.sing.masc.of Χριστός, apposition) 4.
καὶ (adjunctive conjunction joining nouns) 14.
ἡ (nom.sing.fem.of the article in agreement with ἀγάπη) 9.
ἀγάπη (nom.sing.fem.of ἀγάπη, subject of ἔστω understood) 1490.
τοῦ (abl.sing.masc.of the article in agreement with θεοῦ) 9.
θεοῦ (abl.sing.masc.of θεός, source) 124.
καὶ (adjunctive conjunction joining nouns) 14.
ἡ (nom.sing.fem.of the article in agreement with κοινωνία) 9.
κοινωνία (nom.sing.fem.of κοινωνία, subject of ἔστω understood) 3001.
τοῦ (abl.sing.neut.of the article in agreement with πνεύματος) 9.
ἁγίου (abl.sing.neut.of ἅγιος, in agreement with πνεύματος) 84.
πνεύματος (abl.sing.neut.of πνεῦμα, source) 83.
μετὰ (preposition with the genitive of accompaniment) 50.
πάντων (gen.pl.masc.of πᾶς, in agreement with ὑμῶν) 67.
ὑμῶν (gen.pl.masc.of σύ, accompaniment) 104.

Translation - "*The grace from the Lord Jesus Christ and the love from God and the fellowship from the Holy Spirit be with all of you.*"

Comment: These ablatives speak of source. Grace from the Lord Jesus (2 Cor.8:9). Love from God (John 3:16). Participation in it all from the Holy Spirit

(1 Cor.12:13). God's love, Christ's gift and the Holy Spirit's fellowship are all that any sinner needs. Thus we come to the end of two major epistles from Paul to the Corinthian church. Clearly the Corinthians were beset with many problems. Paul's attempts to deal with them drove him to emotional excesses which resulted in his writing much that is less than polished Greek. But his meaning, always intense, is always clear. He is far more analytical in the remainder of his epistles.

Paul's Epistle to the Galatians

Salutation

(Galatians 1:1-5)

Galatians 1:1 - "Paul, an apostle, (not of men, neither by man, but by Jesus Christ, and God the Father, who raised him from the dead:)"

Παῦλος ἀπόστολος, οὐκ ἀπ' ἀνθρώπων οὐδὲ δι' ἀνθρώπου ἀλλὰ διὰ Ἰησοῦ Χριστοῦ καὶ θεοῦ πατρὸς τοῦ ἐγείραντος αὐτὸν ἐκ νεκρῶν.

"PAUL AN APOSTLE — NOT FROM MEN nor through man, but through Jesus Christ and God the Father, who raised him from the dead — " ... RSV

Παῦλος (nom.sing.masc.of Παῦλος, nominative absolute) 3284.
ἀπόστολος (nom.sing.masc.of ἀπόστολος, apposition) 844.
οὐκ (negative conjunction with the indicative understood) 130.
ἀπ' (preposition with the ablative of source) 70.
ἀνθρώπων (abl.pl.masc.of ἄνθρωπος, source) 341.
οὐδὲ (disjunctive) 452.
δι' (preposition with the ablative of agent) 118.
ἀνθρώπου (abl.sing.masc.of ἄνθρωπος, agent) 341.
ἀλλὰ (alternative conjunction) 342.
διὰ (preposition with the ablative of agent) 118.
Ἰησοῦ (abl.sing.masc.of Ἰησοῦς, agent) 3.
Χριστοῦ (abl.sing.masc.of Χριστός, apposition) 4.
καὶ (adjunctive conjunction joining nouns) 14.
θεοῦ (abl.sing.masc.of θεός, source) 124.
πατρὸς (abl.sing.masc.of πατήρ, apposition) 238.
τοῦ (abl.sing.masc.of the article in agreement with ἐγείραντος) 9.

ἐγείραντος (aor.act.part.abl.sing.masc.of ἐγείρω, apposition) 125.

αὐτὸν (acc.sing.masc.of αὐτός, direct object of ἐγείραντος) 16.

ἐκ (preposition with the ablative of separation) 19.

νεκρῶν (abl.pl.masc.of νεκρός, separation) 749.

Translation - "Paul, an Apostle (not from a human source nor by a single human agent, but by the joint agency of Jesus Christ and God, the Father Who raised Him from the dead,"

Comment: Παῦλος is a nominative absolute in the salutation. Immediately he asserts that he is an Apostle, and he defends the supernatural authority of his commission. Neither the source (οὐκ) nor the agency (οὐδὲ) are human. No man nor any group of men created his apostleship, nor did any human being act in establishing him as such. ἀλλὰ is in contrast to οὐκ ... οὐδὲ - "Neither ... nor ... but ... κ.τ.λ." The divine agents were Jesus Christ and God, the Father, Who is further identified in apposition (τοῦ ἐγείραντος) as "the One Who raised Jesus from the dead.

Paul first visited Galatia on his second missionary journey (Acts 16:5,6). He was in the area (Acts 14:6) on his first journey but did not go as far north as Galatia (#4257). He visited Galatia again on his second trip into Asia Minor (Acts 18:23).

Between his first and second visits to the Galatian churches, they were beset with false teachers. Compare Gal.4:13,14, where we learn that the Galatians accepted Paul without reservation on his first visit (Acts 16:5,6). The epistle was probably written from Ephesus in the year A.D.54 or shortly after. This was not long after he paid the Galatians his second visit, when he learned of their defection from the gospel. The epistle is written to refute the heresy spread by the Judaizers (Acts 15:1-29) who had followed Paul into Galatian country after his first visit and taught Paul's converts (1) that salvation was available only to those who had the faith which Paul preached, and who then supplemented that faith by human works or merit, including circumcision, (2) that Paul was not one of the original twelve Apostles and hence not divinely commissioned and that his authority was not on a par with that of the other Apostles, and (3) that Peter disagreed with Paul, as was evidenced by Peter's refusal to fellowship with uncircumcised believers at the Lord's table.

Galatianism is in varying degrees associated with Legalism, Judaism, Pelagianism, Arminianism, the Romanism of the Jesuits (not the Jansenists), Thomism and Modernism. This heresy has been opposed by Jesus, Paul, Augustine, Calvin, Luther and the Reformed Theology of modern times. It teaches that the salvation equation is God's work to be sure, but only as supplemented by man's merit. It teaches salvation by works, however often they use the term grace, in the sense that they say that if man's merit is not a part of the equation no salvation is possible. Paul shows that he is in the line of Jesus, the other Apostles and the Jerusalem church as standing against the legalists. The line continues in church history from Paul to Augustine, who was opposed by Pelagius), Calvin and Luther (as opposed by Arminius and the Jesuits) and the Reformed theologians (Van Til, Buswell, Warfield, Hodge, Kuyper, Bavinck,

Berkhoff, *et al*), as opposed to Barth, Brunner, Fosdick, Tillich and others. Martin Luther said, "The Epistle to the Galatians is my epistle. I have betrothed myself to it. It is my wife." Luther's work, *The Bondage of the Will*, as opposed to Desiderius Erasmus who wrote *The Freedom of the Will* and his work in expounding Galatians are prominent bases for the Protestant Reformation. The epistemology is that of Augustine, not that of Aquinas; the theology is grace rather than works. John Bunyan said, "I do prefer this book of Martin Luther upon the Galatians, excepting the Holy Bible, before all books that I have ever seen, as most fit for a wounded conscience." Luther's commentary was written in 1519.

No man, nor any group of man had called Paul to his role as an Apostle. On the contrary, the God and Father of the Lord Jesus Christ, Whom He had raised from the dead, and Christ Himself are the twin sources of Paul's position. *Cf.* Rom.1:1-5.

Three New Testament epistles quote Habakkuk 2:4. See Rom.1:17 where the emphasis is upon justification; Gal.3:11 where the emphasis is upon the fact that those justified (as defined in Romans) *shall live* by faith. They shall not die. Finally in Heb.10:38 the emphasis is upon the fact that the just shall live *by faith* - the kind of faith that produced the kind of Old Testament saints mentioned in Hebrews 11 - the faith of which Christ is the Author and Finisher (Heb.12:2). Romans 1-8 defines the just man. Galatians argues that such a man will live forever by virtue of God's gift of justification, plus nothing. The writer of Hebrews agrees but stresses the fact that the faith by which the just shall live forever is ethically operative for good. In Galatians the spot light is upon the second couplet - "The just SHALL LIVE by faith." (Gal.3:11).

Verse 2 - "And all the brethren which are with me, unto the churches of Galatia."

καὶ οἱ σὺν ἐμοὶ πάντες ἀδελφοί, ταῖς ἐκκλησίαις τῆς Γαλατίας.

"and all the brethren who are with me, To the churches of Galatia:" ... RSV

καὶ (adjunctive conjunction joining nouns) 14.
οἱ (nom.pl.masc.of the article in agreement with ἀδελφοί) 9.
σὺν (preposition with the instrumental of association) 1542.
ἐμοὶ (instru.sing.masc.of ἐμός, association) 1267.
πάντες (nom.pl.masc.of πᾶς, in agreement with ἀδελφοί) 67.
ἀδελφοί (nom.pl.masc.of ἀδελφός, nominative absolute) 15.
ταῖς (dat.pl.fem.of the article in agreement with ἐκκλησίαις) 9.
ἐκκλησίαις (dat.pl.fem.of ἐκκλησία, indirect object) 1204.
τῆς (gen.sing.fem.of the article in agreement with Γαλατίας) 9.
Γαλατίας (gen.sing.fem.of Γαλατία, description) 4257.

Translation - ". . . and all the brethren with me to the churches of Galatia."

Comment: Παῦλος (verse 1) and all the brethren associated with him in Ephesus at the time of writing, some of whom perhaps are mentioned in Acts 20:4, in greeting to the Christians of the various little local church groups throughout the region of Galatia. *Cf.*#4257 for a geographical description.

Note that the epistle is addressed not to the "Church of Galatia" in the episcopal sense, but to the "churches of Galatia" in the congregational sense.

Verse 3 - "Grace be to you, and peace from God the Father, and from our Lord Jesus Christ."

χάρις ὑμῖν καὶ εἰρήνη ἀπὸ θεοῦ πατρὸς ἡμῶν καὶ κυρίου Ἰησοῦ Χριστοῦ.

"Grace to you and peace from God the Father and our Lord Jesus Christ."...
RSV

χάρις (nom.sing.fem.of χάρις, subject of ἔστω understood) 1700.
ὑμῖν (dat.pl.masc.of σύ, personal advantage) 104.
καὶ (adjunctive conjunction joining nouns) 14.
εἰρήνη (nom.sing.fem.of εἰρήνη, subject of ἔστω understood) 865.
ἀπὸ (preposition with the ablative of source) 70.
θεοῦ (abl.sing.masc.of θεός, source) 124.
πατρὸς (abl.sing.masc.of πατήρ, apposition) 238.
ἡμῶν (gen.pl.masc.of ἐγώ, relationship) 123.
καὶ (adjunctive conjunction joining nouns) 14.
κυρίου (abl.sing.masc.of κύριος, source) 97.
Ἰησοῦ (abl.sing.masc.of Ἰησοῦς, apposition) 3.
Χριστοῦ (abl.sing.masc.of Χριστός, apposition) 4.

Translation - "Grace unto you and peace from God our Father and from the Lord Jesus Christ."

Comment: Variant MSS readings have πατρὸς καὶ κυρίου; πατρὸς καὶ κυρίου or πατρὸς ἡμῶν καὶ κυρίου ἡμῶν.

Certainly the Galatians, who had been misled by false teaching into the insecurity of legalism were in great need of understanding grace (χάρις) without which there can be no peace (εἰρήνη), either soteriologically or psychologically. The personal insecurity of the legalist is constantly manifested by the gusto and bravado with which he announces his determination to gain salvation by his own merit. Witness his fanatical adherence to a self-imposed standard or ethics and religious observance, for which he really feels no great degree of personal enthusiasm. His grim determination to save himself from sin is evidence in the face of one who has never known the joy of deliverance through the sacrifice of a Saviour, of whom Paul now speaks in

Verse 4 - "Who gave himself for our sins, that he might deliver us from this present evil world, according to the will of God and our Father."

τοῦ δόντος ἑαυτὸν ὑπὲρ τῶν ἁμαρτιῶν ἡμῶν ὅπως ἐξέληται ἡμᾶς ἐκ τοῦ αἰωνος τοῦ ἐνεστῶτος πονηροῦ κατὰ τὸ θέλημα τοῦ θεοῦ καὶ πατρὸς ἡμῶν,

"who gave himself for our sins to deliver us from the present evil age, according to the will of our Lord and Father;" ... RSV

τοῦ (abl.sing.masc.of the article in agreement with δόντος) 9.

δόντος (2d.aor.act.part.abl.sing.masc.of δίδωμι, substantival, apposition) 362.

ἑαυτὸν (acc.sing.masc.of ἑαυτός, direct object of δόντος) 288.

ὑπέρ (preposition with the genitive "in behalf of") 545.

τῶν (gen.pl.fem.of the article in agreement with ἁμαρτιῶν) 9.

ἁμαρτιῶν (gen.pl.fem.of ἁμαρτία, "in behalf of") 111.

ἡμῶν (gen.pl.masc.of ἐγώ, possession) 123.

ὅπως (conjunction with the subjunctive in a sub-final clause) 177.

ἐξέληται (3d.per.sing.2d.aor.mid.subj.of ἐξαιρέω, sub-final) 504.

ἡμᾶς (acc.pl.masc.of ἐγώ, direct object of ἐξέληται) 123

ἐκ (preposition with the ablative of separation) 19.

τοῦ (abl.sing.masc.of the article in agreement with αἰῶνος) 9.

αἰῶνος (abl.sing.masc.of αἰών, separation) 1002.

τοῦ (abl.sing.masc.of the article in agreement with αἰῶνος) 9.

ἐνεστῶτος (perf.part.abl.sing.masc.of ἐνίστημι, adjectival, ascriptive in agreement with αἰῶνος) 3954.

πονηροῦ (abl.sing.masc.of πονηρός, in agreement with αἰῶνος) 438.

κατά (preposition with the accusative, standard) 98.

τό (acc.sing.neut.of the article in agreement with θέλημα) 9.

θέλημα (acc.sing.neut.of θέλημα, standard) 577.

τοῦ (gen.sing.masc.of the article in agreement with θεοῦ) 9.

θεοῦ (gen.sing.masc.of θεός, possession) 124.

καί (adjunctive conjunction joining nouns) 14.

πατρὸς (gen.sing.masc.of πατήρ, possession) 238.

ἡμῶν (gen.pl.masc.of ἐγώ, relationship) 123.

Translation - "Who gave Himself for our sins in order (and with the result) that he might rescue us from this current age of evil, in accord with the will of God, even our Father."

Comment: Note the prominence given to Christ in Paul's opening salutation. On a par with the Father (verse 1) He is also alive from the dead (verse 1); again in verse 3 He and the Father are co-Sources of χάρις καὶ εἰρήνη. Thus deity and hence equality with God the Father are ascribed to Jesus. The Judaizers tended to denigrate Jesus as one who really brought nothing new to the old Judaism. Indeed if, as they were saying, salvation is the result of human merit, then Jesus, at best, is nothing more than another good prophet of whom the world already had many. But if He is God, Who gave Himself for our sins with the divine purpose in view, *viz.* that He would rescue those for whom He died from the current order of evil, and if this substitutionary death with its redemptive result is according to the will of God, Who now becomes Father to the believer (John 1:12, *contra* John 8:44), then indeed Christianity, as preached by Paul (not the Judaizers) is a unique system of truth. Christ gave Himself (Gal.2:20; Rom.5:7-11; 2 Cor.5:21; 1 Pet.2:24; Rev.5:9-10). Why? ὑπὲρ τῶν ἁμαρτιῶν ἡμῶν (Isa.53:5,6).

This act was deliberate. Christ was not forced to Calvary against His will

(John 10:10,11; 17-18). His act of dying was the deliberate execution of a divine plan in which God the Father and the Holy Spirit concurred (Heb.9:14). Why? What purpose did the Godhead expect to achieve by this drastic act of self-sacrifice? ὅπως ἐξέληται ἡμᾶς ἐκ . . . πονηροῦ. The sub-final clause speaks of rescue from a current world system that is evil, sociologically, economically, philosophically and politically.

Legalism has little evil to say about the world. Man is in it, an integral part of it. He is not lost but quite capable of cooperating with his world and working out a system of salvation for it. For the legalist there is really nothing to be saved from, for men are not really lost - only temporarily misguided. Paul says that the age is evil. It has men in its grasp who are helpless until rescued by the Holy Spirit in response to the death and resurrection of Jesus Christ. It is significant that the moral influence theory of the atonement with its teaching that Jesus was only trying to show us how to be good, is always associated with some brand of legalism, while Paul's view, expressed in verse 4 is associated with Anselm and the Reformed theology.

Verse 5 - "To whom be glory forever and ever. Amen."

ᾧ ἡ δόξα εἰς τοὺς αἰῶνας τῶν αἰώνων. ἀμήν.

"to whom be the glory for ever and ever. Amen." . . . RSV

ᾧ (dat.sing.masc.of ὅς, relative pronoun, personal advantage) 65.
ἡ (nom.sing.fem.of the article in agreement with δόξα) 9.
δόξα (nom.sing.fem.of δόξα, subject of ἔστω, understood) 361.
εἰς (preposition with the accusative of time extent) 140.
τοὺς (acc.pl.masc.of the article in agreement with αἰῶνας) 9.
αἰῶνας (acc.pl.masc.of αἰών, time extent) 1002.
τῶν (gen.pl.masc.of the article in agreement with αἰώνων) 9.
αἰώνων (gen.pl.masc.of αἰών, description) 1002.
ἀμήν (explicative) 466.

Translation - "To whom be glory into the ages of the ages. Amen."

Comment: This present age is evil - a monster with helpless mankind in its grip, from whose slavery we can be rescued only by the sacrificial death of the Son of God (verse 4). This evil age murdered the Son of God. The future ages will be characterized by glory (δόξα) to Him Who died to save us from this present evil age. The present age rejected God's Son. Every future age will praise Him.

It is notable that Karl Marx, after a searching analysis of the age of capitalism in which he lived (Adam Smith, Malthus, Ricardo, Mill, Bentham) pronounced it incurably evil also and predicted its utter collapse. But Marx's materialism did not provide the deliverance of a Saviour as did Paul. It will be our Lord in the day of His glory, when He returns to earth to take His rightful place on David's throne, who will bring the philosophical, political, social and economic revolutions which His mother predicted in Luke 1:51-53. We had Marx's "law of increasing misery" long before he predicted it. Indeed, we have had it since God pronounced a curse upon earth, since thorn infested and now unable to provide sufficient food to feed the unfortunates who result from the population explosion of the late 20th century.

Legalism in all of its forms is offended when the Reformed theology of Jesus, Paul, Augustine, Luther, Calvin and the 20th century evangelicals pronounce this age as wicked. The "head-in-the-sound" ostrichism of the social gospel addict insists that after all, this is a beautiful world. Even the environmentalists, with their gloom, have not been able to shake the misguided credulity which the Polly Annas call faith. On the other hand Calvinists who understand the theological interpretation of history are not "bleeding hearts." Indeed we have the only viable solution to the ills of this "present evil age." It is the second coming of Messiah, Whose coming is delayed only by the fact that the last elect soul for whom He died has not yet been incorporated into the "church which is His Body." Indeed he may not even yet be born. In the meantime we "have need of patience, that, after (we) have done the will of God, (we) might receive the promise, for yet a little while, and he that shall come will come and will not tarry" (Heb.10:36,37).

There is No Other Gospel

(Galatians 1:6-10)

Verse 6 - "I marvel that ye are so soon removed from him that called you into the grace of Christ unto another gospel."

Θαυμάζω ὅτι οὕτως ταχέως μετατίθεσθε ἀπὸ τοῦ καλέσαντος ὑμᾶς ἐν χάριτι (Χριστοῦ) εἰς ἕτερον εὐαγγέλιον,

"I am astonished that you are so quickly deserting him who called you in the grace of Christ and turning to a different gospel — " . . . RSV

Θαυμάζω (1st.per.sing.pres.act.ind.of θαυμάζω, present progressive duration) 726.

ὅτι (conjunction introducing an object clause in indirect discourse) 211.

οὕτως (demonstrative adverb) 74.

ταχέως (adverbial) 2531.

μετατίθεσθε (2d.per.pl.pres.pass.ind.of μετατίθημι, present progressive duration) 3112.

ἀπὸ (preposition with the ablative of separation) 70.

τοῦ (abl.sing.masc.of the article in agreement with καλέσαντος) 9.

καλέσαντος (aor.act.part.abl.sing.masc.of καλέω, substantival, separation) 107.

ὑμᾶς (acc.pl.masc.of σύ, direct object of καλέσαντος) 104.

ἐν (preposition with the instrumental of means) 80.

χάριτι (instru.sing.fem.of χάρις, means) 1700.

Χριστοῦ (abl.sing.masc.of Χριστός, source) 4.

εἰς (preposition with the accusative of extent, predicate use) 140.
ἕτερον (acc.sing.neut.of ἕτερος, in agreement with εὐαγγέλιον) 605.
εὐαγγέλιον (acc.sing.neut.of εὐαγγέλιον, extent) 405.

Translation - "I am amazed that you are so quickly removed from the One Who called you by the grace of God unto another gospel."

Comment: Θαυμάζω with the objective ὅτι seeks a direct reason. Followed by εἰ it seeks a hypothetical explanation. There was no doubt that the Galatians had turned away from the theology which Paul had preached to them, by which they became Christians. Hence, "I am amazed that . . . " μετατίθεσθε is a progressive durative present, with a retroactive twist, as is Paul's Θαυμάζω. The heresy had been present for some time and Paul had been amazed at its development since first he heard of it. "I have been wondering . . . since I first learned that you have been rejecting the truth which I preached to you."

Ramsay shows numerous examples of ἕτερος in contrast to ἄλλος as we have it here in verses 6 and 7. In such contrast ἕτερος does not mean "different" but "another" of the same type. This distinction seems to hold here since Paul denies that the "other" gospel is not "another gospel."

The gospel preached by Jesus and by Paul would be ἕτερος/ἄλλος - another sermon of the same gospel message. But Paul says that the theology which the Galatians have accepted is not another gospel of the same doctrine. Indeed there is no "good news" in the doctrine that fallen man must work his way to heaven and save himself by his own good works.

Verse 7 - ". . . which is not another; but there be some that trouble you, and would pervert the gospel of Christ."

ὃ οὐκ ἔστιν ἄλλο. εἰ μή τινές εἰσιν οἱ ταράσσοντες ὑμᾶς καὶ θέλοντες μεταστρέφαι τὸ εὐαγγέλιον τοῦ Χριστοῦ.

"not that there is another gospel, but there are some who trouble you and want to pervert the gospel of Christ." . . . RSV

ὃ (acc.sing.neut.of ὅς, relative pronoun, in agreement with εὐαγγέλιον) 65.
οὐκ (negative conjunction with the indicative) 130.
ἔστιν (3d.per.sing.pres.ind.of εἰμί, aoristic) 86.
ἄλλο (nom.sing.neut.of ἄλλος, predicate nominative) 198.
εἰ (conditional particle, simple logical condition) 337.
μή (negative conjunction in a simple logical condition, *cf.* comment *infra*) 87.
τινές (nom.pl.masc.of τις, indefinite pronoun, subject of εἰσιν) 486.
εἰσιν (3d.per.pl.pres.ind.of εἰμί, present progressive duration) 86.
οἱ (nom.pl.masc.of the article in agreement with ταράσσοντες and θέλοντες) 9.
ταράσσοντες (pres.act.part.nom.pl.masc.of ταράσσω, substantival, apposition) 149.
ὑμᾶς (acc.pl.masc.of σύ, direct object of ταράσσοντες) 104.
καὶ (adjunctive conjunction joining participles) 14.

θέλοντες (pres.act.part.nom.pl.masc.of θέλω, apposition) 88.

μεταστρέψαι (aor.act.inf.of μεταστρέφω, complementary) 2987.

τό (acc.sing.neut.of the article in agreement with εὐαγγέλιον) 9.

εὐαγγέλιον (acc.sing.neut.of εὐαγγέλιον, direct object of μεταστρέψαι) 405.

τοῦ (gen.sing.masc.of the article in agreement with Χριστοῦ) 9.

Χριστοῦ (gen.sing.masc.of Χριστός, description) 4.

Translation - ". . . which is not another of the same type, but there are some who are agitating you and wishing to change the character of the gospel of Christ."

Comment: The relative pronoun clause ὅ οὐκ ἔστιν ἄλλο belongs to the previous clause. Paul has just called the legalism of the Judaizers another gospel, but hastens to add that it is not ἄλλο (another instance of the same gospel). There are other gospel sermons (*i.e.* sermons preached on other occasions and/or by other preachers) which preach the same theology that Paul preached, but what the Judaizers were peddling in Galatia was not another gospel in the ἄλλος sense.

But there was a problem - εἰ μή - a first-class condition. There are only four other such instances of εἰ μή in a first-class condition. *Cf.* Mk.6:5; 1 Cor.15:2; 2 Cor.13:5; Gal.1:7; 1 Tim.6:3. Normally the negative in a first-class condition is οὐκ not μή. "The negative of the protasis in the first class condition is practially always οὐ in the N.T. We have εἰ οὐ as a rule, not εἰ μή. In the classic Greek the rule was to use εἰ μή, and εἰ οὐ appeared only where the οὐ coalesced with the single word (the verb generally) or for sharp antithesis or emphasis." (Winer-Thayer, 477, as cited in Robertson, *Grammar*, 1011). "But in the N.T., as in the κοινή generally and occasionally in the Attic (Jannaris, *A Historical Greek Grammar*, 429, as cited in *Ibid.*) we meet εἰ οὐ in the condition of the first class." (*Ibid.*).

Certain persons in Galatia were agitating the saints. *Cf.* Acts 15:24; 17:13; Gal.5:10.

Paul's enemies also accused him of agitating the people with his gospel (Acts 17:8). To the conservative mind (and most people are too intellectually lazy to be otherwise) any new philosophy that challenges what he believes is agitating. New ideas challenge the normal mind. They do not agitate it. The Judaizers wanted to change the character of the gospel of Christ. *Cf.* #2987. This change is not simply one of emphasis. It is a fundamental change in the essence of the message. The modern spirit, which is misnamed "liberalism" pretends to be tolerant of all points of view, as if all philosophies were as good as all others, and that truth is to be found nowhere. Paul, in possession of a supernaturally revealed message of grace, was intolerant of a message of human merit. Whoever changes the character of the gospel of Christ has changed good news into bad news. The gospel of Christ cannot be perverted if it is to remain the gospel of Christ. The truth of the gospel is not subject to relativism. Paul felt strongly about this.

Verse 8 - "But though we, or an angel from heaven, preach any other gospel unto you than that which we have preached unto you, let him be accursed."

ἀλλὰ καὶ ἐὰν ἡμεῖς ἢ ἄγγελος ἐξ οὐρανοῦ (ὑμῖν) εὐαγγελίζηται παρ' ὃ
εὐηγγελισάμεθα ὑμῖν, ἀνάθεμα ἔστω.

"But even if we, or an angel from heaven, should preach to you a gospel
contrary to that which we preached to you, let him be accursed." . . . RSV

ἀλλὰ (adversative conjunction) 342.
καὶ (ascensive conjunction) 14.
ἐὰν (conditional particle with the subjunctive in a third-class condition) 363.
ἡμεῖς (nom.pl.masc.of ἐγώ, subject of εὐαγγελίζηται) 123.
ἢ (disjunctive) 465.
ἄγγελος (nom.sing.masc.of ἄγγελος, subject of εὐαγγελίηται) 96.
ἐξ (preposition with the ablative of source) 19.
οὐρανοῦ (abl.sing.masc.of οὐρανός, source) 254.
(ὑμῖν) (dat.pl.masc.of σύ, indirect object of εὐαγγελίζηται) 104.
εὐαγγελίζηται (3d.per.sing.pres.mid.subj.of εὐαγγελίζομαι, third-class
condition) 909.
παρ' (preposition with the accusative, opposition) 154.
ὃ (acc.sing.neut.of ὅς, relative pronoun, opposition) 65.
εὐηγγελισάμεθα (1st.per.pl.aor.mid.ind.of εὐαγγελίζω, constative) 909.
ὑμῖν (dat.pl.masc.of σύ, indirect object of εὐηγγελισάμεθα) 104.
ἀνάθεμα (nom.sing.neut.of ἀνάθεμα, predicate nominative) 3597.
ἔστω (3d.per.sing.pres.impv.of εἰμί, command) 86.

Translation - "*But even though we or an angel from heaven should preach to you
in opposition to that which we have preached to you, let him be cursed.*"

Comment: The ἐὰν clause is a third-class condition, as Paul expresses doubt that
either he or an angel from heaven would ever do what he suggests. It is also
concessive, with καὶ added in an ascensive sense. If such an improbability should
occur, the curse would rest upon them. So great was Paul's certainty that what he
had always preached in Galatian country was the true gospel that he warns them
even against himself or an angel who might pervert it. This lays to rest any notion
that an "apostle" or other highly regarded official has authority to present
something new, if it is out of harmony with what has already been presented.
Witness the Mormon heresy, with its view that certain "elders" of the church
have authority to receive revelations which then become the dogma of the
church. The *ex cathedra* Papal Infallability dogma comes under the same
accursed heading. Paul disclaims any further revelatory capacity in matters that
would effect the essence of his gospel, although his gift of prophecy enabled him
to give further light from heaven on peripheral matters. He even extends his ban
against false preaching to angels from heaven.

The television airwaves are full of preachers who "say they are apostles, and
are not" (Rev.2:2) and who mislead their viewers into accepting their false
doctrines and enriching them with their financial contributions. Paul
pronounces a curse upon the preacher whose message is parallel to (παρ' ὃ), and
therefore not in line with the gospel which is written in the New Testament. This

is the intolerance which Christianity imposes upon Christians. But Christianity is a theocracy, not a democracy. In a democratic state, under our first amendment freedoms, each may preach that which he wishes, but he has no right to call it the gospel of Christ unless it conforms to Paul's theology. Paul made no effort to impose the power of the Roman Empire upon pagans to prevent them from preaching paganism. He here calls down a curse from heaven upon a pagan who preaches paganism and represents it as the gospel of Christ. Modernists who openly scoff at Paul's theology and present their own legalistic humanism in the name of the gospel have Paul's curse upon them.

παρά here with the accusative in the sense of opposition. *Cf.* #154. *Cf.* James 2:15 — ἐὰν ἀδελφὸς ἢ ἀδελφὴ γυμνοὶ ὑπάρχωσιν, as another example of a double singular subject with a plural verb as we here have ἐὰν ἡμεῖς ἢ ἄγγελος ἐξ οὐρανοῦ with εὐηγγελισάμεθα.

Paul felt the revulsion against perversion of the gospel so strongly that he repeated the curse for emphasis in

Verse 9 - "As we said before, so say I now again, If any man preach any other gospel unto you than that ye have received, let him be accursed."

ὡς προειρήκαμεν, καὶ ἄρτι πάλιν λέγω, εἴ τις ὑμᾶς εὐαγγελίζεται παρ' ὃ παρελάβετε, ἀνάθεμα ἔστω.

"As we have said before, so now I say again, If any one is preaching to you a gospel contrary to that which you received, let him be accursed." . . . RSV

ὡς (comparative particle) 128.
προειρήκαμεν (1st.per.pl.perf.act.ind.of προεῖπον, consummative) 1501.
καὶ (adjunctive conjunction joining verbs) 14.
ἄρτι (temporal adverb) 320.
πάλιν (adverbial) 355.
λέγω (1st.per.sing.pres.act.ind.of λέγω, aoristic) 66.
εἴ (conditional particle in a first-class condition) 337.
τις (nom.sing.masc.of τις, indefinite pronoun, subject of εὐαγγελίζεται) 486.
ὑμᾶς (acc.pl.masc.of σύ, direct object of εὐαγγελίζεται) 104.
εὐαγγελίζεται (3d.per.sing.pres.mid.ind.of εὐαγγελίζω, first-class condition) 909.
παρ' (preposition with the accusative, opposition) 154.
ὃ (acc.sing.neut.of ὅς, relative pronoun, opposition) 65.
παρελάβετε (2d.per.pl.aor.act.ind.of παραλαμβάνω, culminative) 102.
ἀνάθεμα (nom.sing.neut.of ἀνάθεμα, predicate nominative) 3597.
ἔστω (3d.per.sing.pres.impv.of εἰμί, command) 86.

Translation - "As we have said before, also now I am saying again, 'If anyone is preaching to you that which is contrary to what you have received, let him be cursed.' "

Comment: In verse 8 we have a third-class condition with ἐὰν and the subjunctive, while in verse 9 we have a first-class condition with εἴ and the indicative. The third-class condition expresses doubt about the premise. Paul was quite certain that neither he nor an angel from heaven would preach legalism. The first-class condition in verse 9 assumes that the premise is true. Paul was very certain that someone was perverting the gospel of Christ in Galatia. We could have translated, "Since (no doubt about it) someone is preaching a false gospel to you let him be cursed." This curse is specific. The curse in verse 8 is general. The Galatians had received Paul's gospel. Any other philosophy in contradistinction to it is heresy.

Verse 10 - "For do I now persuade men, or God? Or do I seek to please men? For if I yet pleased men, I should not be the servant of Christ."

Ἄρτι γὰρ ἀνθρώπους πείθω ἢ τὸν θεόν; ἢ ζητῶ ἀνθρώποις ἀρέσκειν; εἰ ἔτι ἀνθρώποις ἤρεσκον, Χριστοῦ δοῦλος οὐκ ἂν ἤμην.

"Am I now seeking the favor of men, or God? Or am I trying to please men? If I were still pleasing men, I should not be a servant of Christ." . . . RSV

Ἄρτι (temporal adverb) 320.
γὰρ (causal conjunction) 105.
ἀνθρώπους (acc.pl.masc.of ἄνθρωπος, direct object of πείθω) 341.
πείθω (1st.per.sing.pres.act.ind.of πείθω, direct question) 1929.
ἢ (disjunctive) 465.
τὸν (acc.sing.masc.of the article in agreement with θεόν) 9.
θεόν (acc.sing.masc.of θεός, direct object of πείθω) 124.
ἢ (disjunctive) 465.
ζητῶ (1st.per.sing.pres.act.ind.of ζητέω, direct question) 207.
ἀνθρώποις (dat.pl.masc.of ἄνθρωπος, personal interest) 341.
ἀρέσκειν (pres.act.inf.of ἀρέσκω, complementary) 1110.
εἰ (conditional particle in a second-class condition, contrary to fact) 337.
ἔτι (temporal adverb) 448.
ἀνθρώποις (dat.pl.masc.of ἄνθρωπος, personal interest) 341.
ἤρεσκον (1st.per.sing.imp.act.ind.of ἀρέσκω, second-class condition, progressive description) 1110.
Χριστοῦ (gen.sing.masc.of Χριστός, relationship) 4.
δοῦλος (nom.sing.masc.of δοῦλος, predicate nominative) 725.
οὐκ (negative conjunction with the indicative) 130.
ἂν (contingent particle in a second-class condition, contrary to fact) 205.
ἤμην (1st.per.sing.imp.ind.of εἰμί, voluntative) 86.

Translation - "Because am I now persuading men or God? Or am I trying to please men? If I had been pleasing men, I would not have been a servant of Christ."

Comment: Paul here raises the question that every evangelist/soul winner should face. Whom are we trying to convince? It is clear that unregenerate man can do nothing to save himself. His will is as dead in sin as his intellect and emotional nature (John 6:44; Eph.2:1). The prime mover is God. To whom then should the preacher appeal with his persuasive powers? Mary and Martha made no appeal to Lazarus. He was dead. They did appeal to Incarnate Deity, and they got results. Since God, the Holy Spirit alone can convince the lost (John 16:7-11) all attempts to persuade the sinner, except those directed to the Holy Spirit, are futile. The evangelist who wishes to be popular will gain friends, but not converts. If we wish to sell soap or Fuller brushes we should learn how to make friends and influence people. But if we wish to win souls to Christ we must learn what to preach and how to preach it so that the Holy Spirit will be pleased to cooperate with us. He is the only one who can do anything about man's lost estate.

The most effective way to offend God is to pervert His gospel. That is what the Judaizers in Galatia were doing, for if they were correct in saying that righteousness is by the law, then Christ died in vain (Gal.2:21). Paul had been ruthless in castigating them (verses 7-9).

The preacher who wishes to please God had better not try to please men. Preaching "in the flesh" is the preaching that stoops to an attempt to appeal to the audience on a human basis. Such a preacher dresses in a manner to attract attention, speaks good English, tries to be funny, flatters his audience. Such preaching can never please God (Rom.8:8).

The εἰ clause with the secondary tenses in both protasis and apodosis is a second-class condition of the unreal indicative. If Paul had ever tried to please man when he preached, it was at such a time that he could not quality as the servant of Christ. The only preaching that pleases God is unpopular with lost men. No preacher can have it both ways. The Judaizers were flattering the Galatians by telling them that there was some merit in them that God could and would accept. They could become Jewish prosylytes; they could accept circumcision; they could follow the Mosaic code to the best of their ability; they could fast twice in the week and give tithes of all that they possessed; they could make broad their phylacteries and pray standing on the corners of the streets. All of these things the Pharisees did and they did it very well and before great audiences. Paul went to Galatian country and told the people that they were hoplessly lost and totally at the mercy of God who loved them and would save them, but only if they admitted that they were lost and threw themselves without reservation upon His mercy and grace. *Cf.* Gal.5:11.

How Paul Became an Apostle

(Galatians 1:11-24)

Verse 11 - "But I certify you, brethren, that the gospel which was preached of me is not after men."

Γνωρίζω δὲ ὑμῖν, ἀδελφοί, τὸ εὐαγγέλιον τὸ εὐαγγελισθὲν ὑπ' ἐμοῦ ὅτι οὐκ ἔστιν κατὰ ἄνθρωπον.

"For I would have you know, brethren, that the gospel which was preached by me is not man's gospel." . . . RSV

Γνωρίζω (1st.per.sing.pres.act.ind.of γνωρίζω, aoristic) 1882.

δὲ (adversative conjunction) 11.

ὑμῖν (dat.pl.masc.of σύ, indirect object of γνωρίζω) 104.

ἀδελφοί (voc.pl.masc.of ἀδελφός, address) 15.

τὸ (nom.sing.neut.of the article in agreement with εὐαγγέλιον) 9.

εὐαγγέλιον (nom.sing.neut.of εὐαγγέλιον, subject of ἔστιν) 405.

τὸ (nom.sing.neut.of the article in agreement with εὐαγγέλιον) 9.

εὐαγγελισθὲν (aor.pass.part.nom.sing.neut.of εὐαγγελίζω, adjectival, ascriptive, in agreement with εὐαγγέλιον) 909.

ὑπ' (preposition with the ablative of agent) 117.

ἐμοῦ (abl.sing.masc.of ἐμός, agent) 1267.

ὅτι (conjunction introducing an object clause in indirect discourse) 211.

οὐκ (negative conjunction with the indicative) 130.

ἔστιν (3d.per.sing.pres.ind.of εἰμί, aoristic) 86.

κατὰ (preposition with the accusative, standard) 98.

ἄνθρωπον (acc.sing.masc.of ἄνθρωπος, standard) 341.

Translation - "But I am telling you, brethren, that the gospel which was preached by me is not in keeping with human philosophy."

Comment: Paul was so little concerned with pleasing the Galatians, as such — indeed, he feared that he would please them, and thus displease Christ — that he took adversative steps (adversative δὲ). He gave them a positive guarantee. Γνωρίζω has the ὅτι object clause in indirect discourse. The subject is τὸ εὐαγγέλιον τὸ εὐαγγελισθὲν ὑπ' ἐμοῦ - "the gospel, the having been preached by me gospel." The predicate says that it is not of human origin or design and is not to be judged by human standards (κατὰ ἄνθρωπον). It comports in no way with human intellectual ideas (Isa.55:8-11; 1 Cor.2:9-16).

How different this is from Thomas Aquinas and the attempt of the Scholastics to show that revealed religion is really a highly rationalized approach to the thinking of a natural man. The Medieval Scholastics perpetuated their doctrine that the intellect of man was not involved in Adam's fall through Arminius, Erasmus and the Jesuits and now is proclaimed by the secular humanists. It had already been preached by Paul's enemies, the Judaizers in Galatia and at a later time by Pelagius, the opponent of Augustine.

Even some who call themselves Calvinists, albeit with only scant justification, make futile attempts to reach the sinner's heart through his head. The author recalls, with regret and confusion of face, his own oft repeated attempts, as an evangelist to "convince" his audiences with intellectual argumentation that Christ could save. How often the audience was treated to a closely reasoned rebuttal of the swoon, stolen body and hallucination theories of the resurrection of Jesus! This kind of Bible teaching has its place in the curriculum of Christian Education after the elect have been saved and immersed. It has no place in an evangelistic campaign. Charles Haddon Spurgeon, a Reformed theologian, preached the κατὰ θεόν gospel always with great evangelistic results.

Paul is beginning to refute the charge of his critics that he was not divinely commissioned as an Apostle. Indeed he was not one of the original twelve as his critics liked to point out, but this fact in no way invalidated his claim to Apostleship. Indeed he had an experience that none of the others had had, although John was also to be caught up to heaven before he died (Rev.4:1,2). His critics also said that Paul did not have the endorsement of the other eleven. This was false.

Verse 12 - "For I neither received it of man, neither was I taught it, but by the revelation of Jesus Christ."

οὐδὲ γὰρ ἐγὼ παρὰ ἀνθρώπου παρέλαβον αὐτό, οὔτε ἐδιδάχθην, ἀλλὰ δι' ἀποκαλύψεως Ἰησοῦ Χριστοῦ.

"For I did not receive it from man, nor was I taught it, but it came through a revelation of Jesus Christ." . . . RSV

οὐδὲ (compound negative conjunction) 452.

γὰρ (causal conjunction) 105.

ἐγὼ (nom.sing.masc.of ἐγώ, subject of παρέλαβον) 123.

παρὰ (preposition with the ablative of agent) 154.

ἀνθρώπου (abl.sing.masc.of ἄνθρωπος, agent) 341.

παρέλαβον (1st.per.sing.aor.act.ind.of παραλαμβάνω, constative) 102.

αὐτό (acc.sing.neut.of αὐτός, direct object of παρέλαβον) 16.

οὔτε (compound disjunctive) 598.

ἐδιδάχθην (1st.per.sing.aor.pass.ind.of διδάσκω, constative) 403.

ἀλλὰ (adversative conjunction) 342.

δι' (preposition with the ablative of agent) 118.

ἀποκαλύψεως (abl.sing.fem.of ἀποκάλυψις, agent) 1902.

Ἰησοῦ (gen.sing.masc.of Ἰησοῦς, description) 3.

Χριστοῦ (gen.sing.masc.of Χριστός, apposition) 4.

Translation - "Because I neither received it from man, nor was I taught, but by a revelation of Jesus Christ."

Comment: γὰρ is causal as Paul defends his statement of verse 11. The reason Paul's gospel did not come to him from human sources was simple. He had no contact with any Christian except Ananias and his friends in Damascus, before he started preaching, except as their persecutor (Acts 9:1-2). He did not go to school to any of the Apostles. And he was saved only after Jesus' resurrection and ascension. οὔτε ἐδιδάχθην reinforces the preceding clause. Note οὐδὲ . . . οὔτε. . . ἀλλὰ - "Not by . . . nor . . . but by . . . κ.τ.λ." The agency by which Paul learned what to preach was a personal visit with Jesus Christ. He described this experience in 2 Cor.12:1-7 and Eph.3:1-7. Thus Paul identifies himself as the man of 2 Cor.12:1-7, although in that passage he did not do so, except by implication.

So Paul also, as did the other Apostles, got his theology from the Lord Jesus Christ, the difference being only in terms of geographic locale. Whether Jesus taught His disciples by the Sea of Galilee, on a mountainside or in the Temple, as He had taught the Eleven, or at the right hand of God's throne in heaven, as he taught Paul, the divine Source, the commission and the message was the same. Had Paul admitted that he learned his theology from Peter, James, John or the other Apostles, he would have been taking a subordinate place to them, and his later dispute with Peter (Gal.2:11-14) would have been viewed as an improper insubordination of student to teacher. It was important for Paul to show that he had no contact, as a student of theology, with any Christian, until after his rapture to glory and the theological revelation which was there received as recorded by him in 2 Cor.12:1-7. This he procedes to do in the remainder of the chapter.

Verse 13 - "For ye have heard of my conversation in time past in the Jews' religion, how that beyond measure I persecuted the church of God, and wasted it."

Ἠκούσατε γὰρ τὴν ἐμὴν ἀναστροφήν ποτε ἐν τῷ Ἰουδαϊσμῷ, ὅτι καθ' ὑπερβολὴν ἐδίωκον τὴν ἐκκλησίαν τοῦ θεοῦ καὶ ἐπόρθουν αὐτήν.

"For you have heard of my former life in Judaism, how I persecuted the church of God violently and tried to destroy it;" . . . RSV

Ἠκούσατε (2d.per.pl.aor.act.ind.of ἀκούω, constative) 148.
γὰρ (explanatory conjunction) 105.
τὴν (acc.sing.fem.of the article in agreement with ἀναστροφήν) 9.
ἐμὴν (acc.sing.fem.of ἐμός, in agreement with ἀναστροφήν) 1267.

#4412 ἀναστροφήν (acc.sing.fem.of ἀναστροφή, direct object of Ἠκούσατε).

King James Version

conversation - Gal.1:13; Eph.4:22; 1 Tim.4:12; Heb.13:7; Jam.3:13; 1 Pet.1:15,18; 2:12; 3:1,2,16; 2 Pet.2:7; 3:11.

Revised Standard Version

life - Gal.1:13; Heb.13:7; Jam.3:13.
manner of life - Eph.4:22.
conduct - 1 Tim.4:12; 1 Pet.1:15; 2:12.
way - 1 Pet.1:18.
behavior - 1 Pet.3:1,2,16.
licentiousness - 2 Pet.2:7.
lives - 2 Pet.3:11.

Meaning: Cf. ἀναστρέφω (#3061). Manner of life; ethical code by which behavior is dictated. Conduct. With reference to Saul's way of life before regeneration - Gal.1:13; the unregenerate life - Eph.4:22; 1 Pet.1:18; 2 Pet.2:7; the life of the believer - 1 Tim.4:12; Heb.13:7; Jam.3:13; 1 Pet.1:15; 2:12; 3:1,2,16; 2 Pet.3:11.

ποτε (temporal particle) 2399.

ἐν (preposition with the locative of sphere) 80.

τῷ (loc.sing.masc.of the article in agreement with ʼΙουδαϊσμῷ) 9.

#4413 ʼΙουδαϊσμῷ (loc.sing.masc.of ʼΙουδαϊσμός, sphere).

King James Version

Jews' religion - Gal.1:13,14.

Revised Standard Version

Judaism - Gal.1:13,14.

Meaning: Cf. ʼΙουδαῖος (#143). The doctrine and practice of the religion of Judaism - Gal.1:13,14.

ὅτι (conjunction introducing an object clause in indirect discourse) 211.

καθ' (preposition with the accusative, standard/measure) 98.

ὑπερβολὴν (acc.sing.fem.of ὑπερβολή, standard/measure) 3923.

ἐδίωκον (1st.per.sing.imp.act.ind.of διώκω, iterative) 434.

τὴν (acc.sing.fem.of the article in agreement with ἐκκλησίαν) 9.

ἐκκλησίαν (acc.sing.fem.of ἐκκλησία, direct object of ἐδίωκον) 1204.

τοῦ (gen.sing.masc.of the article in agreement with θεοῦ) 9.

θεοῦ (gen.sing.masc.of θεός, possession) 124.

καὶ (adjunctive conjunction joining verbs) 14.

ἐπόρθουν (1st.per.sing.imp.act.ind.of πορθέω, tendential) 3192.

αὐτήν (acc.sing.fem.of αὐτός, direct object of ἐπόρθουν) 16.

Translation - "Now you have heard about my previous life style with reference to the Jewish religion, that beyond all limits repeatedly I pursued the church of God and tried to devastate it."

Comment: γὰρ is explanatory as Paul begins his proof that whatever he knows of Christian theology, he did not learn it from other Christians. On the contrary again and again (iterative imperfect in ἐδίωκον) he pursued the Christians with a view to their destruction. He tried unsuccessfully (tendential imperfect in ἐπόρθουν) to destroy Christianity, and failed only because he was in conflict with the sovereign Head of the church.

Note ἐμήν in the attributive position, like an adjective. *Cf.*#1267. ποτε the enclitic particle, indicates time. Paul's former life style as a zealous Jew and Pharisee was characterized by his belief that it was his duty to God to stamp out Christianity, which he regarded as heresy. There is no question as to his sincerity (Phil.3:5,6; Acts 26:5; 9-12). καθ' ὑπερβολήν - "beyond all restraints or bounds." He was so sincere that he was beside himself with fury (Acts 9:1-2, 21).

Verse 14 - "And profited in the Jews' religion above many my equals in mine own nation, being more exceedingly zealous of the traditions of my fathers."

καὶ προέκοπτον ἐν τῷ ʼΙουδαϊσμῷ ὑπὲρ πολλοὺς συνηλικιώτας ἐν τῷ γένει μου, περισσοτέρως ζηλωτὴς ὑπάρχων τῶν πατρικῶν μου παραδόσεων.

"and I advanced in Judaism beyond many of my own age among my people, so extremely zealous was I for the traditions of my fathers." . . . RSV

καὶ (adjunctive conjunction joining verbs) 14.

προέκοπτον (1st.per.sing.imp.act.ind.of προκόπτω, progressive description) 1923.

ἐν (preposition with the locative of sphere) 80.

τῷ (loc.sing.masc.of the article in agreement with Ἰουδαϊσμῷ) 9.

Ἰουδαϊσμῷ (loc.sing.masc.of Ἰουδαϊσμός, sphere) 4413.

ὑπὲρ (preposition with the accusative of extent - "more than") 545.

πολλοὺς (acc.pl.masc.of πολύς, in agreement with συνηλικιώτας) 228.

#4414 συνηλικιώτας (acc.pl.masc.of συνηλικιώτης, extent, "more than").

King James Version

equal - Gal.1:14.

Revised Standard Version

my own age - Gal.1:14.

Meaning: A combination of σύν (#1542) and ἡλικία (#622). Hence, one of the same age; generation; peer - Gal.1:14.

ἐν (preposition with the locative of sphere) 80.

τῷ (loc.sing.masc.of the article in agreement with γένει) 9.

γένει (loc.sing.masc.of γένος, sphere) 1090.

μου (gen.sing.masc.of ἐγώ, possession) 123.

περισσοτέρως (adverbial, comparative of περισσός) 525.

ζηλωτὴς (nom.sing.masc.of ζηλοτής, predicate adjective) 2120.

ὑπάρχων (pres.part.nom.sing.masc.of ὑπάρχω, adverbial, causal) 1303.

τῶν (gen.pl.fem.of the article in agreement with παραδοσέων) 9.

#4415 πατρικῶν (gen.pl.fem.of πατρικός, description).

King James Version

of my fathers - Gal.1:14.

Revised Standard Version

of my fathers - Gal.1:14.

Meaning: Cf. πατρίς (#1096); πατρῷος (#3576); πάτρια (#1870); πατήρ (#238). Hence, handed down from one's fathers - traditional - Gal.1:14.

μου (gen.sing.masc.of ἐγώ, relationship) 123.

παραδοσέων (gen.pl.fem.of παράδοσις, reference) 1140.

Translation - "And I continued to make progress in Judaism, more than my peers in my nation, because I was more zealous about the traditions of my fathers."

Comment: Paul goes further in discussing his former life style as he tells how he persecuted the Christians, tried to destroy Christianity and (adjunctive καὶ) made more progress in Judaism than most others. Note the progressive description in προέκοπτον. Paul continued to chop his way forward in the forest of Judaistic traditions. His progress was greater than that of most of his peers (ὑπὲρ . . . γένει μου) because (causal participle in ὑπάρχων) he was more zealous with reference to the traditions which had been handed down to him from his ancestors. As one trained in the school of jurisprudence of Gamaliel, Saul of Tarsus believed in *stare decisis*.

Since Saul of Tarsus was making all of this progress in Judaism, both in its theology and in its practice, it is obvious that he was not studying Christian theology from some one of the Christians whom he was trying to kill.

From whom, then, did Paul get his Christian theology? He addresses this question in Galatians 1:15-2:11.

Verse 15 - "But when it pleased God who separated me from my mother's womb, and called me by his grace."

ὅτε δὲ εὐδόκησεν ὁ ἀφορίσας με ἐκ κοιλίας μητρός μου καὶ καλέσας διὰ τῆς χάριτος αὐτοῦ

"But when he who had set me apart before I was born, and had called me through his grace, . . . " . . . RSV

ὅτε (conjunction in a definite temporal clause, contemporaneous time) 703.

δὲ (adversative conjunction) 11.

εὐδόκησεν (3d.per.sing.aor.act.ind.of εὐδοκέω, constative) 328.

ὁ (nom.sing.masc.of the article in agreement with ἀφορίσας and καλέσας) 9.

ἀφορίσας (aor.act.part.nom.sing.masc.of ἀφορίζω, subject of εὐδόκησεν) 1093.

με (acc.sing.masc.of ἐγώ, direct object of ἀφορίσας and καλέσας) 123.

ἐκ (preposition with the ablative of separation) 19.

κοιλίας (abl.sing.fem.of κοιλία, separation) 1008.

μητρός (gen.sing.fem.of μήτηρ, possession) 76.

μου (gen.sing.masc.of ἐγώ, relationship) 123.

καὶ (adjunctive conjunction joining substantives) 14.

καλέσας (aor.act.part.nom.sing.masc.of καλέω, substantival, subject of εὐδόκησεν) 107.

διὰ (preposition with the genitive, means) 118.

τῆς (gen.sing.fem.of the article in agreement with χάριτος) 9.

χάριτος (gen.sing.fem.of χάρις, means) 1700.

αὐτοῦ (gen.sing.masc.of αὐτός, possession) 16.

Translation - "But when He Who had chosen me for service before I was born and called me by His grace thought it proper . . . "

Comment: δὲ is strongly adversative. Saul of Tarsus had set a course and was following it with all consuming zeal and vigor, but (δὲ) God had other plans.

God is introduced as the One Who, at the time that Paul was born, had already called him to salvation and Christian service. The main verb of this long sentence is ἀπῆλθον of verse 17. The aorist participles ἀφορίσας and καλέσας are the substantival subjects of εὐδόκησεν. They are antecedent in time to the main verb. ἀφορίσας can refer to the physical birth of Paul, but it can also be taken in the sense of Rom.1:1 and Acts 13:2. *Cf.*#1093. The ὅτε clause is definite, since it has the indicative, and it indicates contemporaneous time with that of ἀπῆλθον. It was when God saw fit to reveal His Son in Paul, the great revelation that resulted in his regeneration, that Paul chose not to confer with other Christians nor to go up to Jerusalem, but to go to Arabia.

There is no reason why we cannot take ἀφορίσας both to mean God's eternal call to salvation and service for Paul and also the time of his physical birth, since Scripture clearly teaches the theological interpretation of history (Eph.1:11). God had set Paul apart for salvation and the preaching of the gospel before he was born and He also chose the time when he should be born. His birth took place at a point in time, but his spiritual separation was from eternity. We do well to remember that God is not subject to chronology.

There is much in this passage which is fundamental to Paul's theology. First, God does what He does when it pleases Him - ὅτε δὲ εὐδόκησεν. One cannot hurry the eternal God. His plans for Paul were eternally conceived (Eph.1:4,5; Jude 1).

Secondly, God superintends the entire history of His elect. God chose to separate Paul from his mother's womb at that time and at no other time before or after. Paul was born "on time" which was God's time. God was the divine obstetrician.

Thirdly, it was God Who called Paul, but He did not implement His divine call until He had allowed Saul to carry on the activities described in verses 13-14. God could have prevented Saul's fanatical attack upon the Christians, as He did in Timothy's case (2 Tim.1:5). But just as Paul was born by God's decree and in God's time, so he was called to salvation in God's time, with the intervening period of unregenerate antiChristian activity permitted in the divine wisdom. *Cf.* #328 for what God pleases to do when He pleases to do it. This is sovereignty at its best. *Cf.* Luke 12:32; 1 Cor.1:21. The fact that God conducts His affairs only as it pleases Him, and that His will is always good, is the theme that runs through all of Paul's theology. Fallen man, by his degenerate will, can initiate nothing that is viable in a moral universe. But God can.

Chosen (Eph.1:3), separated unto the gospel (Rom.1:1), born physically (Gal.1:15) and called (Gal.1:15), Paul now has God's Son revealed in him (Gal.1:16).

Verse 16 - "... to reveal his son in me that I might preach him among the heathen, immediately I conferred not with flesh and blood."

ἀποκαλύψαι τὸν υἱὸν αὐτοῦ ἐν ἐμοὶ ἵνα εὐαγγελίζωμαι αὐτὸν ἐν τοῖς ἔθνεσιν, εὐθέως οὐ προσανεθέμην σαρκὶ καὶ αἵματι,

"was pleased to reveal his Son to me, in order that I might preach him among

the Gentiles, I did not confer with flesh and blood, . . . " . . . RSV

ἀποκαλύφαι (aor.act.inf.of ἀποκαλύπτω, complementary) 886.
τὸν (acc.sing.masc.of the article in agreement with υἱὸν) 9.
υἱὸν (acc.sing.masc.of υἱός, direct object of ἀποκαλύφαι) 5.
αὐτοῦ (gen.sing.masc.of αὐτός, relationship) 16.
ἐν (preposition with the locative, metaphorical place) 80.
ἐμοὶ (loc.sing.masc.of ἐμός, metaphorical place) 1267.
ἵνα (conjunction with the subjunctive in a sub-final clause) 114.
εὐαγγελίζωμαι (1st.per.sing.pres.mid.subj.of εὐαγγελίζομαι, sub-final)
909.
αὐτὸν (acc.sing.masc.of αὐτός, direct object of εὐαγγελίζωμαι) 16.
ἐν (preposition with the locative with plural nouns) 80.
τοῖς (loc.pl.neut.of the article in agreement with ἔθνεσιν) 9.
ἔθνεσιν (loc.pl.neut.of ἔθνος, place) 376.
εὐθέως (temporal adverb) 392.
οὐ (negative conjunction with the indicative) 130.

#4416 προσανεθέμην (1st.per.sing.2d.aor.mid.ind.of προσανατίθημι,
ingressive).

King James Version

add in conference - Gal.2:6.
confer - Gal.1:16.

Revised Standard Version

confer - Gal.1:16.
add - Gal.2:6.

Meaning: A combination of πρός (#197), ἀνά (#1059) and τίθημι (#455).
Hence, in the middle voice, to place oneself (τίθημι) up (ἀνά) against (πρός)
another. To approach another for whatever purpose the context demands. For
consultation - Gal.1:16. To add new truth in a discussion - Gal.2:6.

σαρκὶ (instru.sing.fem.of σάρξ, association, after πρός in composition) 1202.
καὶ (adjunctive conjunction joining nouns) 14.
αἵματι (instru.sing.fem.of αἷμα, association, after πρός in composition)
1203.

*Translation - ". . . to reveal His Son in me in order (and with the result) that I
might preach Him among the Gentiles, forthwith I sought no conference with
human advisors, . . . "*

Comment: ἀποκαλύφαι completes εὐδόκησεν. It pleased God, the separator
and the caller (verse 15) also to be the revealer. He revealed Christ to Paul. This
expression ἀποκαλύφαι τὸν υἱὸν αὐτοῦ is a good definition of regeneration, for
that is what regeneration is. Why does God regenerate His elect? (1) That God

may be praised (Eph.2:7); (2) that man may be saved (Eph.2:8), and (3) that the child of God may perform the ministry which has been assigned to him (Eph.2:10). Paul was the Apostle chosen with the special mission of carrying the gospel to the Gentile, although he also preached to the Jews (Rom.1:16; Acts 9:6,15,16,17). Thus the sovereign God continued to be pleased to work in Paul's life before and after he was saved (Phil.1:6; 2 Tim.4:6-8; Eph.2:10).

Now that Paul was saved, what did he do? He tells us precisely what he did not do. Immediately (εὐθέως) he determined to seek no conference with any of the Apostles of Christianity nor with any other Christian. Paul is determined to demonstrate to the Galatians that his standing as an Apostle can be traced only to Christ Himself. Thus his claim to apostleship was as good as theirs. Thus he refuted the claims of his enemies who were misleading the Galatians.

Verse 17 - "Neither went I up to Jerusalem to them which were apostles before me; but I went into Arabia, and returned again unto Damascus."

οὐδὲ ἀνῆλθον εἰς Ἱεροσόλυμα πρὸς τοὺς πρὸ ἐμοῦ ἀποστόλους, ἀλλὰ ἀπῆλθον εἰς Ἀραβίαν, καὶ πάλιν ὑπέστρεφα εἰς Δαμασκόν.

"nor did I go up to Jerusalem to those who were apostles before me, but I went away into Arabia; and again I returned to Damascus." . . . RSV

οὐδὲ (compound disjunctive particle) 452.
ἀνῆλθον (1st.per.sing.aor.mid.ind.of ἀνέρχομαι, constative) 2273.
εἰς (preposition with the accusative of extent) 140.
Ἱεροσόλυμα (acc.sing.masc.of Ἱεροσολύμων, extent) 141.
πρὸς (preposition with the accusative of extent) 197.
τοὺς (acc.pl.masc.of the article in agreement with ἀποστόλους) 9.
πρὸ (preposition with the ablative of time separation) 442.
ἐμοῦ (abl.sing.masc.of ἐμός, time separation) 1267.
ἀποστόλους (acc.pl.masc.of ἀπόστολος, extent) 844.
ἀλλὰ (alternative conjunction) 342.
ἀπῆλθον (1st.per.sing.aor.mid.ind.of ἀπέρχομαι, constative) 239.
εἰς (preposition with the accusative of extent) 140.

#4417 Ἀραβίαν (acc.sing.fem.of Ἀραβία, extent).

King James Version

Arabia - Gal.1:17; 4:25.

Revised Standard Version

Arabia - Gal.1:17; 4:25.

Meaning: Arabia - Gal.1:17; associated in Gal.4:25 with Mount Sinai.

καὶ (adjunctive conjunction joining verbs) 14.
πάλιν (adverbial) 355.

ὑπέστρεφα (1st.per.sing.aor.act.ind.of ὑποστρέφω, constative) 1838.
εἰς (preposition with the accusative of extent) 140.
Δαμασκόν (acc.sing.masc.of Δαμασκός, extent) 3181.

Translation - *"Nor did I go up to Jerusalem to those who preceded me in the Apostleship, but I went away into Arabia, and again I returned to Damascus."*

Comment: The history of Paul's life immediately after his conversion can be fitted into the Acts 9:1-31 story. Had Paul left Straight Street in Damascus immediately after his immersion (Acts 9:18) and gone to Jerusalem, to place himself under the tutelage of Peter, James, John and the other Apostles, his position as their subordinate would have been robbed him of the prestige which is fact he enjoyed as their coordinate. He needed to sit at Jesus' feet as had they. It is probable that it was during his trip into the Arabian desert that the experience of 2 Cor.12:1-7 occurred. The text does not tell us but Paul may have gone down to the Sinai peninsula in order to visit the mountain where the law which had been so much a part of his religion before his conversion was given to Moses. There God came down to Moses, but Paul went up to meet his ascended Lord, as Christ could not leave His seat at the right hand of the Father until His enemies have been made His footstool (Psalm 110:1). Christ could descend to Sinai to give the law to Moses, and He could descend to Bethlehem to become the incarnate Lamb of God, but once dead on the cross and risen from the grave He ascended into heaven there to remain until His second coming in power and great glory. The "until" in Psalm 110:1 makes impossible the view that seven years before His enemies become His footstool at the battle of Armageddon, He will "descend from heaven" in a pretribulation rapture (1 Thess.4:16).

Note the οὐ ... οὐδὲ ... ἀλλὰ sequence. "Not ... nor ... but...." He sought no conferences on theological questions. This indicates that he did not discuss theology with Ananias, nor any other Christian in Damascus, but he went away to Arabia. Later, after his desert sojourn he returned to Damascus, after which, having escaped the police he came to Jerusalem (Acts 9:22-31). It was three years after his return to Damascus before he went up to Jerusalem to see Peter. This we learn in

Verse 18 - *"Then after three years I went up to Jerusalem to see Peter, and abode with him fifteen days."*

Ἔπειτα μετὰ τρία ἔτη ἀνῆλθον εἰς Ἱεροσόλυμα ἱστορῆσαι Κηφᾶν, καὶ ἐπέμεινα πρὸς αὐτὸν ἡμέρας δεκαπέντε.

"Then after three years I went up to Jerusalem to visit Cephas, and remained with him fifteen days." ... RSV

Ἔπειτα (temporal adverb) 2566.
μετὰ (preposition with the accusative, time extent) 50.
τρία (acc.pl.fem.of τρεῖς, in agreement with ἔτη) 1010.
ἔτη (acc.pl.fem.of ἔτος, time extent) 821.
ἀνῆλθον (1st.per.sing.aor.mid.ind.of ἀνέρχομαι, constative) 2273.
εἰς (preposition with the accusative of extent) 140.

Ἱεροσόλυμα (acc.sing.masc.of Ἱεροσολύμων, extent) 141.

#4418 ἱστορῆσαι (aor.act.inf.of ἱστορέω, purpose).

King James Version

see - Gal.1:18.

Revised Standard Version

visit - Gal.1:18.

Meaning: to visit. In Paul's case for the purpose of becoming acquainted with Peter in Jerusalem - Gal.1:18.

Κηφᾶν (acc.sing.masc.of Κηφᾶς, direct object of ἱστορῆσαι) 1964.
καὶ (adjunctive conjunction joining verbs) 14.
ἐπέμεινα (1st.per.sing.aor.act.ind.of ἐπιμένω, constative) 2379.
πρὸς (preposition with the accusative, "near to" "with") 197.
αὐτὸν (acc.sing.masc.of αὐτός, extent) 16.
ἡμέρας (acc.pl.fem.of ἡμέρα, time extent) 135.
δεκαπέντε (numeral) 2601.

Translation - "Then, three years later, I went up to Jerusalem to get acquainted with Cephas and I stayed with him for fifteen days."

Comment: After μετὰ we have the accusative of time extent. Also ἡμέρας δεκαπέντε. This is not the conference recorded in Acts 15, but the one of Acts 9. Luke does not say that Paul met all of the Apostles (Acts 9:27). Paul adds in Gal.1:19 that the two he saw were Peter and James, the Lord's brother. It was during this two weeks visit that Barnabas introduced Paul to the Christians who until reassured were afraid of Paul. His ministry among the Greeks brought the plot to kill him, and he returned to Tarsus (Acts 9:30). *Cf.*Acts 22:6-21.

Verse 19 - "But other of the apostles saw I none, save James the Lord's brother."

ἕτερον δὲ τῶν ἀποστόλων οὐκ εἶδον, εἰ μὴ Ἰάκωβον τὸν ἀδελφὸν τοῦ κυρίου.

"But I saw none of the other apostles except James the Lord's brother." . . .
RSV

ἕτερον (acc.sing.masc.of ἕτερος, direct object of εἶδον) 605.
δὲ (adversative conjunction) 11.
τῶν (gen.pl.masc.of the article in agreement with ἀποστόλων) 9.
ἀποστόλων (gen.pl.masc.of ἀπόστολος, partitive genitive) 844.
οὐκ (negative conjunction with the indicative) 130.
εἶδον (1st.per.sing.aor.act.ind.of ὁράω, constative) 144a.
εἰ (conditional particle in an elliptical first-class condition) 337.
μὴ (negative conjunction in an elliptical first-class condition) 87.
Ἰάκωβον (acc.sing.masc.of Ἰάκωβος, direct object of εἶδον) 1098.
τὸν (acc.sing.masc.of the article in agreement with ἀδελφὸν) 9.

ἀδελφὸν (acc.sing.masc.of ἀδελφός, apposition) 15.
τοῦ (gen.sing.masc.of the article in agreement with κυρίου) 9.
κυρίου (gen.sing.masc.of κύριος, relationship) 97.

Translation - "But I saw none of the other Apostles except James, the brother of the Lord."

Comment: This statement of Paul verifies Luke's use of the plural in Acts 9:27 - τοὺς ἀποστόλους. They were Peter and James.

Verse 20 - "Now the things which I write unto you, behold, before God, I lie not."

ἃ δὲ γράφω ὑμῖν, ἰδοὺ ἐνώπιον τοῦ θεοῦ ὅτι οὐ ψεύδομαι.

"(In what I am writing to you, before God, I do not lie!)" . . . RSV

ἃ (acc.pl.neut.of ὅς, relative pronoun, general reference) 65.
δὲ (explanatory conjunction) 11.
γράφω (1st.per.sing.pres.act.ind.of γράφω, aoristic) 156.
ὑμῖν (dat.pl.masc.of σύ, indirect object of γράφω) 104.
ἰδοὺ (exclamatory) 95
ἐνώπιον (preposition with the genitive, place description) 1798.
τοῦ (gen.sing.masc.of the article in agreement with θεοῦ) 9.
θεοῦ (gen.sing.masc.of θεός, place description) 124.
ὅτι (conjunction introducing an elliptical object clause in indirect discourse) 211.
οὐ (negative conjunction with the indicative) 130.
ψεύδομαι (1st.per.sing.pres.mid.ind.of ψεύδομαι, aoristic) 439.

Translation - "Now with reference to the things which I am writing to you, behold, before God I swear that I am not lying."

Comment: This solemn oath indicates the depth of Paul's feeling and his great desire that the Galatians believe his testimony.

Verse 21 - "Afterwards I came into the regions of Syria and Cilicia."

ἔπειτα ἦλθον εἰς τὰ κλίματα τῆς Συρίας καὶ τῆς Κιλικίας.

"Then I went into the regions of Syria and Cilicia." . . . RSV

ἔπειτα (temporal adverb) 2566.
ἦλθον (1st.per.sing.aor.mid.ind.of ἔρχομαι, constative) 146.
εἰς (preposition with the accusative of extent) 140.
τὰ (acc.pl.neut.of the article in agreement with κλίματα) 9.
κλίματα (acc.pl.neut.of κλίμα, extent) 4055.
τῆς (gen.sing.fem.of the article in agreement with Συρίας) 9.
Συρίας (gen.sing.fem.of Συρία, description) 410.
καὶ (adjunctive conjunction joining nouns) 14.
τῆς (gen.sing.fem.of the article in agreement with Κιλικίας) 9.
Κιλικίας (gen.sing.fem.of Κιλικία, description) 3092.

Translation - "Then I came into the regions of Syria and Cilicia."

Comment: *Cf.* Acts 9:30. This departure from Jerusalem was due to the attempt of the Jews to kill him (Acts 9:29) and to his vision while in Jerusalem (Acts 22:17-21). Paul's next visit to Jerusalem came fourteen years later. During these fourteen years he had no personal contact with Jerusalem.

Verse 22 - "And was unknown by face unto the churches of Judea which were in Christ."

ἤμην δὲ ἀγνοούμενος τῷ προσώπῳ ταῖς ἐκκλησίαις τῆς Ἰουδαίας ταῖς ἐν Χριστῷ,

"And I was still not known by sight to the churches of Christ in Judea;" . . . *RSV*

ἤμην (1st.per.sing.imp.ind.of εἰμί, progressive description) 86.
δὲ (adversative conjunction) 11.
ἀγνοούμενος (pres.pass.part.nom.sing.masc.of ἀγνοέω, adjectival in the predicate) 2345.
τῷ (loc.sing.neut.of the article in agreement with προσώπῳ) 9.
προσώπῳ (loc.sing.neut.of πρόσωπον, sphere) 588.
ταῖς (dat.pl.fem.of the article in agreement with ἐκκλησίαις) 9.
ἐκκλησίαις (dat.pl.fem.of ἐκκλησία, personal interest) 1204.
τῆς (gen.sing.fem.of the article in agreement with Ἰουδαίας) 9.
Ἰουδαίας (gen.sing.fem.of Ἰουδαίας, description) 134.
ταῖς (dat.pl.fem.of the article in agreement with ἐκκλησίαις) 9.
ἐν (preposition with the instrumental of association) 80.
Χριστῷ (instru.sing.masc.of Χριστός, association) 4.

Translation - "But I was unknown by face to the churches in Christ of Judea."

Comment: Paul's intent is to demonstrate to his readers his total independence of any other Christian for his theology. Though he did visit Jerusalem to meet Peter and James for fifteen days, this was after his rapture experience of 2 Cor.12:1-7. On that visit he saw none of the other Apostles. In the intervening fourteen years between his first and second visit to Jerusalem he had no personal contact with any of the Judean churches. He did not visit them again, nor did they visit him. They heard about his work up north and glorified God because of it, but they made no intellectual contribution to his development. This information he adds in verses 23,24.

Verse 23 - "But they had heard only, That he which persecuted us in times past now preacheth the faith which once he destroyed."

μόνον δὲ ἀκούοντες ἦσαν ὅτι Ὁ διώκων ἡμᾶς ποτε νῦν εὐαγγελίζεται τὴν πίστιν ἣν ποτε ἐπόρθει,

"they only heard it said, 'He who once persecuted us is now preaching the faith he once tried to destroy.'" . . . *RSV*

μόνον (acc.sing.neut.of μόνος, adverbial) 339.

δὲ (adversative conjunction) 11.

ἀκούοντες (pres.act.part.nom.pl.masc.of ἀκούω, imperfect periphrastic) 148.

ἦσαν (3d.per.pl.imp.ind.of εἰμί, imperfect periphrastic) 86.

ὅτι (recitative) 211.

Ὁ (nom.sing.masc.of the article in agreement with διώκων) 9.

διώκων (pres.act.part.nom.sing.masc.of διώκω, substantival, subject of εὐαγγελίζεται) 434.

ὑμᾶς (acc.pl.masc.of ἐγώ, direct object of διώκων) 123.

ποτε (temporal particle) 2399.

νῦν (temporal adverb) 1497.

εὐαγγελίζεται (3d.per.sing.pres.mid.ind.of εὐαγγελίζομαι, present progressive duration retroactive) 909.

τὴν (acc.sing.fem.of the article in agreement with πίστιν) 9.

πίστιν (acc.sing.fem.of πίστις, direct object of εὐαγγελίζεται) 728.

ἣν (acc.sing.fem.of ὅς, relative pronoun, direct object of ἐπόρθει) 65.

ποτε (temporal particle) 2399.

ἐπόρθει (3d.per.sing.imp.act.ind.of πορθέω, progressive description) 3192.

Translation - "But they only were hearing again and again, 'He who persecuted us before is now preaching the faith which once he devastated.'"

Comment: The Judean Christians never once saw Paul's face during the intervening fourteen years, as the imperfect periphrastic ἤμην . . . ἀγνοούμενος (durative action) indicates, but (adversative δὲ) they heard again and again (iterative action in the imperfect periphrastic ἀκούοντες ἦσαν) the report, which we have hear in direct discourse.

Occasionally the context demands antecedent time for the present participle as we have it here in Ὁ διώκων. Robertson *(Grammar,* 892) cites John 9:25; Mt.2:20; John 12:17; Acts 4:34; 10:7; Mk.1:4 as other examples. He calls it a sort of "imperfect" participle, denoting former continuous action. What they meant is "He who formerly persecuted . . . is now preaching. . . κ.τ.λ." Note that both Ὁ διώκων and εὐαγγελίζεται are present tense, but ποτε joined to διώκων indicates antecedence, while νῦν, joined to εὐαγγελίζεται indicates contemporaneity. The former persecutor is now the preacher of the faith. What faith? The relative pronoun tell us - ἣν ποτε ἐπόρθει - "which formerly he was always laying waste." The rumors of Paul's work during his first missionary journey (Acts 13-14) were constantly drifting back to Judea. Before Saul was always devastating (ἐπόρθει). Now Paul was always preaching (εὐαγγελίζεται). And they were always hearing about it (ἀκούοντες ἦσαν). But not once did any Apostle or any other Christian visit Paul to instruct him in his theology.

Verse 24 - "And they glorified God in me."

καὶ ἐδόξαζον ἐν ἐμοὶ τὸν θεόν.

"And they glorified God because of me." . . . RSV

καὶ (continuative conjunction) 14.

ἐδόξαζον (3d.per.pl.imp.act.ind.of δοξάζω, progressive description) 461.

ἐν (preposition with the instrumental of cause) 80.

ἐμοὶ (instru.sing.masc.of ἐμός, cause) 1267.

τὸν (acc.sing.masc.of the article in agreement with θεόν) 9.

θεόν (acc.sing.masc.of θεός, direct object of ἐδόξαζον) 124.

Translation - "And they were always glorifying God because of me."

Comment: Paul continues to use the durative imperfect in verses 22-24. While Paul was out preaching in his first missionary journey what he later preached to the Galatians when he first visited them on his second missionary journey, the Judean Christians, whom the Judaizers said did not endorse Paul, were back in Judea applauding him and glorifying God. Thus Paul continues to attack the notion that his theology, received only by Christ's revelation to him alone, was different from that of the original Jerusalem church, as taught by the other Apostles.

INDEX